AND
NOW
I SPILL
THE
FAMILY
SECRETS

AND NOW I SPILL THE FAMILY SECRETS

An Illustrated Memoir

MARGARET KIMBALL

HarperOne
An Imprint of HarperCollinsPublishers

FIRST EDITION

DESIGNED BY MARGARET KIMBALL
FONTS COPYRIGHT © 2021 BY MARGARET KIMBALL

LIBRARY OF CONGRESS CATALOGING-IN-PUBLICATION DATA
HAS BEEN APPLIED FOR.

ISBN 978-0-06-300744-4

21 22 23 24 25 IMAGO 10 9 8 7 6 5 4 3 2 1

AUTHOR'S NOTE

THIS IS A WORK OF NONFICTION. THE EXPERIENCES I WRITE ABOUT IN THIS BOOK ARE TRUE AND RENDERED AS I REMEMBER THEM TO THE BEST OF MY ABILITY. THE STORIES ARE TOLD ACCORDING TO MY MEMORY, MY MOM'S MEMORY, AND ANY VERIFYING DOCUMENTATION I COULD FIND (DIARIES, NEWSPAPER ARTICLES, VIDEOS, ETC.). I REORDERED A FEW MINOR EVENTS—AND COMPRESSED THE TIME BETWEEN THEM—IN SERVICE OF A COHERENT NARRATIVE.

MY FAMILY MEMBERS ASKED ME TO CHANGE THEIR NAMES, SO I DID. I ALSO CHANGED THE PHYSICAL DESCRIPTION OF ONE CHARACTER. THE CONVERSATIONS IN THE BOOK ARE SOMETIMES TAKEN FROM MY DIARIES AND OTHER TIMES DESCRIBED FROM MY MEMORY WITH THE HELP OF MEMORIES FROM MY BROTHERS AND PARENTS. THEY DON'T REPRESENT WORD-FOR-WORD DOCUMENTATION. INSTEAD, I'VE RETOLD THEM SO THAT THEY CONVEY THE MEANING OF WHAT WAS SAID, IN KEEPING WITH THE ESSENCE OF EACH EXPERIENCE OR EVENT.

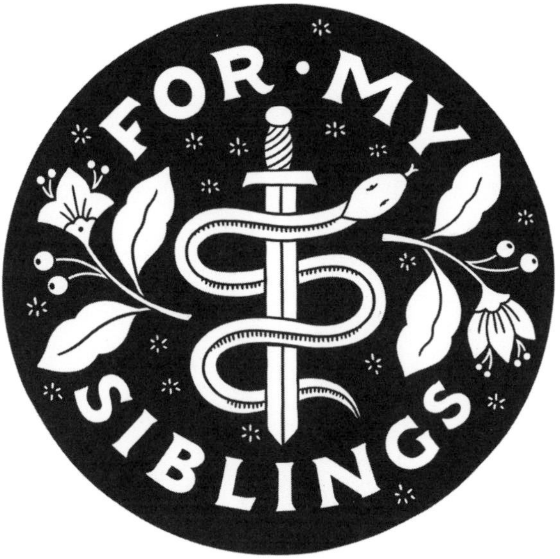
FOR · MY
SIBLINGS

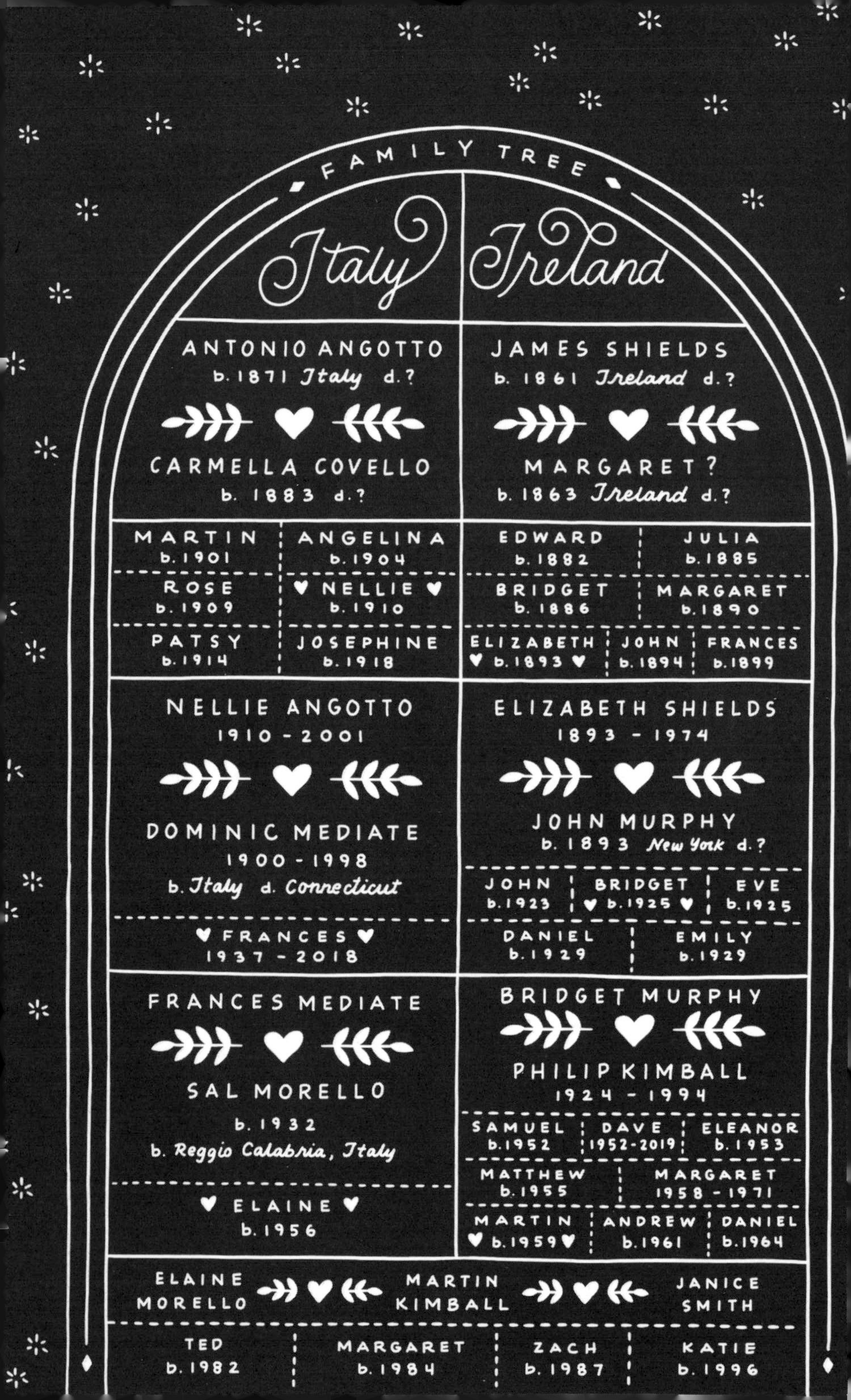
FAMILY TREE
Italy
Ireland
ANTONIO ANGOTTO
b. 1871 Italy d. ?
CARMELLA COVELLO
b. 1883 d. ?
JAMES SHIELDS
b. 1861 Ireland d. ?
MARGARET ?
b. 1863 Ireland d. ?
MARTIN b. 1901
ANGELINA b. 1904
ROSE b. 1909
NELLIE b. 1910
PATSY b. 1914
JOSEPHINE b. 1918
EDWARD b. 1882
JULIA b. 1885
BRIDGET b. 1886
MARGARET b. 1890
ELIZABETH b. 1893
JOHN b. 1894
FRANCES b. 1899
NELLIE ANGOTTO
1910 - 2001
DOMINIC MEDIATE
1900 - 1998
b. Italy d. Connecticut
FRANCES
1937 - 2018
ELIZABETH SHIELDS
1893 - 1974
JOHN MURPHY
b. 1893 New York d. ?
JOHN b. 1923
BRIDGET b. 1925
EVE b. 1925
DANIEL b. 1929
EMILY b. 1929
FRANCES MEDIATE
SAL MORELLO
b. 1932
b. Reggio Calabria, Italy
ELAINE
b. 1956
BRIDGET MURPHY
PHILIP KIMBALL
1924 - 1994
SAMUEL b. 1952
DAVE 1952-2019
ELEANOR b. 1953
MATTHEW b. 1955
MARGARET 1958 - 1971
MARTIN b. 1959
ANDREW b. 1961
DANIEL b. 1964
ELAINE MORELLO
MARTIN KIMBALL
JANICE SMITH
TED b. 1982
MARGARET b. 1984
ZACH b. 1987
KATIE b. 1996

TABLE OF CONTENTS

Life is all arrivals and departures.

· KAREN JOY FOWLER ·

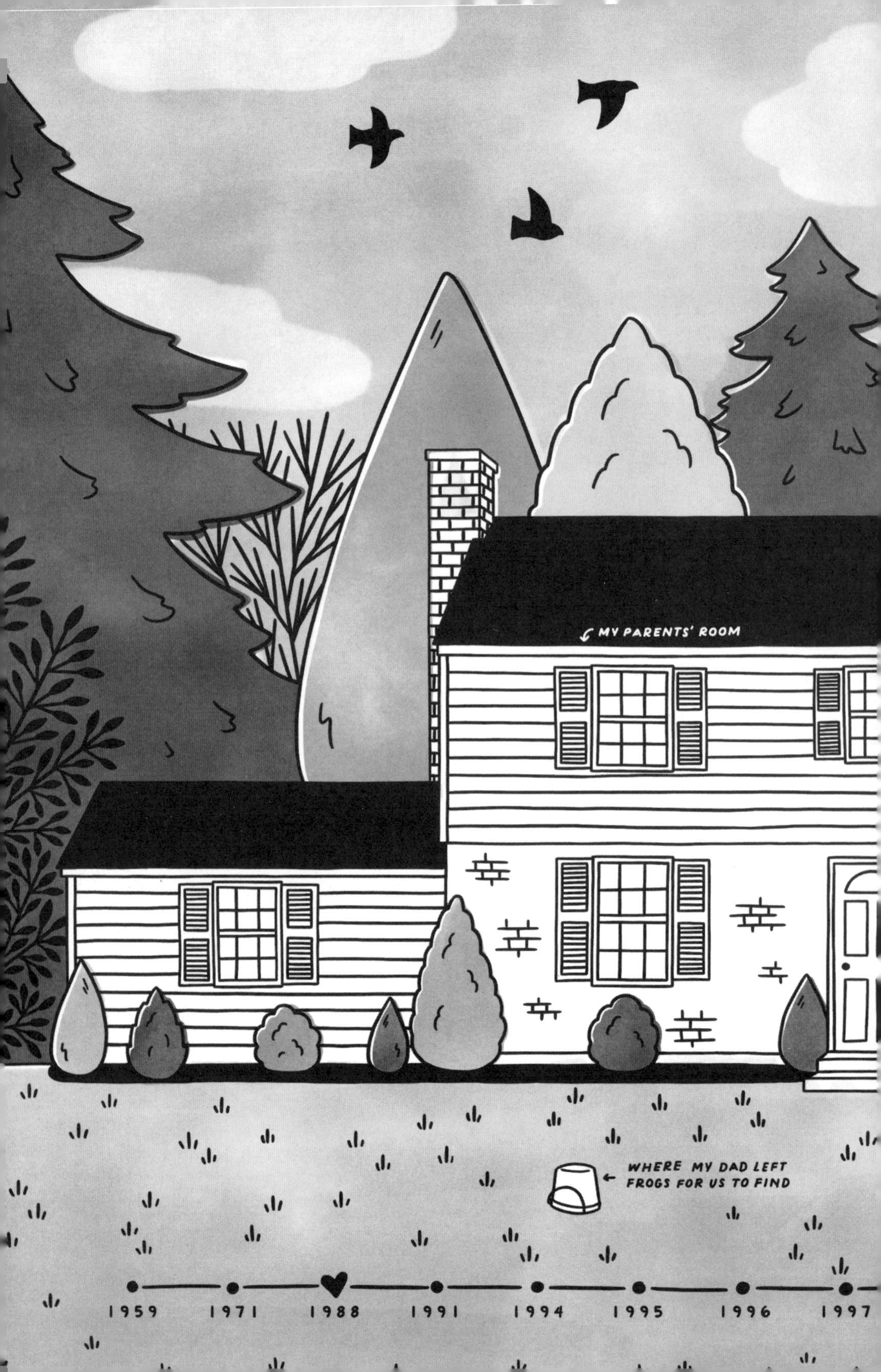
MY PARENTS' ROOM
WHERE MY DAD LEFT FROGS FOR US TO FIND
1959
1971
1988
1991
1994
1995
1996
1997

CHAPTER 01

The Secret

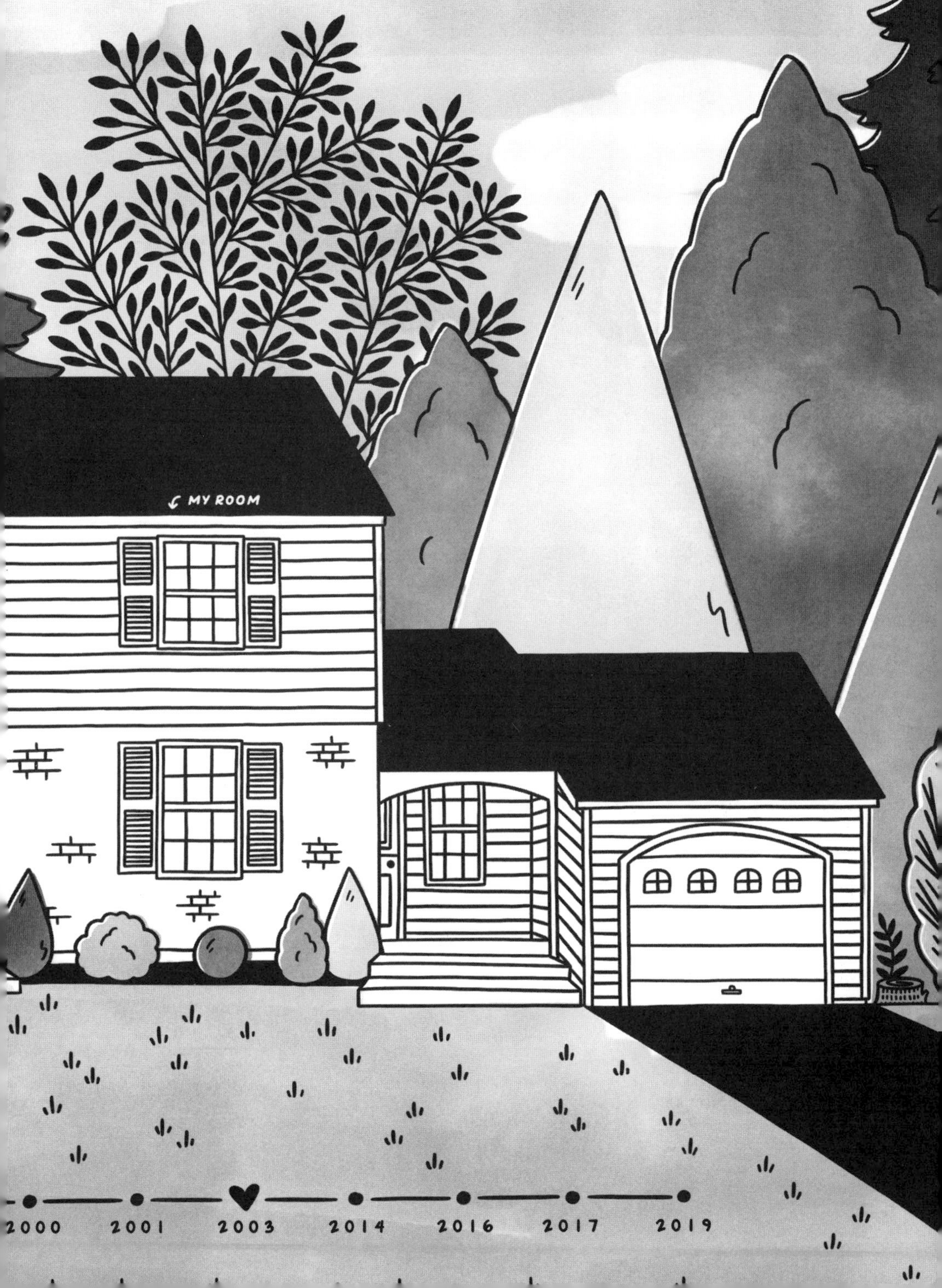
MY ROOM
2000
2001
2003
2014
2016
2017
2019

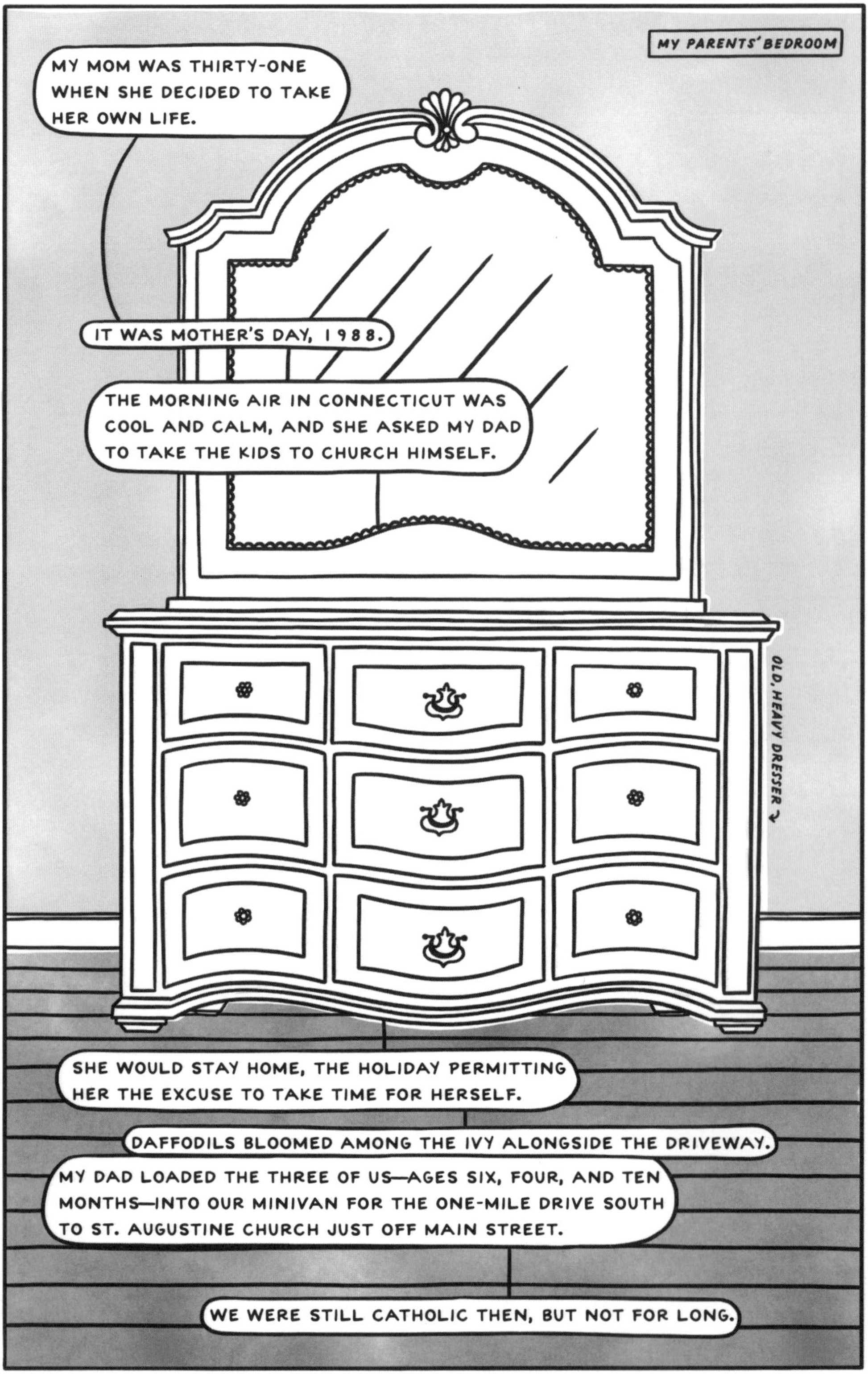
MY PARENTS' BEDROOM
MY MOM WAS THIRTY-ONE WHEN SHE DECIDED TO TAKE HER OWN LIFE.
IT WAS MOTHER'S DAY, 1988.
THE MORNING AIR IN CONNECTICUT WAS COOL AND CALM, AND SHE ASKED MY DAD TO TAKE THE KIDS TO CHURCH HIMSELF.
OLD, HEAVY DRESSER
SHE WOULD STAY HOME, THE HOLIDAY PERMITTING HER THE EXCUSE TO TAKE TIME FOR HERSELF.
DAFFODILS BLOOMED AMONG THE IVY ALONGSIDE THE DRIVEWAY.
MY DAD LOADED THE THREE OF US—AGES SIX, FOUR, AND TEN MONTHS—INTO OUR MINIVAN FOR THE ONE-MILE DRIVE SOUTH TO ST. AUGUSTINE CHURCH JUST OFF MAIN STREET.
WE WERE STILL CATHOLIC THEN, BUT NOT FOR LONG.

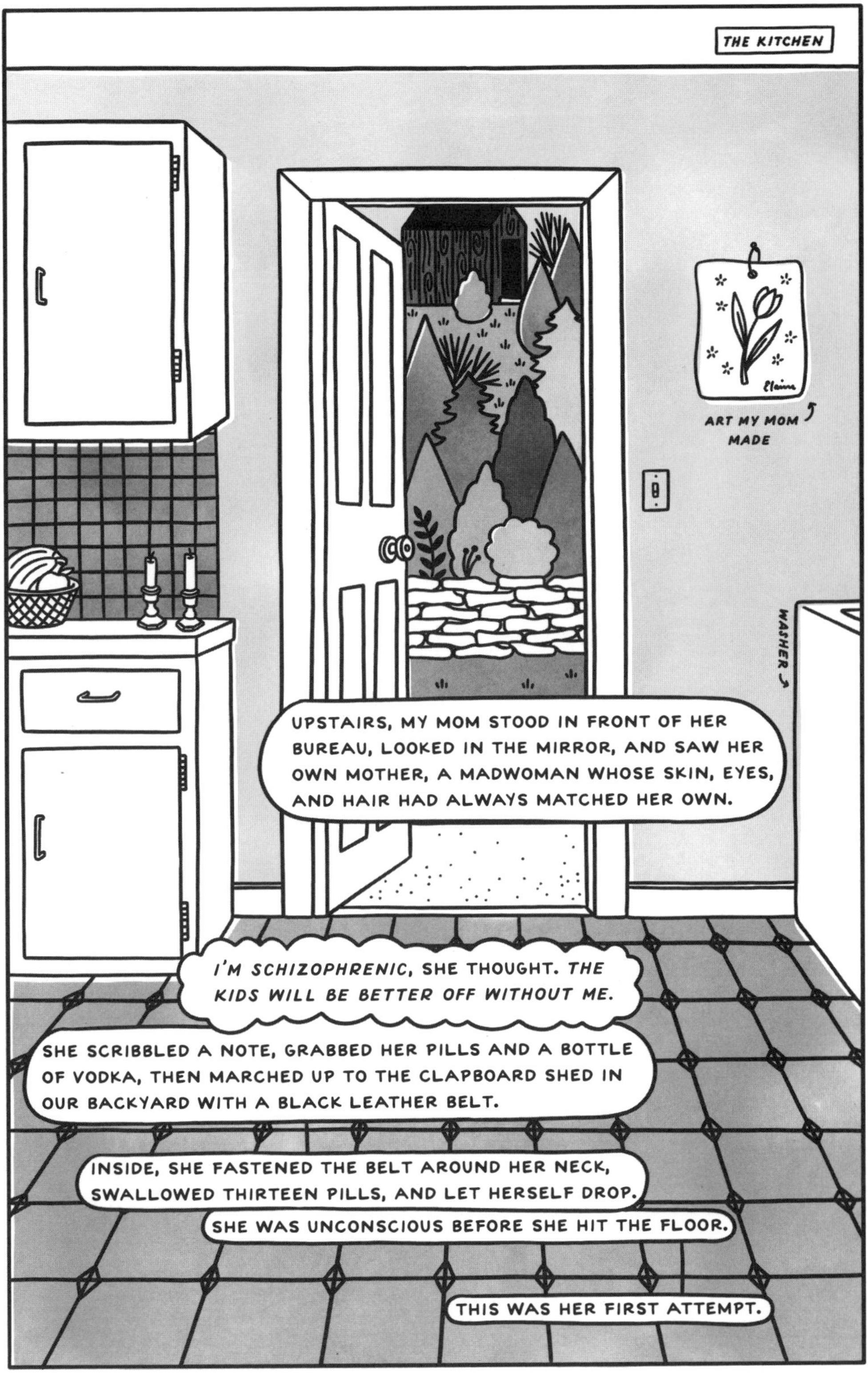
THE KITCHEN
ART MY MOM MADE
Elaine
WASHER
UPSTAIRS, MY MOM STOOD IN FRONT OF HER BUREAU, LOOKED IN THE MIRROR, AND SAW HER OWN MOTHER, A MADWOMAN WHOSE SKIN, EYES, AND HAIR HAD ALWAYS MATCHED HER OWN.
I'M SCHIZOPHRENIC, SHE THOUGHT. *THE KIDS WILL BE BETTER OFF WITHOUT ME.*
SHE SCRIBBLED A NOTE, GRABBED HER PILLS AND A BOTTLE OF VODKA, THEN MARCHED UP TO THE CLAPBOARD SHED IN OUR BACKYARD WITH A BLACK LEATHER BELT.
INSIDE, SHE FASTENED THE BELT AROUND HER NECK, SWALLOWED THIRTEEN PILLS, AND LET HERSELF DROP.
SHE WAS UNCONSCIOUS BEFORE SHE HIT THE FLOOR.
THIS WAS HER FIRST ATTEMPT.

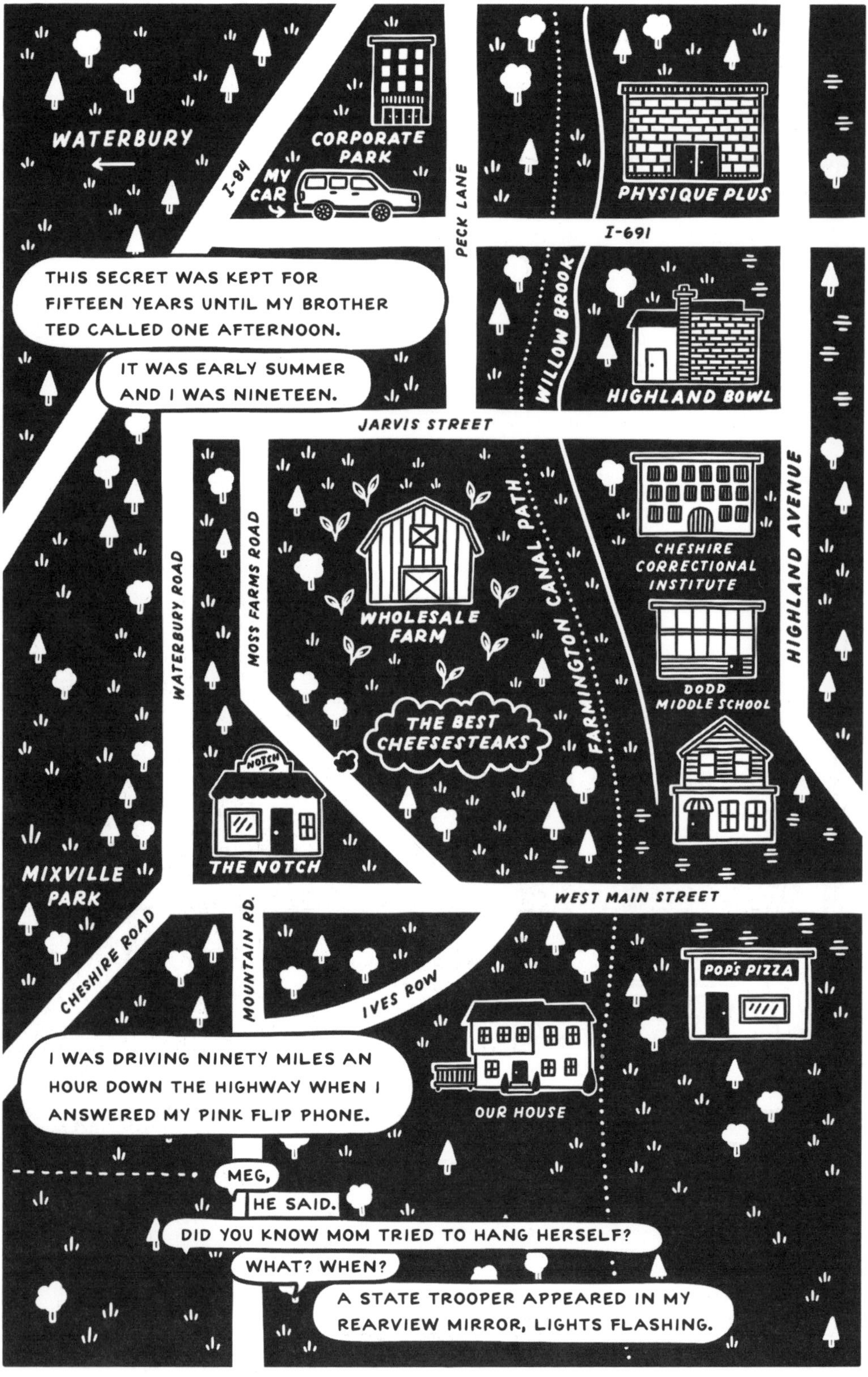
WATERBURY
I-84
CORPORATE PARK
MY CAR
PECK LANE
PHYSIQUE PLUS
I-691
THIS SECRET WAS KEPT FOR FIFTEEN YEARS UNTIL MY BROTHER TED CALLED ONE AFTERNOON.
IT WAS EARLY SUMMER AND I WAS NINETEEN.
WILLOW BROOK
HIGHLAND BOWL
JARVIS STREET
HIGHLAND AVENUE
CHESHIRE CORRECTIONAL INSTITUTE
DODD MIDDLE SCHOOL
WATERBURY ROAD
MOSS FARMS ROAD
WHOLESALE FARM
FARMINGTON CANAL PATH
THE BEST CHEESESTEAKS
NOTCH
THE NOTCH
MIXVILLE PARK
WEST MAIN STREET
CHESHIRE ROAD
MOUNTAIN RD.
IVES ROW
POP'S PIZZA
OUR HOUSE
I WAS DRIVING NINETY MILES AN HOUR DOWN THE HIGHWAY WHEN I ANSWERED MY PINK FLIP PHONE.
MEG,
HE SAID.
DID YOU KNOW MOM TRIED TO HANG HERSELF?
WHAT? WHEN?
A STATE TROOPER APPEARED IN MY REARVIEW MIRROR, LIGHTS FLASHING.

THIS IS A FAMILY NICKNAME. AS A CHILD I WORSHIPPED MY COUSIN MEGHAN AND DEMANDED THAT EVERYONE CALL ME "MEG"

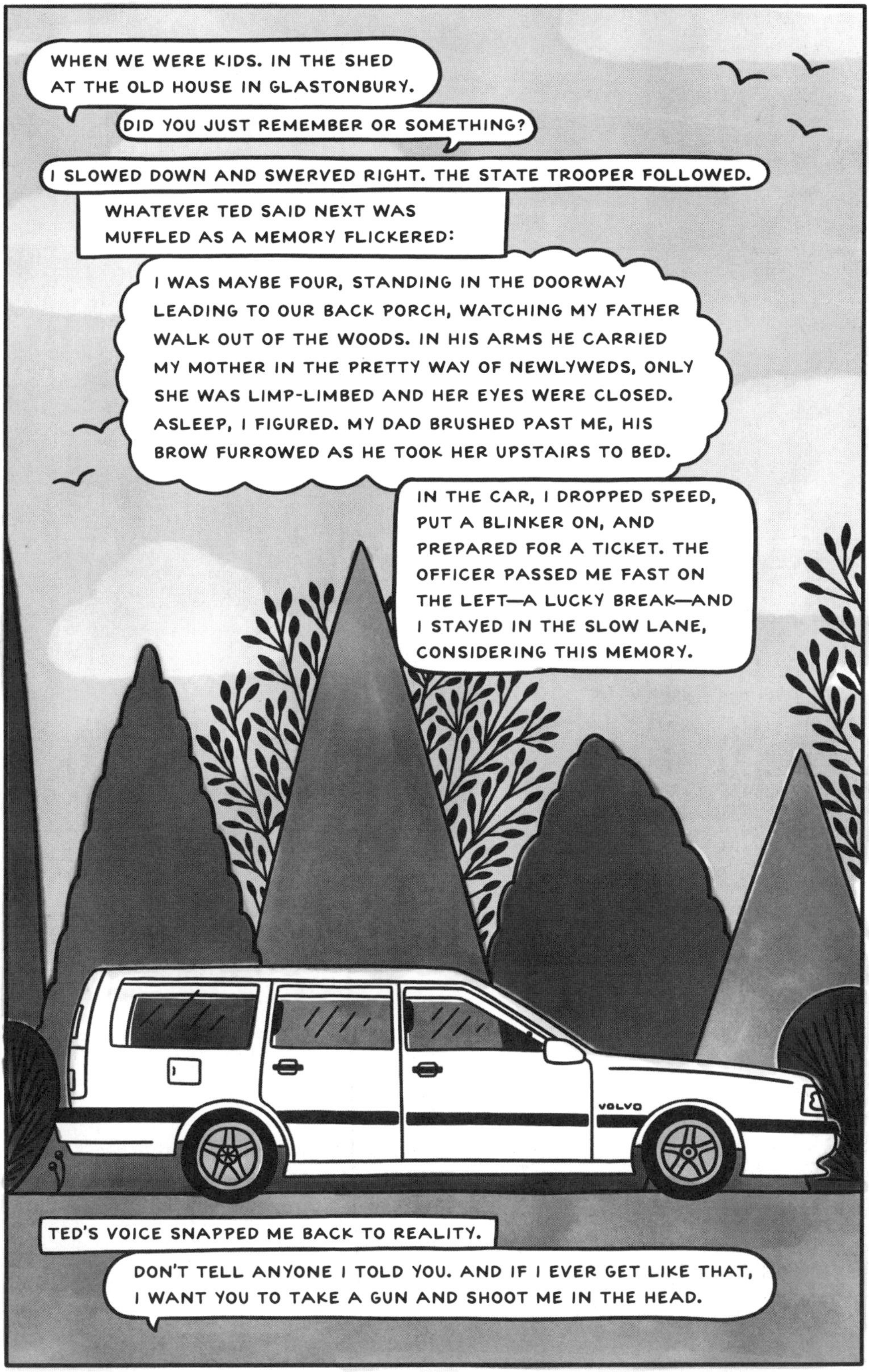
WHEN WE WERE KIDS. IN THE SHED AT THE OLD HOUSE IN GLASTONBURY.
DID YOU JUST REMEMBER OR SOMETHING?
I SLOWED DOWN AND SWERVED RIGHT. THE STATE TROOPER FOLLOWED.
WHATEVER TED SAID NEXT WAS MUFFLED AS A MEMORY FLICKERED:
I WAS MAYBE FOUR, STANDING IN THE DOORWAY LEADING TO OUR BACK PORCH, WATCHING MY FATHER WALK OUT OF THE WOODS. IN HIS ARMS HE CARRIED MY MOTHER IN THE PRETTY WAY OF NEWLYWEDS, ONLY SHE WAS LIMP-LIMBED AND HER EYES WERE CLOSED. ASLEEP, I FIGURED. MY DAD BRUSHED PAST ME, HIS BROW FURROWED AS HE TOOK HER UPSTAIRS TO BED.
IN THE CAR, I DROPPED SPEED, PUT A BLINKER ON, AND PREPARED FOR A TICKET. THE OFFICER PASSED ME FAST ON THE LEFT—A LUCKY BREAK—AND I STAYED IN THE SLOW LANE, CONSIDERING THIS MEMORY.
VOLVO
TED'S VOICE SNAPPED ME BACK TO REALITY.
DON'T TELL ANYONE I TOLD YOU. AND IF I EVER GET LIKE THAT, I WANT YOU TO TAKE A GUN AND SHOOT ME IN THE HEAD.

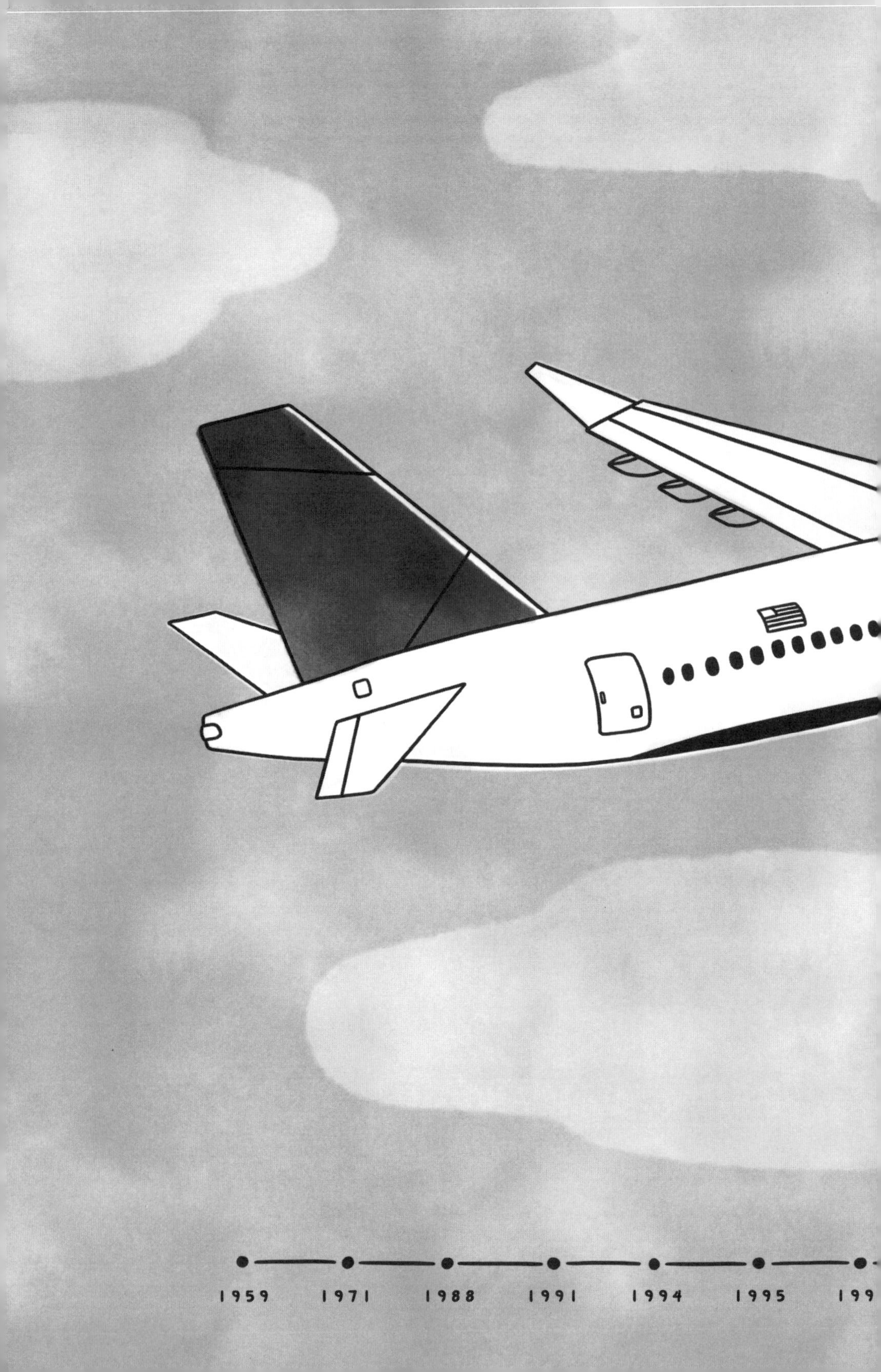
1959
1971
1988
1991
1994
1995

CHAPTER 02
The Trip Home

PART I

1997   2000   2001   2003   2014   2016   2017   2019

IN 2016, THIRTEEN YEARS AFTER MY BROTHER
SPILLED THE SECRET, I BIT MY LIP AS I WAITED FOR
HIM AT THE AIRPORT IN CONNECTICUT.

SINCE TED'S PHONE CALL IN 2003 I'D CIRCLED THE
SUBJECT OF MY FAMILY LIKE A TIGER CHAINED TO A
POLE, SCRATCHING AT OUR HISTORY, WONDERING WHAT
HAD HAPPENED TO MY MOM, AND, AS A RESULT, TO US.

MY PARENTS HAD KEPT SECRET THAT FIRST SUICIDE
ATTEMPT FOR SO LONG, WHAT ELSE WERE THEY HIDING?

WHAT ELSE DIDN'T I KNOW? A TRIP HOME MEANT
ANOTHER CHANCE TO ASK QUESTIONS.

FLIGHT Nº DELTA AIRLINES 3725	DESTINATION CLE → BDL	PASSENGER M KIMBALL	FLIGHT DELTA AIR 3725

PASSENGER
MARGARET KIMBALL

PASSENGER
M/KIMBALL

| GATE A12 | DEPARTURE 6:30 PM 3 NOV 2016 | ZONE D5 | SEAT 24C | DEPARTURE 6:30 PM |

TRACKING
4 507 659 3919 633

OPTIONS
CARRY

OPTIONS
CARRY

△ DELTA   △ DELTA

TED PULLED UP TO THE CURB AND POPPED THE TRUNK.

HE REMAINED IN THE DRIVER'S SEAT, HIS HEAD HUNG LOW
OVER THE CELL PHONE CRADLED IN HIS HANDS.

A PULLED-UP HOODIE OBSCURED HIS FACE.

HIS PUPPY LAY WITH ITS HEAD
DOWN IN THE PASSENGER SEAT,
GLOOMY AND LETHARGIC.

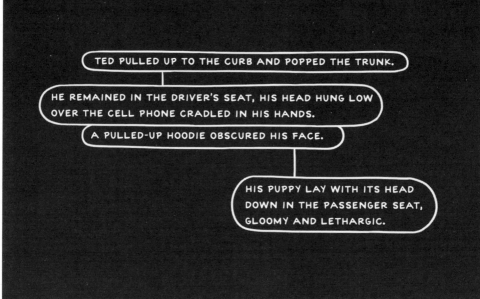

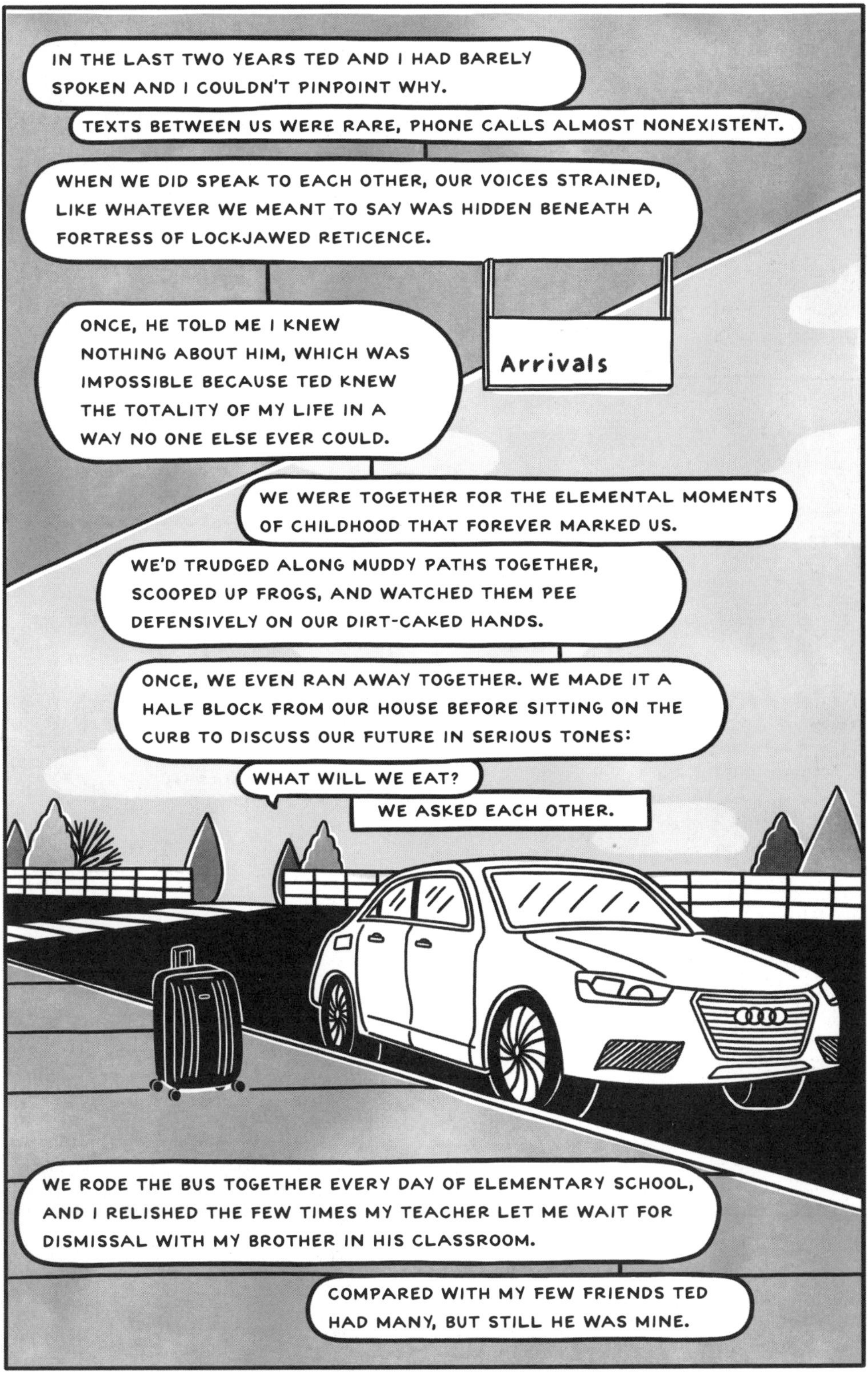
IN THE LAST TWO YEARS TED AND I HAD BARELY SPOKEN AND I COULDN'T PINPOINT WHY.
TEXTS BETWEEN US WERE RARE, PHONE CALLS ALMOST NONEXISTENT.
WHEN WE DID SPEAK TO EACH OTHER, OUR VOICES STRAINED, LIKE WHATEVER WE MEANT TO SAY WAS HIDDEN BENEATH A FORTRESS OF LOCKJAWED RETICENCE.
Arrivals
ONCE, HE TOLD ME I KNEW NOTHING ABOUT HIM, WHICH WAS IMPOSSIBLE BECAUSE TED KNEW THE TOTALITY OF MY LIFE IN A WAY NO ONE ELSE EVER COULD.
WE WERE TOGETHER FOR THE ELEMENTAL MOMENTS OF CHILDHOOD THAT FOREVER MARKED US.
WE'D TRUDGED ALONG MUDDY PATHS TOGETHER, SCOOPED UP FROGS, AND WATCHED THEM PEE DEFENSIVELY ON OUR DIRT-CAKED HANDS.
ONCE, WE EVEN RAN AWAY TOGETHER. WE MADE IT A HALF BLOCK FROM OUR HOUSE BEFORE SITTING ON THE CURB TO DISCUSS OUR FUTURE IN SERIOUS TONES:
WHAT WILL WE EAT?
WE ASKED EACH OTHER.
WE RODE THE BUS TOGETHER EVERY DAY OF ELEMENTARY SCHOOL, AND I RELISHED THE FEW TIMES MY TEACHER LET ME WAIT FOR DISMISSAL WITH MY BROTHER IN HIS CLASSROOM.
COMPARED WITH MY FEW FRIENDS TED HAD MANY, BUT STILL HE WAS MINE.

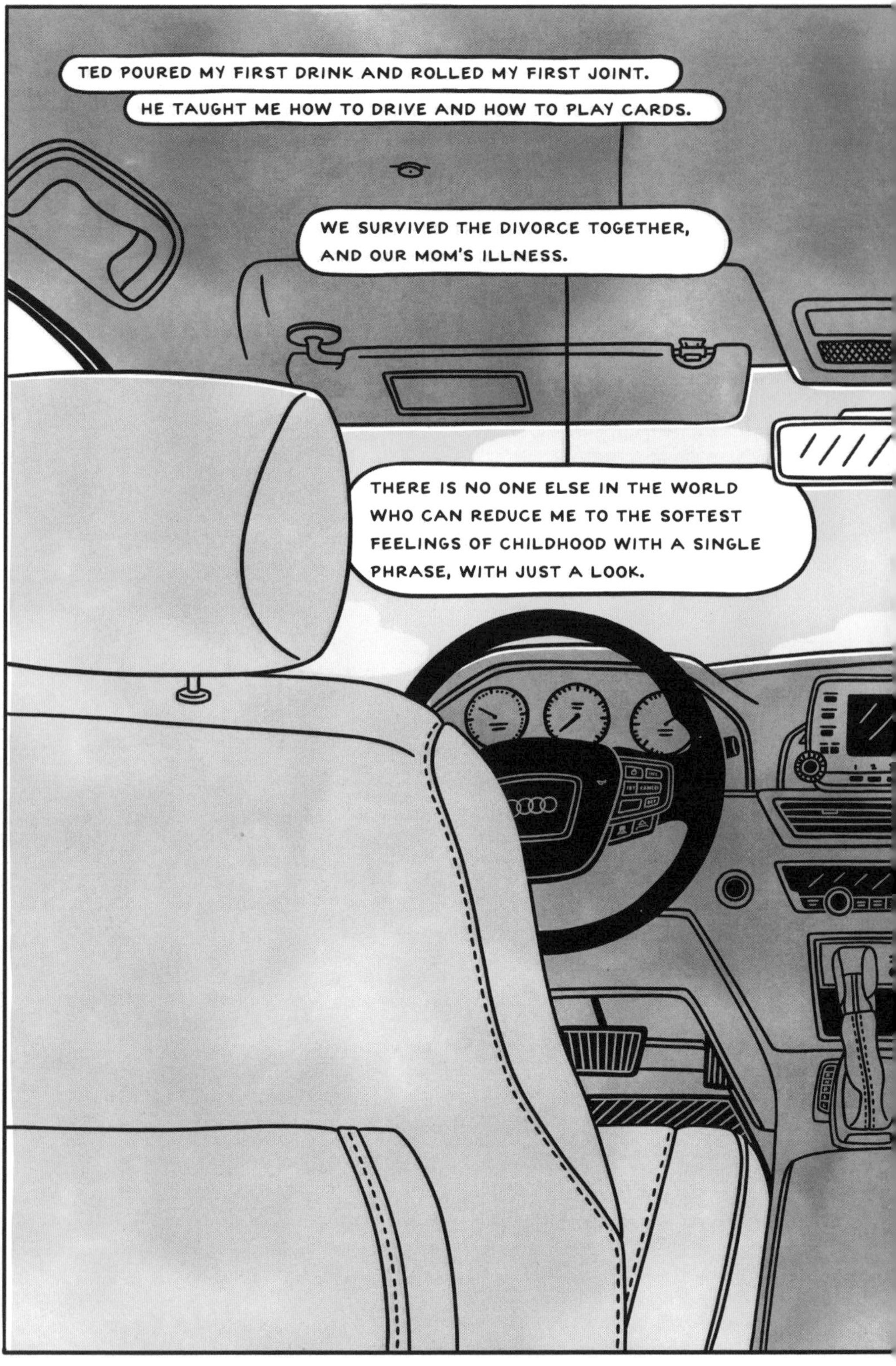
TED POURED MY FIRST DRINK AND ROLLED MY FIRST JOINT.
HE TAUGHT ME HOW TO DRIVE AND HOW TO PLAY CARDS.
WE SURVIVED THE DIVORCE TOGETHER, AND OUR MOM'S ILLNESS.
THERE IS NO ONE ELSE IN THE WORLD WHO CAN REDUCE ME TO THE SOFTEST FEELINGS OF CHILDHOOD WITH A SINGLE PHRASE, WITH JUST A LOOK.

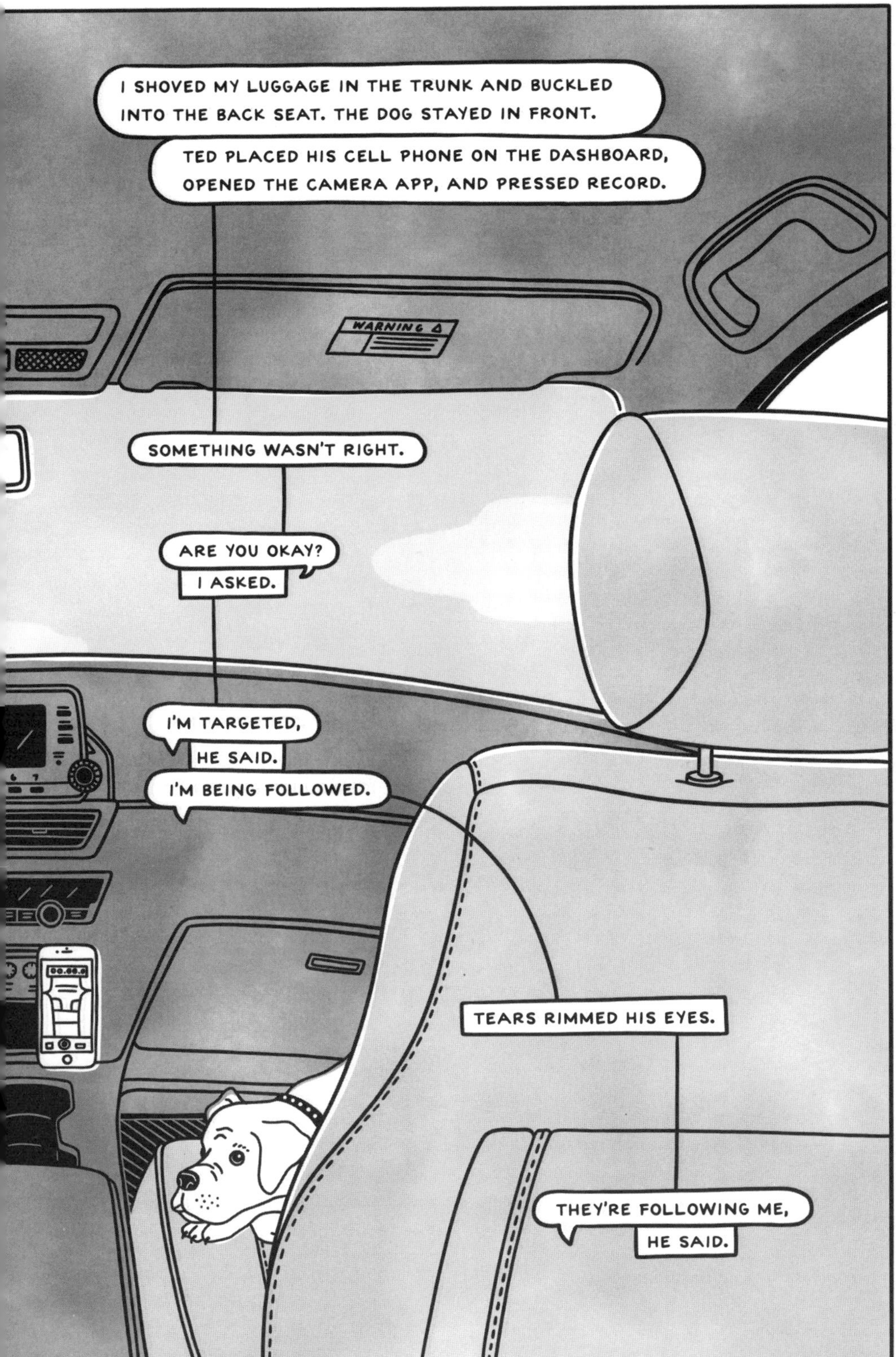
I SHOVED MY LUGGAGE IN THE TRUNK AND BUCKLED INTO THE BACK SEAT. THE DOG STAYED IN FRONT.
TED PLACED HIS CELL PHONE ON THE DASHBOARD, OPENED THE CAMERA APP, AND PRESSED RECORD.
WARNING
SOMETHING WASN'T RIGHT.
ARE YOU OKAY?
I ASKED.
I'M TARGETED,
HE SAID.
I'M BEING FOLLOWED.
TEARS RIMMED HIS EYES.
THEY'RE FOLLOWING ME,
HE SAID.

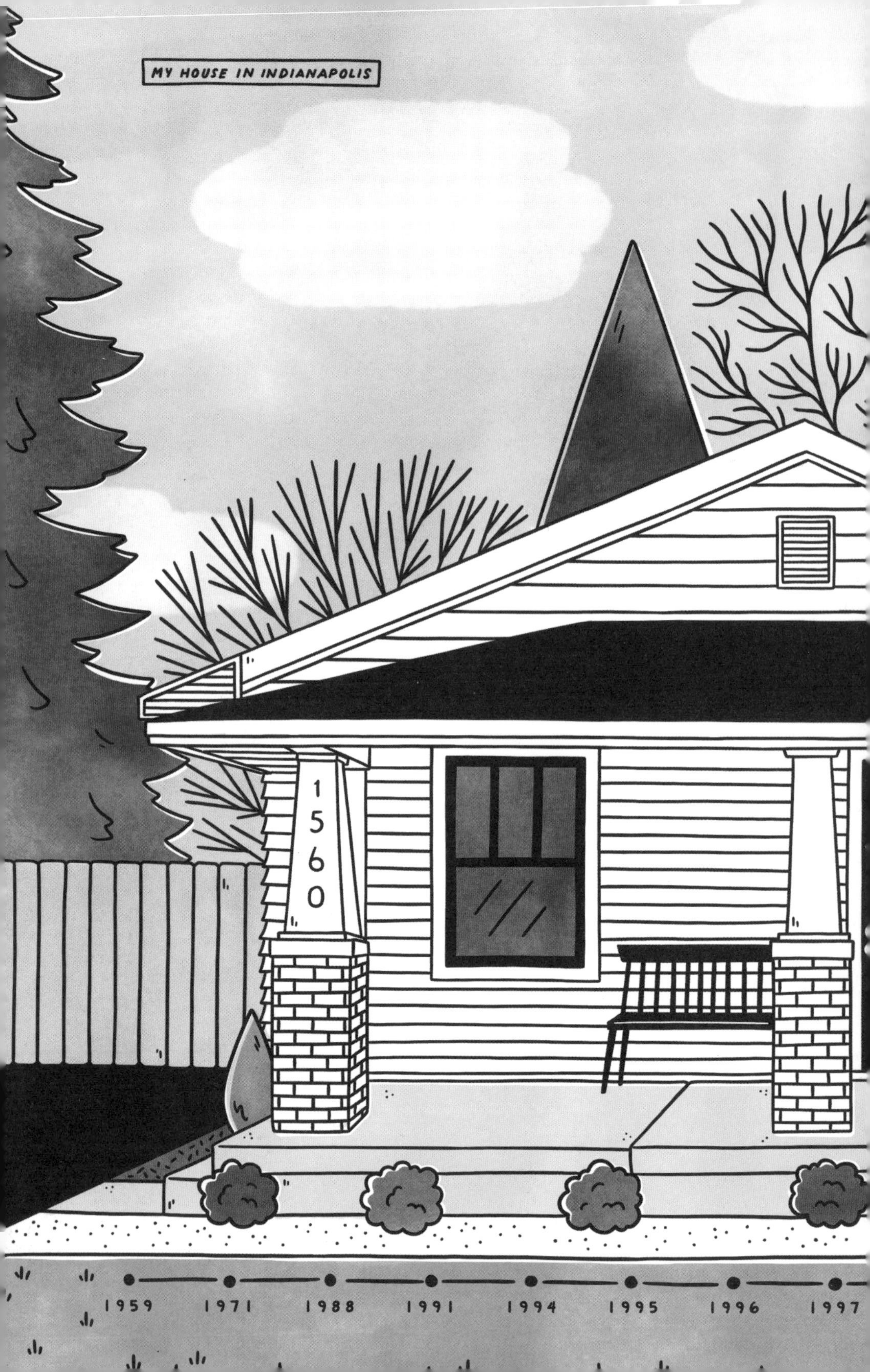

MY HOUSE IN INDIANAPOLIS
1560
1959
1971
1988
1991
1994
1995
1996
1997

CHAPTER 03

The Videos

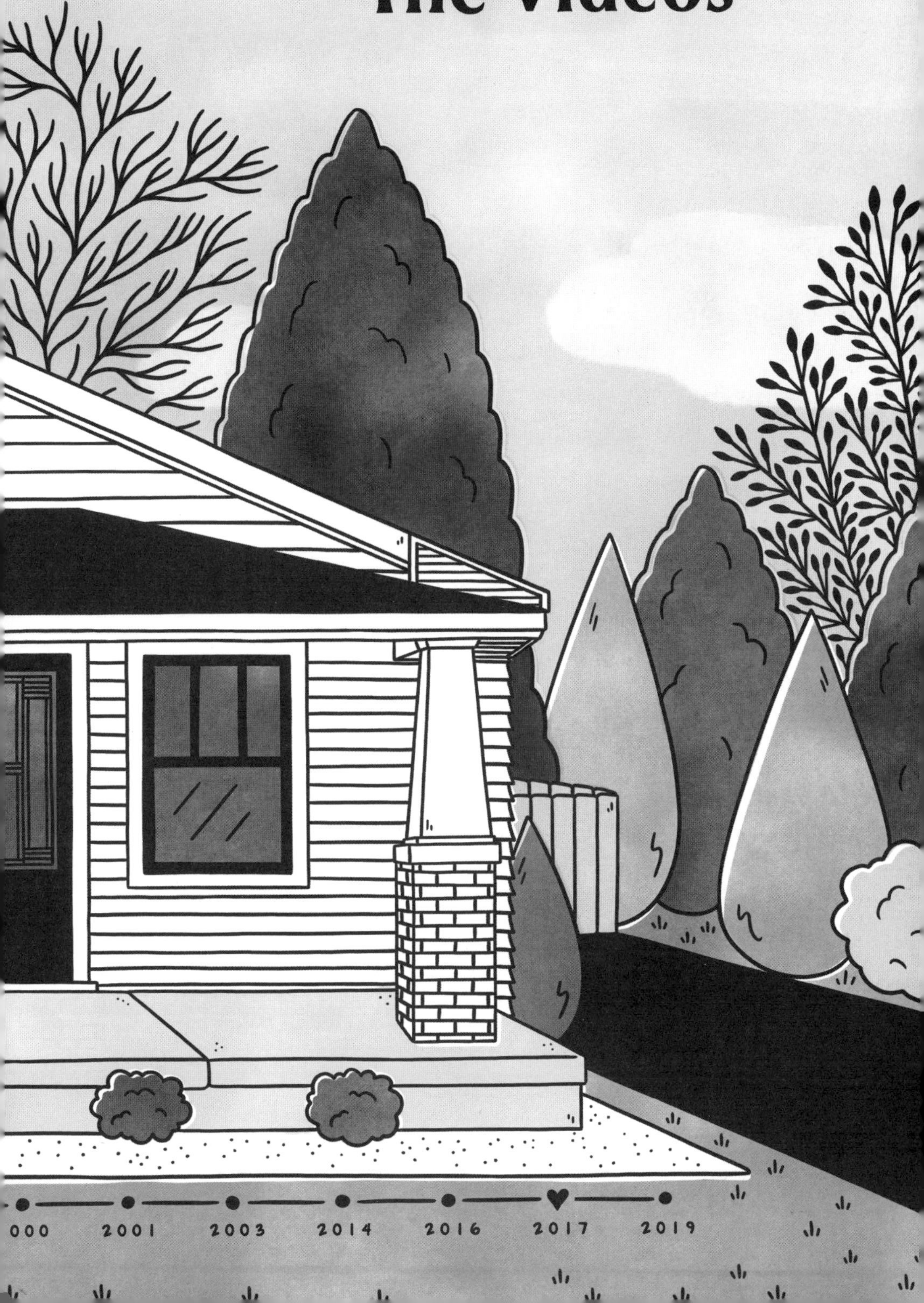
000
2001
2003
2014
2016
2017
2019

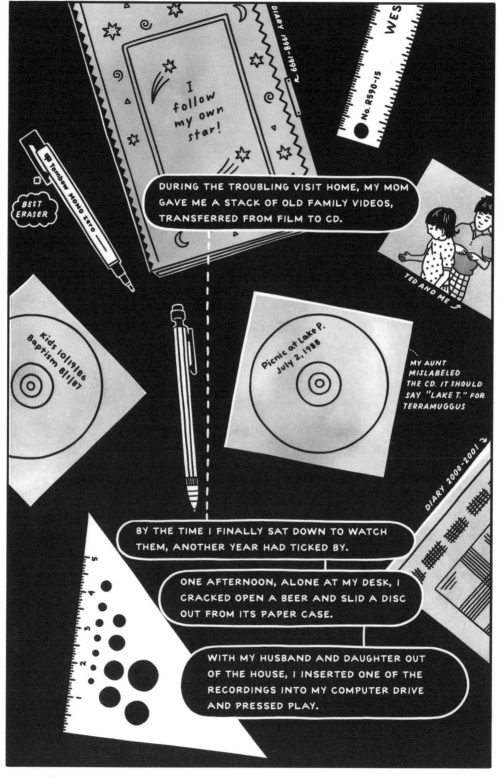

DIARY 1998-1999

I follow my own star!

WES

No. R590-15

BEST ERASER

Tombow MONO zero

DURING THE TROUBLING VISIT HOME, MY MOM GAVE ME A STACK OF OLD FAMILY VIDEOS, TRANSFERRED FROM FILM TO CD.

TED AND ME →

Kids 10/19/86 Baptism 8/1/87

Picnic at Lake P. July 2, 1988

MY AUNT MISLABELED THE CD. IT SHOULD SAY "LAKE T." FOR TERRAMUGGUS

DIARY 2000-2001 →

BY THE TIME I FINALLY SAT DOWN TO WATCH THEM, ANOTHER YEAR HAD TICKED BY.

ONE AFTERNOON, ALONE AT MY DESK, I CRACKED OPEN A BEER AND SLID A DISC OUT FROM ITS PAPER CASE.

WITH MY HUSBAND AND DAUGHTER OUT OF THE HOUSE, I INSERTED ONE OF THE RECORDINGS INTO MY COMPUTER DRIVE AND PRESSED PLAY.

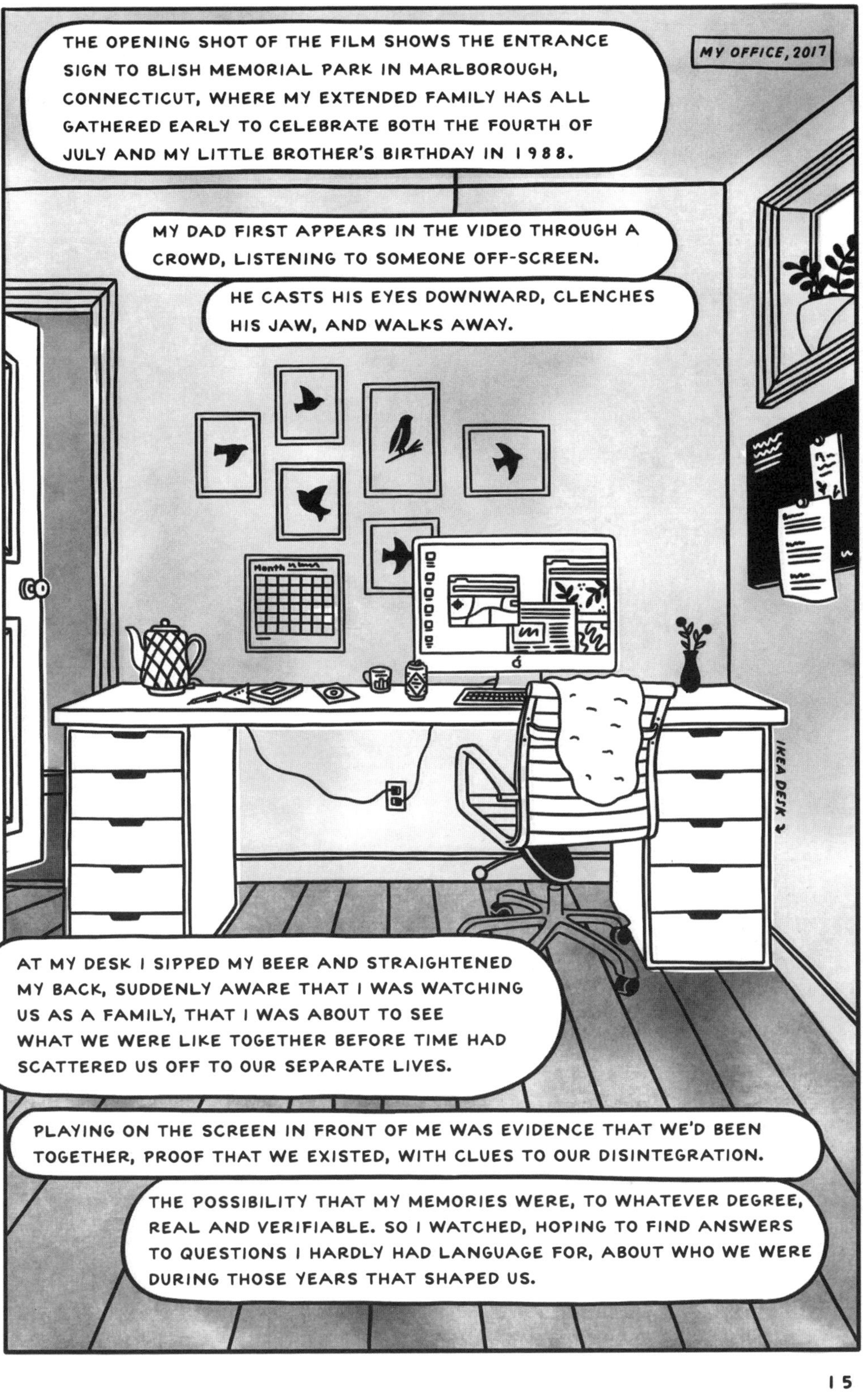
THE OPENING SHOT OF THE FILM SHOWS THE ENTRANCE SIGN TO BLISH MEMORIAL PARK IN MARLBOROUGH, CONNECTICUT, WHERE MY EXTENDED FAMILY HAS ALL GATHERED EARLY TO CELEBRATE BOTH THE FOURTH OF JULY AND MY LITTLE BROTHER'S BIRTHDAY IN 1988.
MY OFFICE, 2017
MY DAD FIRST APPEARS IN THE VIDEO THROUGH A CROWD, LISTENING TO SOMEONE OFF-SCREEN.
HE CASTS HIS EYES DOWNWARD, CLENCHES HIS JAW, AND WALKS AWAY.
IKEA DESK
AT MY DESK I SIPPED MY BEER AND STRAIGHTENED MY BACK, SUDDENLY AWARE THAT I WAS WATCHING US AS A FAMILY, THAT I WAS ABOUT TO SEE WHAT WE WERE LIKE TOGETHER BEFORE TIME HAD SCATTERED US OFF TO OUR SEPARATE LIVES.
PLAYING ON THE SCREEN IN FRONT OF ME WAS EVIDENCE THAT WE'D BEEN TOGETHER, PROOF THAT WE EXISTED, WITH CLUES TO OUR DISINTEGRATION.
THE POSSIBILITY THAT MY MEMORIES WERE, TO WHATEVER DEGREE, REAL AND VERIFIABLE. SO I WATCHED, HOPING TO FIND ANSWERS TO QUESTIONS I HARDLY HAD LANGUAGE FOR, ABOUT WHO WE WERE DURING THOSE YEARS THAT SHAPED US.

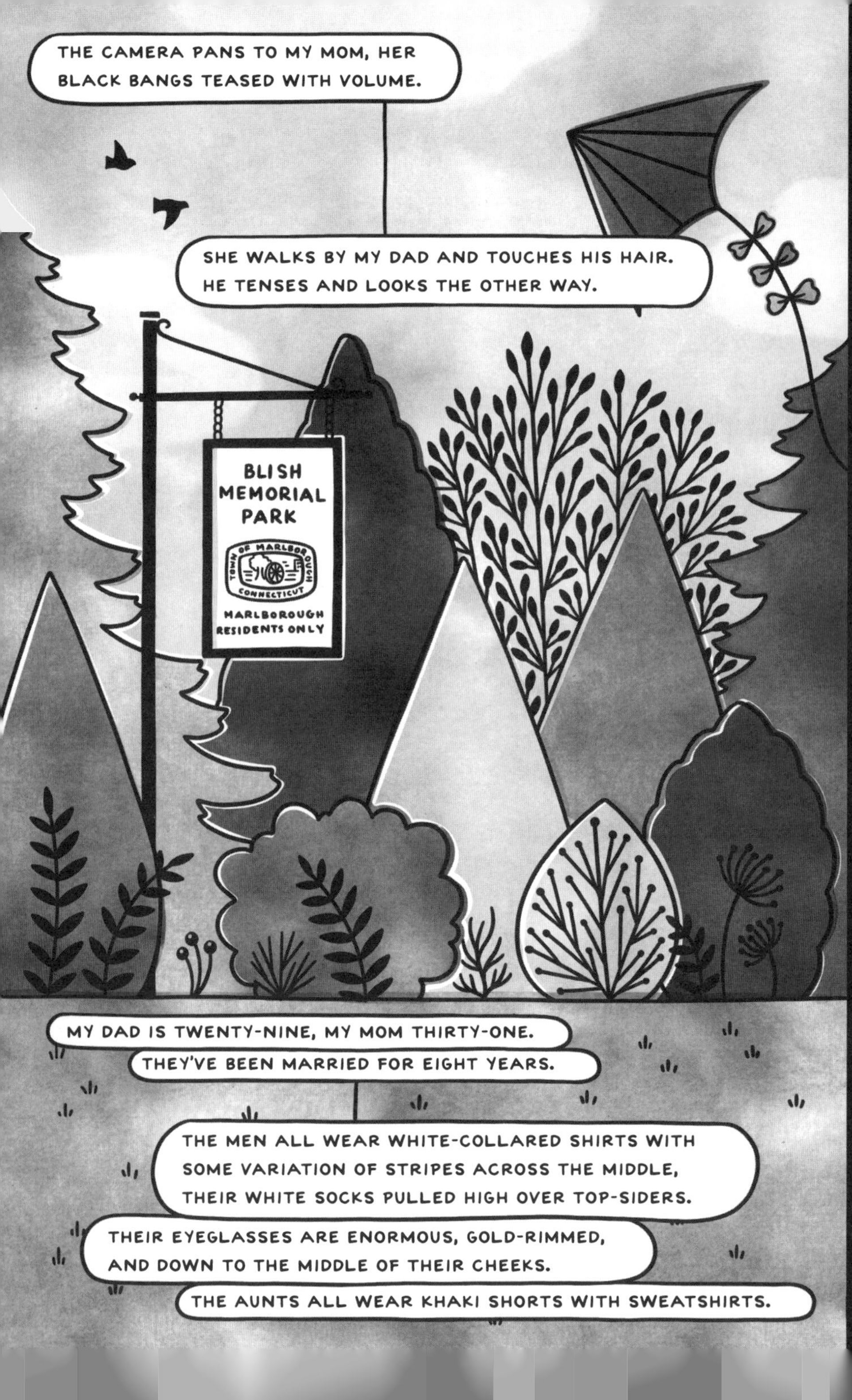
THE CAMERA PANS TO MY MOM, HER BLACK BANGS TEASED WITH VOLUME.
SHE WALKS BY MY DAD AND TOUCHES HIS HAIR. HE TENSES AND LOOKS THE OTHER WAY.
BLISH MEMORIAL PARK
TOWN OF MARLBOROUGH CONNECTICUT
MARLBOROUGH RESIDENTS ONLY
MY DAD IS TWENTY-NINE, MY MOM THIRTY-ONE.
THEY'VE BEEN MARRIED FOR EIGHT YEARS.
THE MEN ALL WEAR WHITE-COLLARED SHIRTS WITH SOME VARIATION OF STRIPES ACROSS THE MIDDLE, THEIR WHITE SOCKS PULLED HIGH OVER TOP-SIDERS.
THEIR EYEGLASSES ARE ENORMOUS, GOLD-RIMMED, AND DOWN TO THE MIDDLE OF THEIR CHEEKS.
THE AUNTS ALL WEAR KHAKI SHORTS WITH SWEATSHIRTS.

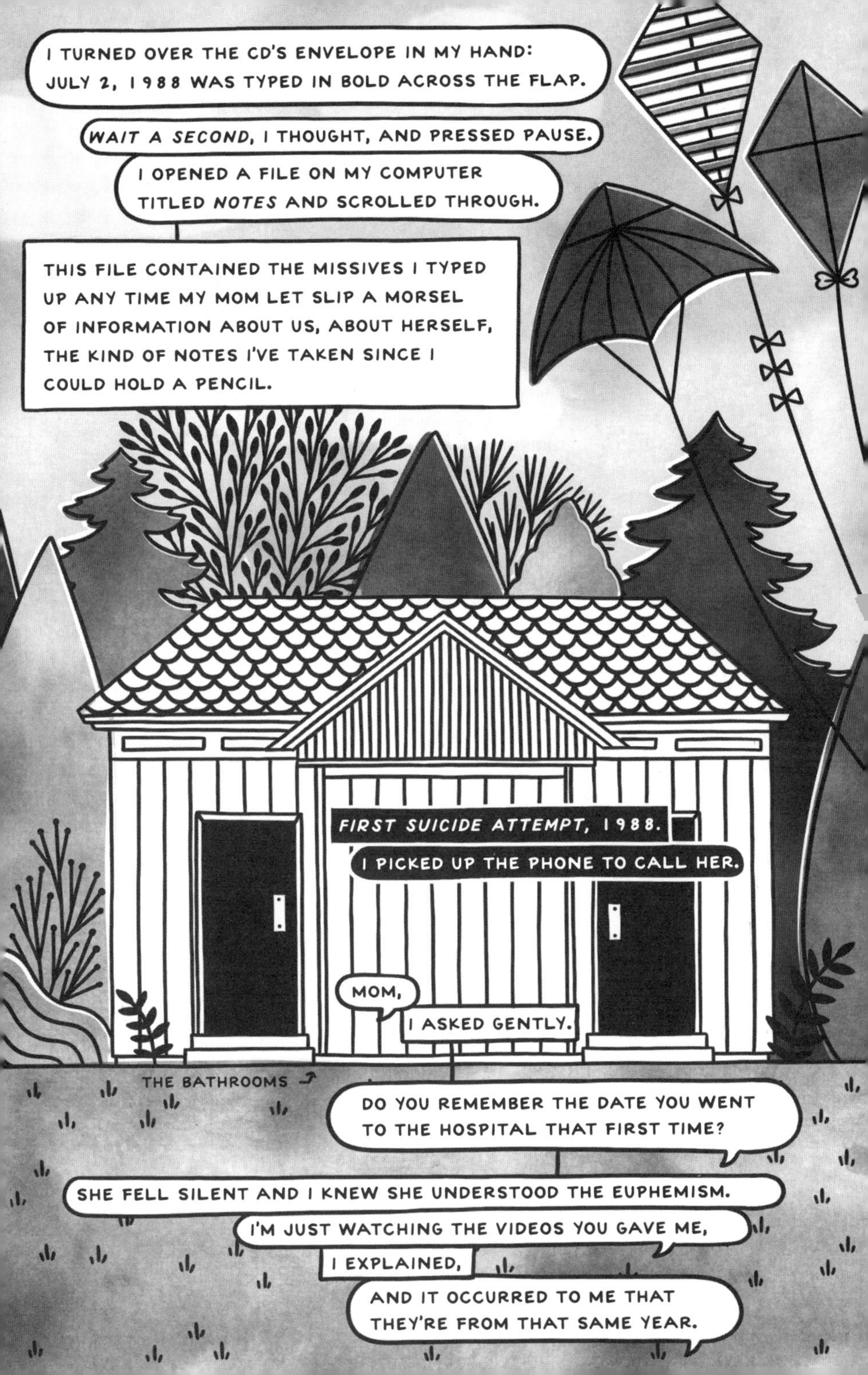
I TURNED OVER THE CD'S ENVELOPE IN MY HAND: JULY 2, 1988 WAS TYPED IN BOLD ACROSS THE FLAP.
WAIT A SECOND, I THOUGHT, AND PRESSED PAUSE.
I OPENED A FILE ON MY COMPUTER TITLED *NOTES* AND SCROLLED THROUGH.
THIS FILE CONTAINED THE MISSIVES I TYPED UP ANY TIME MY MOM LET SLIP A MORSEL OF INFORMATION ABOUT US, ABOUT HERSELF, THE KIND OF NOTES I'VE TAKEN SINCE I COULD HOLD A PENCIL.
FIRST SUICIDE ATTEMPT, 1988.
I PICKED UP THE PHONE TO CALL HER.
MOM,
I ASKED GENTLY.
THE BATHROOMS
DO YOU REMEMBER THE DATE YOU WENT TO THE HOSPITAL THAT FIRST TIME?
SHE FELL SILENT AND I KNEW SHE UNDERSTOOD THE EUPHEMISM.
I'M JUST WATCHING THE VIDEOS YOU GAVE ME,
I EXPLAINED,
AND IT OCCURRED TO ME THAT THEY'RE FROM THAT SAME YEAR.

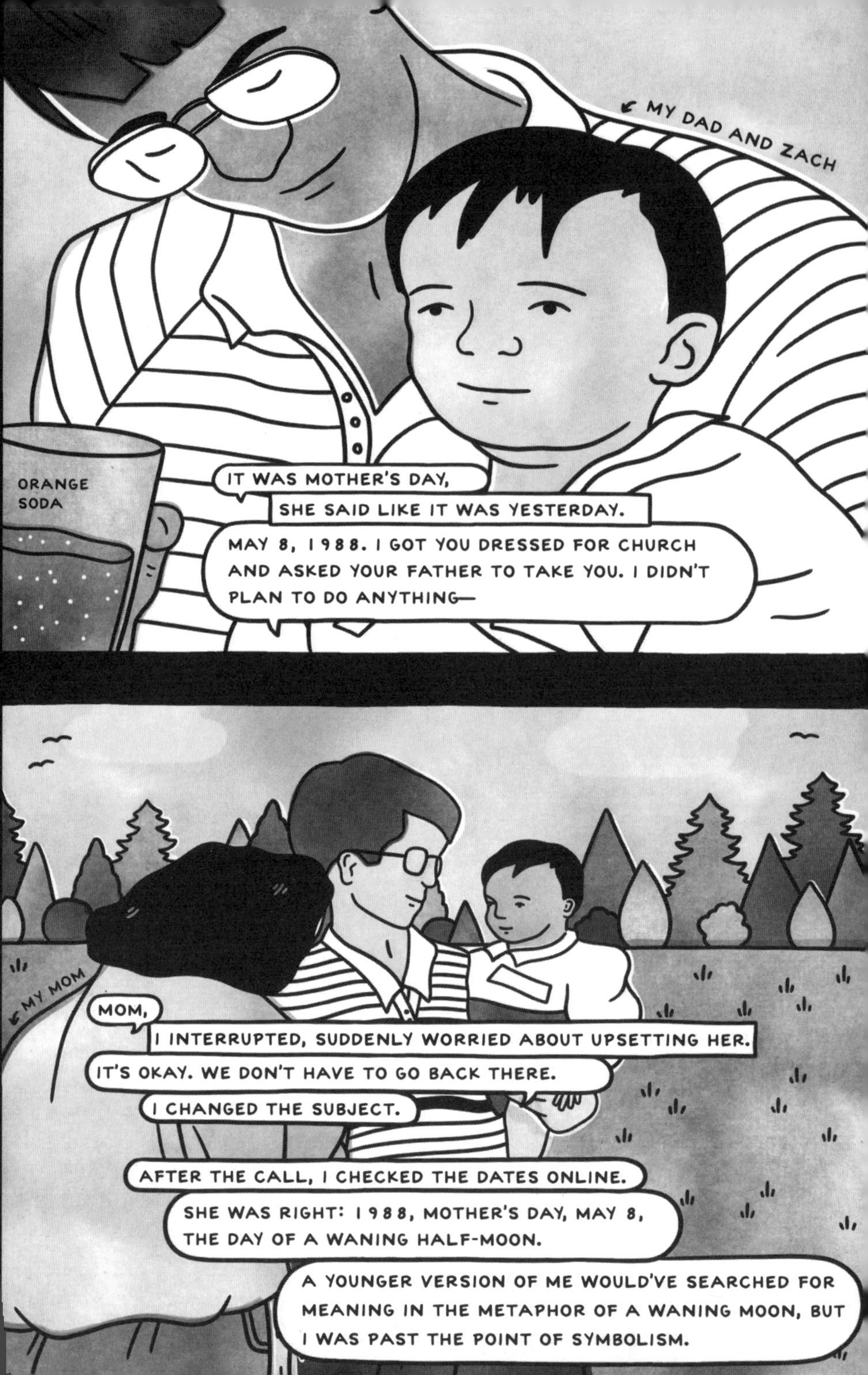
MY DAD AND ZACH
ORANGE SODA
IT WAS MOTHER'S DAY,
SHE SAID LIKE IT WAS YESTERDAY.
MAY 8, 1988. I GOT YOU DRESSED FOR CHURCH AND ASKED YOUR FATHER TO TAKE YOU. I DIDN'T PLAN TO DO ANYTHING—
MY MOM
MOM,
I INTERRUPTED, SUDDENLY WORRIED ABOUT UPSETTING HER.
IT'S OKAY. WE DON'T HAVE TO GO BACK THERE.
I CHANGED THE SUBJECT.
AFTER THE CALL, I CHECKED THE DATES ONLINE.
SHE WAS RIGHT: 1988, MOTHER'S DAY, MAY 8, THE DAY OF A WANING HALF-MOON.
A YOUNGER VERSION OF ME WOULD'VE SEARCHED FOR MEANING IN THE METAPHOR OF A WANING MOON, BUT I WAS PAST THE POINT OF SYMBOLISM.

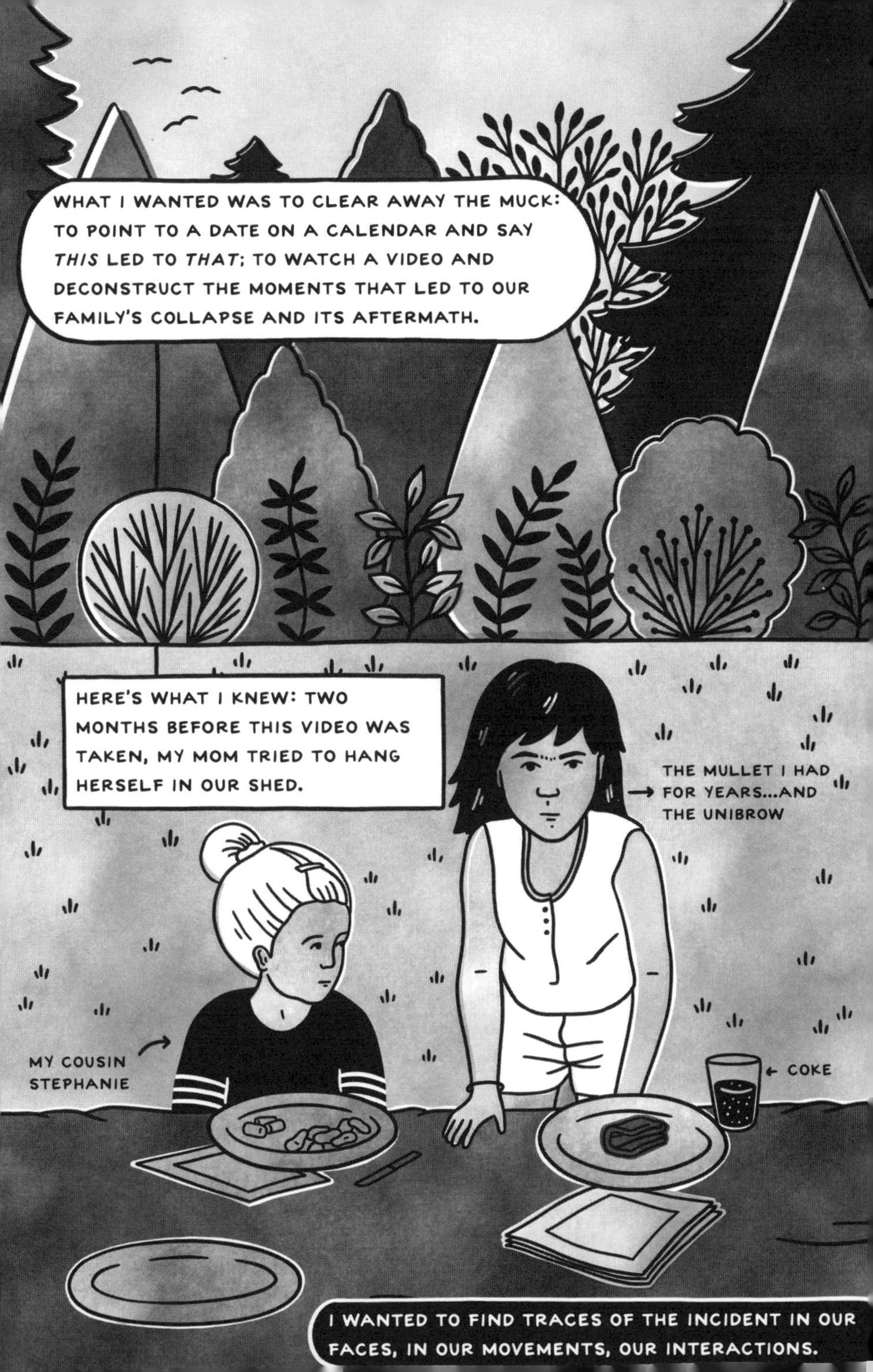
WHAT I WANTED WAS TO CLEAR AWAY THE MUCK: TO POINT TO A DATE ON A CALENDAR AND SAY *THIS* LED TO *THAT*; TO WATCH A VIDEO AND DECONSTRUCT THE MOMENTS THAT LED TO OUR FAMILY'S COLLAPSE AND ITS AFTERMATH.
HERE'S WHAT I KNEW: TWO MONTHS BEFORE THIS VIDEO WAS TAKEN, MY MOM TRIED TO HANG HERSELF IN OUR SHED.
THE MULLET I HAD FOR YEARS...AND THE UNIBROW
MY COUSIN STEPHANIE
COKE
I WANTED TO FIND TRACES OF THE INCIDENT IN OUR FACES, IN OUR MOVEMENTS, OUR INTERACTIONS.

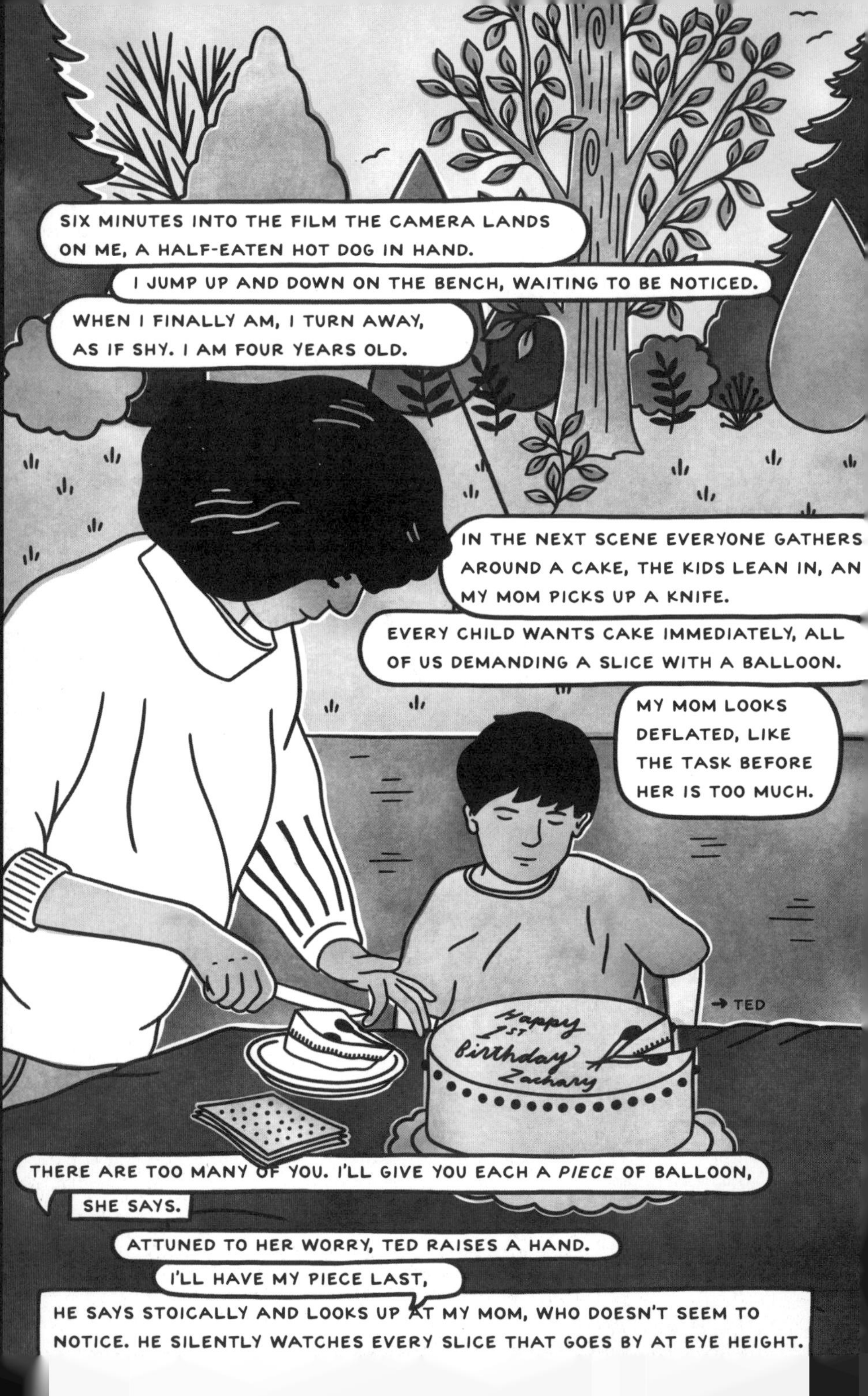
SIX MINUTES INTO THE FILM THE CAMERA LANDS ON ME, A HALF-EATEN HOT DOG IN HAND.
I JUMP UP AND DOWN ON THE BENCH, WAITING TO BE NOTICED.
WHEN I FINALLY AM, I TURN AWAY, AS IF SHY. I AM FOUR YEARS OLD.
IN THE NEXT SCENE EVERYONE GATHERS AROUND A CAKE, THE KIDS LEAN IN, AN MY MOM PICKS UP A KNIFE.
EVERY CHILD WANTS CAKE IMMEDIATELY, ALL OF US DEMANDING A SLICE WITH A BALLOON.
MY MOM LOOKS DEFLATED, LIKE THE TASK BEFORE HER IS TOO MUCH.
→ TED
Happy 1st Birthday Zachary
THERE ARE TOO MANY OF YOU. I'LL GIVE YOU EACH A *PIECE* OF BALLOON,
SHE SAYS.
ATTUNED TO HER WORRY, TED RAISES A HAND.
I'LL HAVE MY PIECE LAST,
HE SAYS STOICALLY AND LOOKS UP AT MY MOM, WHO DOESN'T SEEM TO NOTICE. HE SILENTLY WATCHES EVERY SLICE THAT GOES BY AT EYE HEIGHT.

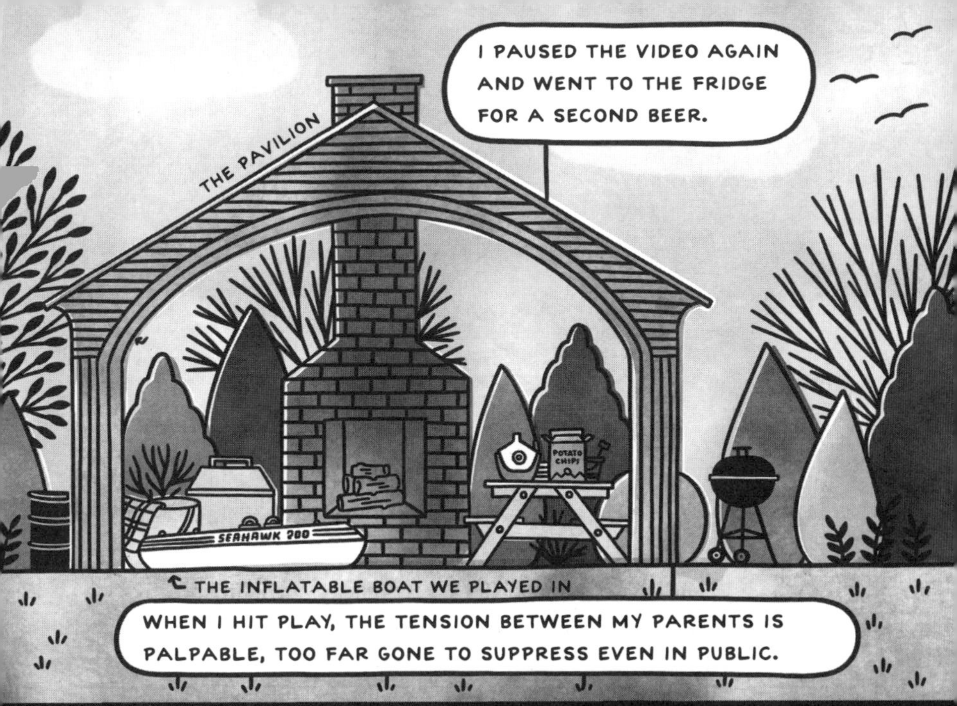
I PAUSED THE VIDEO AGAIN AND WENT TO THE FRIDGE FOR A SECOND BEER.
THE PAVILION
POTATO CHIPS
SEAHAWK 200
THE INFLATABLE BOAT WE PLAYED IN
WHEN I HIT PLAY, THE TENSION BETWEEN MY PARENTS IS PALPABLE, TOO FAR GONE TO SUPPRESS EVEN IN PUBLIC.

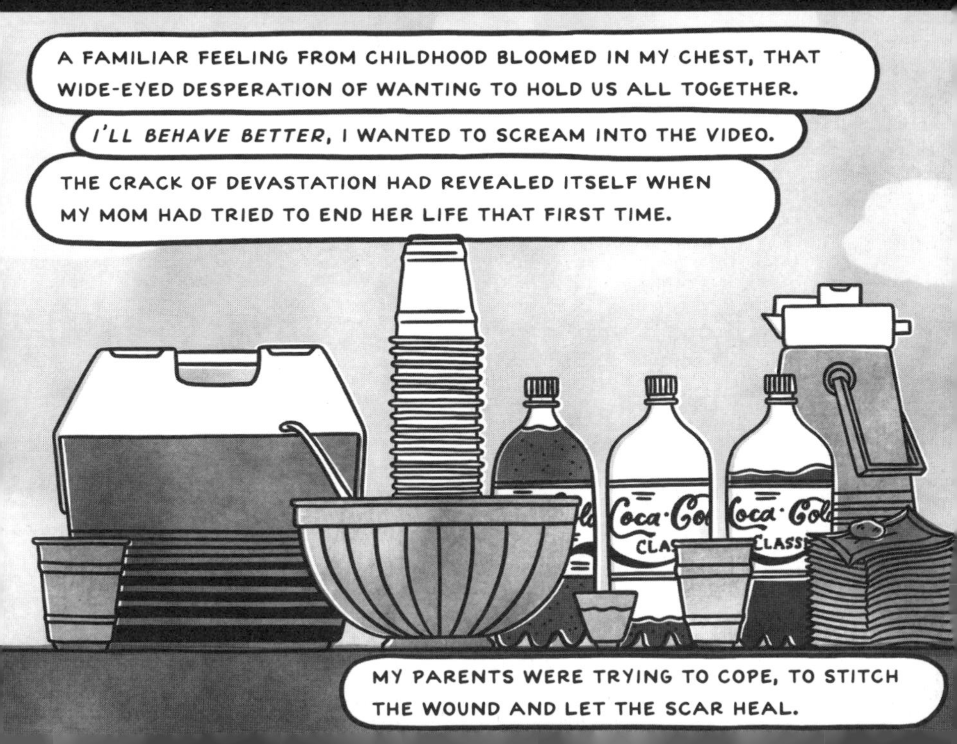
A FAMILIAR FEELING FROM CHILDHOOD BLOOMED IN MY CHEST, THAT WIDE-EYED DESPERATION OF WANTING TO HOLD US ALL TOGETHER.
I'LL BEHAVE BETTER, I WANTED TO SCREAM INTO THE VIDEO.
THE CRACK OF DEVASTATION HAD REVEALED ITSELF WHEN MY MOM HAD TRIED TO END HER LIFE THAT FIRST TIME.
MY PARENTS WERE TRYING TO COPE, TO STITCH THE WOUND AND LET THE SCAR HEAL.

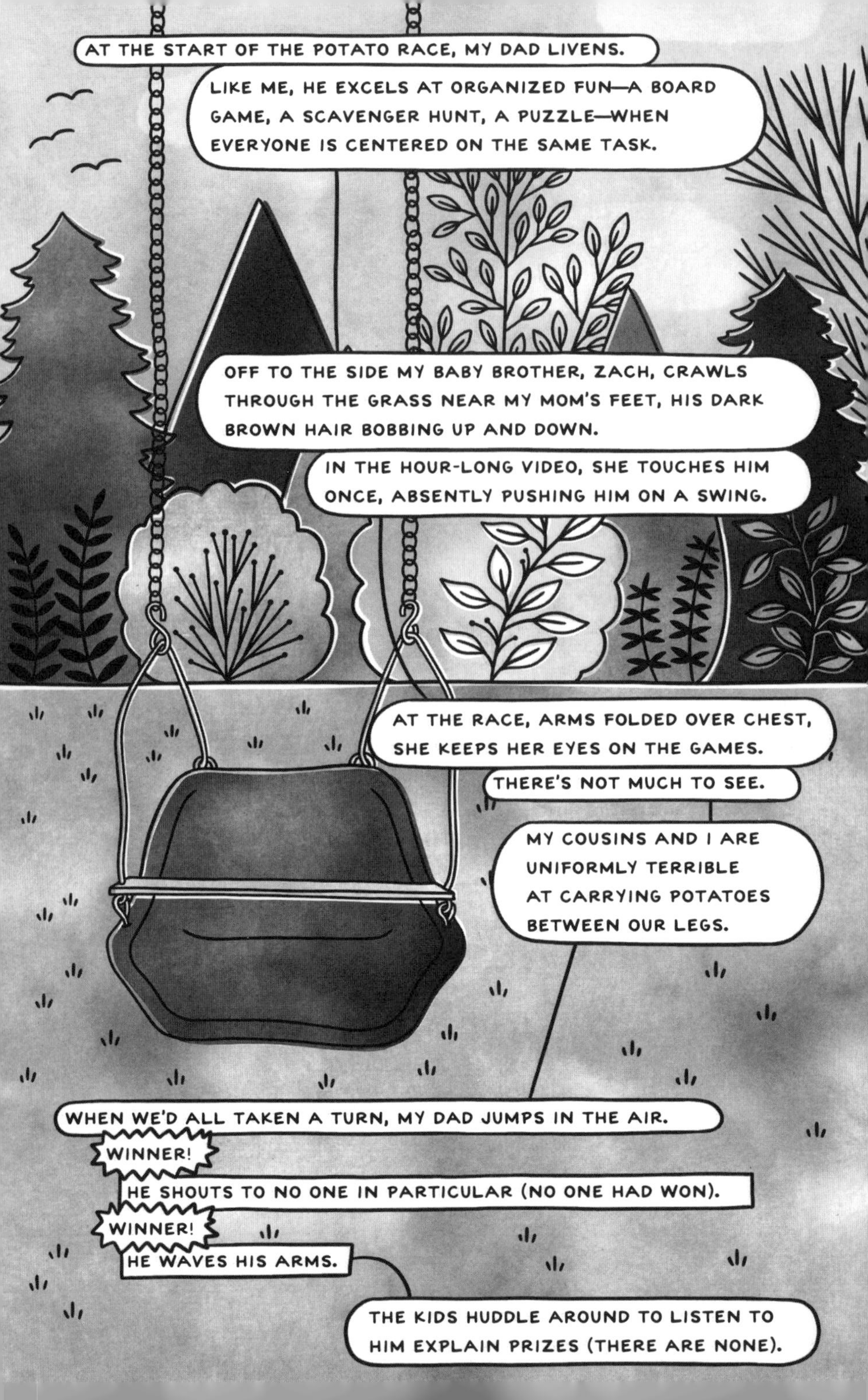
AT THE START OF THE POTATO RACE, MY DAD LIVENS.
LIKE ME, HE EXCELS AT ORGANIZED FUN—A BOARD GAME, A SCAVENGER HUNT, A PUZZLE—WHEN EVERYONE IS CENTERED ON THE SAME TASK.
OFF TO THE SIDE MY BABY BROTHER, ZACH, CRAWLS THROUGH THE GRASS NEAR MY MOM'S FEET, HIS DARK BROWN HAIR BOBBING UP AND DOWN.
IN THE HOUR-LONG VIDEO, SHE TOUCHES HIM ONCE, ABSENTLY PUSHING HIM ON A SWING.
AT THE RACE, ARMS FOLDED OVER CHEST, SHE KEEPS HER EYES ON THE GAMES.
THERE'S NOT MUCH TO SEE.
MY COUSINS AND I ARE UNIFORMLY TERRIBLE AT CARRYING POTATOES BETWEEN OUR LEGS.
WHEN WE'D ALL TAKEN A TURN, MY DAD JUMPS IN THE AIR.
WINNER!
HE SHOUTS TO NO ONE IN PARTICULAR (NO ONE HAD WON).
WINNER!
HE WAVES HIS ARMS.
THE KIDS HUDDLE AROUND TO LISTEN TO HIM EXPLAIN PRIZES (THERE ARE NONE).

MARTIN!

MY MOM CALLS AND THE CAMERA ZOOMS OVER TO HER.

HOW MANY PERCOCETS DID YOU HAVE TODAY? SHE ASKS, THEN CHUCKLES.

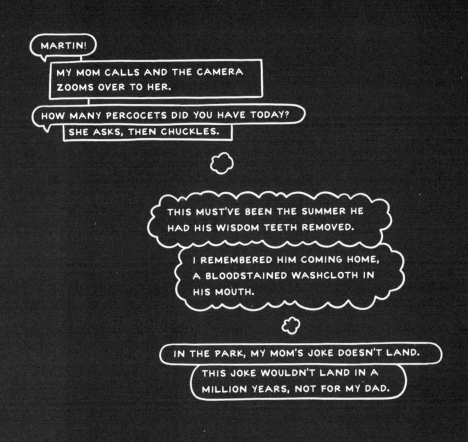

THIS MUST'VE BEEN THE SUMMER HE HAD HIS WISDOM TEETH REMOVED.

I REMEMBERED HIM COMING HOME, A BLOODSTAINED WASHCLOTH IN HIS MOUTH.

IN THE PARK, MY MOM'S JOKE DOESN'T LAND.

THIS JOKE WOULDN'T LAND IN A MILLION YEARS, NOT FOR MY DAD.

NONE,

HE SAYS, NOT LOOKING UP.

I'M ON A NATURAL HIGH.

SHE DOESN'T SEEM TO REGISTER HIS IRRITATION.

SOON AFTER, THE VIDEO FADES TO BLACK.

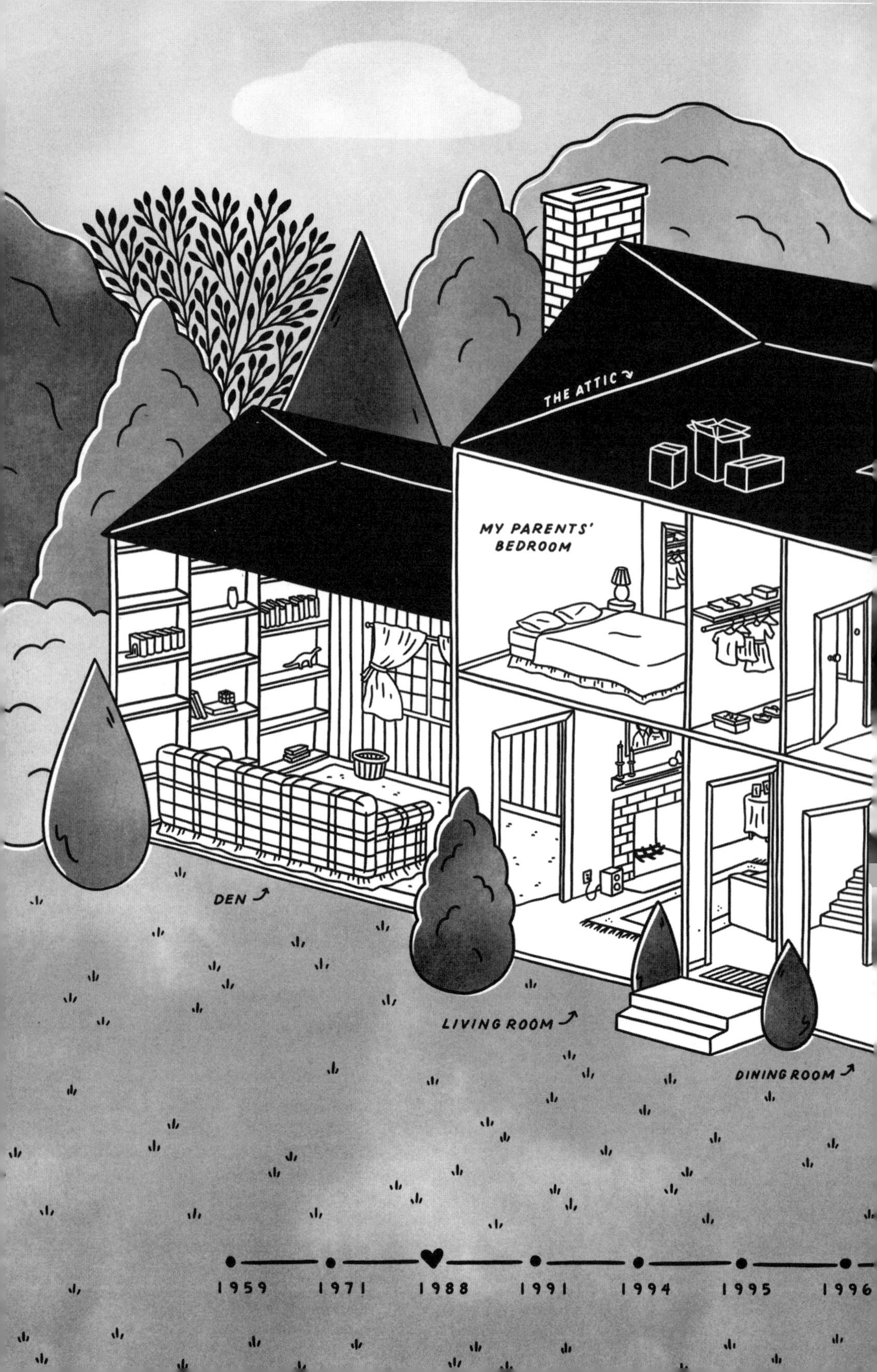
THE ATTIC
MY PARENTS' BEDROOM
DEN
LIVING ROOM
DINING ROOM
1959
1971
1988
1991
1994
1995
1996

CHAPTER 04

The Event

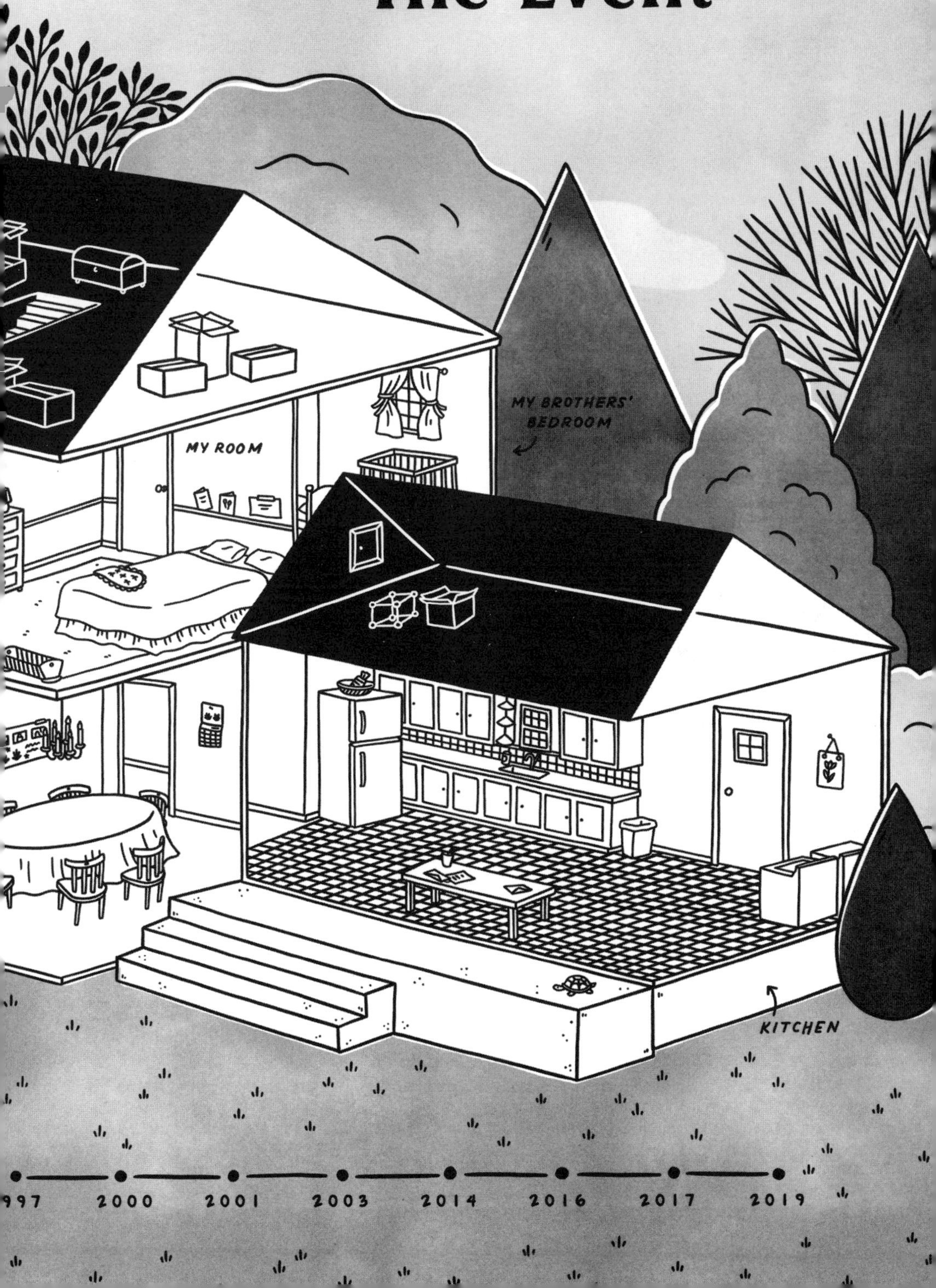
MY BROTHERS' BEDROOM
MY ROOM
KITCHEN
997
2000
2001
2003
2014
2016
2017
2019

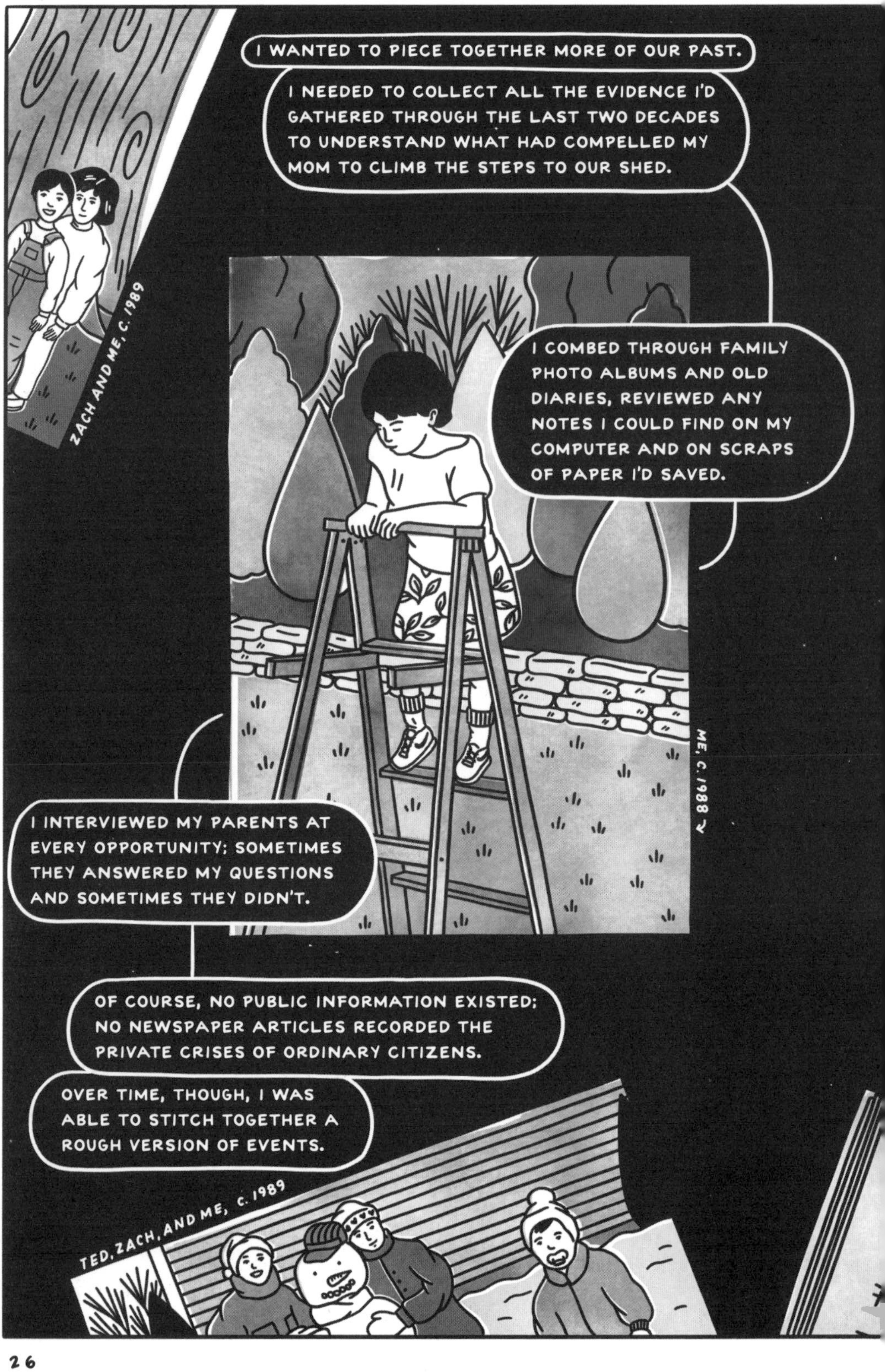
I WANTED TO PIECE TOGETHER MORE OF OUR PAST.
I NEEDED TO COLLECT ALL THE EVIDENCE I'D GATHERED THROUGH THE LAST TWO DECADES TO UNDERSTAND WHAT HAD COMPELLED MY MOM TO CLIMB THE STEPS TO OUR SHED.
ZACH AND ME, C. 1989
I COMBED THROUGH FAMILY PHOTO ALBUMS AND OLD DIARIES, REVIEWED ANY NOTES I COULD FIND ON MY COMPUTER AND ON SCRAPS OF PAPER I'D SAVED.
ME, C. 1988
I INTERVIEWED MY PARENTS AT EVERY OPPORTUNITY: SOMETIMES THEY ANSWERED MY QUESTIONS AND SOMETIMES THEY DIDN'T.
OF COURSE, NO PUBLIC INFORMATION EXISTED: NO NEWSPAPER ARTICLES RECORDED THE PRIVATE CRISES OF ORDINARY CITIZENS.
OVER TIME, THOUGH, I WAS ABLE TO STITCH TOGETHER A ROUGH VERSION OF EVENTS.
TED, ZACH, AND ME, C. 1989

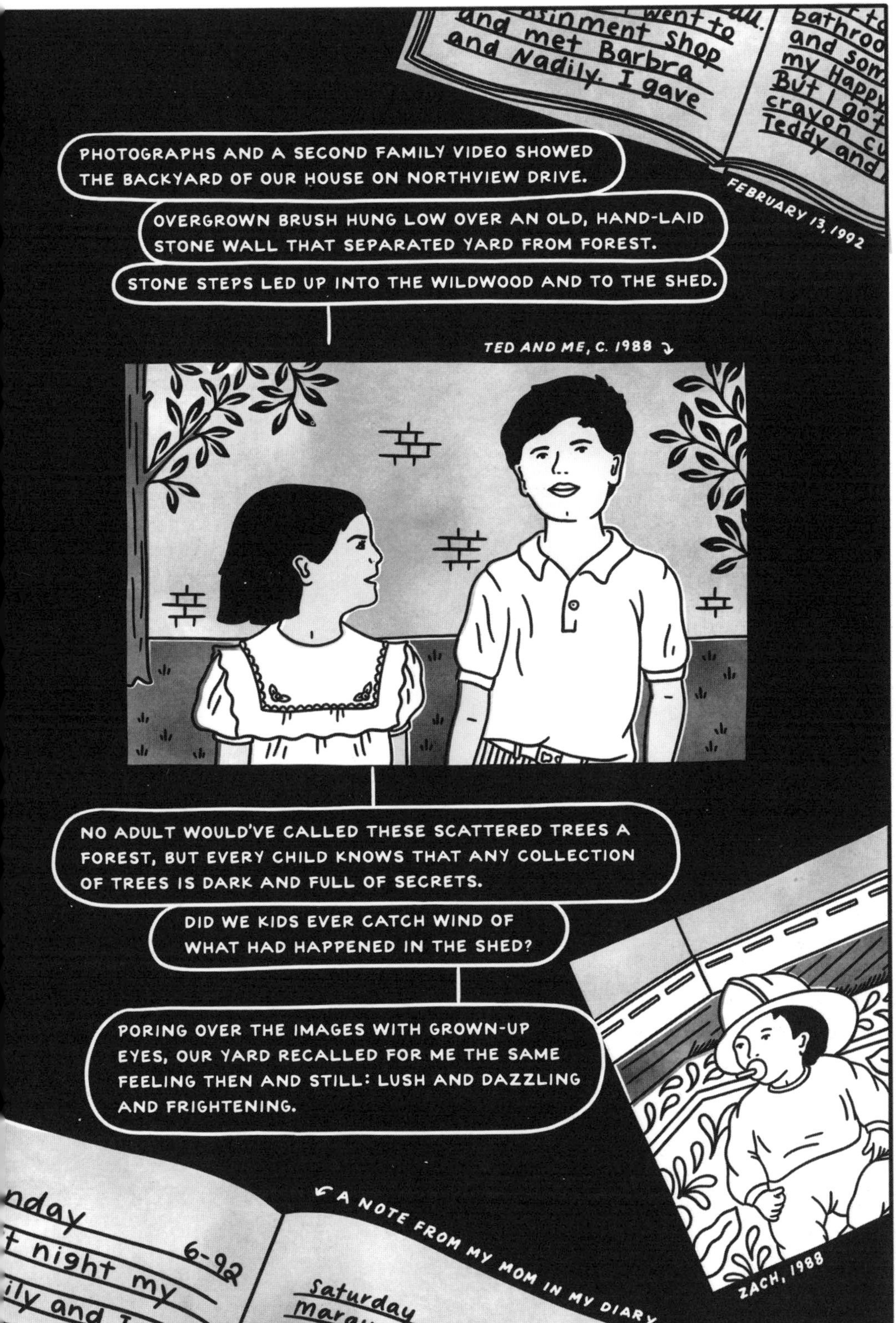
and met Barbra
and Nadily. I gave
FEBRUARY 13, 1992
PHOTOGRAPHS AND A SECOND FAMILY VIDEO SHOWED THE BACKYARD OF OUR HOUSE ON NORTHVIEW DRIVE.
OVERGROWN BRUSH HUNG LOW OVER AN OLD, HAND-LAID STONE WALL THAT SEPARATED YARD FROM FOREST.
STONE STEPS LED UP INTO THE WILDWOOD AND TO THE SHED.
TED AND ME, C. 1988
NO ADULT WOULD'VE CALLED THESE SCATTERED TREES A FOREST, BUT EVERY CHILD KNOWS THAT ANY COLLECTION OF TREES IS DARK AND FULL OF SECRETS.
DID WE KIDS EVER CATCH WIND OF WHAT HAD HAPPENED IN THE SHED?
PORING OVER THE IMAGES WITH GROWN-UP EYES, OUR YARD RECALLED FOR ME THE SAME FEELING THEN AND STILL: LUSH AND DAZZLING AND FRIGHTENING.
ZACH, 1988
6-92
Saturday
A NOTE FROM MY MOM IN MY DIARY

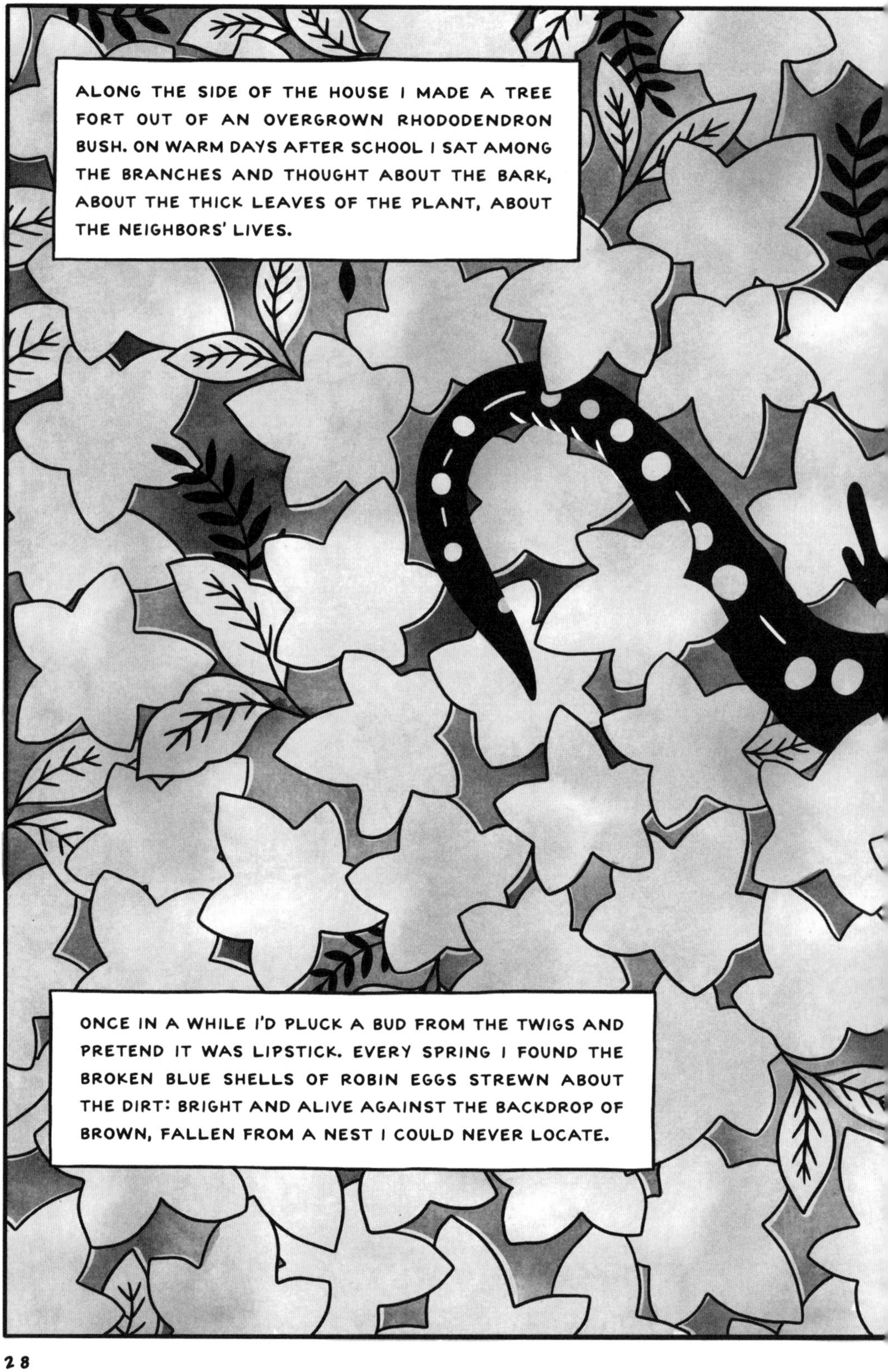
ALONG THE SIDE OF THE HOUSE I MADE A TREE FORT OUT OF AN OVERGROWN RHODODENDRON BUSH. ON WARM DAYS AFTER SCHOOL I SAT AMONG THE BRANCHES AND THOUGHT ABOUT THE BARK, ABOUT THE THICK LEAVES OF THE PLANT, ABOUT THE NEIGHBORS' LIVES.
ONCE IN A WHILE I'D PLUCK A BUD FROM THE TWIGS AND PRETEND IT WAS LIPSTICK. EVERY SPRING I FOUND THE BROKEN BLUE SHELLS OF ROBIN EGGS STREWN ABOUT THE DIRT: BRIGHT AND ALIVE AGAINST THE BACKDROP OF BROWN, FALLEN FROM A NEST I COULD NEVER LOCATE.

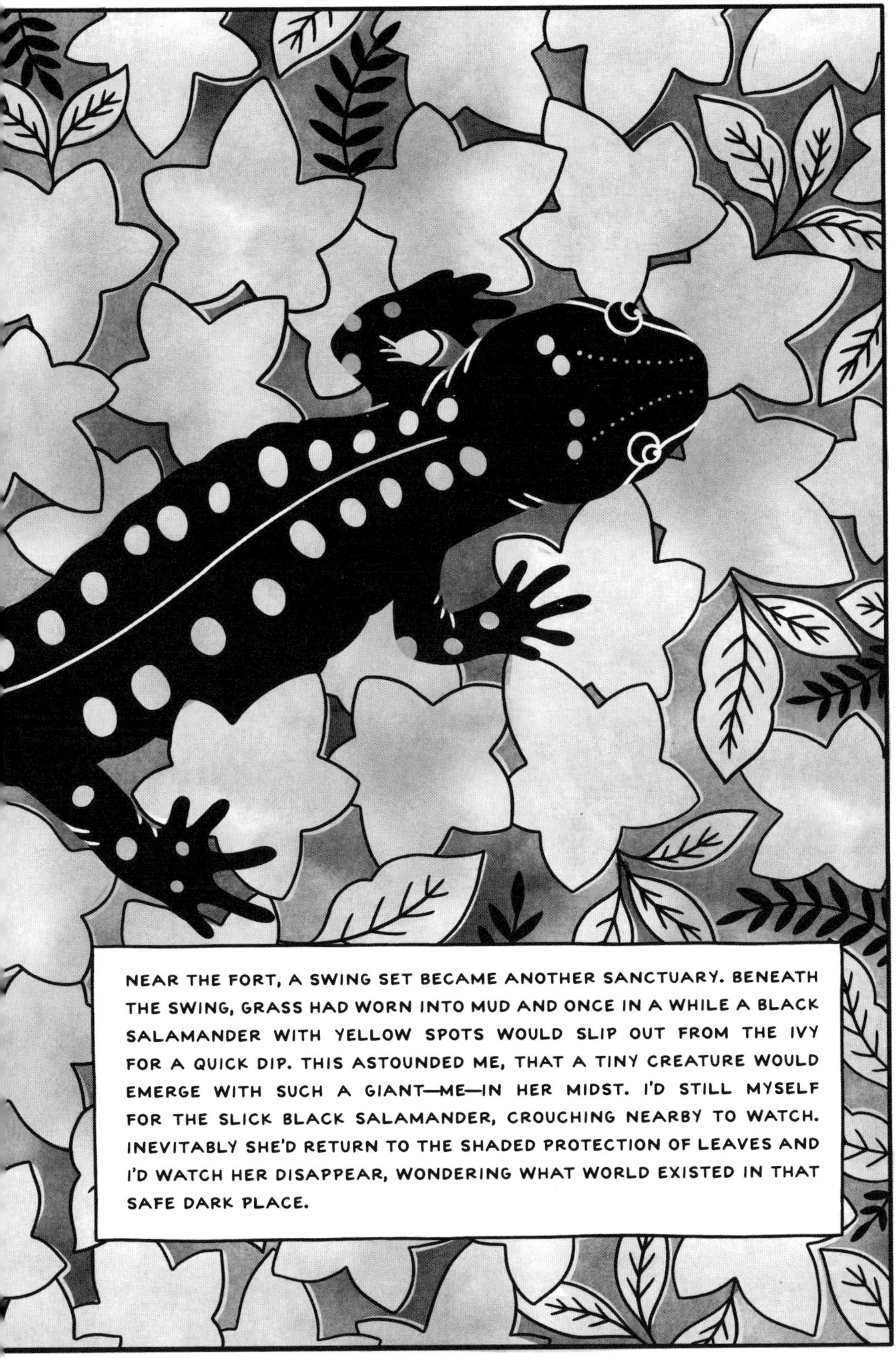
NEAR THE FORT, A SWING SET BECAME ANOTHER SANCTUARY. BENEATH THE SWING, GRASS HAD WORN INTO MUD AND ONCE IN A WHILE A BLACK SALAMANDER WITH YELLOW SPOTS WOULD SLIP OUT FROM THE IVY FOR A QUICK DIP. THIS ASTOUNDED ME, THAT A TINY CREATURE WOULD EMERGE WITH SUCH A GIANT—ME—IN HER MIDST. I'D STILL MYSELF FOR THE SLICK BLACK SALAMANDER, CROUCHING NEARBY TO WATCH. INEVITABLY SHE'D RETURN TO THE SHADED PROTECTION OF LEAVES AND I'D WATCH HER DISAPPEAR, WONDERING WHAT WORLD EXISTED IN THAT SAFE DARK PLACE.

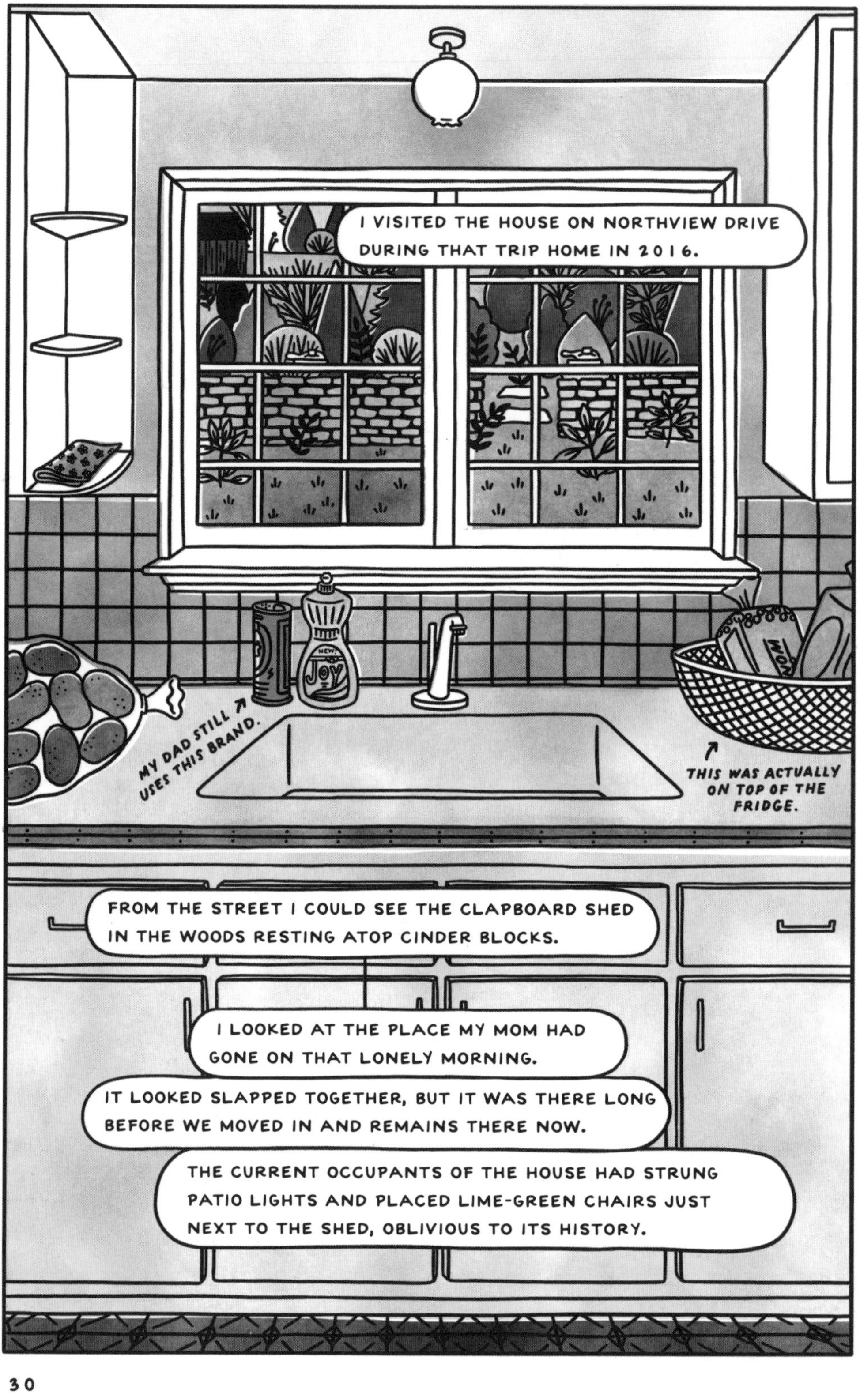
I VISITED THE HOUSE ON NORTHVIEW DRIVE DURING THAT TRIP HOME IN 2016.
NEW! JOY
MY DAD STILL USES THIS BRAND.
THIS WAS ACTUALLY ON TOP OF THE FRIDGE.
FROM THE STREET I COULD SEE THE CLAPBOARD SHED IN THE WOODS RESTING ATOP CINDER BLOCKS.
I LOOKED AT THE PLACE MY MOM HAD GONE ON THAT LONELY MORNING.
IT LOOKED SLAPPED TOGETHER, BUT IT WAS THERE LONG BEFORE WE MOVED IN AND REMAINS THERE NOW.
THE CURRENT OCCUPANTS OF THE HOUSE HAD STRUNG PATIO LIGHTS AND PLACED LIME-GREEN CHAIRS JUST NEXT TO THE SHED, OBLIVIOUS TO ITS HISTORY.

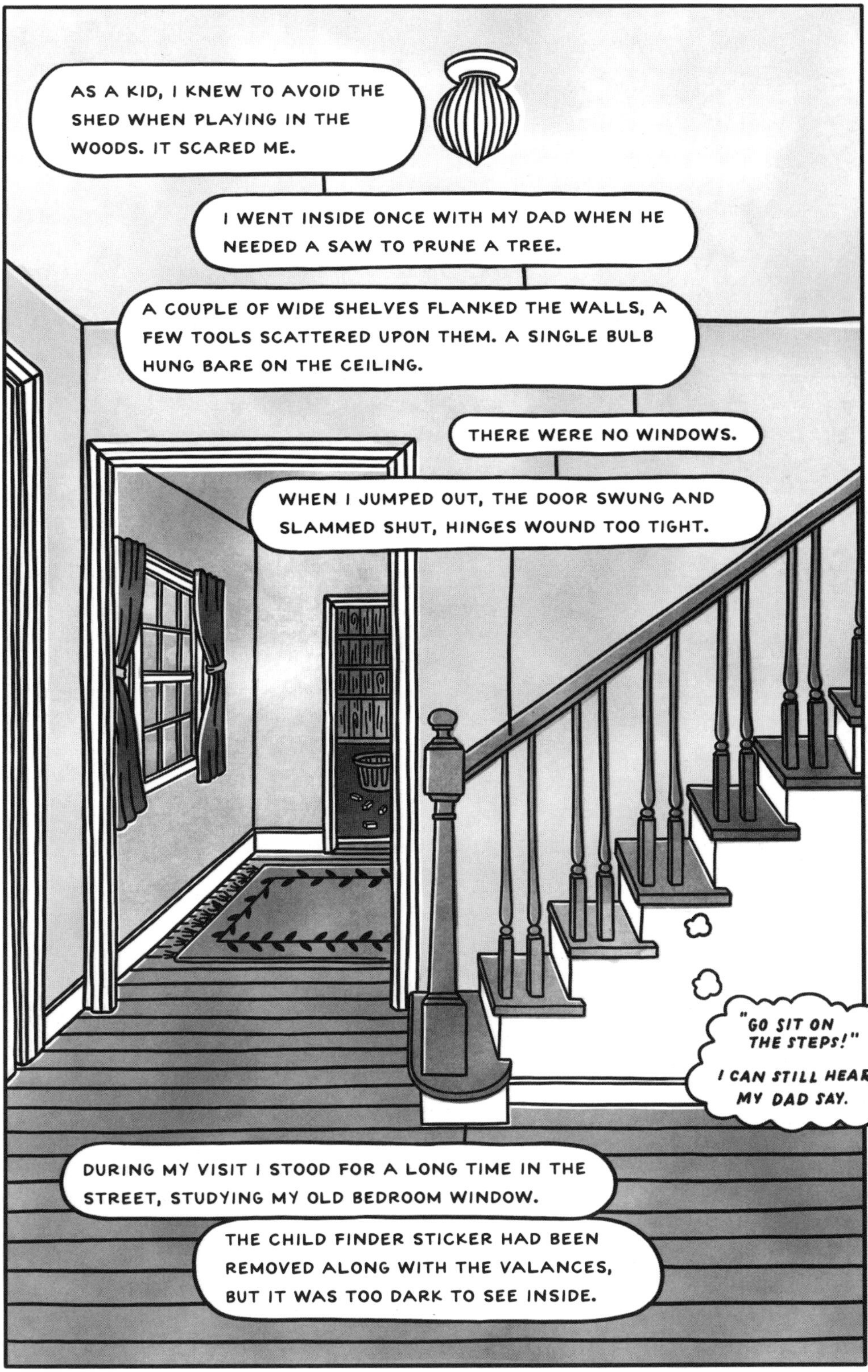
AS A KID, I KNEW TO AVOID THE SHED WHEN PLAYING IN THE WOODS. IT SCARED ME.
I WENT INSIDE ONCE WITH MY DAD WHEN HE NEEDED A SAW TO PRUNE A TREE.
A COUPLE OF WIDE SHELVES FLANKED THE WALLS, A FEW TOOLS SCATTERED UPON THEM. A SINGLE BULB HUNG BARE ON THE CEILING.
THERE WERE NO WINDOWS.
WHEN I JUMPED OUT, THE DOOR SWUNG AND SLAMMED SHUT, HINGES WOUND TOO TIGHT.
"GO SIT ON THE STEPS!"
I CAN STILL HEAR MY DAD SAY.
DURING MY VISIT I STOOD FOR A LONG TIME IN THE STREET, STUDYING MY OLD BEDROOM WINDOW.
THE CHILD FINDER STICKER HAD BEEN REMOVED ALONG WITH THE VALANCES, BUT IT WAS TOO DARK TO SEE INSIDE.

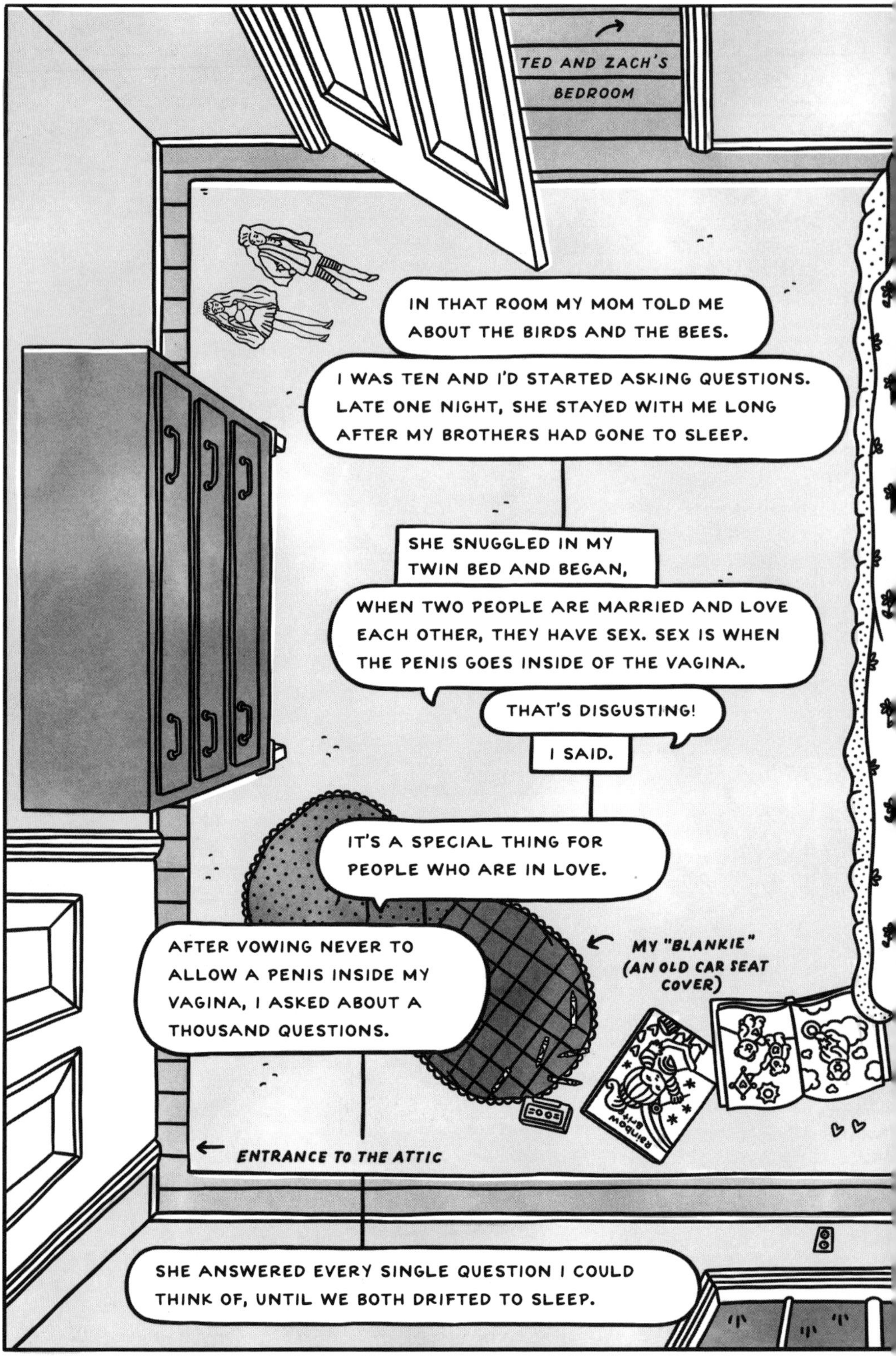
TED AND ZACH'S BEDROOM
IN THAT ROOM MY MOM TOLD ME ABOUT THE BIRDS AND THE BEES.
I WAS TEN AND I'D STARTED ASKING QUESTIONS. LATE ONE NIGHT, SHE STAYED WITH ME LONG AFTER MY BROTHERS HAD GONE TO SLEEP.
SHE SNUGGLED IN MY TWIN BED AND BEGAN,
WHEN TWO PEOPLE ARE MARRIED AND LOVE EACH OTHER, THEY HAVE SEX. SEX IS WHEN THE PENIS GOES INSIDE OF THE VAGINA.
THAT'S DISGUSTING!
I SAID.
IT'S A SPECIAL THING FOR PEOPLE WHO ARE IN LOVE.
AFTER VOWING NEVER TO ALLOW A PENIS INSIDE MY VAGINA, I ASKED ABOUT A THOUSAND QUESTIONS.
MY "BLANKIE" (AN OLD CAR SEAT COVER)
Rainbow Brite
ENTRANCE TO THE ATTIC
SHE ANSWERED EVERY SINGLE QUESTION I COULD THINK OF, UNTIL WE BOTH DRIFTED TO SLEEP.

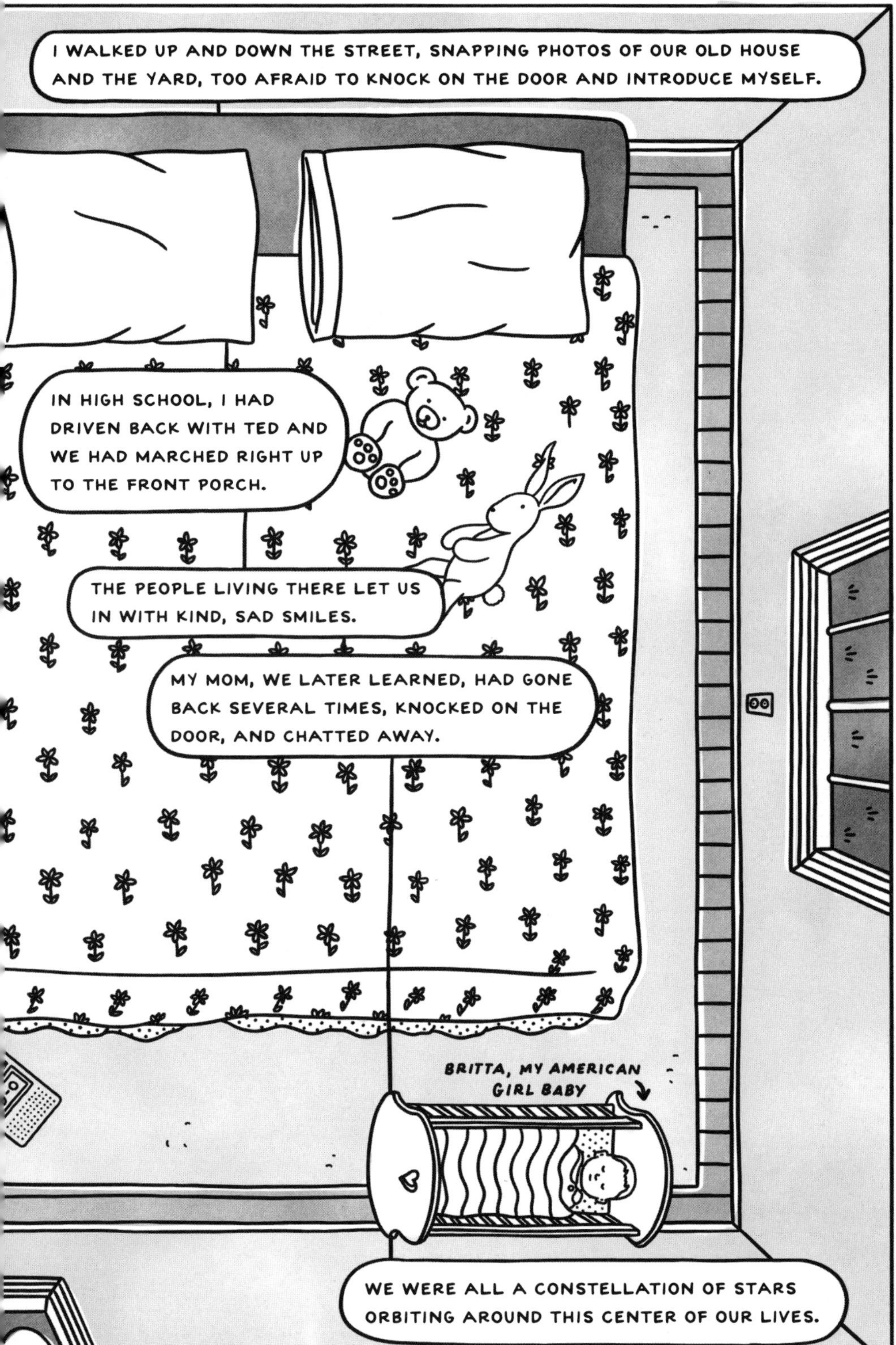
I WALKED UP AND DOWN THE STREET, SNAPPING PHOTOS OF OUR OLD HOUSE AND THE YARD, TOO AFRAID TO KNOCK ON THE DOOR AND INTRODUCE MYSELF.
IN HIGH SCHOOL, I HAD DRIVEN BACK WITH TED AND WE HAD MARCHED RIGHT UP TO THE FRONT PORCH.
THE PEOPLE LIVING THERE LET US IN WITH KIND, SAD SMILES.
MY MOM, WE LATER LEARNED, HAD GONE BACK SEVERAL TIMES, KNOCKED ON THE DOOR, AND CHATTED AWAY.
BRITTA, MY AMERICAN GIRL BABY
WE WERE ALL A CONSTELLATION OF STARS ORBITING AROUND THIS CENTER OF OUR LIVES.

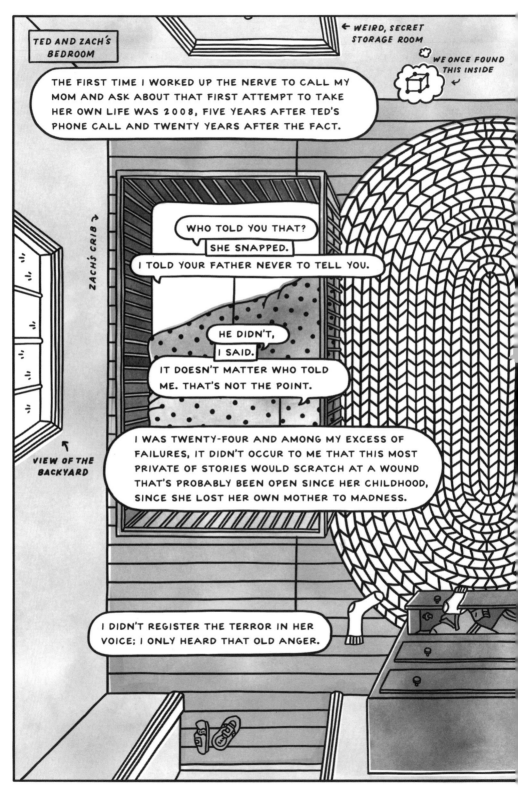

TED AND ZACH'S BEDROOM

← WEIRD, SECRET STORAGE ROOM

WE ONCE FOUND THIS INSIDE

THE FIRST TIME I WORKED UP THE NERVE TO CALL MY MOM AND ASK ABOUT THAT FIRST ATTEMPT TO TAKE HER OWN LIFE WAS 2008, FIVE YEARS AFTER TED'S PHONE CALL AND TWENTY YEARS AFTER THE FACT.

ZACH'S CRIB →

WHO TOLD YOU THAT? SHE SNAPPED. I TOLD YOUR FATHER NEVER TO TELL YOU.

HE DIDN'T, I SAID. IT DOESN'T MATTER WHO TOLD ME. THAT'S NOT THE POINT.

I WAS TWENTY-FOUR AND AMONG MY EXCESS OF FAILURES, IT DIDN'T OCCUR TO ME THAT THIS MOST PRIVATE OF STORIES WOULD SCRATCH AT A WOUND THAT'S PROBABLY BEEN OPEN SINCE HER CHILDHOOD, SINCE SHE LOST HER OWN MOTHER TO MADNESS.

↑ VIEW OF THE BACKYARD

I DIDN'T REGISTER THE TERROR IN HER VOICE; I ONLY HEARD THAT OLD ANGER.

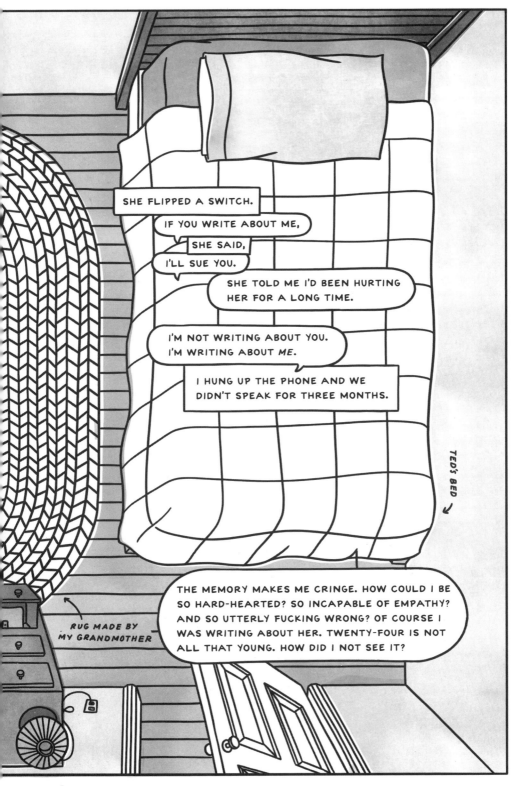

SHE FLIPPED A SWITCH.

IF YOU WRITE ABOUT ME,

SHE SAID,

I'LL SUE YOU.

SHE TOLD ME I'D BEEN HURTING HER FOR A LONG TIME.

I'M NOT WRITING ABOUT YOU. I'M WRITING ABOUT *ME*.

I HUNG UP THE PHONE AND WE DIDN'T SPEAK FOR THREE MONTHS.

TED'S BED →

RUG MADE BY MY GRANDMOTHER

THE MEMORY MAKES ME CRINGE. HOW COULD I BE SO HARD-HEARTED? SO INCAPABLE OF EMPATHY? AND SO UTTERLY FUCKING WRONG? OF COURSE I WAS WRITING ABOUT HER. TWENTY-FOUR IS NOT ALL THAT YOUNG. HOW DID I NOT SEE IT?

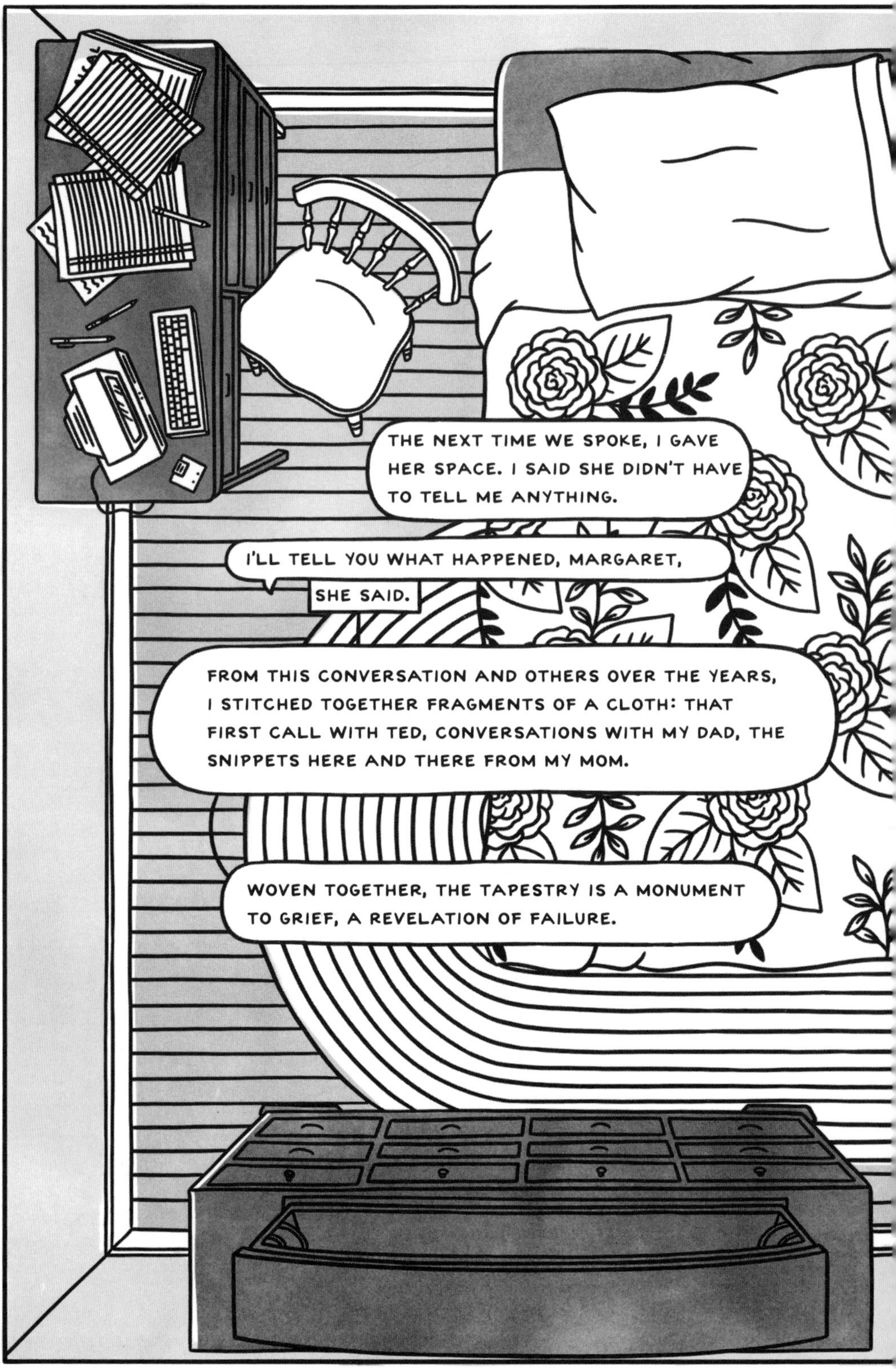
THE NEXT TIME WE SPOKE, I GAVE HER SPACE. I SAID SHE DIDN'T HAVE TO TELL ME ANYTHING.
I'LL TELL YOU WHAT HAPPENED, MARGARET,
SHE SAID.
FROM THIS CONVERSATION AND OTHERS OVER THE YEARS, I STITCHED TOGETHER FRAGMENTS OF A CLOTH: THAT FIRST CALL WITH TED, CONVERSATIONS WITH MY DAD, THE SNIPPETS HERE AND THERE FROM MY MOM.
WOVEN TOGETHER, THE TAPESTRY IS A MONUMENT TO GRIEF, A REVELATION OF FAILURE.

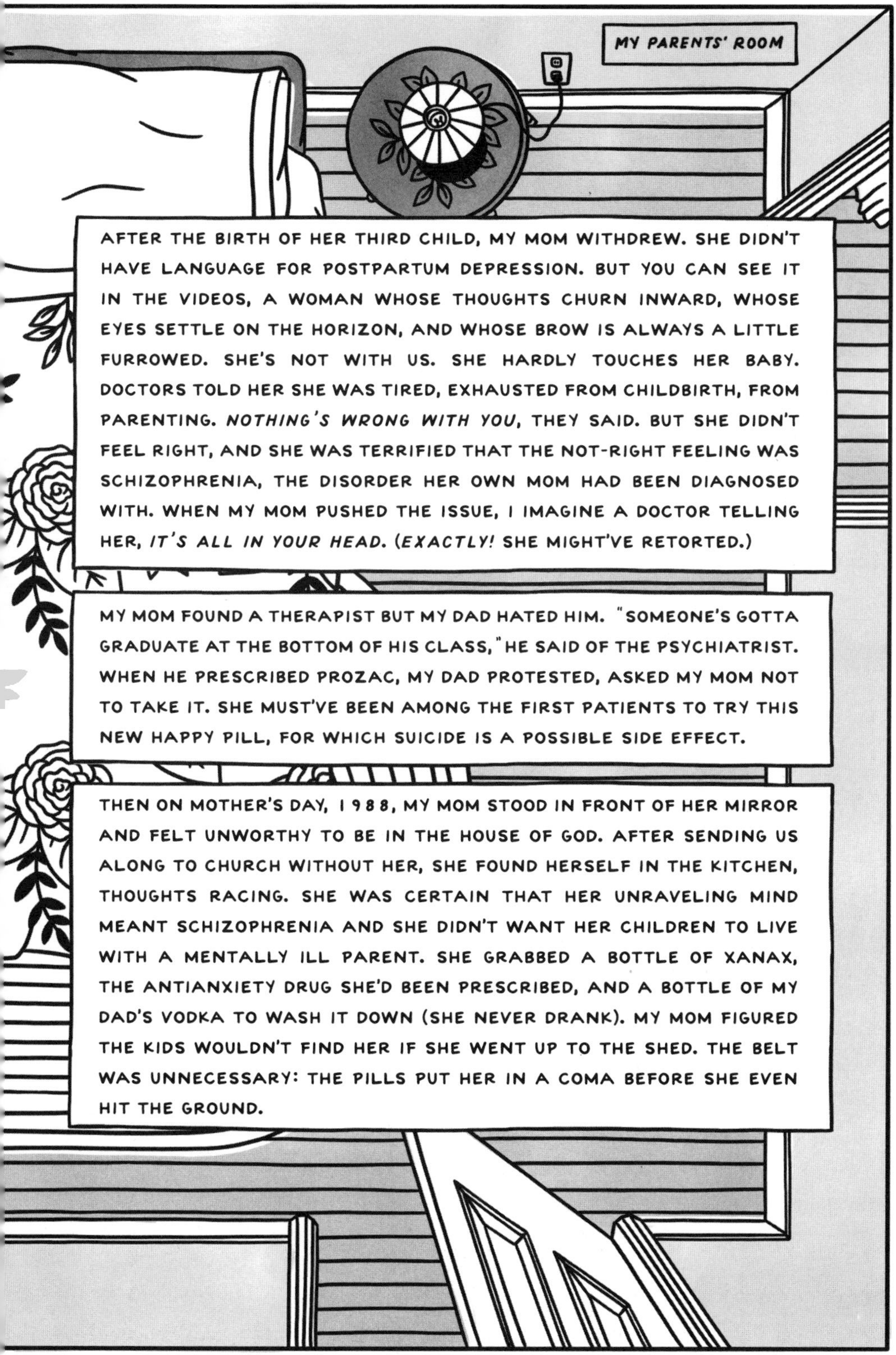
MY PARENTS' ROOM
AFTER THE BIRTH OF HER THIRD CHILD, MY MOM WITHDREW. SHE DIDN'T HAVE LANGUAGE FOR POSTPARTUM DEPRESSION. BUT YOU CAN SEE IT IN THE VIDEOS, A WOMAN WHOSE THOUGHTS CHURN INWARD, WHOSE EYES SETTLE ON THE HORIZON, AND WHOSE BROW IS ALWAYS A LITTLE FURROWED. SHE'S NOT WITH US. SHE HARDLY TOUCHES HER BABY. DOCTORS TOLD HER SHE WAS TIRED, EXHAUSTED FROM CHILDBIRTH, FROM PARENTING. *NOTHING'S WRONG WITH YOU*, THEY SAID. BUT SHE DIDN'T FEEL RIGHT, AND SHE WAS TERRIFIED THAT THE NOT-RIGHT FEELING WAS SCHIZOPHRENIA, THE DISORDER HER OWN MOM HAD BEEN DIAGNOSED WITH. WHEN MY MOM PUSHED THE ISSUE, I IMAGINE A DOCTOR TELLING HER, *IT'S ALL IN YOUR HEAD*. (*EXACTLY!* SHE MIGHT'VE RETORTED.)
MY MOM FOUND A THERAPIST BUT MY DAD HATED HIM. "SOMEONE'S GOTTA GRADUATE AT THE BOTTOM OF HIS CLASS," HE SAID OF THE PSYCHIATRIST. WHEN HE PRESCRIBED PROZAC, MY DAD PROTESTED, ASKED MY MOM NOT TO TAKE IT. SHE MUST'VE BEEN AMONG THE FIRST PATIENTS TO TRY THIS NEW HAPPY PILL, FOR WHICH SUICIDE IS A POSSIBLE SIDE EFFECT.
THEN ON MOTHER'S DAY, 1988, MY MOM STOOD IN FRONT OF HER MIRROR AND FELT UNWORTHY TO BE IN THE HOUSE OF GOD. AFTER SENDING US ALONG TO CHURCH WITHOUT HER, SHE FOUND HERSELF IN THE KITCHEN, THOUGHTS RACING. SHE WAS CERTAIN THAT HER UNRAVELING MIND MEANT SCHIZOPHRENIA AND SHE DIDN'T WANT HER CHILDREN TO LIVE WITH A MENTALLY ILL PARENT. SHE GRABBED A BOTTLE OF XANAX, THE ANTIANXIETY DRUG SHE'D BEEN PRESCRIBED, AND A BOTTLE OF MY DAD'S VODKA TO WASH IT DOWN (SHE NEVER DRANK). MY MOM FIGURED THE KIDS WOULDN'T FIND HER IF SHE WENT UP TO THE SHED. THE BELT WAS UNNECESSARY: THE PILLS PUT HER IN A COMA BEFORE SHE EVEN HIT THE GROUND.

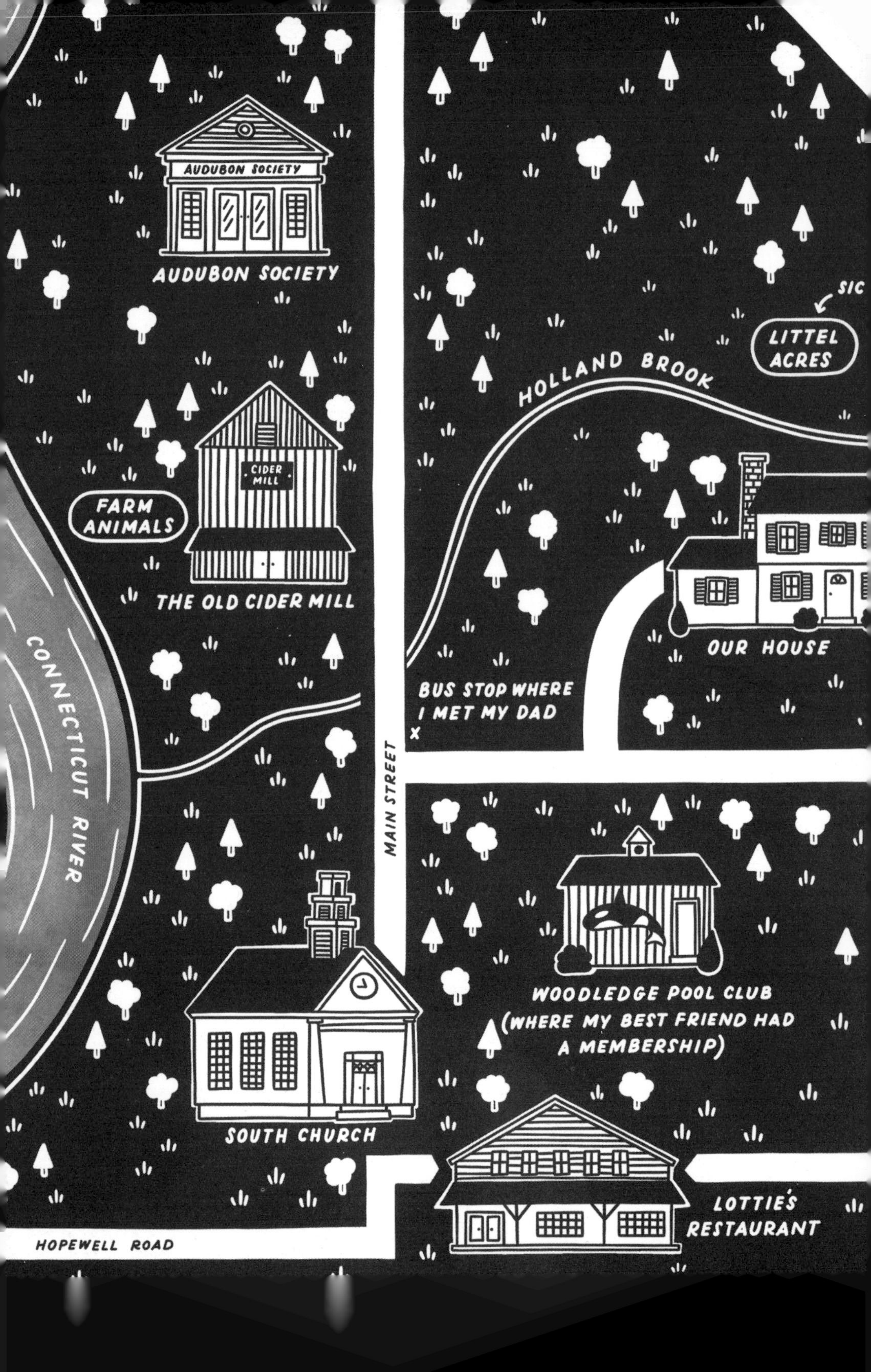
AUDUBON SOCIETY
AUDUBON SOCIETY
SIC
LITTEL ACRES
HOLLAND BROOK
CIDER MILL
FARM ANIMALS
THE OLD CIDER MILL
OUR HOUSE
CONNECTICUT RIVER
BUS STOP WHERE I MET MY DAD
X
MAIN STREET
WOODLEDGE POOL CLUB (WHERE MY BEST FRIEND HAD A MEMBERSHIP)
SOUTH CHURCH
LOTTIE'S RESTAURANT
HOPEWELL ROAD

CHAPTER 05

The Year

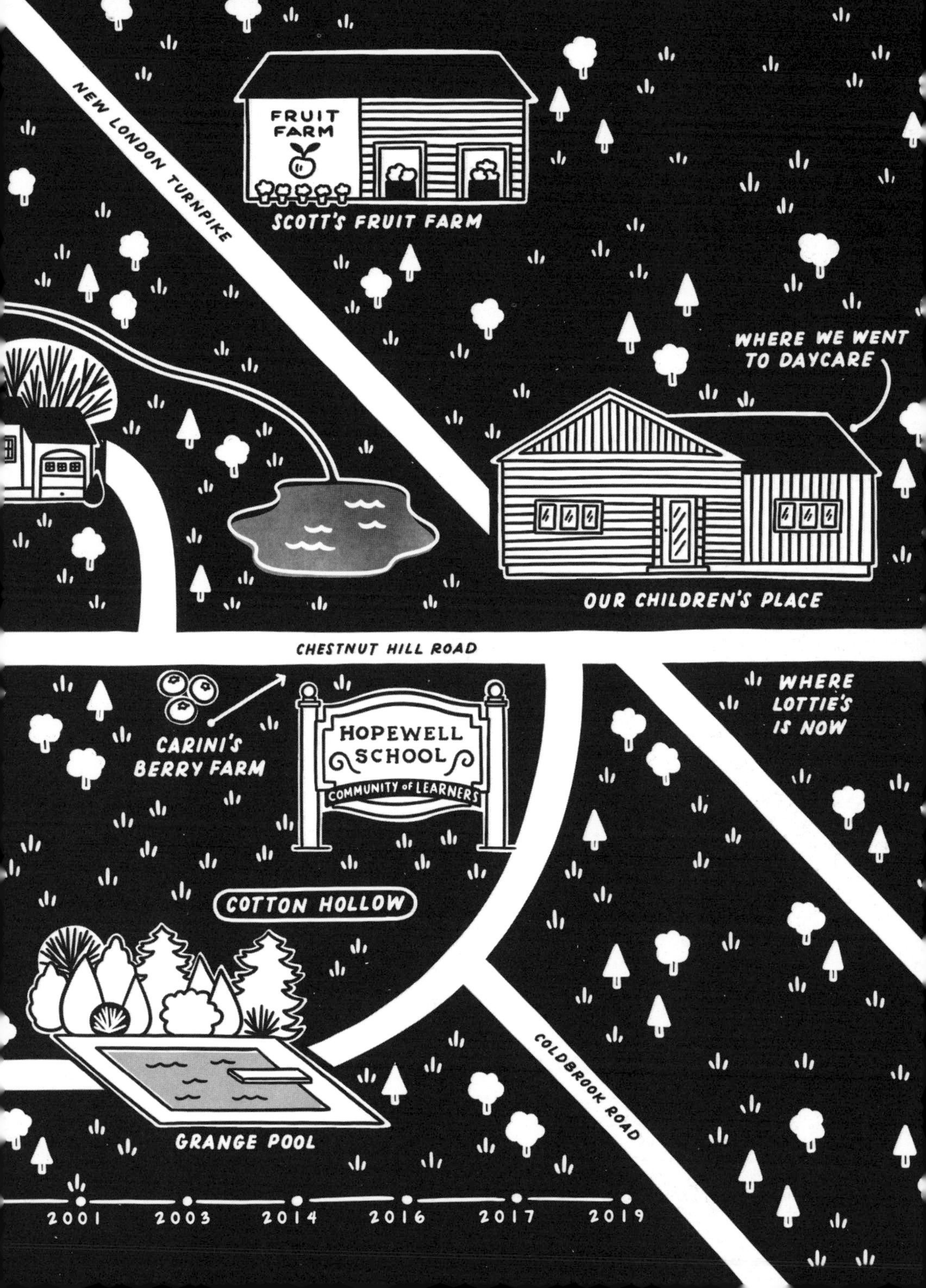
NEW LONDON TURNPIKE
FRUIT FARM
SCOTT'S FRUIT FARM
WHERE WE WENT TO DAYCARE
OUR CHILDREN'S PLACE
CHESTNUT HILL ROAD
CARINI'S BERRY FARM
HOPEWELL SCHOOL
COMMUNITY of LEARNERS
WHERE LOTTIE'S IS NOW
COTTON HOLLOW
COLDBROOK ROAD
GRANGE POOL
2001
2003
2014
2016
2017
2019

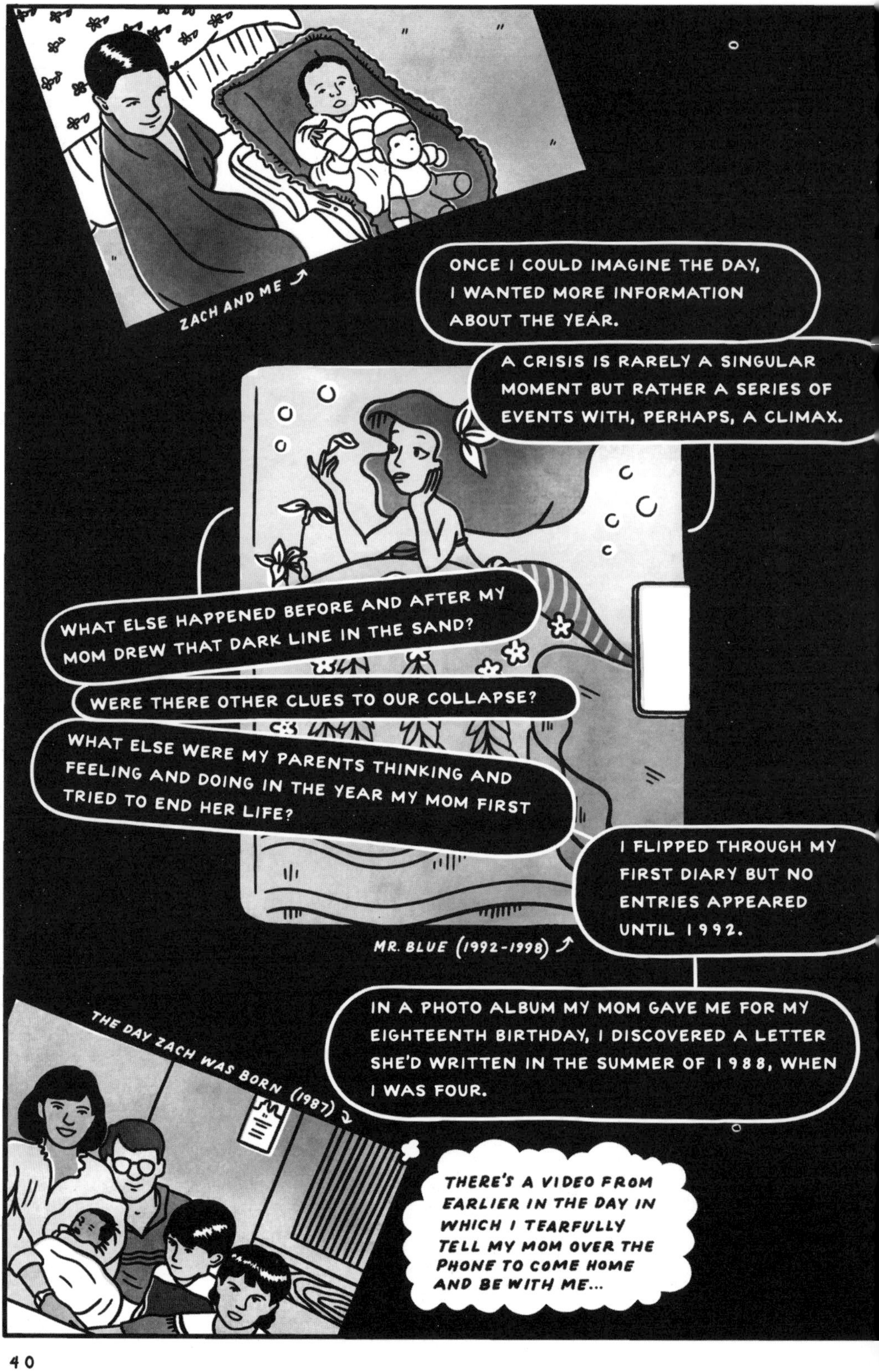
ZACH AND ME
ONCE I COULD IMAGINE THE DAY, I WANTED MORE INFORMATION ABOUT THE YEAR.
A CRISIS IS RARELY A SINGULAR MOMENT BUT RATHER A SERIES OF EVENTS WITH, PERHAPS, A CLIMAX.
WHAT ELSE HAPPENED BEFORE AND AFTER MY MOM DREW THAT DARK LINE IN THE SAND?
WERE THERE OTHER CLUES TO OUR COLLAPSE?
WHAT ELSE WERE MY PARENTS THINKING AND FEELING AND DOING IN THE YEAR MY MOM FIRST TRIED TO END HER LIFE?
I FLIPPED THROUGH MY FIRST DIARY BUT NO ENTRIES APPEARED UNTIL 1992.
MR. BLUE (1992-1998)
IN A PHOTO ALBUM MY MOM GAVE ME FOR MY EIGHTEENTH BIRTHDAY, I DISCOVERED A LETTER SHE'D WRITTEN IN THE SUMMER OF 1988, WHEN I WAS FOUR.
THE DAY ZACH WAS BORN (1987)
THERE'S A VIDEO FROM EARLIER IN THE DAY IN WHICH I TEARFULLY TELL MY MOM OVER THE PHONE TO COME HOME AND BE WITH ME...

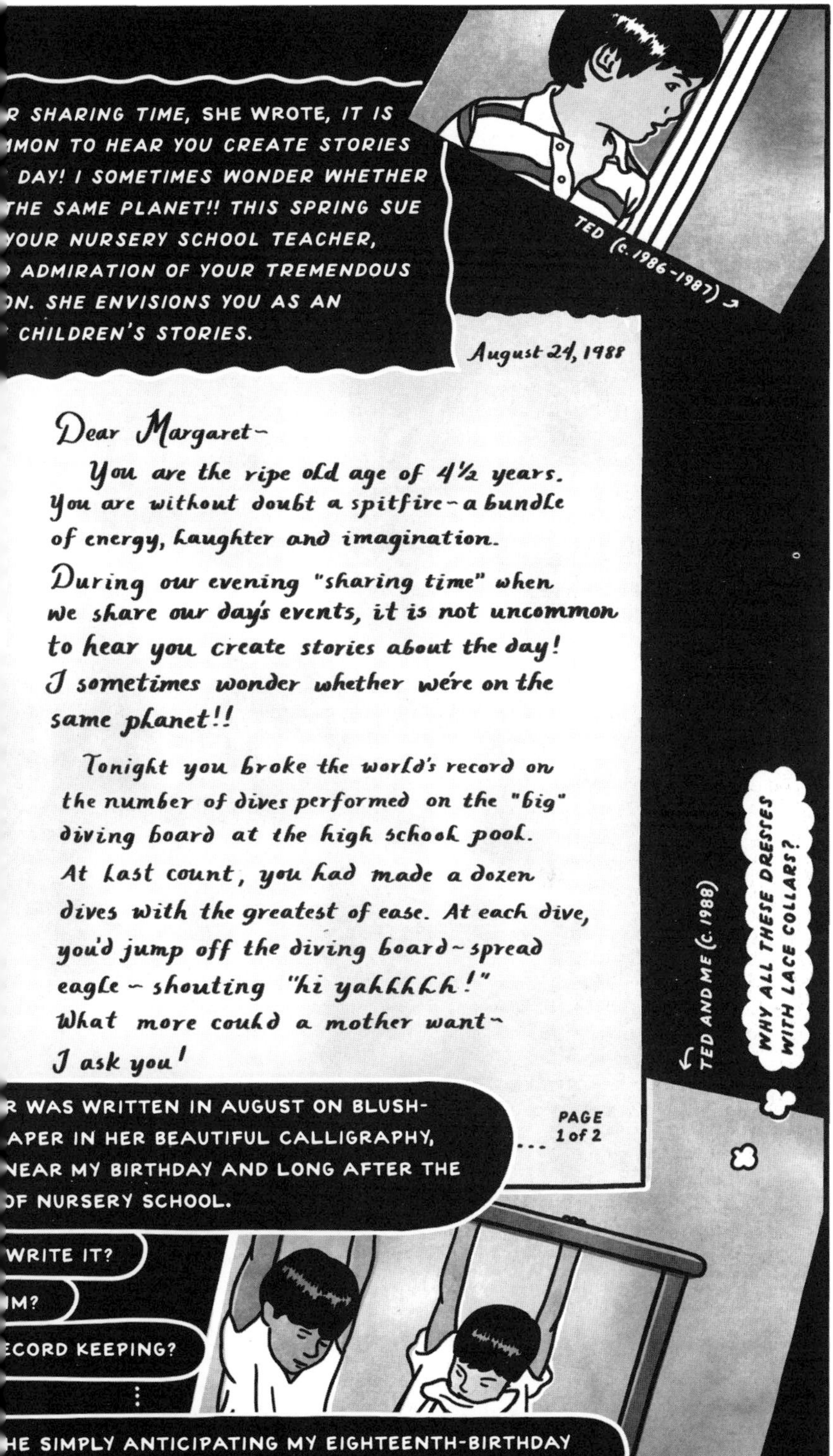
R SHARING TIME, SHE WROTE, IT IS
IMON TO HEAR YOU CREATE STORIES
DAY! I SOMETIMES WONDER WHETHER
THE SAME PLANET!! THIS SPRING SUE
YOUR NURSERY SCHOOL TEACHER,
ADMIRATION OF YOUR TREMENDOUS
ON. SHE ENVISIONS YOU AS AN
CHILDREN'S STORIES.
TED (c. 1986-1987)
August 24, 1988
Dear Margaret-
You are the ripe old age of 4½ years. You are without doubt a spitfire-a bundle of energy, laughter and imagination.
During our evening "sharing time" when we share our day's events, it is not uncommon to hear you create stories about the day! I sometimes wonder whether we're on the same planet!!
Tonight you broke the world's record on the number of dives performed on the "big" diving board at the high school pool. At last count, you had made a dozen dives with the greatest of ease. At each dive, you'd jump off the diving board~spread eagle-shouting "hi yahhhhh!" What more could a mother want-I ask you!
PAGE 1 of 2
TED AND ME (c. 1988)
WHY ALL THESE DRESSES WITH LACE COLLARS?
R WAS WRITTEN IN AUGUST ON BLUSH-
APER IN HER BEAUTIFUL CALLIGRAPHY,
NEAR MY BIRTHDAY AND LONG AFTER THE
OF NURSERY SCHOOL.
WRITE IT?
IM?
ECORD KEEPING?
HE SIMPLY ANTICIPATING MY EIGHTEENTH-BIRTHDAY
, OR WAS SHE PLANNING SOMETHING DARKER?

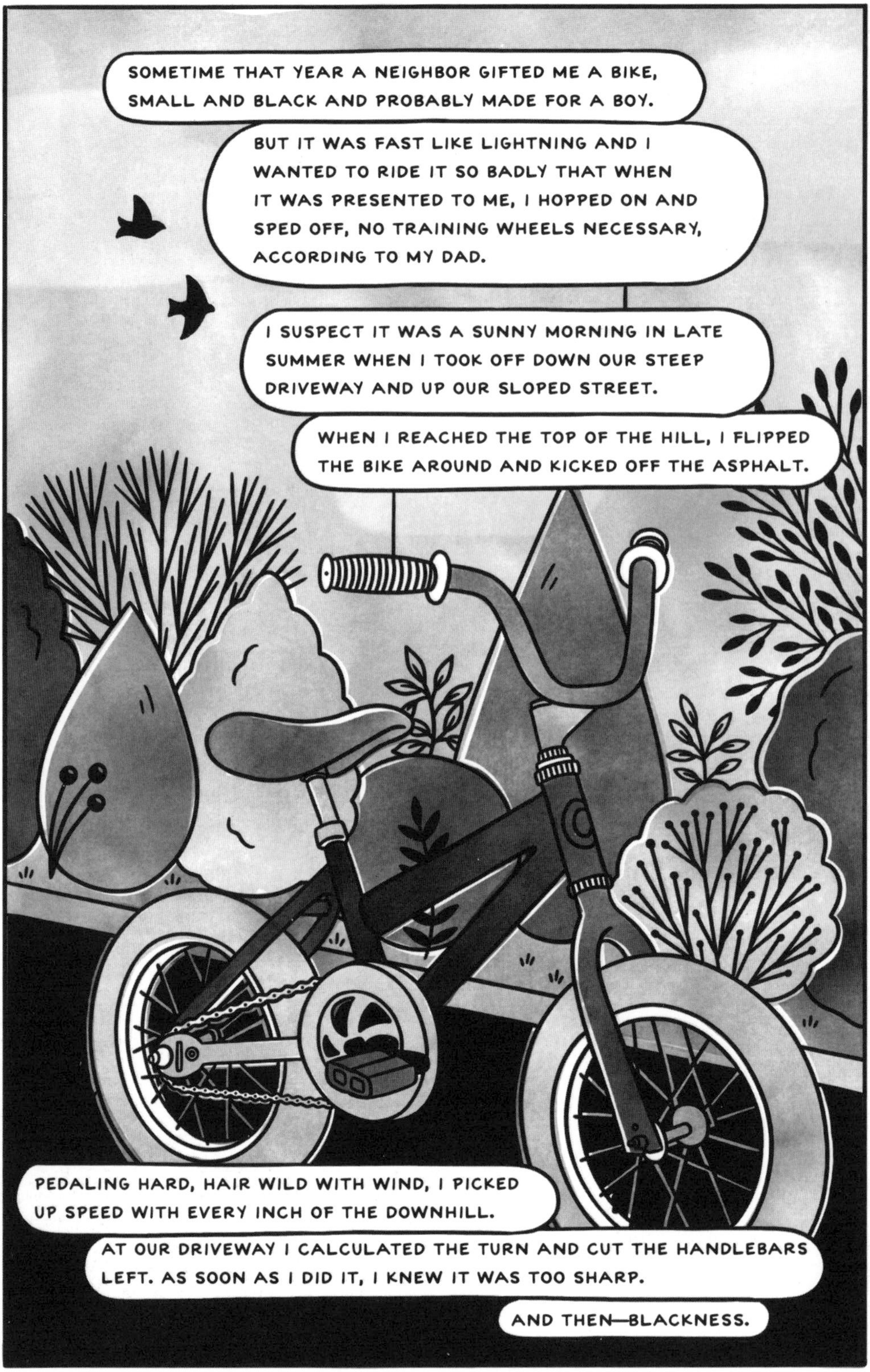
SOMETIME THAT YEAR A NEIGHBOR GIFTED ME A BIKE, SMALL AND BLACK AND PROBABLY MADE FOR A BOY.
BUT IT WAS FAST LIKE LIGHTNING AND I WANTED TO RIDE IT SO BADLY THAT WHEN IT WAS PRESENTED TO ME, I HOPPED ON AND SPED OFF, NO TRAINING WHEELS NECESSARY, ACCORDING TO MY DAD.
I SUSPECT IT WAS A SUNNY MORNING IN LATE SUMMER WHEN I TOOK OFF DOWN OUR STEEP DRIVEWAY AND UP OUR SLOPED STREET.
WHEN I REACHED THE TOP OF THE HILL, I FLIPPED THE BIKE AROUND AND KICKED OFF THE ASPHALT.
PEDALING HARD, HAIR WILD WITH WIND, I PICKED UP SPEED WITH EVERY INCH OF THE DOWNHILL.
AT OUR DRIVEWAY I CALCULATED THE TURN AND CUT THE HANDLEBARS LEFT. AS SOON AS I DID IT, I KNEW IT WAS TOO SHARP.
AND THEN—BLACKNESS.

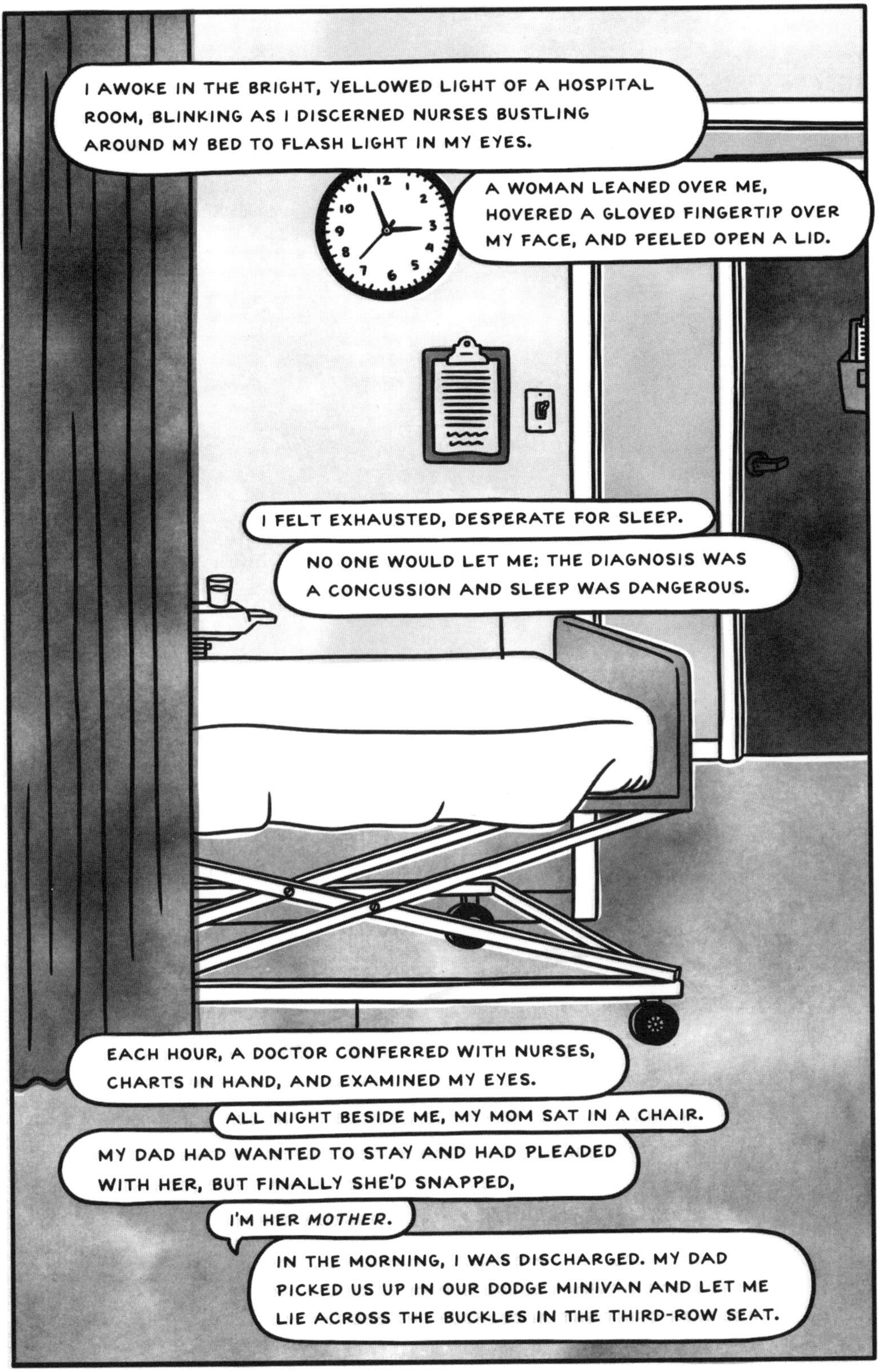
I AWOKE IN THE BRIGHT, YELLOWED LIGHT OF A HOSPITAL ROOM, BLINKING AS I DISCERNED NURSES BUSTLING AROUND MY BED TO FLASH LIGHT IN MY EYES.
A WOMAN LEANED OVER ME, HOVERED A GLOVED FINGERTIP OVER MY FACE, AND PEELED OPEN A LID.
I FELT EXHAUSTED, DESPERATE FOR SLEEP.
NO ONE WOULD LET ME; THE DIAGNOSIS WAS A CONCUSSION AND SLEEP WAS DANGEROUS.
EACH HOUR, A DOCTOR CONFERRED WITH NURSES, CHARTS IN HAND, AND EXAMINED MY EYES.
ALL NIGHT BESIDE ME, MY MOM SAT IN A CHAIR.
MY DAD HAD WANTED TO STAY AND HAD PLEADED WITH HER, BUT FINALLY SHE'D SNAPPED,
I'M HER *MOTHER*.
IN THE MORNING, I WAS DISCHARGED. MY DAD PICKED US UP IN OUR DODGE MINIVAN AND LET ME LIE ACROSS THE BUCKLES IN THE THIRD-ROW SEAT.

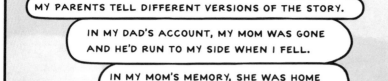

MY PARENTS TELL DIFFERENT VERSIONS OF THE STORY.

IN MY DAD'S ACCOUNT, MY MOM WAS GONE AND HE'D RUN TO MY SIDE WHEN I FELL.

IN MY MOM'S MEMORY, SHE WAS HOME MAKING US LUNCH WHEN IT HAPPENED.

BOTH ACCOUNTS REINFORCE THEIR NOTIONS OF SELF (MY DAD TENDING TO US ALONE; MY MOM FOREVER MINDING THE FAMILY DUTIES) AND BOTH STRIKE ME AS SUPREMELY LONELY: TWO PEOPLE FOR WHOM PARENTING WAS A SOLITARY ACT.

THE ONLY POINT THEY AGREE ON IS THAT MY DAD HAD PLEADED TO STAY WITH ME IN THE HOSPITAL BUT MY MOTHER PUT HER FOOT DOWN.

WHEN I RECENTLY ASKED HER TO RECOUNT THE EVENT, EXASPERATION WAS HOT ON HER BREATH.

I MEAN, OF *COURSE* I'D BE THE ONE TO STAY. I'M YOUR *MOTHER*.

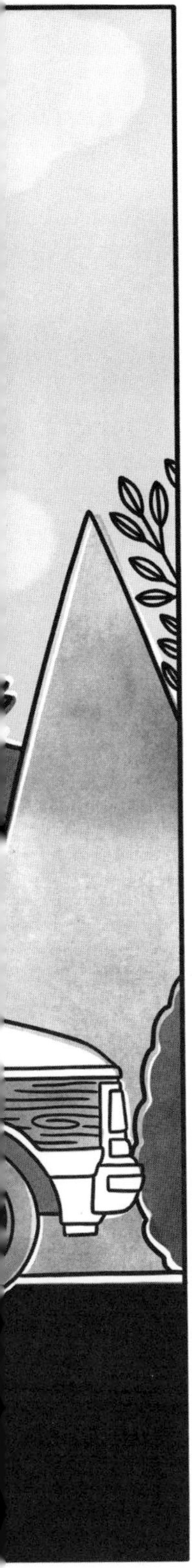

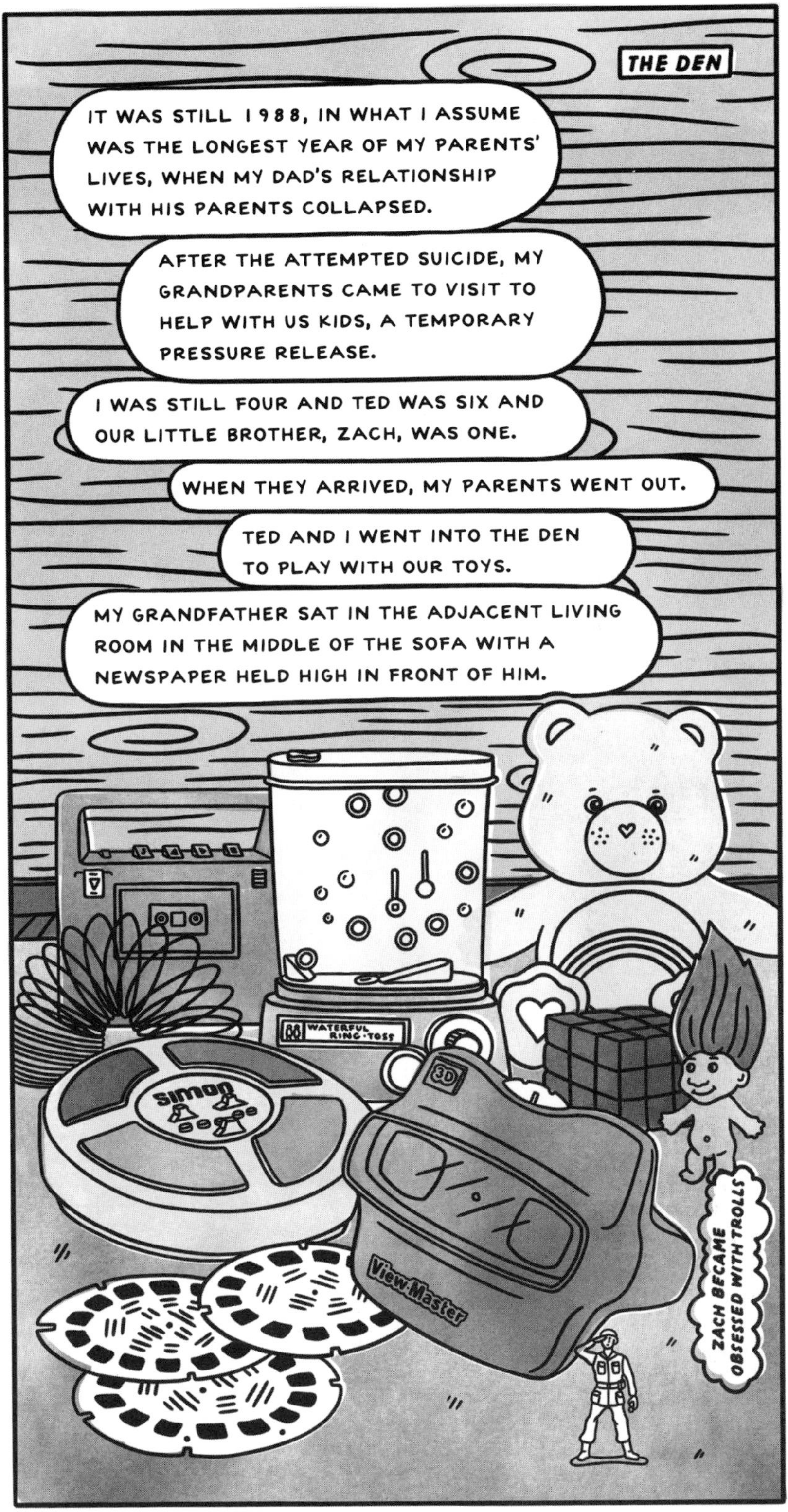
THE DEN
IT WAS STILL 1988, IN WHAT I ASSUME WAS THE LONGEST YEAR OF MY PARENTS' LIVES, WHEN MY DAD'S RELATIONSHIP WITH HIS PARENTS COLLAPSED.
AFTER THE ATTEMPTED SUICIDE, MY GRANDPARENTS CAME TO VISIT TO HELP WITH US KIDS, A TEMPORARY PRESSURE RELEASE.
I WAS STILL FOUR AND TED WAS SIX AND OUR LITTLE BROTHER, ZACH, WAS ONE.
WHEN THEY ARRIVED, MY PARENTS WENT OUT.
TED AND I WENT INTO THE DEN TO PLAY WITH OUR TOYS.
MY GRANDFATHER SAT IN THE ADJACENT LIVING ROOM IN THE MIDDLE OF THE SOFA WITH A NEWSPAPER HELD HIGH IN FRONT OF HIM.
WATERFUL RING-TOSS
SIMON
3D
View-Master
ZACH BECAME OBSESSED WITH TROLLS

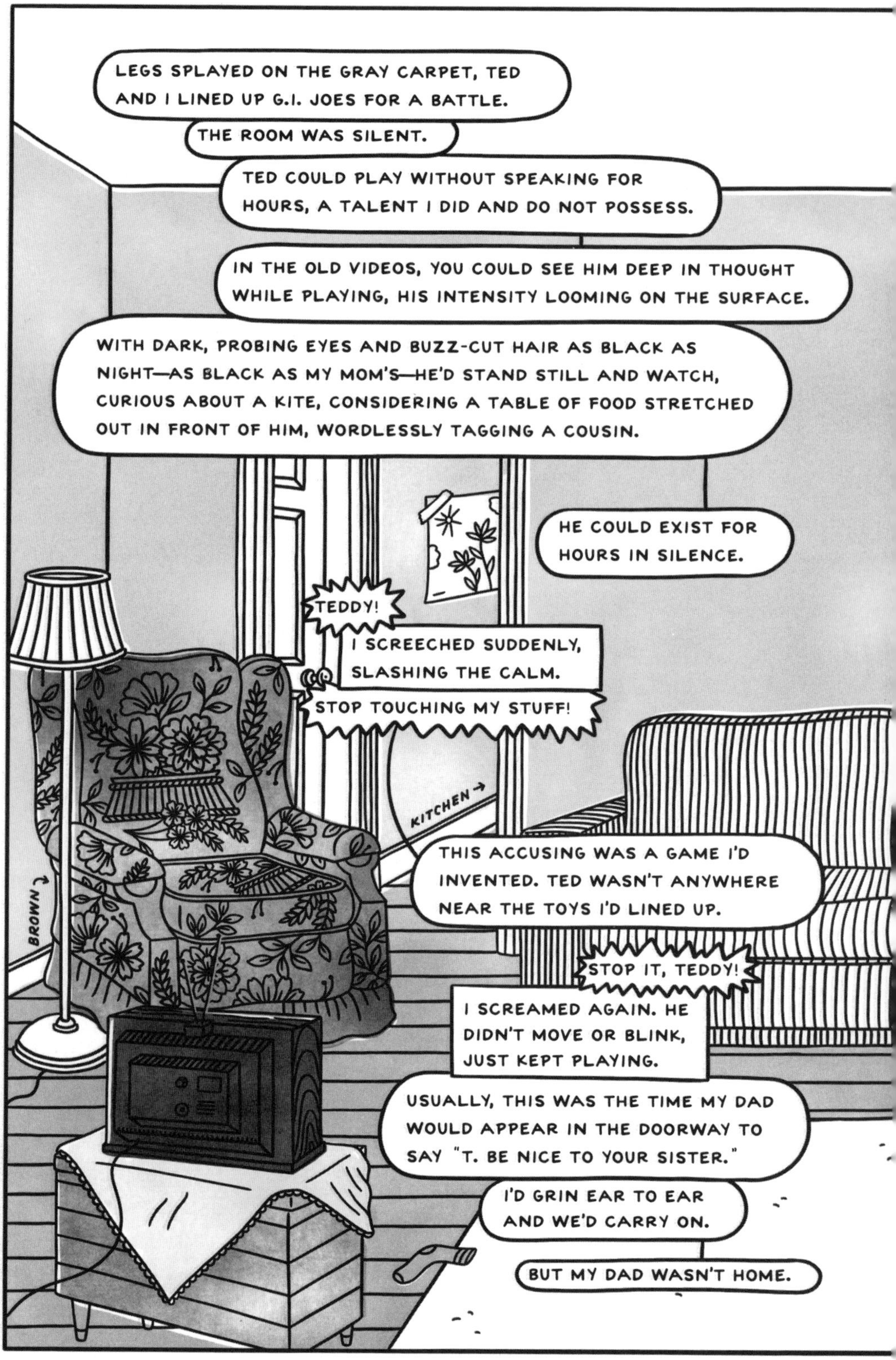
LEGS SPLAYED ON THE GRAY CARPET, TED AND I LINED UP G.I. JOES FOR A BATTLE.
THE ROOM WAS SILENT.
TED COULD PLAY WITHOUT SPEAKING FOR HOURS, A TALENT I DID AND DO NOT POSSESS.
IN THE OLD VIDEOS, YOU COULD SEE HIM DEEP IN THOUGHT WHILE PLAYING, HIS INTENSITY LOOMING ON THE SURFACE.
WITH DARK, PROBING EYES AND BUZZ-CUT HAIR AS BLACK AS NIGHT—AS BLACK AS MY MOM'S—HE'D STAND STILL AND WATCH, CURIOUS ABOUT A KITE, CONSIDERING A TABLE OF FOOD STRETCHED OUT IN FRONT OF HIM, WORDLESSLY TAGGING A COUSIN.
HE COULD EXIST FOR HOURS IN SILENCE.
TEDDY!
I SCREECHED SUDDENLY, SLASHING THE CALM.
STOP TOUCHING MY STUFF!
KITCHEN →
BROWN
THIS ACCUSING WAS A GAME I'D INVENTED. TED WASN'T ANYWHERE NEAR THE TOYS I'D LINED UP.
STOP IT, TEDDY!
I SCREAMED AGAIN. HE DIDN'T MOVE OR BLINK, JUST KEPT PLAYING.
USUALLY, THIS WAS THE TIME MY DAD WOULD APPEAR IN THE DOORWAY TO SAY "T. BE NICE TO YOUR SISTER."
I'D GRIN EAR TO EAR AND WE'D CARRY ON.
BUT MY DAD WASN'T HOME.

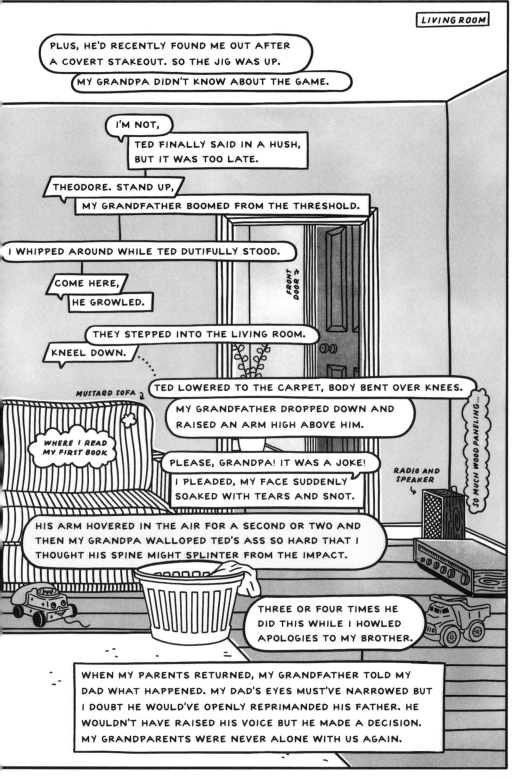

PLUS, HE'D RECENTLY FOUND ME OUT AFTER A COVERT STAKEOUT. SO THE JIG WAS UP.

MY GRANDPA DIDN'T KNOW ABOUT THE GAME.

I'M NOT,

TED FINALLY SAID IN A HUSH, BUT IT WAS TOO LATE.

THEODORE. STAND UP,

MY GRANDFATHER BOOMED FROM THE THRESHOLD.

I WHIPPED AROUND WHILE TED DUTIFULLY STOOD.

COME HERE,

HE GROWLED.

THEY STEPPED INTO THE LIVING ROOM.

KNEEL DOWN.

FRONT DOOR →

MUSTARD SOFA

TED LOWERED TO THE CARPET, BODY BENT OVER KNEES.

MY GRANDFATHER DROPPED DOWN AND RAISED AN ARM HIGH ABOVE HIM.

WHERE I READ MY FIRST BOOK

PLEASE, GRANDPA! IT WAS A JOKE!

I PLEADED, MY FACE SUDDENLY SOAKED WITH TEARS AND SNOT.

RADIO AND SPEAKER →

SO MUCH WOOD PANELING...

HIS ARM HOVERED IN THE AIR FOR A SECOND OR TWO AND THEN MY GRANDPA WALLOPED TED'S ASS SO HARD THAT I THOUGHT HIS SPINE MIGHT SPLINTER FROM THE IMPACT.

THREE OR FOUR TIMES HE DID THIS WHILE I HOWLED APOLOGIES TO MY BROTHER.

WHEN MY PARENTS RETURNED, MY GRANDFATHER TOLD MY DAD WHAT HAPPENED. MY DAD'S EYES MUST'VE NARROWED BUT I DOUBT HE WOULD'VE OPENLY REPRIMANDED HIS FATHER. HE WOULDN'T HAVE RAISED HIS VOICE BUT HE MADE A DECISION. MY GRANDPARENTS WERE NEVER ALONE WITH US AGAIN.

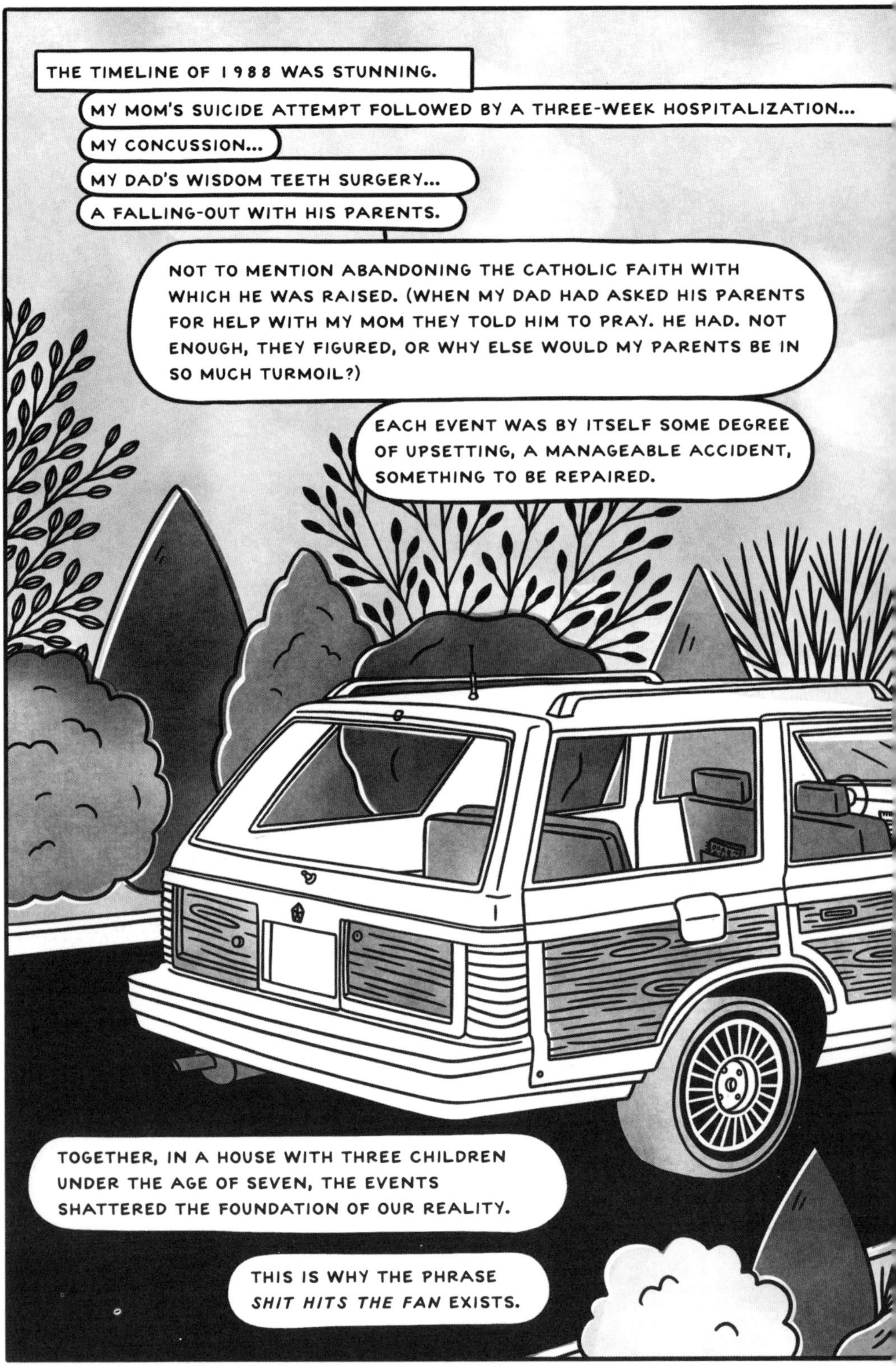
THE TIMELINE OF 1988 WAS STUNNING.
MY MOM'S SUICIDE ATTEMPT FOLLOWED BY A THREE-WEEK HOSPITALIZATION...
MY CONCUSSION...
MY DAD'S WISDOM TEETH SURGERY...
A FALLING-OUT WITH HIS PARENTS.
NOT TO MENTION ABANDONING THE CATHOLIC FAITH WITH WHICH HE WAS RAISED. (WHEN MY DAD HAD ASKED HIS PARENTS FOR HELP WITH MY MOM THEY TOLD HIM TO PRAY. HE HAD. NOT ENOUGH, THEY FIGURED, OR WHY ELSE WOULD MY PARENTS BE IN SO MUCH TURMOIL?)
EACH EVENT WAS BY ITSELF SOME DEGREE OF UPSETTING, A MANAGEABLE ACCIDENT, SOMETHING TO BE REPAIRED.
TOGETHER, IN A HOUSE WITH THREE CHILDREN UNDER THE AGE OF SEVEN, THE EVENTS SHATTERED THE FOUNDATION OF OUR REALITY.
THIS IS WHY THE PHRASE *SHIT HITS THE FAN* EXISTS.

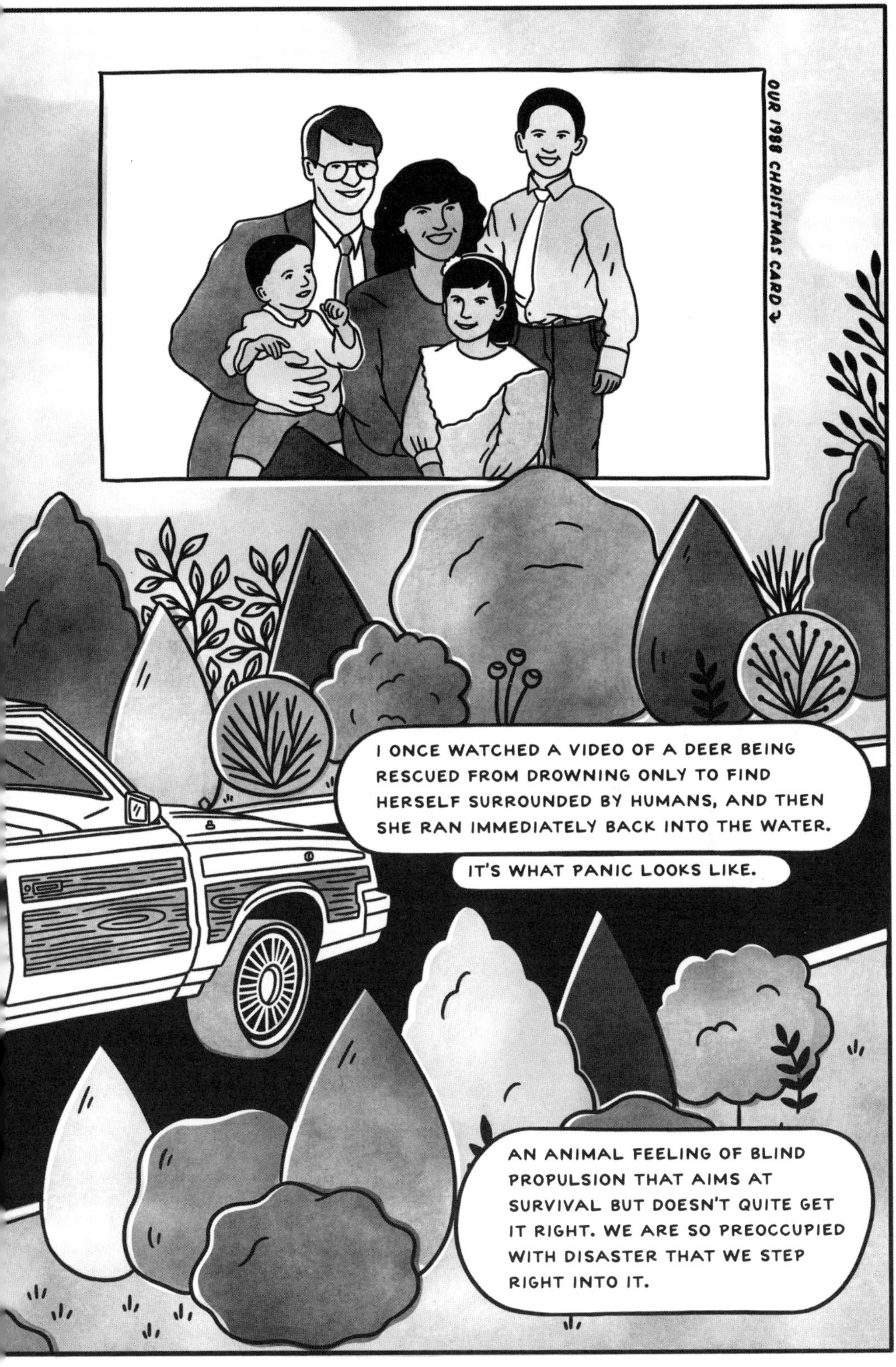
OUR 1988 CHRISTMAS CARD
I ONCE WATCHED A VIDEO OF A DEER BEING RESCUED FROM DROWNING ONLY TO FIND HERSELF SURROUNDED BY HUMANS, AND THEN SHE RAN IMMEDIATELY BACK INTO THE WATER.
IT'S WHAT PANIC LOOKS LIKE.
AN ANIMAL FEELING OF BLIND PROPULSION THAT AIMS AT SURVIVAL BUT DOESN'T QUITE GET IT RIGHT. WE ARE SO PREOCCUPIED WITH DISASTER THAT WE STEP RIGHT INTO IT.

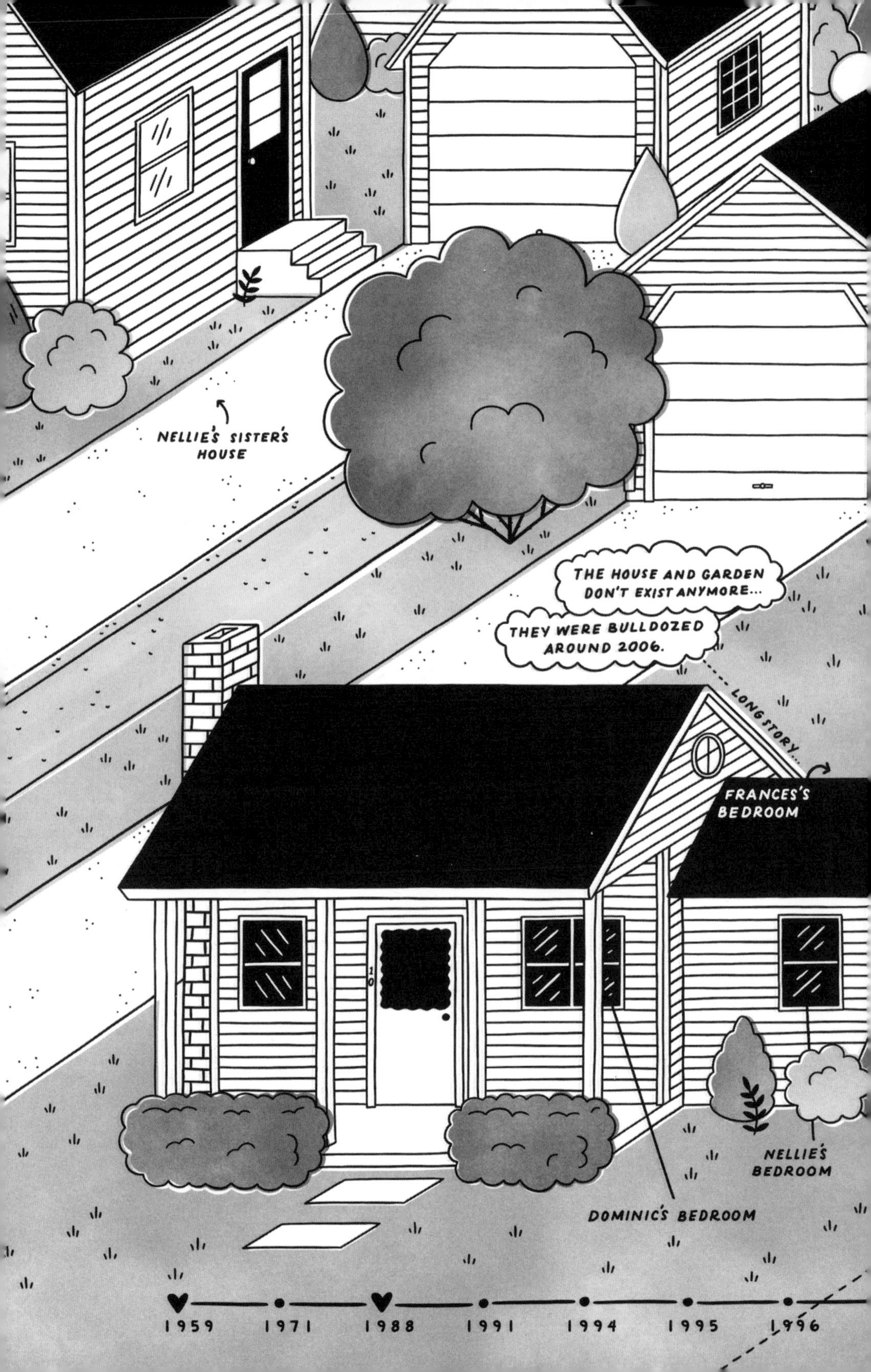
NELLIE'S SISTER'S HOUSE
THE HOUSE AND GARDEN DON'T EXIST ANYMORE...
THEY WERE BULLDOZED AROUND 2006.
LONG STORY...
FRANCES'S BEDROOM
10
NELLIE'S BEDROOM
DOMINIC'S BEDROOM
1959
1971
1988
1991
1994
1995
1996

CHAPTER 06

The History

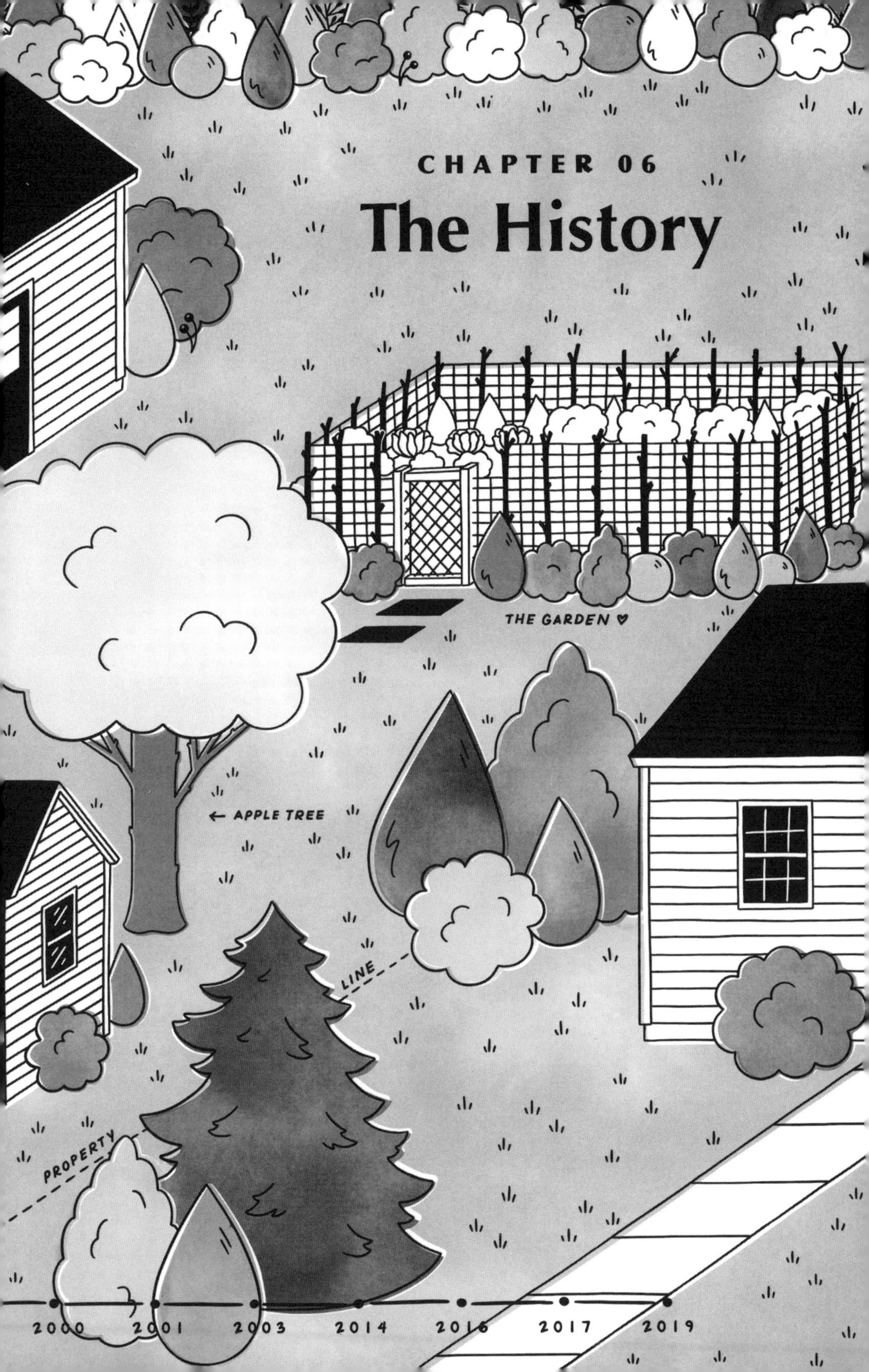
THE GARDEN ♥
← APPLE TREE
PROPERTY LINE
2000
2001
2003
2014
2016
2017
2019

A SURVEY MADE FOR THE TRANSFER OF SOME PROPERTY

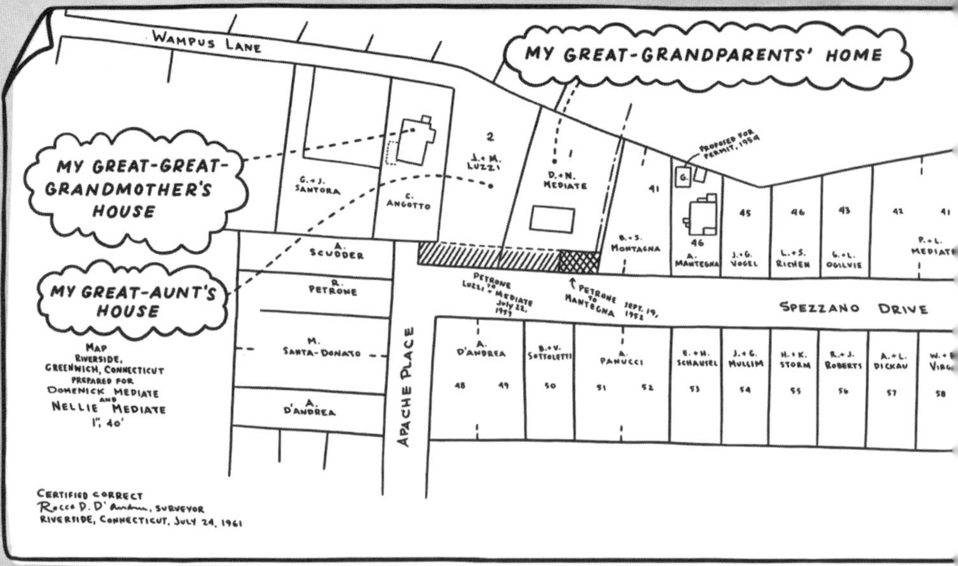

WAMPUS LANE
MY GREAT-GRANDPARENTS' HOME
MY GREAT-GREAT-GRANDMOTHER'S HOUSE
MY GREAT-AUNT'S HOUSE
2
J. + M. LUZZI
G. + J. SANTORA
C. ANGOTTO
D. + N. MEDIATE
1
41
PROPOSED FOR PERMIT, 1954
G.
45
46
43
42
41
46
B. + S. MONTAGNA
A. MANTEGNA
J. + G. VOGEL
L. + S. RICHEN
G. + L. OGILVIE
P. + L. MEDIATE
A. SCUDDER
R. PETRONE
PETRONE LUZZI TO MEDIATE July 22, 1957
PETRONE TO MANTEGNA SEPT. 19, 1952
SPEZZANO DRIVE
M. SANTA-DONATO
APACHE PLACE
A. D'ANDREA
B. + V. SOTTOLETTI
A. PANUCCI
E. + H. SCHAUSEL
J. + G. MULLIM
H. + K. STORM
R. + J. ROBERTS
A. + L. DICKAU
48
49
50
51
52
53
54
55
56
57
58
A. D'ANDREA
MAP RIVERSIDE, GREENWICH, CONNECTICUT PREPARED FOR DOMENICK MEDIATE AND NELLIE MEDIATE
1", 40'
CERTIFIED CORRECT
Rocco D. D'Andrea, SURVEYOR
RIVERSIDE, CONNECTICUT, JULY 24, 1961

NELLIE AND DOMINIC SAVED A SURPRISING AMOUNT OF MONEY

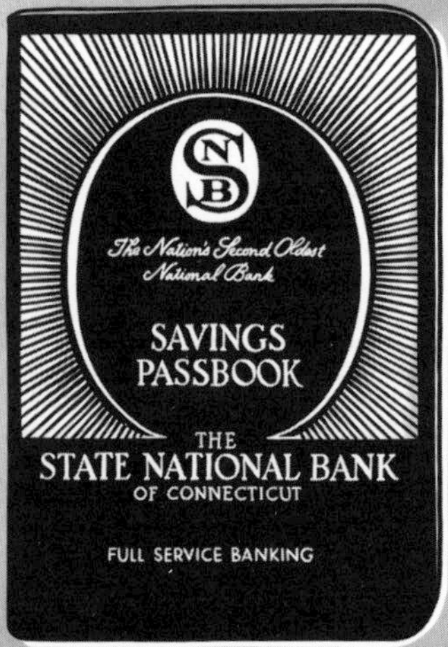

SNB
The Nation's Second Oldest National Bank
SAVINGS PASSBOOK
THE STATE NATIONAL BANK OF CONNECTICUT
FULL SERVICE BANKING

CORRESPONDENCE REGARDING THE IMMIGRATION OF MY GREAT-GREAT-UNCLES FROM ITALY

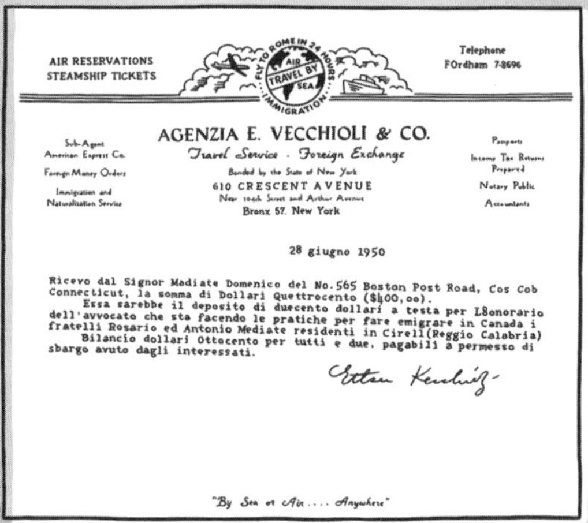

AIR RESERVATIONS
STEAMSHIP TICKETS

FLY TO ROME IN 24 HOURS — AIR — TRAVEL BY — SEA — IMMIGRATION

Telephone
FOrdham 7-8696

AGENZIA E. VECCHIOLI & CO.
Travel Service - Foreign Exchange
Bonded by the State of New York
610 CRESCENT AVENUE
Near 186th Street and Arthur Avenue
Bronx 57, New York

Sub-Agent American Express Co.
Foreign Money Orders
Immigration and Naturalization Service

Passports
Income Tax Returns Prepared
Notary Public
Accountants

28 giugno 1950

Ricevo dal Signor Mediate Domenico del No.565 Boston Post Road, Cos Cob Connecticut, la somma di Dollari Quattrocento ($400,oo).
Essa sarebbe il deposito di duecento dollari a testa per l8onorario dell'avvocato che sta facendo le pratiche per fare emigrare in Canada i fratelli Rosario ed Antonio Mediate residenti in Cirell(Reggio Calabria)
Bilancio dollari Ottocento per tutti e due, pagabili a permesso di sbargo avuto dagli interessati.

"By Sea or Air . . . . Anywhere"

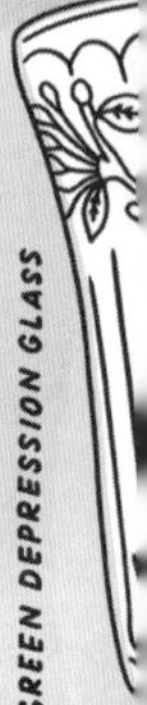

GREEN DEPRESSION GLASS

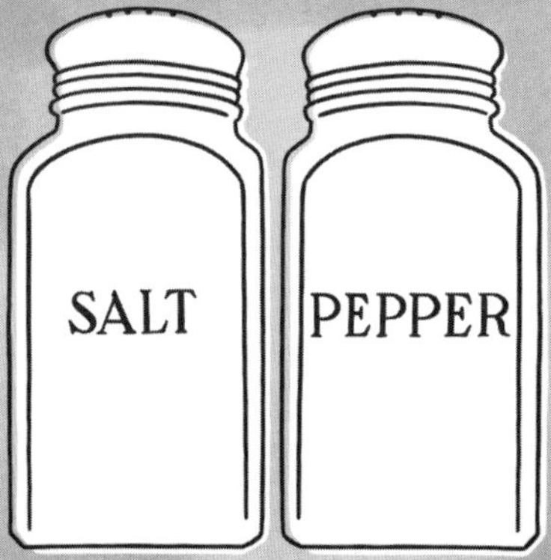

SALT
PEPPER

THESE REMIND ME OF NELLIE'S KITCHEN

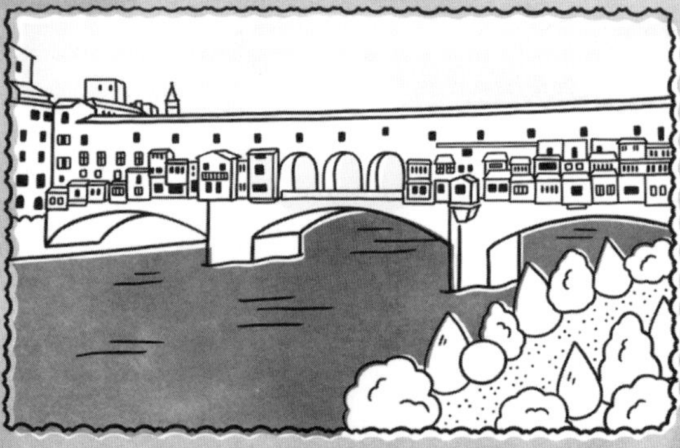

PHOTO OF PONTE VECCHIO IN FLORENCE, ITALY (OCTOBER 6, 1952 — WE DON'T KNOW WHO TOOK THE PICTURE)

MY GRANDMOTHER AND GREAT-GRANDPARENTS

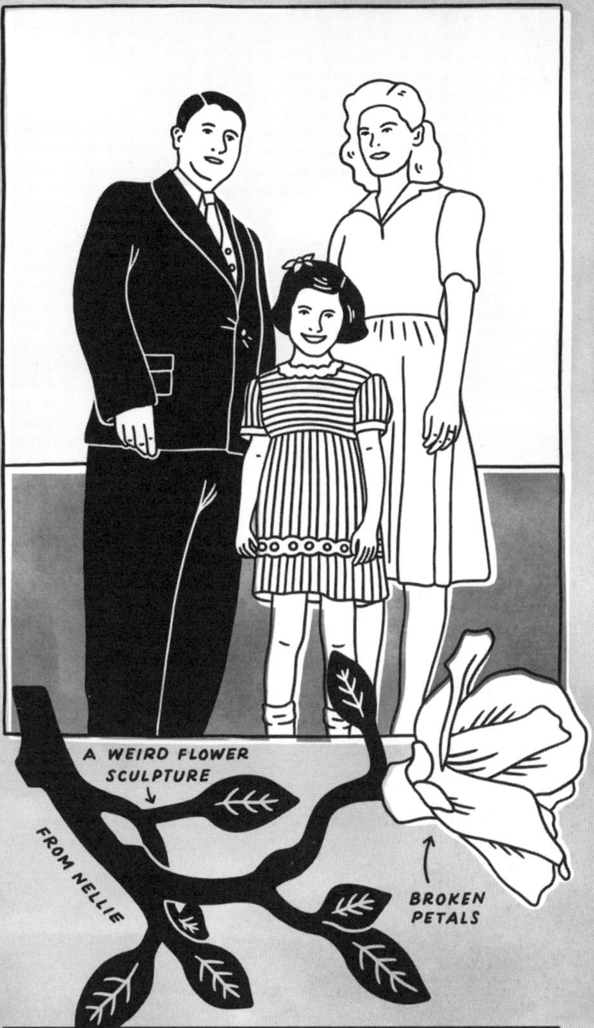
A WEIRD FLOWER SCULPTURE
FROM NELLIE
BROKEN PETALS

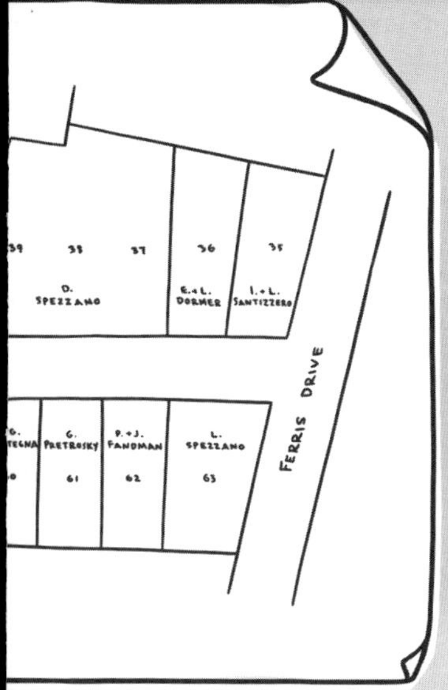
39
38
37
36
35
D. SPEZZANO
E. + L. DORMER
I. + L. SANTIZZERO
FERRIS DRIVE
G. PRETROSKY
P. + J. FANDMAN
L. SPEZZANO
61
62
63

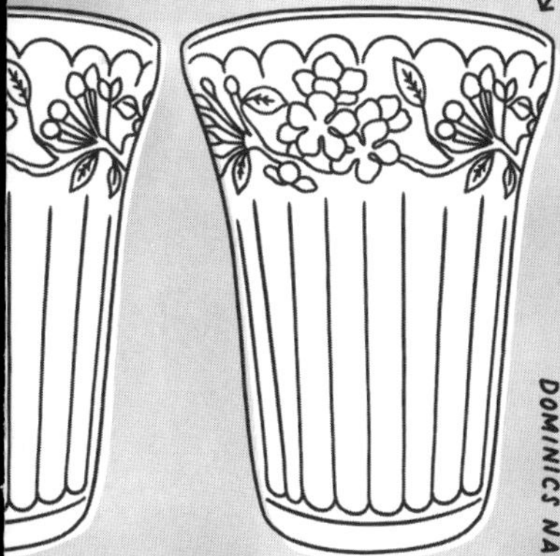

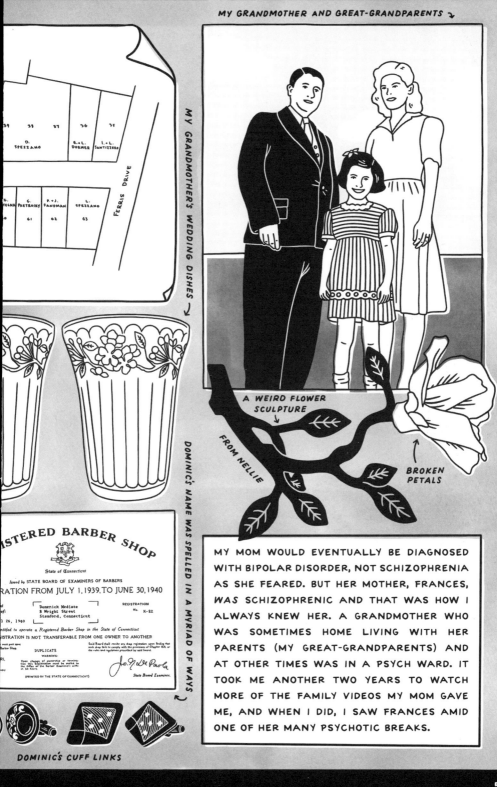

MY GRANDMOTHER'S WEDDING DISHES

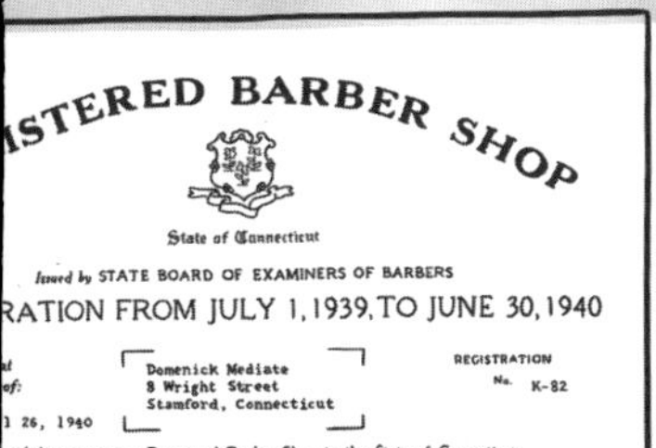
ISTERED BARBER SHOP

State of Connecticut

Issued by STATE BOARD OF EXAMINERS OF BARBERS

RATION FROM JULY 1, 1939, TO JUNE 30, 1940

Domenick Mediate
8 Wright Street
Stamford, Connecticut

REGISTRATION No. K-82

1 26, 1940

ntitled to operate a Registered Barber Shop in the State of Connecticut

ISTRATION IS NOT TRANSFERABLE FROM ONE OWNER TO ANOTHER

DUPLICATE

WARNING:

Upon change of ownership or termination this Registration must be mailed to the Office of the Barber Examiners within 24 hours.

Said Board shall revoke any shop registration upon finding that such shop fails to comply with the provisions of Chapter 164, or the rules and regulations prescribed by said board.

(PRINTED BY THE STATE OF CONNECTICUT)

State Board Examiner.

DOMINIC'S NAME WAS SPELLED IN A MYRIAD OF WAYS

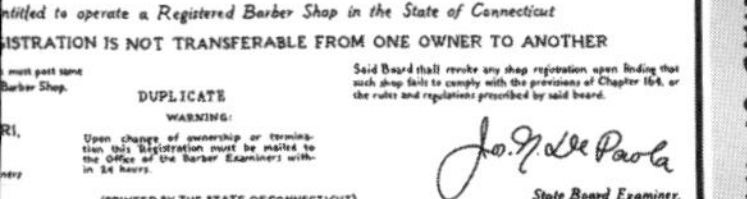

DOMINIC'S CUFF LINKS

MY MOM WOULD EVENTUALLY BE DIAGNOSED WITH BIPOLAR DISORDER, NOT SCHIZOPHRENIA AS SHE FEARED. BUT HER MOTHER, FRANCES, *WAS* SCHIZOPHRENIC AND THAT WAS HOW I ALWAYS KNEW HER. A GRANDMOTHER WHO WAS SOMETIMES HOME LIVING WITH HER PARENTS (MY GREAT-GRANDPARENTS) AND AT OTHER TIMES WAS IN A PSYCH WARD. IT TOOK ME ANOTHER TWO YEARS TO WATCH MORE OF THE FAMILY VIDEOS MY MOM GAVE ME, AND WHEN I DID, I SAW FRANCES AMID ONE OF HER MANY PSYCHOTIC BREAKS.

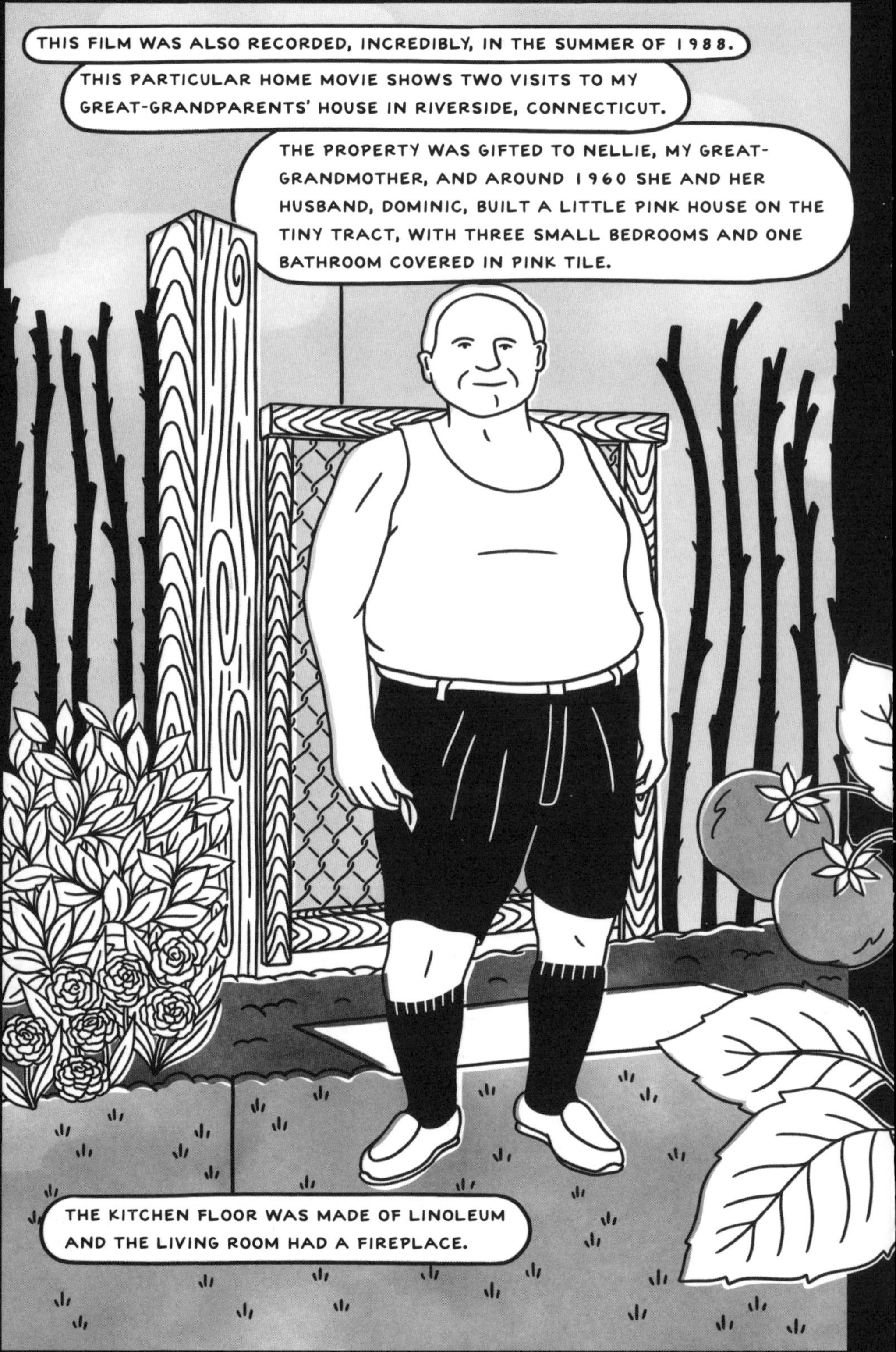
THIS FILM WAS ALSO RECORDED, INCREDIBLY, IN THE SUMMER OF 1988.
THIS PARTICULAR HOME MOVIE SHOWS TWO VISITS TO MY GREAT-GRANDPARENTS' HOUSE IN RIVERSIDE, CONNECTICUT.
THE PROPERTY WAS GIFTED TO NELLIE, MY GREAT-GRANDMOTHER, AND AROUND 1960 SHE AND HER HUSBAND, DOMINIC, BUILT A LITTLE PINK HOUSE ON THE TINY TRACT, WITH THREE SMALL BEDROOMS AND ONE BATHROOM COVERED IN PINK TILE.
THE KITCHEN FLOOR WAS MADE OF LINOLEUM AND THE LIVING ROOM HAD A FIREPLACE.

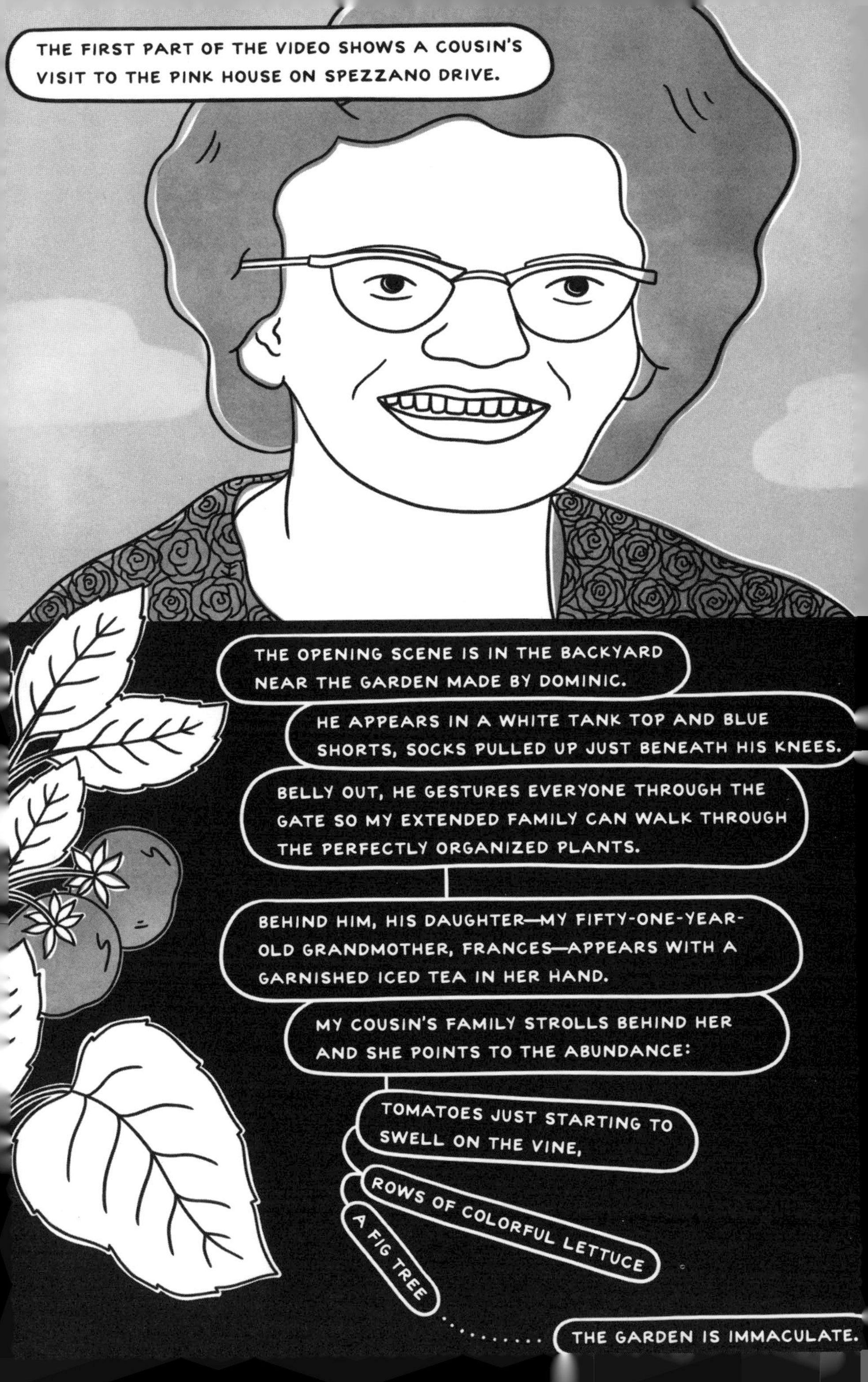

THE FIRST PART OF THE VIDEO SHOWS A COUSIN'S VISIT TO THE PINK HOUSE ON SPEZZANO DRIVE.
THE OPENING SCENE IS IN THE BACKYARD NEAR THE GARDEN MADE BY DOMINIC.
HE APPEARS IN A WHITE TANK TOP AND BLUE SHORTS, SOCKS PULLED UP JUST BENEATH HIS KNEES.
BELLY OUT, HE GESTURES EVERYONE THROUGH THE GATE SO MY EXTENDED FAMILY CAN WALK THROUGH THE PERFECTLY ORGANIZED PLANTS.
BEHIND HIM, HIS DAUGHTER—MY FIFTY-ONE-YEAR-OLD GRANDMOTHER, FRANCES—APPEARS WITH A GARNISHED ICED TEA IN HER HAND.
MY COUSIN'S FAMILY STROLLS BEHIND HER AND SHE POINTS TO THE ABUNDANCE:
TOMATOES JUST STARTING TO SWELL ON THE VINE,
ROWS OF COLORFUL LETTUCE
A FIG TREE
THE GARDEN IS IMMACULATE.

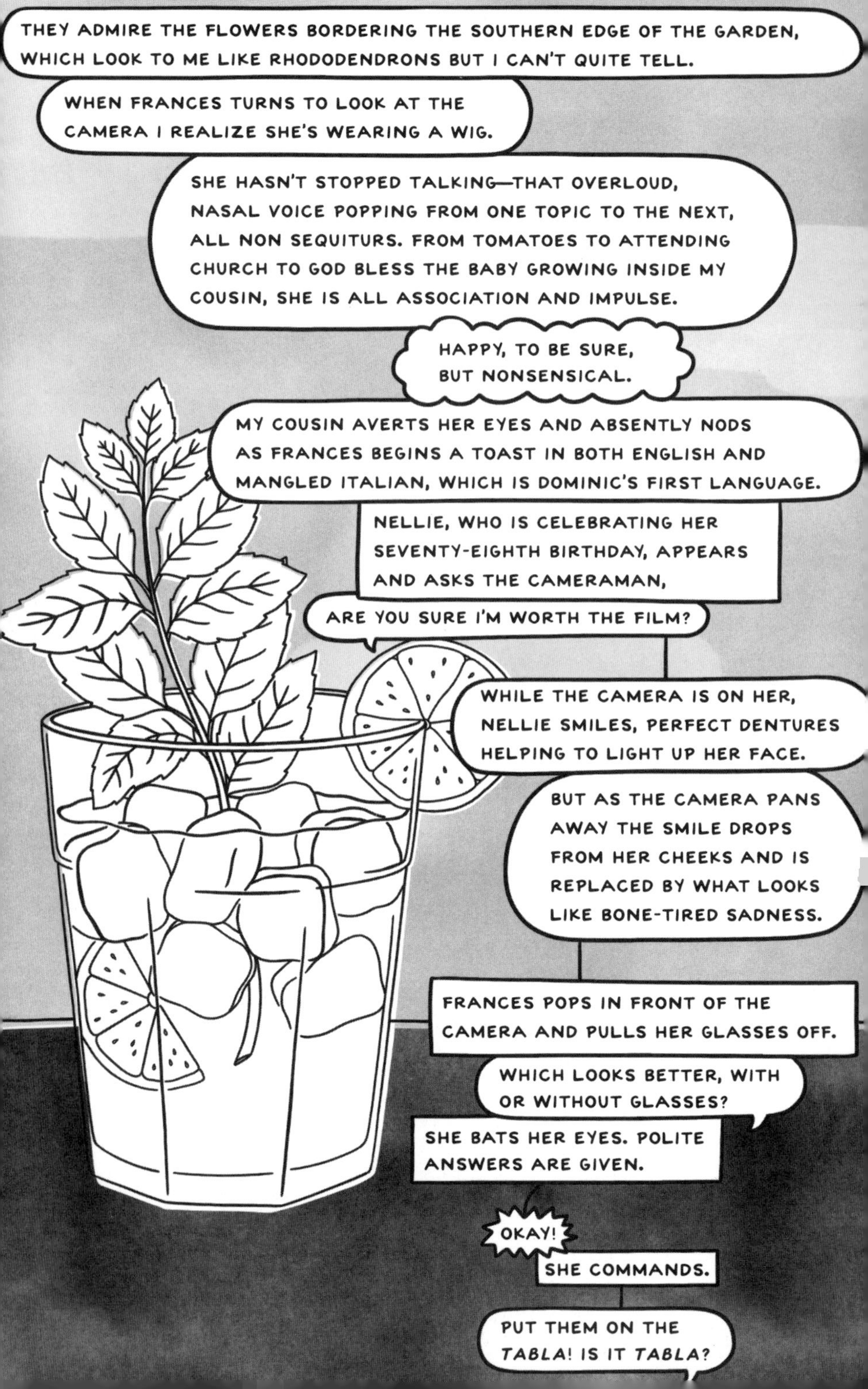
THEY ADMIRE THE FLOWERS BORDERING THE SOUTHERN EDGE OF THE GARDEN, WHICH LOOK TO ME LIKE RHODODENDRONS BUT I CAN'T QUITE TELL.
WHEN FRANCES TURNS TO LOOK AT THE CAMERA I REALIZE SHE'S WEARING A WIG.
SHE HASN'T STOPPED TALKING—THAT OVERLOUD, NASAL VOICE POPPING FROM ONE TOPIC TO THE NEXT, ALL NON SEQUITURS. FROM TOMATOES TO ATTENDING CHURCH TO GOD BLESS THE BABY GROWING INSIDE MY COUSIN, SHE IS ALL ASSOCIATION AND IMPULSE.
HAPPY, TO BE SURE, BUT NONSENSICAL.
MY COUSIN AVERTS HER EYES AND ABSENTLY NODS AS FRANCES BEGINS A TOAST IN BOTH ENGLISH AND MANGLED ITALIAN, WHICH IS DOMINIC'S FIRST LANGUAGE.
NELLIE, WHO IS CELEBRATING HER SEVENTY-EIGHTH BIRTHDAY, APPEARS AND ASKS THE CAMERAMAN,
ARE YOU SURE I'M WORTH THE FILM?
WHILE THE CAMERA IS ON HER, NELLIE SMILES, PERFECT DENTURES HELPING TO LIGHT UP HER FACE.
BUT AS THE CAMERA PANS AWAY THE SMILE DROPS FROM HER CHEEKS AND IS REPLACED BY WHAT LOOKS LIKE BONE-TIRED SADNESS.
FRANCES POPS IN FRONT OF THE CAMERA AND PULLS HER GLASSES OFF.
WHICH LOOKS BETTER, WITH OR WITHOUT GLASSES?
SHE BATS HER EYES. POLITE ANSWERS ARE GIVEN.
OKAY!
SHE COMMANDS.
PUT THEM ON THE *TABLA*! IS IT *TABLA*?

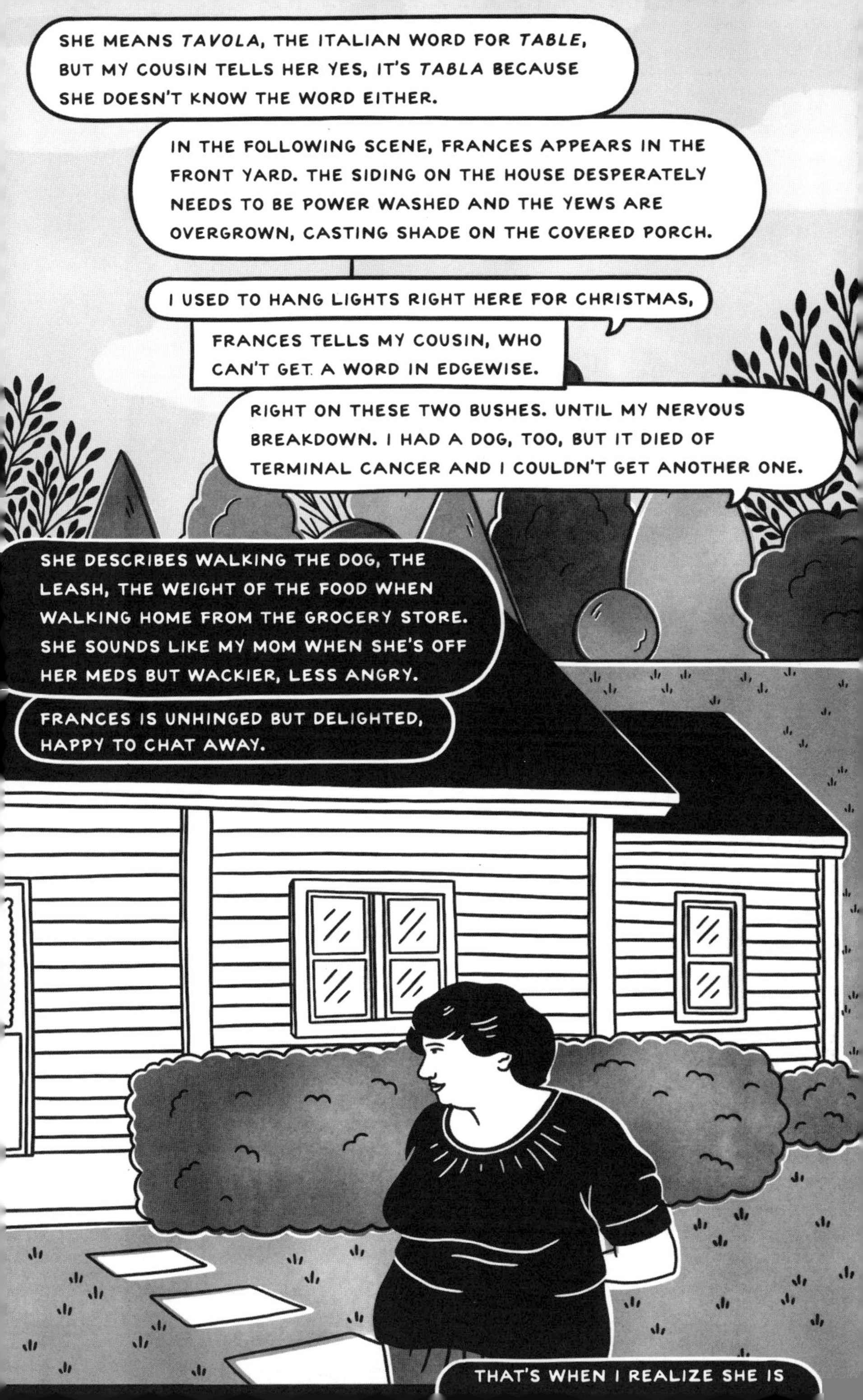
SHE MEANS *TAVOLA*, THE ITALIAN WORD FOR *TABLE*, BUT MY COUSIN TELLS HER YES, IT'S *TABLA* BECAUSE SHE DOESN'T KNOW THE WORD EITHER.
IN THE FOLLOWING SCENE, FRANCES APPEARS IN THE FRONT YARD. THE SIDING ON THE HOUSE DESPERATELY NEEDS TO BE POWER WASHED AND THE YEWS ARE OVERGROWN, CASTING SHADE ON THE COVERED PORCH.
I USED TO HANG LIGHTS RIGHT HERE FOR CHRISTMAS,
FRANCES TELLS MY COUSIN, WHO CAN'T GET A WORD IN EDGEWISE.
RIGHT ON THESE TWO BUSHES. UNTIL MY NERVOUS BREAKDOWN. I HAD A DOG, TOO, BUT IT DIED OF TERMINAL CANCER AND I COULDN'T GET ANOTHER ONE.
SHE DESCRIBES WALKING THE DOG, THE LEASH, THE WEIGHT OF THE FOOD WHEN WALKING HOME FROM THE GROCERY STORE. SHE SOUNDS LIKE MY MOM WHEN SHE'S OFF HER MEDS BUT WACKIER, LESS ANGRY.
FRANCES IS UNHINGED BUT DELIGHTED, HAPPY TO CHAT AWAY.
THAT'S WHEN I REALIZE SHE IS

IN 1956, ALMOST THIRTY YEARS BEFORE THIS VIDEO WAS FILMED, FRANCES WAS TWENTY-ONE AND NEWLY MARRIED TO MY GRANDFATHER SAL AND PREGNANT WITH MY MOM.

NELLIE WENT TO VISIT HER DAUGHTER IN THE NEXT TOWN AND REALIZED THERE WAS NO FOOD IN THE REFRIGERATOR.

FRANCES HAD LOST WEIGHT.

THIS WAS THE FIRST SIGN THAT SOMETHING WAS WRONG.

LESS THAN THREE YEARS LATER, FRANCES WAS SENT TO FAIRFIELD HILLS, A NOW-DEFUNCT HOSPITAL ORIGINALLY ERECTED FOR THE CRIMINALLY INSANE BUT LATER OPENED TO NONCRIMINAL PSYCHIATRIC PATIENTS.

MY MOM DOESN'T KNOW WHAT SPECIFIC BEHAVIOR GOT FRANCES SENT TO THE HOSPITAL AND, ACCORDING TO THE ARCHIVIST AT THE CONNECTICUT STATE LIBRARY, THE PATIENT FILES WERE DESTROYED.

↙ ONE OF THE ADMINISTRATION BUILDINGS

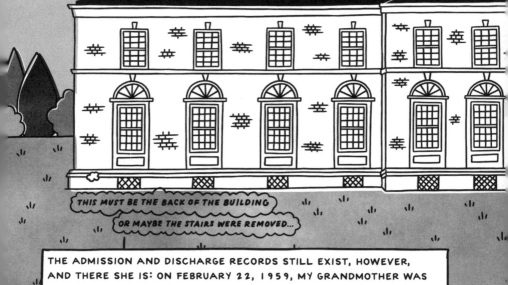

THIS MUST BE THE BACK OF THE BUILDING

OR MAYBE THE STAIRS WERE REMOVED...

THE ADMISSION AND DISCHARGE RECORDS STILL EXIST, HOWEVER, AND THERE SHE IS: ON FEBRUARY 22, 1959, MY GRANDMOTHER WAS ADMITTED TO WARD CO 3D AT FAIRFIELD HILLS HOSPITAL. I CAN'T TELL IF THE DISCHARGE DATE IS JULY 2, 1959, OR MARCH 11, 1961.

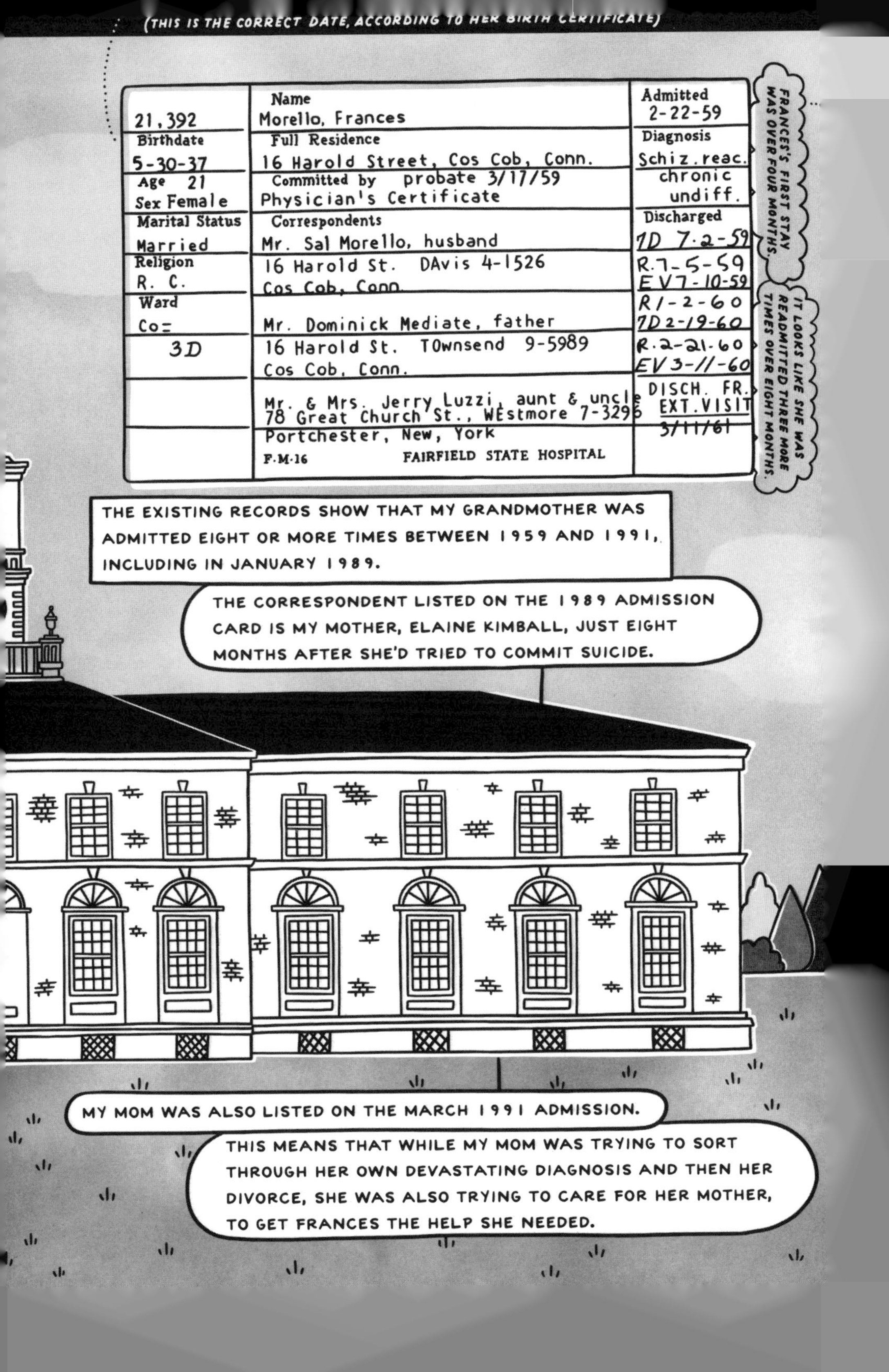

	Name	Admitted
21,392	Morello, Frances	2-22-59
Birthdate	**Full Residence**	**Diagnosis**
5-30-37	16 Harold Street, Cos Cob, Conn.	Schiz. reac.
Age 21	**Committed by** probate 3/17/59	chronic
Sex Female	Physician's Certificate	undiff.
Marital Status	**Correspondents**	**Discharged**
Married	Mr. Sal Morello, husband	7D 7-2-59
Religion	16 Harold St. DAvis 4-1526	R. 7-5-59
R. C.	Cos Cob, Conn.	E V7-10-59
Ward		R 1-2-60
Co=	Mr. Dominick Mediate, father	7D 2-19-60
3D	16 Harold St. TOwnsend 9-5989	R. 2-21-60
	Cos Cob, Conn.	EV 3-11-60
	Mr. & Mrs. Jerry Luzzi, aunt & uncle	DISCH. FR.
	78 Great Church St., WEstmore 7-3296	EXT. VISIT
	Portchester, New, York	3/11/61
	F·M·16 FAIRFIELD STATE HOSPITAL	

FRANCES'S FIRST STAY WAS OVER FOUR MONTHS.

IT LOOKS LIKE SHE WAS READMITTED THREE MORE TIMES OVER EIGHT MONTHS.

THE EXISTING RECORDS SHOW THAT MY GRANDMOTHER WAS ADMITTED EIGHT OR MORE TIMES BETWEEN 1959 AND 1991, INCLUDING IN JANUARY 1989.

THE CORRESPONDENT LISTED ON THE 1989 ADMISSION CARD IS MY MOTHER, ELAINE KIMBALL, JUST EIGHT MONTHS AFTER SHE'D TRIED TO COMMIT SUICIDE.

MY MOM WAS ALSO LISTED ON THE MARCH 1991 ADMISSION.

THIS MEANS THAT WHILE MY MOM WAS TRYING TO SORT THROUGH HER OWN DEVASTATING DIAGNOSIS AND THEN HER DIVORCE, SHE WAS ALSO TRYING TO CARE FOR HER MOTHER, TO GET FRANCES THE HELP SHE NEEDED.

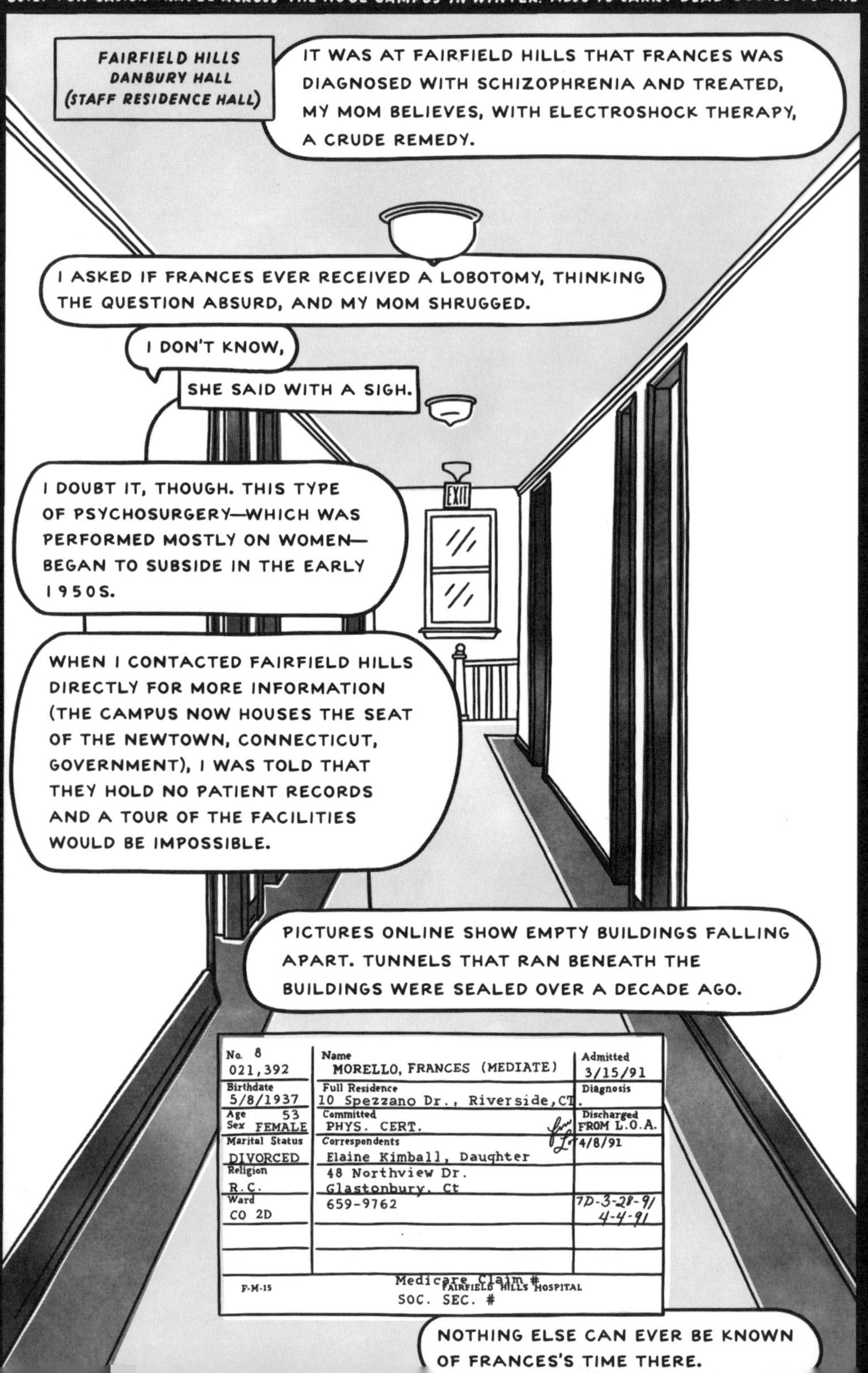
FAIRFIELD HILLS
DANBURY HALL
(STAFF RESIDENCE HALL)
IT WAS AT FAIRFIELD HILLS THAT FRANCES WAS DIAGNOSED WITH SCHIZOPHRENIA AND TREATED, MY MOM BELIEVES, WITH ELECTROSHOCK THERAPY, A CRUDE REMEDY.
I ASKED IF FRANCES EVER RECEIVED A LOBOTOMY, THINKING THE QUESTION ABSURD, AND MY MOM SHRUGGED.
I DON'T KNOW,
SHE SAID WITH A SIGH.
I DOUBT IT, THOUGH. THIS TYPE OF PSYCHOSURGERY—WHICH WAS PERFORMED MOSTLY ON WOMEN—BEGAN TO SUBSIDE IN THE EARLY 1950S.
WHEN I CONTACTED FAIRFIELD HILLS DIRECTLY FOR MORE INFORMATION (THE CAMPUS NOW HOUSES THE SEAT OF THE NEWTOWN, CONNECTICUT, GOVERNMENT), I WAS TOLD THAT THEY HOLD NO PATIENT RECORDS AND A TOUR OF THE FACILITIES WOULD BE IMPOSSIBLE.
PICTURES ONLINE SHOW EMPTY BUILDINGS FALLING APART. TUNNELS THAT RAN BENEATH THE BUILDINGS WERE SEALED OVER A DECADE AGO.
No. 8
021,392
Name
MORELLO, FRANCES (MEDIATE)
Admitted
3/15/91
Birthdate
5/8/1937
Full Residence
10 Spezzano Dr., Riverside, CT.
Diagnosis
Age 53
Sex FEMALE
Committed
PHYS. CERT.
Discharged
FROM L.O.A.
4/8/91
Marital Status
DIVORCED
Correspondents
Elaine Kimball, Daughter
48 Northview Dr.
Glastonbury, Ct
659-9762
Religion
R.C.
Ward
CO 2D
7D-3-28-91
4-4-91
F-M-15
Medicare Claim #
FAIRFIELD HILLS HOSPITAL
SOC. SEC. #
NOTHING ELSE CAN EVER BE KNOWN OF FRANCES'S TIME THERE.

FROM PHOTOS FOUND ONLINE. UP UNTIL 2007 YOU COULD TRESPASS INTO THE DI

INCLUDING THE UNDERGROUND TUNNELS BUILT FOR EASIER TRAVEL ACROSS THE HUGE CAMPUS IN WINTER. ALSO TO CARRY DEAD BODIES TO THE MORGUE. I DIDN'T LEARN OF MY GRANDMOTHER'S STAY THERE UNTIL AFTER THE BUILDINGS WERE LOCKED AND PATIENT RECORDS DESTROYED.

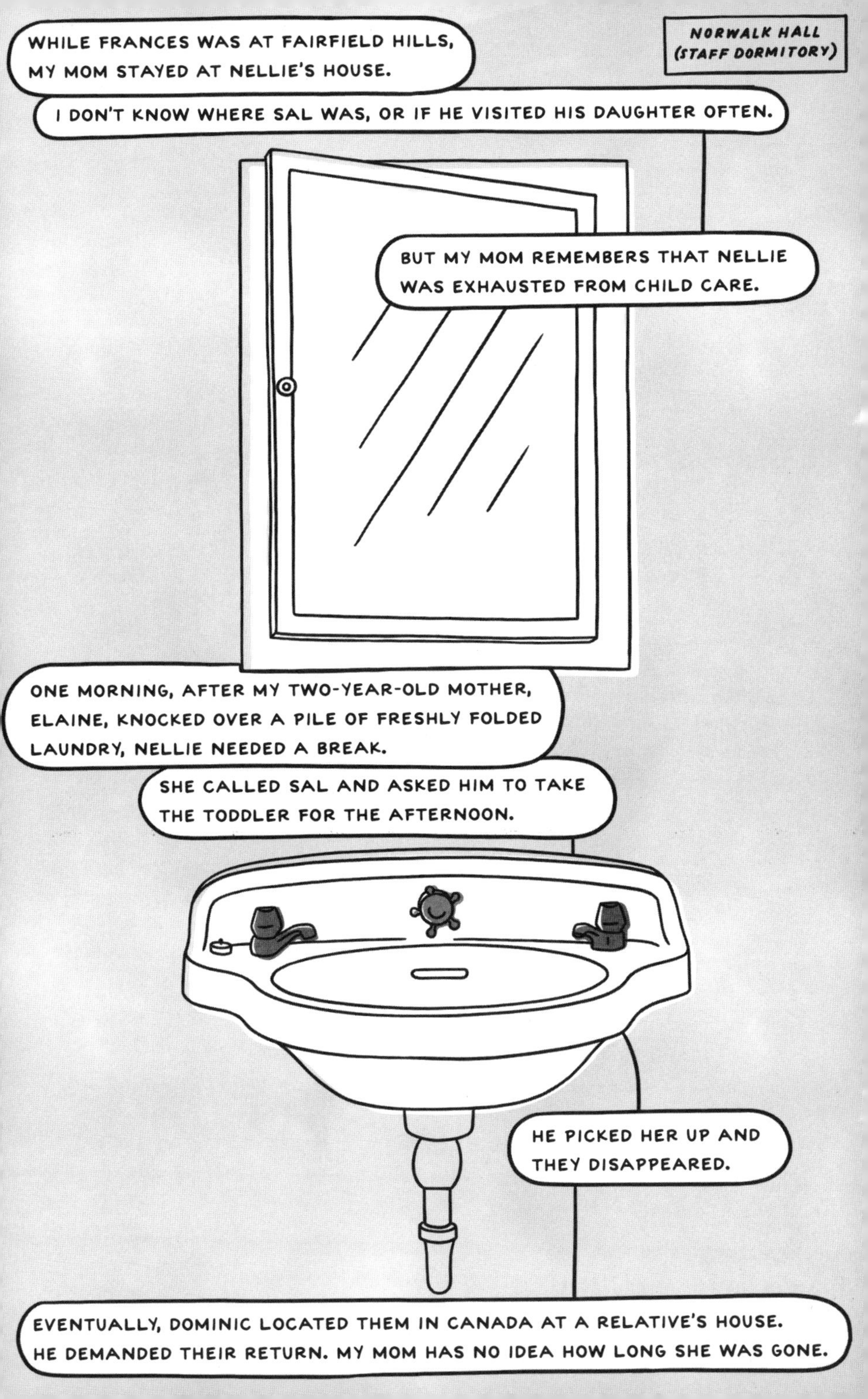
WHILE FRANCES WAS AT FAIRFIELD HILLS, MY MOM STAYED AT NELLIE'S HOUSE.
NORWALK HALL (STAFF DORMITORY)
I DON'T KNOW WHERE SAL WAS, OR IF HE VISITED HIS DAUGHTER OFTEN.
BUT MY MOM REMEMBERS THAT NELLIE WAS EXHAUSTED FROM CHILD CARE.
ONE MORNING, AFTER MY TWO-YEAR-OLD MOTHER, ELAINE, KNOCKED OVER A PILE OF FRESHLY FOLDED LAUNDRY, NELLIE NEEDED A BREAK.
SHE CALLED SAL AND ASKED HIM TO TAKE THE TODDLER FOR THE AFTERNOON.
HE PICKED HER UP AND THEY DISAPPEARED.
EVENTUALLY, DOMINIC LOCATED THEM IN CANADA AT A RELATIVE'S HOUSE. HE DEMANDED THEIR RETURN. MY MOM HAS NO IDEA HOW LONG SHE WAS GONE.

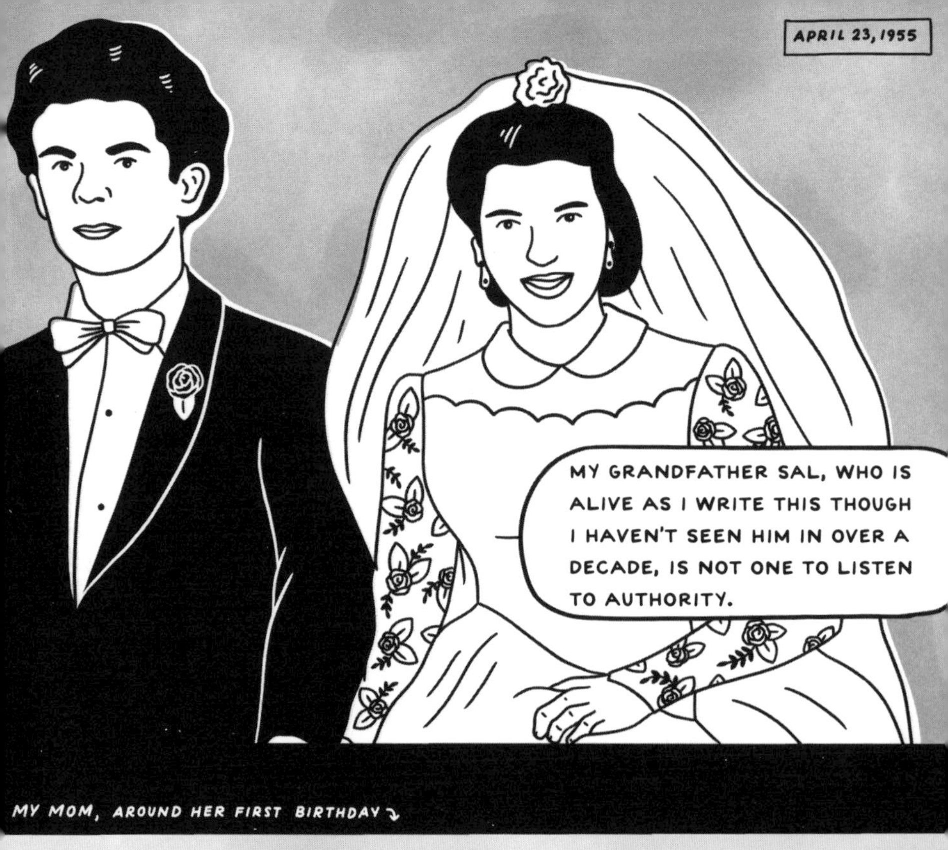
APRIL 23, 1955
MY GRANDFATHER SAL, WHO IS ALIVE AS I WRITE THIS THOUGH I HAVEN'T SEEN HIM IN OVER A DECADE, IS NOT ONE TO LISTEN TO AUTHORITY.
MY MOM, AROUND HER FIRST BIRTHDAY

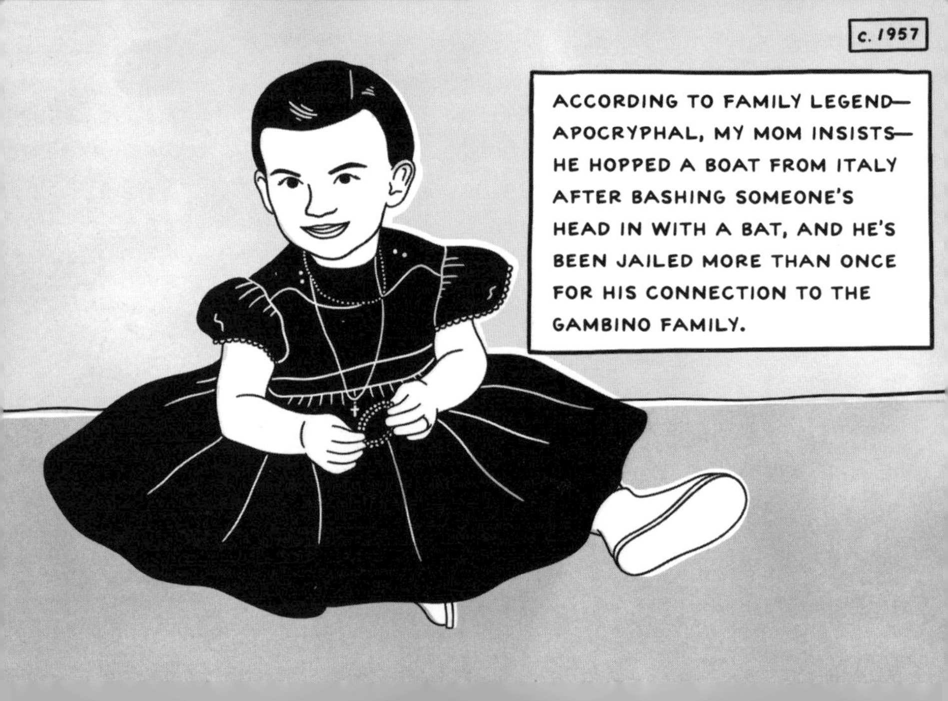
c. 1957
ACCORDING TO FAMILY LEGEND—APOCRYPHAL, MY MOM INSISTS—HE HOPPED A BOAT FROM ITALY AFTER BASHING SOMEONE'S HEAD IN WITH A BAT, AND HE'S BEEN JAILED MORE THAN ONCE FOR HIS CONNECTION TO THE GAMBINO FAMILY.

ADA STORY IS ALWAYS TOLD AS A KIDNAPPING, BUT I WONDER IF MY
ATHER REALIZED FRANCES WOULD NEVER BE FULLY ABLE TO CARE FOR T
ND FIGURED HIS SISTER COULD BE A SURROGATE MOTHER, SOMEONE TO GI
HTER A STABLE HOME, A FAMILY FULL OF COUSINS, FOOD ON THE TABLE

FACT THAT HE WAS REACHABLE, THAT HE AGREED
RETURN MY MOTHER AFTER NO-ONE-KNOWS-HOW-
G TELLS ME THAT THIS WAS SOMETHING SOFTER
N A KIDNAPPING, SOMETHING WITH A TINGE OF
PERATION SURROUNDING IT.

No. 5395

SALVATORE MORELLO	)	SUPERIOR COURT AT STAMFORD
vs.	)	COUNTY OF FAIRFIELD
FRANCES MEDIATE MORELLO	)	MARCH 5, 1964

Present: Hon. Joseph W. Bogdanski, Judge

JUDGMENT

This action by writ and complaint, dated November 9,
1962, claiming a divorce, annulment, and custody of minor child,
as on file, came to this court on the first Tuesday of December,
1962, when the defendant appeared, and thence to November 28, 1962
when the defendant filed an answer and cross complaint, claiming a
divorce, annulment, custody and support of minor child, alimony and
counsel fees, thence to December 18, 1962 when the plaintiff filed
an answer to the cross complaint, and thence to April 5, 1963 when
the parties being at issue, the case was ordered referred to the
Hon. Samuel Mellitz, State Referee, to hear the facts and report to
the court, and thence to November 27, 1963 when a substituted complaint was filed, and thence to January 20, 1964 when an answer and
cross complaint to the substituted complaint was filed, and thence to
February 19, 1964 when the report of the Referee was filed, and
thence to the present time when, no exceptions to the report having
been filed, the court accepts the same.

The court finds that at the date of said complaint, the defendant was a resident of Greenwich in the State of Connecticut, and
that said writ and complaint was served on the defendant, as appears
by the officer's
complaint has be
the return day :
pending in this
filing thereof.

A FEW YEARS AFTER MY MOTHER WAS RETURN
TO NELLIE AND DOMINIC AND FRANCES, DIVOR
PAPERS WERE DRAWN UP. ON MARCH 5, 1964, S
WAS ORDERED TO PAY FORTY DOLLARS PER WEEK
BOTH ALIMONY AND CHILD SUPPORT, PLUS LEG
FEES. HE WAS ALLOWED TO SEE MY MOM EV
SUNDAY, ALTERNATE BIRTHDAYS, AND LEGAL HOLID
BETWEEN 11:30 A.M. AND 6:30 P.M., PLUS ONE W
IN THE SUMMER FOR VACATION. IN A GOOD YEAR T
WOULD BE A TOTAL OF ABOUT SIXTY-FIVE DAYS,
17.8 PERCENT OF THE TIME.

IT WASN'T UNTIL SHE WAS THIRTEEN THAT MY MOM FOUND OUT THAT HER MOTHER WAS MENTALLY ILL.

FOR MORE THAN A DECADE FRANCES HAD STABILIZED, HAD BOUGHT MY MOM NEW CLOTHES EVERY YEAR BEFORE SCHOOL, AND LINED HER BACKPACK WITH THE APPROPRIATE SUPPLIES.

SHE NEVER WORKED BUT SHE PICKED UP GROCERIES AT THE NEARBY A&P AND CARTED THEM HOME; SOMETIMES SHE COOKED.

AND THEN SHE WAS SUDDENLY GONE AGAIN, THIS TIME TO STAMFORD HOSPITAL.

AFTER FRANCES'S DEATH, I CALLED THE HOSPITAL TO REQUEST THE MEDICAL RECORDS BUT ONLY MY MOM, WHOSE NAME IS ON THE DEATH CERTIFICATE, CAN ACCESS THEM.

MY MOM HAD SOME OF HER OWN RECORDS EXPUNGED FROM THE 1988 HOSPITALIZATION—SO MY UNDERSTANDING OF THE EVENT WILL ALWAYS BE ONLY WHAT SHE TELLS ME.

SHE WON'T, SHE SAYS, OUT OF RESPECT FOR HER MOTHER'S PRIVACY.

THERE'S THAT FAMILY SILENCE AGAIN, HELD BENEATH A BLANKET OF SHAME, THESE SECRETS MY FOREBEARS WANT DISAPPEARED.

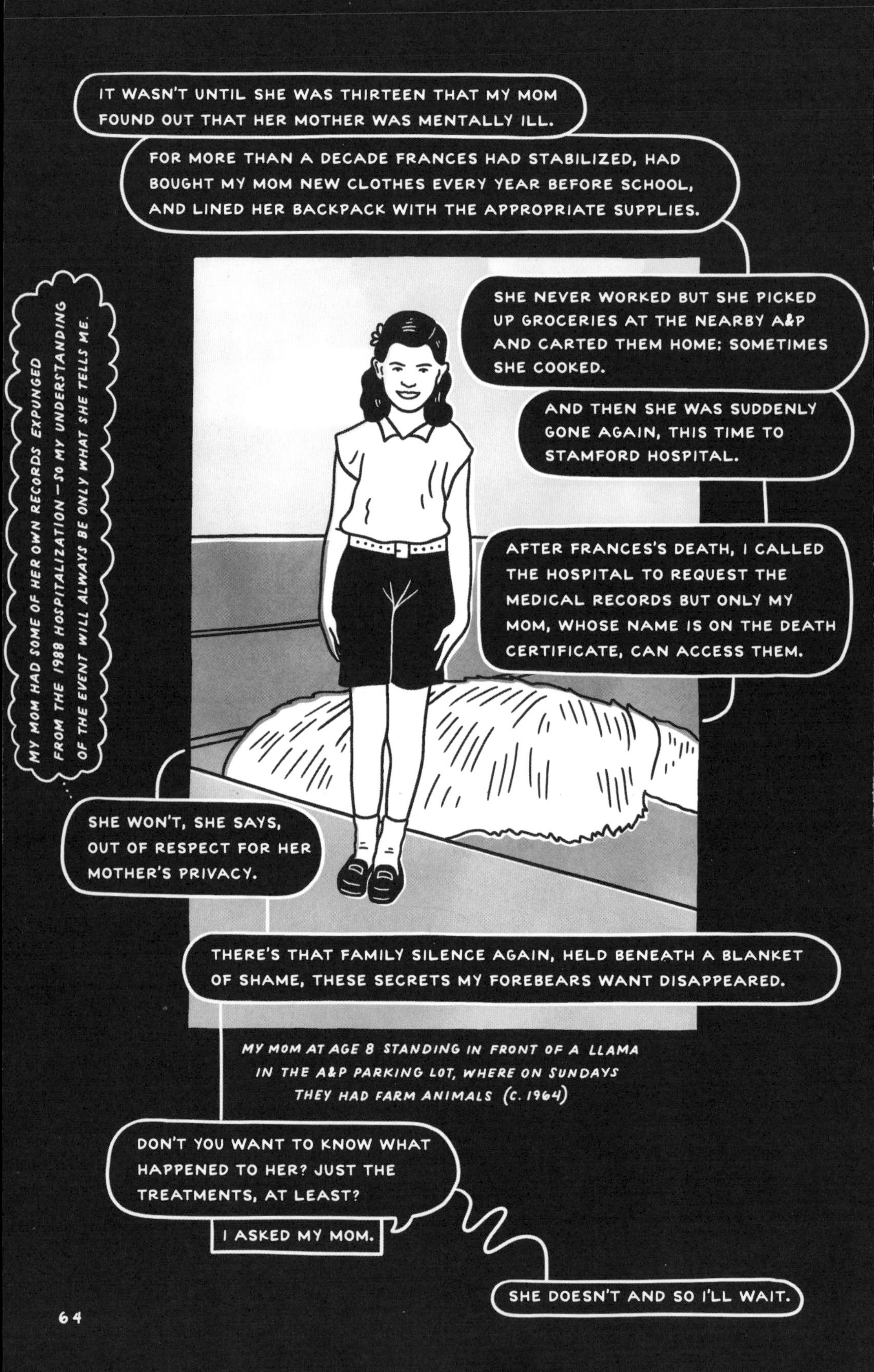

MY MOM AT AGE 8 STANDING IN FRONT OF A LLAMA IN THE A&P PARKING LOT, WHERE ON SUNDAYS THEY HAD FARM ANIMALS (C. 1964)

DON'T YOU WANT TO KNOW WHAT HAPPENED TO HER? JUST THE TREATMENTS, AT LEAST?

I ASKED MY MOM.

SHE DOESN'T AND SO I'LL WAIT.

[WH]EN FRANCES RETURNED FROM STAMFORD HOSPITAL, SHE [RE]SEARCHED THE RELATIONSHIP OF FOOD TO MENTAL HEALTH.

SHE PURCHASED BOOKS AND READ PAMPHLETS AND COMBED THROUGH ENCYCLOPEDIAS, IN THE HOPES THAT A BALANCED DIET WOULD PRESERVE HER SANITY.

A WOMAN WHOSE LIFE WAS RIPPED OUT FROM UNDER HER, WHO UNDERSTOOD WHAT SHE'D WANTED HER LIFE T[O] BE—CAPABLE MOTHER, WIFE—ONLY TO BE TRAPPED IN TH[E] PRISON OF HER OWN DUPLICITOUS MIND.

A WOMAN WHO [COULD] NOT ESCAPE TH[E] CONFINES OF H[ER] BUT WHO SAW [HER] DAUGHTER EVER[Y] THE EVIDENCE [OF] OTHER LIFE.

FRANCES, NELLIE, MY MOM, AND ME (C. 1986)

IF WE GROW UP IN A SAFE HOME, WE EXPECT SECURITY AND IMAGINE NO OTHER POSSIBILITY. FRANCES, STUNNINGLY BEAUTIFUL AS A YOUNG WOMAN, HELD IN HER GRASP THAT DREAMED-OF STABLE LIFE ONLY TO BE BETRAYED BY HER OWN BRAIN, TO HAVE BEEN SPUN AND SWIRLED AND TORNADOED UNTIL SHE WAS HALTED BY, IT SEEMED, ELECTROSHOCK THERAPY AND PHYSICAL RESTRAINTS AND, WHAT? LITHIUM? CHLORPROMAZINE? I'M SURE SHE DIDN'T WANT TO BE SCHIZOPHRENIC BUT SHE LIVED WITH THE KNOWLEDGE THAT SOMETHING INSIDE HER WAS THE CAUSE OF HER OWN CATASTROPHIC UNDOING.

I'VE NO DOUBT MY GRANDFATHER WOULD'VE LEFT HER, A[ND] BUT SHE MAY HAVE NEVER UNDERSTOOD OR BELIEVED T[HAT]

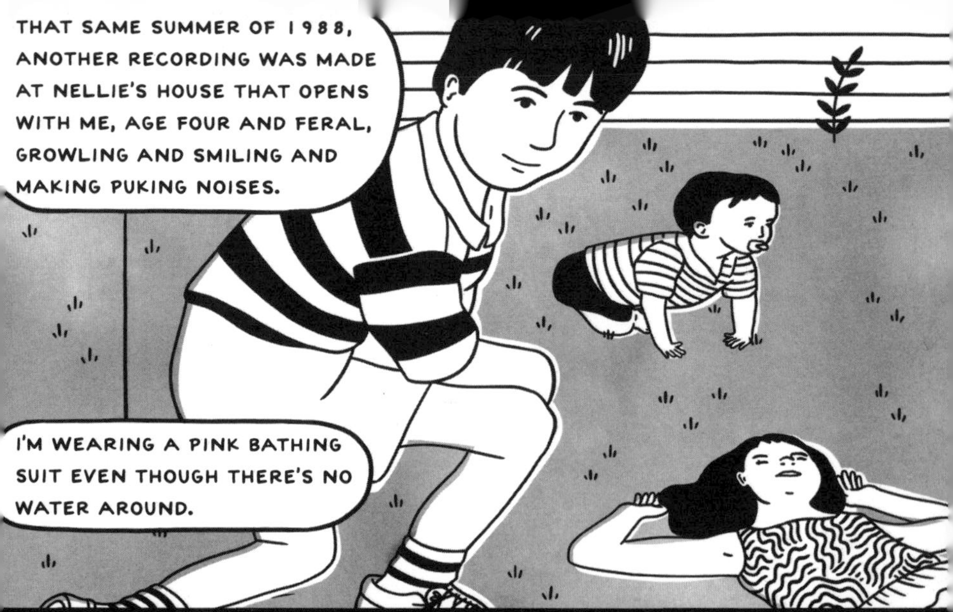
THAT SAME SUMMER OF 1988, ANOTHER RECORDING WAS MADE AT NELLIE'S HOUSE THAT OPENS WITH ME, AGE FOUR AND FERAL, GROWLING AND SMILING AND MAKING PUKING NOISES.
I'M WEARING A PINK BATHING SUIT EVEN THOUGH THERE'S NO WATER AROUND.

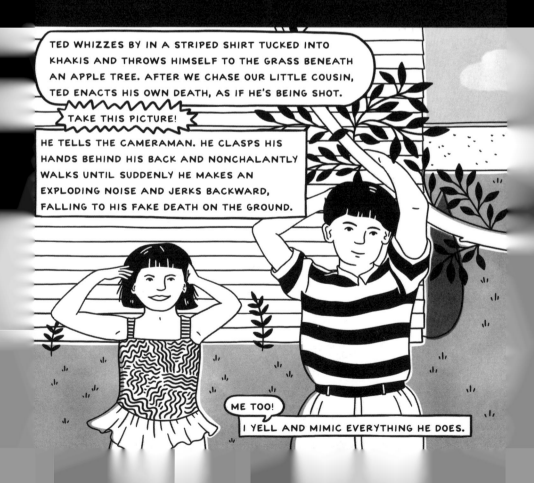

THE THREE OF US. ZACH IS IN THE MIDDLE OF HIS VERY STRANGE, ONE-LEGGED CRAWL.

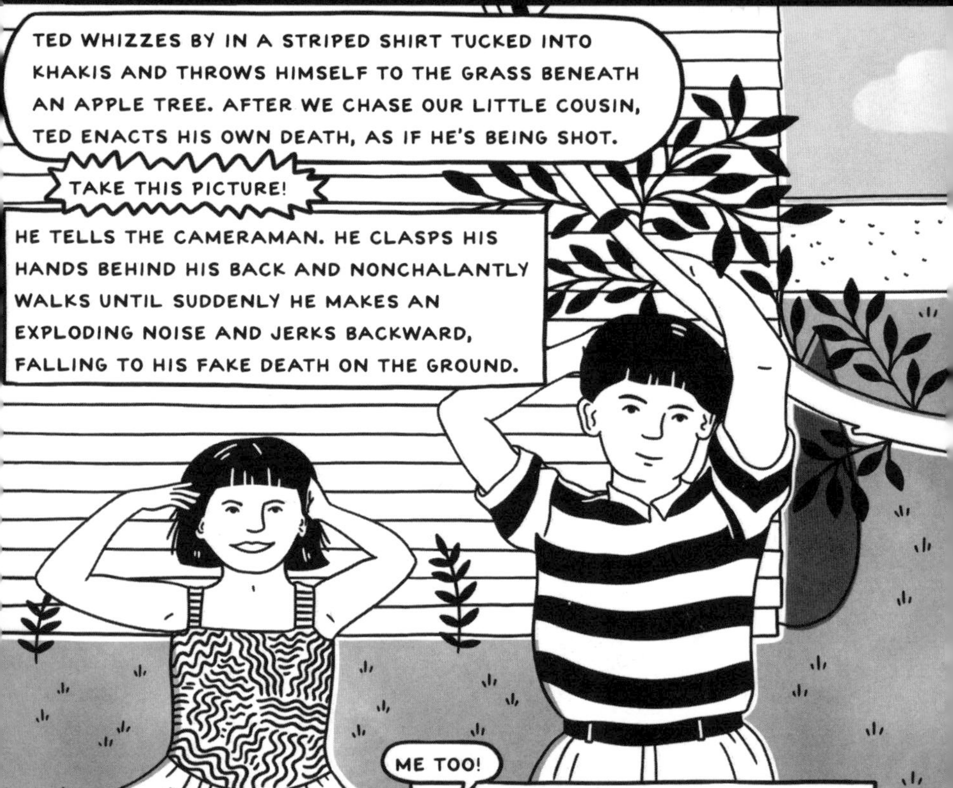
TED WHIZZES BY IN A STRIPED SHIRT TUCKED INTO KHAKIS AND THROWS HIMSELF TO THE GRASS BENEATH AN APPLE TREE. AFTER WE CHASE OUR LITTLE COUSIN, TED ENACTS HIS OWN DEATH, AS IF HE'S BEING SHOT.
TAKE THIS PICTURE!
HE TELLS THE CAMERAMAN. HE CLASPS HIS HANDS BEHIND HIS BACK AND NONCHALANTLY WALKS UNTIL SUDDENLY HE MAKES AN EXPLODING NOISE AND JERKS BACKWARD, FALLING TO HIS FAKE DEATH ON THE GROUND.
ME TOO!
I YELL AND MIMIC EVERYTHING HE DOES.

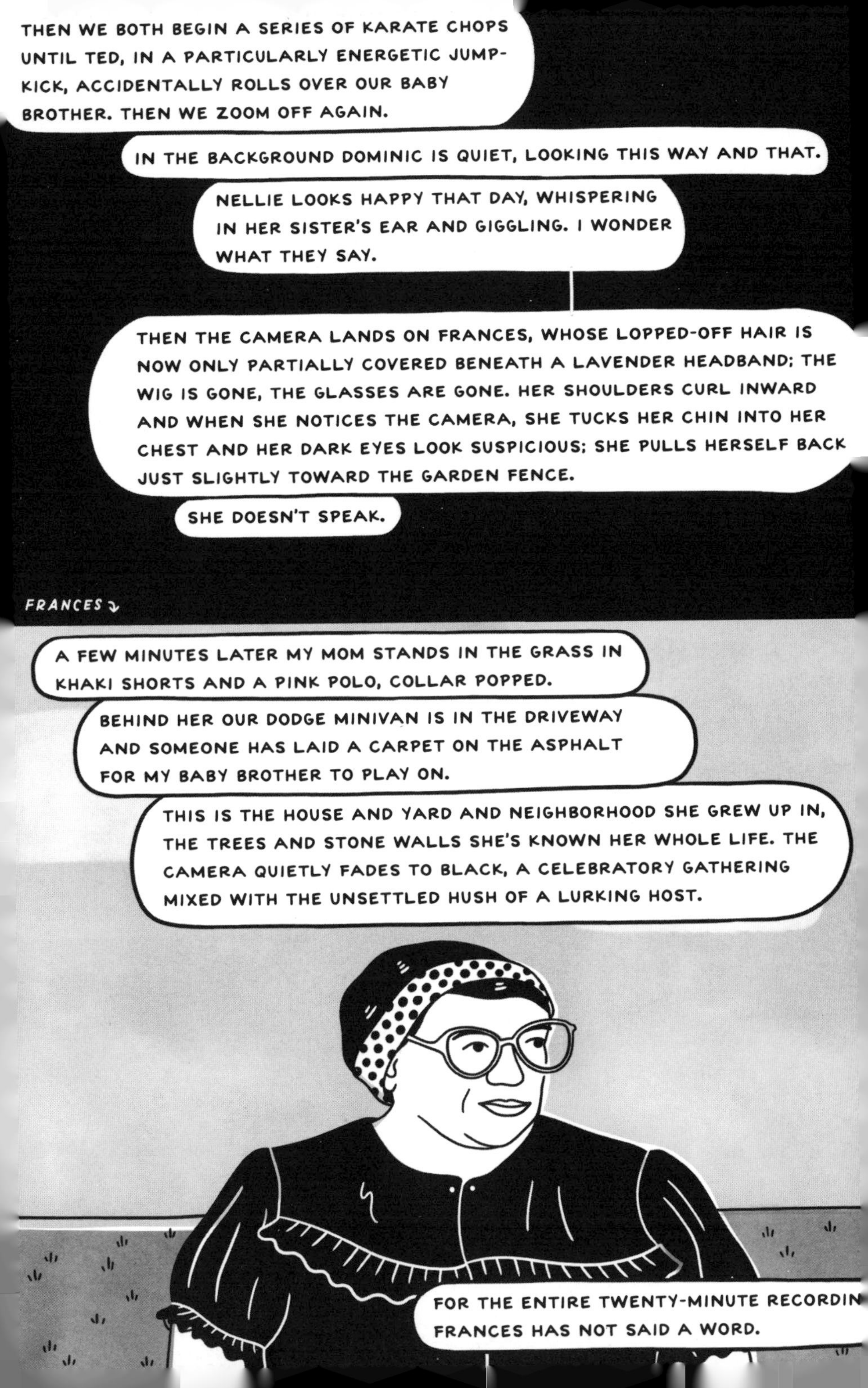
THEN WE BOTH BEGIN A SERIES OF KARATE CHOPS UNTIL TED, IN A PARTICULARLY ENERGETIC JUMP-KICK, ACCIDENTALLY ROLLS OVER OUR BABY BROTHER. THEN WE ZOOM OFF AGAIN.
IN THE BACKGROUND DOMINIC IS QUIET, LOOKING THIS WAY AND THAT.
NELLIE LOOKS HAPPY THAT DAY, WHISPERING IN HER SISTER'S EAR AND GIGGLING. I WONDER WHAT THEY SAY.
THEN THE CAMERA LANDS ON FRANCES, WHOSE LOPPED-OFF HAIR IS NOW ONLY PARTIALLY COVERED BENEATH A LAVENDER HEADBAND; THE WIG IS GONE, THE GLASSES ARE GONE. HER SHOULDERS CURL INWARD AND WHEN SHE NOTICES THE CAMERA, SHE TUCKS HER CHIN INTO HER CHEST AND HER DARK EYES LOOK SUSPICIOUS; SHE PULLS HERSELF BACK JUST SLIGHTLY TOWARD THE GARDEN FENCE.
SHE DOESN'T SPEAK.
FRANCES
A FEW MINUTES LATER MY MOM STANDS IN THE GRASS IN KHAKI SHORTS AND A PINK POLO, COLLAR POPPED.
BEHIND HER OUR DODGE MINIVAN IS IN THE DRIVEWAY AND SOMEONE HAS LAID A CARPET ON THE ASPHALT FOR MY BABY BROTHER TO PLAY ON.
THIS IS THE HOUSE AND YARD AND NEIGHBORHOOD SHE GREW UP IN, THE TREES AND STONE WALLS SHE'S KNOWN HER WHOLE LIFE. THE CAMERA QUIETLY FADES TO BLACK, A CELEBRATORY GATHERING MIXED WITH THE UNSETTLED HUSH OF A LURKING HOST.
FOR THE ENTIRE TWENTY-MINUTE RECORDIN
FRANCES HAS NOT SAID A WORD.

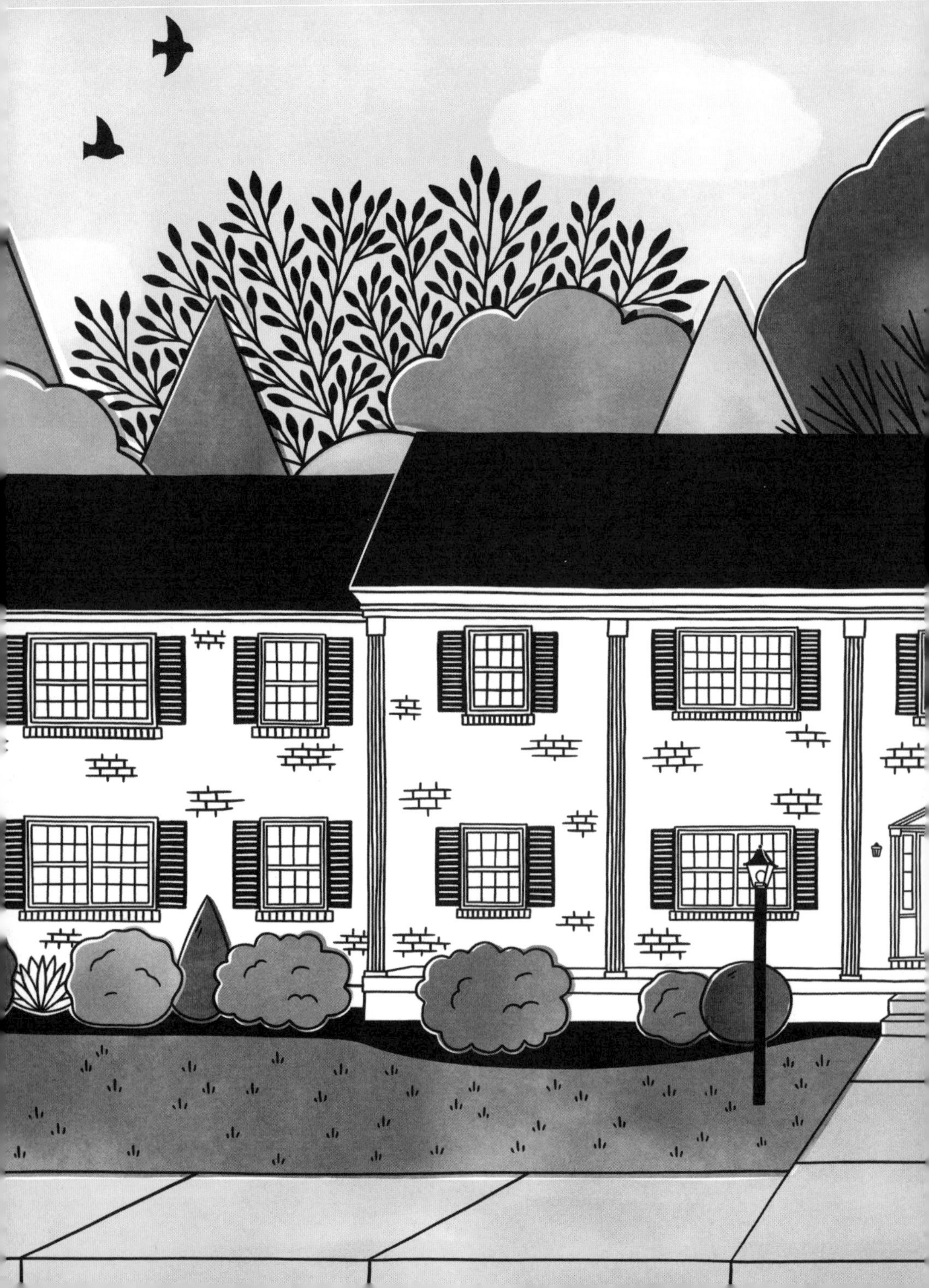

CHAPTER 07

The Silence

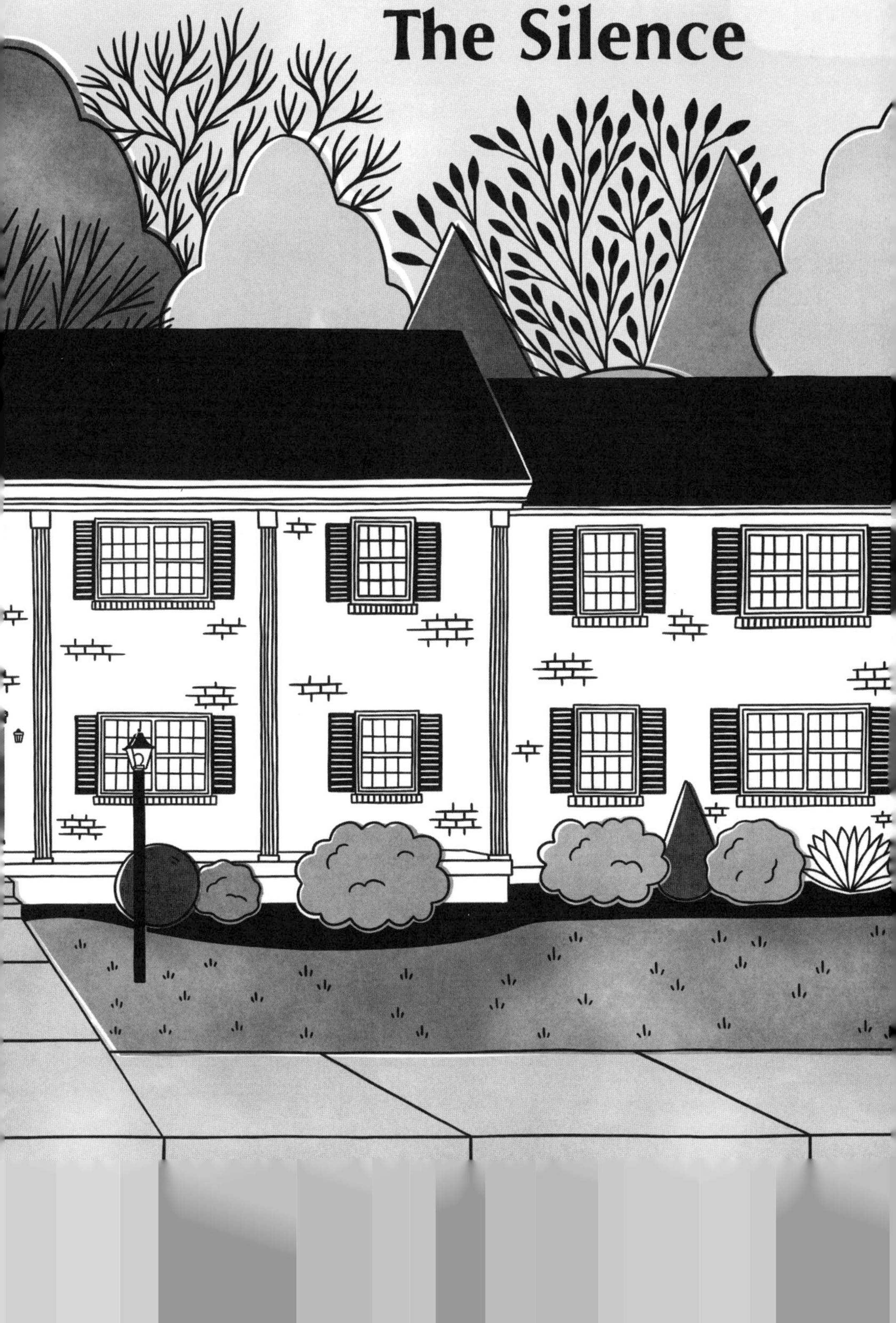

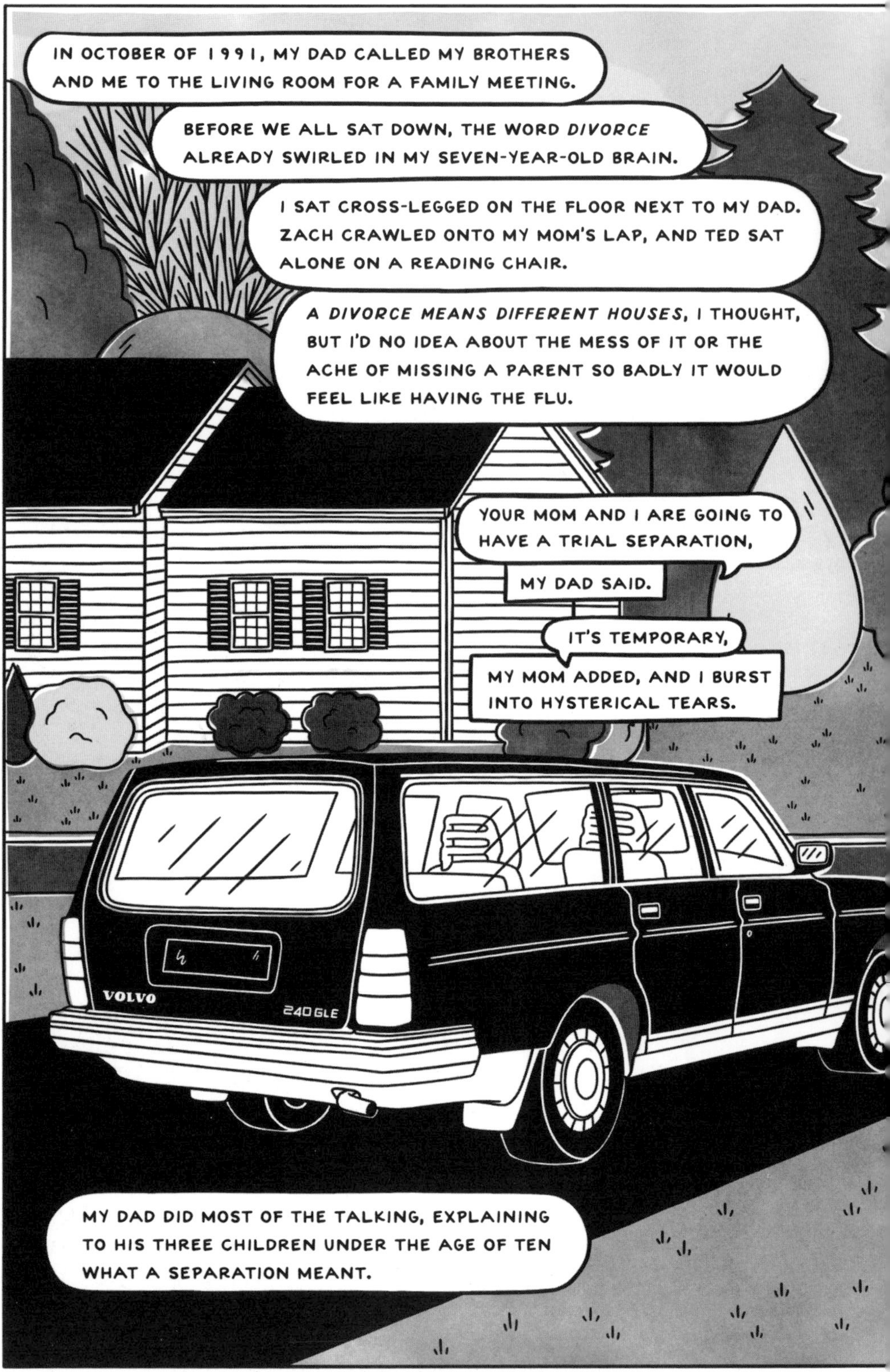
IN OCTOBER OF 1991, MY DAD CALLED MY BROTHERS AND ME TO THE LIVING ROOM FOR A FAMILY MEETING.
BEFORE WE ALL SAT DOWN, THE WORD *DIVORCE* ALREADY SWIRLED IN MY SEVEN-YEAR-OLD BRAIN.
I SAT CROSS-LEGGED ON THE FLOOR NEXT TO MY DAD. ZACH CRAWLED ONTO MY MOM'S LAP, AND TED SAT ALONE ON A READING CHAIR.
A *DIVORCE MEANS DIFFERENT HOUSES*, I THOUGHT, BUT I'D NO IDEA ABOUT THE MESS OF IT OR THE ACHE OF MISSING A PARENT SO BADLY IT WOULD FEEL LIKE HAVING THE FLU.
YOUR MOM AND I ARE GOING TO HAVE A TRIAL SEPARATION,
MY DAD SAID.
IT'S TEMPORARY,
MY MOM ADDED, AND I BURST INTO HYSTERICAL TEARS.
VOLVO
240GLE
MY DAD DID MOST OF THE TALKING, EXPLAINING TO HIS THREE CHILDREN UNDER THE AGE OF TEN WHAT A SEPARATION MEANT.

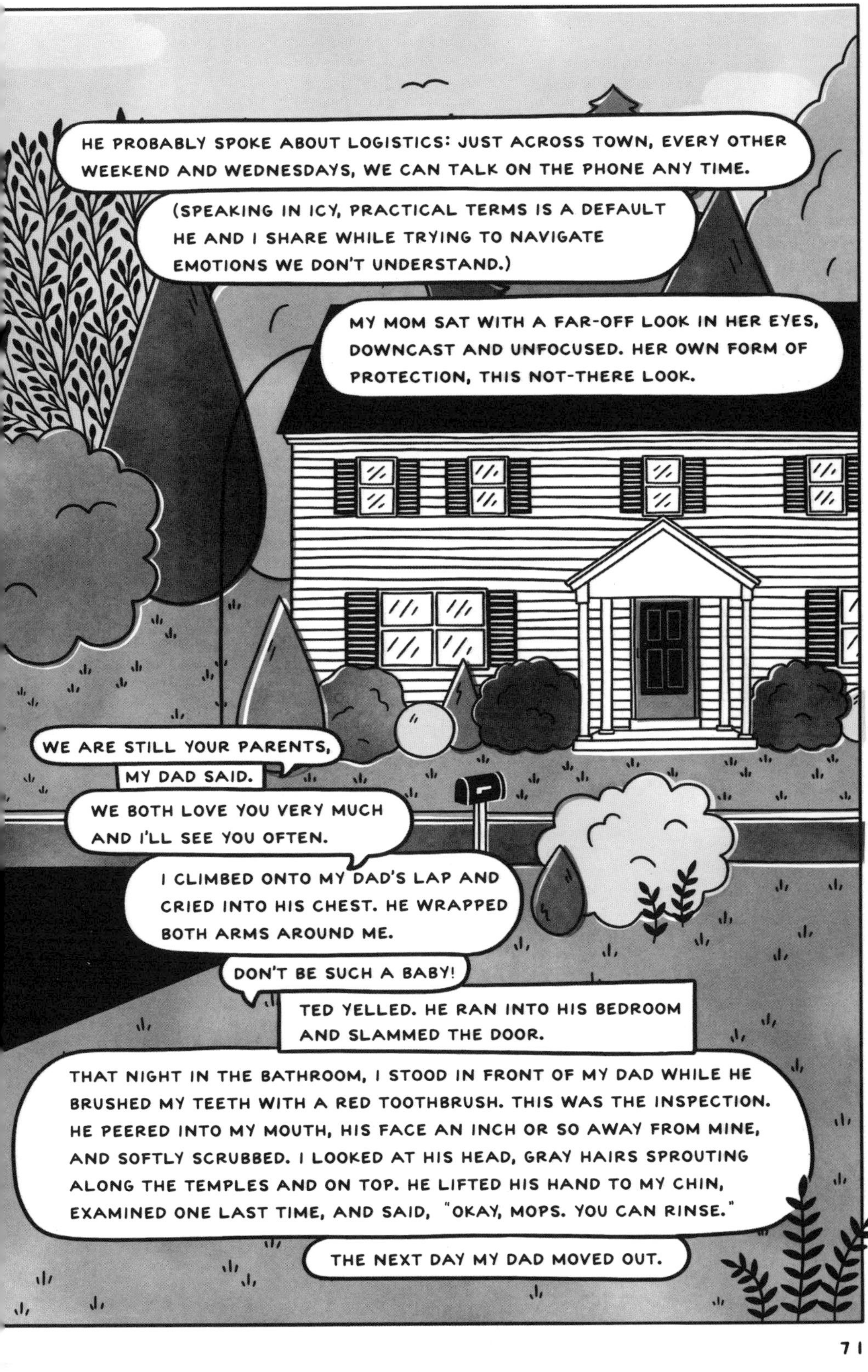
HE PROBABLY SPOKE ABOUT LOGISTICS: JUST ACROSS TOWN, EVERY OTHER WEEKEND AND WEDNESDAYS, WE CAN TALK ON THE PHONE ANY TIME.
(SPEAKING IN ICY, PRACTICAL TERMS IS A DEFAULT HE AND I SHARE WHILE TRYING TO NAVIGATE EMOTIONS WE DON'T UNDERSTAND.)
MY MOM SAT WITH A FAR-OFF LOOK IN HER EYES, DOWNCAST AND UNFOCUSED. HER OWN FORM OF PROTECTION, THIS NOT-THERE LOOK.
WE ARE STILL YOUR PARENTS,
MY DAD SAID.
WE BOTH LOVE YOU VERY MUCH AND I'LL SEE YOU OFTEN.
I CLIMBED ONTO MY DAD'S LAP AND CRIED INTO HIS CHEST. HE WRAPPED BOTH ARMS AROUND ME.
DON'T BE SUCH A BABY!
TED YELLED. HE RAN INTO HIS BEDROOM AND SLAMMED THE DOOR.
THAT NIGHT IN THE BATHROOM, I STOOD IN FRONT OF MY DAD WHILE HE BRUSHED MY TEETH WITH A RED TOOTHBRUSH. THIS WAS THE INSPECTION. HE PEERED INTO MY MOUTH, HIS FACE AN INCH OR SO AWAY FROM MINE, AND SOFTLY SCRUBBED. I LOOKED AT HIS HEAD, GRAY HAIRS SPROUTING ALONG THE TEMPLES AND ON TOP. HE LIFTED HIS HAND TO MY CHIN, EXAMINED ONE LAST TIME, AND SAID, "OKAY, MOPS. YOU CAN RINSE."
THE NEXT DAY MY DAD MOVED OUT.

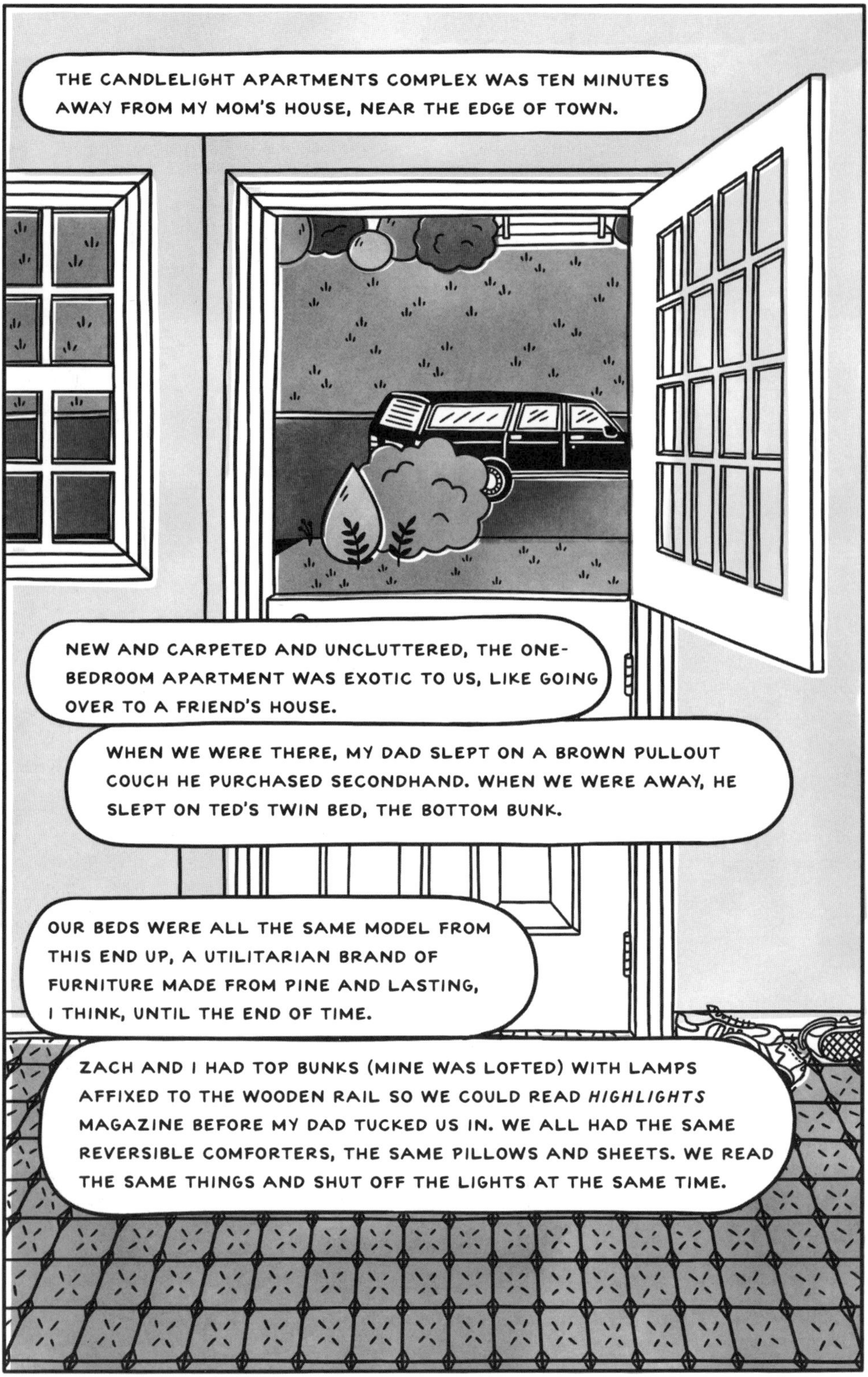
THE CANDLELIGHT APARTMENTS COMPLEX WAS TEN MINUTES AWAY FROM MY MOM'S HOUSE, NEAR THE EDGE OF TOWN.
NEW AND CARPETED AND UNCLUTTERED, THE ONE-BEDROOM APARTMENT WAS EXOTIC TO US, LIKE GOING OVER TO A FRIEND'S HOUSE.
WHEN WE WERE THERE, MY DAD SLEPT ON A BROWN PULLOUT COUCH HE PURCHASED SECONDHAND. WHEN WE WERE AWAY, HE SLEPT ON TED'S TWIN BED, THE BOTTOM BUNK.
OUR BEDS WERE ALL THE SAME MODEL FROM THIS END UP, A UTILITARIAN BRAND OF FURNITURE MADE FROM PINE AND LASTING, I THINK, UNTIL THE END OF TIME.
ZACH AND I HAD TOP BUNKS (MINE WAS LOFTED) WITH LAMPS AFFIXED TO THE WOODEN RAIL SO WE COULD READ *HIGHLIGHTS* MAGAZINE BEFORE MY DAD TUCKED US IN. WE ALL HAD THE SAME REVERSIBLE COMFORTERS, THE SAME PILLOWS AND SHEETS. WE READ THE SAME THINGS AND SHUT OFF THE LIGHTS AT THE SAME TIME.

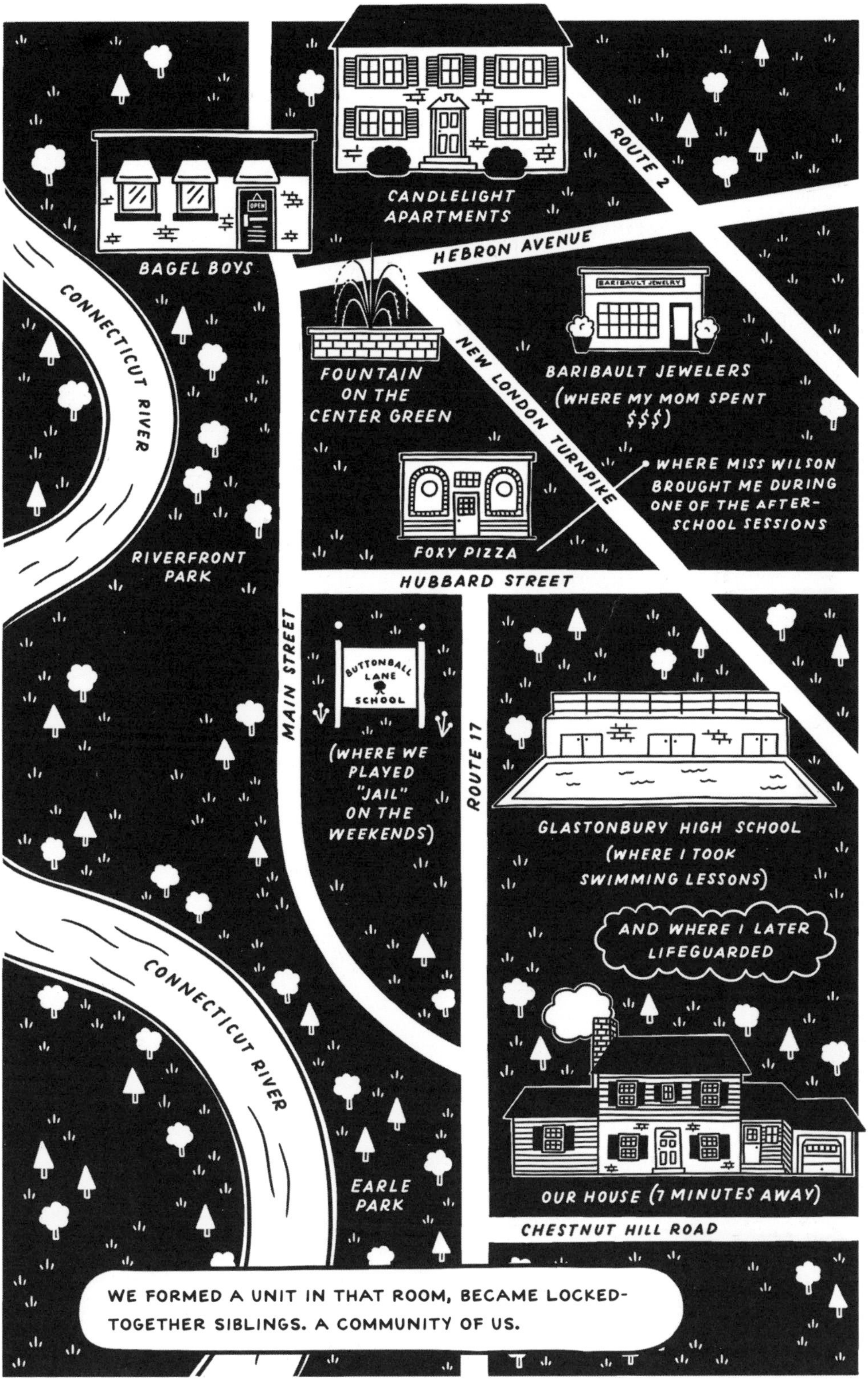
CANDLELIGHT APARTMENTS
ROUTE 2
OPEN
BAGEL BOYS
HEBRON AVENUE
BARIBAULT JEWELRY
CONNECTICUT RIVER
NEW LONDON TURNPIKE
FOUNTAIN ON THE CENTER GREEN
BARIBAULT JEWELERS
(WHERE MY MOM SPENT $$$)
WHERE MISS WILSON BROUGHT ME DURING ONE OF THE AFTER-SCHOOL SESSIONS
FOXY PIZZA
RIVERFRONT PARK
HUBBARD STREET
MAIN STREET
BUTTONBALL LANE SCHOOL
ROUTE 17
(WHERE WE PLAYED "JAIL" ON THE WEEKENDS)
GLASTONBURY HIGH SCHOOL
(WHERE I TOOK SWIMMING LESSONS)
AND WHERE I LATER LIFEGUARDED
CONNECTICUT RIVER
EARLE PARK
OUR HOUSE (7 MINUTES AWAY)
CHESTNUT HILL ROAD
WE FORMED A UNIT IN THAT ROOM, BECAME LOCKED-TOGETHER SIBLINGS. A COMMUNITY OF US.

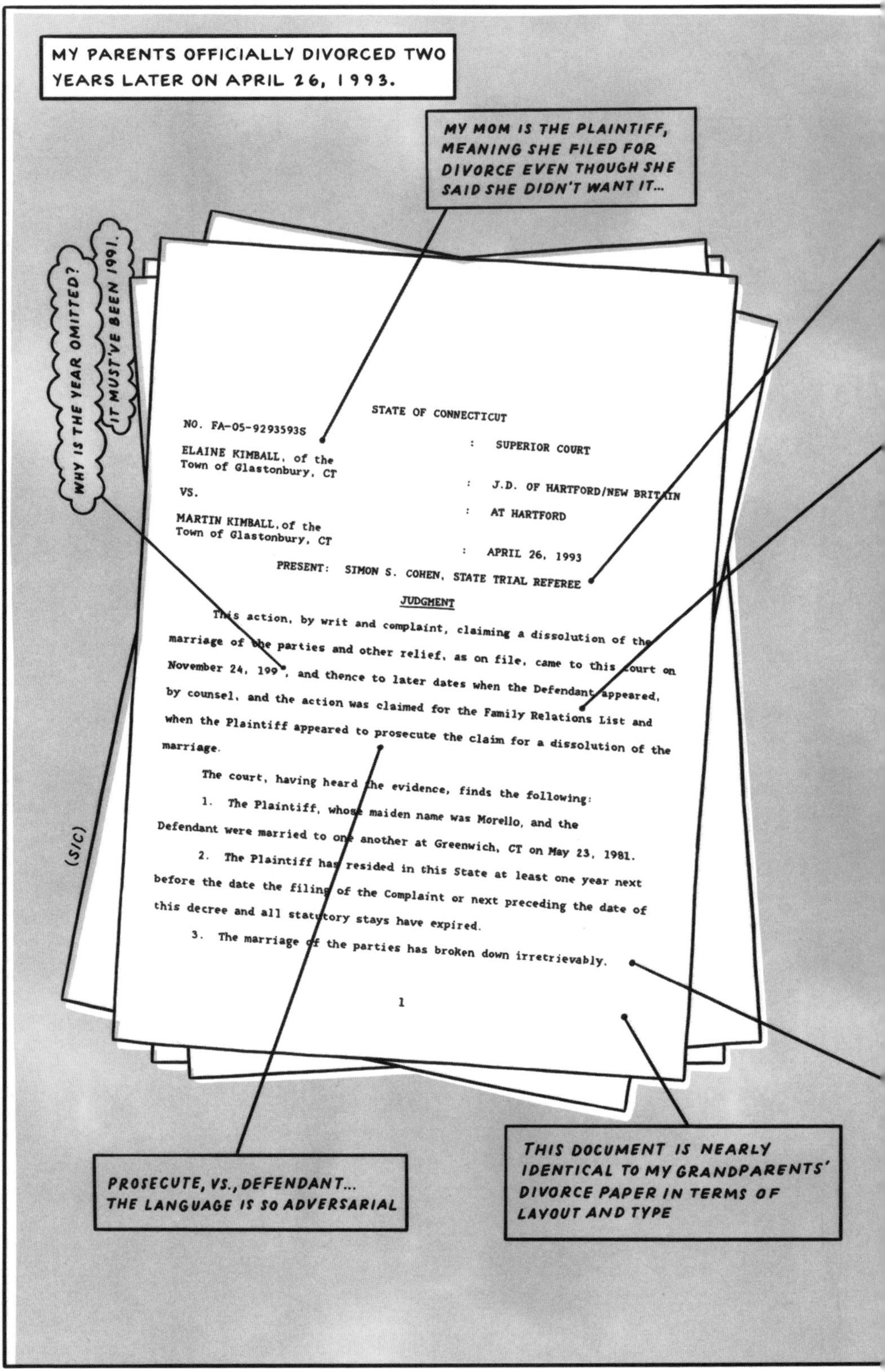
MY PARENTS OFFICIALLY DIVORCED TWO YEARS LATER ON APRIL 26, 1993.
MY MOM IS THE PLAINTIFF, MEANING SHE FILED FOR DIVORCE EVEN THOUGH SHE SAID SHE DIDN'T WANT IT...
WHY IS THE YEAR OMITTED?
IT MUST'VE BEEN 1991.
STATE OF CONNECTICUT
NO. FA-05-92935935
ELAINE KIMBALL, of the Town of Glastonbury, CT
VS.
MARTIN KIMBALL, of the Town of Glastonbury, CT
: SUPERIOR COURT
: J.D. OF HARTFORD/NEW BRITAIN
: AT HARTFORD
: APRIL 26, 1993
PRESENT: SIMON S. COHEN, STATE TRIAL REFEREE
JUDGMENT
This action, by writ and complaint, claiming a dissolution of the marriage of the parties and other relief, as on file, came to this court on November 24, 199 , and thence to later dates when the Defendant appeared, by counsel, and the action was claimed for the Family Relations List and when the Plaintiff appeared to prosecute the claim for a dissolution of the marriage.
The court, having heard the evidence, finds the following:
1. The Plaintiff, whose maiden name was Morello, and the Defendant were married to one another at Greenwich, CT on May 23, 1981.
2. The Plaintiff has resided in this State at least one year next before the date the filing of the Complaint or next preceding the date of this decree and all statutory stays have expired.
3. The marriage of the parties has broken down irretrievably.
1
(SIC)
PROSECUTE, VS., DEFENDANT... THE LANGUAGE IS SO ADVERSARIAL
THIS DOCUMENT IS NEARLY IDENTICAL TO MY GRANDPARENTS' DIVORCE PAPER IN TERMS OF LAYOUT AND TYPE

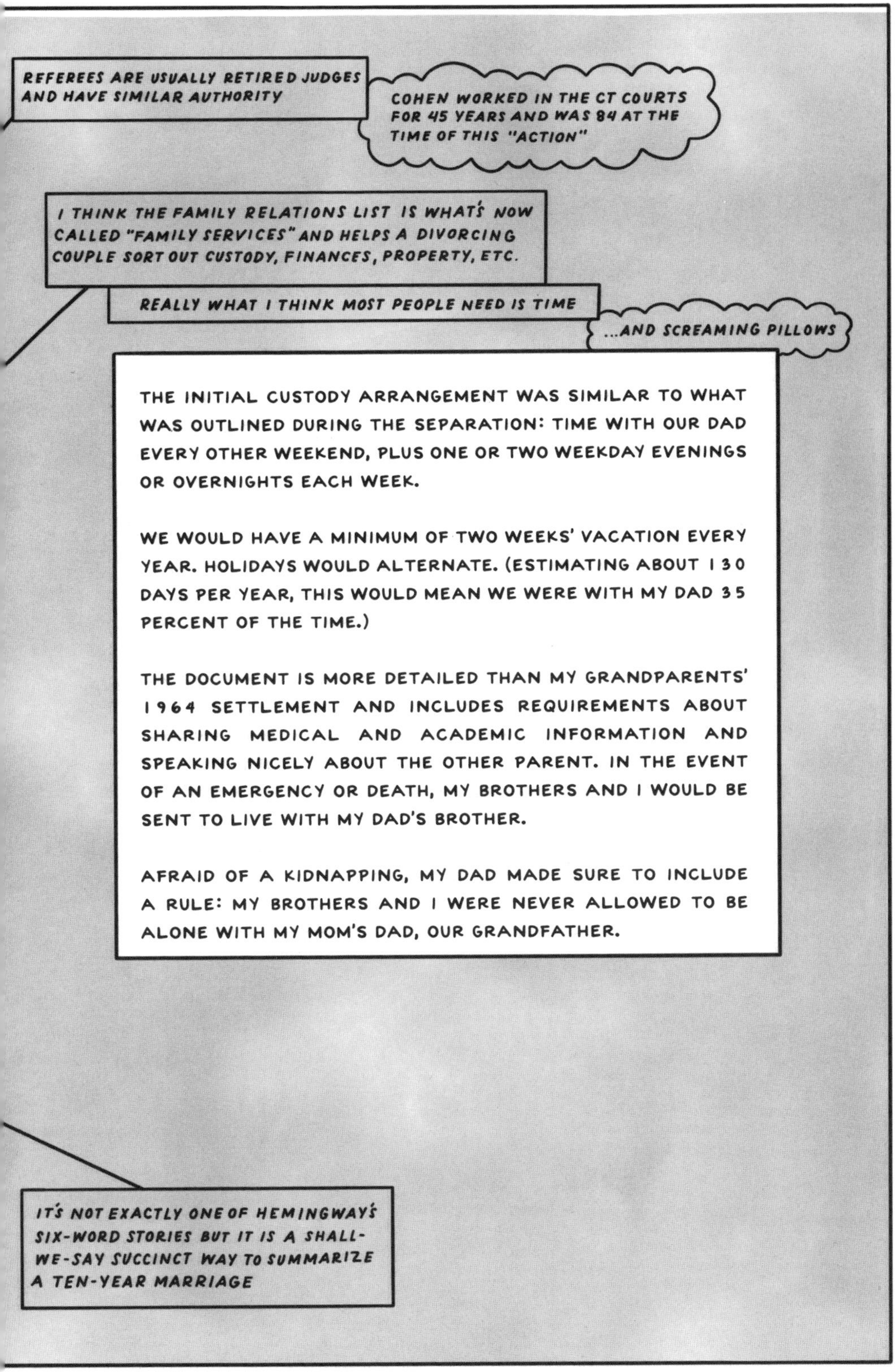
REFEREES ARE USUALLY RETIRED JUDGES AND HAVE SIMILAR AUTHORITY
COHEN WORKED IN THE CT COURTS FOR 45 YEARS AND WAS 84 AT THE TIME OF THIS "ACTION"
I THINK THE FAMILY RELATIONS LIST IS WHAT'S NOW CALLED "FAMILY SERVICES" AND HELPS A DIVORCING COUPLE SORT OUT CUSTODY, FINANCES, PROPERTY, ETC.
REALLY WHAT I THINK MOST PEOPLE NEED IS TIME
...AND SCREAMING PILLOWS
THE INITIAL CUSTODY ARRANGEMENT WAS SIMILAR TO WHAT WAS OUTLINED DURING THE SEPARATION: TIME WITH OUR DAD EVERY OTHER WEEKEND, PLUS ONE OR TWO WEEKDAY EVENINGS OR OVERNIGHTS EACH WEEK.
WE WOULD HAVE A MINIMUM OF TWO WEEKS' VACATION EVERY YEAR. HOLIDAYS WOULD ALTERNATE. (ESTIMATING ABOUT 130 DAYS PER YEAR, THIS WOULD MEAN WE WERE WITH MY DAD 35 PERCENT OF THE TIME.)
THE DOCUMENT IS MORE DETAILED THAN MY GRANDPARENTS' 1964 SETTLEMENT AND INCLUDES REQUIREMENTS ABOUT SHARING MEDICAL AND ACADEMIC INFORMATION AND SPEAKING NICELY ABOUT THE OTHER PARENT. IN THE EVENT OF AN EMERGENCY OR DEATH, MY BROTHERS AND I WOULD BE SENT TO LIVE WITH MY DAD'S BROTHER.
AFRAID OF A KIDNAPPING, MY DAD MADE SURE TO INCLUDE A RULE: MY BROTHERS AND I WERE NEVER ALLOWED TO BE ALONE WITH MY MOM'S DAD, OUR GRANDFATHER.
IT'S NOT EXACTLY ONE OF HEMINGWAY'S SIX-WORD STORIES BUT IT IS A SHALL-WE-SAY SUCCINCT WAY TO SUMMARIZE A TEN-YEAR MARRIAGE

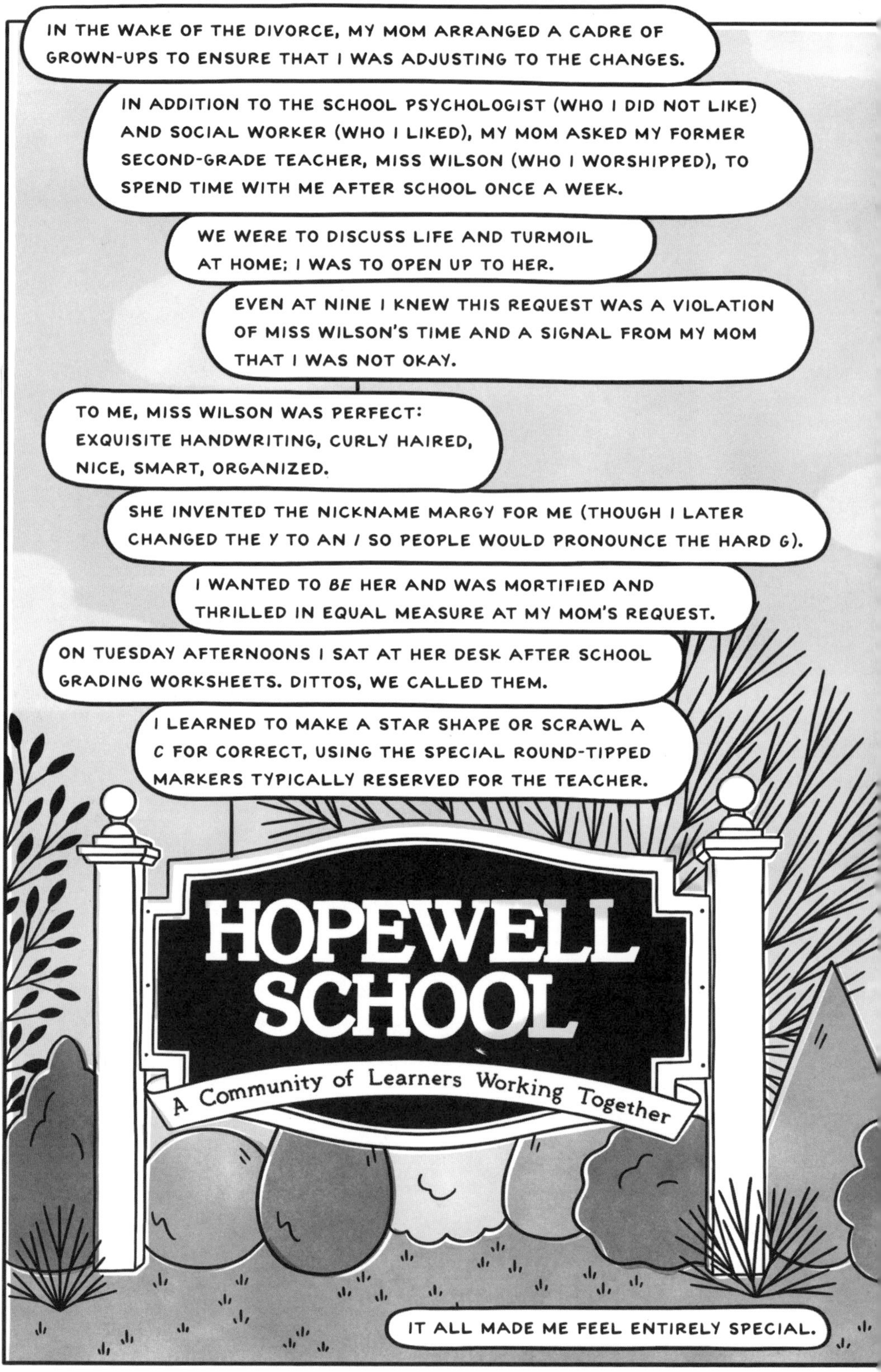
IN THE WAKE OF THE DIVORCE, MY MOM ARRANGED A CADRE OF GROWN-UPS TO ENSURE THAT I WAS ADJUSTING TO THE CHANGES.
IN ADDITION TO THE SCHOOL PSYCHOLOGIST (WHO I DID NOT LIKE) AND SOCIAL WORKER (WHO I LIKED), MY MOM ASKED MY FORMER SECOND-GRADE TEACHER, MISS WILSON (WHO I WORSHIPPED), TO SPEND TIME WITH ME AFTER SCHOOL ONCE A WEEK.
WE WERE TO DISCUSS LIFE AND TURMOIL AT HOME; I WAS TO OPEN UP TO HER.
EVEN AT NINE I KNEW THIS REQUEST WAS A VIOLATION OF MISS WILSON'S TIME AND A SIGNAL FROM MY MOM THAT I WAS NOT OKAY.
TO ME, MISS WILSON WAS PERFECT: EXQUISITE HANDWRITING, CURLY HAIRED, NICE, SMART, ORGANIZED.
SHE INVENTED THE NICKNAME MARGY FOR ME (THOUGH I LATER CHANGED THE *Y* TO AN *I* SO PEOPLE WOULD PRONOUNCE THE HARD *G*).
I WANTED TO *BE* HER AND WAS MORTIFIED AND THRILLED IN EQUAL MEASURE AT MY MOM'S REQUEST.
ON TUESDAY AFTERNOONS I SAT AT HER DESK AFTER SCHOOL GRADING WORKSHEETS. DITTOS, WE CALLED THEM.
I LEARNED TO MAKE A STAR SHAPE OR SCRAWL A *C* FOR CORRECT, USING THE SPECIAL ROUND-TIPPED MARKERS TYPICALLY RESERVED FOR THE TEACHER.
HOPEWELL SCHOOL
A Community of Learners Working Together
IT ALL MADE ME FEEL ENTIRELY SPECIAL.

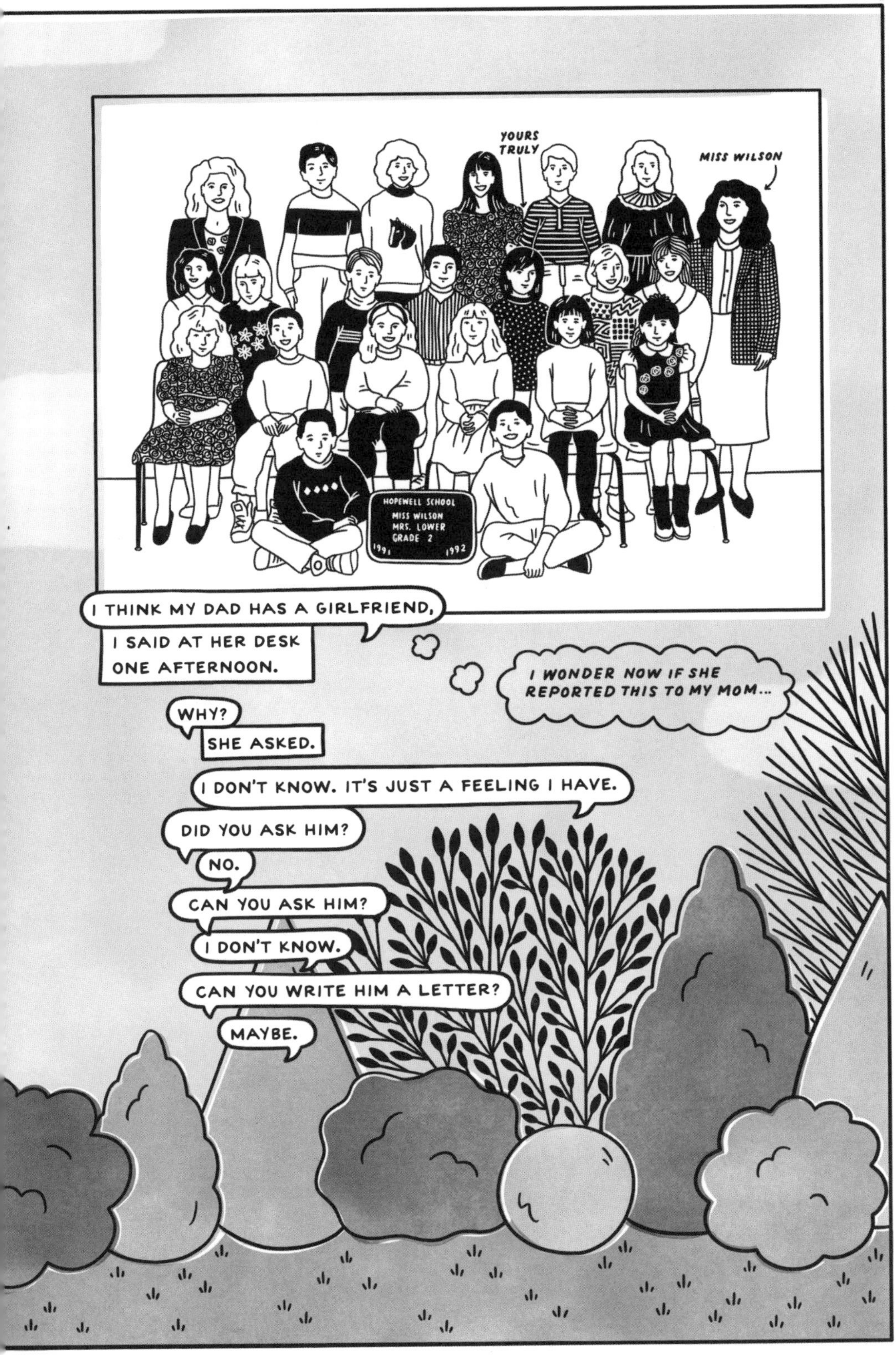
YOURS TRULY
MISS WILSON
HOPEWELL SCHOOL
MISS WILSON
MRS. LOWER
GRADE 2
1991 1992
I THINK MY DAD HAS A GIRLFRIEND,
I SAID AT HER DESK ONE AFTERNOON.
I WONDER NOW IF SHE REPORTED THIS TO MY MOM...
WHY?
SHE ASKED.
I DON'T KNOW. IT'S JUST A FEELING I HAVE.
DID YOU ASK HIM?
NO.
CAN YOU ASK HIM?
I DON'T KNOW.
CAN YOU WRITE HIM A LETTER?
MAYBE.

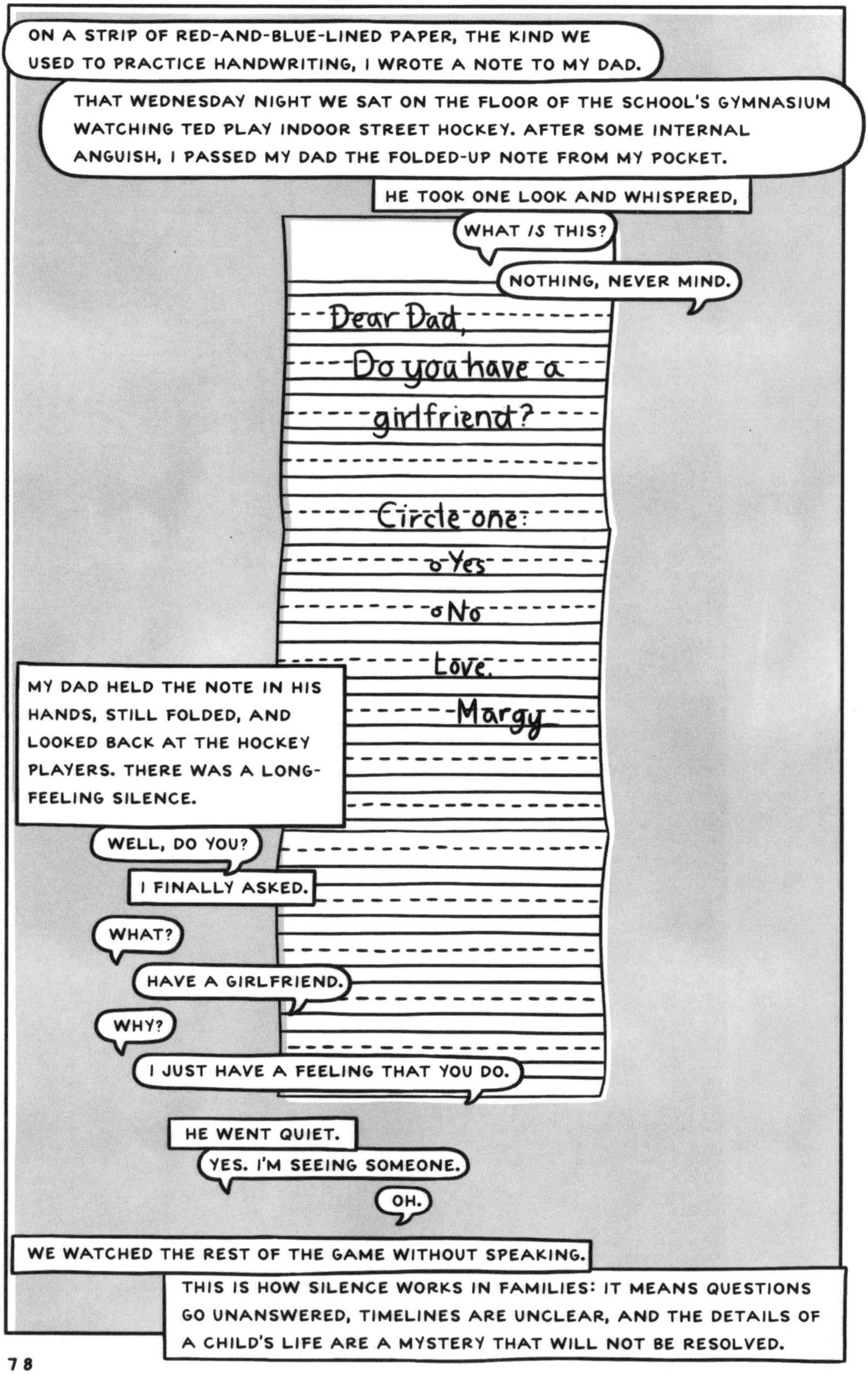
ON A STRIP OF RED-AND-BLUE-LINED PAPER, THE KIND WE USED TO PRACTICE HANDWRITING, I WROTE A NOTE TO MY DAD.
THAT WEDNESDAY NIGHT WE SAT ON THE FLOOR OF THE SCHOOL'S GYMNASIUM WATCHING TED PLAY INDOOR STREET HOCKEY. AFTER SOME INTERNAL ANGUISH, I PASSED MY DAD THE FOLDED-UP NOTE FROM MY POCKET.
HE TOOK ONE LOOK AND WHISPERED,
WHAT *IS* THIS?
NOTHING, NEVER MIND.
Dear Dad,
Do you have a girlfriend?
Circle one:
o Yes
o No
Love,
Margy
MY DAD HELD THE NOTE IN HIS HANDS, STILL FOLDED, AND LOOKED BACK AT THE HOCKEY PLAYERS. THERE WAS A LONG-FEELING SILENCE.
WELL, DO YOU?
I FINALLY ASKED.
WHAT?
HAVE A GIRLFRIEND.
WHY?
I JUST HAVE A FEELING THAT YOU DO.
HE WENT QUIET.
YES. I'M SEEING SOMEONE.
OH.
WE WATCHED THE REST OF THE GAME WITHOUT SPEAKING.
THIS IS HOW SILENCE WORKS IN FAMILIES: IT MEANS QUESTIONS GO UNANSWERED, TIMELINES ARE UNCLEAR, AND THE DETAILS OF A CHILD'S LIFE ARE A MYSTERY THAT WILL NOT BE RESOLVED.

UNDERSTAND MY FATHER'S PENCHANT FOR SILENCE
STER PEGGY WHO DROWNED IN A LAKE AT AGE THIR

S A NICKNAME FOR MARGARET; SHE IS MY NAMES

PON HER DEATH MY DAD SAID NO ONE TALKED ABC
T, THAT THE HOUSE SEEMED TO FALL SILENT.

RARELY TALKS ABOUT HER BUT SHE IS CLEARLY O
T HE KEEPS A RIVER ROCK SHE GAVE HIM OVER FOR
RE SHE PAINTED HANGS ON THE WALL IN HIS ENTR

↑ *PEGGY'S PAINTING*

GRANDPARENTS MIGHT'VE BEEN
EATH BUT THEY WEREN'T QUIET.

OKED THEM UP, I FOUND LETTERS TO THE EDITOR
HOUTING THEIR OPINIONS TO ALL OF BRIDGEPORT,
CUT (CHILDREN SHOULDN'T GET FREE LUNCHES,
SHOULD TEACH RELIGION, ETC.).

GRANDMOTHER REGULARLY HOSTED REPUBLICAN V
AS IN HER HOME. THESE WERE ANNOUNCED IN THE

SHE AND MY GRANDFATHER READ AND ARGUED
AND SPOKE, JUST NOT ABOUT PRIVATE FEELING

THINKING LIVES AND MAJOR CHOICES SEEMED
ST IN SERVICE TO THEIR RELIGIOUS BELIEFS.

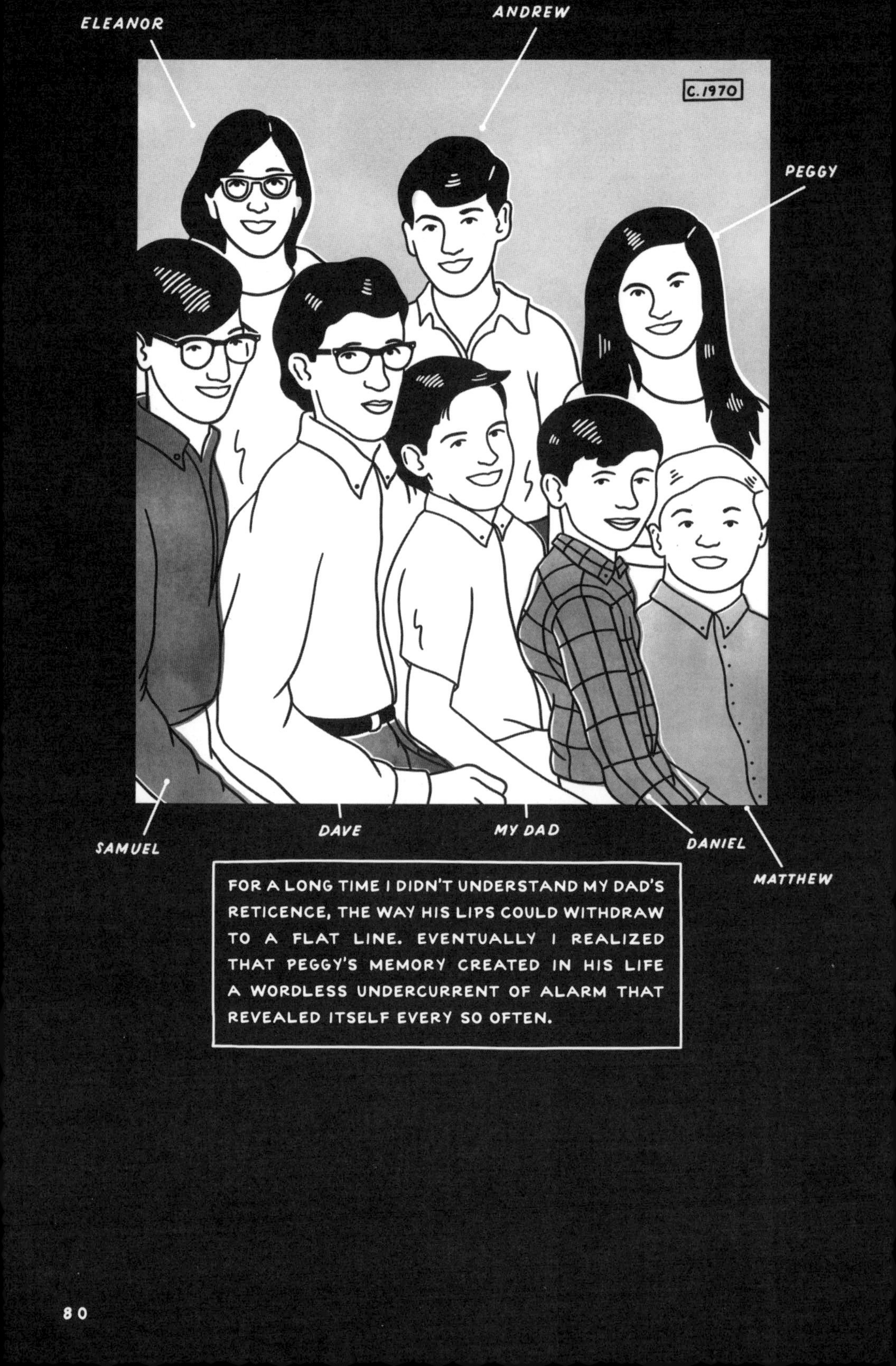
ELEANOR
ANDREW
C.1970
PEGGY
SAMUEL
DAVE
MY DAD
DANIEL
MATTHEW

FOR A LONG TIME I DIDN'T UNDERSTAND MY DAD'S RETICENCE, THE WAY HIS LIPS COULD WITHDRAW TO A FLAT LINE. EVENTUALLY I REALIZED THAT PEGGY'S MEMORY CREATED IN HIS LIFE A WORDLESS UNDERCURRENT OF ALARM THAT REVEALED ITSELF EVERY SO OFTEN.

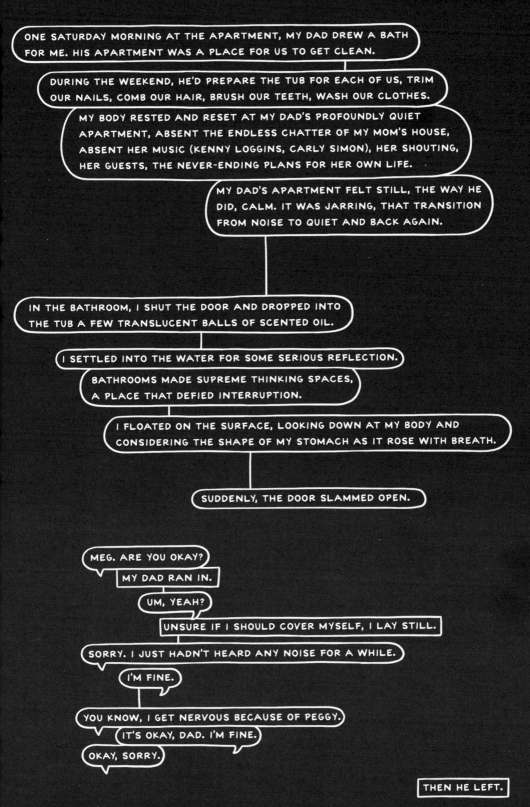

ONE SATURDAY MORNING AT THE APARTMENT, MY DAD DREW A BATH FOR ME. HIS APARTMENT WAS A PLACE FOR US TO GET CLEAN.

DURING THE WEEKEND, HE'D PREPARE THE TUB FOR EACH OF US, TRIM OUR NAILS, COMB OUR HAIR, BRUSH OUR TEETH, WASH OUR CLOTHES.

MY BODY RESTED AND RESET AT MY DAD'S PROFOUNDLY QUIET APARTMENT, ABSENT THE ENDLESS CHATTER OF MY MOM'S HOUSE, ABSENT HER MUSIC (KENNY LOGGINS, CARLY SIMON), HER SHOUTING, HER GUESTS, THE NEVER-ENDING PLANS FOR HER OWN LIFE.

MY DAD'S APARTMENT FELT STILL, THE WAY HE DID, CALM. IT WAS JARRING, THAT TRANSITION FROM NOISE TO QUIET AND BACK AGAIN.

IN THE BATHROOM, I SHUT THE DOOR AND DROPPED INTO THE TUB A FEW TRANSLUCENT BALLS OF SCENTED OIL.

I SETTLED INTO THE WATER FOR SOME SERIOUS REFLECTION.

BATHROOMS MADE SUPREME THINKING SPACES, A PLACE THAT DEFIED INTERRUPTION.

I FLOATED ON THE SURFACE, LOOKING DOWN AT MY BODY AND CONSIDERING THE SHAPE OF MY STOMACH AS IT ROSE WITH BREATH.

SUDDENLY, THE DOOR SLAMMED OPEN.

MEG. ARE YOU OKAY?

MY DAD RAN IN.

UM, YEAH?

UNSURE IF I SHOULD COVER MYSELF, I LAY STILL.

SORRY. I JUST HADN'T HEARD ANY NOISE FOR A WHILE.

I'M FINE.

YOU KNOW, I GET NERVOUS BECAUSE OF PEGGY.

IT'S OKAY, DAD. I'M FINE.

OKAY, SORRY.

THEN HE LEFT.

ROWNED IN LAKE WARAMAUG IN WESTERN
TICUT, WHERE I'VE NEVER BEEN.

HOTOGRAPHS REVEAL A PRETTY PLACE. THICK
ECIDUOUS TREES CONTAIN THE LAKE'S SPRAWL
ND DEEP AND CALL TO MIND PICNICS AND
AUGHTER AND THE SOUNDS OF BIRDS.

THE ENTIRE FAMILY WAS THERE THE DAY SHE DIED (JULY 18, 1971).

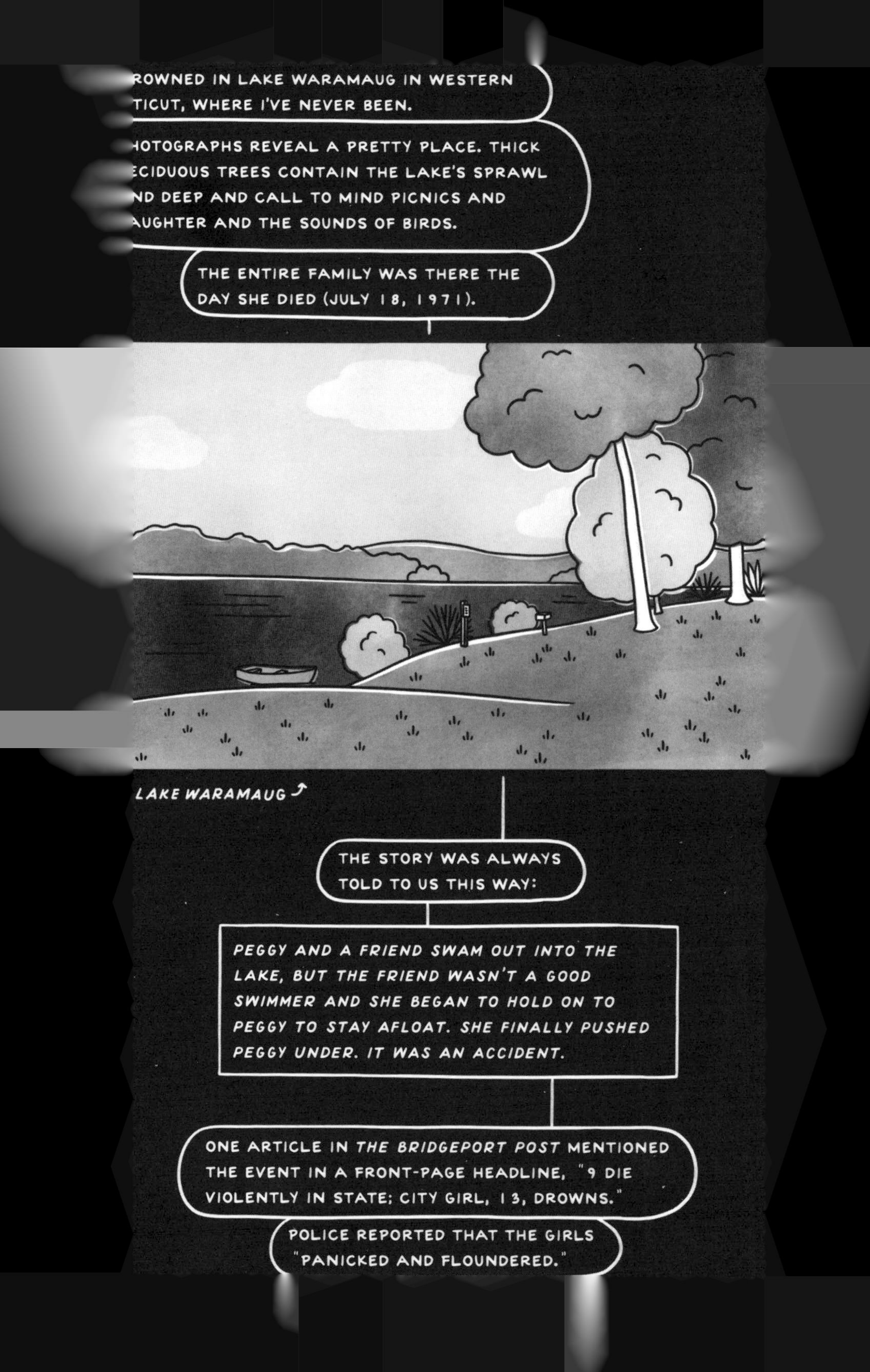

LAKE WARAMAUG

THE STORY WAS ALWAYS TOLD TO US THIS WAY:

PEGGY AND A FRIEND SWAM OUT INTO THE LAKE, BUT THE FRIEND WASN'T A GOOD SWIMMER AND SHE BEGAN TO HOLD ON TO PEGGY TO STAY AFLOAT. SHE FINALLY PUSHED PEGGY UNDER. IT WAS AN ACCIDENT.

ONE ARTICLE IN *THE BRIDGEPORT POST* MENTIONED THE EVENT IN A FRONT-PAGE HEADLINE, "9 DIE VIOLENTLY IN STATE; CITY GIRL, 13, DROWNS."

POLICE REPORTED THAT THE GIRLS "PANICKED AND FLOUNDERED."

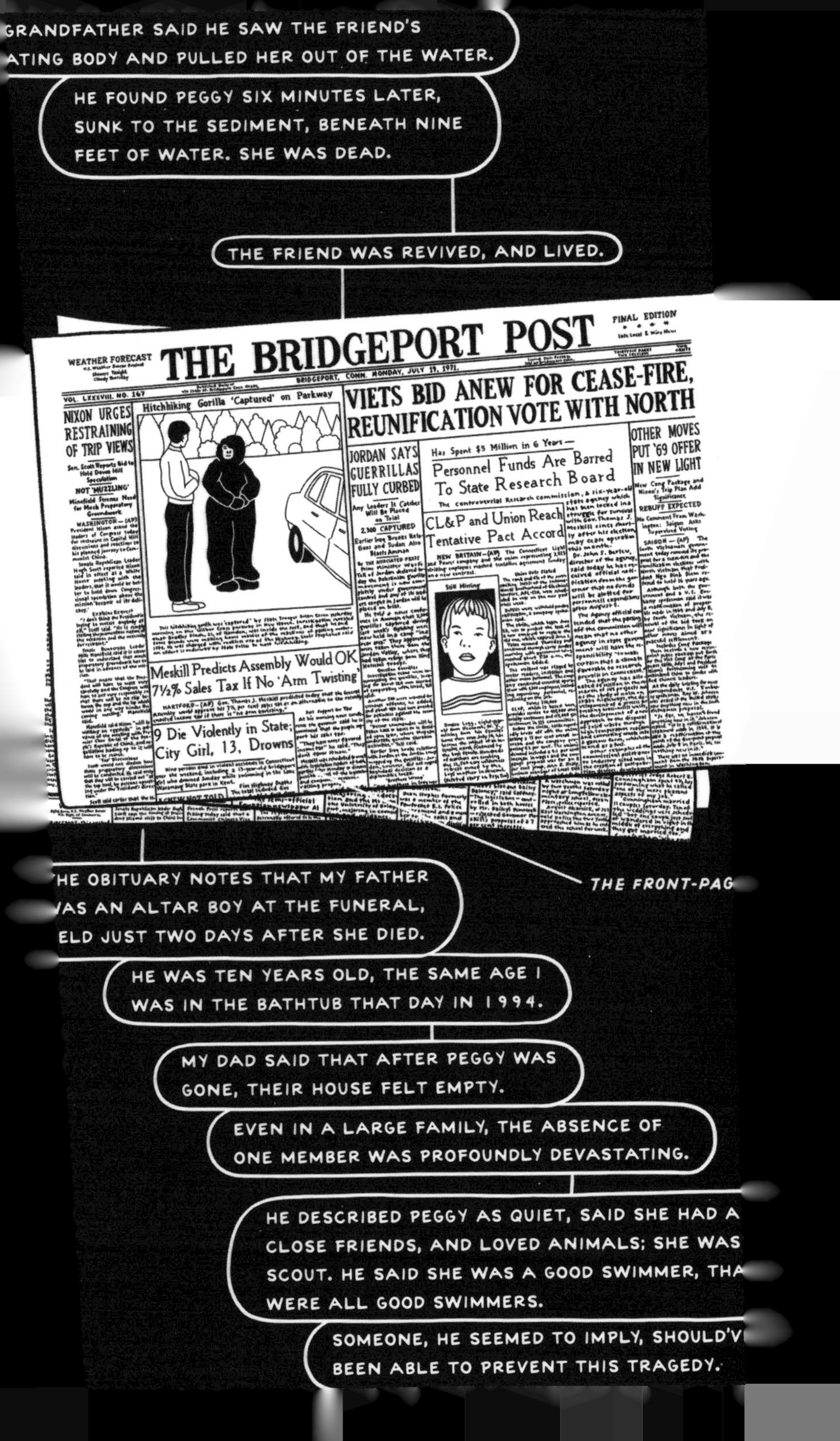

GRANDFATHER SAID HE SAW THE FRIEND'S
ATING BODY AND PULLED HER OUT OF THE WATER.
HE FOUND PEGGY SIX MINUTES LATER, SUNK TO THE SEDIMENT, BENEATH NINE FEET OF WATER. SHE WAS DEAD.
THE FRIEND WAS REVIVED, AND LIVED.
THE BRIDGEPORT POST
FINAL EDITION
WEATHER FORECAST
BRIDGEPORT, CONN. MONDAY, JULY 19, 1971.
VIETS BID ANEW FOR CEASE-FIRE, REUNIFICATION VOTE WITH NORTH
NIXON URGES RESTRAINING OF TRIP VIEWS
Hitchhiking Gorilla 'Captured' on Parkway
JORDAN SAYS GUERRILLAS FULLY CURBED
Has Spent $5 Million in 6 Years —
Personnel Funds Are Barred To State Research Board
OTHER MOVES PUT '69 OFFER IN NEW LIGHT
CL&P and Union Reach Tentative Pact Accord
Still Missing
Meskill Predicts Assembly Would OK 7½% Sales Tax If No 'Arm Twisting'
9 Die Violently in State; City Girl, 13, Drowns
THE FRONT-PAG
HE OBITUARY NOTES THAT MY FATHER
VAS AN ALTAR BOY AT THE FUNERAL,
ELD JUST TWO DAYS AFTER SHE DIED.
HE WAS TEN YEARS OLD, THE SAME AGE I WAS IN THE BATHTUB THAT DAY IN 1994.
MY DAD SAID THAT AFTER PEGGY WAS GONE, THEIR HOUSE FELT EMPTY.
EVEN IN A LARGE FAMILY, THE ABSENCE OF ONE MEMBER WAS PROFOUNDLY DEVASTATING.
HE DESCRIBED PEGGY AS QUIET, SAID SHE HAD A
CLOSE FRIENDS, AND LOVED ANIMALS; SHE WAS
SCOUT. HE SAID SHE WAS A GOOD SWIMMER, THA
WERE ALL GOOD SWIMMERS.
SOMEONE, HE SEEMED TO IMPLY, SHOULD'V
BEEN ABLE TO PREVENT THIS TRAGEDY.

THE BRIDGEPORT HOUSE NOW (ACCORDING TO THE INTERNET) ↘

HIS CATHOLIC PARENTS, DEVOUT ATTENDEES OF LATIN MASS, FELT
THAT GOD HAD WILLED PEGGY'S DEATH. GOD'S PLAN WAS BEYOND THE
UNDERSTANDING OF MORTALS SO THERE WAS NO NEED TO DISCUSS
IT. WHAT KIND OF GOD, MY DAD MUST'VE WONDERED, WOULD'VE
WANTED A CHILD TO DIE?

WHEN I THINK OF MY DAD'S CAPACITY FOR SILENCE, I THINK OF THE
FEAR STRUCK IN HIM BY THE FINALITY OF HIS SISTER'S UNEXPECTED
DEATH. I THINK OF THE SLOW, YEARS-LONG REVELATION THAT NO
ONE HAD BEEN ABLE TO HELP HER. THE REALIZATION THAT HER
PASSING WAS ARBITRARY, WITHOUT REASON. RATHER THAN TALK
ABOUT HIS EXPERIENCE OF THE EVENT, HE WENT QUIET. AN ARDENT
READER AND LOVER OF WORDS, MY DAD STILL HAS NOT FOUND A
WAY TO PUT LANGUAGE TO FEELING.

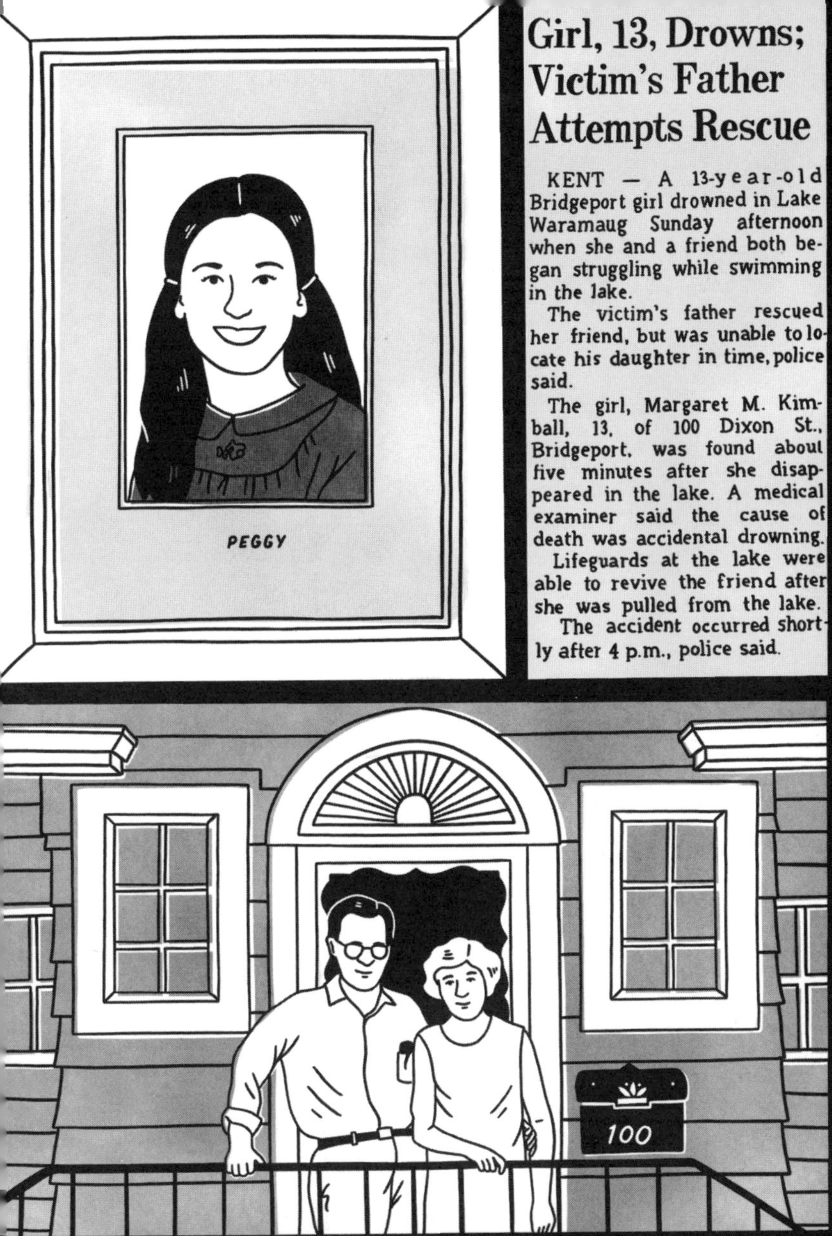
PEGGY
Girl, 13, Drowns; Victim's Father Attempts Rescue
KENT — A 13-year-old Bridgeport girl drowned in Lake Waramaug Sunday afternoon when she and a friend both began struggling while swimming in the lake.
The victim's father rescued her friend, but was unable to locate his daughter in time, police said.
The girl, Margaret M. Kimball, 13, of 100 Dixon St., Bridgeport, was found about five minutes after she disappeared in the lake. A medical examiner said the cause of death was accidental drowning.
Lifeguards at the lake were able to revive the friend after she was pulled from the lake.
The accident occurred shortly after 4 p.m., police said.
100

HAT DAY IN THE BATH WHEN MY DAD BURST THROUGH THE DOOR IN A PANIC, E WAS TRYING TO PRECLUDE DISASTER. HE'D BEEN UNABLE TO HELP PEGGY, NABLE TO FORESTALL MY MOM'S SUICIDE ATTEMPT. IN EITHER CASE THERE VAS NOTHING HE COULD'VE DONE, BUT STILL HE VIEWED THE EVENTS AS AILURES. THE MEMORY OF BEING A BYSTANDER TO CRISIS BECAME THE RUISE THAT WOULD NEVER HEAL. MOVING HIMSELF OUT OF THE HOUSE—AND, ATER, MY BROTHERS AND ME—WAS HIS BEST IDEA FOR PROTECTING US, AND M SURE HE PROMISED HIMSELF WE'D NEVER GET HURT ON HIS WATCH.

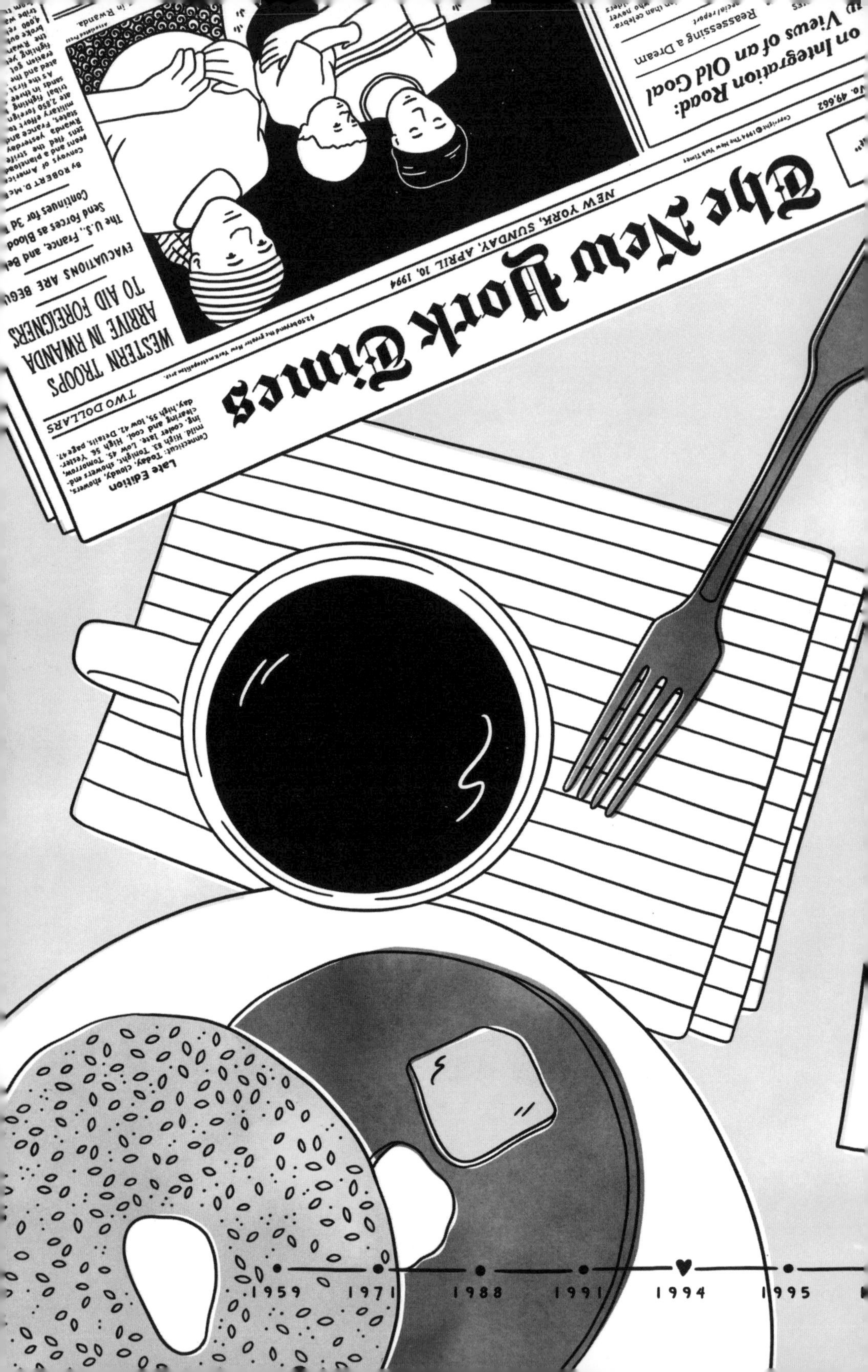
The New York Times
NEW YORK, SUNDAY, APRIL 10, 1994
TWO DOLLARS
Late Edition
WESTERN TROOPS ARRIVE IN RWANDA TO AID FOREIGNERS
Reassessing a Dream
1959
1971
1988
1991
1994
1995

CHAPTER 08

The Proposal

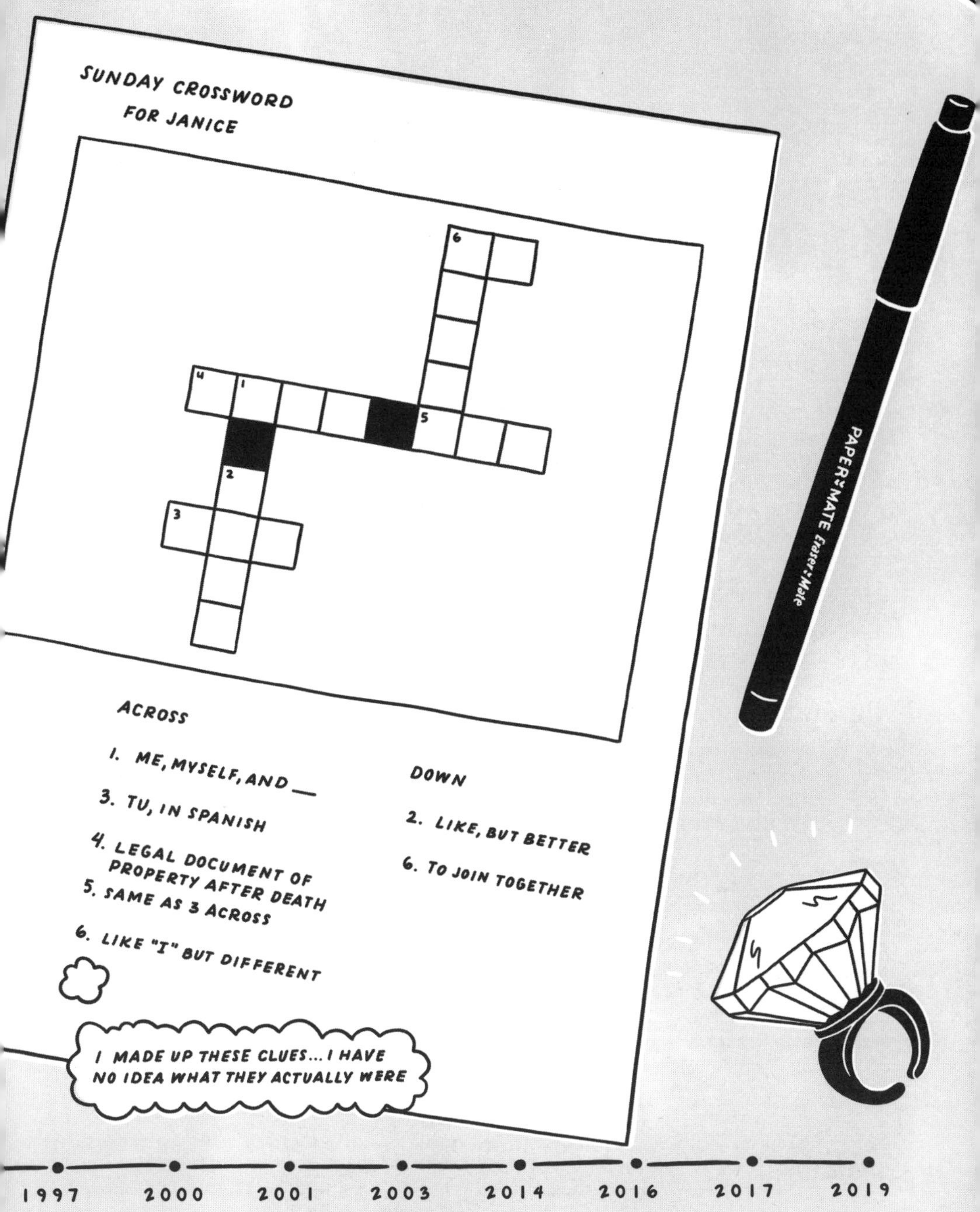
SUNDAY CROSSWORD
FOR JANICE
ACROSS
1. ME, MYSELF, AND ___
3. TU, IN SPANISH
4. LEGAL DOCUMENT OF PROPERTY AFTER DEATH
5. SAME AS 3 ACROSS
6. LIKE "I" BUT DIFFERENT
DOWN
2. LIKE, BUT BETTER
6. TO JOIN TOGETHER
I MADE UP THESE CLUES... I HAVE NO IDEA WHAT THEY ACTUALLY WERE
PAPER:MATE Eraser:Mate
1997
2000
2001
2003
2014
2016
2017
2019

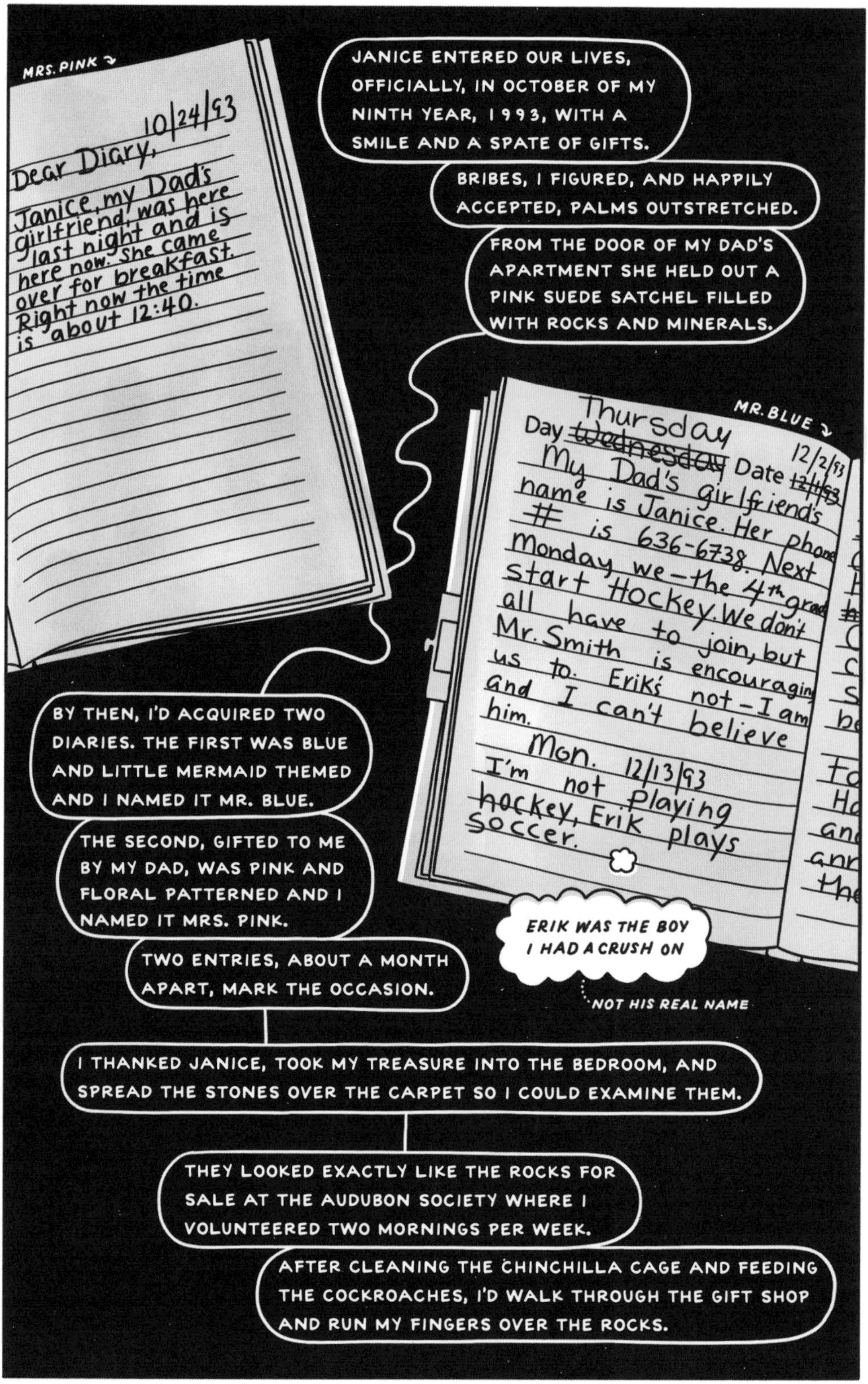
MRS. PINK
10/24/93
Dear Diary,
Janice, my Dad's girlfriend, was here last night and is here now. She came over for breakfast. Right now the time is about 12:40.
JANICE ENTERED OUR LIVES, OFFICIALLY, IN OCTOBER OF MY NINTH YEAR, 1993, WITH A SMILE AND A SPATE OF GIFTS.
BRIBES, I FIGURED, AND HAPPILY ACCEPTED, PALMS OUTSTRETCHED.
FROM THE DOOR OF MY DAD'S APARTMENT SHE HELD OUT A PINK SUEDE SATCHEL FILLED WITH ROCKS AND MINERALS.
MR. BLUE
Day ~~Wednesday~~ Thursday Date ~~12/1/93~~ 12/2/93
My Dad's girlfriend's name is Janice. Her phone # is 636-6738. Next Monday we—the 4th grade start Hockey. We don't all have to join, but Mr. Smith is encouraging us to. Erik's not—I am and I can't believe him.
Mon. 12/13/93
I'm not playing hockey, Erik plays soccer.
ERIK WAS THE BOY I HAD A CRUSH ON
NOT HIS REAL NAME
BY THEN, I'D ACQUIRED TWO DIARIES. THE FIRST WAS BLUE AND LITTLE MERMAID THEMED AND I NAMED IT MR. BLUE.
THE SECOND, GIFTED TO ME BY MY DAD, WAS PINK AND FLORAL PATTERNED AND I NAMED IT MRS. PINK.
TWO ENTRIES, ABOUT A MONTH APART, MARK THE OCCASION.
I THANKED JANICE, TOOK MY TREASURE INTO THE BEDROOM, AND SPREAD THE STONES OVER THE CARPET SO I COULD EXAMINE THEM.
THEY LOOKED EXACTLY LIKE THE ROCKS FOR SALE AT THE AUDUBON SOCIETY WHERE I VOLUNTEERED TWO MORNINGS PER WEEK.
AFTER CLEANING THE CHINCHILLA CAGE AND FEEDING THE COCKROACHES, I'D WALK THROUGH THE GIFT SHOP AND RUN MY FINGERS OVER THE ROCKS.

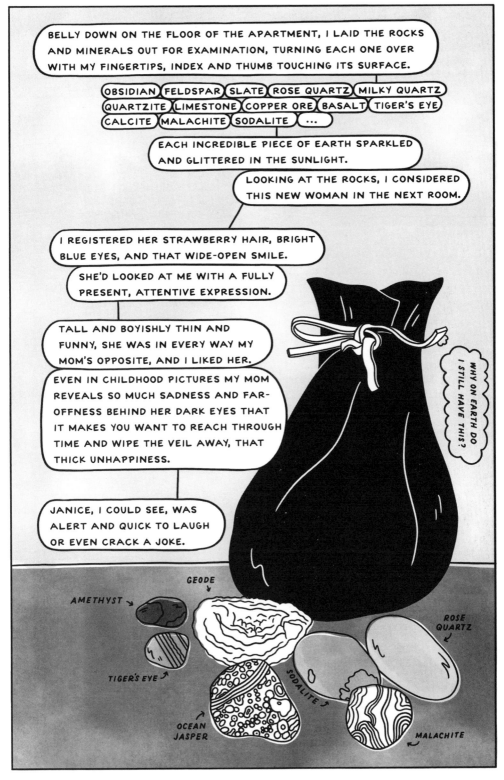

BELLY DOWN ON THE FLOOR OF THE APARTMENT, I LAID THE ROCKS AND MINERALS OUT FOR EXAMINATION, TURNING EACH ONE OVER WITH MY FINGERTIPS, INDEX AND THUMB TOUCHING ITS SURFACE.

OBSIDIAN FELDSPAR SLATE ROSE QUARTZ MILKY QUARTZ QUARTZITE LIMESTONE COPPER ORE BASALT TIGER'S EYE CALCITE MALACHITE SODALITE ...

EACH INCREDIBLE PIECE OF EARTH SPARKLED AND GLITTERED IN THE SUNLIGHT.

LOOKING AT THE ROCKS, I CONSIDERED THIS NEW WOMAN IN THE NEXT ROOM.

I REGISTERED HER STRAWBERRY HAIR, BRIGHT BLUE EYES, AND THAT WIDE-OPEN SMILE.

SHE'D LOOKED AT ME WITH A FULLY PRESENT, ATTENTIVE EXPRESSION.

TALL AND BOYISHLY THIN AND FUNNY, SHE WAS IN EVERY WAY MY MOM'S OPPOSITE, AND I LIKED HER.

EVEN IN CHILDHOOD PICTURES MY MOM REVEALS SO MUCH SADNESS AND FAR-OFFNESS BEHIND HER DARK EYES THAT IT MAKES YOU WANT TO REACH THROUGH TIME AND WIPE THE VEIL AWAY, THAT THICK UNHAPPINESS.

JANICE, I COULD SEE, WAS ALERT AND QUICK TO LAUGH OR EVEN CRACK A JOKE.

WHY ON EARTH DO I STILL HAVE THIS?

AMETHYST

GEODE

ROSE QUARTZ

TIGER'S EYE

SODALITE

OCEAN JASPER

MALACHITE

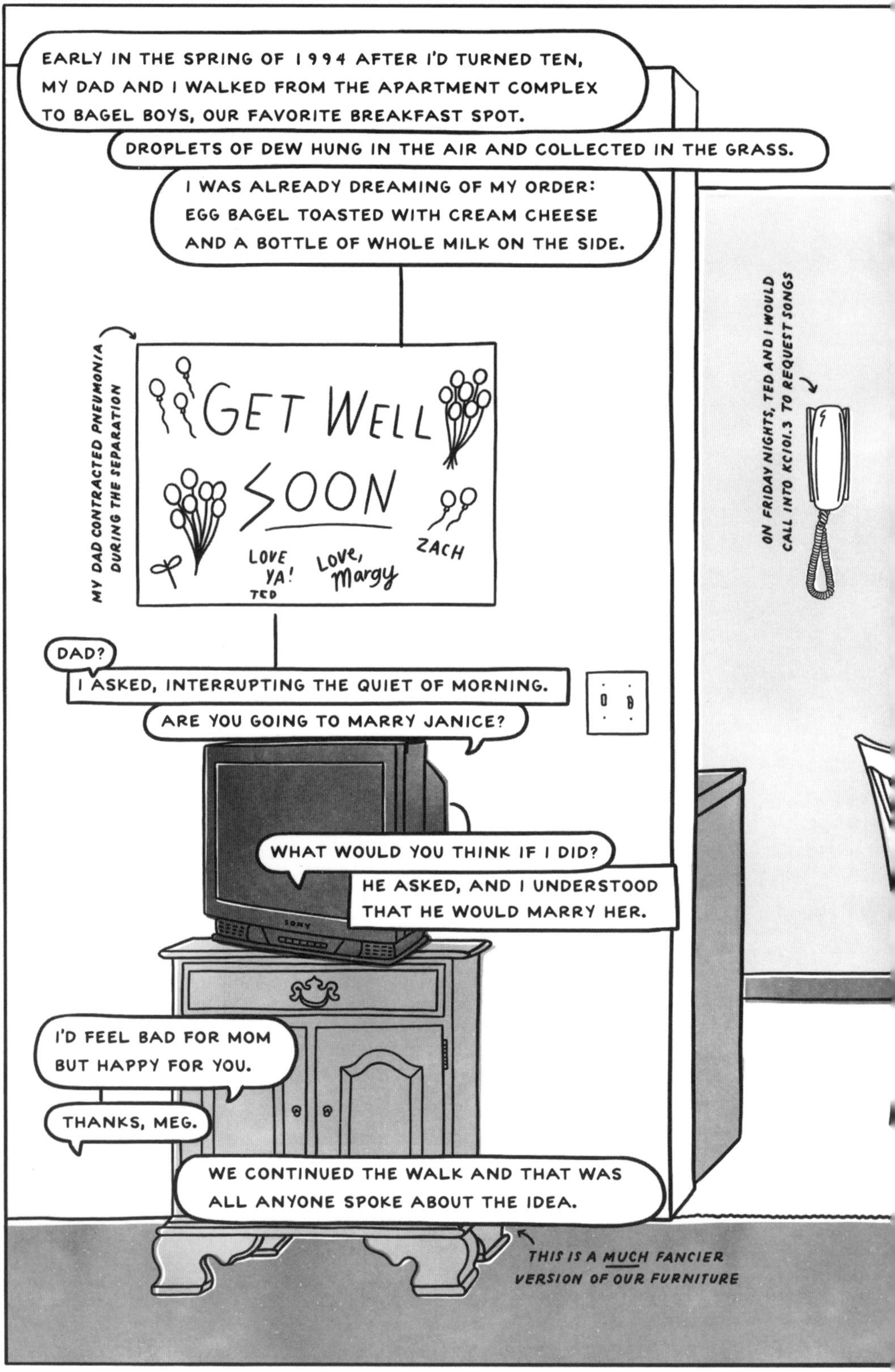
EARLY IN THE SPRING OF 1994 AFTER I'D TURNED TEN, MY DAD AND I WALKED FROM THE APARTMENT COMPLEX TO BAGEL BOYS, OUR FAVORITE BREAKFAST SPOT.
DROPLETS OF DEW HUNG IN THE AIR AND COLLECTED IN THE GRASS.
I WAS ALREADY DREAMING OF MY ORDER: EGG BAGEL TOASTED WITH CREAM CHEESE AND A BOTTLE OF WHOLE MILK ON THE SIDE.
MY DAD CONTRACTED PNEUMONIA DURING THE SEPARATION
GET WELL SOON
LOVE YA! TED
Love, Margy
ZACH
ON FRIDAY NIGHTS, TED AND I WOULD CALL INTO KC101.3 TO REQUEST SONGS
DAD?
I ASKED, INTERRUPTING THE QUIET OF MORNING.
ARE YOU GOING TO MARRY JANICE?
WHAT WOULD YOU THINK IF I DID?
HE ASKED, AND I UNDERSTOOD THAT HE WOULD MARRY HER.
I'D FEEL BAD FOR MOM BUT HAPPY FOR YOU.
THANKS, MEG.
WE CONTINUED THE WALK AND THAT WAS ALL ANYONE SPOKE ABOUT THE IDEA.
THIS IS A MUCH FANCIER VERSION OF OUR FURNITURE

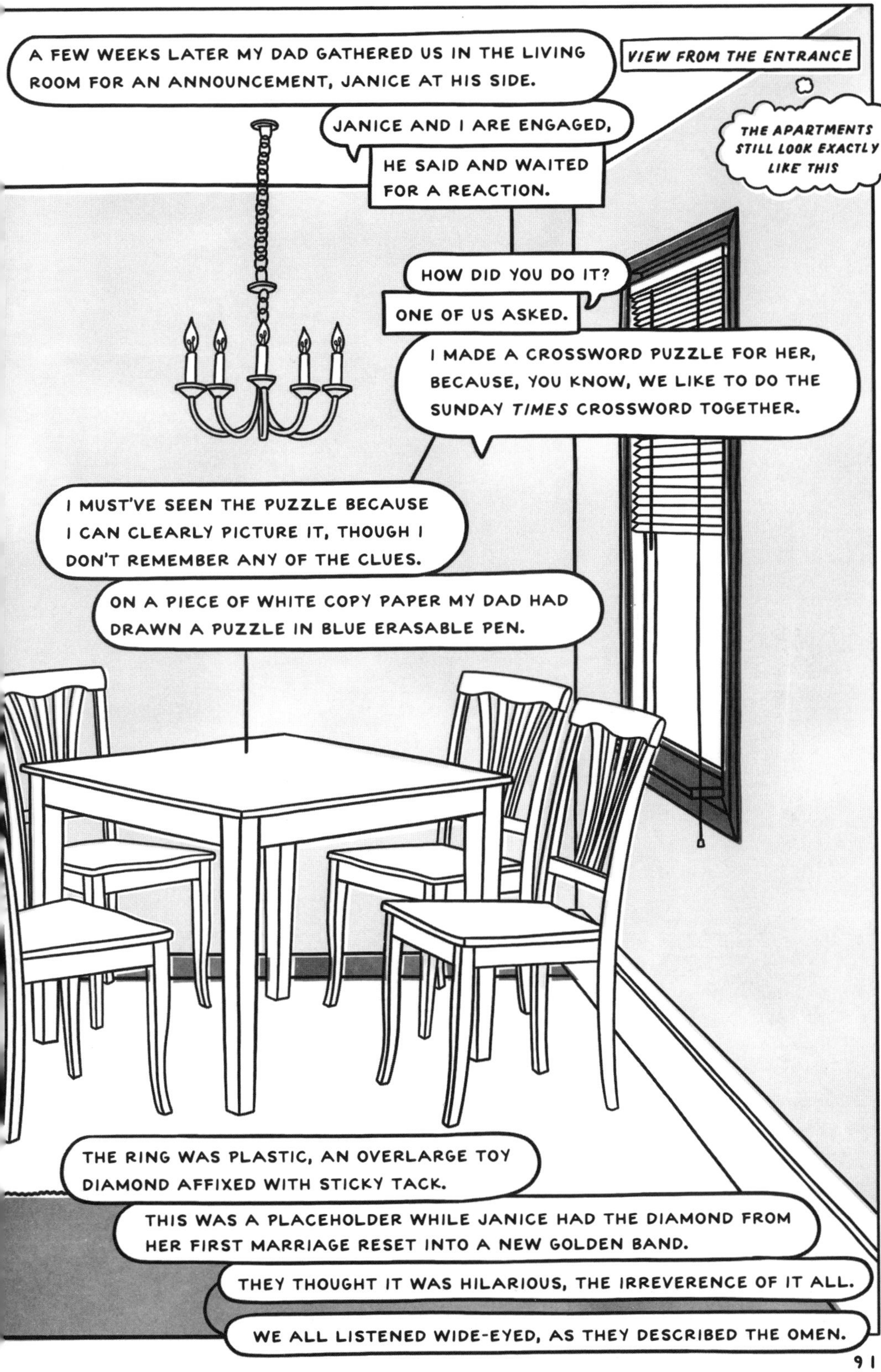
A FEW WEEKS LATER MY DAD GATHERED US IN THE LIVING ROOM FOR AN ANNOUNCEMENT, JANICE AT HIS SIDE.
VIEW FROM THE ENTRANCE
JANICE AND I ARE ENGAGED,
HE SAID AND WAITED FOR A REACTION.
THE APARTMENTS STILL LOOK EXACTLY LIKE THIS
HOW DID YOU DO IT?
ONE OF US ASKED.
I MADE A CROSSWORD PUZZLE FOR HER, BECAUSE, YOU KNOW, WE LIKE TO DO THE SUNDAY *TIMES* CROSSWORD TOGETHER.
I MUST'VE SEEN THE PUZZLE BECAUSE I CAN CLEARLY PICTURE IT, THOUGH I DON'T REMEMBER ANY OF THE CLUES.
ON A PIECE OF WHITE COPY PAPER MY DAD HAD DRAWN A PUZZLE IN BLUE ERASABLE PEN.
THE RING WAS PLASTIC, AN OVERLARGE TOY DIAMOND AFFIXED WITH STICKY TACK.
THIS WAS A PLACEHOLDER WHILE JANICE HAD THE DIAMOND FROM HER FIRST MARRIAGE RESET INTO A NEW GOLDEN BAND.
THEY THOUGHT IT WAS HILARIOUS, THE IRREVERENCE OF IT ALL.
WE ALL LISTENED WIDE-EYED, AS THEY DESCRIBED THE OMEN.

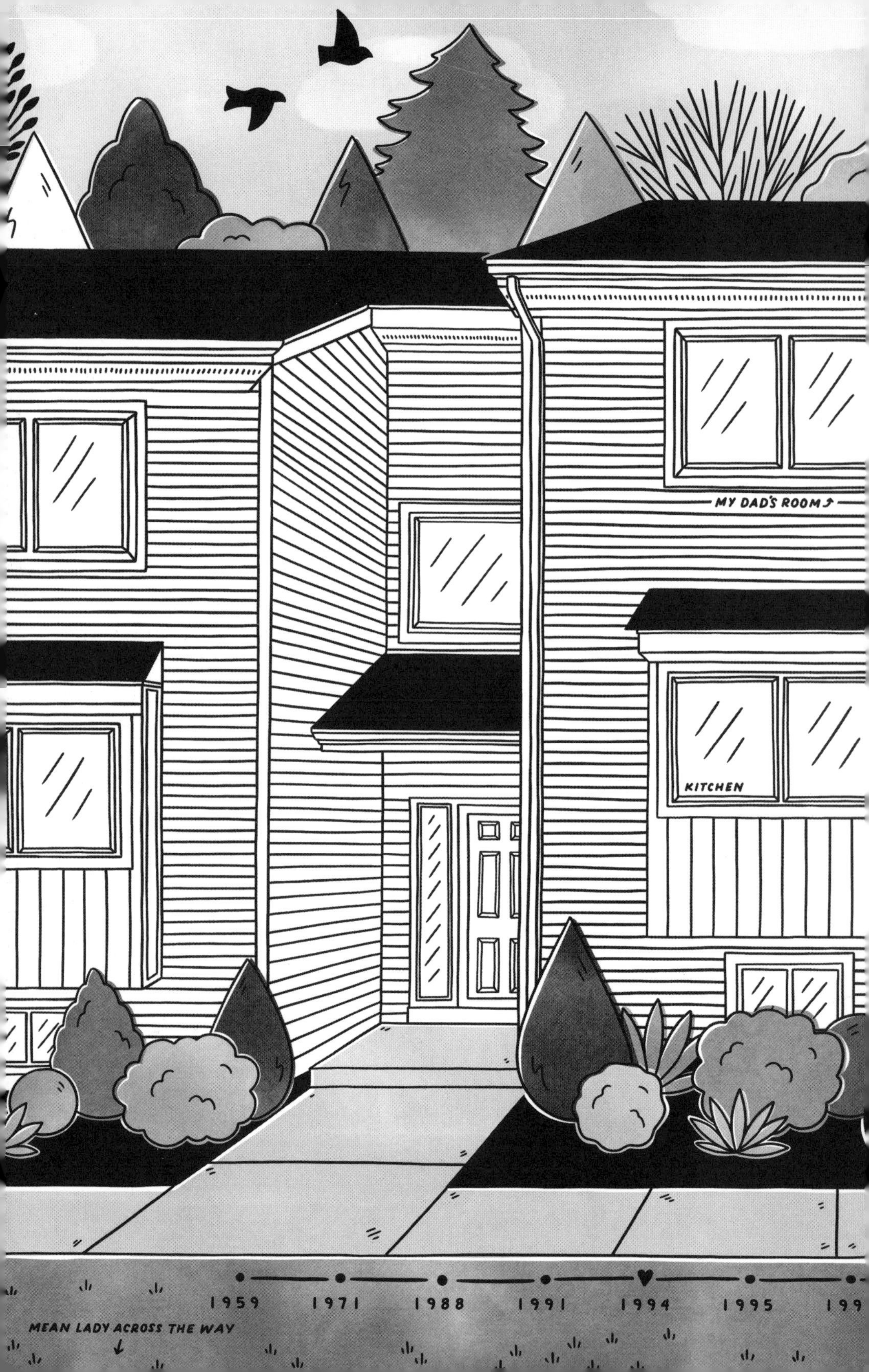
MY DAD'S ROOM
KITCHEN
1959
1971
1988
1991
1994
1995
MEAN LADY ACROSS THE WAY

CHAPTER 09
The Wedding

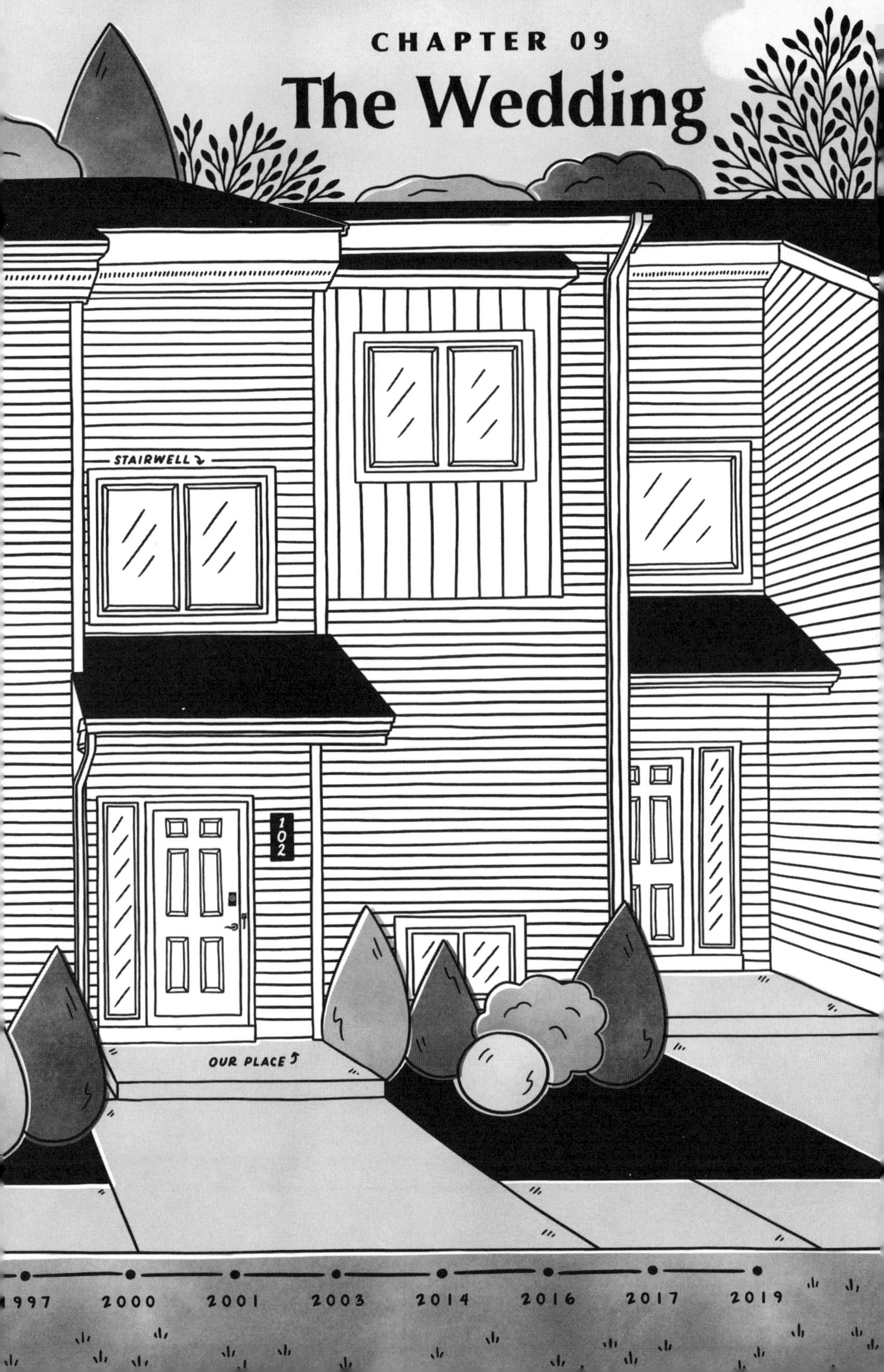
STAIRWELL
102
OUR PLACE
1997
2000
2001
2003
2014
2016
2017
2019

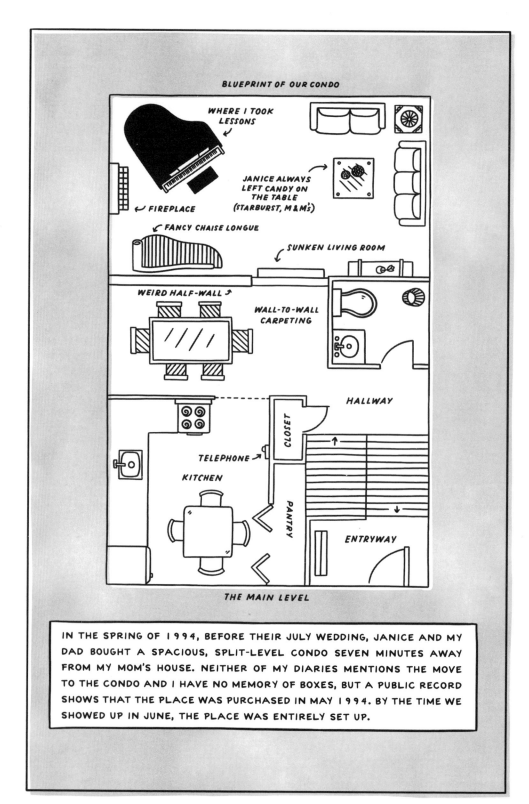

BLUEPRINT OF OUR CONDO

WHERE I TOOK LESSONS

JANICE ALWAYS LEFT CANDY ON THE TABLE (STARBURST, M&M's)

← FIREPLACE

← FANCY CHAISE LONGUE

← SUNKEN LIVING ROOM

WEIRD HALF-WALL →

WALL-TO-WALL CARPETING

HALLWAY

CLOSET

TELEPHONE →

KITCHEN

PANTRY

ENTRYWAY

THE MAIN LEVEL

IN THE SPRING OF 1994, BEFORE THEIR JULY WEDDING, JANICE AND MY DAD BOUGHT A SPACIOUS, SPLIT-LEVEL CONDO SEVEN MINUTES AWAY FROM MY MOM'S HOUSE. NEITHER OF MY DIARIES MENTIONS THE MOVE TO THE CONDO AND I HAVE NO MEMORY OF BOXES, BUT A PUBLIC RECORD SHOWS THAT THE PLACE WAS PURCHASED IN MAY 1994. BY THE TIME WE SHOWED UP IN JUNE, THE PLACE WAS ENTIRELY SET UP.

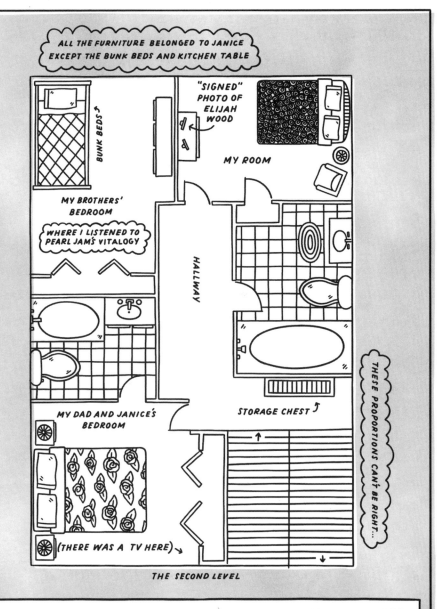

ALL THE FURNITURE BELONGED TO JANICE EXCEPT THE BUNK BEDS AND KITCHEN TABLE

BUNK BEDS

"SIGNED" PHOTO OF ELIJAH WOOD

MY ROOM

MY BROTHERS' BEDROOM

WHERE I LISTENED TO PEARL JAM'S VITALOGY

HALLWAY

THESE PROPORTIONS CAN'T BE RIGHT...

STORAGE CHEST

MY DAD AND JANICE'S BEDROOM

(THERE WAS A TV HERE)

THE SECOND LEVEL

DIVIDED INTO THREE LEVELS, THE TOP FLOOR CONTAINED ALL THREE BEDROOMS. MY BROTHERS SLEPT IN THE BUNKS FROM THE APARTMENT. I HAD MY OWN ROOM, AND JANICE HAD GIVEN ME HER FULL-SIZE BED. EVERY TIME I SHOWED UP, THE ROOM SMELLED CRISP AND THE WHITE CARPETED FLOOR WAS VACUUMED. "I WILL ALWAYS HAVE CLEAN SHEETS FOR YOU," MY DAD SAID, AND IT FELT MIRACULOUS, LIKE RENEWAL, TO SLEEP IN A ROOM THAT SMELLED OF FRESH AIR AND LAUNDERED FABRIC. THE SIMPLE ACT MADE ME FEEL CARED FOR AND SAFE. EVEN TODAY I SLEEP BEST AT MY DAD'S HOUSE.

WHEN JANICE GIFTED ME THE DRESS, I KNEW IT WASN'T COOL. INEXPLICABLY, I'VE KEPT IT. MY DAUGHTER USES IT TO DRESS UP AS AN OLD-FASHIONED GIRL.

← FRENCH BRAID

I LOOKED LIKE A 90-YEAR-OLD

FLORAL DRESS

WHITE LACEY TIGHTS →

THE WEDDING WAS HELD ON JULY 2, SIX YEARS TO THE DAY AFTER THAT 1988 FAMILY VIDEO WAS FILMED AT BLISH MEMORIAL PARK.

JANICE ASKED ME TO BE HER MAID OF HONOR.

I THOUGHT OF MY MOM AND THE PAIN IT WOULD CAUSE HER BUT UNDERSTOOD THAT THIS WAS MORE OF A REQUEST THAN AN INVITATION. COME HELL OR HIGH WATER WE WOULD SMASH OURSELVES INTO A FAMILY.

IT WAS TEMPTING, TOO, THIS IDEA THAT WE MIGHT BECOME A SOLITARY UNIT CONTAINED UNDER ONE ROOF, WITHOUT THE HOLLOWED-OUT FEELING THAT COMES WITH A FOREVER-ABSENT PARENT.

THERE WOULD BE A NEW DRESS, TOO, WITH THIS POSITION AS MAID OF HONOR. AND I WANTED A NEW DRESS.

I AGREED TO DO IT AND WONDERED HOW I'D TELL MY MOM. I DID, AND SHE TOOK IT IN UNUSUAL STRIDE, BY NODDING AND SAYING NOTHING. IT WAS ONLY MUCH LATER THAT SHE FELL APART.

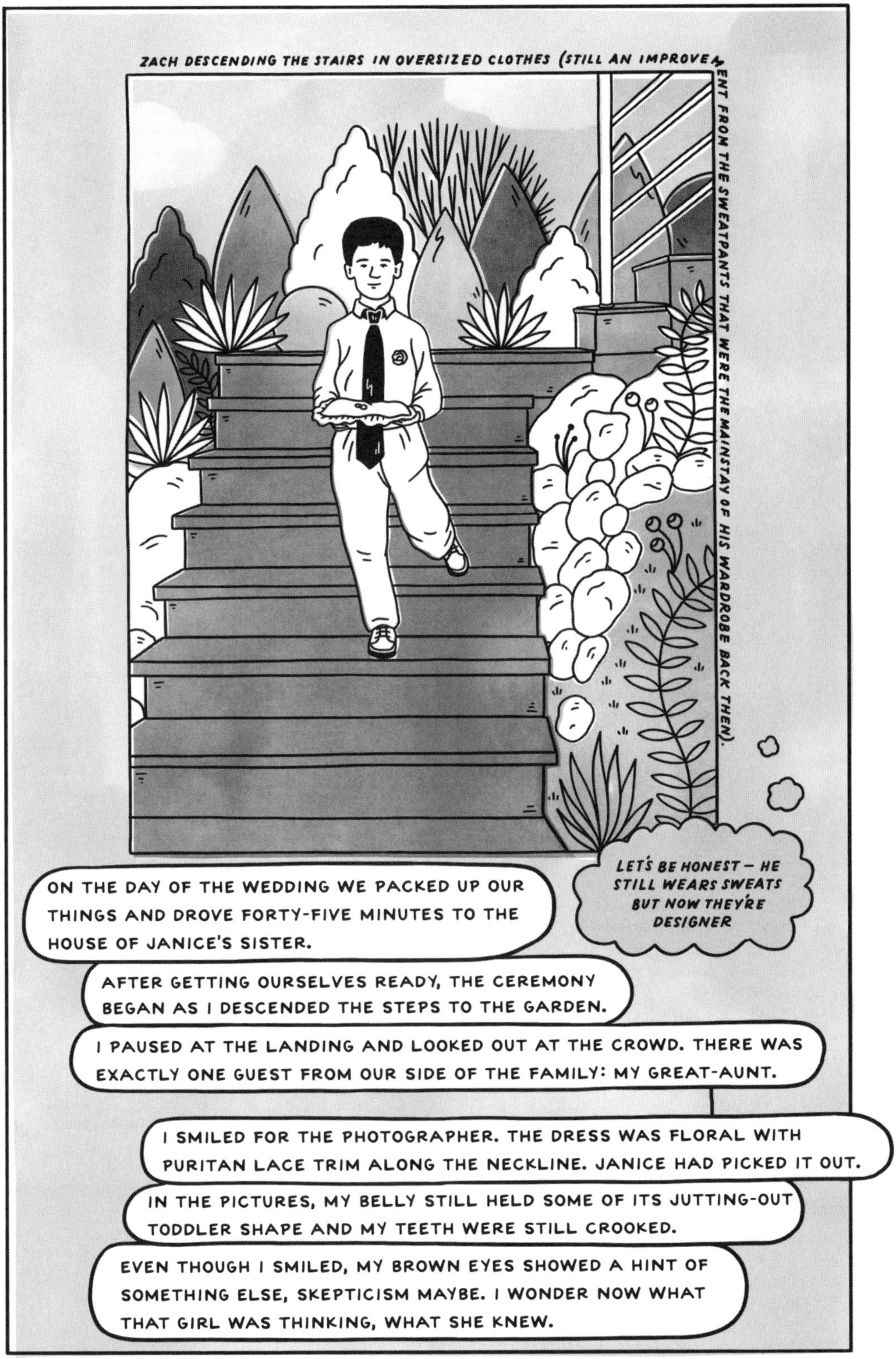
ZACH DESCENDING THE STAIRS IN OVERSIZED CLOTHES (STILL AN IMPROVEMENT FROM THE SWEATPANTS THAT WERE THE MAINSTAY OF HIS WARDROBE BACK THEN).
ON THE DAY OF THE WEDDING WE PACKED UP OUR THINGS AND DROVE FORTY-FIVE MINUTES TO THE HOUSE OF JANICE'S SISTER.
LET'S BE HONEST — HE STILL WEARS SWEATS BUT NOW THEY'RE DESIGNER
AFTER GETTING OURSELVES READY, THE CEREMONY BEGAN AS I DESCENDED THE STEPS TO THE GARDEN.
I PAUSED AT THE LANDING AND LOOKED OUT AT THE CROWD. THERE WAS EXACTLY ONE GUEST FROM OUR SIDE OF THE FAMILY: MY GREAT-AUNT.
I SMILED FOR THE PHOTOGRAPHER. THE DRESS WAS FLORAL WITH PURITAN LACE TRIM ALONG THE NECKLINE. JANICE HAD PICKED IT OUT.
IN THE PICTURES, MY BELLY STILL HELD SOME OF ITS JUTTING-OUT TODDLER SHAPE AND MY TEETH WERE STILL CROOKED.
EVEN THOUGH I SMILED, MY BROWN EYES SHOWED A HINT OF SOMETHING ELSE, SKEPTICISM MAYBE. I WONDER NOW WHAT THAT GIRL WAS THINKING, WHAT SHE KNEW.

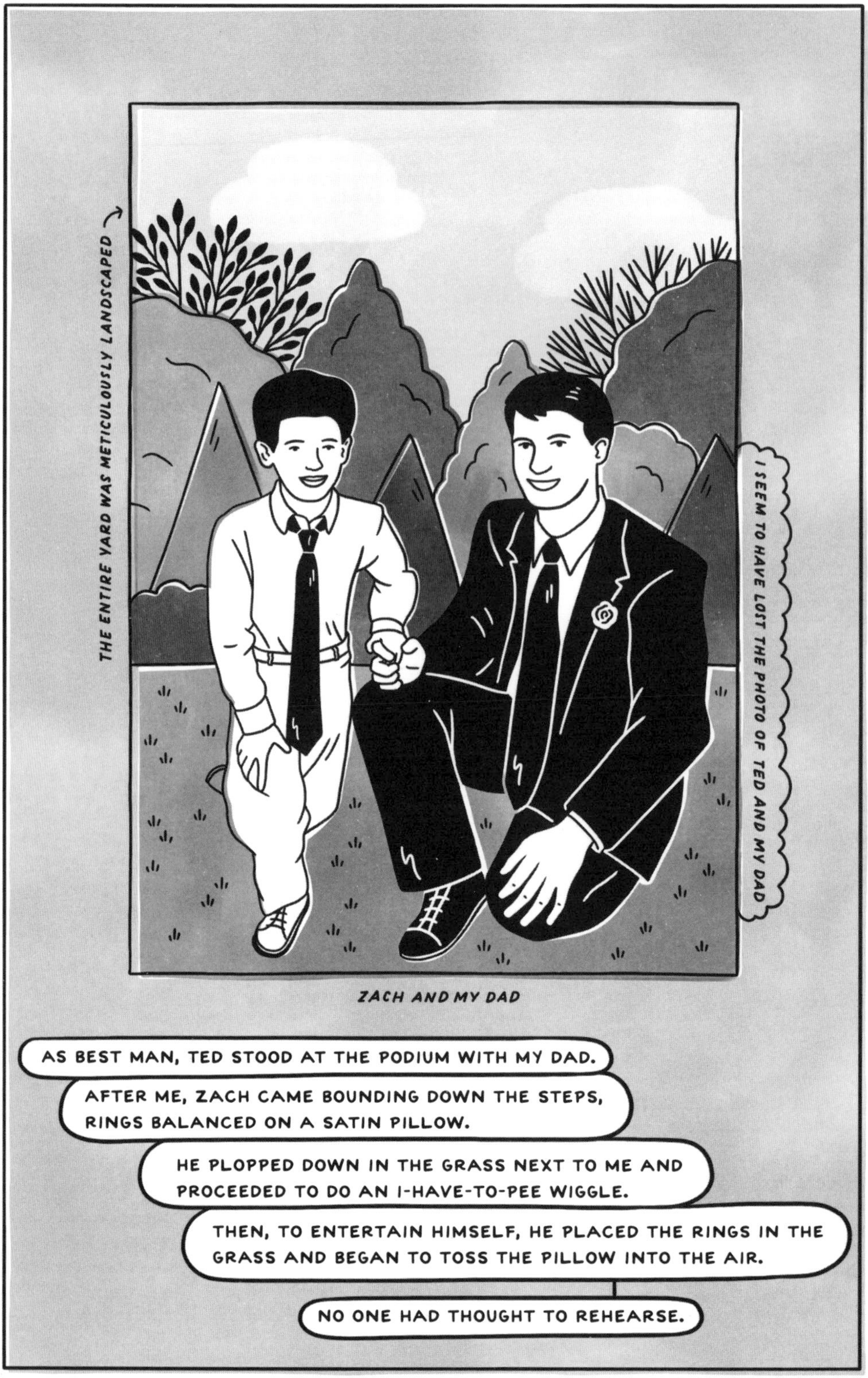
THE ENTIRE YARD WAS METICULOUSLY LANDSCAPED
I SEEM TO HAVE LOST THE PHOTO OF TED AND MY DAD
ZACH AND MY DAD
AS BEST MAN, TED STOOD AT THE PODIUM WITH MY DAD.
AFTER ME, ZACH CAME BOUNDING DOWN THE STEPS, RINGS BALANCED ON A SATIN PILLOW.
HE PLOPPED DOWN IN THE GRASS NEXT TO ME AND PROCEEDED TO DO AN I-HAVE-TO-PEE WIGGLE.
THEN, TO ENTERTAIN HIMSELF, HE PLACED THE RINGS IN THE GRASS AND BEGAN TO TOSS THE PILLOW INTO THE AIR.
NO ONE HAD THOUGHT TO REHEARSE.

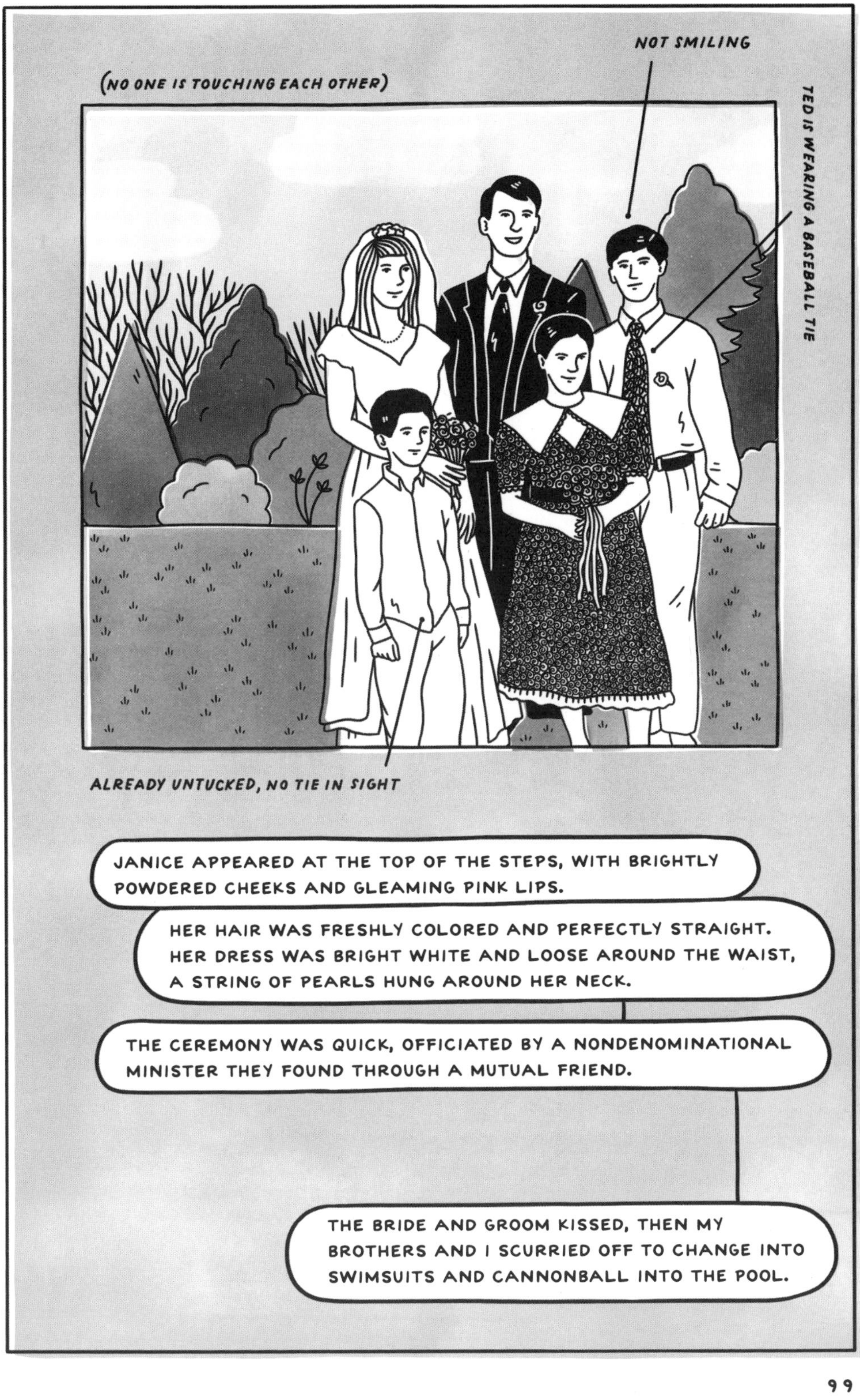
(NO ONE IS TOUCHING EACH OTHER)
NOT SMILING
TED IS WEARING A BASEBALL TIE
ALREADY UNTUCKED, NO TIE IN SIGHT
JANICE APPEARED AT THE TOP OF THE STEPS, WITH BRIGHTLY POWDERED CHEEKS AND GLEAMING PINK LIPS.
HER HAIR WAS FRESHLY COLORED AND PERFECTLY STRAIGHT. HER DRESS WAS BRIGHT WHITE AND LOOSE AROUND THE WAIST, A STRING OF PEARLS HUNG AROUND HER NECK.
THE CEREMONY WAS QUICK, OFFICIATED BY A NONDENOMINATIONAL MINISTER THEY FOUND THROUGH A MUTUAL FRIEND.
THE BRIDE AND GROOM KISSED, THEN MY BROTHERS AND I SCURRIED OFF TO CHANGE INTO SWIMSUITS AND CANNONBALL INTO THE POOL.

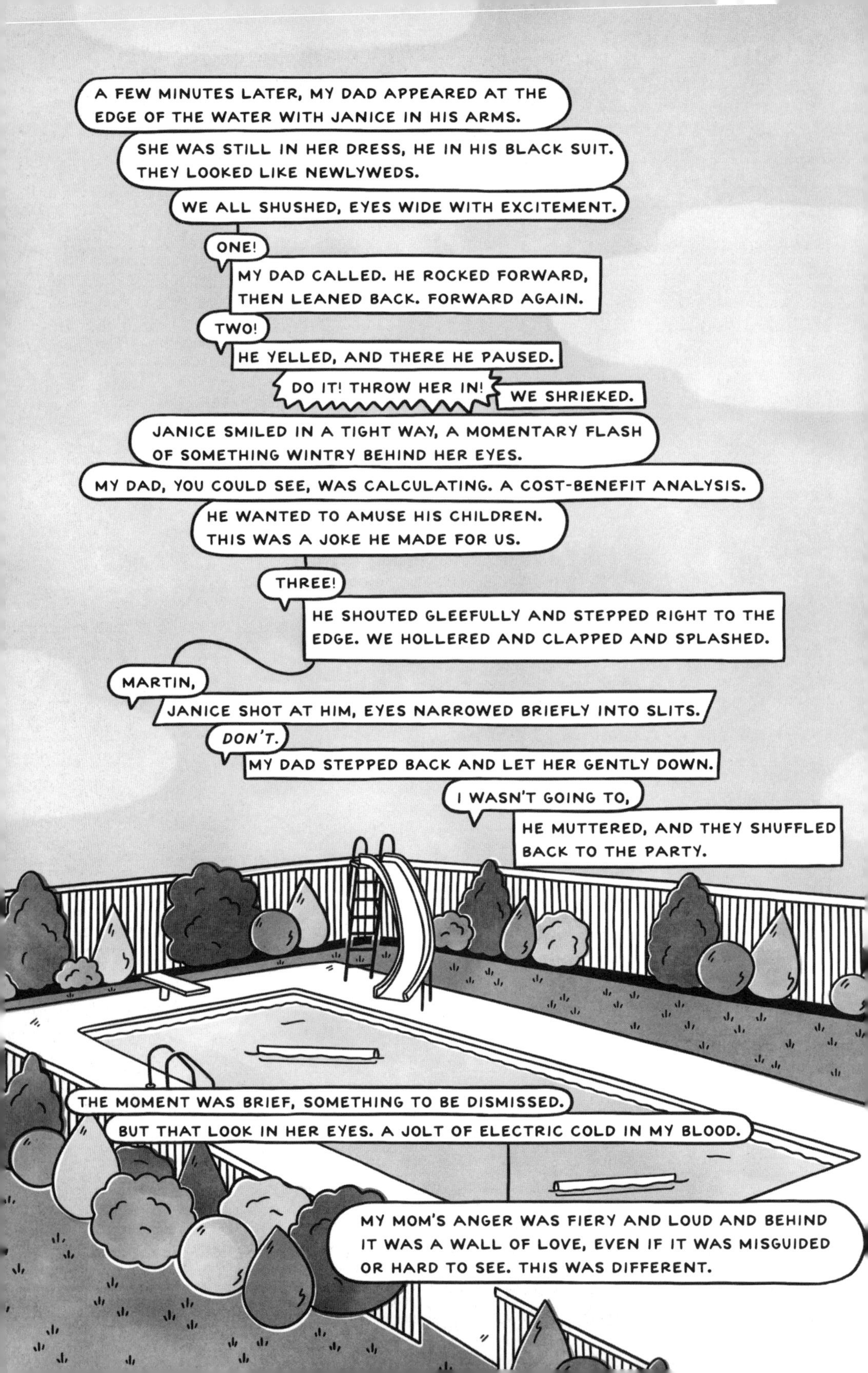

A FEW MINUTES LATER, MY DAD APPEARED AT THE EDGE OF THE WATER WITH JANICE IN HIS ARMS.
SHE WAS STILL IN HER DRESS, HE IN HIS BLACK SUIT. THEY LOOKED LIKE NEWLYWEDS.
WE ALL SHUSHED, EYES WIDE WITH EXCITEMENT.
ONE!
MY DAD CALLED. HE ROCKED FORWARD, THEN LEANED BACK. FORWARD AGAIN.
TWO!
HE YELLED, AND THERE HE PAUSED.
DO IT! THROW HER IN!
WE SHRIEKED.
JANICE SMILED IN A TIGHT WAY, A MOMENTARY FLASH OF SOMETHING WINTRY BEHIND HER EYES.
MY DAD, YOU COULD SEE, WAS CALCULATING. A COST-BENEFIT ANALYSIS.
HE WANTED TO AMUSE HIS CHILDREN. THIS WAS A JOKE HE MADE FOR US.
THREE!
HE SHOUTED GLEEFULLY AND STEPPED RIGHT TO THE EDGE. WE HOLLERED AND CLAPPED AND SPLASHED.
MARTIN,
JANICE SHOT AT HIM, EYES NARROWED BRIEFLY INTO SLITS.
DON'T.
MY DAD STEPPED BACK AND LET HER GENTLY DOWN.
I WASN'T GOING TO,
HE MUTTERED, AND THEY SHUFFLED BACK TO THE PARTY.
THE MOMENT WAS BRIEF, SOMETHING TO BE DISMISSED.
BUT THAT LOOK IN HER EYES. A JOLT OF ELECTRIC COLD IN MY BLOOD.
MY MOM'S ANGER WAS FIERY AND LOUD AND BEHIND IT WAS A WALL OF LOVE, EVEN IF IT WAS MISGUIDED OR HARD TO SEE. THIS WAS DIFFERENT.

A FEW WEEKS AFTER THE START OF FIFTH GRADE, MY MOM LOST HER MIND.

ENTRIES IN BOTH MY DIARIES DESCRIBED A HARBINGER.

THE LOCAL JEWELRY STORE WAS RUNNING A SPECIAL. IF IT RAINED NINE AND A HALF INCHES IN ONE DAY, ANYONE WHO BOUGHT JEWELRY IN THE LAST MONTH WOULD GET THEIR MONEY BACK.

AN OCCUPATIONAL HAZARD OF HAVING AN OLDER BROTHER... INAPPROPRIATE QUESTIONS FROM INQUISITIVE GIRLFRIENDS

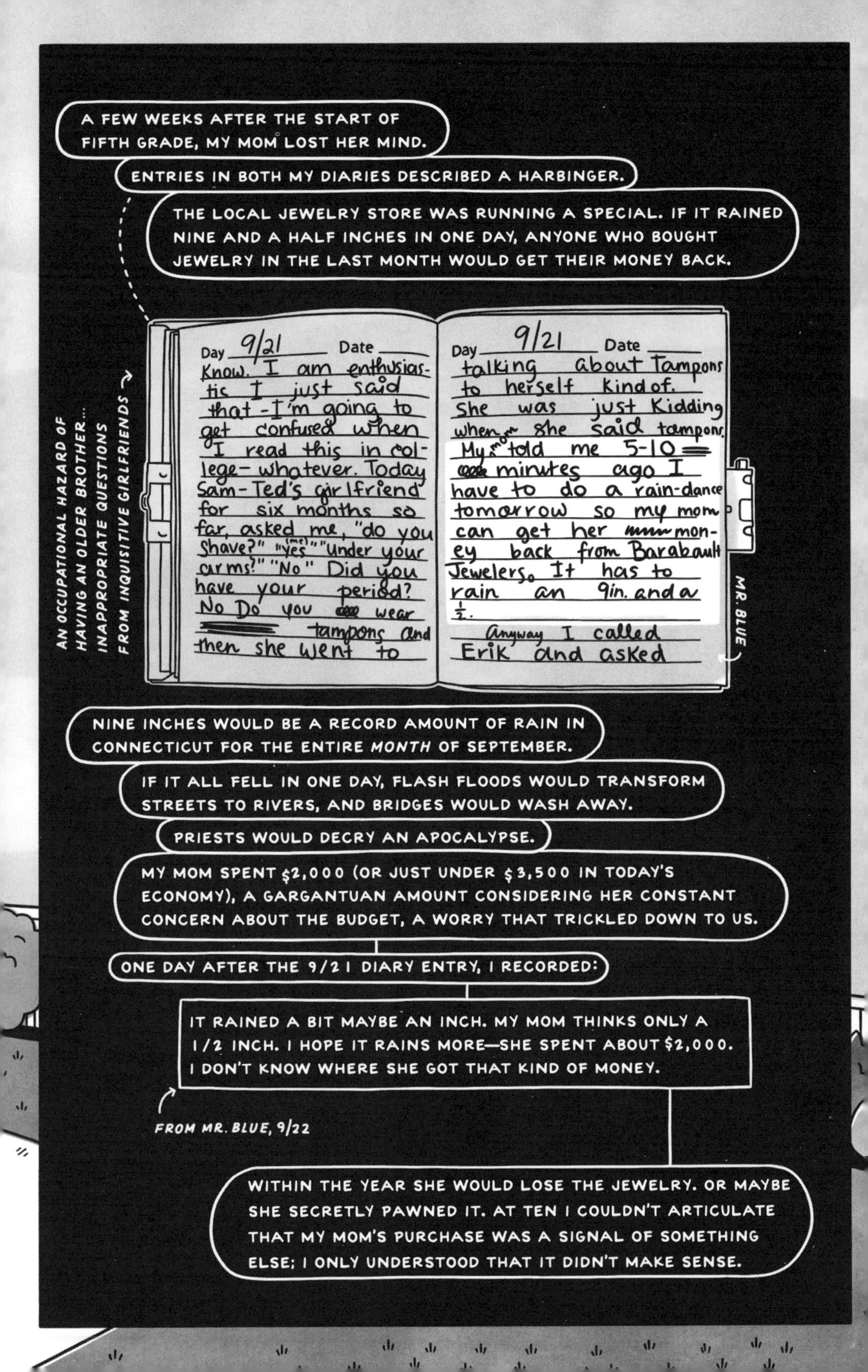

Day 9/21 Date
Know. I am enthusiastic I just said that - I'm going to get confused when I read this in college - whatever. Today Sam-Ted's girlfriend for six months so far, asked me, "do you Shave?" "yes" (me) "Under your arms?" "No" Did you have your period? No Do you wear tampons and then she went to
Day 9/21 Date
talking about Tampons to herself kind of. She was just Kidding when she said tampons. My mom told me 5-10 minutes ago I have to do a rain-dance tomorrow so my mom can get her money back from Barabault Jewelers. It has to rain an 9in. and a 1/2.
Anyway I called Erik and asked

MR. BLUE

NINE INCHES WOULD BE A RECORD AMOUNT OF RAIN IN CONNECTICUT FOR THE ENTIRE *MONTH* OF SEPTEMBER.

IF IT ALL FELL IN ONE DAY, FLASH FLOODS WOULD TRANSFORM STREETS TO RIVERS, AND BRIDGES WOULD WASH AWAY.

PRIESTS WOULD DECRY AN APOCALYPSE.

MY MOM SPENT $2,000 (OR JUST UNDER $3,500 IN TODAY'S ECONOMY), A GARGANTUAN AMOUNT CONSIDERING HER CONSTANT CONCERN ABOUT THE BUDGET, A WORRY THAT TRICKLED DOWN TO US.

ONE DAY AFTER THE 9/21 DIARY ENTRY, I RECORDED:

IT RAINED A BIT MAYBE AN INCH. MY MOM THINKS ONLY A 1/2 INCH. I HOPE IT RAINS MORE—SHE SPENT ABOUT $2,000. I DON'T KNOW WHERE SHE GOT THAT KIND OF MONEY.

FROM MR. BLUE, 9/22

WITHIN THE YEAR SHE WOULD LOSE THE JEWELRY. OR MAYBE SHE SECRETLY PAWNED IT. AT TEN I COULDN'T ARTICULATE THAT MY MOM'S PURCHASE WAS A SIGNAL OF SOMETHING ELSE; I ONLY UNDERSTOOD THAT IT DIDN'T MAKE SENSE.

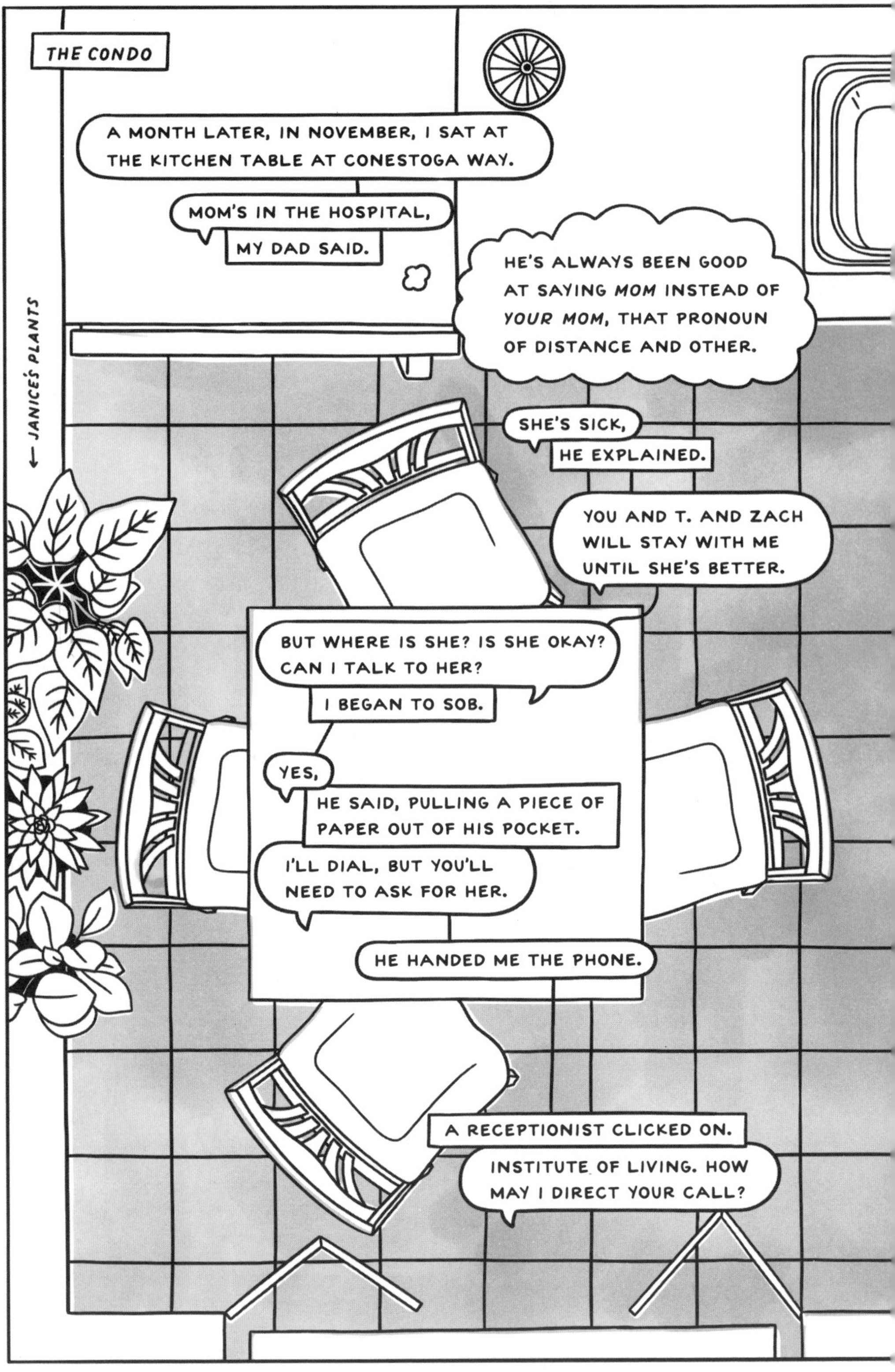
THE CONDO
A MONTH LATER, IN NOVEMBER, I SAT AT THE KITCHEN TABLE AT CONESTOGA WAY.
MOM'S IN THE HOSPITAL,
MY DAD SAID.
HE'S ALWAYS BEEN GOOD AT SAYING *MOM* INSTEAD OF *YOUR MOM*, THAT PRONOUN OF DISTANCE AND OTHER.
← JANICE'S PLANTS
SHE'S SICK,
HE EXPLAINED.
YOU AND T. AND ZACH WILL STAY WITH ME UNTIL SHE'S BETTER.
BUT WHERE IS SHE? IS SHE OKAY? CAN I TALK TO HER?
I BEGAN TO SOB.
YES,
HE SAID, PULLING A PIECE OF PAPER OUT OF HIS POCKET.
I'LL DIAL, BUT YOU'LL NEED TO ASK FOR HER.
HE HANDED ME THE PHONE.
A RECEPTIONIST CLICKED ON.
INSTITUTE OF LIVING. HOW MAY I DIRECT YOUR CALL?

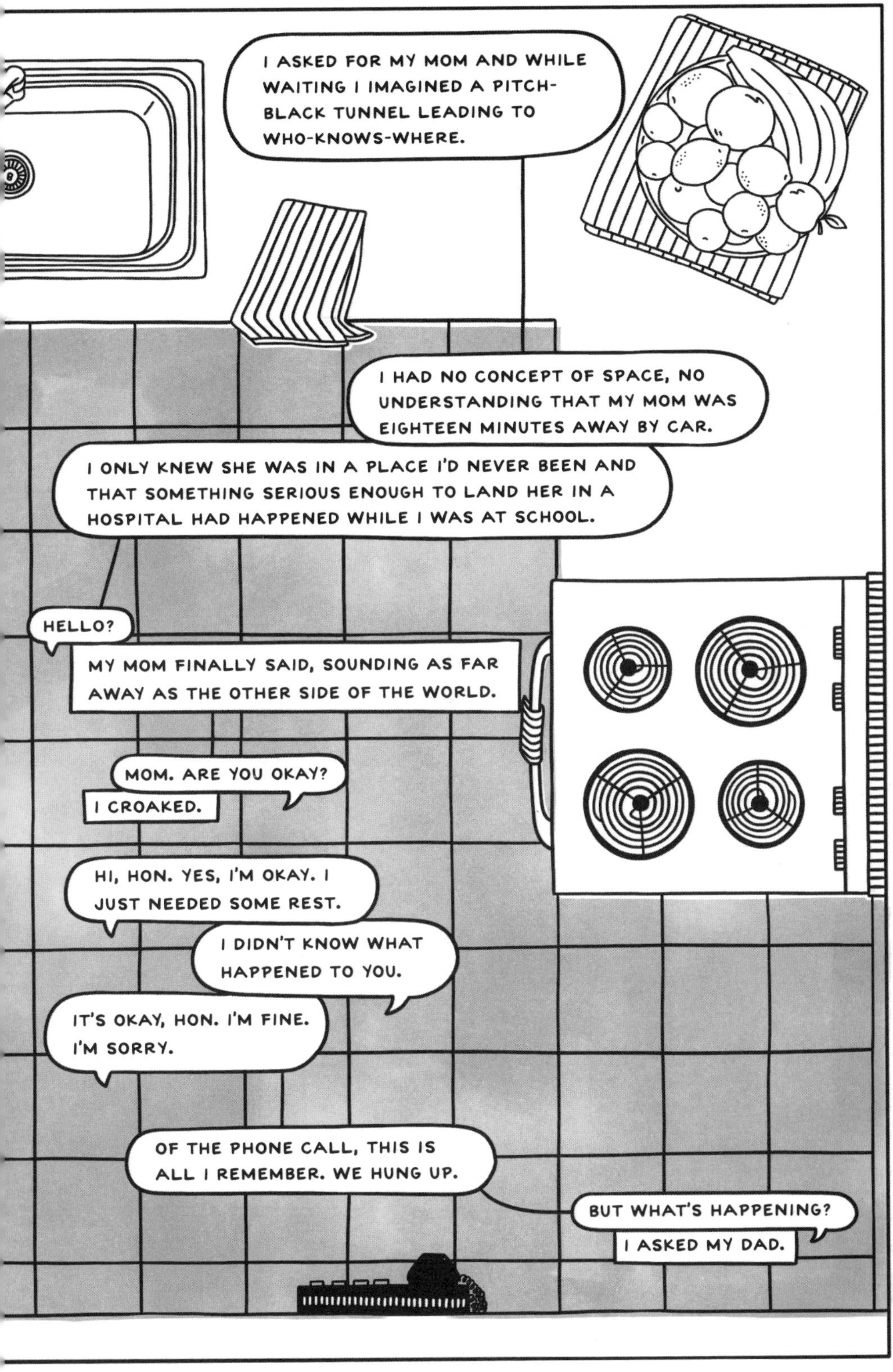
I ASKED FOR MY MOM AND WHILE WAITING I IMAGINED A PITCH-BLACK TUNNEL LEADING TO WHO-KNOWS-WHERE.
I HAD NO CONCEPT OF SPACE, NO UNDERSTANDING THAT MY MOM WAS EIGHTEEN MINUTES AWAY BY CAR.
I ONLY KNEW SHE WAS IN A PLACE I'D NEVER BEEN AND THAT SOMETHING SERIOUS ENOUGH TO LAND HER IN A HOSPITAL HAD HAPPENED WHILE I WAS AT SCHOOL.
HELLO?
MY MOM FINALLY SAID, SOUNDING AS FAR AWAY AS THE OTHER SIDE OF THE WORLD.
MOM. ARE YOU OKAY?
I CROAKED.
HI, HON. YES, I'M OKAY. I JUST NEEDED SOME REST.
I DIDN'T KNOW WHAT HAPPENED TO YOU.
IT'S OKAY, HON. I'M FINE. I'M SORRY.
OF THE PHONE CALL, THIS IS ALL I REMEMBER. WE HUNG UP.
BUT WHAT'S HAPPENING?
I ASKED MY DAD.

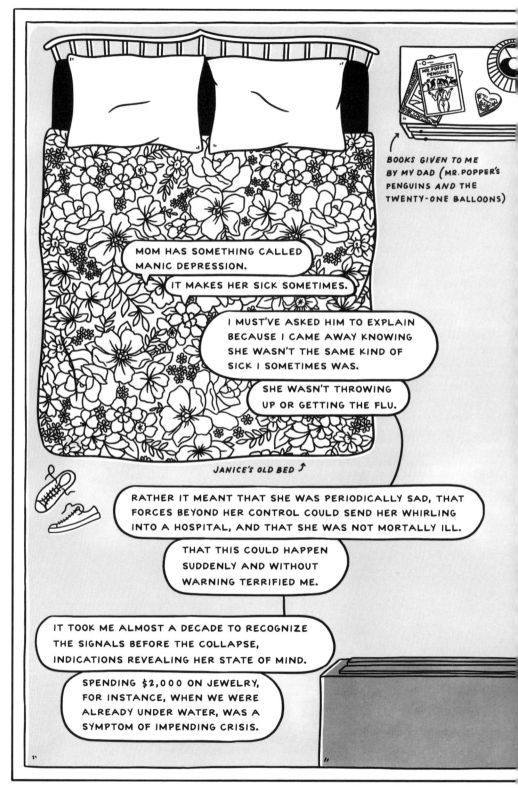

BOOKS GIVEN TO ME BY MY DAD (MR. POPPER'S PENGUINS AND THE TWENTY-ONE BALLOONS)

MOM HAS SOMETHING CALLED MANIC DEPRESSION.

IT MAKES HER SICK SOMETIMES.

I MUST'VE ASKED HIM TO EXPLAIN BECAUSE I CAME AWAY KNOWING SHE WASN'T THE SAME KIND OF SICK I SOMETIMES WAS.

SHE WASN'T THROWING UP OR GETTING THE FLU.

JANICE'S OLD BED ↑

RATHER IT MEANT THAT SHE WAS PERIODICALLY SAD, THAT FORCES BEYOND HER CONTROL COULD SEND HER WHIRLING INTO A HOSPITAL, AND THAT SHE WAS NOT MORTALLY ILL.

THAT THIS COULD HAPPEN SUDDENLY AND WITHOUT WARNING TERRIFIED ME.

IT TOOK ME ALMOST A DECADE TO RECOGNIZE THE SIGNALS BEFORE THE COLLAPSE, INDICATIONS REVEALING HER STATE OF MIND.

SPENDING $2,000 ON JEWELRY, FOR INSTANCE, WHEN WE WERE ALREADY UNDER WATER, WAS A SYMPTOM OF IMPENDING CRISIS.

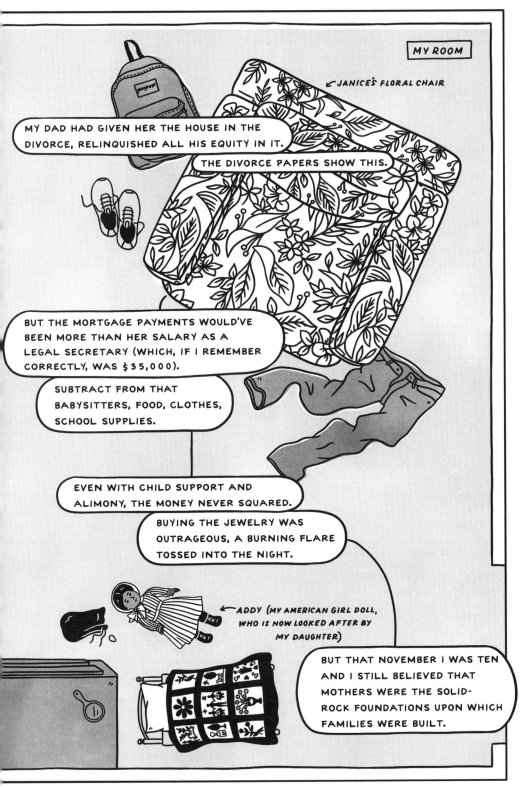

← JANICE'S FLORAL CHAIR

MY DAD HAD GIVEN HER THE HOUSE IN THE DIVORCE, RELINQUISHED ALL HIS EQUITY IN IT.

THE DIVORCE PAPERS SHOW THIS.

BUT THE MORTGAGE PAYMENTS WOULD'VE BEEN MORE THAN HER SALARY AS A LEGAL SECRETARY (WHICH, IF I REMEMBER CORRECTLY, WAS $35,000).

SUBTRACT FROM THAT BABYSITTERS, FOOD, CLOTHES, SCHOOL SUPPLIES.

EVEN WITH CHILD SUPPORT AND ALIMONY, THE MONEY NEVER SQUARED.

BUYING THE JEWELRY WAS OUTRAGEOUS, A BURNING FLARE TOSSED INTO THE NIGHT.

← ADDY (MY AMERICAN GIRL DOLL, WHO IS NOW LOOKED AFTER BY MY DAUGHTER)

BUT THAT NOVEMBER I WAS TEN AND I STILL BELIEVED THAT MOTHERS WERE THE SOLID-ROCK FOUNDATIONS UPON WHICH FAMILIES WERE BUILT.

THE INSTITUTE OF LIVING BECAME PART OF HARTFORD HOSPITAL THE SAME YEAR MY MOM WAS ADMITTED, 1994. BEFORE THAT THE PLACE WAS CALLED THE HARTFORD RETREAT FOR THE INSANE. THE GROUNDS WERE ORIGINALLY DESIGNED BY FREDERICK LAW OLMSTED IN THE 1860s.

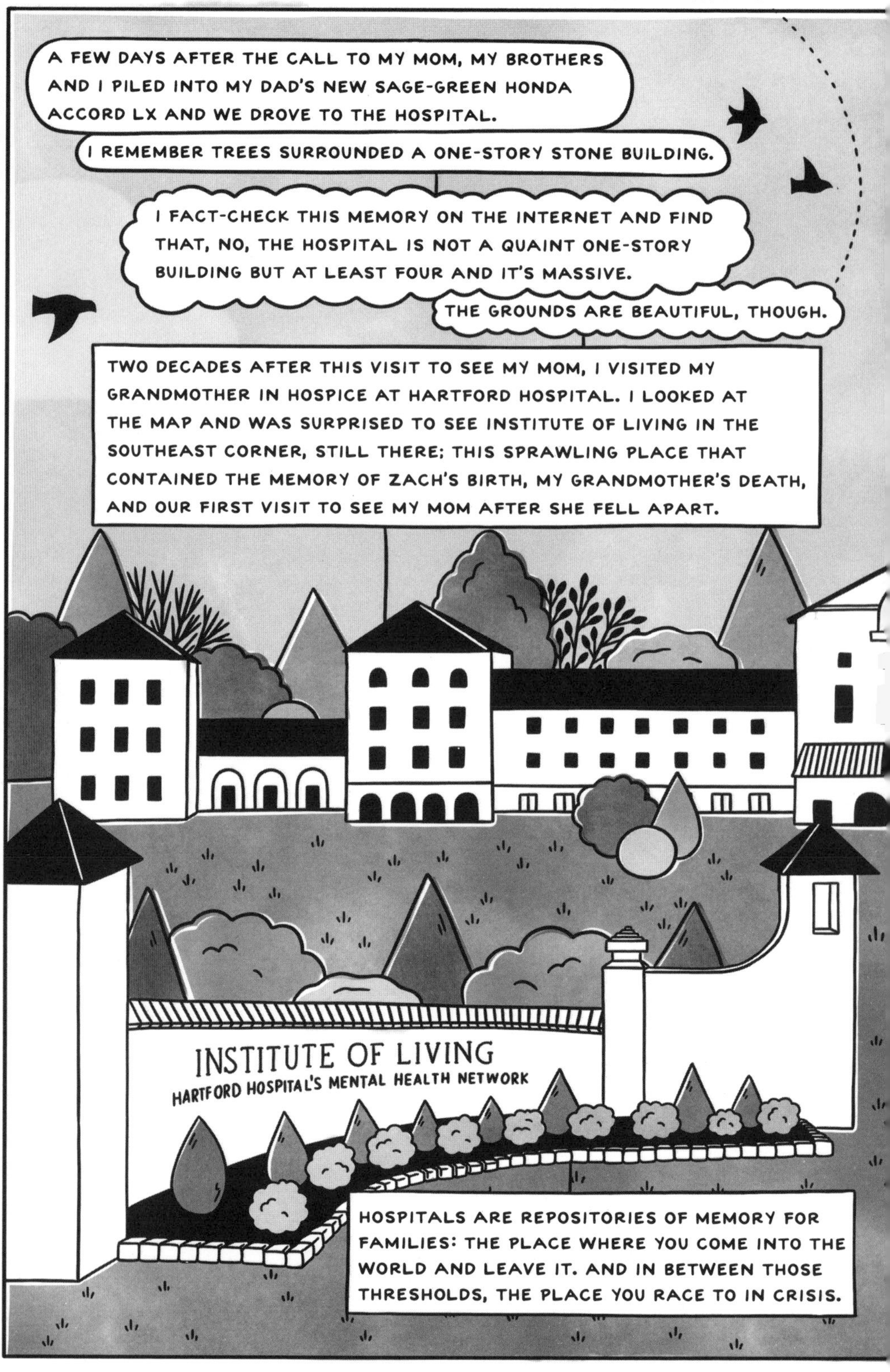
A FEW DAYS AFTER THE CALL TO MY MOM, MY BROTHERS AND I PILED INTO MY DAD'S NEW SAGE-GREEN HONDA ACCORD LX AND WE DROVE TO THE HOSPITAL.
I REMEMBER TREES SURROUNDED A ONE-STORY STONE BUILDING.
I FACT-CHECK THIS MEMORY ON THE INTERNET AND FIND THAT, NO, THE HOSPITAL IS NOT A QUAINT ONE-STORY BUILDING BUT AT LEAST FOUR AND IT'S MASSIVE.
THE GROUNDS ARE BEAUTIFUL, THOUGH.
TWO DECADES AFTER THIS VISIT TO SEE MY MOM, I VISITED MY GRANDMOTHER IN HOSPICE AT HARTFORD HOSPITAL. I LOOKED AT THE MAP AND WAS SURPRISED TO SEE INSTITUTE OF LIVING IN THE SOUTHEAST CORNER, STILL THERE; THIS SPRAWLING PLACE THAT CONTAINED THE MEMORY OF ZACH'S BIRTH, MY GRANDMOTHER'S DEATH, AND OUR FIRST VISIT TO SEE MY MOM AFTER SHE FELL APART.
INSTITUTE OF LIVING
HARTFORD HOSPITAL'S MENTAL HEALTH NETWORK
HOSPITALS ARE REPOSITORIES OF MEMORY FOR FAMILIES: THE PLACE WHERE YOU COME INTO THE WORLD AND LEAVE IT. AND IN BETWEEN THOSE THRESHOLDS, THE PLACE YOU RACE TO IN CRISIS.

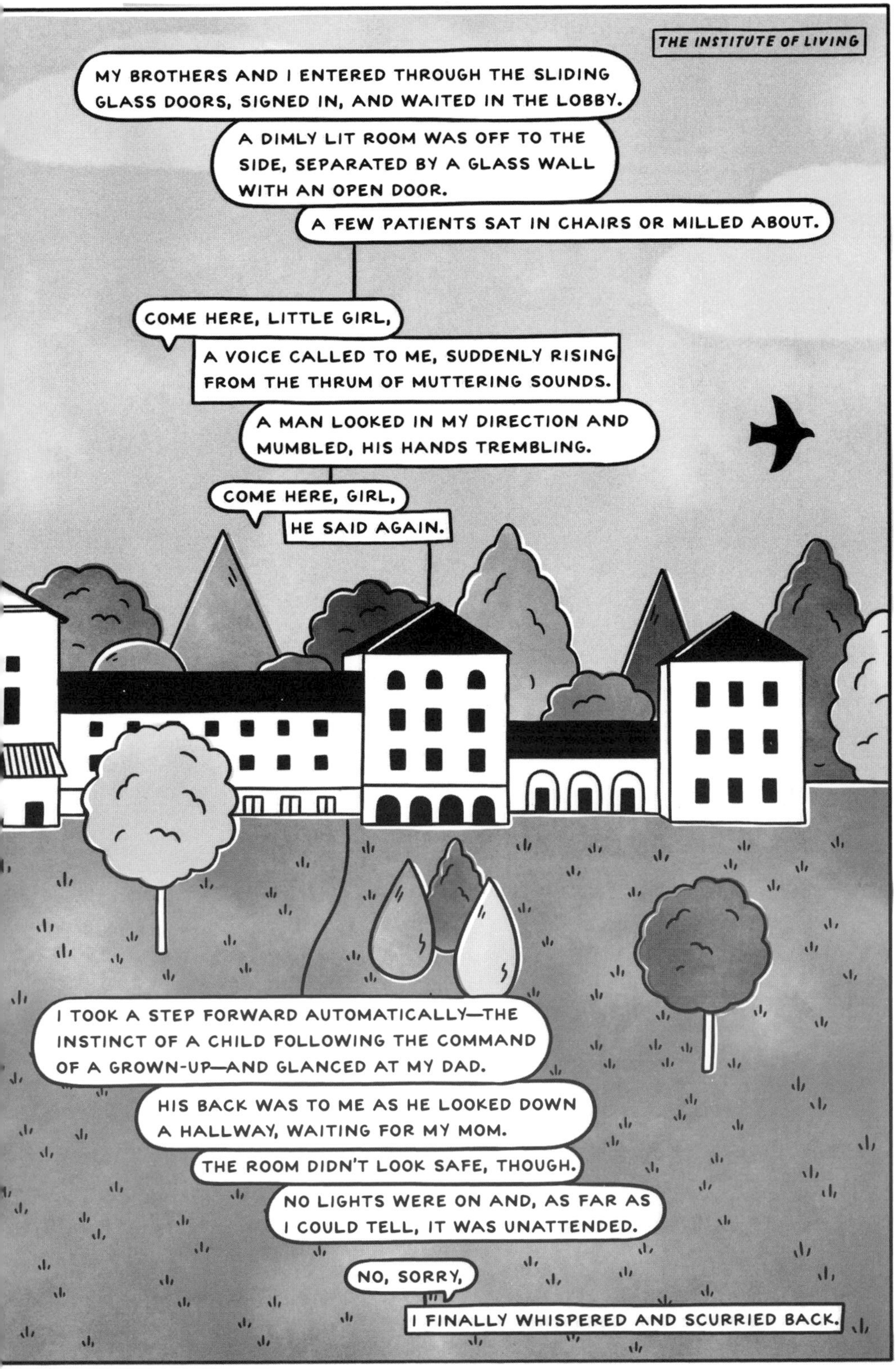
THE INSTITUTE OF LIVING
MY BROTHERS AND I ENTERED THROUGH THE SLIDING GLASS DOORS, SIGNED IN, AND WAITED IN THE LOBBY.
A DIMLY LIT ROOM WAS OFF TO THE SIDE, SEPARATED BY A GLASS WALL WITH AN OPEN DOOR.
A FEW PATIENTS SAT IN CHAIRS OR MILLED ABOUT.
COME HERE, LITTLE GIRL,
A VOICE CALLED TO ME, SUDDENLY RISING FROM THE THRUM OF MUTTERING SOUNDS.
A MAN LOOKED IN MY DIRECTION AND MUMBLED, HIS HANDS TREMBLING.
COME HERE, GIRL,
HE SAID AGAIN.
I TOOK A STEP FORWARD AUTOMATICALLY—THE INSTINCT OF A CHILD FOLLOWING THE COMMAND OF A GROWN-UP—AND GLANCED AT MY DAD.
HIS BACK WAS TO ME AS HE LOOKED DOWN A HALLWAY, WAITING FOR MY MOM.
THE ROOM DIDN'T LOOK SAFE, THOUGH.
NO LIGHTS WERE ON AND, AS FAR AS I COULD TELL, IT WAS UNATTENDED.
NO, SORRY,
I FINALLY WHISPERED AND SCURRIED BACK.

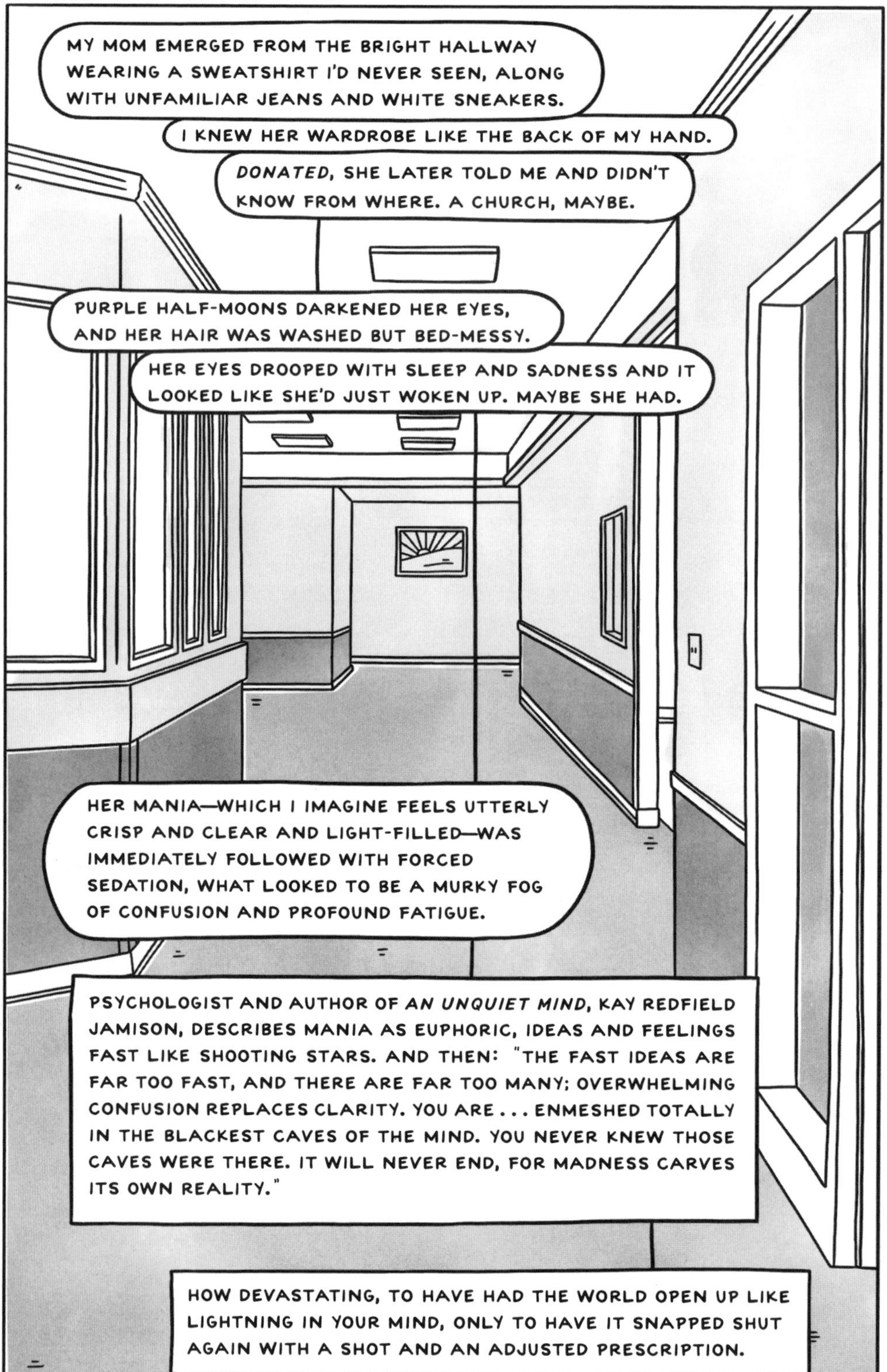
MY MOM EMERGED FROM THE BRIGHT HALLWAY WEARING A SWEATSHIRT I'D NEVER SEEN, ALONG WITH UNFAMILIAR JEANS AND WHITE SNEAKERS.
I KNEW HER WARDROBE LIKE THE BACK OF MY HAND.
DONATED, SHE LATER TOLD ME AND DIDN'T KNOW FROM WHERE. A CHURCH, MAYBE.
PURPLE HALF-MOONS DARKENED HER EYES, AND HER HAIR WAS WASHED BUT BED-MESSY.
HER EYES DROOPED WITH SLEEP AND SADNESS AND IT LOOKED LIKE SHE'D JUST WOKEN UP. MAYBE SHE HAD.
HER MANIA—WHICH I IMAGINE FEELS UTTERLY CRISP AND CLEAR AND LIGHT-FILLED—WAS IMMEDIATELY FOLLOWED WITH FORCED SEDATION, WHAT LOOKED TO BE A MURKY FOG OF CONFUSION AND PROFOUND FATIGUE.
PSYCHOLOGIST AND AUTHOR OF *AN UNQUIET MIND*, KAY REDFIELD JAMISON, DESCRIBES MANIA AS EUPHORIC, IDEAS AND FEELINGS FAST LIKE SHOOTING STARS. AND THEN: "THE FAST IDEAS ARE FAR TOO FAST, AND THERE ARE FAR TOO MANY; OVERWHELMING CONFUSION REPLACES CLARITY. YOU ARE . . . ENMESHED TOTALLY IN THE BLACKEST CAVES OF THE MIND. YOU NEVER KNEW THOSE CAVES WERE THERE. IT WILL NEVER END, FOR MADNESS CARVES ITS OWN REALITY."
HOW DEVASTATING, TO HAVE HAD THE WORLD OPEN UP LIKE LIGHTNING IN YOUR MIND, ONLY TO HAVE IT SNAPPED SHUT AGAIN WITH A SHOT AND AN ADJUSTED PRESCRIPTION.

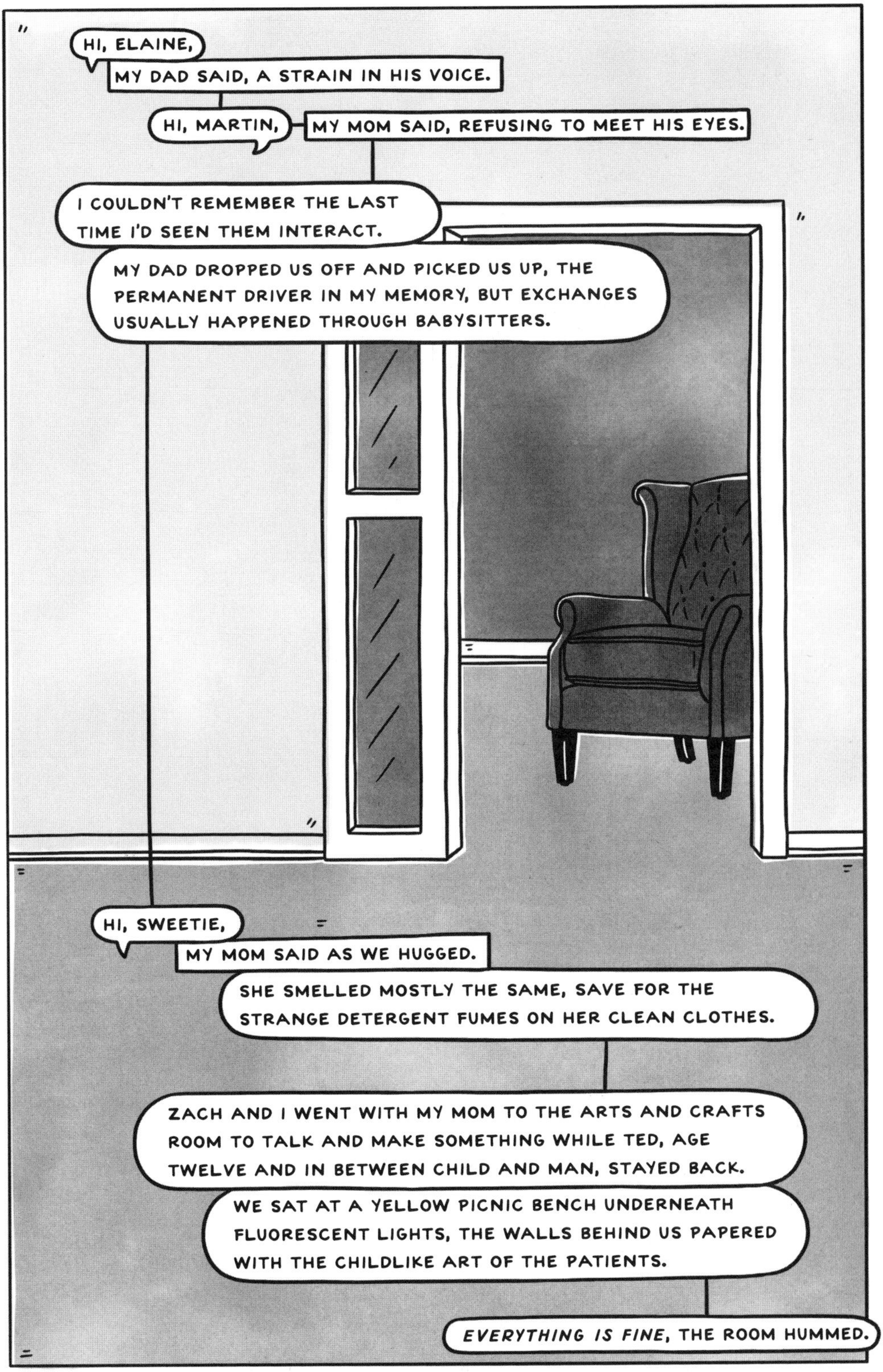
HI, ELAINE,
MY DAD SAID, A STRAIN IN HIS VOICE.
HI, MARTIN,
MY MOM SAID, REFUSING TO MEET HIS EYES.
I COULDN'T REMEMBER THE LAST TIME I'D SEEN THEM INTERACT.
MY DAD DROPPED US OFF AND PICKED US UP, THE PERMANENT DRIVER IN MY MEMORY, BUT EXCHANGES USUALLY HAPPENED THROUGH BABYSITTERS.
HI, SWEETIE,
MY MOM SAID AS WE HUGGED.
SHE SMELLED MOSTLY THE SAME, SAVE FOR THE STRANGE DETERGENT FUMES ON HER CLEAN CLOTHES.
ZACH AND I WENT WITH MY MOM TO THE ARTS AND CRAFTS ROOM TO TALK AND MAKE SOMETHING WHILE TED, AGE TWELVE AND IN BETWEEN CHILD AND MAN, STAYED BACK.
WE SAT AT A YELLOW PICNIC BENCH UNDERNEATH FLUORESCENT LIGHTS, THE WALLS BEHIND US PAPERED WITH THE CHILDLIKE ART OF THE PATIENTS.
EVERYTHING IS FINE, THE ROOM HUMMED.

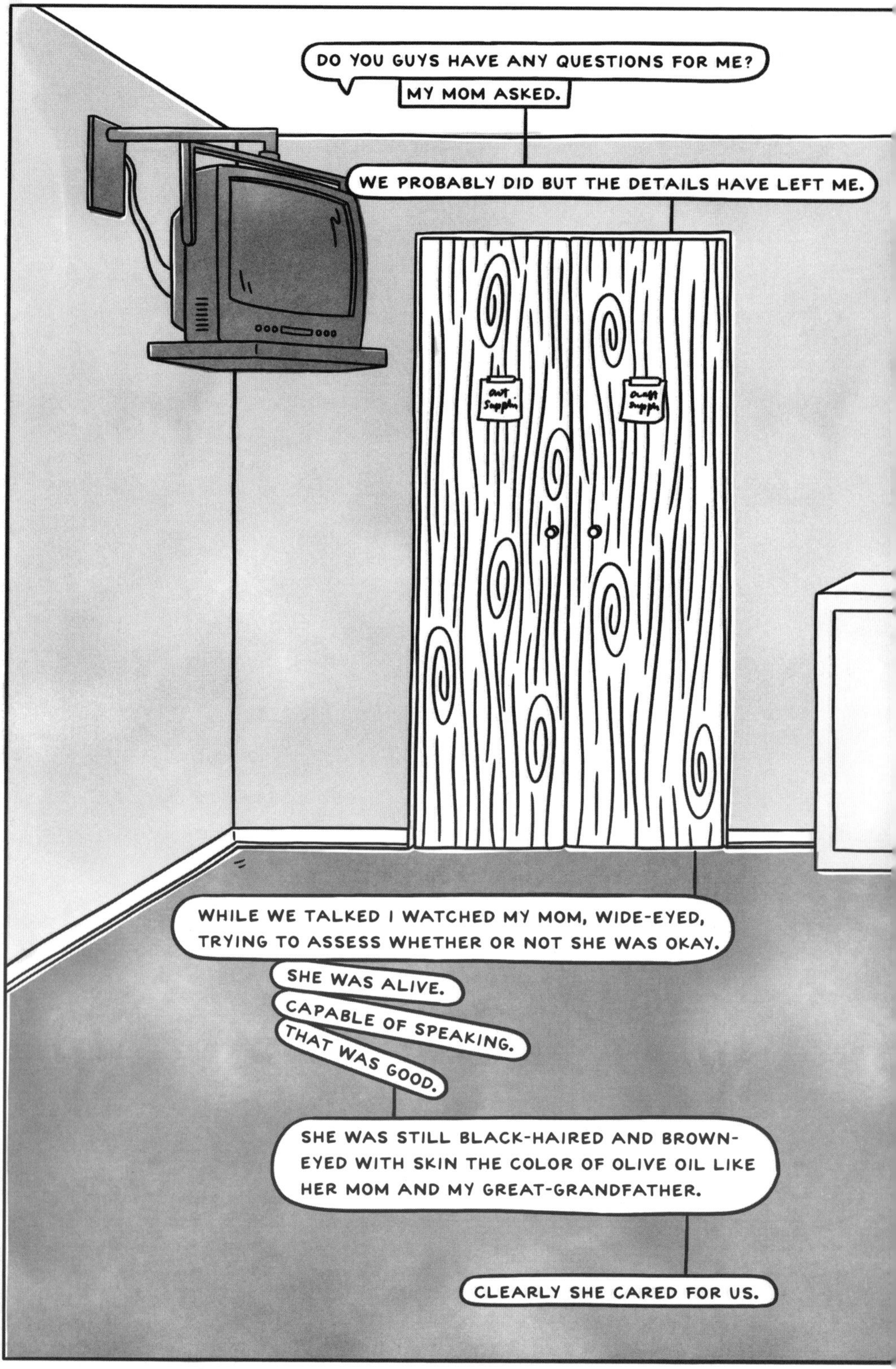
DO YOU GUYS HAVE ANY QUESTIONS FOR ME?
MY MOM ASKED.
WE PROBABLY DID BUT THE DETAILS HAVE LEFT ME.
WHILE WE TALKED I WATCHED MY MOM, WIDE-EYED, TRYING TO ASSESS WHETHER OR NOT SHE WAS OKAY.
SHE WAS ALIVE.
CAPABLE OF SPEAKING.
THAT WAS GOOD.
SHE WAS STILL BLACK-HAIRED AND BROWN-EYED WITH SKIN THE COLOR OF OLIVE OIL LIKE HER MOM AND MY GREAT-GRANDFATHER.
CLEARLY SHE CARED FOR US.

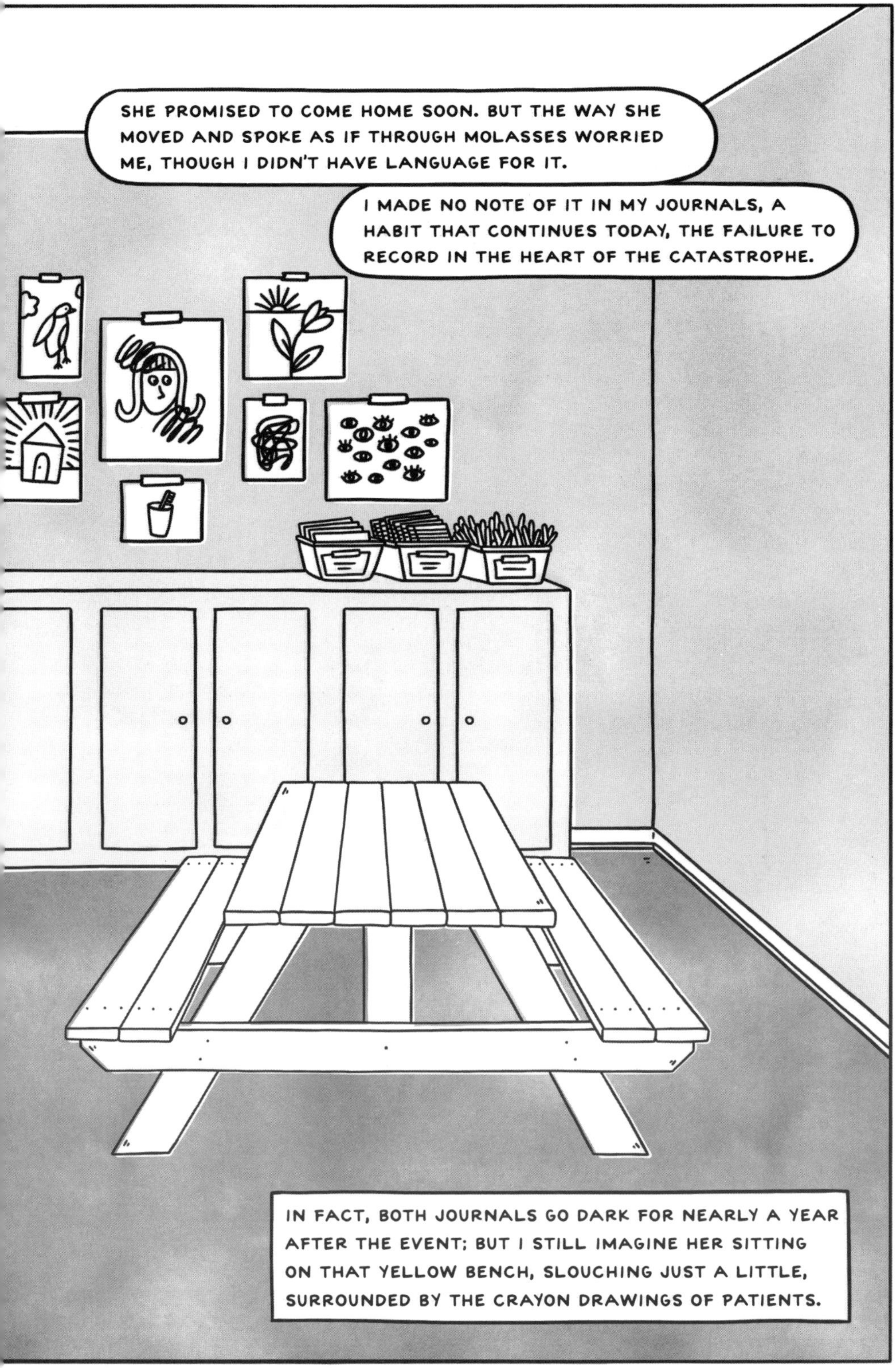
SHE PROMISED TO COME HOME SOON. BUT THE WAY SHE MOVED AND SPOKE AS IF THROUGH MOLASSES WORRIED ME, THOUGH I DIDN'T HAVE LANGUAGE FOR IT.
I MADE NO NOTE OF IT IN MY JOURNALS, A HABIT THAT CONTINUES TODAY, THE FAILURE TO RECORD IN THE HEART OF THE CATASTROPHE.
IN FACT, BOTH JOURNALS GO DARK FOR NEARLY A YEAR AFTER THE EVENT; BUT I STILL IMAGINE HER SITTING ON THAT YELLOW BENCH, SLOUCHING JUST A LITTLE, SURROUNDED BY THE CRAYON DRAWINGS OF PATIENTS.

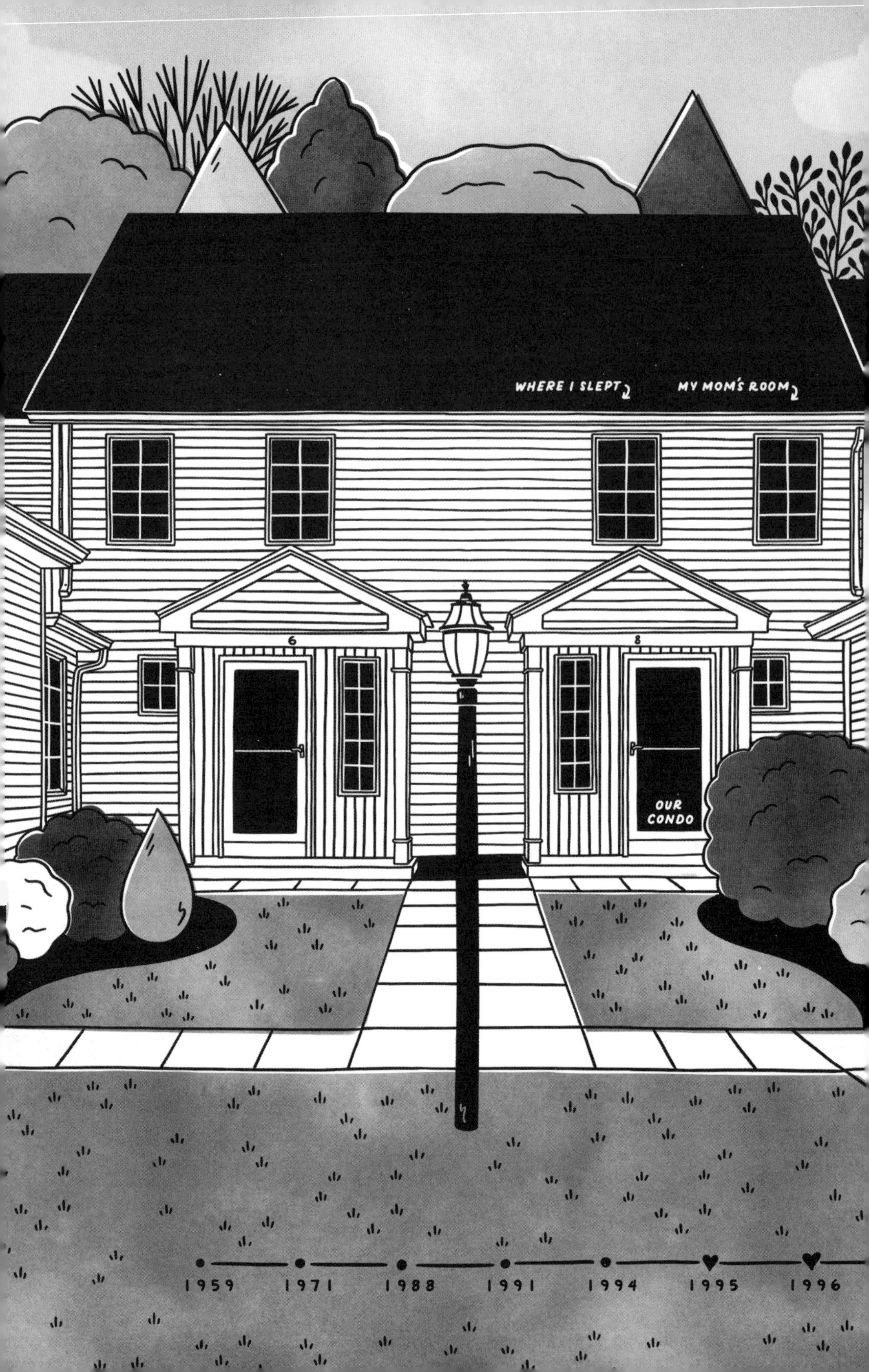
WHERE I SLEPT
MY MOM'S ROOM
6
8
OUR CONDO
1959
1971
1988
1991
1994
1995
1996

CHAPTER 10

The Custody Battles

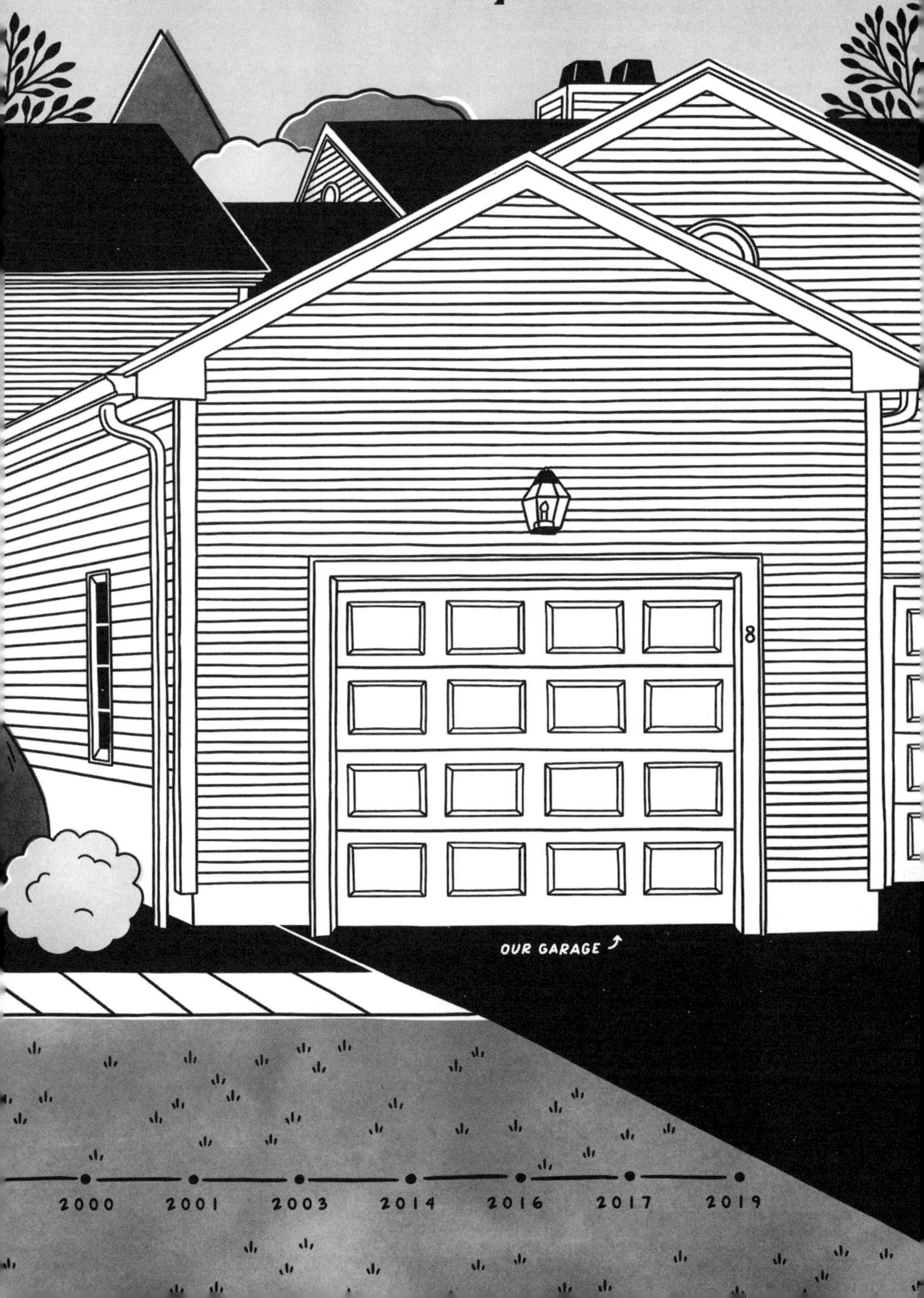
8
OUR GARAGE
2000
2001
2003
2014
2016
2017
2019

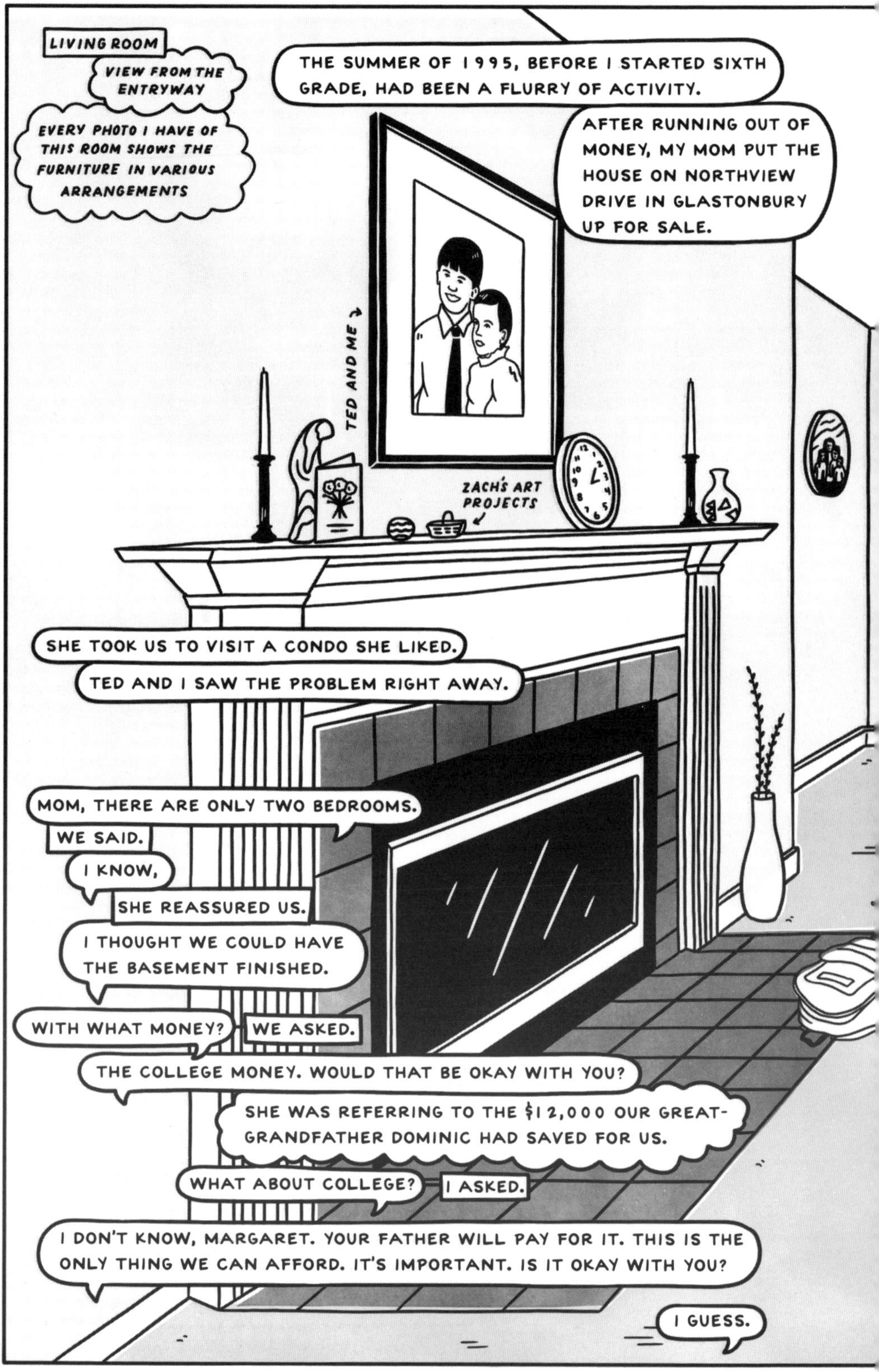

LIVING ROOM
VIEW FROM THE ENTRYWAY
EVERY PHOTO I HAVE OF THIS ROOM SHOWS THE FURNITURE IN VARIOUS ARRANGEMENTS
THE SUMMER OF 1995, BEFORE I STARTED SIXTH GRADE, HAD BEEN A FLURRY OF ACTIVITY.
AFTER RUNNING OUT OF MONEY, MY MOM PUT THE HOUSE ON NORTHVIEW DRIVE IN GLASTONBURY UP FOR SALE.
TED AND ME
ZACH'S ART PROJECTS
SHE TOOK US TO VISIT A CONDO SHE LIKED.
TED AND I SAW THE PROBLEM RIGHT AWAY.
MOM, THERE ARE ONLY TWO BEDROOMS.
WE SAID.
I KNOW,
SHE REASSURED US.
I THOUGHT WE COULD HAVE THE BASEMENT FINISHED.
WITH WHAT MONEY?
WE ASKED.
THE COLLEGE MONEY. WOULD THAT BE OKAY WITH YOU?
SHE WAS REFERRING TO THE $12,000 OUR GREAT-GRANDFATHER DOMINIC HAD SAVED FOR US.
WHAT ABOUT COLLEGE?
I ASKED.
I DON'T KNOW, MARGARET. YOUR FATHER WILL PAY FOR IT. THIS IS THE ONLY THING WE CAN AFFORD. IT'S IMPORTANT. IS IT OKAY WITH YOU?
I GUESS.

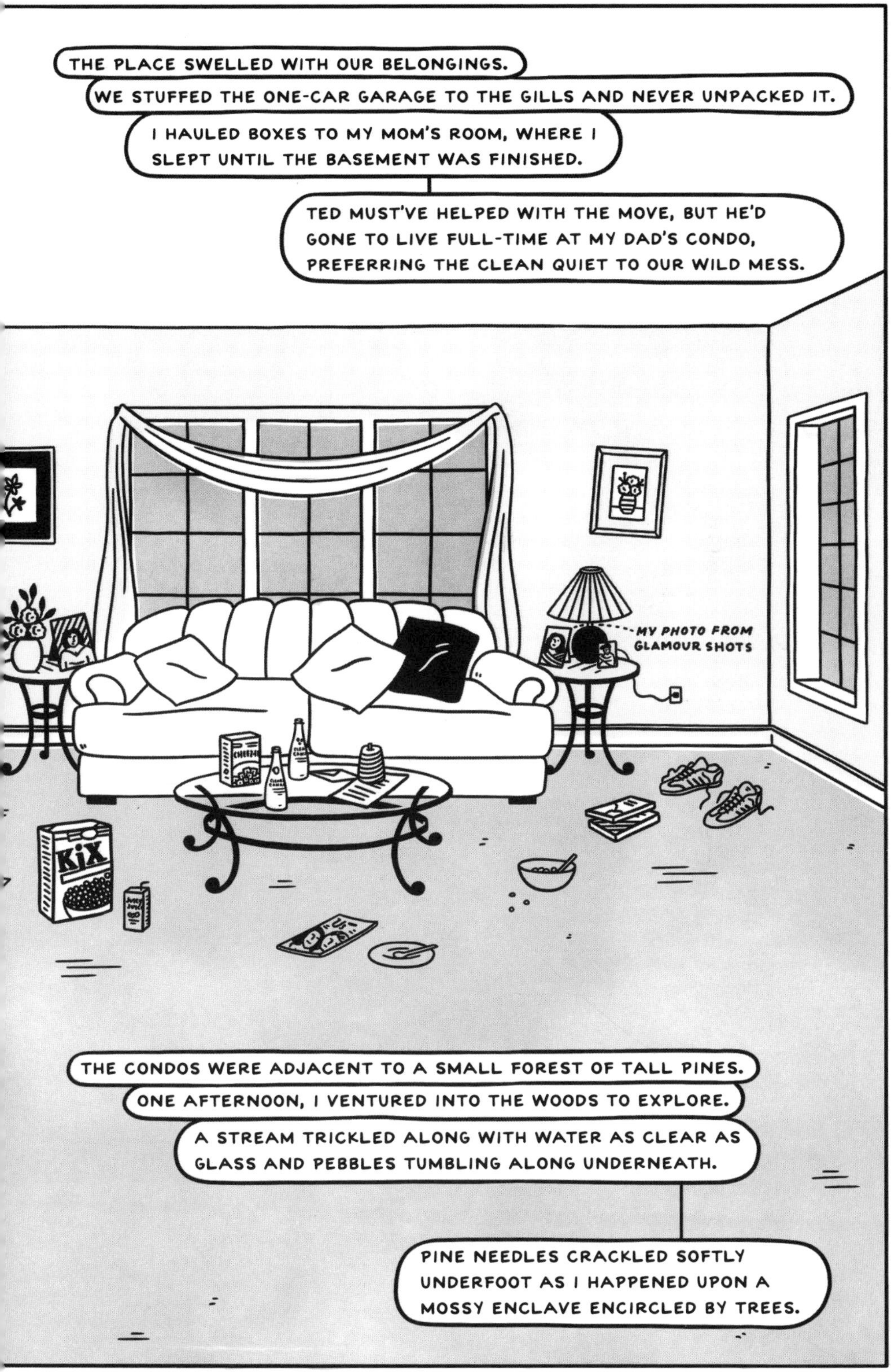
THE PLACE SWELLED WITH OUR BELONGINGS.
WE STUFFED THE ONE-CAR GARAGE TO THE GILLS AND NEVER UNPACKED IT.
I HAULED BOXES TO MY MOM'S ROOM, WHERE I SLEPT UNTIL THE BASEMENT WAS FINISHED.
TED MUST'VE HELPED WITH THE MOVE, BUT HE'D GONE TO LIVE FULL-TIME AT MY DAD'S CONDO, PREFERRING THE CLEAN QUIET TO OUR WILD MESS.
MY PHOTO FROM GLAMOUR SHOTS
KIX
THE CONDOS WERE ADJACENT TO A SMALL FOREST OF TALL PINES.
ONE AFTERNOON, I VENTURED INTO THE WOODS TO EXPLORE.
A STREAM TRICKLED ALONG WITH WATER AS CLEAR AS GLASS AND PEBBLES TUMBLING ALONG UNDERNEATH.
PINE NEEDLES CRACKLED SOFTLY UNDERFOOT AS I HAPPENED UPON A MOSSY ENCLAVE ENCIRCLED BY TREES.

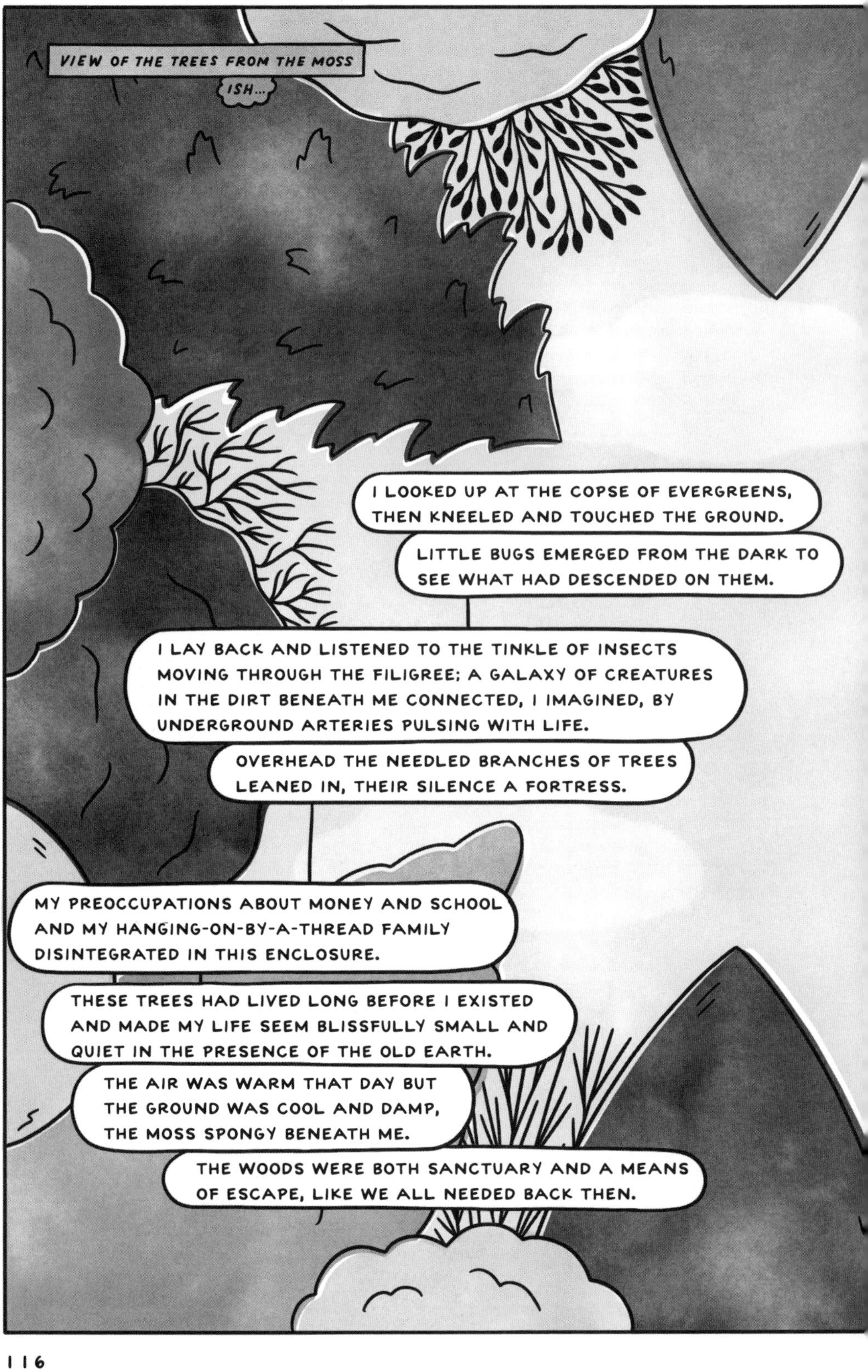
VIEW OF THE TREES FROM THE MOSS
ISH...
I LOOKED UP AT THE COPSE OF EVERGREENS, THEN KNEELED AND TOUCHED THE GROUND.
LITTLE BUGS EMERGED FROM THE DARK TO SEE WHAT HAD DESCENDED ON THEM.
I LAY BACK AND LISTENED TO THE TINKLE OF INSECTS MOVING THROUGH THE FILIGREE; A GALAXY OF CREATURES IN THE DIRT BENEATH ME CONNECTED, I IMAGINED, BY UNDERGROUND ARTERIES PULSING WITH LIFE.
OVERHEAD THE NEEDLED BRANCHES OF TREES LEANED IN, THEIR SILENCE A FORTRESS.
MY PREOCCUPATIONS ABOUT MONEY AND SCHOOL AND MY HANGING-ON-BY-A-THREAD FAMILY DISINTEGRATED IN THIS ENCLOSURE.
THESE TREES HAD LIVED LONG BEFORE I EXISTED AND MADE MY LIFE SEEM BLISSFULLY SMALL AND QUIET IN THE PRESENCE OF THE OLD EARTH.
THE AIR WAS WARM THAT DAY BUT THE GROUND WAS COOL AND DAMP, THE MOSS SPONGY BENEATH ME.
THE WOODS WERE BOTH SANCTUARY AND A MEANS OF ESCAPE, LIKE WE ALL NEEDED BACK THEN.

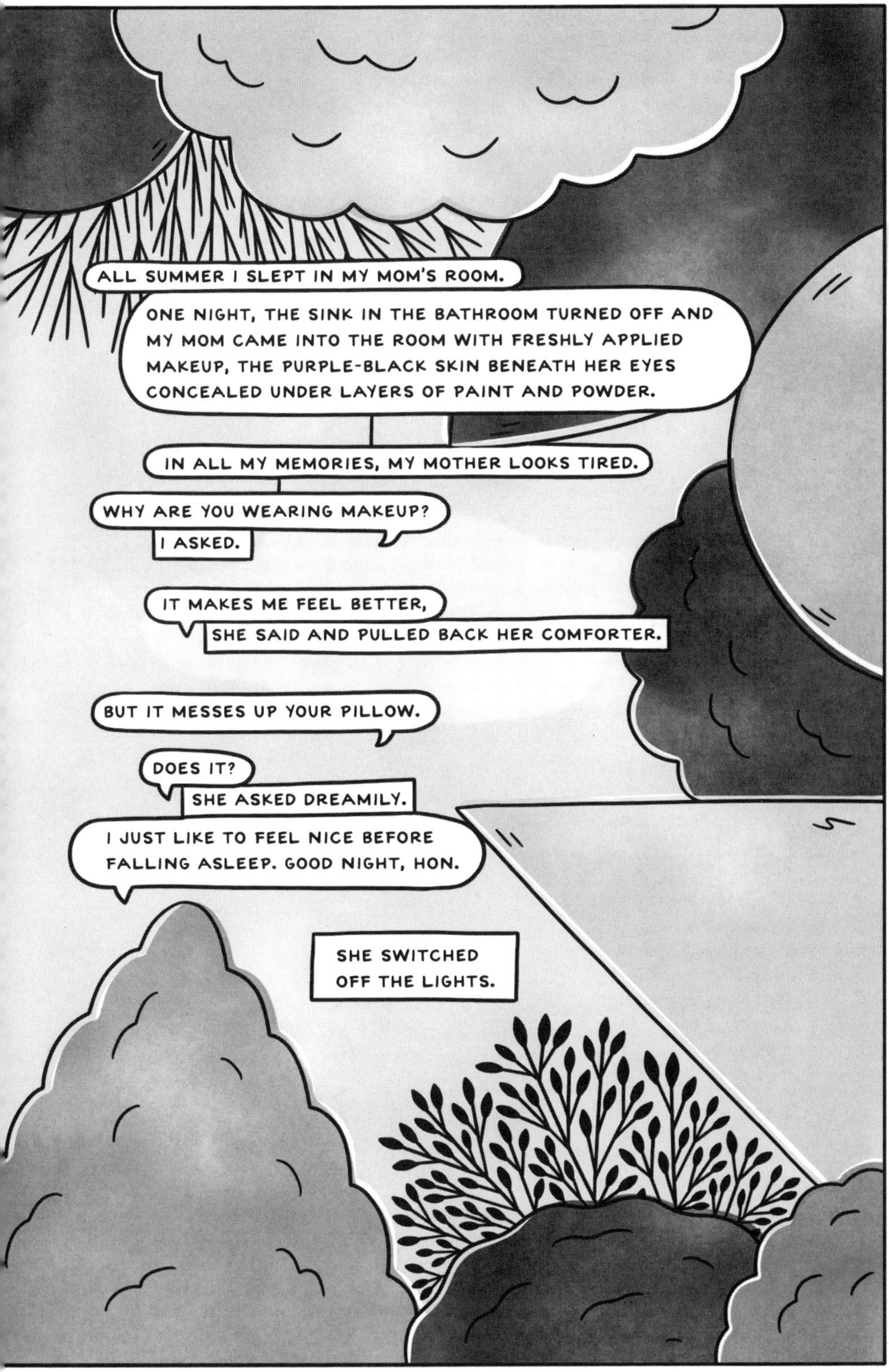
ALL SUMMER I SLEPT IN MY MOM'S ROOM.
ONE NIGHT, THE SINK IN THE BATHROOM TURNED OFF AND MY MOM CAME INTO THE ROOM WITH FRESHLY APPLIED MAKEUP, THE PURPLE-BLACK SKIN BENEATH HER EYES CONCEALED UNDER LAYERS OF PAINT AND POWDER.
IN ALL MY MEMORIES, MY MOTHER LOOKS TIRED.
WHY ARE YOU WEARING MAKEUP?
I ASKED.
IT MAKES ME FEEL BETTER,
SHE SAID AND PULLED BACK HER COMFORTER.
BUT IT MESSES UP YOUR PILLOW.
DOES IT?
SHE ASKED DREAMILY.
I JUST LIKE TO FEEL NICE BEFORE FALLING ASLEEP. GOOD NIGHT, HON.
SHE SWITCHED OFF THE LIGHTS.

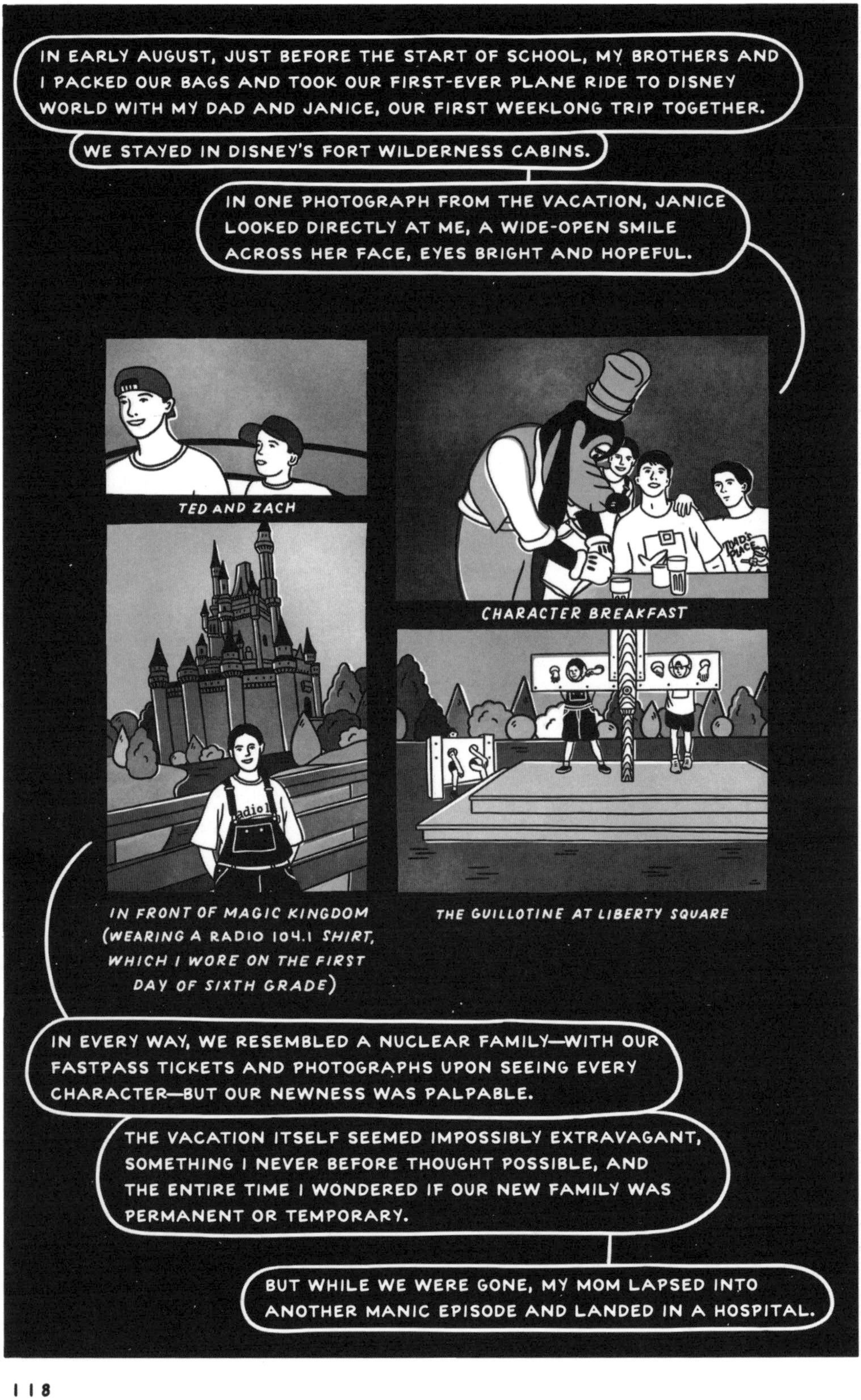
IN EARLY AUGUST, JUST BEFORE THE START OF SCHOOL, MY BROTHERS AND I PACKED OUR BAGS AND TOOK OUR FIRST-EVER PLANE RIDE TO DISNEY WORLD WITH MY DAD AND JANICE, OUR FIRST WEEKLONG TRIP TOGETHER.
WE STAYED IN DISNEY'S FORT WILDERNESS CABINS.
IN ONE PHOTOGRAPH FROM THE VACATION, JANICE LOOKED DIRECTLY AT ME, A WIDE-OPEN SMILE ACROSS HER FACE, EYES BRIGHT AND HOPEFUL.
TED AND ZACH
CHARACTER BREAKFAST
IN FRONT OF MAGIC KINGDOM (WEARING A RADIO 104.1 SHIRT, WHICH I WORE ON THE FIRST DAY OF SIXTH GRADE)
THE GUILLOTINE AT LIBERTY SQUARE
IN EVERY WAY, WE RESEMBLED A NUCLEAR FAMILY—WITH OUR FASTPASS TICKETS AND PHOTOGRAPHS UPON SEEING EVERY CHARACTER—BUT OUR NEWNESS WAS PALPABLE.
THE VACATION ITSELF SEEMED IMPOSSIBLY EXTRAVAGANT, SOMETHING I NEVER BEFORE THOUGHT POSSIBLE, AND THE ENTIRE TIME I WONDERED IF OUR NEW FAMILY WAS PERMANENT OR TEMPORARY.
BUT WHILE WE WERE GONE, MY MOM LAPSED INTO ANOTHER MANIC EPISODE AND LANDED IN A HOSPITAL.

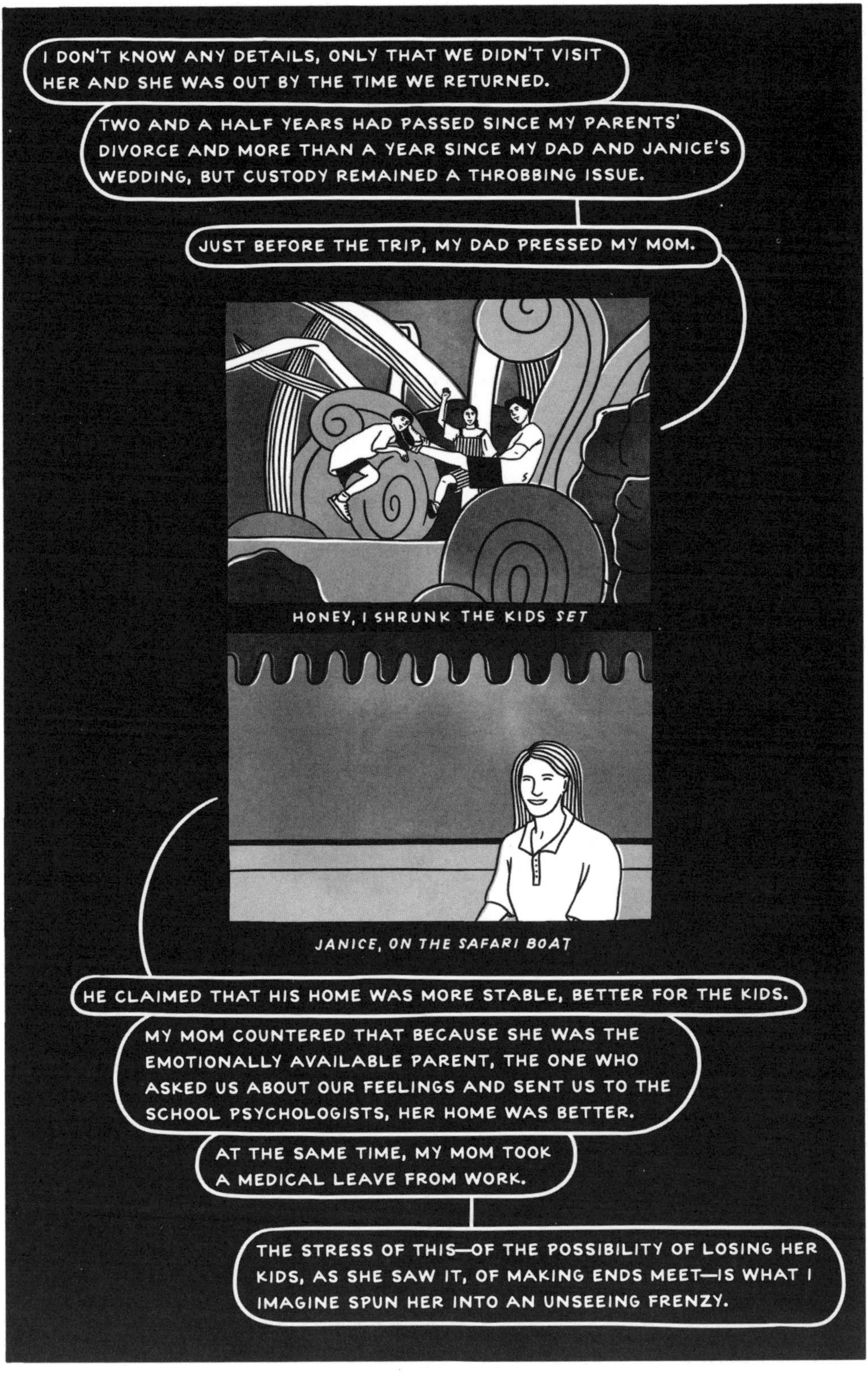
I DON'T KNOW ANY DETAILS, ONLY THAT WE DIDN'T VISIT HER AND SHE WAS OUT BY THE TIME WE RETURNED.
TWO AND A HALF YEARS HAD PASSED SINCE MY PARENTS' DIVORCE AND MORE THAN A YEAR SINCE MY DAD AND JANICE'S WEDDING, BUT CUSTODY REMAINED A THROBBING ISSUE.
JUST BEFORE THE TRIP, MY DAD PRESSED MY MOM.
HONEY, I SHRUNK THE KIDS *SET*
JANICE, ON THE SAFARI BOAT
HE CLAIMED THAT HIS HOME WAS MORE STABLE, BETTER FOR THE KIDS.
MY MOM COUNTERED THAT BECAUSE SHE WAS THE EMOTIONALLY AVAILABLE PARENT, THE ONE WHO ASKED US ABOUT OUR FEELINGS AND SENT US TO THE SCHOOL PSYCHOLOGISTS, HER HOME WAS BETTER.
AT THE SAME TIME, MY MOM TOOK A MEDICAL LEAVE FROM WORK.
THE STRESS OF THIS—OF THE POSSIBILITY OF LOSING HER KIDS, AS SHE SAW IT, OF MAKING ENDS MEET—IS WHAT I IMAGINE SPUN HER INTO AN UNSEEING FRENZY.

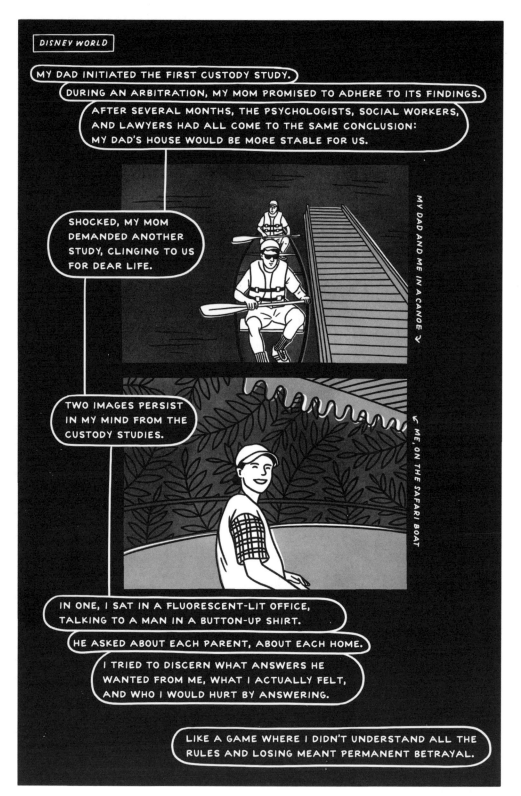

DISNEY WORLD

MY DAD INITIATED THE FIRST CUSTODY STUDY.

DURING AN ARBITRATION, MY MOM PROMISED TO ADHERE TO ITS FINDINGS.

AFTER SEVERAL MONTHS, THE PSYCHOLOGISTS, SOCIAL WORKERS, AND LAWYERS HAD ALL COME TO THE SAME CONCLUSION: MY DAD'S HOUSE WOULD BE MORE STABLE FOR US.

SHOCKED, MY MOM DEMANDED ANOTHER STUDY, CLINGING TO US FOR DEAR LIFE.

MY DAD AND ME IN A CANOE

TWO IMAGES PERSIST IN MY MIND FROM THE CUSTODY STUDIES.

ME, ON THE SAFARI BOAT

IN ONE, I SAT IN A FLUORESCENT-LIT OFFICE, TALKING TO A MAN IN A BUTTON-UP SHIRT.

HE ASKED ABOUT EACH PARENT, ABOUT EACH HOME.

I TRIED TO DISCERN WHAT ANSWERS HE WANTED FROM ME, WHAT I ACTUALLY FELT, AND WHO I WOULD HURT BY ANSWERING.

LIKE A GAME WHERE I DIDN'T UNDERSTAND ALL THE RULES AND LOSING MEANT PERMANENT BETRAYAL.

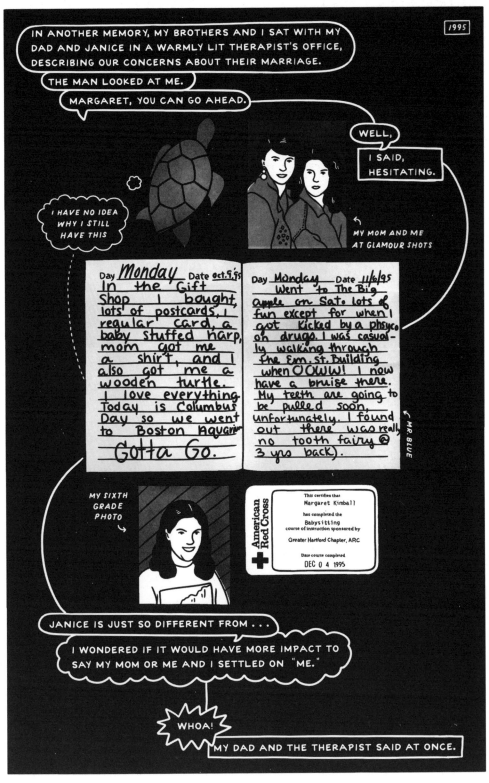

IN ANOTHER MEMORY, MY BROTHERS AND I SAT WITH MY DAD AND JANICE IN A WARMLY LIT THERAPIST'S OFFICE, DESCRIBING OUR CONCERNS ABOUT THEIR MARRIAGE.

THE MAN LOOKED AT ME.

MARGARET, YOU CAN GO AHEAD.

WELL,

I SAID, HESITATING.

I HAVE NO IDEA WHY I STILL HAVE THIS

MY MOM AND ME AT GLAMOUR SHOTS

Day **Monday** Date oct.9,95
In the Gift Shop I bought, lots of postcards, I regular card, a baby stuffed harp, mom got me a shirt, and I also got me a wooden turtle. I love everything Today is Columbus Day so we went to Boston Aquarium Gotta Go.

Day Monday Date 11/6/95
Went to The Big apple on Sat. lots of fun except for when I got kicked by a phsyco on drugs. I was casually walking through the Em. st. building when OOWW! I now have a bruise there. My teeth are going to be pulled soon, unfortunately. I found out there was really no tooth fairy @ 3 yrs back).

← MR. BLUE

MY SIXTH GRADE PHOTO →

This certifies that
Margaret Kimball
has completed the
Babysitting
course of instruction sponsored by
Greater Hartford Chapter, ARC

Date course completed
DEC 0 4 1995

American Red Cross

JANICE IS JUST SO DIFFERENT FROM . . .

I WONDERED IF IT WOULD HAVE MORE IMPACT TO SAY MY MOM OR ME AND I SETTLED ON "ME."

WHOA!

MY DAD AND THE THERAPIST SAID AT ONCE.

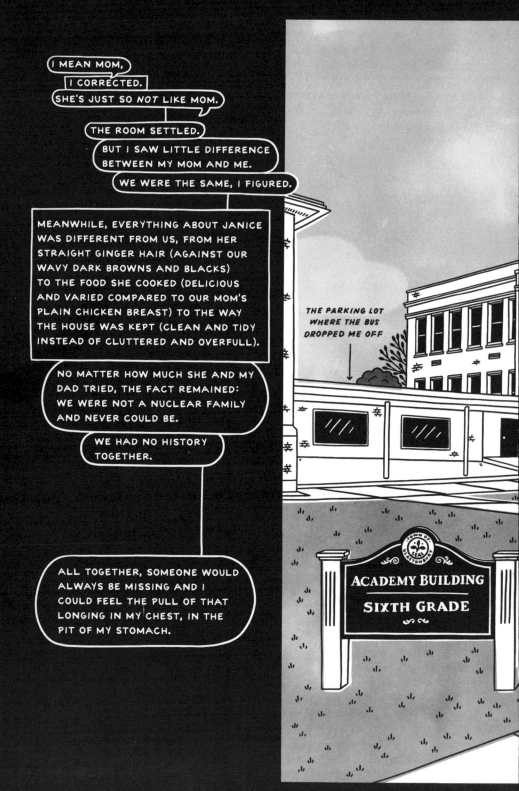

I MEAN MOM,

I CORRECTED.

SHE'S JUST SO *NOT* LIKE MOM.

THE ROOM SETTLED.

BUT I SAW LITTLE DIFFERENCE BETWEEN MY MOM AND ME.

WE WERE THE SAME, I FIGURED.

MEANWHILE, EVERYTHING ABOUT JANICE WAS DIFFERENT FROM US, FROM HER STRAIGHT GINGER HAIR (AGAINST OUR WAVY DARK BROWNS AND BLACKS) TO THE FOOD SHE COOKED (DELICIOUS AND VARIED COMPARED TO OUR MOM'S PLAIN CHICKEN BREAST) TO THE WAY THE HOUSE WAS KEPT (CLEAN AND TIDY INSTEAD OF CLUTTERED AND OVERFULL).

NO MATTER HOW MUCH SHE AND MY DAD TRIED, THE FACT REMAINED: WE WERE NOT A NUCLEAR FAMILY AND NEVER COULD BE.

WE HAD NO HISTORY TOGETHER.

THE PARKING LOT WHERE THE BUS DROPPED ME OFF
TOWN OF GLASTONBURY SEAL
ACADEMY BUILDING
SIXTH GRADE

ALL TOGETHER, SOMEONE WOULD ALWAYS BE MISSING AND I COULD FEEL THE PULL OF THAT LONGING IN MY CHEST, IN THE PIT OF MY STOMACH.

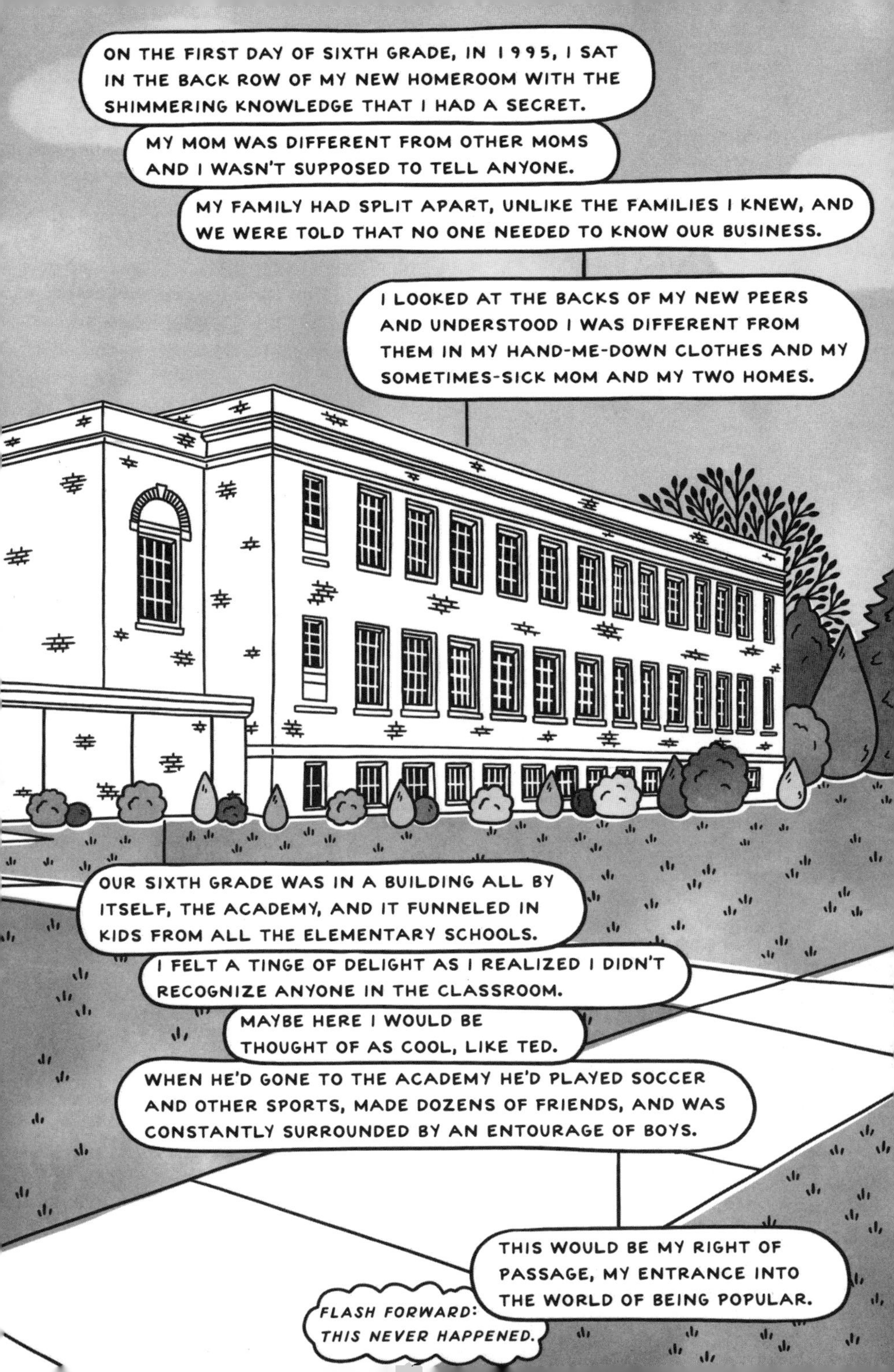
ON THE FIRST DAY OF SIXTH GRADE, IN 1995, I SAT IN THE BACK ROW OF MY NEW HOMEROOM WITH THE SHIMMERING KNOWLEDGE THAT I HAD A SECRET.
MY MOM WAS DIFFERENT FROM OTHER MOMS AND I WASN'T SUPPOSED TO TELL ANYONE.
MY FAMILY HAD SPLIT APART, UNLIKE THE FAMILIES I KNEW, AND WE WERE TOLD THAT NO ONE NEEDED TO KNOW OUR BUSINESS.
I LOOKED AT THE BACKS OF MY NEW PEERS AND UNDERSTOOD I WAS DIFFERENT FROM THEM IN MY HAND-ME-DOWN CLOTHES AND MY SOMETIMES-SICK MOM AND MY TWO HOMES.
OUR SIXTH GRADE WAS IN A BUILDING ALL BY ITSELF, THE ACADEMY, AND IT FUNNELED IN KIDS FROM ALL THE ELEMENTARY SCHOOLS.
I FELT A TINGE OF DELIGHT AS I REALIZED I DIDN'T RECOGNIZE ANYONE IN THE CLASSROOM.
MAYBE HERE I WOULD BE THOUGHT OF AS COOL, LIKE TED.
WHEN HE'D GONE TO THE ACADEMY HE'D PLAYED SOCCER AND OTHER SPORTS, MADE DOZENS OF FRIENDS, AND WAS CONSTANTLY SURROUNDED BY AN ENTOURAGE OF BOYS.
THIS WOULD BE MY RIGHT OF PASSAGE, MY ENTRANCE INTO THE WORLD OF BEING POPULAR.
FLASH FORWARD: THIS NEVER HAPPENED.

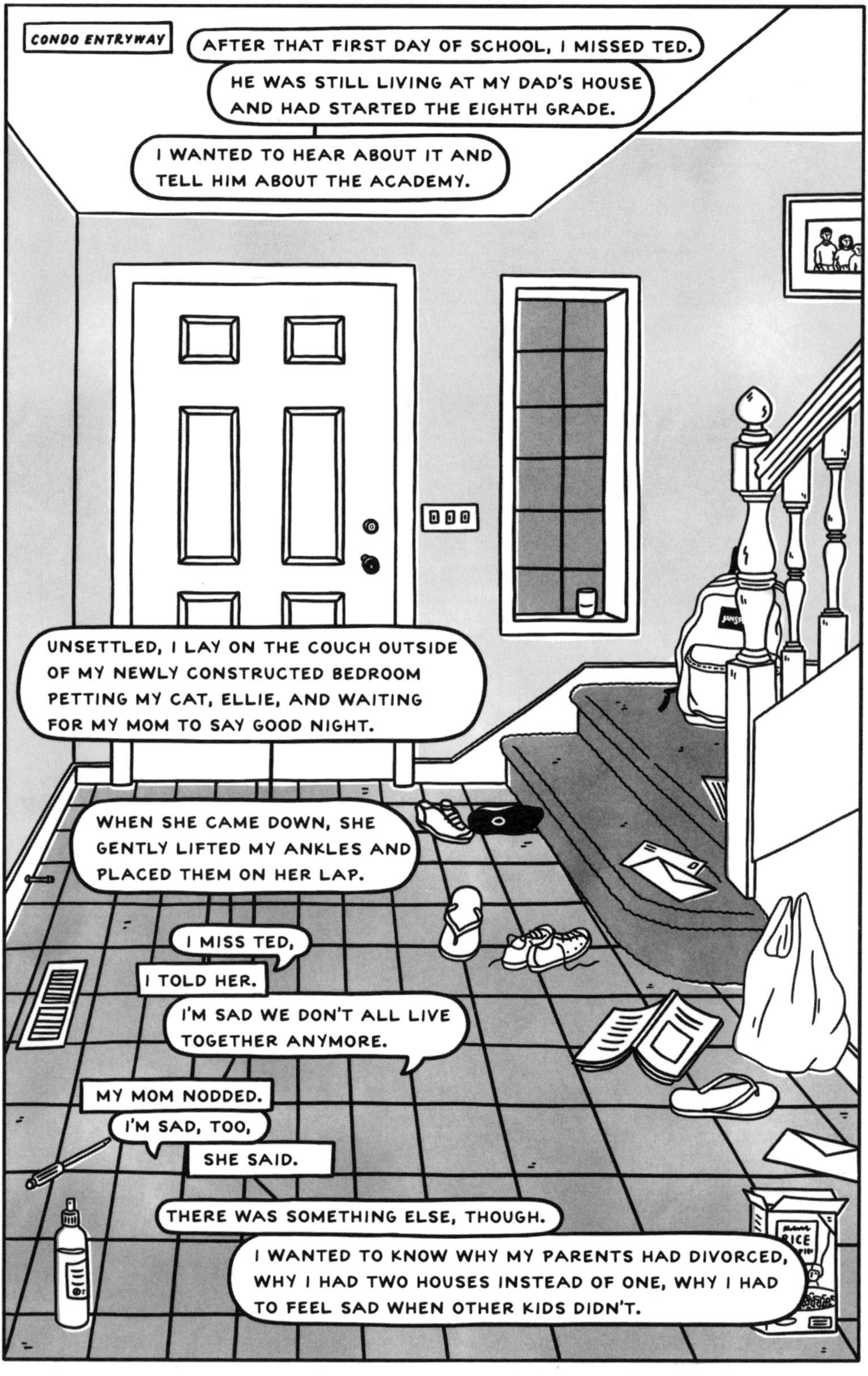
CONDO ENTRYWAY
AFTER THAT FIRST DAY OF SCHOOL, I MISSED TED.
HE WAS STILL LIVING AT MY DAD'S HOUSE AND HAD STARTED THE EIGHTH GRADE.
I WANTED TO HEAR ABOUT IT AND TELL HIM ABOUT THE ACADEMY.
UNSETTLED, I LAY ON THE COUCH OUTSIDE OF MY NEWLY CONSTRUCTED BEDROOM PETTING MY CAT, ELLIE, AND WAITING FOR MY MOM TO SAY GOOD NIGHT.
WHEN SHE CAME DOWN, SHE GENTLY LIFTED MY ANKLES AND PLACED THEM ON HER LAP.
I MISS TED,
I TOLD HER.
I'M SAD WE DON'T ALL LIVE TOGETHER ANYMORE.
MY MOM NODDED.
I'M SAD, TOO,
SHE SAID.
THERE WAS SOMETHING ELSE, THOUGH.
I WANTED TO KNOW WHY MY PARENTS HAD DIVORCED, WHY I HAD TWO HOUSES INSTEAD OF ONE, WHY I HAD TO FEEL SAD WHEN OTHER KIDS DIDN'T.

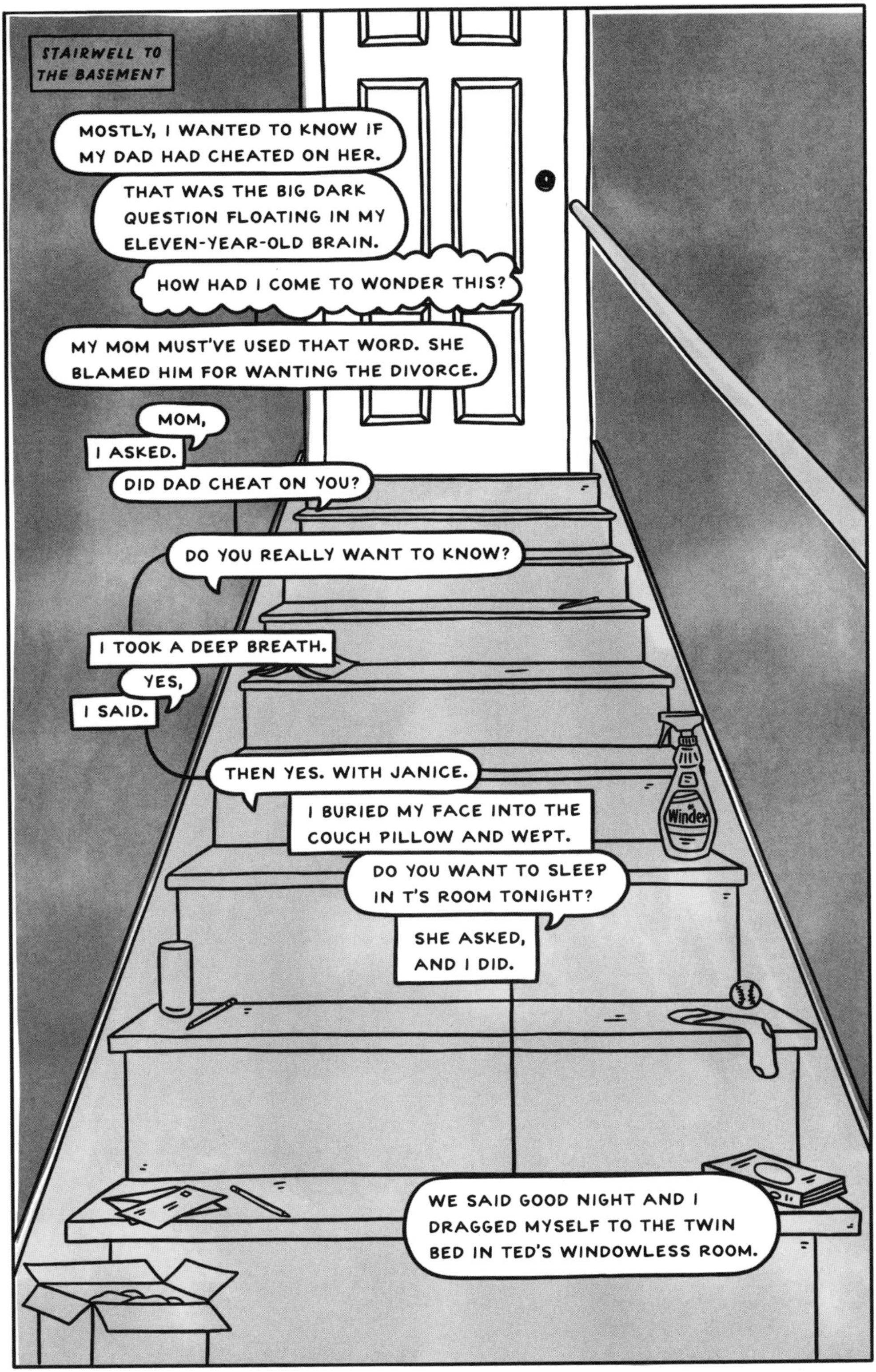
STAIRWELL TO THE BASEMENT
MOSTLY, I WANTED TO KNOW IF MY DAD HAD CHEATED ON HER.
THAT WAS THE BIG DARK QUESTION FLOATING IN MY ELEVEN-YEAR-OLD BRAIN.
HOW HAD I COME TO WONDER THIS?
MY MOM MUST'VE USED THAT WORD. SHE BLAMED HIM FOR WANTING THE DIVORCE.
MOM,
I ASKED.
DID DAD CHEAT ON YOU?
DO YOU REALLY WANT TO KNOW?
I TOOK A DEEP BREATH.
YES,
I SAID.
THEN YES. WITH JANICE.
I BURIED MY FACE INTO THE COUCH PILLOW AND WEPT.
DO YOU WANT TO SLEEP IN T'S ROOM TONIGHT?
SHE ASKED, AND I DID.
WE SAID GOOD NIGHT AND I DRAGGED MYSELF TO THE TWIN BED IN TED'S WINDOWLESS ROOM.

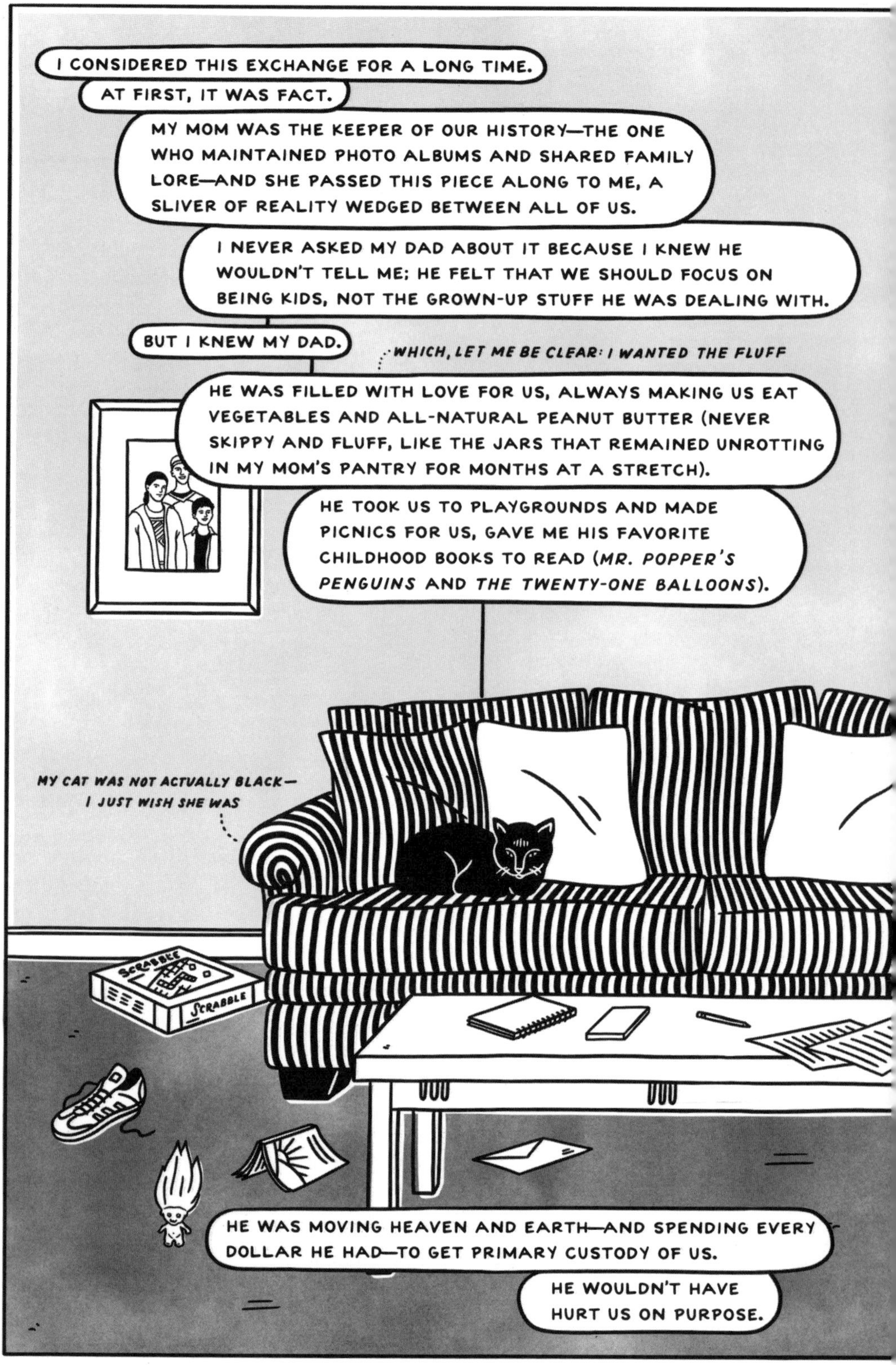

I CONSIDERED THIS EXCHANGE FOR A LONG TIME.
AT FIRST, IT WAS FACT.
MY MOM WAS THE KEEPER OF OUR HISTORY—THE ONE WHO MAINTAINED PHOTO ALBUMS AND SHARED FAMILY LORE—AND SHE PASSED THIS PIECE ALONG TO ME, A SLIVER OF REALITY WEDGED BETWEEN ALL OF US.
I NEVER ASKED MY DAD ABOUT IT BECAUSE I KNEW HE WOULDN'T TELL ME; HE FELT THAT WE SHOULD FOCUS ON BEING KIDS, NOT THE GROWN-UP STUFF HE WAS DEALING WITH.
BUT I KNEW MY DAD.
WHICH, LET ME BE CLEAR: I WANTED THE FLUFF
HE WAS FILLED WITH LOVE FOR US, ALWAYS MAKING US EAT VEGETABLES AND ALL-NATURAL PEANUT BUTTER (NEVER SKIPPY AND FLUFF, LIKE THE JARS THAT REMAINED UNROTTING IN MY MOM'S PANTRY FOR MONTHS AT A STRETCH).
HE TOOK US TO PLAYGROUNDS AND MADE PICNICS FOR US, GAVE ME HIS FAVORITE CHILDHOOD BOOKS TO READ (*MR. POPPER'S PENGUINS* AND *THE TWENTY-ONE BALLOONS*).
MY CAT WAS NOT ACTUALLY BLACK— I JUST WISH SHE WAS
SCRABBLE
HE WAS MOVING HEAVEN AND EARTH—AND SPENDING EVERY DOLLAR HE HAD—TO GET PRIMARY CUSTODY OF US.
HE WOULDN'T HAVE HURT US ON PURPOSE.

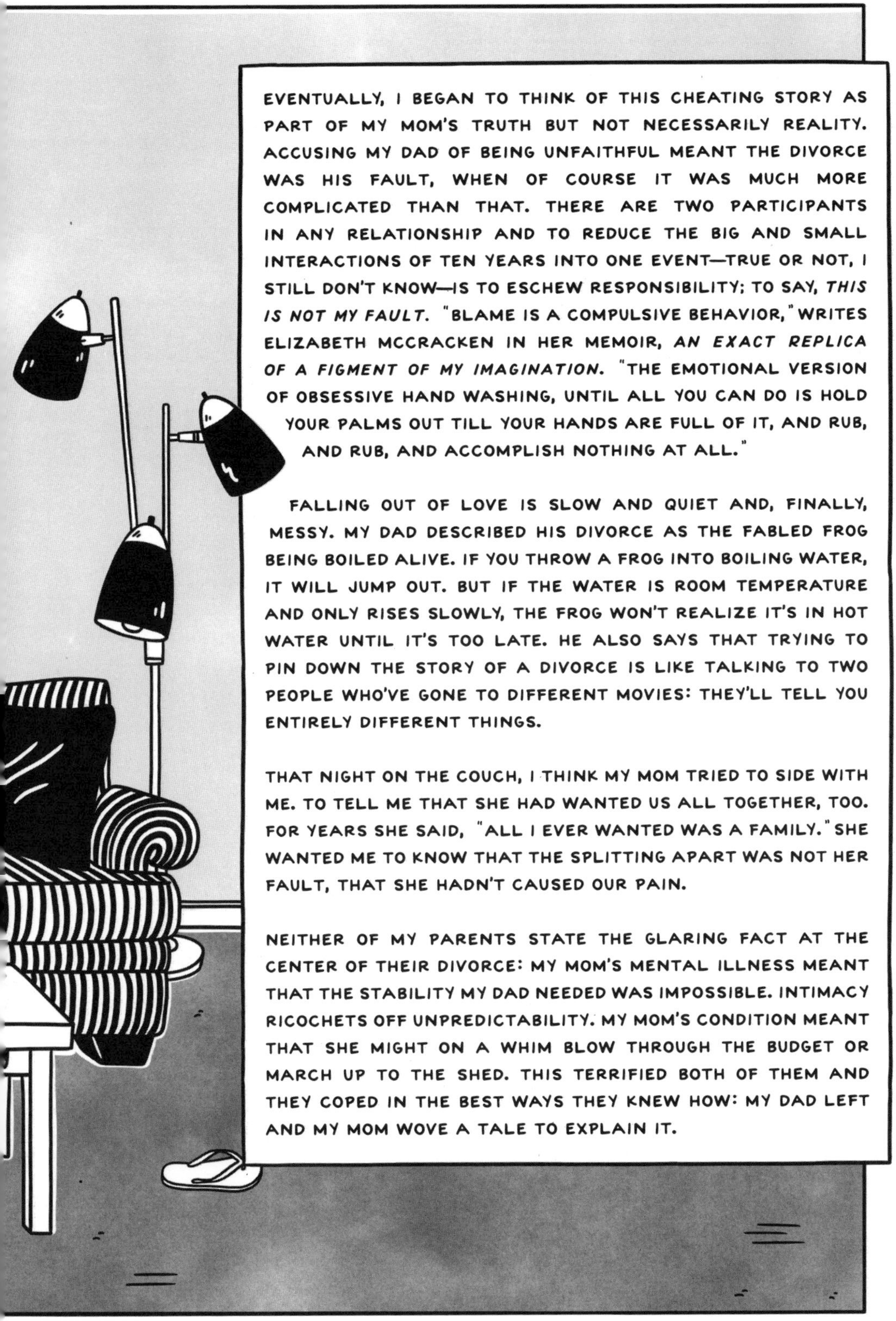
EVENTUALLY, I BEGAN TO THINK OF THIS CHEATING STORY AS PART OF MY MOM'S TRUTH BUT NOT NECESSARILY REALITY. ACCUSING MY DAD OF BEING UNFAITHFUL MEANT THE DIVORCE WAS HIS FAULT, WHEN OF COURSE IT WAS MUCH MORE COMPLICATED THAN THAT. THERE ARE TWO PARTICIPANTS IN ANY RELATIONSHIP AND TO REDUCE THE BIG AND SMALL INTERACTIONS OF TEN YEARS INTO ONE EVENT—TRUE OR NOT, I STILL DON'T KNOW—IS TO ESCHEW RESPONSIBILITY; TO SAY, *THIS IS NOT MY FAULT.* "BLAME IS A COMPULSIVE BEHAVIOR," WRITES ELIZABETH MCCRACKEN IN HER MEMOIR, *AN EXACT REPLICA OF A FIGMENT OF MY IMAGINATION.* "THE EMOTIONAL VERSION OF OBSESSIVE HAND WASHING, UNTIL ALL YOU CAN DO IS HOLD YOUR PALMS OUT TILL YOUR HANDS ARE FULL OF IT, AND RUB, AND RUB, AND ACCOMPLISH NOTHING AT ALL."
FALLING OUT OF LOVE IS SLOW AND QUIET AND, FINALLY, MESSY. MY DAD DESCRIBED HIS DIVORCE AS THE FABLED FROG BEING BOILED ALIVE. IF YOU THROW A FROG INTO BOILING WATER, IT WILL JUMP OUT. BUT IF THE WATER IS ROOM TEMPERATURE AND ONLY RISES SLOWLY, THE FROG WON'T REALIZE IT'S IN HOT WATER UNTIL IT'S TOO LATE. HE ALSO SAYS THAT TRYING TO PIN DOWN THE STORY OF A DIVORCE IS LIKE TALKING TO TWO PEOPLE WHO'VE GONE TO DIFFERENT MOVIES: THEY'LL TELL YOU ENTIRELY DIFFERENT THINGS.
THAT NIGHT ON THE COUCH, I THINK MY MOM TRIED TO SIDE WITH ME. TO TELL ME THAT SHE HAD WANTED US ALL TOGETHER, TOO. FOR YEARS SHE SAID, "ALL I EVER WANTED WAS A FAMILY." SHE WANTED ME TO KNOW THAT THE SPLITTING APART WAS NOT HER FAULT, THAT SHE HADN'T CAUSED OUR PAIN.
NEITHER OF MY PARENTS STATE THE GLARING FACT AT THE CENTER OF THEIR DIVORCE: MY MOM'S MENTAL ILLNESS MEANT THAT THE STABILITY MY DAD NEEDED WAS IMPOSSIBLE. INTIMACY RICOCHETS OFF UNPREDICTABILITY. MY MOM'S CONDITION MEANT THAT SHE MIGHT ON A WHIM BLOW THROUGH THE BUDGET OR MARCH UP TO THE SHED. THIS TERRIFIED BOTH OF THEM AND THEY COPED IN THE BEST WAYS THEY KNEW HOW: MY DAD LEFT AND MY MOM WOVE A TALE TO EXPLAIN IT.

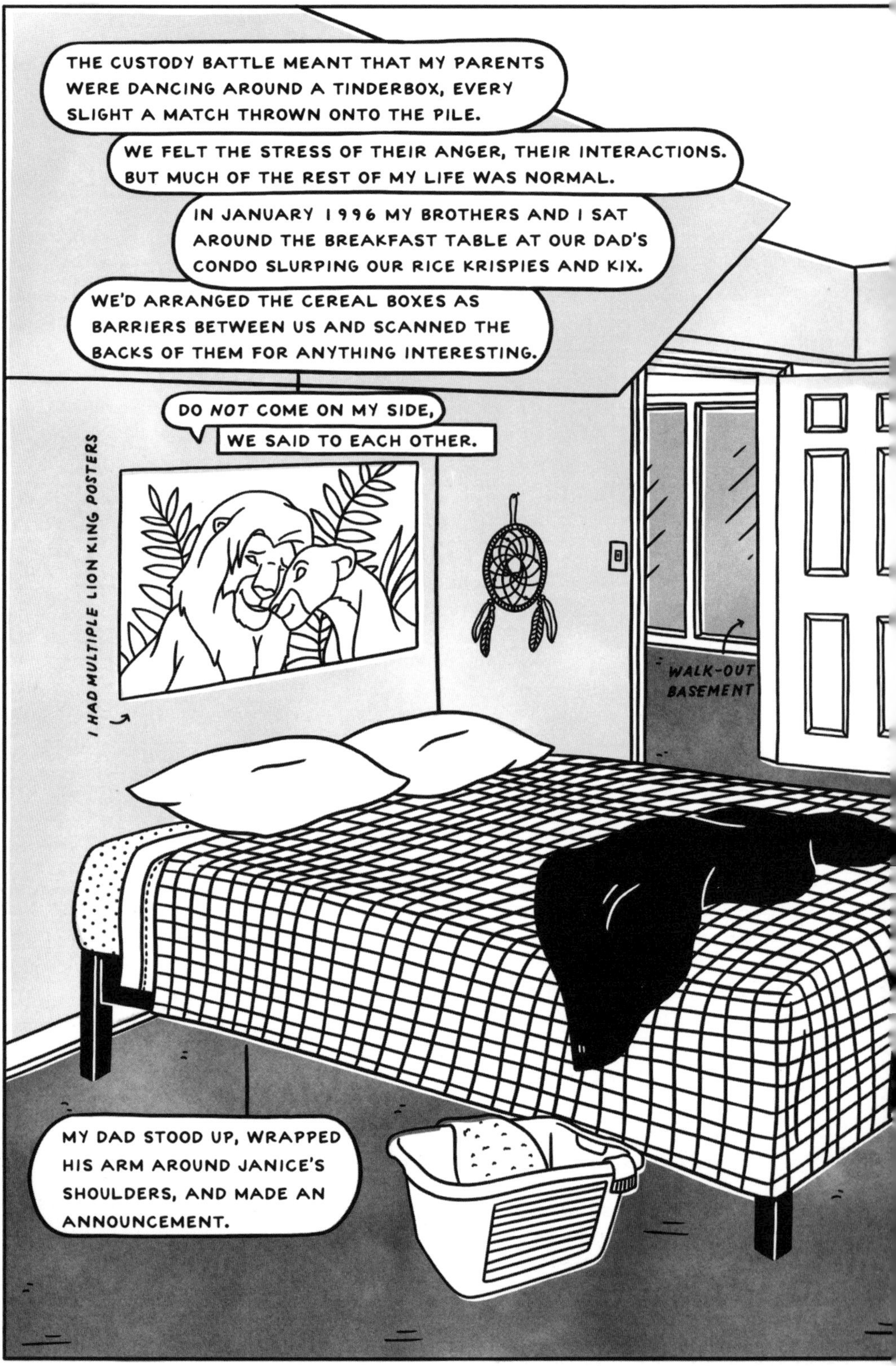
THE CUSTODY BATTLE MEANT THAT MY PARENTS WERE DANCING AROUND A TINDERBOX, EVERY SLIGHT A MATCH THROWN ONTO THE PILE.
WE FELT THE STRESS OF THEIR ANGER, THEIR INTERACTIONS. BUT MUCH OF THE REST OF MY LIFE WAS NORMAL.
IN JANUARY 1996 MY BROTHERS AND I SAT AROUND THE BREAKFAST TABLE AT OUR DAD'S CONDO SLURPING OUR RICE KRISPIES AND KIX.
WE'D ARRANGED THE CEREAL BOXES AS BARRIERS BETWEEN US AND SCANNED THE BACKS OF THEM FOR ANYTHING INTERESTING.
DO *NOT* COME ON MY SIDE,
WE SAID TO EACH OTHER.
I HAD MULTIPLE LION KING *POSTERS*
WALK-OUT BASEMENT
MY DAD STOOD UP, WRAPPED HIS ARM AROUND JANICE'S SHOULDERS, AND MADE AN ANNOUNCEMENT.

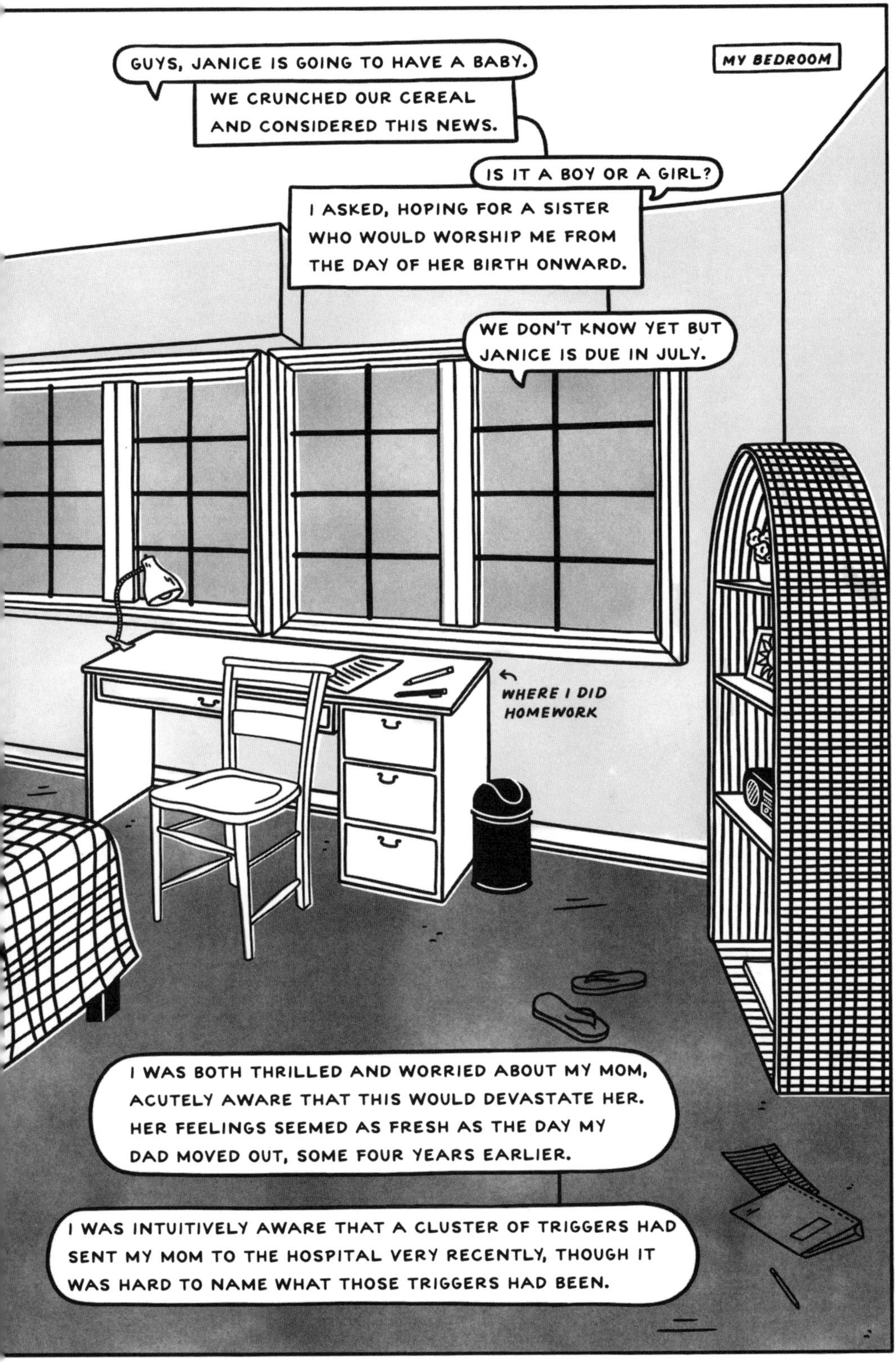
GUYS, JANICE IS GOING TO HAVE A BABY.
WE CRUNCHED OUR CEREAL AND CONSIDERED THIS NEWS.
MY BEDROOM
IS IT A BOY OR A GIRL?
I ASKED, HOPING FOR A SISTER WHO WOULD WORSHIP ME FROM THE DAY OF HER BIRTH ONWARD.
WE DON'T KNOW YET BUT JANICE IS DUE IN JULY.
WHERE I DID HOMEWORK
I WAS BOTH THRILLED AND WORRIED ABOUT MY MOM, ACUTELY AWARE THAT THIS WOULD DEVASTATE HER. HER FEELINGS SEEMED AS FRESH AS THE DAY MY DAD MOVED OUT, SOME FOUR YEARS EARLIER.
I WAS INTUITIVELY AWARE THAT A CLUSTER OF TRIGGERS HAD SENT MY MOM TO THE HOSPITAL VERY RECENTLY, THOUGH IT WAS HARD TO NAME WHAT THOSE TRIGGERS HAD BEEN.

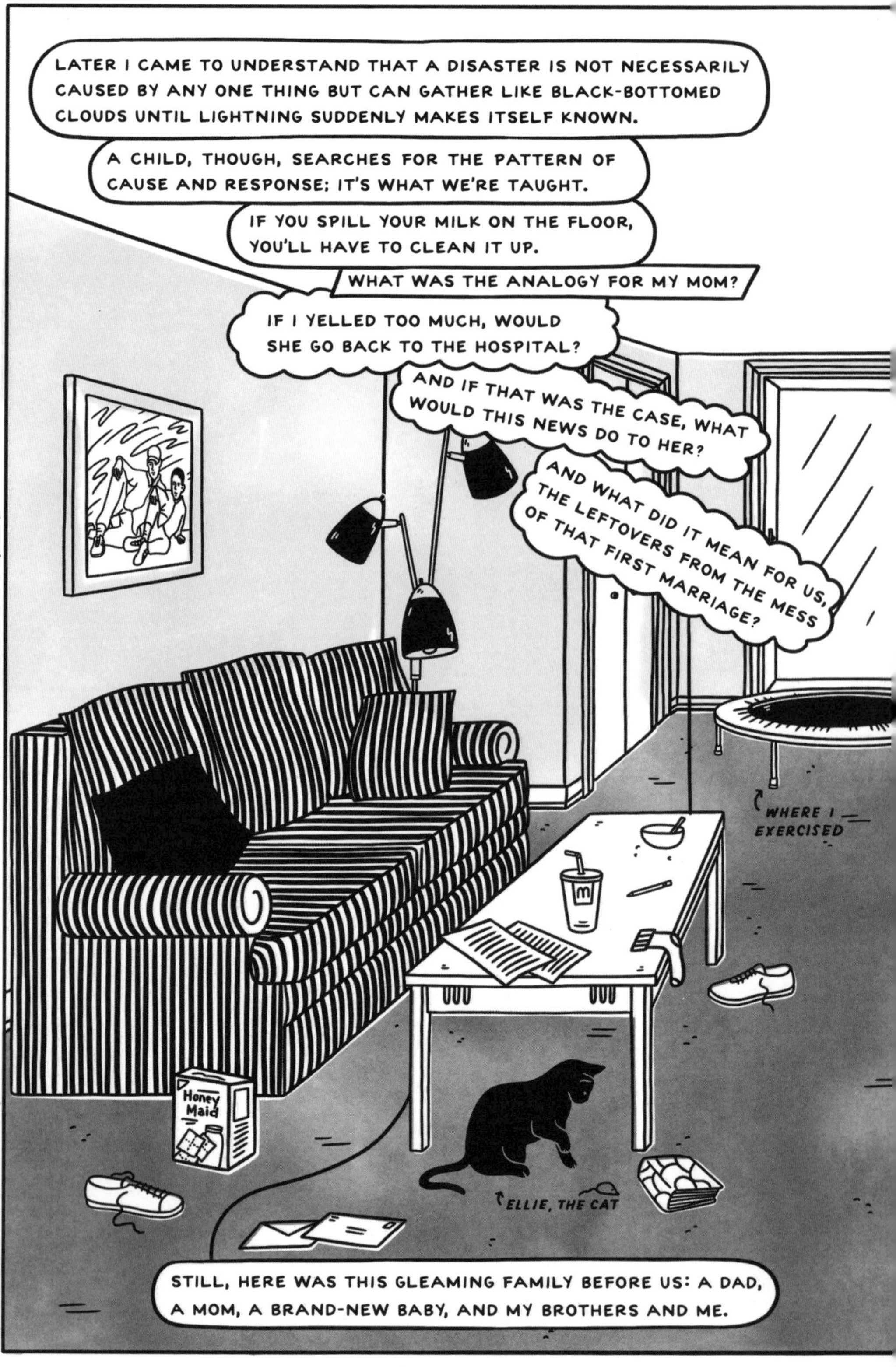
LATER I CAME TO UNDERSTAND THAT A DISASTER IS NOT NECESSARILY CAUSED BY ANY ONE THING BUT CAN GATHER LIKE BLACK-BOTTOMED CLOUDS UNTIL LIGHTNING SUDDENLY MAKES ITSELF KNOWN.
A CHILD, THOUGH, SEARCHES FOR THE PATTERN OF CAUSE AND RESPONSE; IT'S WHAT WE'RE TAUGHT.
IF YOU SPILL YOUR MILK ON THE FLOOR, YOU'LL HAVE TO CLEAN IT UP.
WHAT WAS THE ANALOGY FOR MY MOM?
IF I YELLED TOO MUCH, WOULD SHE GO BACK TO THE HOSPITAL?
AND IF THAT WAS THE CASE, WHAT WOULD THIS NEWS DO TO HER?
AND WHAT DID IT MEAN FOR US, THE LEFTOVERS FROM THE MESS OF THAT FIRST MARRIAGE?
WHERE I EXERCISED
Honey Maid
ELLIE, THE CAT
STILL, HERE WAS THIS GLEAMING FAMILY BEFORE US: A DAD, A MOM, A BRAND-NEW BABY, AND MY BROTHERS AND ME.

THIS CARPET (FROM 1995) IS STILL IN THE CONDO—OR STILL WAS WHEN IT WAS SOLD IN 2016 (ICK...)

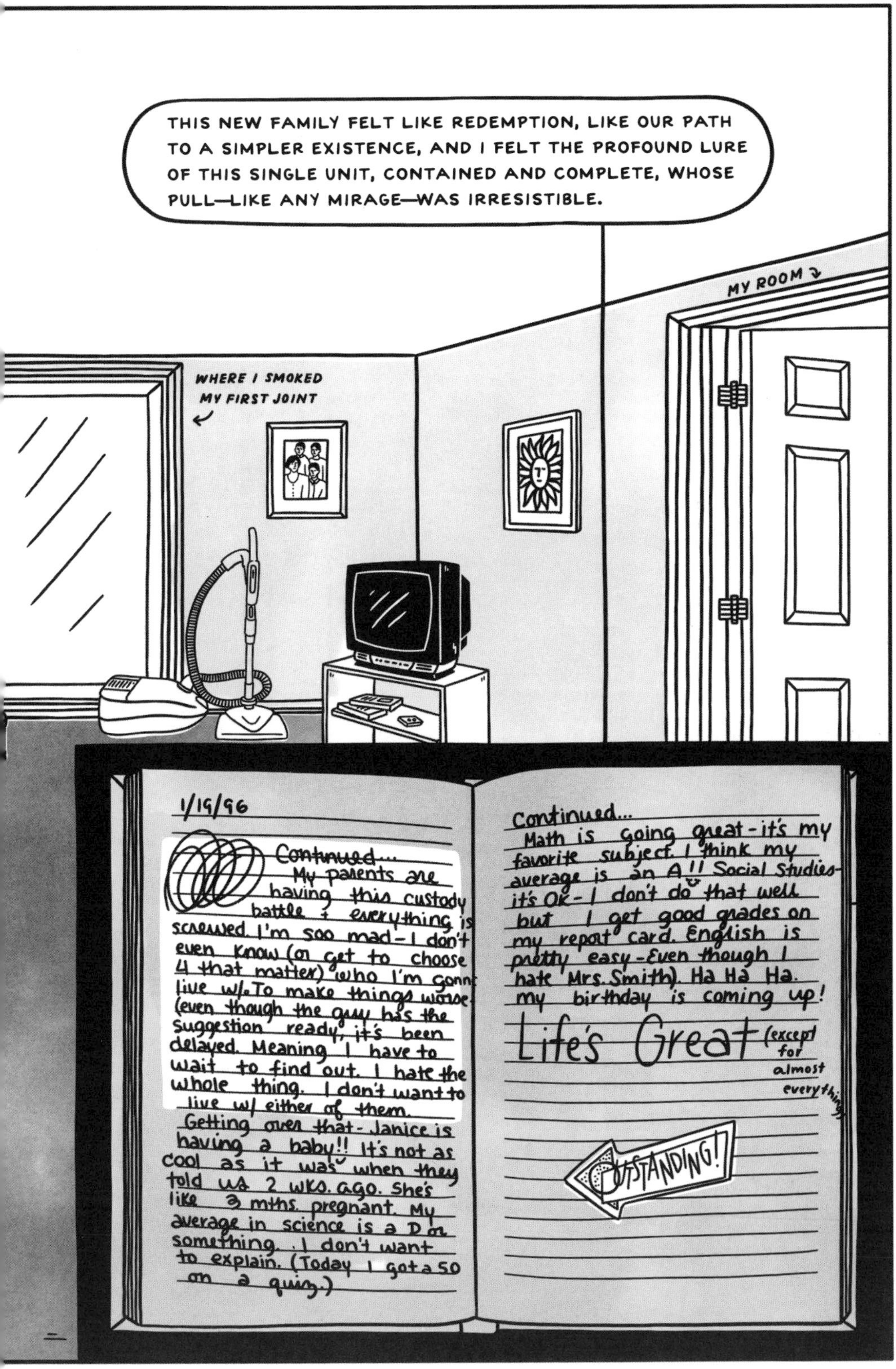
THIS NEW FAMILY FELT LIKE REDEMPTION, LIKE OUR PATH TO A SIMPLER EXISTENCE, AND I FELT THE PROFOUND LURE OF THIS SINGLE UNIT, CONTAINED AND COMPLETE, WHOSE PULL—LIKE ANY MIRAGE—WAS IRRESISTIBLE.
MY ROOM
WHERE I SMOKED MY FIRST JOINT
1/19/96
Continued...
My parents are having this custody battle + everything is screwed. I'm soo mad—I don't even know (or get to choose 4 that matter) who I'm gonna live w/. To make things worse (even though the guy has the suggestion ready, it's been delayed. Meaning I have to wait to find out. I hate the whole thing. I don't want to live w/ either of them.
Getting over that - Janice is having a baby!! It's not as cool as it was when they told us 2 wks. ago. She's like 3 mths. pregnant. My average in science is a D or something. I don't want to explain. (Today I got a 50 on a quiz.)
Continued...
Math is going great - it's my favorite subject. I think my average is an A!! Social Studies - it's OK - I don't do that well but I get good grades on my report card. English is pretty easy - Even though I hate Mrs. Smith). Ha Ha Ha. my birthday is coming up!
Life's Great (except for almost everything)
OUTSTANDING!

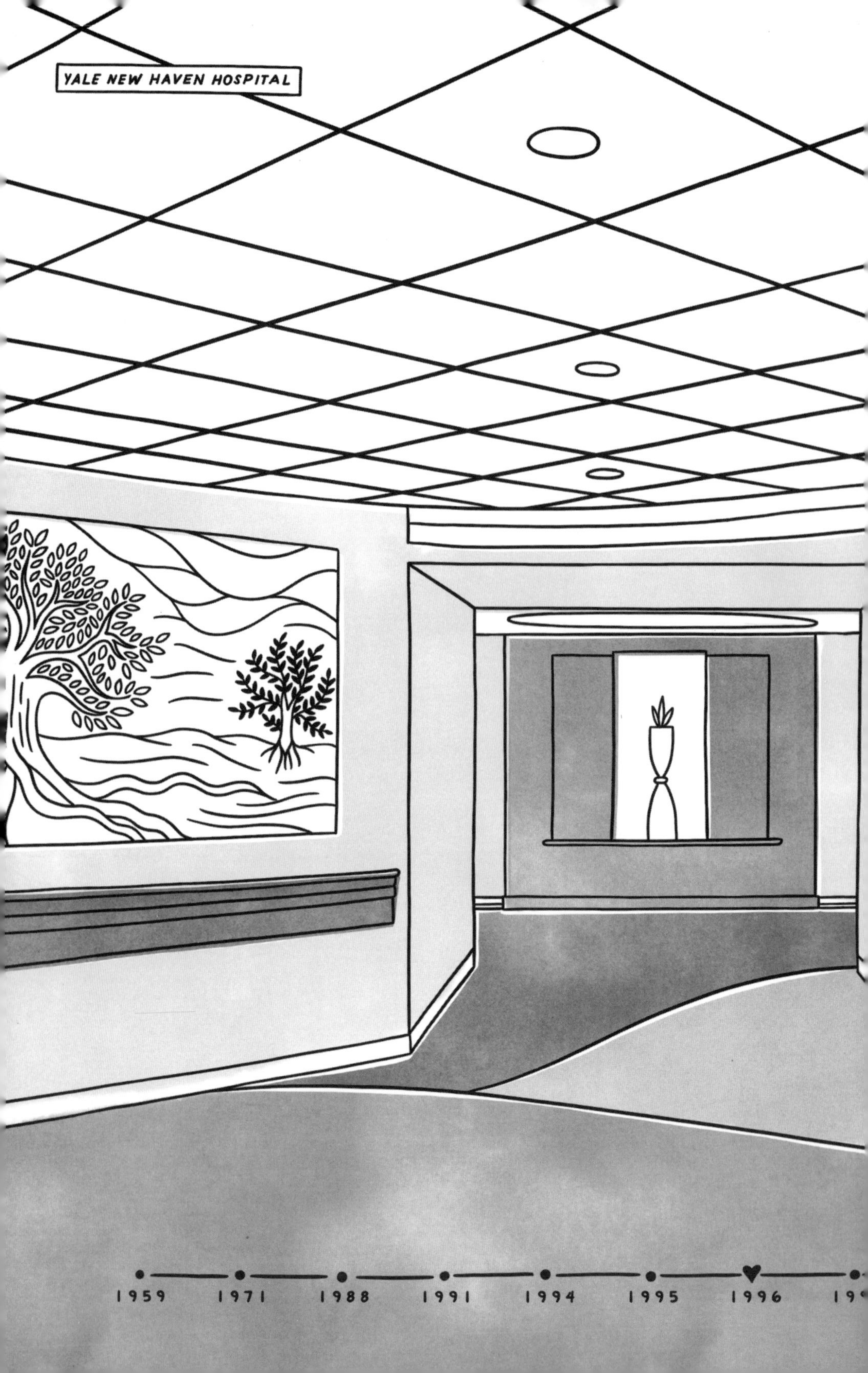

YALE NEW HAVEN HOSPITAL
1959
1971
1988
1991
1994
1995
1996

CHAPTER 11

The Baby

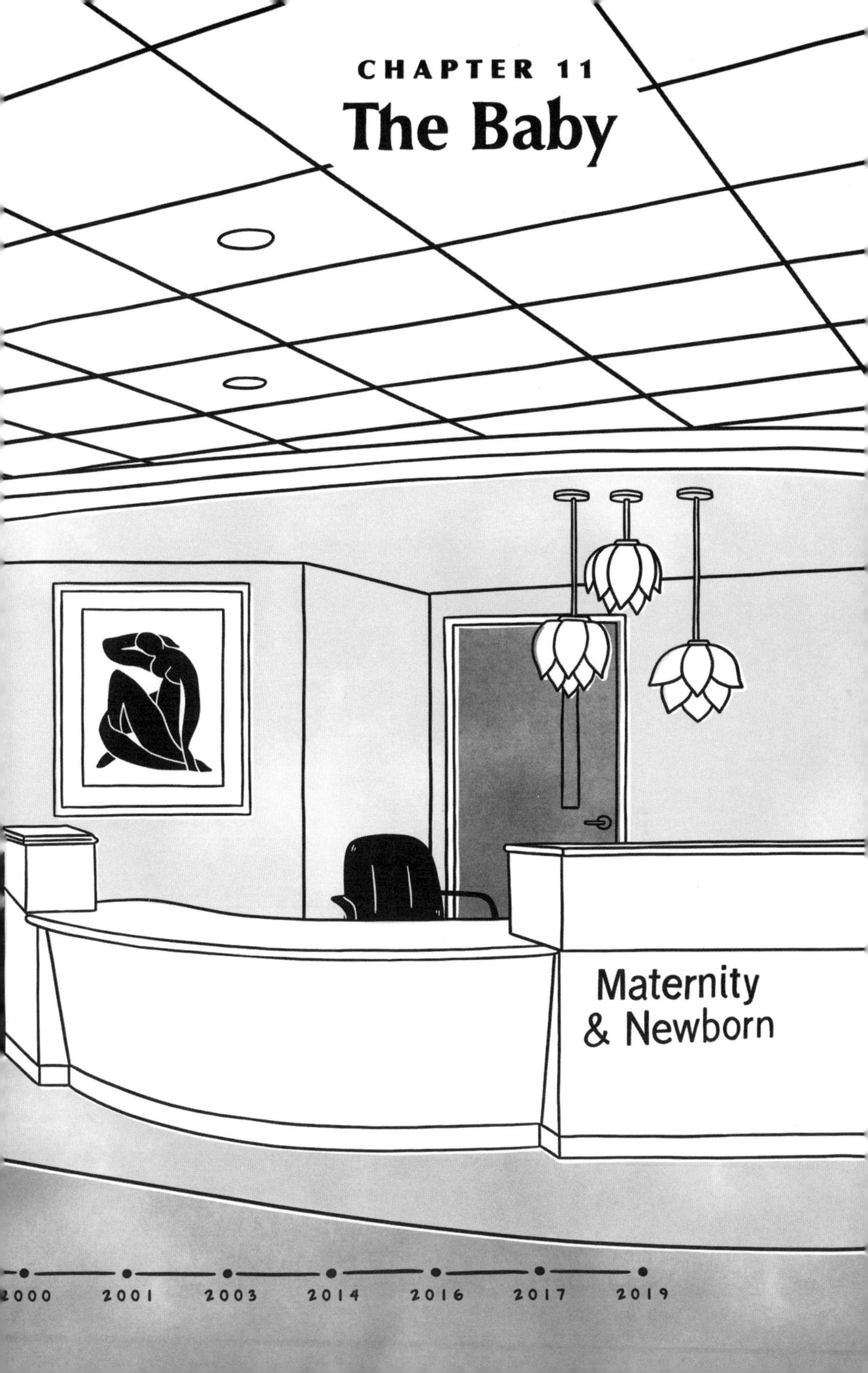
Maternity
& Newborn
2000
2001
2003
2014
2016
2017
2019

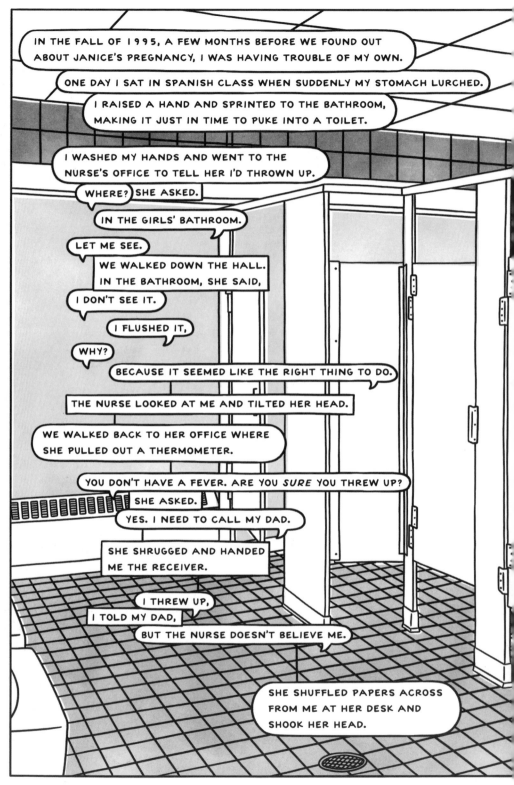

IN THE FALL OF 1995, A FEW MONTHS BEFORE WE FOUND OUT ABOUT JANICE'S PREGNANCY, I WAS HAVING TROUBLE OF MY OWN.

ONE DAY I SAT IN SPANISH CLASS WHEN SUDDENLY MY STOMACH LURCHED.

I RAISED A HAND AND SPRINTED TO THE BATHROOM, MAKING IT JUST IN TIME TO PUKE INTO A TOILET.

I WASHED MY HANDS AND WENT TO THE NURSE'S OFFICE TO TELL HER I'D THROWN UP.

WHERE? SHE ASKED.

IN THE GIRLS' BATHROOM.

LET ME SEE.

WE WALKED DOWN THE HALL. IN THE BATHROOM, SHE SAID,

I DON'T SEE IT.

I FLUSHED IT,

WHY?

BECAUSE IT SEEMED LIKE THE RIGHT THING TO DO.

THE NURSE LOOKED AT ME AND TILTED HER HEAD.

WE WALKED BACK TO HER OFFICE WHERE SHE PULLED OUT A THERMOMETER.

YOU DON'T HAVE A FEVER. ARE YOU *SURE* YOU THREW UP? SHE ASKED.

YES. I NEED TO CALL MY DAD.

SHE SHRUGGED AND HANDED ME THE RECEIVER.

I THREW UP,

I TOLD MY DAD,

BUT THE NURSE DOESN'T BELIEVE ME.

SHE SHUFFLED PAPERS ACROSS FROM ME AT HER DESK AND SHOOK HER HEAD.

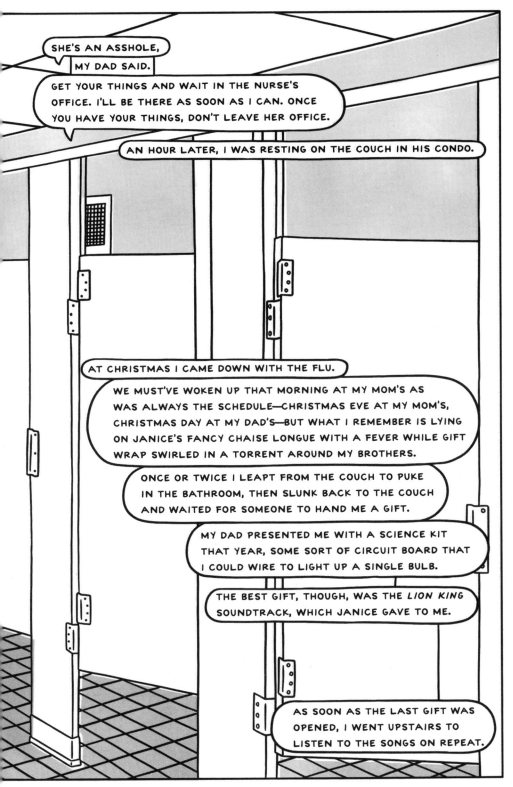

SHE'S AN ASSHOLE, MY DAD SAID.

GET YOUR THINGS AND WAIT IN THE NURSE'S OFFICE. I'LL BE THERE AS SOON AS I CAN. ONCE YOU HAVE YOUR THINGS, DON'T LEAVE HER OFFICE.

AN HOUR LATER, I WAS RESTING ON THE COUCH IN HIS CONDO.

AT CHRISTMAS I CAME DOWN WITH THE FLU.

WE MUST'VE WOKEN UP THAT MORNING AT MY MOM'S AS WAS ALWAYS THE SCHEDULE—CHRISTMAS EVE AT MY MOM'S, CHRISTMAS DAY AT MY DAD'S—BUT WHAT I REMEMBER IS LYING ON JANICE'S FANCY CHAISE LONGUE WITH A FEVER WHILE GIFT WRAP SWIRLED IN A TORRENT AROUND MY BROTHERS.

ONCE OR TWICE I LEAPT FROM THE COUCH TO PUKE IN THE BATHROOM, THEN SLUNK BACK TO THE COUCH AND WAITED FOR SOMEONE TO HAND ME A GIFT.

MY DAD PRESENTED ME WITH A SCIENCE KIT THAT YEAR, SOME SORT OF CIRCUIT BOARD THAT I COULD WIRE TO LIGHT UP A SINGLE BULB.

THE BEST GIFT, THOUGH, WAS THE *LION KING* SOUNDTRACK, WHICH JANICE GAVE TO ME.

AS SOON AS THE LAST GIFT WAS OPENED, I WENT UPSTAIRS TO LISTEN TO THE SONGS ON REPEAT.

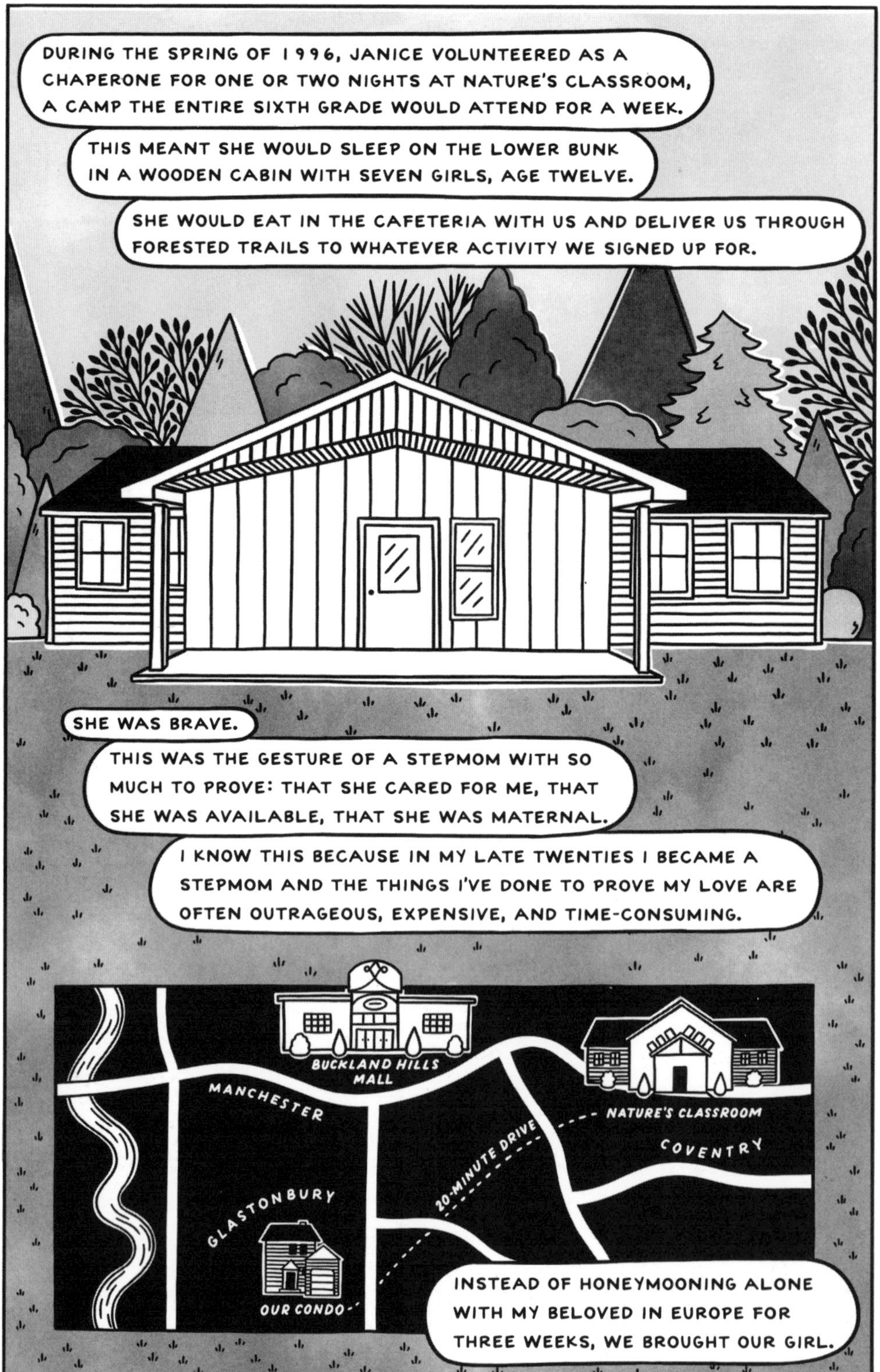
DURING THE SPRING OF 1996, JANICE VOLUNTEERED AS A CHAPERONE FOR ONE OR TWO NIGHTS AT NATURE'S CLASSROOM, A CAMP THE ENTIRE SIXTH GRADE WOULD ATTEND FOR A WEEK.
THIS MEANT SHE WOULD SLEEP ON THE LOWER BUNK IN A WOODEN CABIN WITH SEVEN GIRLS, AGE TWELVE.
SHE WOULD EAT IN THE CAFETERIA WITH US AND DELIVER US THROUGH FORESTED TRAILS TO WHATEVER ACTIVITY WE SIGNED UP FOR.
SHE WAS BRAVE.
THIS WAS THE GESTURE OF A STEPMOM WITH SO MUCH TO PROVE: THAT SHE CARED FOR ME, THAT SHE WAS AVAILABLE, THAT SHE WAS MATERNAL.
I KNOW THIS BECAUSE IN MY LATE TWENTIES I BECAME A STEPMOM AND THE THINGS I'VE DONE TO PROVE MY LOVE ARE OFTEN OUTRAGEOUS, EXPENSIVE, AND TIME-CONSUMING.
BUCKLAND HILLS MALL
MANCHESTER
NATURE'S CLASSROOM
20-MINUTE DRIVE
COVENTRY
GLASTONBURY
OUR CONDO
INSTEAD OF HONEYMOONING ALONE WITH MY BELOVED IN EUROPE FOR THREE WEEKS, WE BROUGHT OUR GIRL.

AFTER MONTHS OF MEASURING AND PLANNING, I BOUGHT HER A NEW BED AND REDECORATED HER ENTIRE ROOM SO SHE COULD HAVE THE DESK SHE WANTED, IN THE COLORS SHE WANTED.

IN FACT, I LIVE IN THE MIDDLE OF THE COUNTRY TO BE NEAR HER (AND MY HUSBAND) WHEN EVERY CELL IN MY BODY ACHES FOR THE EAST COAST, WHERE MY ENTIRE FAMILY LIVES AND HAS LIVED FOR GENERATIONS.

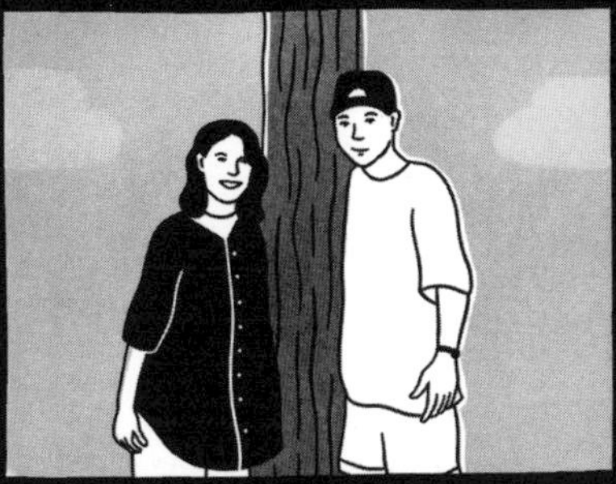

ME, IN A GIANT SHIRT, POSING WITH A BOY I LIKED

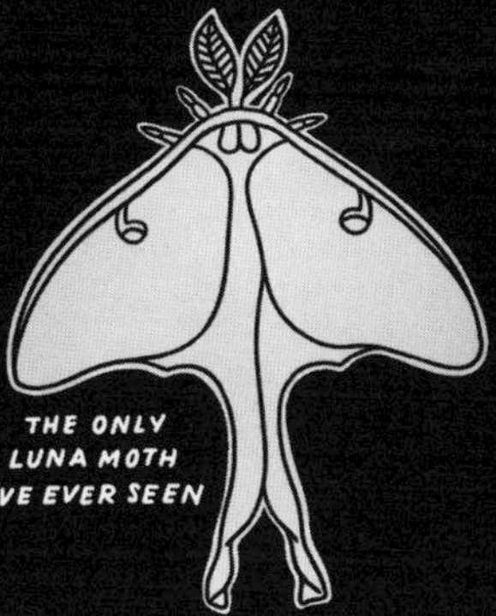

THE ONLY LUNA MOTH I'VE EVER SEEN

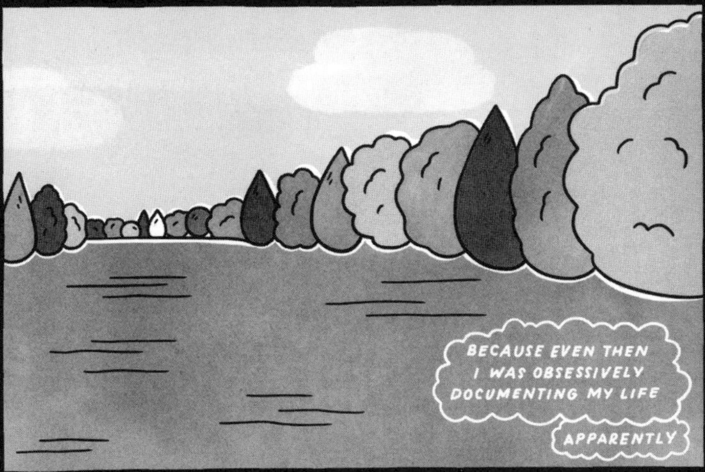
BECAUSE EVEN THEN I WAS OBSESSIVELY DOCUMENTING MY LIFE
APPARENTLY

PHOTOS FROM NATURE'S CLASSROOM

IT'S ABSURD, THE THINGS STEPPARENTS DO TO BE ACKNOWLEDGED AS A TRUE MEMBER OF THE FAMILY; I AM FOREVER TRYING TO MAKE UP FOR THE FACT THAT I AM NOT HER BIOLOGICAL MOTHER.

GEORGE WASHINGTON, A FAMOUS STEPFATHER, REMARKED THAT TO BE A STEPPARENT MEANS THAT NOTHING IS GIVEN AND EVERYTHING IS EARNED.

JANICE WAS TRYING HARD.

SHE WAS CHEERFUL AND LIGHTHEARTED AND DIDN'T YELL WHEN WE BEGGED TO STAY UP LATE, THEN CLIMBED INTO EACH OTHER'S BUNKS TO MAKE HAND SHADOWS WITH FLASHLIGHTS AGAINST THE WALLS.

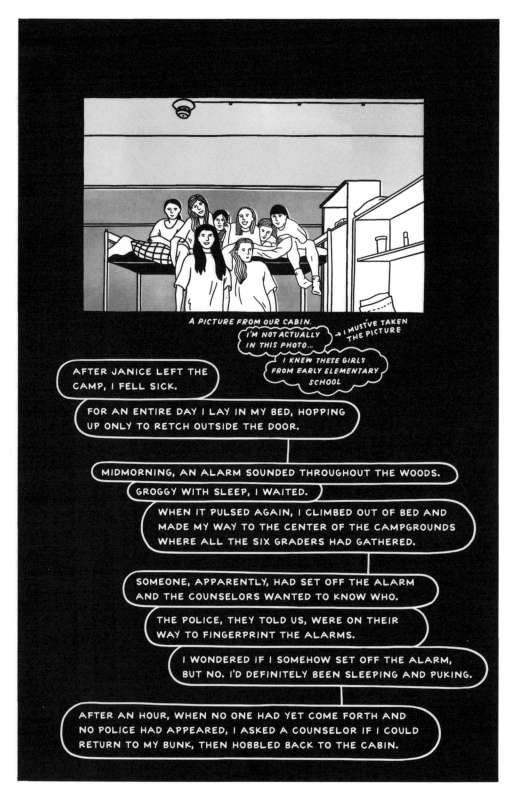

A PICTURE FROM OUR CABIN.

I'M NOT ACTUALLY IN THIS PHOTO... → I MUST'VE TAKEN THE PICTURE

I KNEW THESE GIRLS FROM EARLY ELEMENTARY SCHOOL

AFTER JANICE LEFT THE CAMP, I FELL SICK.

FOR AN ENTIRE DAY I LAY IN MY BED, HOPPING UP ONLY TO RETCH OUTSIDE THE DOOR.

MIDMORNING, AN ALARM SOUNDED THROUGHOUT THE WOODS.

GROGGY WITH SLEEP, I WAITED.

WHEN IT PULSED AGAIN, I CLIMBED OUT OF BED AND MADE MY WAY TO THE CENTER OF THE CAMPGROUNDS WHERE ALL THE SIX GRADERS HAD GATHERED.

SOMEONE, APPARENTLY, HAD SET OFF THE ALARM AND THE COUNSELORS WANTED TO KNOW WHO.

THE POLICE, THEY TOLD US, WERE ON THEIR WAY TO FINGERPRINT THE ALARMS.

I WONDERED IF I SOMEHOW SET OFF THE ALARM, BUT NO. I'D DEFINITELY BEEN SLEEPING AND PUKING.

AFTER AN HOUR, WHEN NO ONE HAD YET COME FORTH AND NO POLICE HAD APPEARED, I ASKED A COUNSELOR IF I COULD RETURN TO MY BUNK, THEN HOBBLED BACK TO THE CABIN.

BACK AT SCHOOL, A DIARY ENTRY NOTES THAT I WAS SICK AGAIN, THIS TIME THROWING UP IN THE HALLWAY.

WHY WAS I SO SICK IN FIFTH AND SIXTH GRADE?

THIS IS THE TIME PERIOD THAT COINCIDED WITH THE INTENSIFICATION OF MY PARENTS' FIGHT FOR CUSTODY.

ONE ENTRY FROM JANUARY 1996 READ:

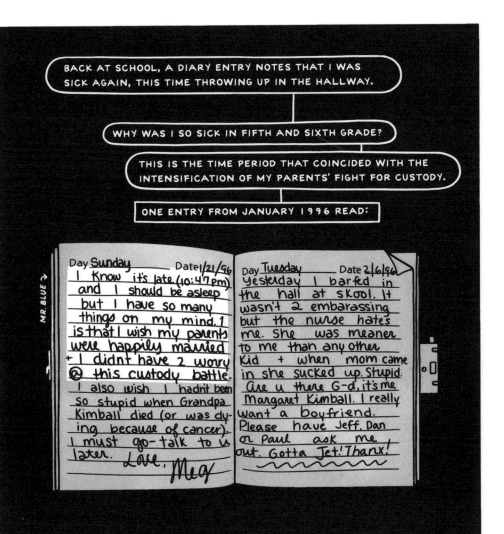

MR. BLUE →

Day Sunday   Date 1/21/96
I know it's late (10:47 pm) and I should be asleep but I have so many things on my mind. 1 is that I wish my parents were happily married + I didn't have 2 worry @ this custody battle. I also wish I hadn't been so stupid when Grandpa Kimball died (or was dying because of cancer). I must go- talk to u later. Love, Meg

Day Tuesday   Date 2/6/96
Yesterday I barfed in the hall at skool. It wasn't 2 embarassing but the nurse hates me. She was meaner to me than any other kid + when mom came in she sucked up. Stupid. Are u there G-d, it's me Margaret Kimball. I really want a boyfriend. Please have Jeff, Dan or Paul ask me out. Gotta Jet! Thanx!

CONFLICT IN ANY PART OF THE FAMILY AFFECTS THE WHOLE. PSYCHOLOGISTS TELL US THAT PARENTS ARE ONLY AS HAPPY AS THE LEAST-HAPPY CHILD, AND I'D ADD THAT CHILDREN ARE ONLY AS HAPPY AS THEIR LEAST-HAPPY PARENT. WHEN A PARENT IS SAD OR ANGRY, THE MOOD IN THE FAMILY SHIFTS TO ACCOMMODATE THOSE FEELINGS; EVERYONE MAKES ROOM FOR THEM. A CHILD GOES QUIET, RETREATS TO HER ROOM, OR SETS OFF IN THE WOODS. THE PARENT TAKES A NAP OR WASHES DISHES FOR HOURS. BENEATH EVERY CONVERSATION, EVERY INTERACTION, THE EMOTION BREATHES ITS OWN LIFE, LETS ITSELF BE KNOWN IN THE CURVE OF A SMILE, AN UNINTENTIONAL SIGH.

WHILE MY PARENTS TRIED TO CONTAIN THEIR FIGHTING TO LAWYERS' OFFICES AND HEATED PHONE CALLS, MY BROTHERS AND I FELT THEIR ANGER. I WAS SO FILLED WITH APPREHENSION OVER WHAT MIGHT HAPPEN TO US THAT I COULDN'T SLEEP AT NIGHT.

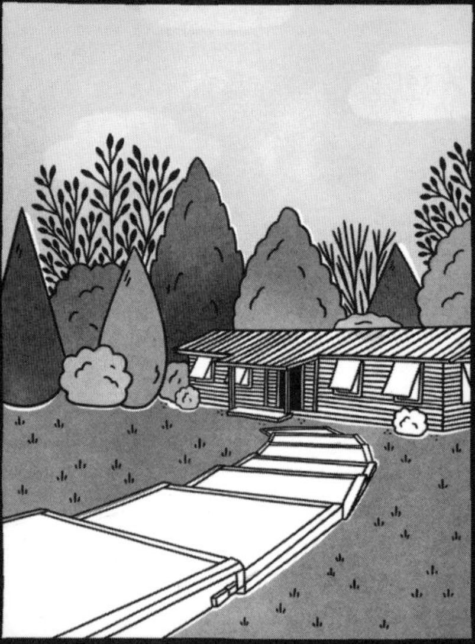

CABIN AT NATURE'S CLASSROOM

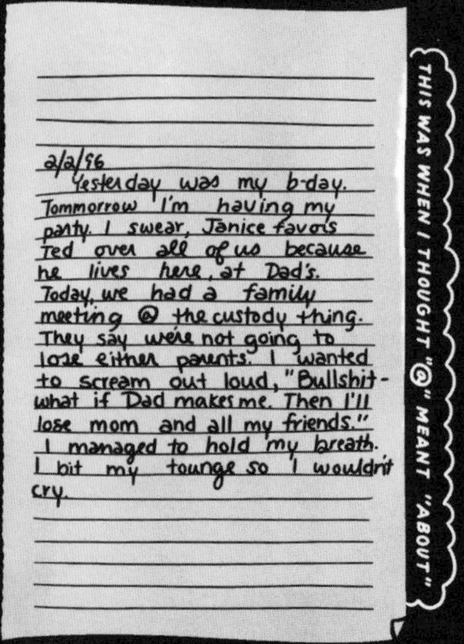

2/2/96
Yesterday was my b-day. Tommorrow I'm having my party. I swear, Janice favors Ted over all of us because he lives here, at Dad's. Today, we had a family meeting @ the custody thing. They say we're not going to lose either parents. I wanted to scream out loud, "Bullshit - what if Dad makes me. Then I'll lose mom and all my friends." I managed to hold my breath. I bit my tounge so I wouldn't cry.

THIS WAS WHEN I THOUGHT "@" MEANT "ABOUT"

EXCERPT FROM MRS. PINK

DURING THE DAY I BECAME SICK WITH THE STRESS OF IT. AS THE QUESTION OF CUSTODY LOOMED OVER US FOR THOSE TWO YEARS, THE KNOT IN MY STOMACH GREW AND GREW. IN MY MOM'S GRIEF SHE BECAME UNABLE TO GUIDE ME AND I DRIFTED AWAY FROM HER, A PEELING APART OF SKIN FROM FRUIT. INSTEAD, I WAS SENT TO COUNSELORS AND TEACHERS, PSYCHOLOGISTS AND EVEN OUR CHURCH'S YOUTH LEADER, WHOSE LOOKS OF CONCERN ONLY EXAGGERATED MY FEAR, MADE BIGGER THE TANGLED-UP MESS INSIDE ME.

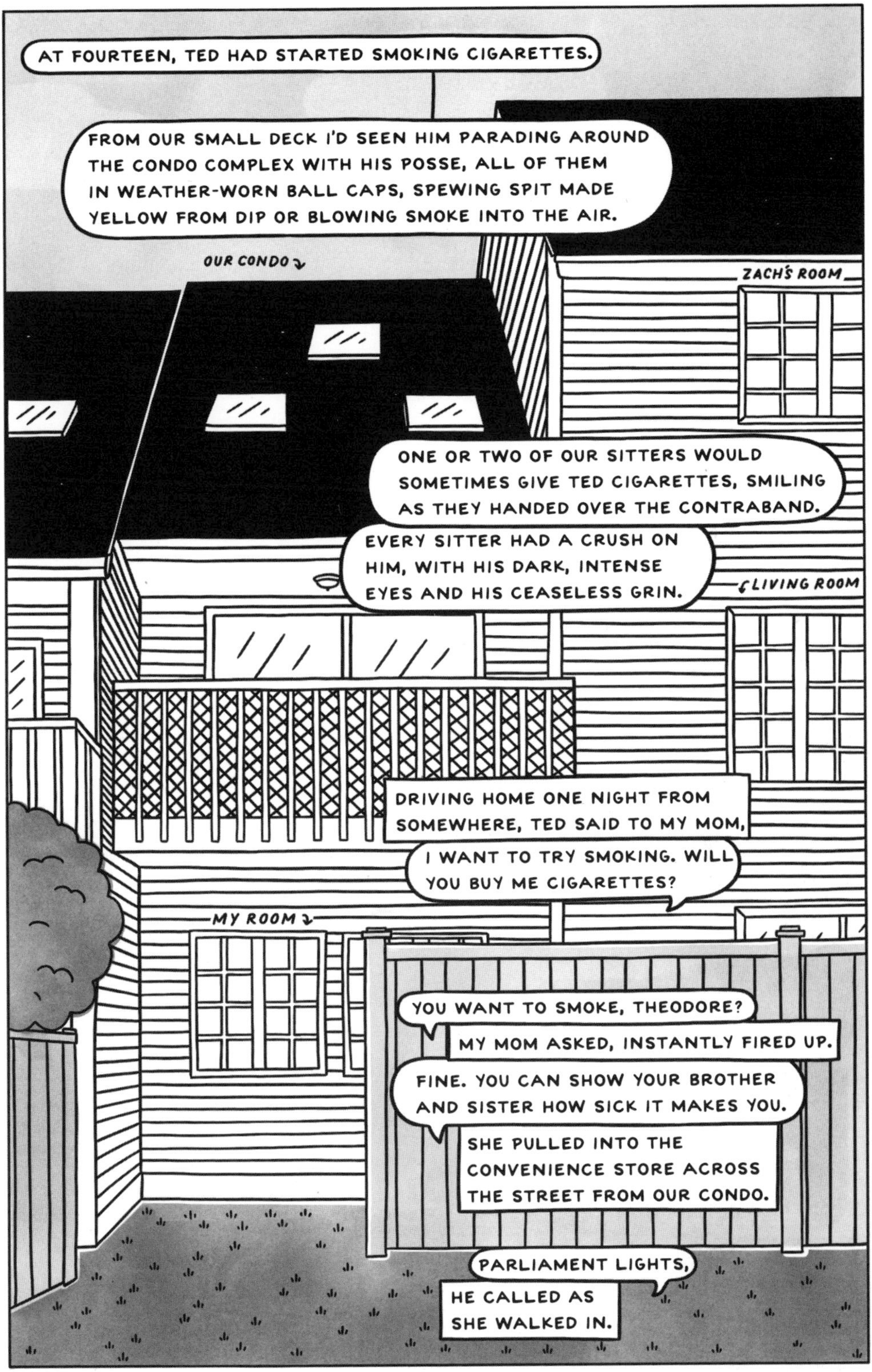
AT FOURTEEN, TED HAD STARTED SMOKING CIGARETTES.
FROM OUR SMALL DECK I'D SEEN HIM PARADING AROUND THE CONDO COMPLEX WITH HIS POSSE, ALL OF THEM IN WEATHER-WORN BALL CAPS, SPEWING SPIT MADE YELLOW FROM DIP OR BLOWING SMOKE INTO THE AIR.
OUR CONDO
ZACH'S ROOM
ONE OR TWO OF OUR SITTERS WOULD SOMETIMES GIVE TED CIGARETTES, SMILING AS THEY HANDED OVER THE CONTRABAND.
EVERY SITTER HAD A CRUSH ON HIM, WITH HIS DARK, INTENSE EYES AND HIS CEASELESS GRIN.
LIVING ROOM
DRIVING HOME ONE NIGHT FROM SOMEWHERE, TED SAID TO MY MOM,
I WANT TO TRY SMOKING. WILL YOU BUY ME CIGARETTES?
MY ROOM
YOU WANT TO SMOKE, THEODORE?
MY MOM ASKED, INSTANTLY FIRED UP.
FINE. YOU CAN SHOW YOUR BROTHER AND SISTER HOW SICK IT MAKES YOU.
SHE PULLED INTO THE CONVENIENCE STORE ACROSS THE STREET FROM OUR CONDO.
PARLIAMENT LIGHTS,
HE CALLED AS SHE WALKED IN.

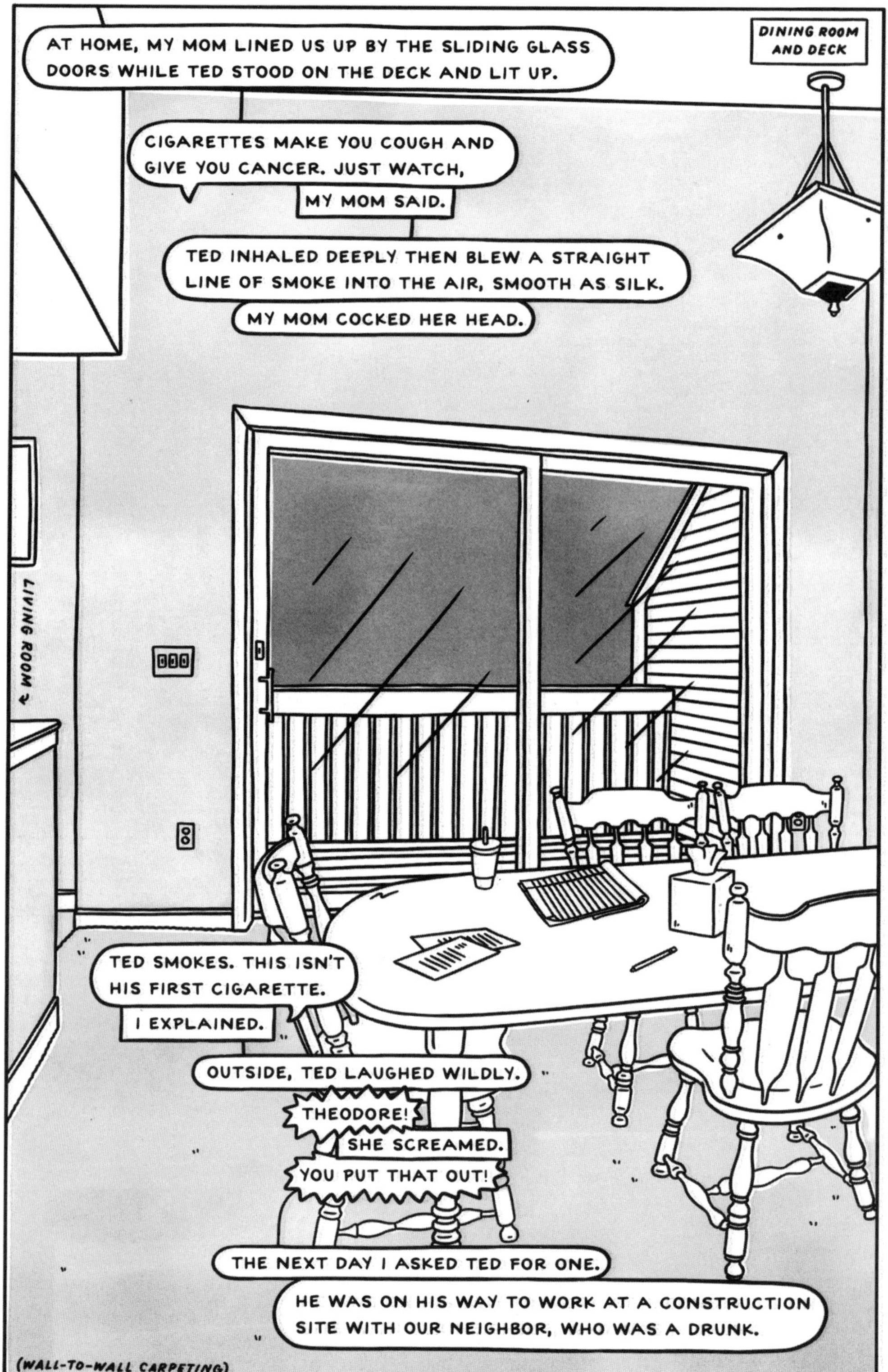
AT HOME, MY MOM LINED US UP BY THE SLIDING GLASS DOORS WHILE TED STOOD ON THE DECK AND LIT UP.
DINING ROOM AND DECK
CIGARETTES MAKE YOU COUGH AND GIVE YOU CANCER. JUST WATCH,
MY MOM SAID.
TED INHALED DEEPLY THEN BLEW A STRAIGHT LINE OF SMOKE INTO THE AIR, SMOOTH AS SILK.
MY MOM COCKED HER HEAD.
LIVING ROOM
TED SMOKES. THIS ISN'T HIS FIRST CIGARETTE.
I EXPLAINED.
OUTSIDE, TED LAUGHED WILDLY.
THEODORE!
SHE SCREAMED.
YOU PUT THAT OUT!
THE NEXT DAY I ASKED TED FOR ONE.
HE WAS ON HIS WAY TO WORK AT A CONSTRUCTION SITE WITH OUR NEIGHBOR, WHO WAS A DRUNK.
(WALL-TO-WALL CARPETING)

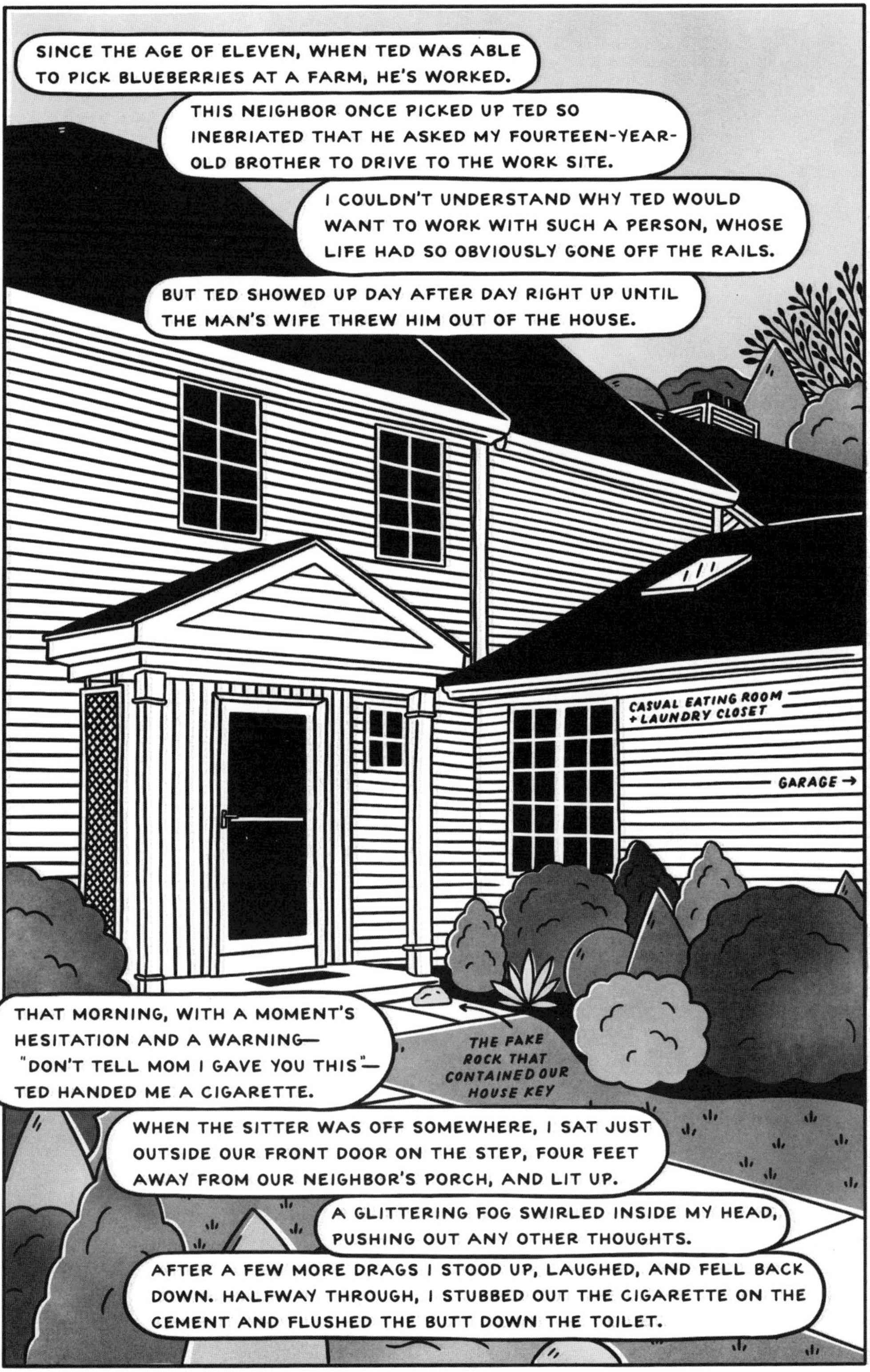
SINCE THE AGE OF ELEVEN, WHEN TED WAS ABLE TO PICK BLUEBERRIES AT A FARM, HE'S WORKED.
THIS NEIGHBOR ONCE PICKED UP TED SO INEBRIATED THAT HE ASKED MY FOURTEEN-YEAR-OLD BROTHER TO DRIVE TO THE WORK SITE.
I COULDN'T UNDERSTAND WHY TED WOULD WANT TO WORK WITH SUCH A PERSON, WHOSE LIFE HAD SO OBVIOUSLY GONE OFF THE RAILS.
BUT TED SHOWED UP DAY AFTER DAY RIGHT UP UNTIL THE MAN'S WIFE THREW HIM OUT OF THE HOUSE.
CASUAL EATING ROOM + LAUNDRY CLOSET
GARAGE →
THAT MORNING, WITH A MOMENT'S HESITATION AND A WARNING—"DON'T TELL MOM I GAVE YOU THIS"—TED HANDED ME A CIGARETTE.
THE FAKE ROCK THAT CONTAINED OUR HOUSE KEY
WHEN THE SITTER WAS OFF SOMEWHERE, I SAT JUST OUTSIDE OUR FRONT DOOR ON THE STEP, FOUR FEET AWAY FROM OUR NEIGHBOR'S PORCH, AND LIT UP.
A GLITTERING FOG SWIRLED INSIDE MY HEAD, PUSHING OUT ANY OTHER THOUGHTS.
AFTER A FEW MORE DRAGS I STOOD UP, LAUGHED, AND FELL BACK DOWN. HALFWAY THROUGH, I STUBBED OUT THE CIGARETTE ON THE CEMENT AND FLUSHED THE BUTT DOWN THE TOILET.

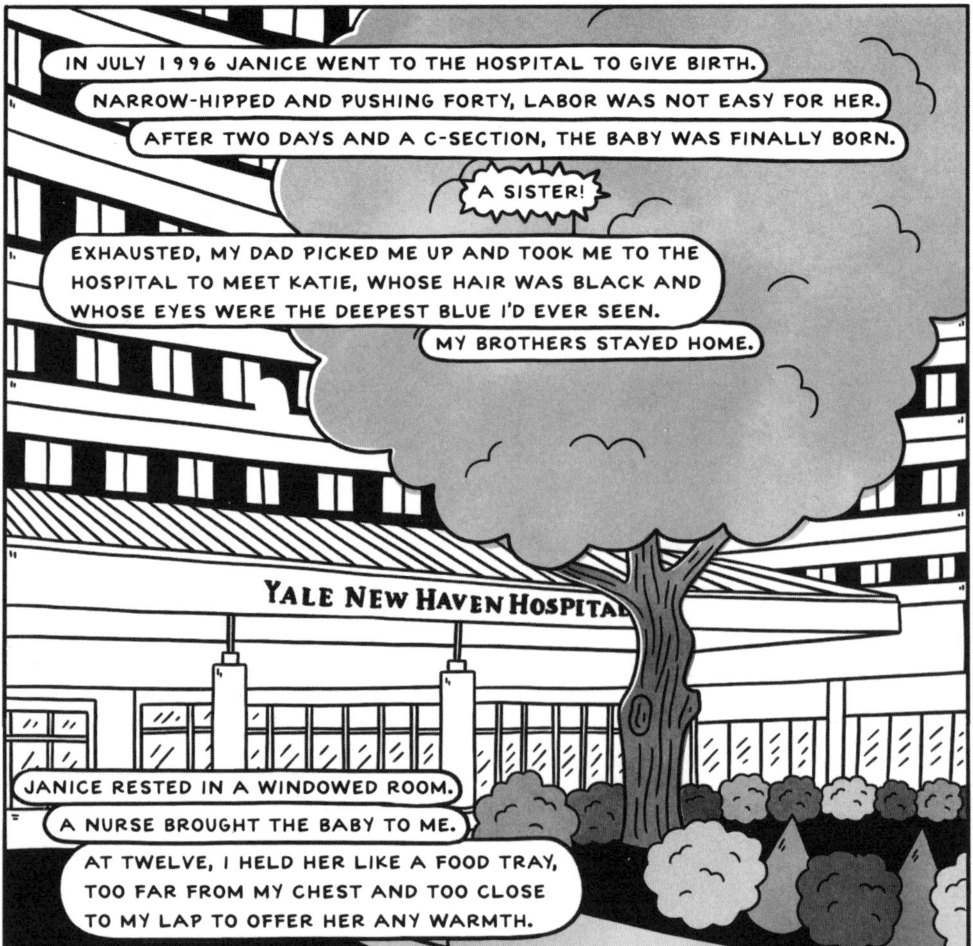
IN JULY 1996 JANICE WENT TO THE HOSPITAL TO GIVE BIRTH.
NARROW-HIPPED AND PUSHING FORTY, LABOR WAS NOT EASY FOR HER.
AFTER TWO DAYS AND A C-SECTION, THE BABY WAS FINALLY BORN.
A SISTER!
EXHAUSTED, MY DAD PICKED ME UP AND TOOK ME TO THE HOSPITAL TO MEET KATIE, WHOSE HAIR WAS BLACK AND WHOSE EYES WERE THE DEEPEST BLUE I'D EVER SEEN.
MY BROTHERS STAYED HOME.
YALE NEW HAVEN HOSPITAL
JANICE RESTED IN A WINDOWED ROOM.
A NURSE BROUGHT THE BABY TO ME.
AT TWELVE, I HELD HER LIKE A FOOD TRAY, TOO FAR FROM MY CHEST AND TOO CLOSE TO MY LAP TO OFFER HER ANY WARMTH.

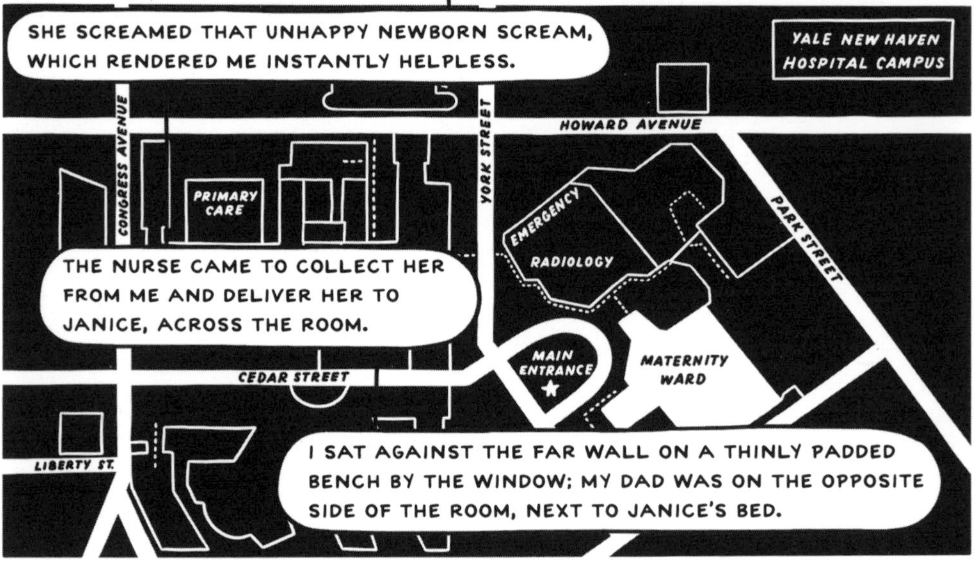
SHE SCREAMED THAT UNHAPPY NEWBORN SCREAM, WHICH RENDERED ME INSTANTLY HELPLESS.
YALE NEW HAVEN HOSPITAL CAMPUS
CONGRESS AVENUE
YORK STREET
HOWARD AVENUE
PRIMARY CARE
EMERGENCY
RADIOLOGY
PARK STREET
THE NURSE CAME TO COLLECT HER FROM ME AND DELIVER HER TO JANICE, ACROSS THE ROOM.
MAIN ENTRANCE
MATERNITY WARD
CEDAR STREET
LIBERTY ST.
I SAT AGAINST THE FAR WALL ON A THINLY PADDED BENCH BY THE WINDOW; MY DAD WAS ON THE OPPOSITE SIDE OF THE ROOM, NEXT TO JANICE'S BED.

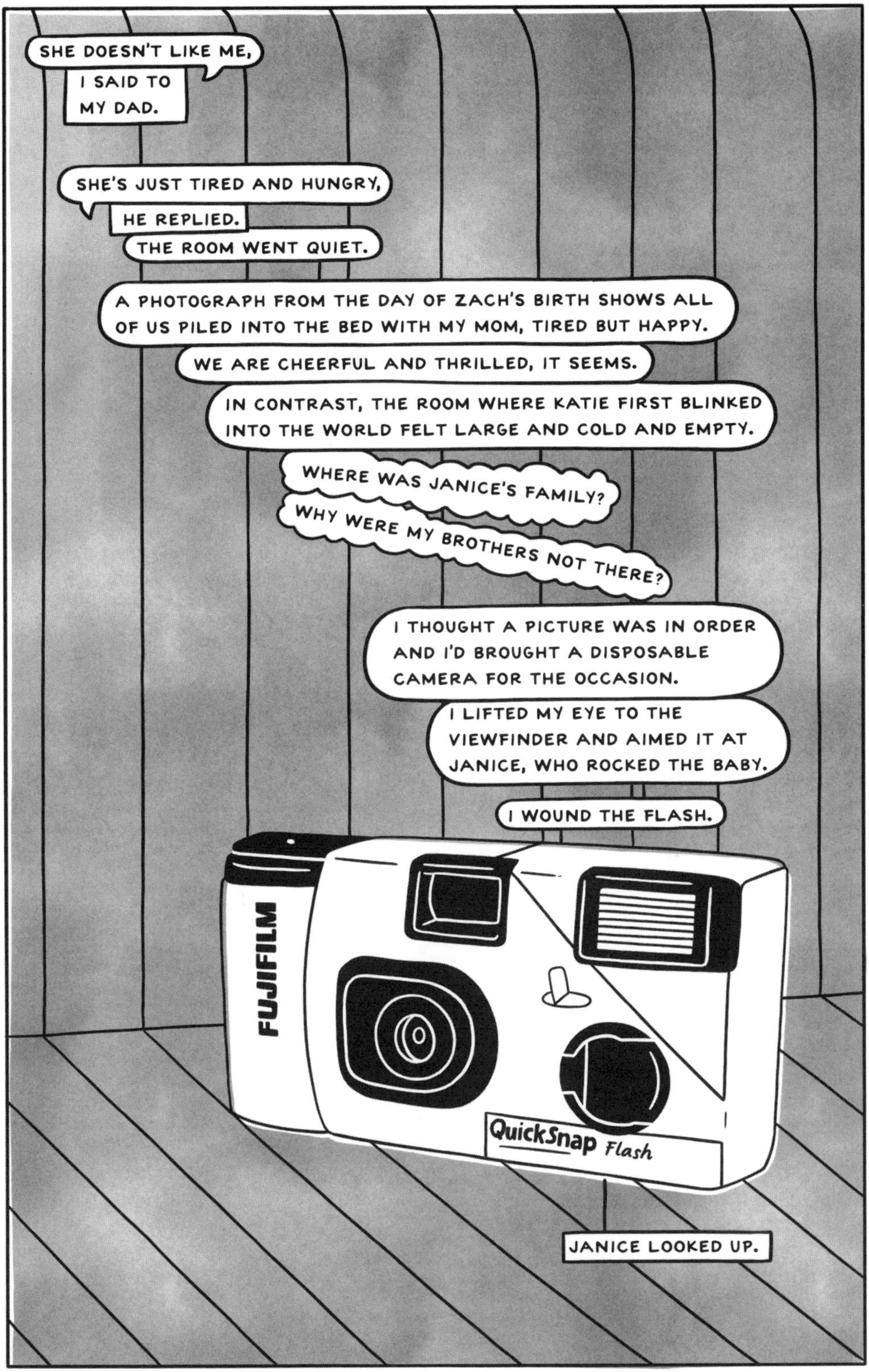
SHE DOESN'T LIKE ME,
I SAID TO MY DAD.
SHE'S JUST TIRED AND HUNGRY,
HE REPLIED.
THE ROOM WENT QUIET.
A PHOTOGRAPH FROM THE DAY OF ZACH'S BIRTH SHOWS ALL OF US PILED INTO THE BED WITH MY MOM, TIRED BUT HAPPY.
WE ARE CHEERFUL AND THRILLED, IT SEEMS.
IN CONTRAST, THE ROOM WHERE KATIE FIRST BLINKED INTO THE WORLD FELT LARGE AND COLD AND EMPTY.
WHERE WAS JANICE'S FAMILY?
WHY WERE MY BROTHERS NOT THERE?
I THOUGHT A PICTURE WAS IN ORDER AND I'D BROUGHT A DISPOSABLE CAMERA FOR THE OCCASION.
I LIFTED MY EYE TO THE VIEWFINDER AND AIMED IT AT JANICE, WHO ROCKED THE BABY.
I WOUND THE FLASH.
FUJIFILM
QuickSnap Flash
JANICE LOOKED UP.

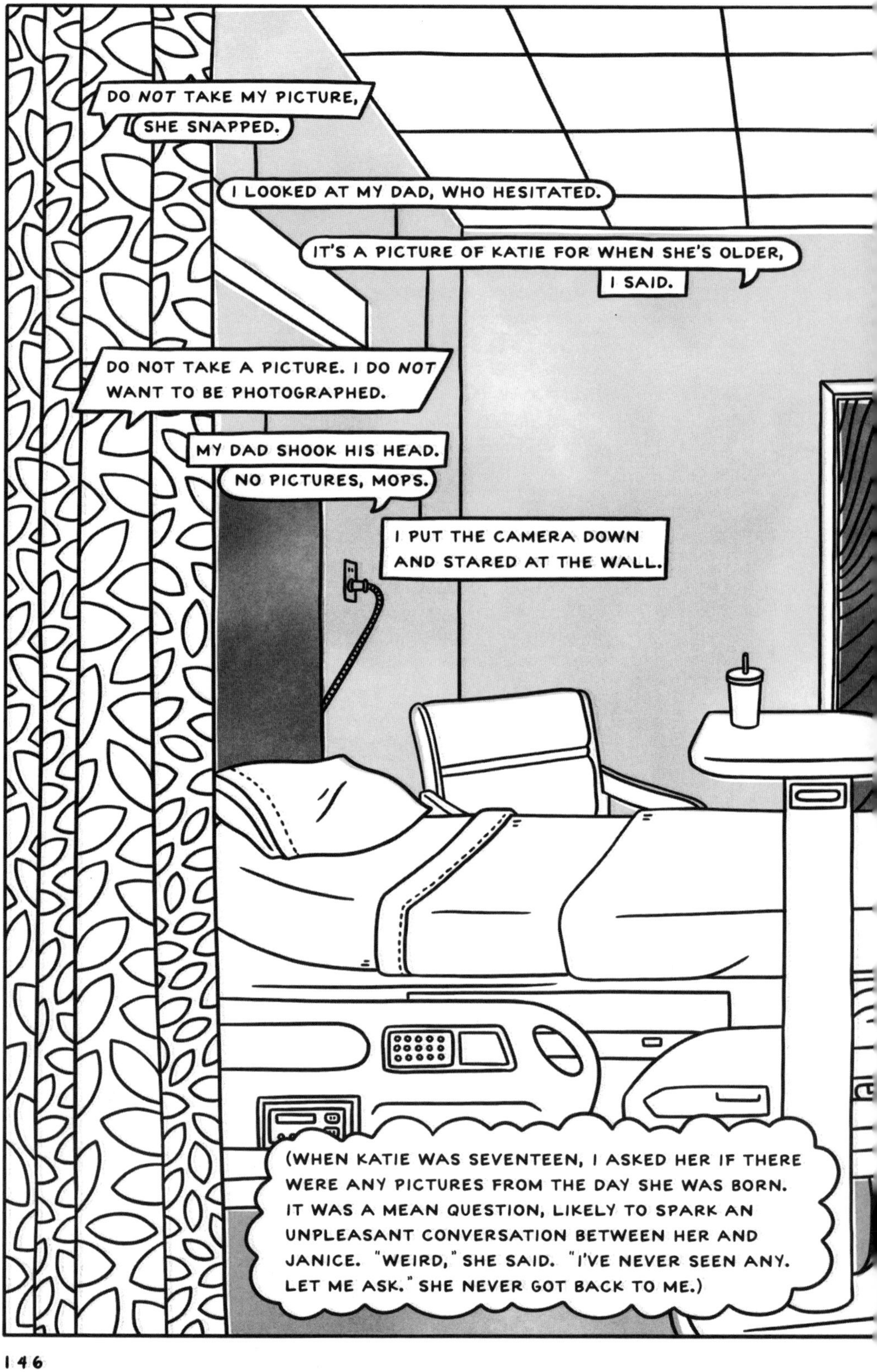
DO *NOT* TAKE MY PICTURE,
SHE SNAPPED.
I LOOKED AT MY DAD, WHO HESITATED.
IT'S A PICTURE OF KATIE FOR WHEN SHE'S OLDER,
I SAID.
DO NOT TAKE A PICTURE. I DO *NOT* WANT TO BE PHOTOGRAPHED.
MY DAD SHOOK HIS HEAD.
NO PICTURES, MOPS.
I PUT THE CAMERA DOWN AND STARED AT THE WALL.
(WHEN KATIE WAS SEVENTEEN, I ASKED HER IF THERE WERE ANY PICTURES FROM THE DAY SHE WAS BORN. IT WAS A MEAN QUESTION, LIKELY TO SPARK AN UNPLEASANT CONVERSATION BETWEEN HER AND JANICE. "WEIRD," SHE SAID. "I'VE NEVER SEEN ANY. LET ME ASK." SHE NEVER GOT BACK TO ME.)

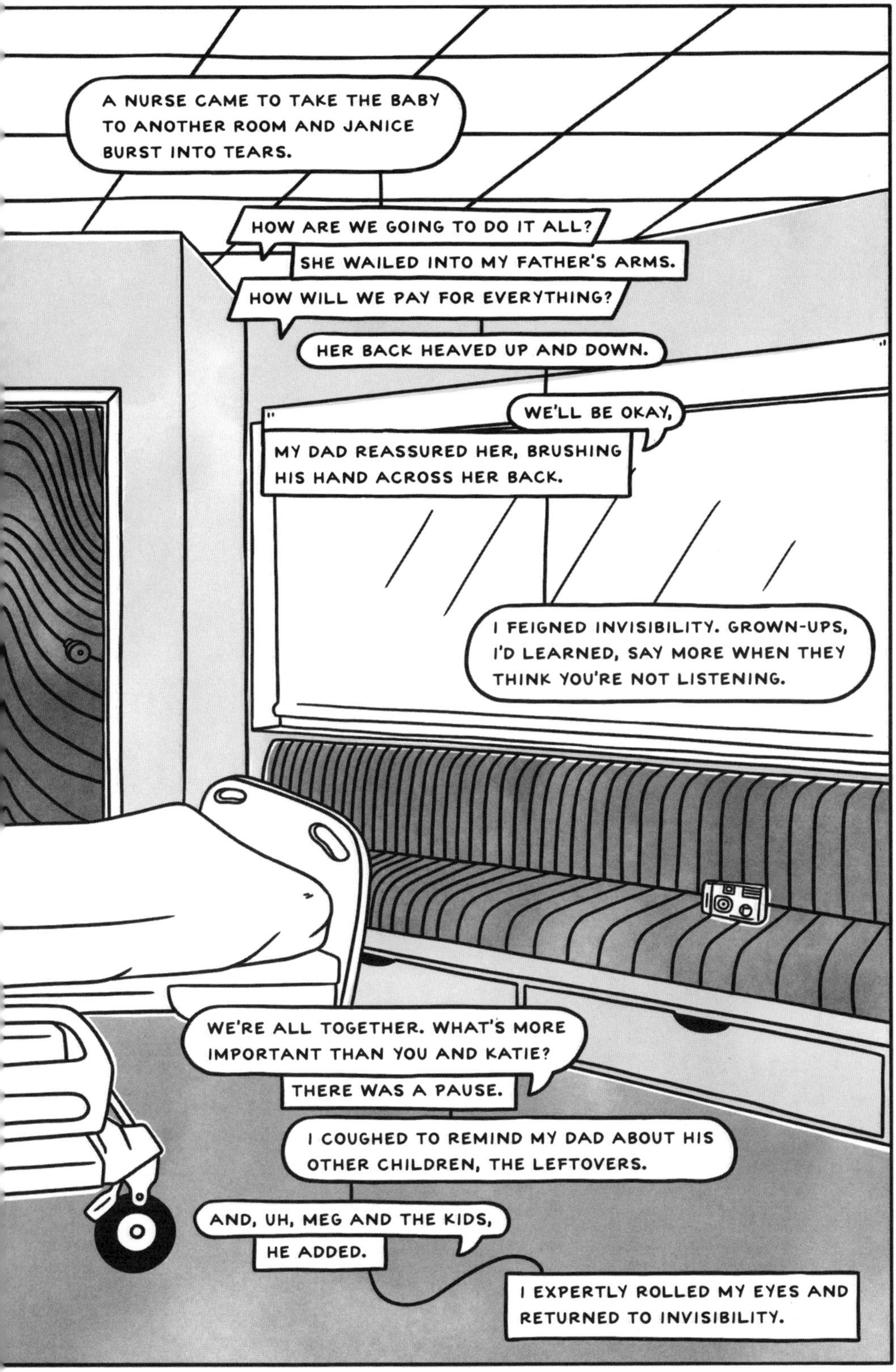
A NURSE CAME TO TAKE THE BABY TO ANOTHER ROOM AND JANICE BURST INTO TEARS.
HOW ARE WE GOING TO DO IT ALL?
SHE WAILED INTO MY FATHER'S ARMS.
HOW WILL WE PAY FOR EVERYTHING?
HER BACK HEAVED UP AND DOWN.
WE'LL BE OKAY,
MY DAD REASSURED HER, BRUSHING HIS HAND ACROSS HER BACK.
I FEIGNED INVISIBILITY. GROWN-UPS, I'D LEARNED, SAY MORE WHEN THEY THINK YOU'RE NOT LISTENING.
WE'RE ALL TOGETHER. WHAT'S MORE IMPORTANT THAN YOU AND KATIE?
THERE WAS A PAUSE.
I COUGHED TO REMIND MY DAD ABOUT HIS OTHER CHILDREN, THE LEFTOVERS.
AND, UH, MEG AND THE KIDS,
HE ADDED.
I EXPERTLY ROLLED MY EYES AND RETURNED TO INVISIBILITY.

MY ROOM AT MY MOM'S CONDO

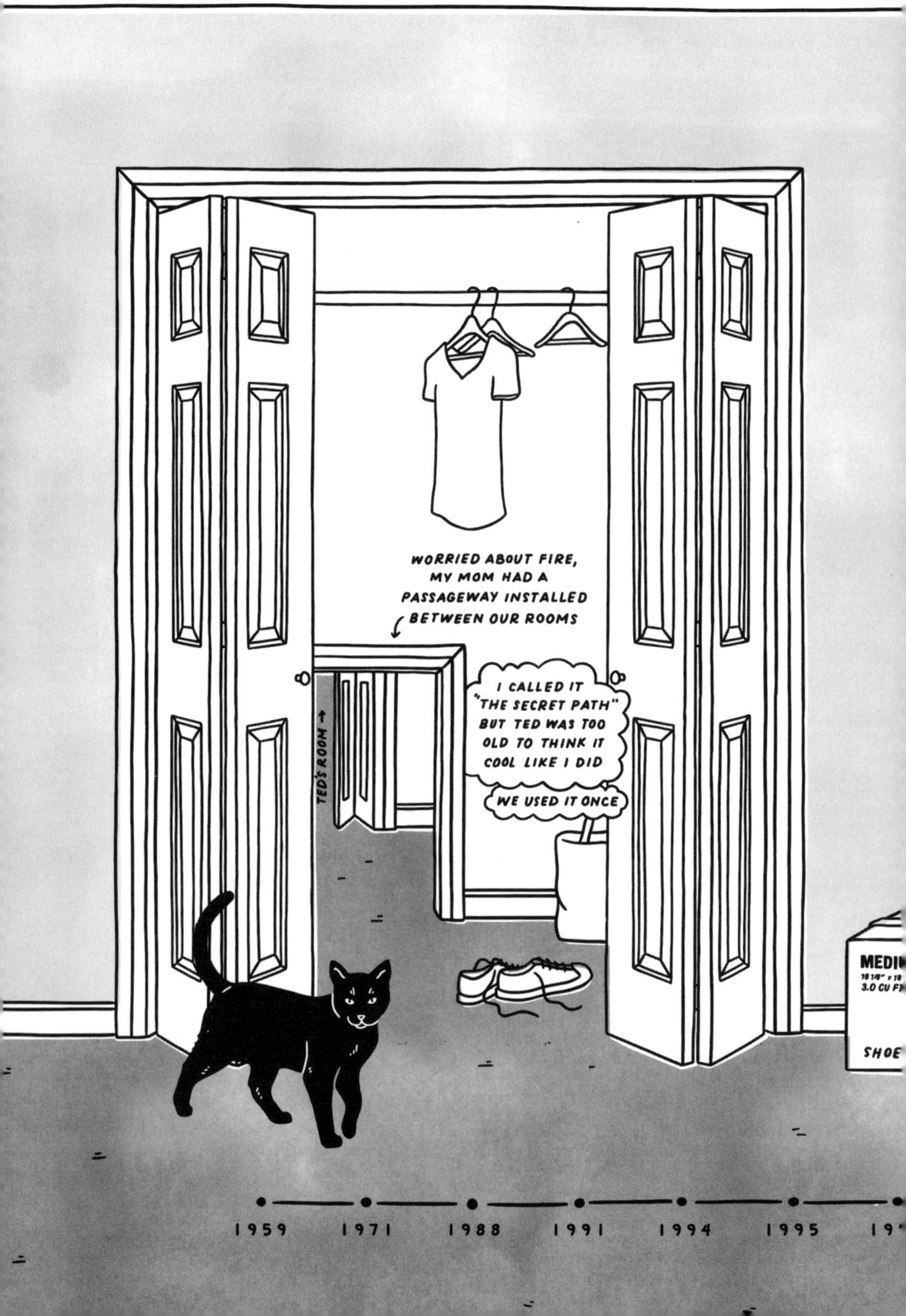
WORRIED ABOUT FIRE, MY MOM HAD A PASSAGEWAY INSTALLED BETWEEN OUR ROOMS
TED'S ROOM
I CALLED IT "THE SECRET PATH" BUT TED WAS TOO OLD TO THINK IT COOL LIKE I DID
WE USED IT ONCE
MEDI
3.0 CU F
SHOE
1959
1971
1988
1991
1994
1995

CHAPTER 12

The Move

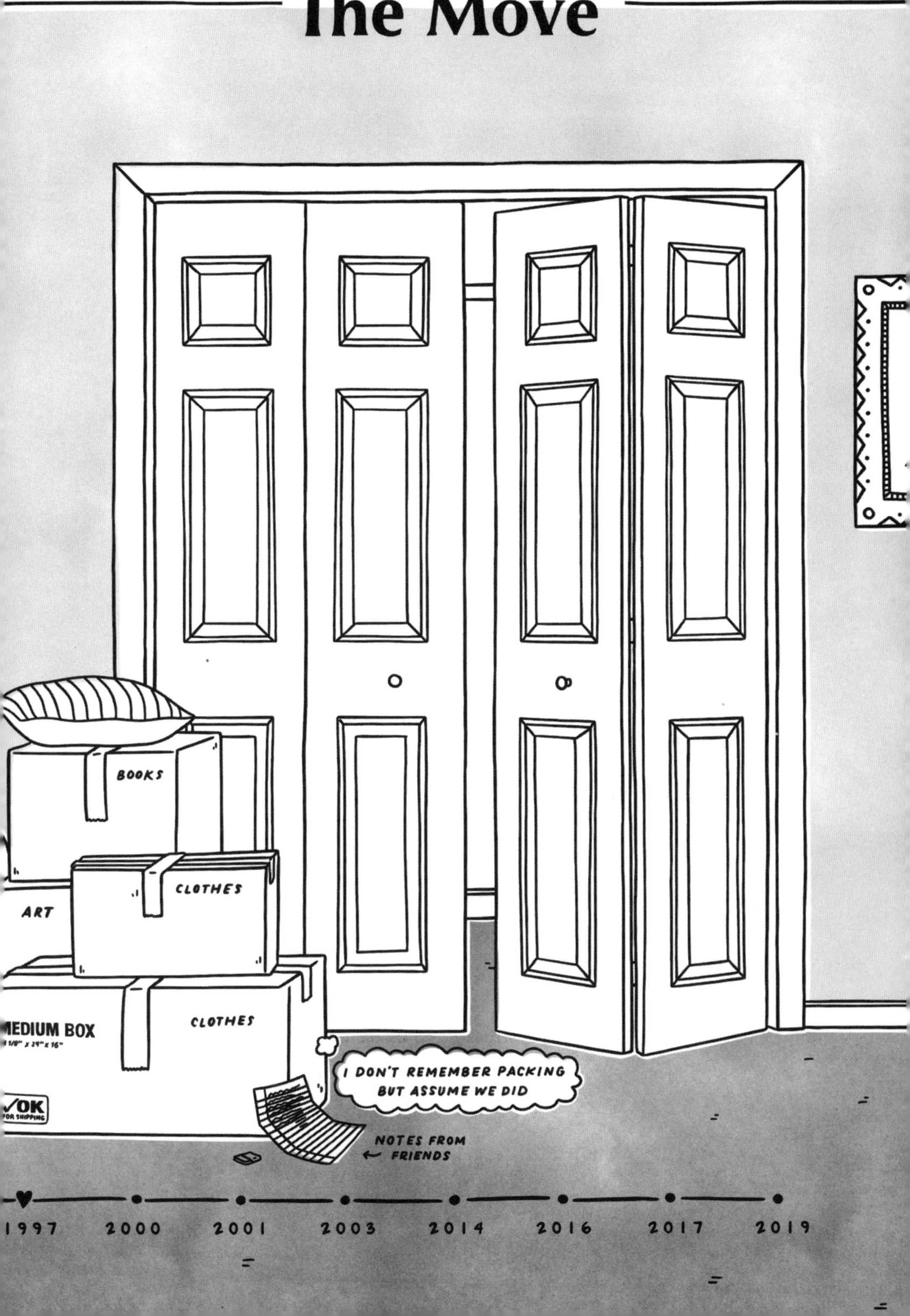
BOOKS
CLOTHES
ART
MEDIUM BOX
CLOTHES
OK FOR SHIPPING
I DON'T REMEMBER PACKING BUT ASSUME WE DID
NOTES FROM FRIENDS
1997
2000
2001
2003
2014
2016
2017
2019

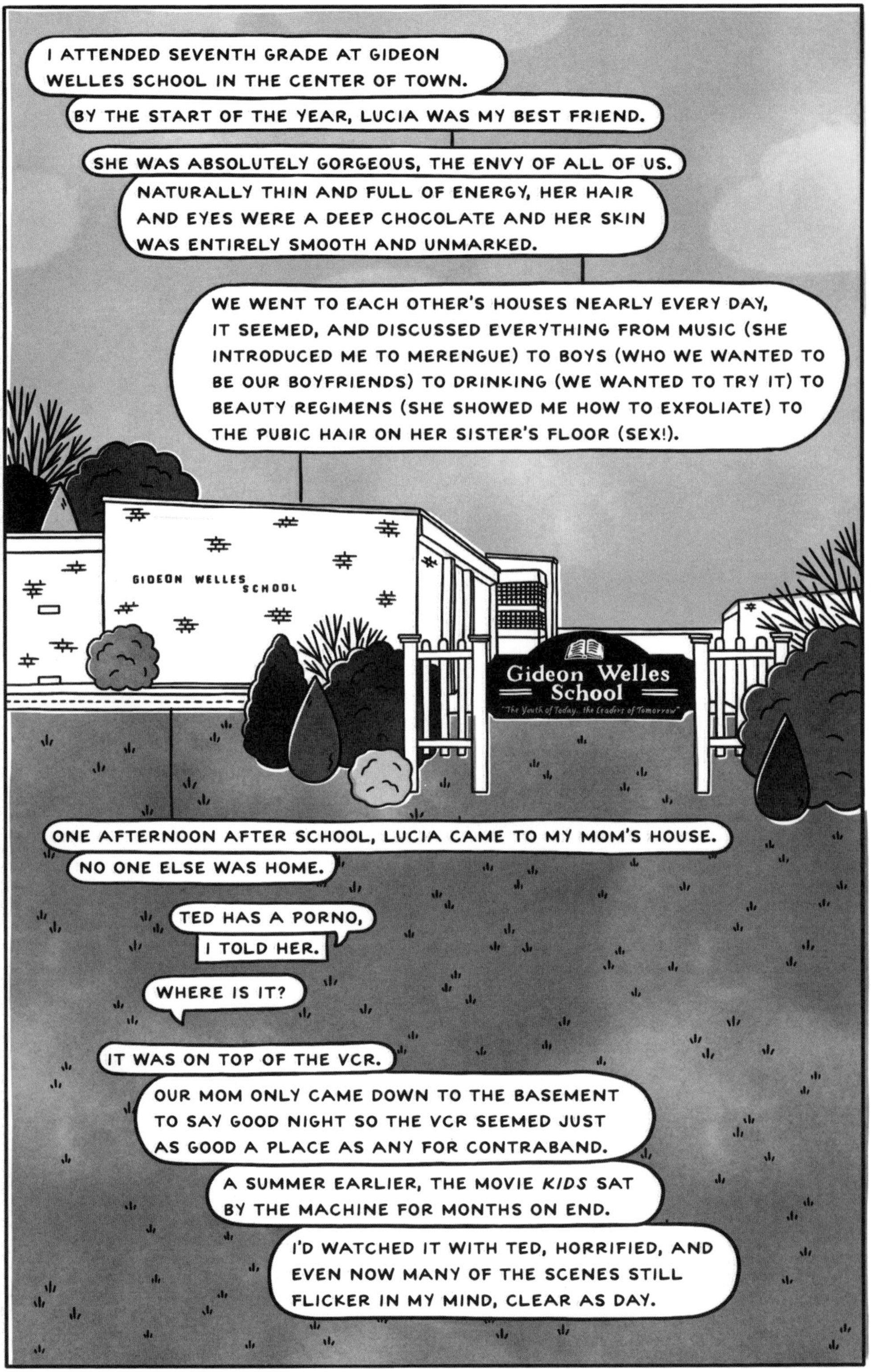
I ATTENDED SEVENTH GRADE AT GIDEON WELLES SCHOOL IN THE CENTER OF TOWN.
BY THE START OF THE YEAR, LUCIA WAS MY BEST FRIEND.
SHE WAS ABSOLUTELY GORGEOUS, THE ENVY OF ALL OF US.
NATURALLY THIN AND FULL OF ENERGY, HER HAIR AND EYES WERE A DEEP CHOCOLATE AND HER SKIN WAS ENTIRELY SMOOTH AND UNMARKED.
WE WENT TO EACH OTHER'S HOUSES NEARLY EVERY DAY, IT SEEMED, AND DISCUSSED EVERYTHING FROM MUSIC (SHE INTRODUCED ME TO MERENGUE) TO BOYS (WHO WE WANTED TO BE OUR BOYFRIENDS) TO DRINKING (WE WANTED TO TRY IT) TO BEAUTY REGIMENS (SHE SHOWED ME HOW TO EXFOLIATE) TO THE PUBIC HAIR ON HER SISTER'S FLOOR (SEX!).
GIDEON WELLES SCHOOL
Gideon Welles School
"The Youth of Today.. the Leaders of Tomorrow"
ONE AFTERNOON AFTER SCHOOL, LUCIA CAME TO MY MOM'S HOUSE.
NO ONE ELSE WAS HOME.
TED HAS A PORNO,
I TOLD HER.
WHERE IS IT?
IT WAS ON TOP OF THE VCR.
OUR MOM ONLY CAME DOWN TO THE BASEMENT TO SAY GOOD NIGHT SO THE VCR SEEMED JUST AS GOOD A PLACE AS ANY FOR CONTRABAND.
A SUMMER EARLIER, THE MOVIE *KIDS* SAT BY THE MACHINE FOR MONTHS ON END.
I'D WATCHED IT WITH TED, HORRIFIED, AND EVEN NOW MANY OF THE SCENES STILL FLICKER IN MY MIND, CLEAR AS DAY.

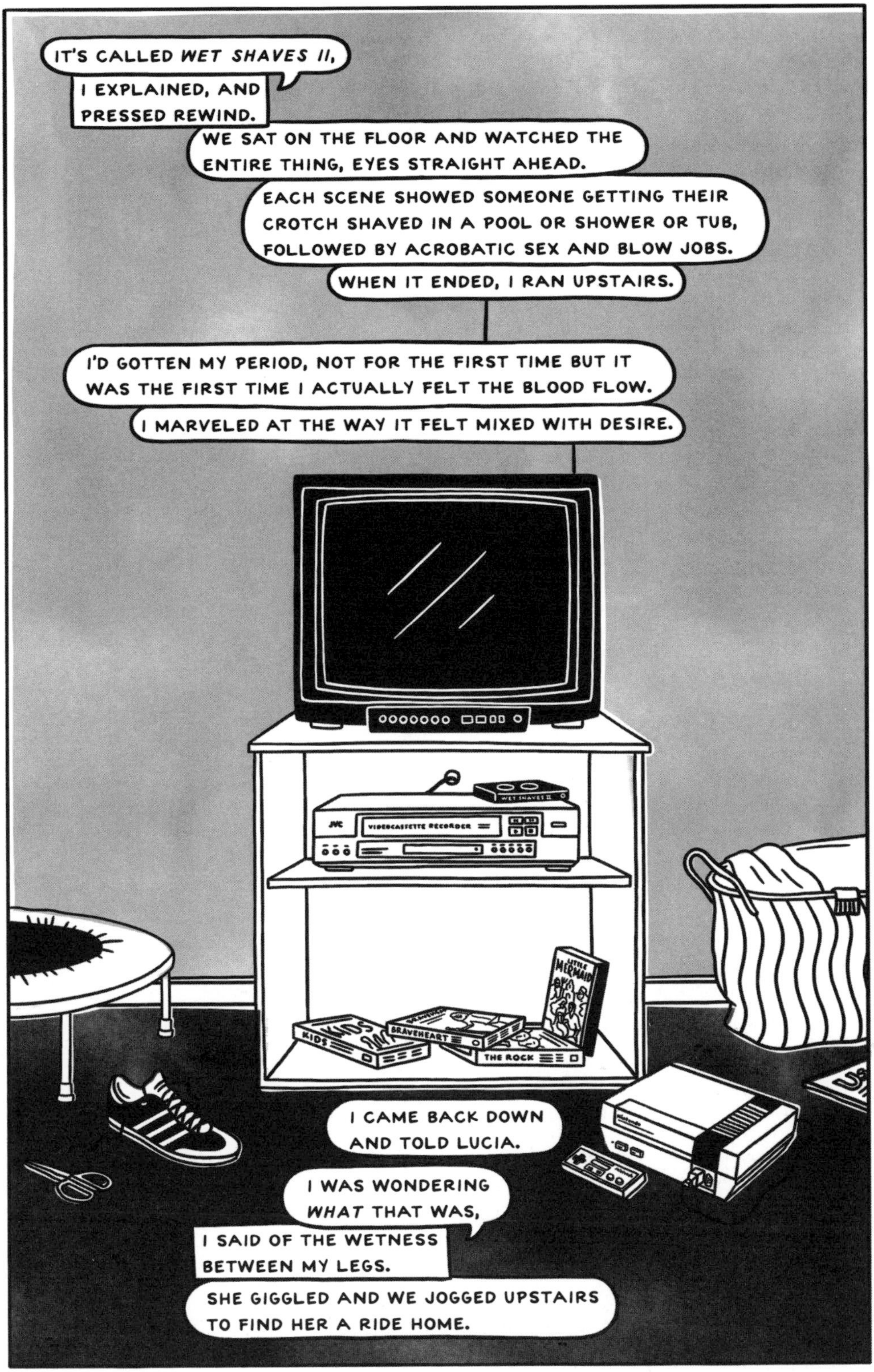

IT'S CALLED *WET SHAVES II*,
I EXPLAINED, AND PRESSED REWIND.
WE SAT ON THE FLOOR AND WATCHED THE ENTIRE THING, EYES STRAIGHT AHEAD.
EACH SCENE SHOWED SOMEONE GETTING THEIR CROTCH SHAVED IN A POOL OR SHOWER OR TUB, FOLLOWED BY ACROBATIC SEX AND BLOW JOBS.
WHEN IT ENDED, I RAN UPSTAIRS.
I'D GOTTEN MY PERIOD, NOT FOR THE FIRST TIME BUT IT WAS THE FIRST TIME I ACTUALLY FELT THE BLOOD FLOW.
I MARVELED AT THE WAY IT FELT MIXED WITH DESIRE.
WET SHAVES II
JVC
VIDEOCASSETTE RECORDER
LITTLE MERMAID
KIDS
BRAVEHEART
THE ROCK
I CAME BACK DOWN AND TOLD LUCIA.
I WAS WONDERING *WHAT* THAT WAS,
I SAID OF THE WETNESS BETWEEN MY LEGS.
SHE GIGGLED AND WE JOGGED UPSTAIRS TO FIND HER A RIDE HOME.

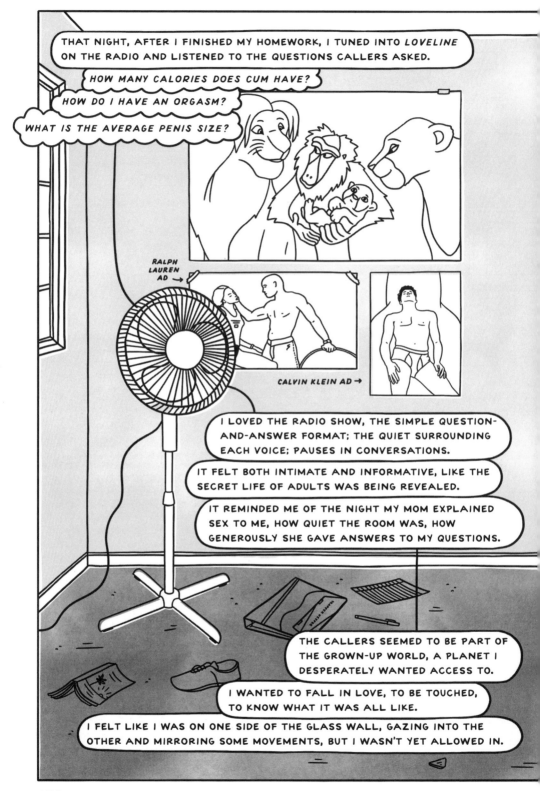

THAT NIGHT, AFTER I FINISHED MY HOMEWORK, I TUNED INTO *LOVELINE* ON THE RADIO AND LISTENED TO THE QUESTIONS CALLERS ASKED.

HOW MANY CALORIES DOES CUM HAVE?

HOW DO I HAVE AN ORGASM?

WHAT IS THE AVERAGE PENIS SIZE?

RALPH LAUREN AD →

CALVIN KLEIN AD →

I LOVED THE RADIO SHOW, THE SIMPLE QUESTION-AND-ANSWER FORMAT; THE QUIET SURROUNDING EACH VOICE; PAUSES IN CONVERSATIONS.

IT FELT BOTH INTIMATE AND INFORMATIVE, LIKE THE SECRET LIFE OF ADULTS WAS BEING REVEALED.

IT REMINDED ME OF THE NIGHT MY MOM EXPLAINED SEX TO ME, HOW QUIET THE ROOM WAS, HOW GENEROUSLY SHE GAVE ANSWERS TO MY QUESTIONS.

THE CALLERS SEEMED TO BE PART OF THE GROWN-UP WORLD, A PLANET I DESPERATELY WANTED ACCESS TO.

I WANTED TO FALL IN LOVE, TO BE TOUCHED, TO KNOW WHAT IT WAS ALL LIKE.

I FELT LIKE I WAS ON ONE SIDE OF THE GLASS WALL, GAZING INTO THE OTHER AND MIRRORING SOME MOVEMENTS, BUT I WASN'T YET ALLOWED IN.

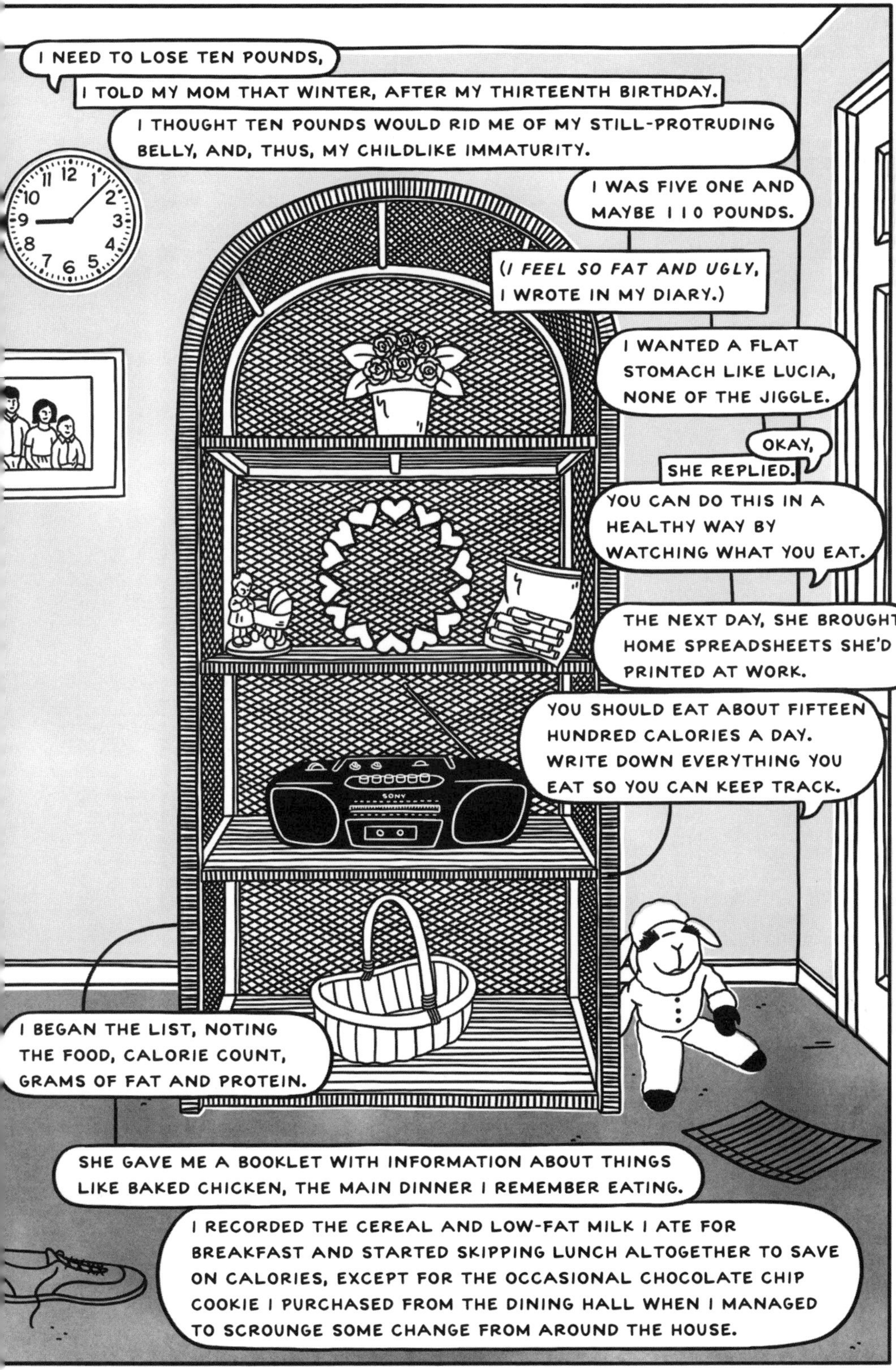

I NEED TO LOSE TEN POUNDS,
I TOLD MY MOM THAT WINTER, AFTER MY THIRTEENTH BIRTHDAY.
I THOUGHT TEN POUNDS WOULD RID ME OF MY STILL-PROTRUDING BELLY, AND, THUS, MY CHILDLIKE IMMATURITY.
I WAS FIVE ONE AND MAYBE 110 POUNDS.
(*I FEEL SO FAT AND UGLY,* I WROTE IN MY DIARY.)
I WANTED A FLAT STOMACH LIKE LUCIA, NONE OF THE JIGGLE.
OKAY,
SHE REPLIED.
YOU CAN DO THIS IN A HEALTHY WAY BY WATCHING WHAT YOU EAT.
THE NEXT DAY, SHE BROUGHT HOME SPREADSHEETS SHE'D PRINTED AT WORK.
YOU SHOULD EAT ABOUT FIFTEEN HUNDRED CALORIES A DAY. WRITE DOWN EVERYTHING YOU EAT SO YOU CAN KEEP TRACK.
I BEGAN THE LIST, NOTING THE FOOD, CALORIE COUNT, GRAMS OF FAT AND PROTEIN.
SHE GAVE ME A BOOKLET WITH INFORMATION ABOUT THINGS LIKE BAKED CHICKEN, THE MAIN DINNER I REMEMBER EATING.
I RECORDED THE CEREAL AND LOW-FAT MILK I ATE FOR BREAKFAST AND STARTED SKIPPING LUNCH ALTOGETHER TO SAVE ON CALORIES, EXCEPT FOR THE OCCASIONAL CHOCOLATE CHIP COOKIE I PURCHASED FROM THE DINING HALL WHEN I MANAGED TO SCROUNGE SOME CHANGE FROM AROUND THE HOUSE.

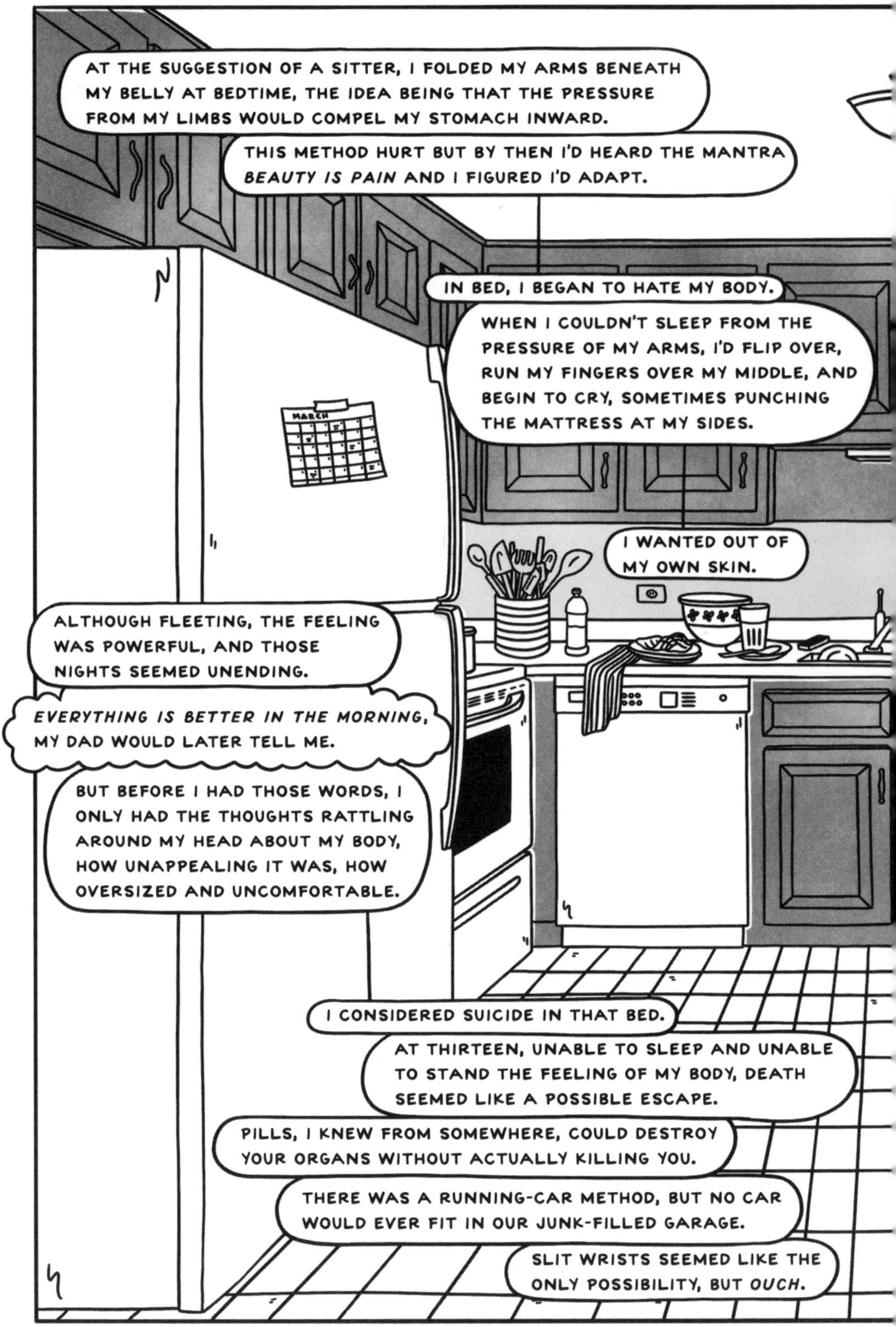
AT THE SUGGESTION OF A SITTER, I FOLDED MY ARMS BENEATH MY BELLY AT BEDTIME, THE IDEA BEING THAT THE PRESSURE FROM MY LIMBS WOULD COMPEL MY STOMACH INWARD.
THIS METHOD HURT BUT BY THEN I'D HEARD THE MANTRA *BEAUTY IS PAIN* AND I FIGURED I'D ADAPT.
IN BED, I BEGAN TO HATE MY BODY.
WHEN I COULDN'T SLEEP FROM THE PRESSURE OF MY ARMS, I'D FLIP OVER, RUN MY FINGERS OVER MY MIDDLE, AND BEGIN TO CRY, SOMETIMES PUNCHING THE MATTRESS AT MY SIDES.
I WANTED OUT OF MY OWN SKIN.
ALTHOUGH FLEETING, THE FEELING WAS POWERFUL, AND THOSE NIGHTS SEEMED UNENDING.
EVERYTHING IS BETTER IN THE MORNING, MY DAD WOULD LATER TELL ME.
BUT BEFORE I HAD THOSE WORDS, I ONLY HAD THE THOUGHTS RATTLING AROUND MY HEAD ABOUT MY BODY, HOW UNAPPEALING IT WAS, HOW OVERSIZED AND UNCOMFORTABLE.
I CONSIDERED SUICIDE IN THAT BED.
AT THIRTEEN, UNABLE TO SLEEP AND UNABLE TO STAND THE FEELING OF MY BODY, DEATH SEEMED LIKE A POSSIBLE ESCAPE.
PILLS, I KNEW FROM SOMEWHERE, COULD DESTROY YOUR ORGANS WITHOUT ACTUALLY KILLING YOU.
THERE WAS A RUNNING-CAR METHOD, BUT NO CAR WOULD EVER FIT IN OUR JUNK-FILLED GARAGE.
SLIT WRISTS SEEMED LIKE THE ONLY POSSIBILITY, BUT *OUCH*.

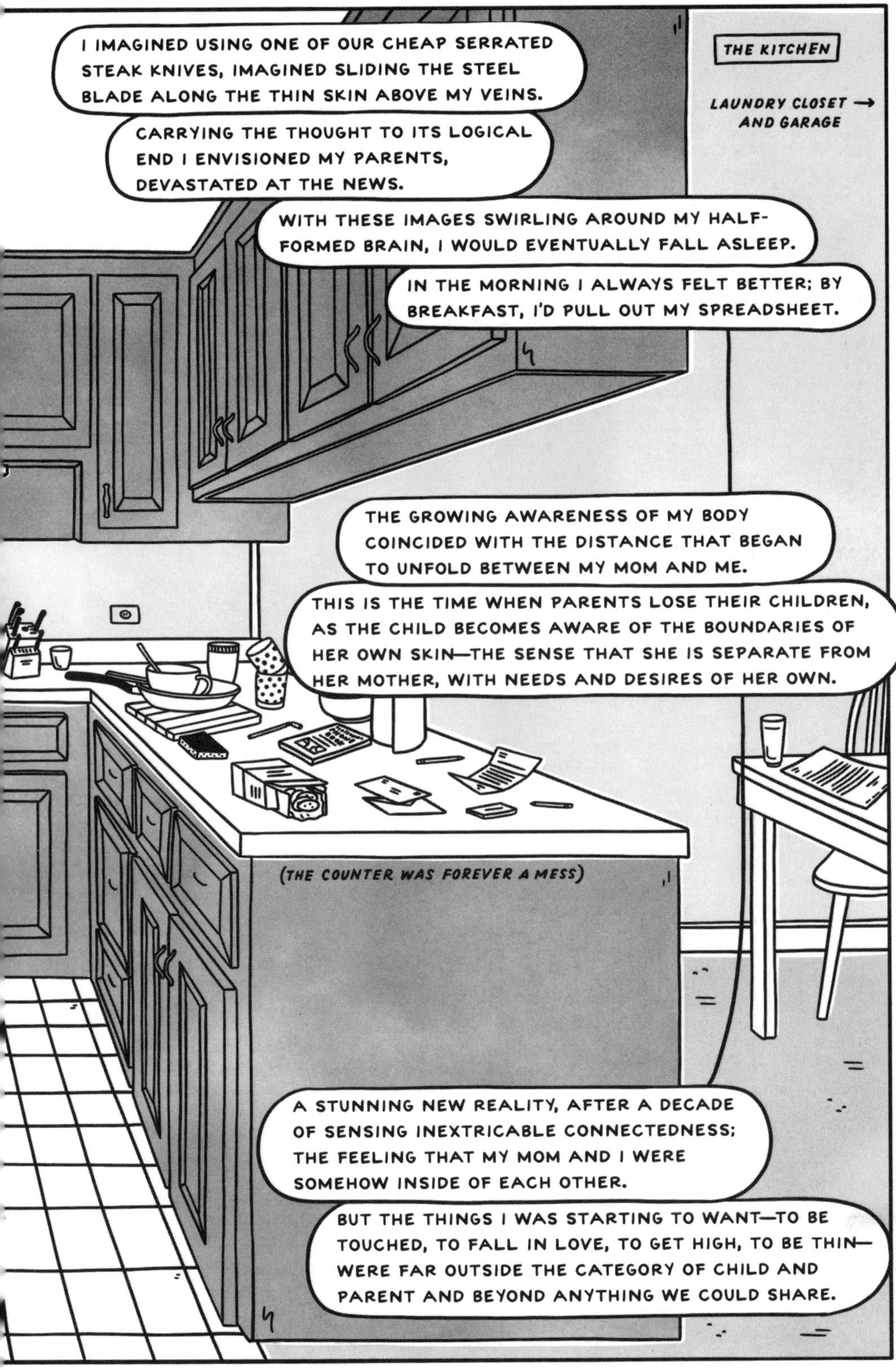

I IMAGINED USING ONE OF OUR CHEAP SERRATED STEAK KNIVES, IMAGINED SLIDING THE STEEL BLADE ALONG THE THIN SKIN ABOVE MY VEINS.
CARRYING THE THOUGHT TO ITS LOGICAL END I ENVISIONED MY PARENTS, DEVASTATED AT THE NEWS.
WITH THESE IMAGES SWIRLING AROUND MY HALF-FORMED BRAIN, I WOULD EVENTUALLY FALL ASLEEP.
IN THE MORNING I ALWAYS FELT BETTER; BY BREAKFAST, I'D PULL OUT MY SPREADSHEET.
THE KITCHEN
LAUNDRY CLOSET AND GARAGE →
THE GROWING AWARENESS OF MY BODY COINCIDED WITH THE DISTANCE THAT BEGAN TO UNFOLD BETWEEN MY MOM AND ME.
THIS IS THE TIME WHEN PARENTS LOSE THEIR CHILDREN, AS THE CHILD BECOMES AWARE OF THE BOUNDARIES OF HER OWN SKIN—THE SENSE THAT SHE IS SEPARATE FROM HER MOTHER, WITH NEEDS AND DESIRES OF HER OWN.
(THE COUNTER WAS FOREVER A MESS)
A STUNNING NEW REALITY, AFTER A DECADE OF SENSING INEXTRICABLE CONNECTEDNESS; THE FEELING THAT MY MOM AND I WERE SOMEHOW INSIDE OF EACH OTHER.
BUT THE THINGS I WAS STARTING TO WANT—TO BE TOUCHED, TO FALL IN LOVE, TO GET HIGH, TO BE THIN—WERE FAR OUTSIDE THE CATEGORY OF CHILD AND PARENT AND BEYOND ANYTHING WE COULD SHARE.

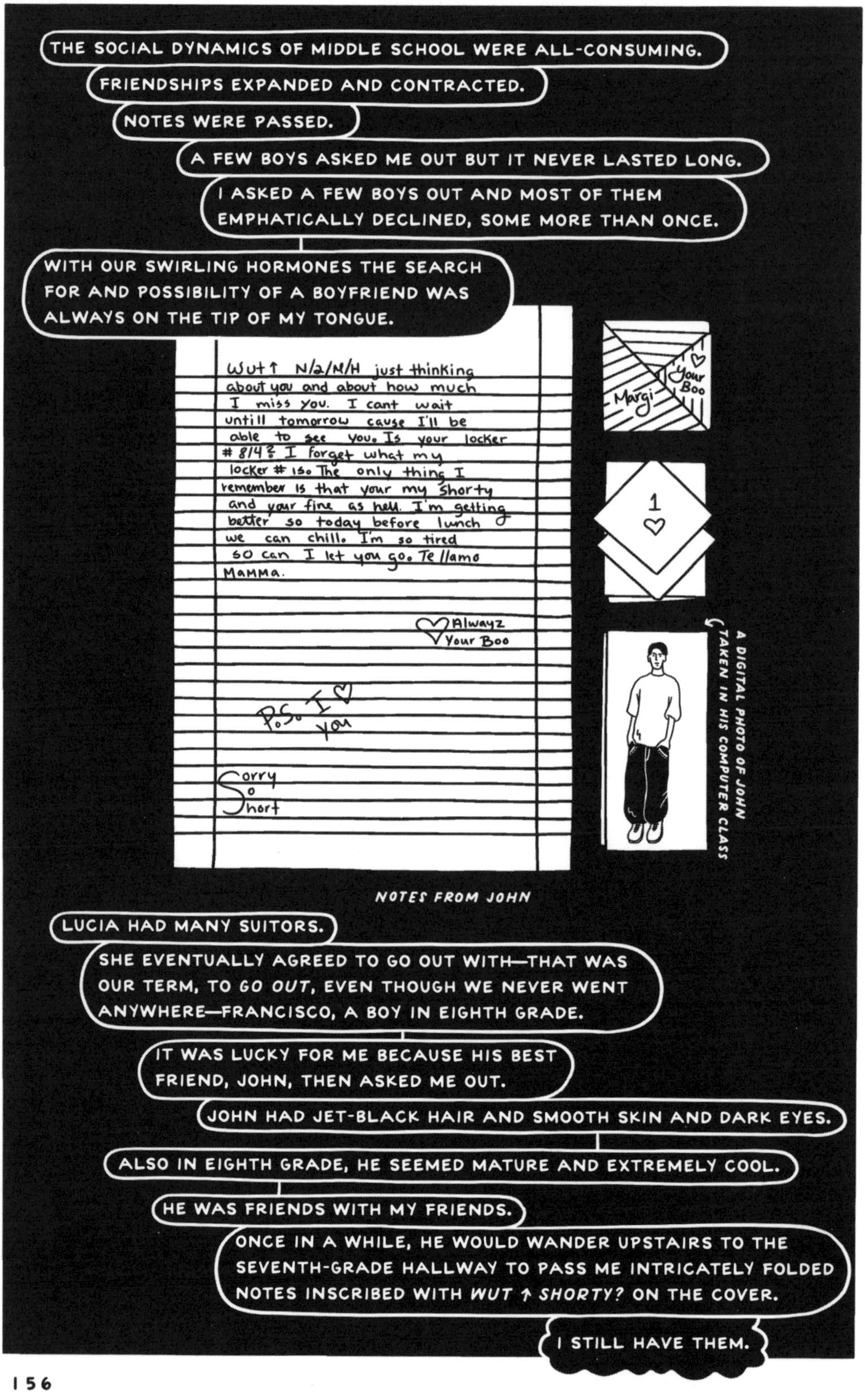
THE SOCIAL DYNAMICS OF MIDDLE SCHOOL WERE ALL-CONSUMING.
FRIENDSHIPS EXPANDED AND CONTRACTED.
NOTES WERE PASSED.
A FEW BOYS ASKED ME OUT BUT IT NEVER LASTED LONG.
I ASKED A FEW BOYS OUT AND MOST OF THEM EMPHATICALLY DECLINED, SOME MORE THAN ONCE.
WITH OUR SWIRLING HORMONES THE SEARCH FOR AND POSSIBILITY OF A BOYFRIEND WAS ALWAYS ON THE TIP OF MY TONGUE.
Wut↑ N/a/N/H just thinking about you and about how much I miss you. I cant wait untill tomorrow cause I'll be able to see you. Is your locker # 814? I forget what my locker # is. The only thing I remember is that your my Shorty and your fine as hell. I'm getting better so today before lunch we can chill. I'm so tired so can I let you go. Te llamo Mamma.
Alwayz Your Boo
P.S. I ♡ you
Sorry So Short
Margi
Your Boo
1
A DIGITAL PHOTO OF JOHN TAKEN IN HIS COMPUTER CLASS
NOTES FROM JOHN
LUCIA HAD MANY SUITORS.
SHE EVENTUALLY AGREED TO GO OUT WITH—THAT WAS OUR TERM, TO *GO OUT*, EVEN THOUGH WE NEVER WENT ANYWHERE—FRANCISCO, A BOY IN EIGHTH GRADE.
IT WAS LUCKY FOR ME BECAUSE HIS BEST FRIEND, JOHN, THEN ASKED ME OUT.
JOHN HAD JET-BLACK HAIR AND SMOOTH SKIN AND DARK EYES.
ALSO IN EIGHTH GRADE, HE SEEMED MATURE AND EXTREMELY COOL.
HE WAS FRIENDS WITH MY FRIENDS.
ONCE IN A WHILE, HE WOULD WANDER UPSTAIRS TO THE SEVENTH-GRADE HALLWAY TO PASS ME INTRICATELY FOLDED NOTES INSCRIBED WITH *WUT ↑ SHORTY?* ON THE COVER.
I STILL HAVE THEM.

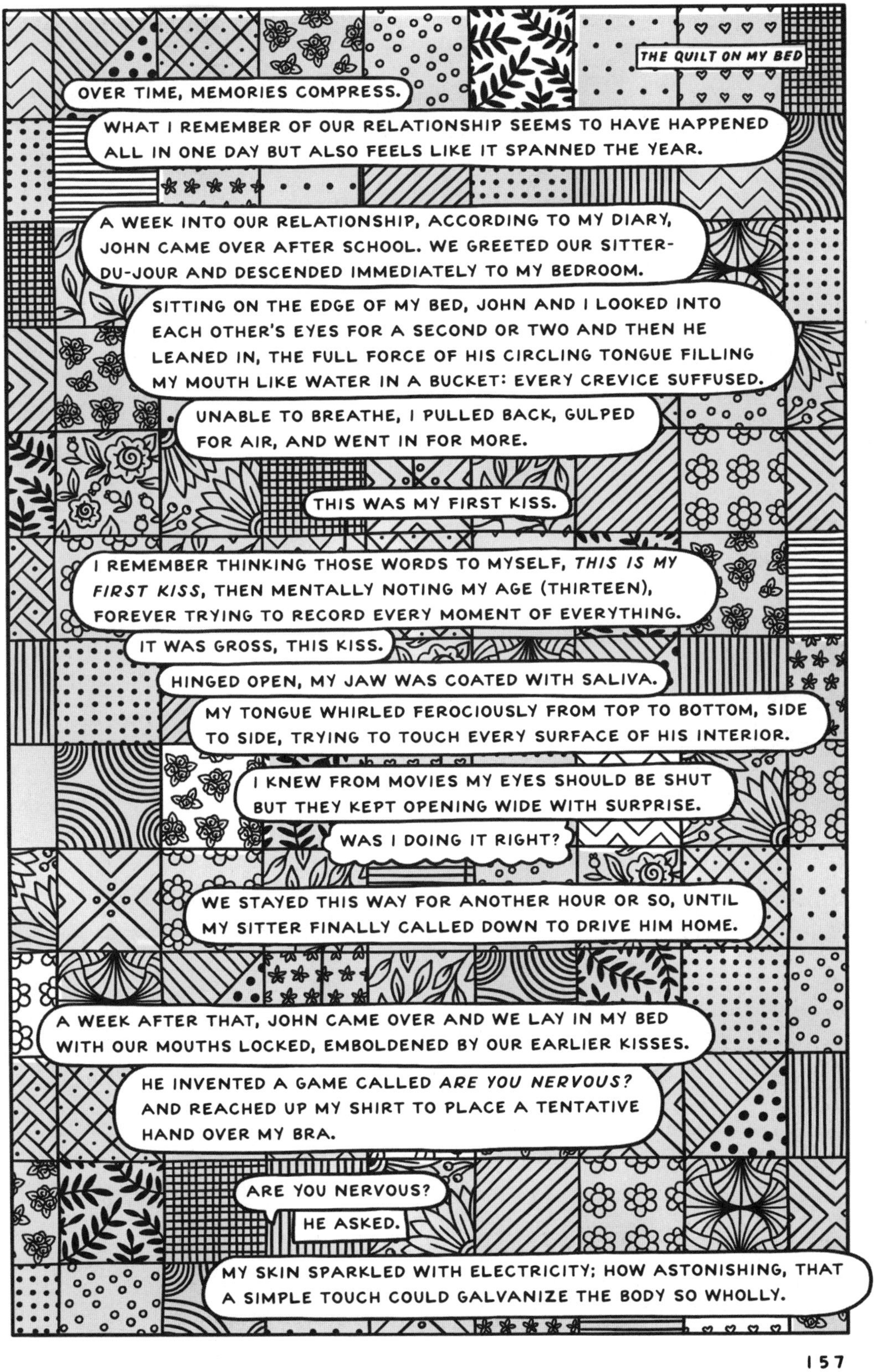
THE QUILT ON MY BED
OVER TIME, MEMORIES COMPRESS.
WHAT I REMEMBER OF OUR RELATIONSHIP SEEMS TO HAVE HAPPENED ALL IN ONE DAY BUT ALSO FEELS LIKE IT SPANNED THE YEAR.
A WEEK INTO OUR RELATIONSHIP, ACCORDING TO MY DIARY, JOHN CAME OVER AFTER SCHOOL. WE GREETED OUR SITTER-DU-JOUR AND DESCENDED IMMEDIATELY TO MY BEDROOM.
SITTING ON THE EDGE OF MY BED, JOHN AND I LOOKED INTO EACH OTHER'S EYES FOR A SECOND OR TWO AND THEN HE LEANED IN, THE FULL FORCE OF HIS CIRCLING TONGUE FILLING MY MOUTH LIKE WATER IN A BUCKET: EVERY CREVICE SUFFUSED.
UNABLE TO BREATHE, I PULLED BACK, GULPED FOR AIR, AND WENT IN FOR MORE.
THIS WAS MY FIRST KISS.
I REMEMBER THINKING THOSE WORDS TO MYSELF, *THIS IS MY FIRST KISS*, THEN MENTALLY NOTING MY AGE (THIRTEEN), FOREVER TRYING TO RECORD EVERY MOMENT OF EVERYTHING.
IT WAS GROSS, THIS KISS.
HINGED OPEN, MY JAW WAS COATED WITH SALIVA.
MY TONGUE WHIRLED FEROCIOUSLY FROM TOP TO BOTTOM, SIDE TO SIDE, TRYING TO TOUCH EVERY SURFACE OF HIS INTERIOR.
I KNEW FROM MOVIES MY EYES SHOULD BE SHUT BUT THEY KEPT OPENING WIDE WITH SURPRISE.
WAS I DOING IT RIGHT?
WE STAYED THIS WAY FOR ANOTHER HOUR OR SO, UNTIL MY SITTER FINALLY CALLED DOWN TO DRIVE HIM HOME.
A WEEK AFTER THAT, JOHN CAME OVER AND WE LAY IN MY BED WITH OUR MOUTHS LOCKED, EMBOLDENED BY OUR EARLIER KISSES.
HE INVENTED A GAME CALLED *ARE YOU NERVOUS?* AND REACHED UP MY SHIRT TO PLACE A TENTATIVE HAND OVER MY BRA.
ARE YOU NERVOUS?
HE ASKED.
MY SKIN SPARKLED WITH ELECTRICITY; HOW ASTONISHING, THAT A SIMPLE TOUCH COULD GALVANIZE THE BODY SO WHOLLY.

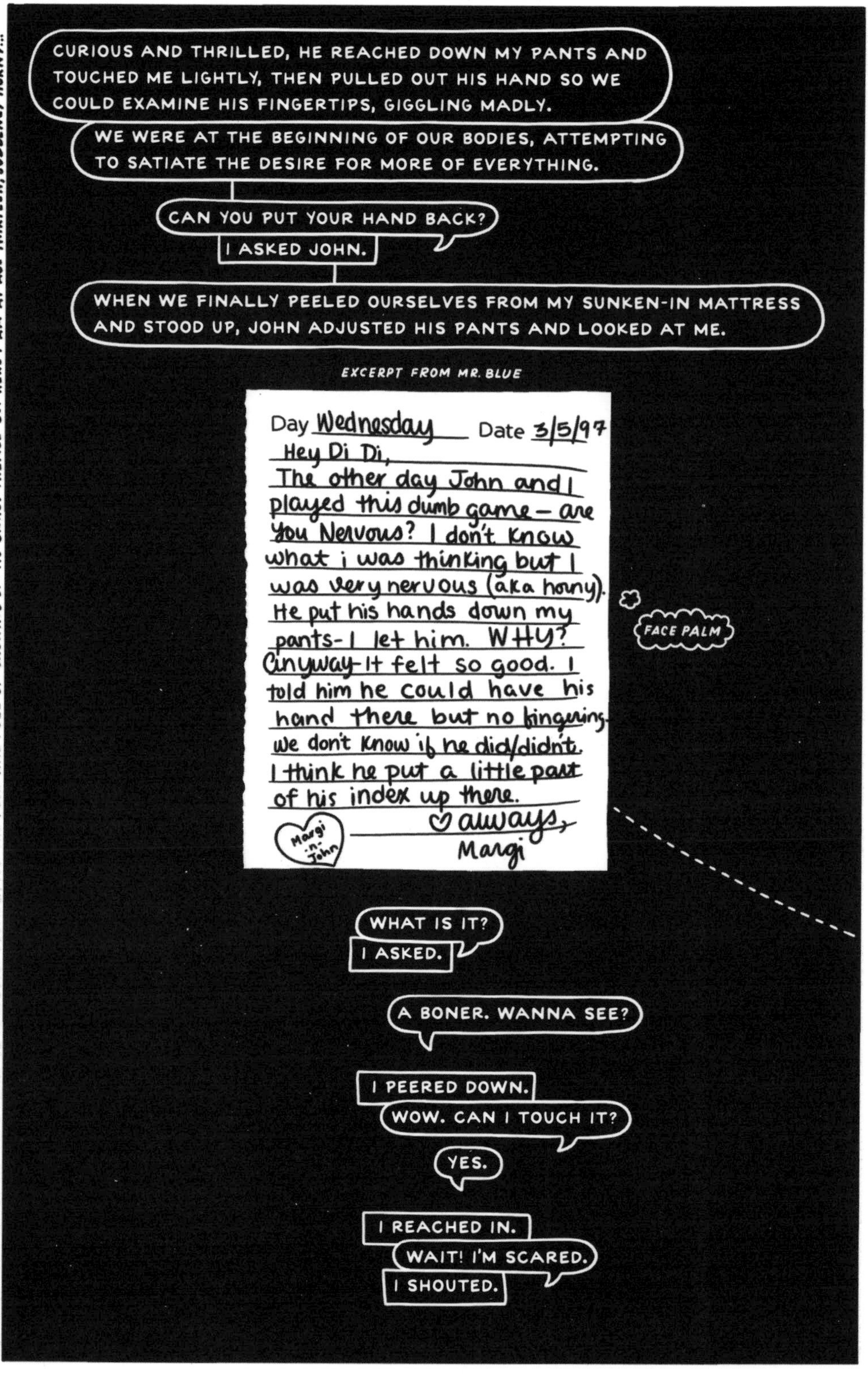

CURIOUS AND THRILLED, HE REACHED DOWN MY PANTS AND TOUCHED ME LIGHTLY, THEN PULLED OUT HIS HAND SO WE COULD EXAMINE HIS FINGERTIPS, GIGGLING MADLY.
WE WERE AT THE BEGINNING OF OUR BODIES, ATTEMPTING TO SATIATE THE DESIRE FOR MORE OF EVERYTHING.
CAN YOU PUT YOUR HAND BACK?
I ASKED JOHN.
WHEN WE FINALLY PEELED OURSELVES FROM MY SUNKEN-IN MATTRESS AND STOOD UP, JOHN ADJUSTED HIS PANTS AND LOOKED AT ME.
EXCERPT FROM MR. BLUE
Day Wednesday Date 3/5/97
Hey Di Di,
The other day John and I played this dumb game – are you Nervous? I don't know what i was thinking but I was very nervous (aka horny). He put his hands down my pants- I let him. WHY? anyway- It felt so good. I told him he could have his hand there but no fingering. we don't know if he did/didn't. I think he put a little part of his index up there.
♡ always,
Margi
Margi-n-John
FACE PALM
WHAT IS IT?
I ASKED.
A BONER. WANNA SEE?
I PEERED DOWN.
WOW. CAN I TOUCH IT?
YES.
I REACHED IN.
WAIT! I'M SCARED.
I SHOUTED.

I LOVE HOW THIS LITTLE MERMAID DIARY SO PERFECTLY EXEMPLIFIES THE PUSH AND PULL OF GROWING UP: IT'S DISNEY THEMED BUT HERE I AM AT AGE THIRTEEN, SUDDENLY HORNY...

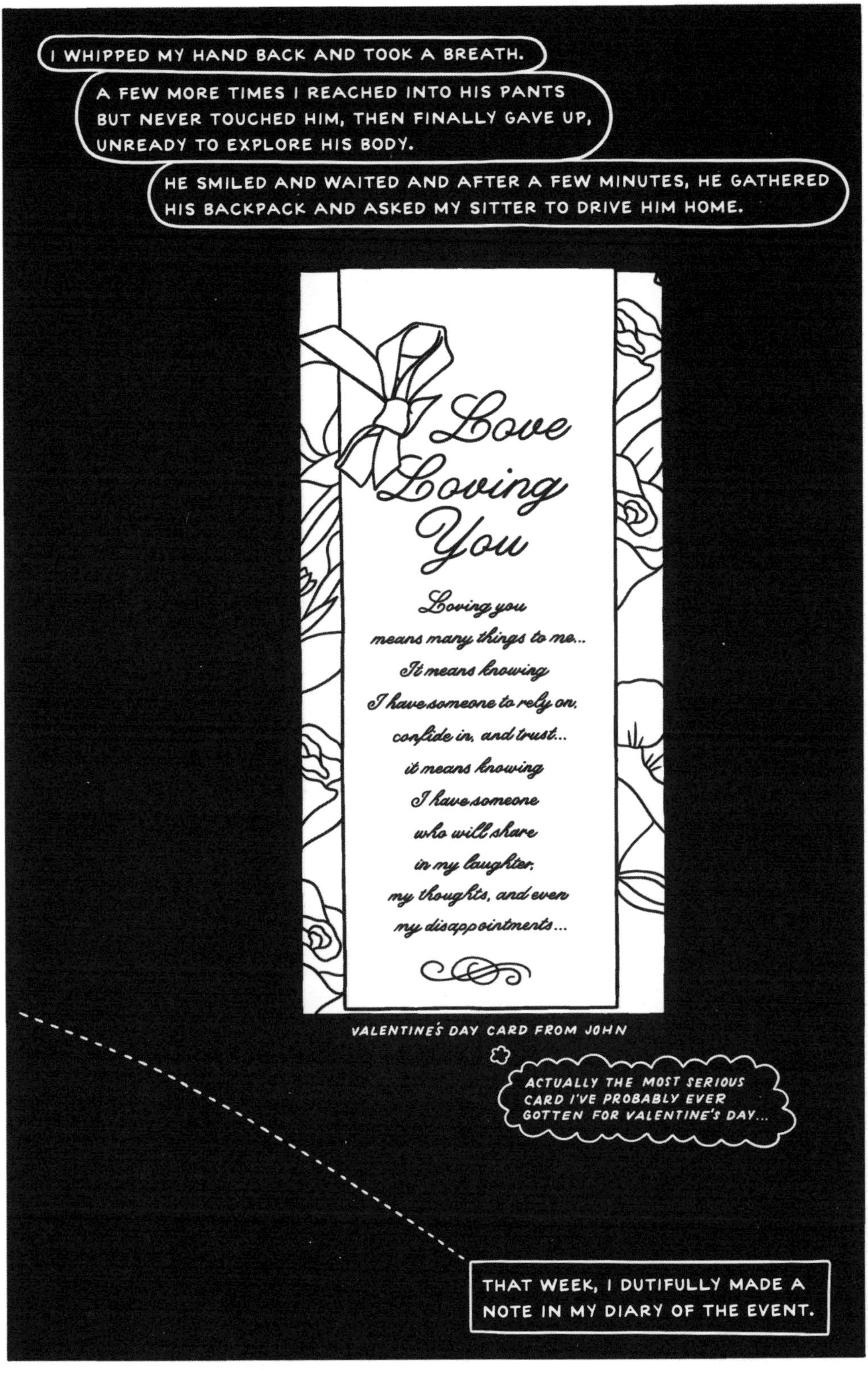
I WHIPPED MY HAND BACK AND TOOK A BREATH.
A FEW MORE TIMES I REACHED INTO HIS PANTS BUT NEVER TOUCHED HIM, THEN FINALLY GAVE UP, UNREADY TO EXPLORE HIS BODY.
HE SMILED AND WAITED AND AFTER A FEW MINUTES, HE GATHERED HIS BACKPACK AND ASKED MY SITTER TO DRIVE HIM HOME.
I Love Loving You
Loving you means many things to me... It means knowing I have someone to rely on, confide in, and trust... it means knowing I have someone who will share in my laughter, my thoughts, and even my disappointments...
VALENTINE'S DAY CARD FROM JOHN
ACTUALLY THE MOST SERIOUS CARD I'VE PROBABLY EVER GOTTEN FOR VALENTINE'S DAY...
THAT WEEK, I DUTIFULLY MADE A NOTE IN MY DIARY OF THE EVENT.

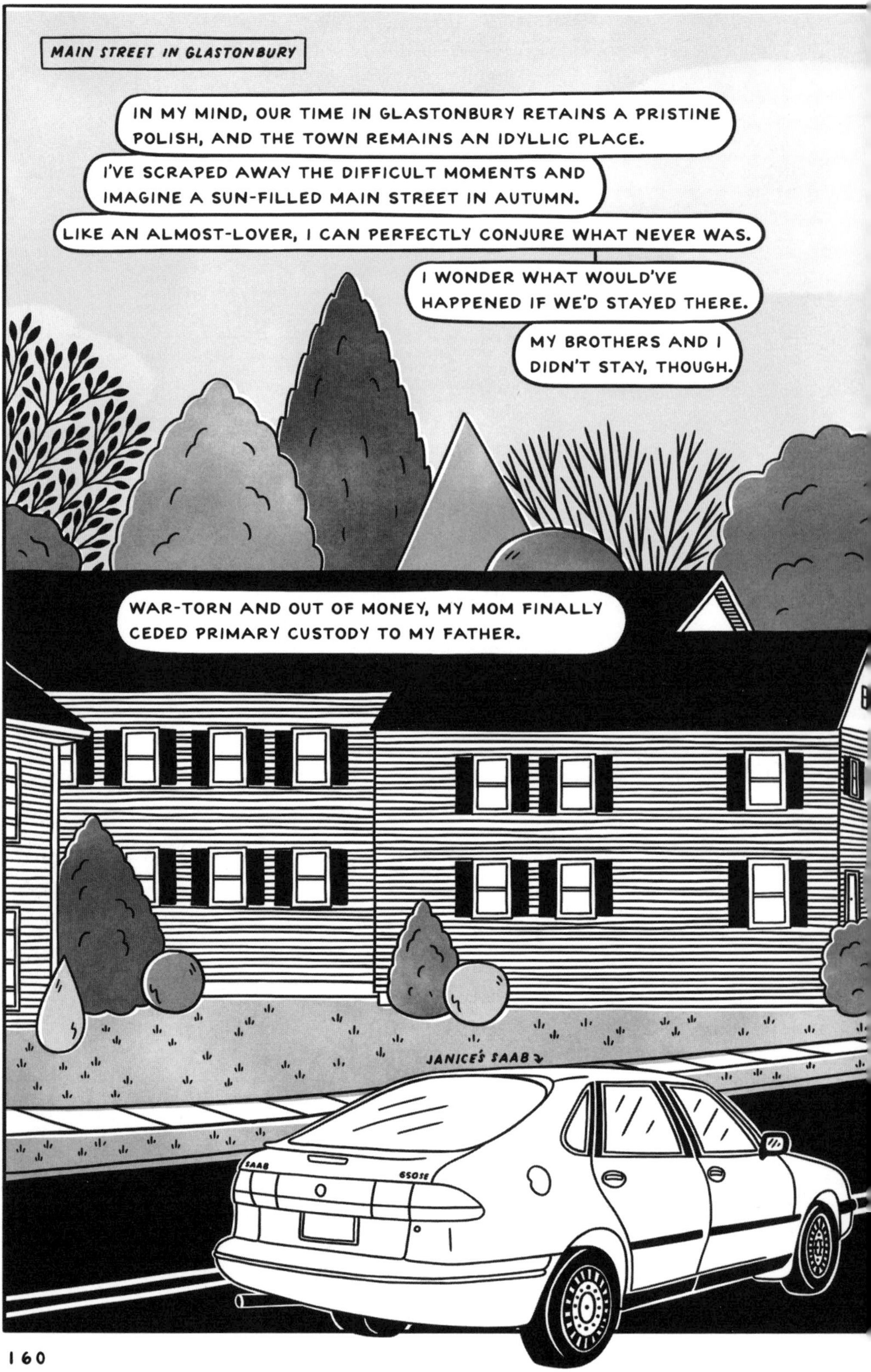
MAIN STREET IN GLASTONBURY
IN MY MIND, OUR TIME IN GLASTONBURY RETAINS A PRISTINE POLISH, AND THE TOWN REMAINS AN IDYLLIC PLACE.
I'VE SCRAPED AWAY THE DIFFICULT MOMENTS AND IMAGINE A SUN-FILLED MAIN STREET IN AUTUMN.
LIKE AN ALMOST-LOVER, I CAN PERFECTLY CONJURE WHAT NEVER WAS.
I WONDER WHAT WOULD'VE HAPPENED IF WE'D STAYED THERE.
MY BROTHERS AND I DIDN'T STAY, THOUGH.
WAR-TORN AND OUT OF MONEY, MY MOM FINALLY CEDED PRIMARY CUSTODY TO MY FATHER.
JANICE'S SAAB
SAAB
9-5 SE

WE WOULD MOVE TO CHESHIRE, A TOWN FORTY-FIVE MINUTES SOUTHEAST OF GLASTONBURY.

A NEW HOUSE HAD BEEN BUILT IN A NEW DEVELOPMENT AND WE'D LIVE IN IT WITH JANICE, MY DAD, AND KATIE, WHO WAS APPROACHING ONE YEAR OLD.

MY CAT WOULD STAY BEHIND, SINCE JANICE WAS ALLERGIC.

MY BROTHERS AND I WOULD VISIT MY MOM ON THE WEEKENDS AND DURING BREAKS, EXEMPTING THE FIRST SUMMER SO WE COULD ATTEND HOLIDAY HILL SUMMER CAMP AND MAKE NEW FRIENDS (FLASH FORWARD: I MADE ZERO FRIENDS).

WHEN I ASKED MY DAD WHY WE HAD TO LEAVE GLASTONBURY, HE SAID CHESHIRE WAS HALFWAY BETWEEN HIS JOB AND JANICE'S.

I WAS FURIOUS.

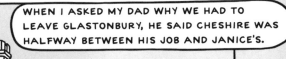

BUT ALSO: MAYBE YOU NEED TO LEAVE THE PLACE WHERE YOUR HEART WAS BROKEN. GLASTONBURY, THOUGH SPARKLING AND BEAUTIFUL IN MY MIND, WOULD ALWAYS CONTAIN THE ROADS THAT LED TO LAWYERS AND PSYCHOLOGISTS AND COURTROOMS THAT DEVASTATED MY PARENTS, THAT RIPPED OPEN WOUNDS THAT LEFT EVERLASTING BRUISES ON BOTH OF THEM. IN A KNOCKDOWN BATTLE FOR CUSTODY EVERYONE LOSES: THE KIDS LOSE THEIR PARENTS TO THE FIGHT; THE PARENTS LOSE SIGHT OF THE KIDS, OF ANY LOVE THEY FELT FOR EACH OTHER; MONEY AVALANCHES OUT OF BANK ACCOUNTS. THAT MY DAD WON PRIMARY TIME-SHARING WAS NO VICTORY; IT WAS JUST THE BEST IDEA HE COULD COME UP WITH IN HIS ATTEMPT TO SHIELD US, TO GIVE US A STABLE LIFE.

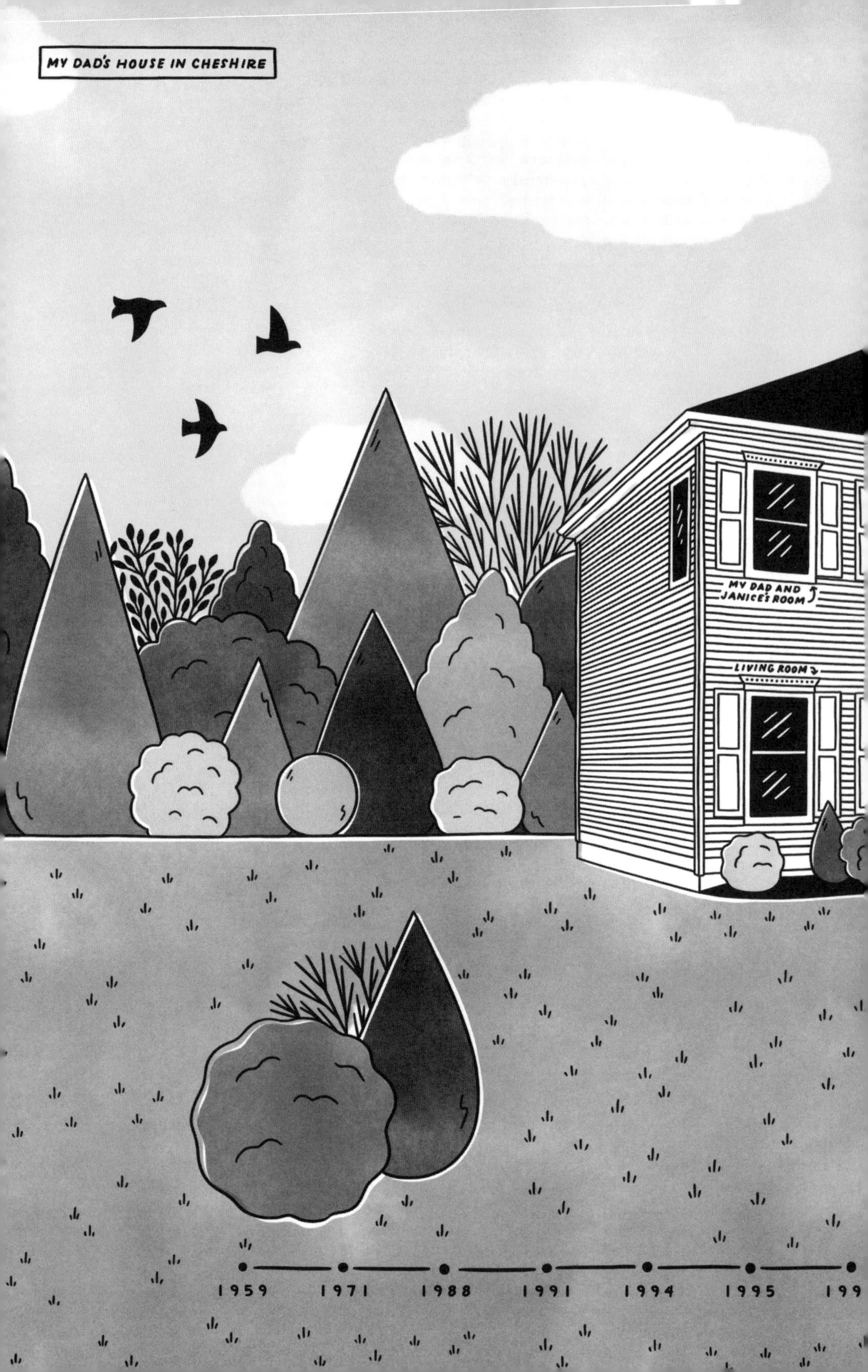
MY DAD'S HOUSE IN CHESHIRE
MY DAD AND JANICE'S ROOM
LIVING ROOM
1959
1971
1988
1991
1994
1995

CHAPTER 13
The Blue House

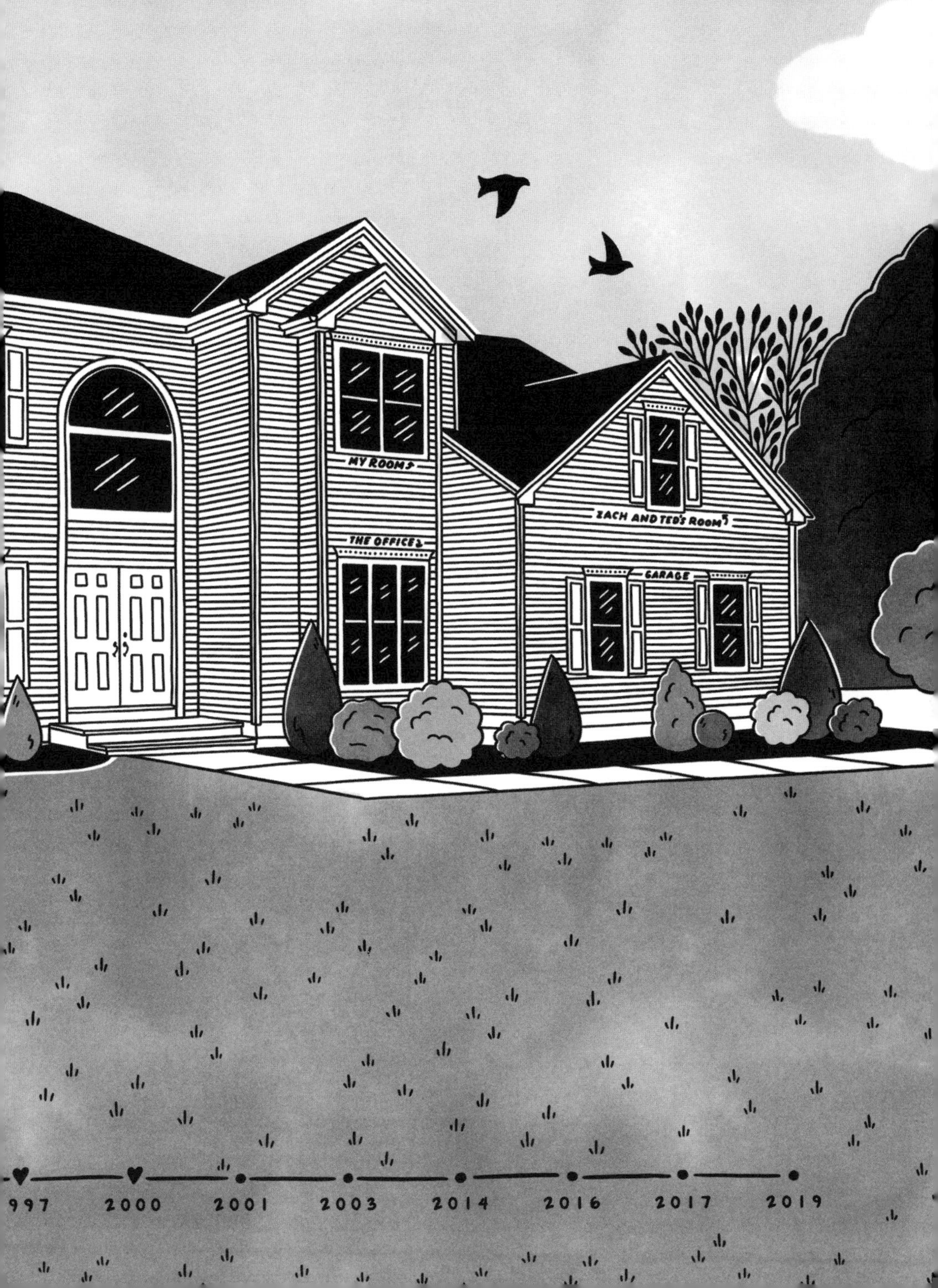
MY ROOM
THE OFFICE
ZACH AND TED'S ROOM
GARAGE
2000
2001
2003
2014
2016
2017
2019

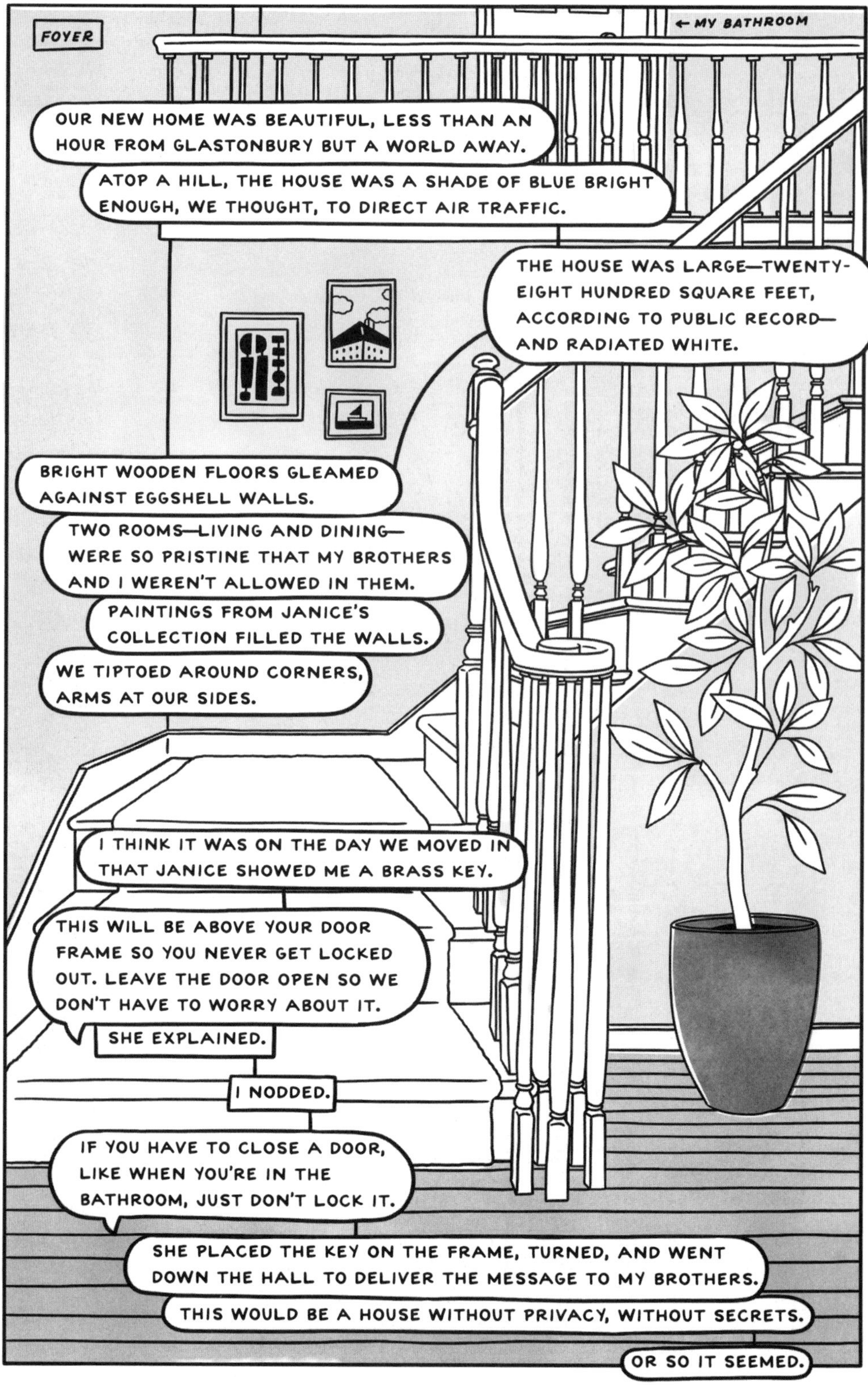
FOYER
← MY BATHROOM
OUR NEW HOME WAS BEAUTIFUL, LESS THAN AN HOUR FROM GLASTONBURY BUT A WORLD AWAY.
ATOP A HILL, THE HOUSE WAS A SHADE OF BLUE BRIGHT ENOUGH, WE THOUGHT, TO DIRECT AIR TRAFFIC.
THE HOUSE WAS LARGE—TWENTY-EIGHT HUNDRED SQUARE FEET, ACCORDING TO PUBLIC RECORD—AND RADIATED WHITE.
BRIGHT WOODEN FLOORS GLEAMED AGAINST EGGSHELL WALLS.
TWO ROOMS—LIVING AND DINING—WERE SO PRISTINE THAT MY BROTHERS AND I WEREN'T ALLOWED IN THEM.
PAINTINGS FROM JANICE'S COLLECTION FILLED THE WALLS.
WE TIPTOED AROUND CORNERS, ARMS AT OUR SIDES.
I THINK IT WAS ON THE DAY WE MOVED IN THAT JANICE SHOWED ME A BRASS KEY.
THIS WILL BE ABOVE YOUR DOOR FRAME SO YOU NEVER GET LOCKED OUT. LEAVE THE DOOR OPEN SO WE DON'T HAVE TO WORRY ABOUT IT.
SHE EXPLAINED.
I NODDED.
IF YOU HAVE TO CLOSE A DOOR, LIKE WHEN YOU'RE IN THE BATHROOM, JUST DON'T LOCK IT.
SHE PLACED THE KEY ON THE FRAME, TURNED, AND WENT DOWN THE HALL TO DELIVER THE MESSAGE TO MY BROTHERS.
THIS WOULD BE A HOUSE WITHOUT PRIVACY, WITHOUT SECRETS.
OR SO IT SEEMED.

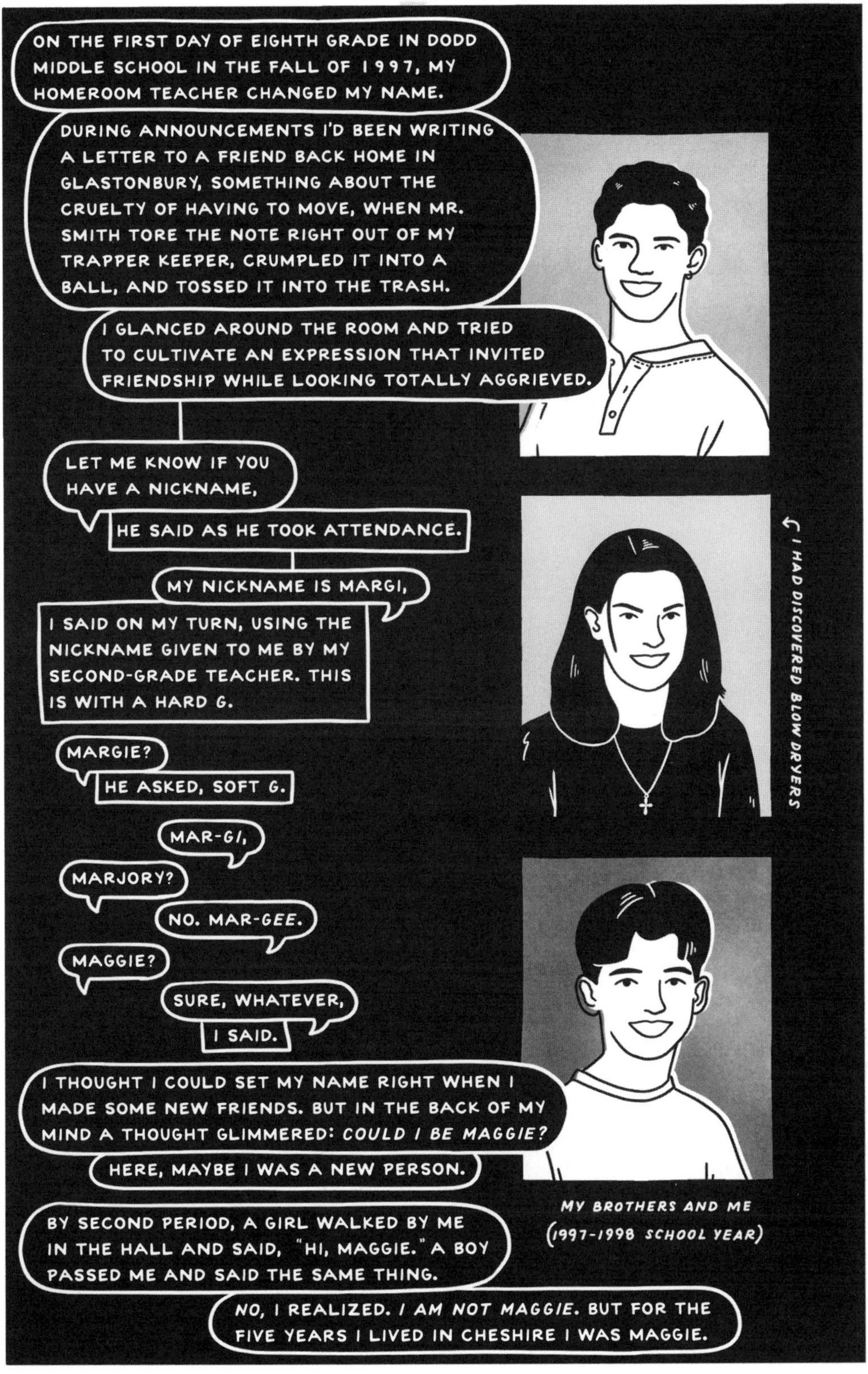

ON THE FIRST DAY OF EIGHTH GRADE IN DODD MIDDLE SCHOOL IN THE FALL OF 1997, MY HOMEROOM TEACHER CHANGED MY NAME.
DURING ANNOUNCEMENTS I'D BEEN WRITING A LETTER TO A FRIEND BACK HOME IN GLASTONBURY, SOMETHING ABOUT THE CRUELTY OF HAVING TO MOVE, WHEN MR. SMITH TORE THE NOTE RIGHT OUT OF MY TRAPPER KEEPER, CRUMPLED IT INTO A BALL, AND TOSSED IT INTO THE TRASH.
I GLANCED AROUND THE ROOM AND TRIED TO CULTIVATE AN EXPRESSION THAT INVITED FRIENDSHIP WHILE LOOKING TOTALLY AGGRIEVED.
LET ME KNOW IF YOU HAVE A NICKNAME,
HE SAID AS HE TOOK ATTENDANCE.
MY NICKNAME IS MARGI,
I SAID ON MY TURN, USING THE NICKNAME GIVEN TO ME BY MY SECOND-GRADE TEACHER. THIS IS WITH A HARD *G*.
MARGIE?
HE ASKED, SOFT *G*.
MAR-*GI*,
MARJORY?
NO. MAR-*GEE*.
MAGGIE?
SURE, WHATEVER,
I SAID.
I THOUGHT I COULD SET MY NAME RIGHT WHEN I MADE SOME NEW FRIENDS. BUT IN THE BACK OF MY MIND A THOUGHT GLIMMERED: *COULD I BE MAGGIE?*
HERE, MAYBE I WAS A NEW PERSON.
BY SECOND PERIOD, A GIRL WALKED BY ME IN THE HALL AND SAID, "HI, MAGGIE." A BOY PASSED ME AND SAID THE SAME THING.
NO, I REALIZED. *I AM NOT MAGGIE*. BUT FOR THE FIVE YEARS I LIVED IN CHESHIRE I WAS MAGGIE.
I HAD DISCOVERED BLOW DRYERS
MY BROTHERS AND ME (1997-1998 SCHOOL YEAR)

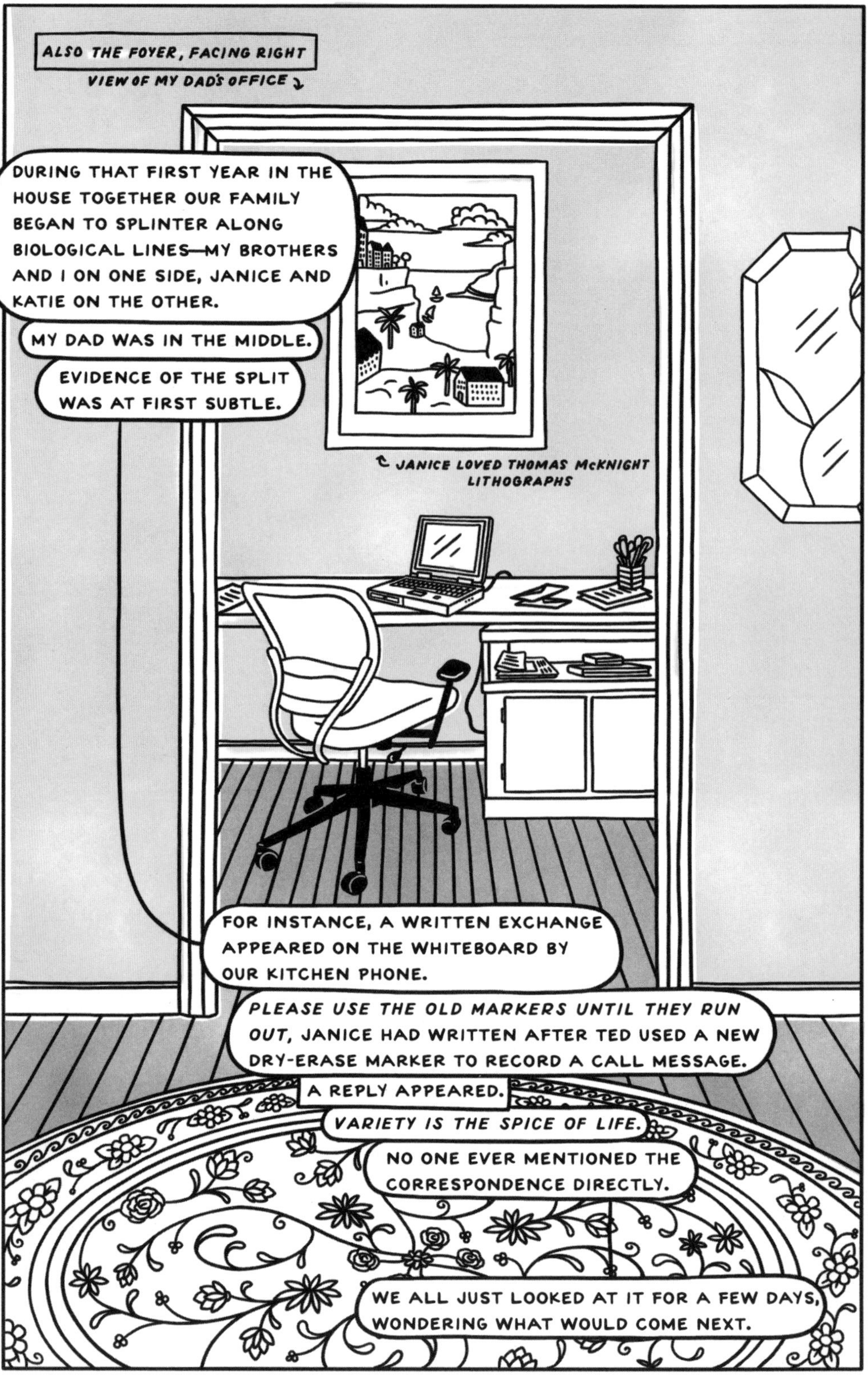
ALSO THE FOYER, FACING RIGHT
VIEW OF MY DAD'S OFFICE
DURING THAT FIRST YEAR IN THE HOUSE TOGETHER OUR FAMILY BEGAN TO SPLINTER ALONG BIOLOGICAL LINES—MY BROTHERS AND I ON ONE SIDE, JANICE AND KATIE ON THE OTHER.
MY DAD WAS IN THE MIDDLE.
EVIDENCE OF THE SPLIT WAS AT FIRST SUBTLE.
JANICE LOVED THOMAS McKNIGHT LITHOGRAPHS
FOR INSTANCE, A WRITTEN EXCHANGE APPEARED ON THE WHITEBOARD BY OUR KITCHEN PHONE.
PLEASE USE THE OLD MARKERS UNTIL THEY RUN OUT, JANICE HAD WRITTEN AFTER TED USED A NEW DRY-ERASE MARKER TO RECORD A CALL MESSAGE.
A REPLY APPEARED.
VARIETY IS THE SPICE OF LIFE.
NO ONE EVER MENTIONED THE CORRESPONDENCE DIRECTLY.
WE ALL JUST LOOKED AT IT FOR A FEW DAYS, WONDERING WHAT WOULD COME NEXT.

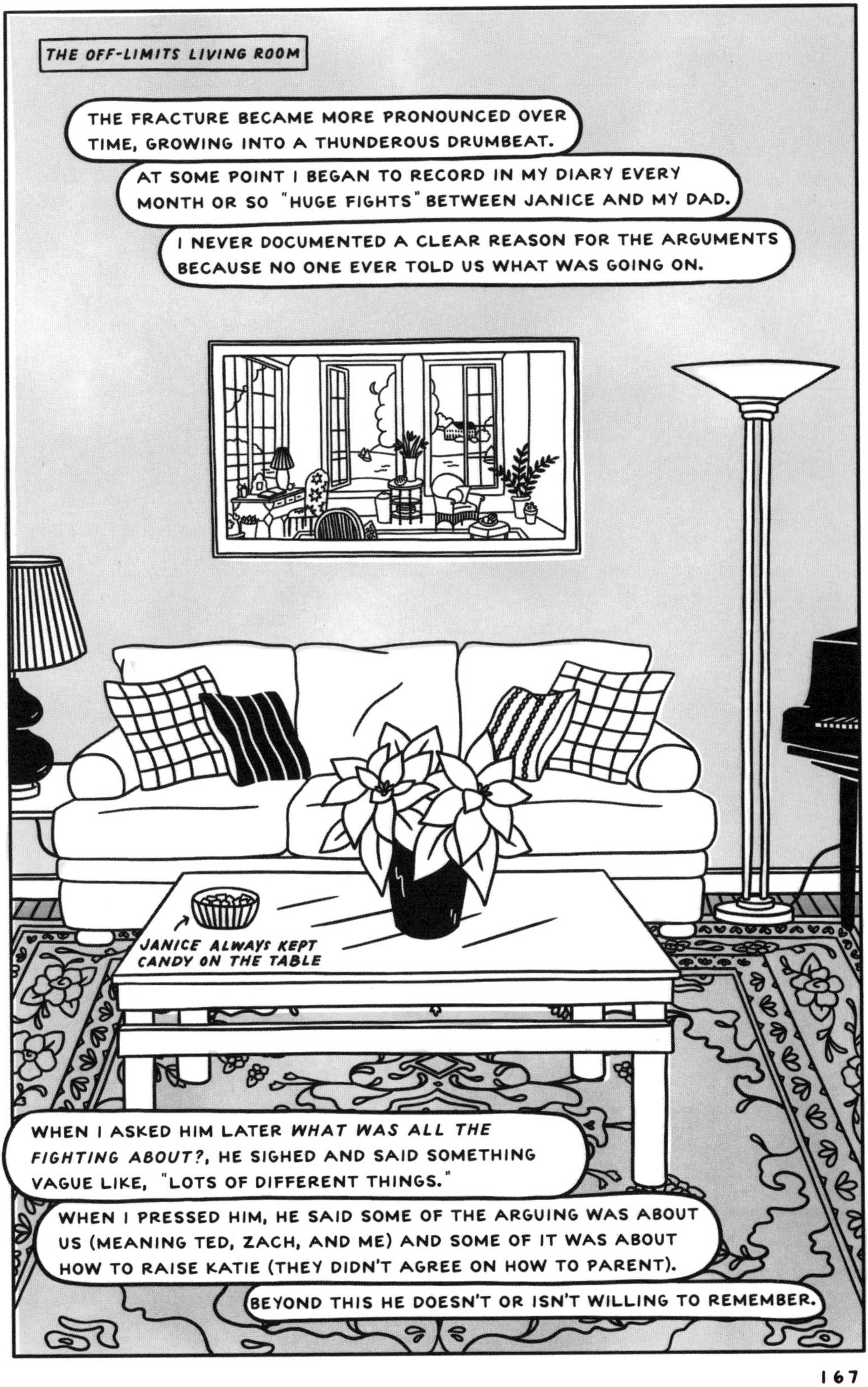
THE OFF-LIMITS LIVING ROOM
THE FRACTURE BECAME MORE PRONOUNCED OVER TIME, GROWING INTO A THUNDEROUS DRUMBEAT.
AT SOME POINT I BEGAN TO RECORD IN MY DIARY EVERY MONTH OR SO "HUGE FIGHTS" BETWEEN JANICE AND MY DAD.
I NEVER DOCUMENTED A CLEAR REASON FOR THE ARGUMENTS BECAUSE NO ONE EVER TOLD US WHAT WAS GOING ON.
JANICE ALWAYS KEPT CANDY ON THE TABLE
WHEN I ASKED HIM LATER *WHAT WAS ALL THE FIGHTING ABOUT?*, HE SIGHED AND SAID SOMETHING VAGUE LIKE, "LOTS OF DIFFERENT THINGS."
WHEN I PRESSED HIM, HE SAID SOME OF THE ARGUING WAS ABOUT US (MEANING TED, ZACH, AND ME) AND SOME OF IT WAS ABOUT HOW TO RAISE KATIE (THEY DIDN'T AGREE ON HOW TO PARENT).
BEYOND THIS HE DOESN'T OR ISN'T WILLING TO REMEMBER.

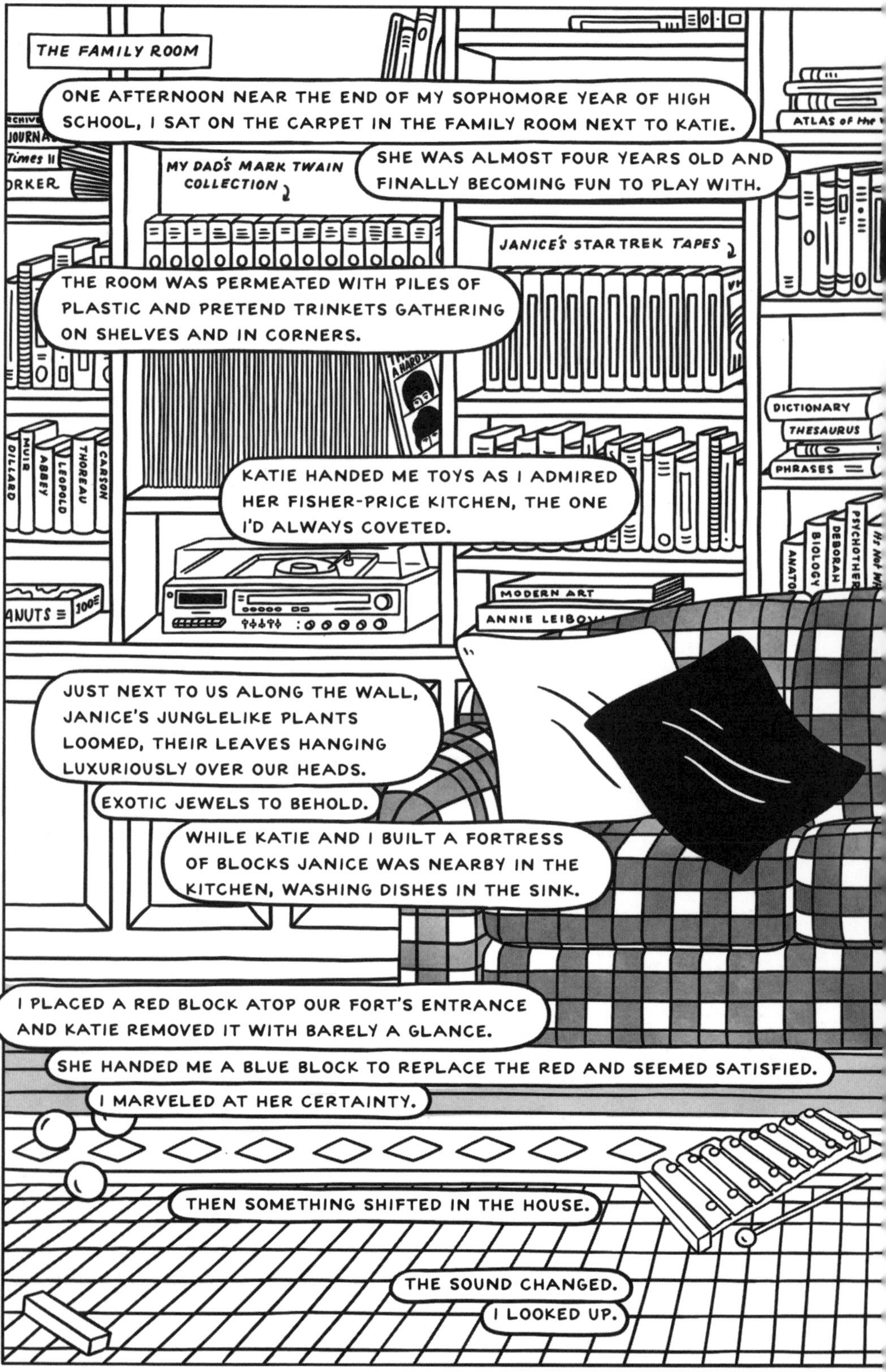
THE FAMILY ROOM
ONE AFTERNOON NEAR THE END OF MY SOPHOMORE YEAR OF HIGH SCHOOL, I SAT ON THE CARPET IN THE FAMILY ROOM NEXT TO KATIE.
MY DAD'S MARK TWAIN COLLECTION
SHE WAS ALMOST FOUR YEARS OLD AND FINALLY BECOMING FUN TO PLAY WITH.
JANICE'S STAR TREK TAPES
THE ROOM WAS PERMEATED WITH PILES OF PLASTIC AND PRETEND TRINKETS GATHERING ON SHELVES AND IN CORNERS.
DICTIONARY
THESAURUS
PHRASES
DILLARD
MUIR
ABBEY
LEOPOLD
THOREAU
CARSON
KATIE HANDED ME TOYS AS I ADMIRED HER FISHER-PRICE KITCHEN, THE ONE I'D ALWAYS COVETED.
BIOLOGY
DEBORAH
MODERN ART
JUST NEXT TO US ALONG THE WALL, JANICE'S JUNGLELIKE PLANTS LOOMED, THEIR LEAVES HANGING LUXURIOUSLY OVER OUR HEADS.
EXOTIC JEWELS TO BEHOLD.
WHILE KATIE AND I BUILT A FORTRESS OF BLOCKS JANICE WAS NEARBY IN THE KITCHEN, WASHING DISHES IN THE SINK.
I PLACED A RED BLOCK ATOP OUR FORT'S ENTRANCE AND KATIE REMOVED IT WITH BARELY A GLANCE.
SHE HANDED ME A BLUE BLOCK TO REPLACE THE RED AND SEEMED SATISFIED.
I MARVELED AT HER CERTAINTY.
THEN SOMETHING SHIFTED IN THE HOUSE.
THE SOUND CHANGED.
I LOOKED UP.

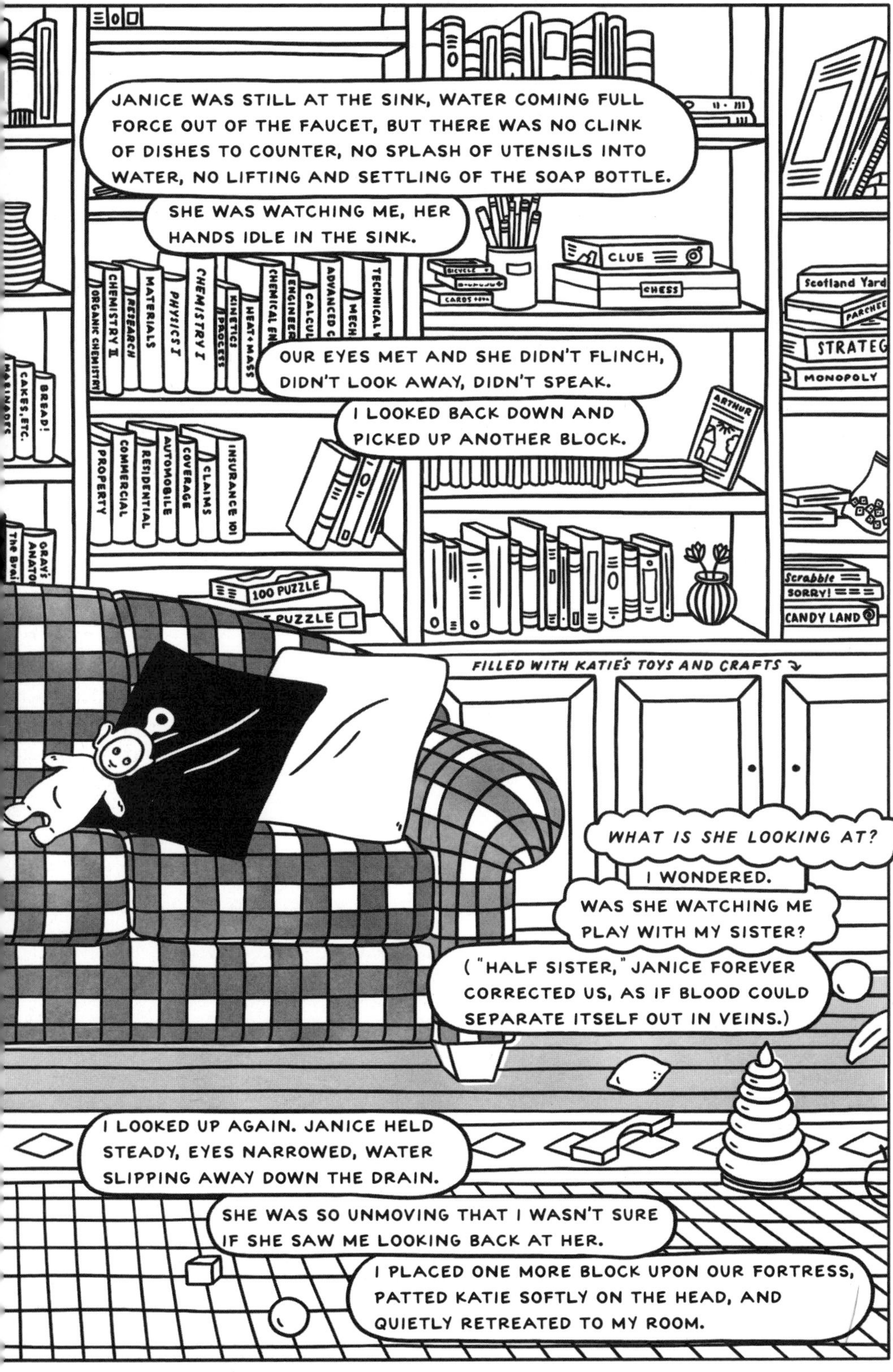
JANICE WAS STILL AT THE SINK, WATER COMING FULL FORCE OUT OF THE FAUCET, BUT THERE WAS NO CLINK OF DISHES TO COUNTER, NO SPLASH OF UTENSILS INTO WATER, NO LIFTING AND SETTLING OF THE SOAP BOTTLE.
SHE WAS WATCHING ME, HER HANDS IDLE IN THE SINK.
OUR EYES MET AND SHE DIDN'T FLINCH, DIDN'T LOOK AWAY, DIDN'T SPEAK.
I LOOKED BACK DOWN AND PICKED UP ANOTHER BLOCK.
CLUE
CHESS
Scotland Yard
MONOPOLY
ARTHUR
100 PUZZLE
Scrabble
SORRY!
CANDY LAND
FILLED WITH KATIE'S TOYS AND CRAFTS
WHAT IS SHE LOOKING AT?
I WONDERED.
WAS SHE WATCHING ME PLAY WITH MY SISTER?
("HALF SISTER," JANICE FOREVER CORRECTED US, AS IF BLOOD COULD SEPARATE ITSELF OUT IN VEINS.)
I LOOKED UP AGAIN. JANICE HELD STEADY, EYES NARROWED, WATER SLIPPING AWAY DOWN THE DRAIN.
SHE WAS SO UNMOVING THAT I WASN'T SURE IF SHE SAW ME LOOKING BACK AT HER.
I PLACED ONE MORE BLOCK UPON OUR FORTRESS, PATTED KATIE SOFTLY ON THE HEAD, AND QUIETLY RETREATED TO MY ROOM.

THAT EVENING MY DAD CAME UPSTAIRS.

JANICE THINKS YOU'RE TOO CLOSE TO KATIE, HE SAID.

WHAT ARE YOU TALKING ABOUT?

IT'S JUST THAT KATIE GOES TO YOU A LOT. SHE WANTS TO SPEND TOO MUCH TIME WITH YOU.

BUT WE'RE SISTERS, I SAID.

I KNOW, MOPS. BUT JANICE WANTED ME TO TALK TO YOU.

HE LEFT AND I FUMED IN MY ROOM, AWARE THAT SOMETHING WAS OFF BUT I DIDN'T KNOW HOW TO DESCRIBE IT.

WHAT WAS THE POINT OF SIBLINGS IF NOT TO BE CLOSE?

WASN'T I *SUPPOSED* TO PLAY WITH A TODDLER?

AND THEN: WAS IT POSSIBLE I *WAS* TOO CLOSE TO KATIE?

WHAT DID THAT EVEN MEAN?

NO, I DECIDED. *I'M RIGHT.*

I MADE NOTE OF THE CONVERSATION IN MY DIARY.

IN A STEPFAMILY THE INVISIBLE LINE BETWEEN BIOLOGICAL AND NOT, BETWEEN OLD AND NEW, IS ALWAYS PRESENT.

A RAISED EYEBROW CAN MEAN *THAT'S NOT THE WAY MY MOM DOES IT*; A SHAKE OF THE HEAD CAN MEAN *YOU'RE NOT MY DAUGHTER.*

IN THE BEST OF TIMES, THE BOUNDARY IS SMALL AND SURMOUNTABLE.

WHEN COMMUNICATION GOES OFF THE RAILS, WHEN THE FAMILY STOPS SEEING EYE TO EYE, THE BOUNDARY WIDENS AND DECLARES ITSELF.

WE DO NOT BELONG TO EACH OTHER, IT SCREAMS.

WITHOUT A SOFTENING OF THE HEART, WITHOUT DAILY ATTENTION, THAT INVISIBLE LINE CAN BECOME A PERMANENT, UNCLIMBABLE MOUNTAIN.

JANICE WANTED ME TO KNOW THAT HER DAUGHTER WAS ON HER SIDE OF THE LINE, NOT MINE.

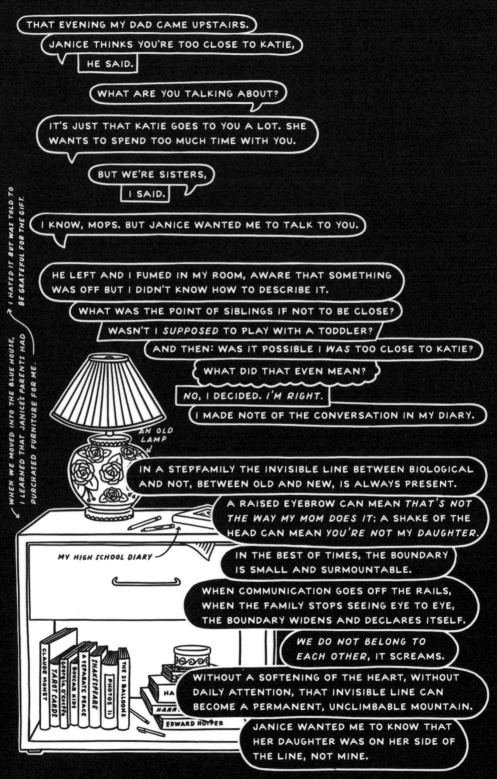

WHEN WE MOVED INTO THE BLUE HOUSE, I LEARNED THAT JANICE'S PARENTS HAD PURCHASED FURNITURE FOR ME. I HATED IT BUT WAS TOLD TO BE GRATEFUL FOR THE GIFT.

AN OLD LAMP

MY HIGH SCHOOL DIARY

CLAUDE MONET

TAROT CARDS

GEORGIA O'KEEFFE

BONZAI KIDS

A SEPARATE PEACE

SHAKESPEARE

PHOTOS II

THE 21 BALLOONS

HA

NARR.

EDWARD HOPPER

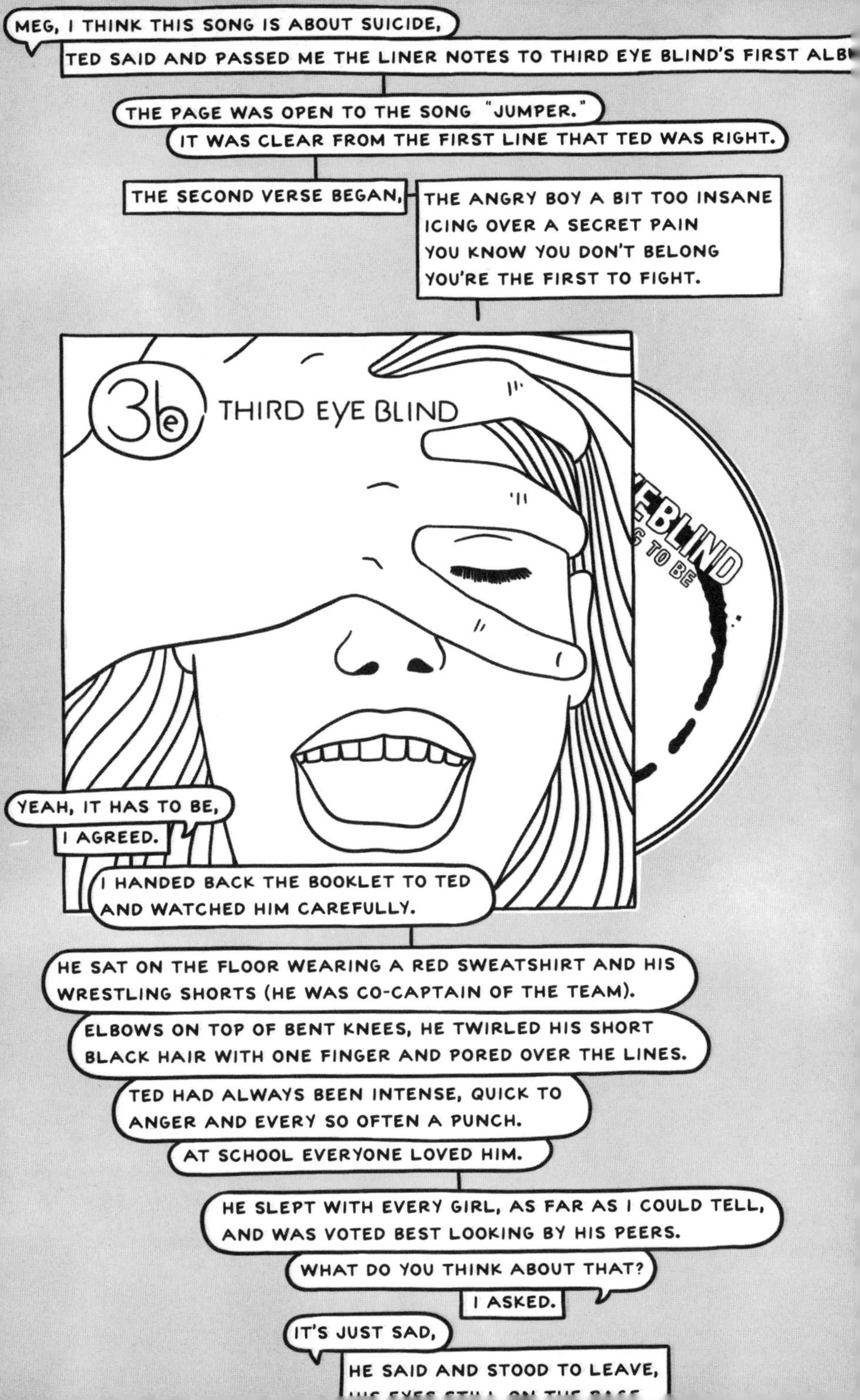
MEG, I THINK THIS SONG IS ABOUT SUICIDE,
TED SAID AND PASSED ME THE LINER NOTES TO THIRD EYE BLIND'S FIRST ALB
THE PAGE WAS OPEN TO THE SONG "JUMPER."
IT WAS CLEAR FROM THE FIRST LINE THAT TED WAS RIGHT.
THE SECOND VERSE BEGAN,
THE ANGRY BOY A BIT TOO INSANE
ICING OVER A SECRET PAIN
YOU KNOW YOU DON'T BELONG
YOU'RE THE FIRST TO FIGHT.
3e THIRD EYE BLIND
YEAH, IT HAS TO BE,
I AGREED.
I HANDED BACK THE BOOKLET TO TED AND WATCHED HIM CAREFULLY.
HE SAT ON THE FLOOR WEARING A RED SWEATSHIRT AND HIS WRESTLING SHORTS (HE WAS CO-CAPTAIN OF THE TEAM).
ELBOWS ON TOP OF BENT KNEES, HE TWIRLED HIS SHORT BLACK HAIR WITH ONE FINGER AND PORED OVER THE LINES.
TED HAD ALWAYS BEEN INTENSE, QUICK TO ANGER AND EVERY SO OFTEN A PUNCH.
AT SCHOOL EVERYONE LOVED HIM.
HE SLEPT WITH EVERY GIRL, AS FAR AS I COULD TELL, AND WAS VOTED BEST LOOKING BY HIS PEERS.
WHAT DO YOU THINK ABOUT THAT?
I ASKED.
IT'S JUST SAD,
HE SAID AND STOOD TO LEAVE,

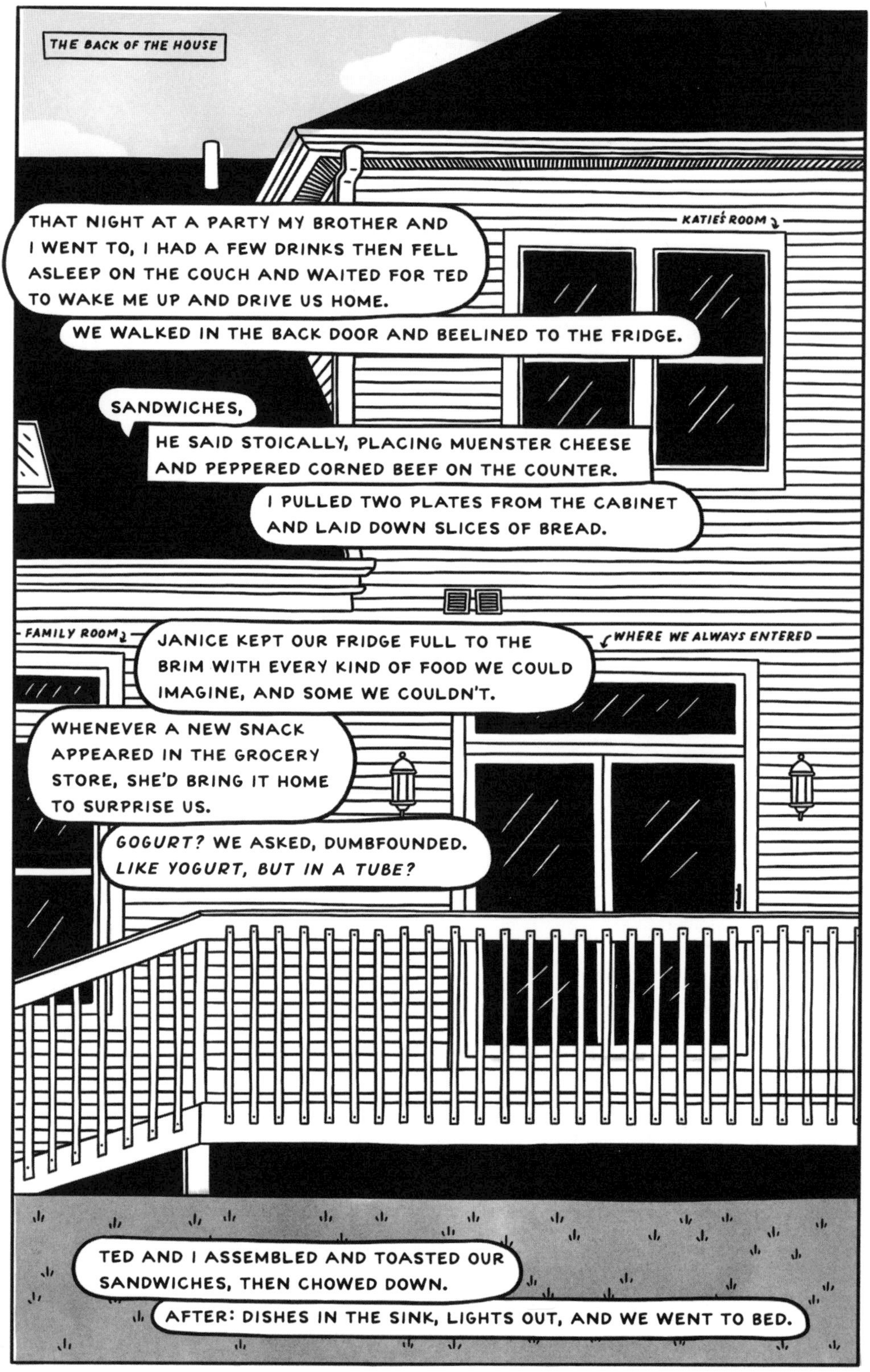
THE BACK OF THE HOUSE
THAT NIGHT AT A PARTY MY BROTHER AND I WENT TO, I HAD A FEW DRINKS THEN FELL ASLEEP ON THE COUCH AND WAITED FOR TED TO WAKE ME UP AND DRIVE US HOME.
WE WALKED IN THE BACK DOOR AND BEELINED TO THE FRIDGE.
KATIE'S ROOM
SANDWICHES,
HE SAID STOICALLY, PLACING MUENSTER CHEESE AND PEPPERED CORNED BEEF ON THE COUNTER.
I PULLED TWO PLATES FROM THE CABINET AND LAID DOWN SLICES OF BREAD.
FAMILY ROOM
JANICE KEPT OUR FRIDGE FULL TO THE BRIM WITH EVERY KIND OF FOOD WE COULD IMAGINE, AND SOME WE COULDN'T.
WHERE WE ALWAYS ENTERED
WHENEVER A NEW SNACK APPEARED IN THE GROCERY STORE, SHE'D BRING IT HOME TO SURPRISE US.
GOGURT? WE ASKED, DUMBFOUNDED. *LIKE YOGURT, BUT IN A TUBE?*
TED AND I ASSEMBLED AND TOASTED OUR SANDWICHES, THEN CHOWED DOWN.
AFTER: DISHES IN THE SINK, LIGHTS OUT, AND WE WENT TO BED.

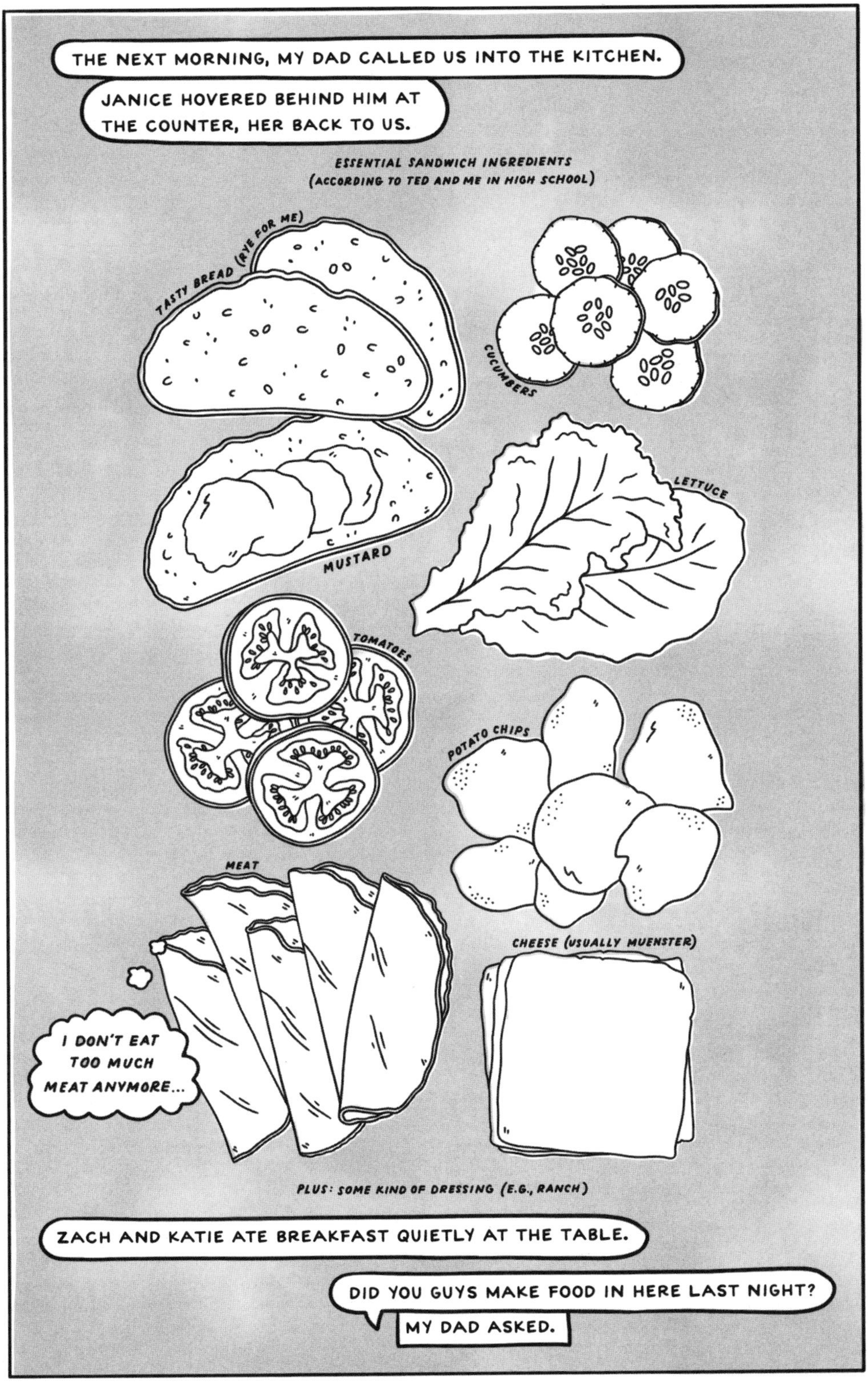

THE NEXT MORNING, MY DAD CALLED US INTO THE KITCHEN.
JANICE HOVERED BEHIND HIM AT THE COUNTER, HER BACK TO US.
ESSENTIAL SANDWICH INGREDIENTS (ACCORDING TO TED AND ME IN HIGH SCHOOL)
TASTY BREAD (RYE FOR ME)
CUCUMBERS
MUSTARD
LETTUCE
TOMATOES
POTATO CHIPS
MEAT
CHEESE (USUALLY MUENSTER)
I DON'T EAT TOO MUCH MEAT ANYMORE...
PLUS: SOME KIND OF DRESSING (E.G., RANCH)
ZACH AND KATIE ATE BREAKFAST QUIETLY AT THE TABLE.
DID YOU GUYS MAKE FOOD IN HERE LAST NIGHT?
MY DAD ASKED.

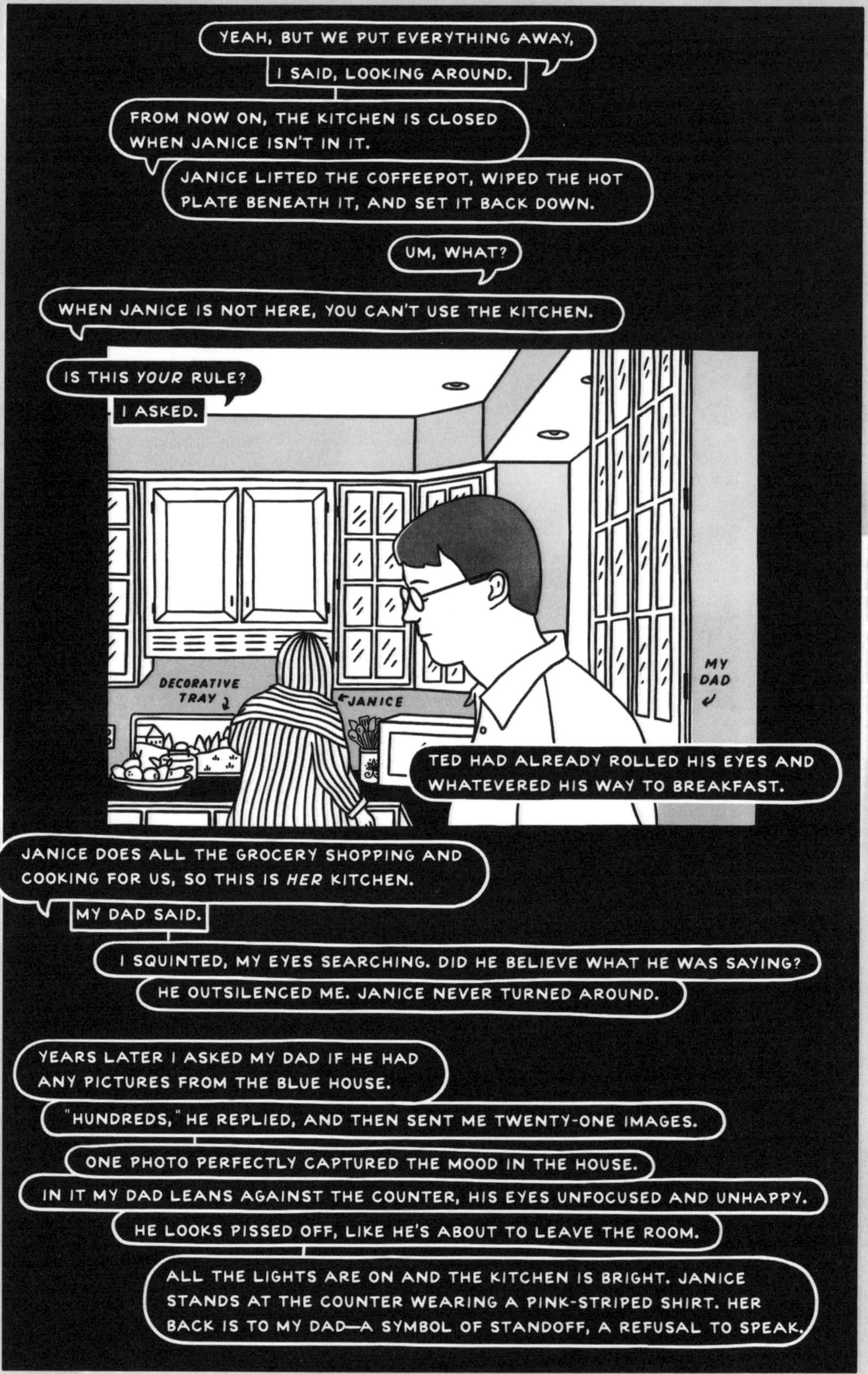
YEAH, BUT WE PUT EVERYTHING AWAY,
I SAID, LOOKING AROUND.
FROM NOW ON, THE KITCHEN IS CLOSED WHEN JANICE ISN'T IN IT.
JANICE LIFTED THE COFFEEPOT, WIPED THE HOT PLATE BENEATH IT, AND SET IT BACK DOWN.
UM, WHAT?
WHEN JANICE IS NOT HERE, YOU CAN'T USE THE KITCHEN.
IS THIS *YOUR* RULE?
I ASKED.
DECORATIVE TRAY
JANICE
MY DAD
TED HAD ALREADY ROLLED HIS EYES AND WHATEVERED HIS WAY TO BREAKFAST.
JANICE DOES ALL THE GROCERY SHOPPING AND COOKING FOR US, SO THIS IS *HER* KITCHEN.
MY DAD SAID.
I SQUINTED, MY EYES SEARCHING. DID HE BELIEVE WHAT HE WAS SAYING?
HE OUTSILENCED ME. JANICE NEVER TURNED AROUND.
YEARS LATER I ASKED MY DAD IF HE HAD ANY PICTURES FROM THE BLUE HOUSE.
"HUNDREDS," HE REPLIED, AND THEN SENT ME TWENTY-ONE IMAGES.
ONE PHOTO PERFECTLY CAPTURED THE MOOD IN THE HOUSE.
IN IT MY DAD LEANS AGAINST THE COUNTER, HIS EYES UNFOCUSED AND UNHAPPY.
HE LOOKS PISSED OFF, LIKE HE'S ABOUT TO LEAVE THE ROOM.
ALL THE LIGHTS ARE ON AND THE KITCHEN IS BRIGHT. JANICE STANDS AT THE COUNTER WEARING A PINK-STRIPED SHIRT. HER BACK IS TO MY DAD—A SYMBOL OF STANDOFF, A REFUSAL TO SPEAK.

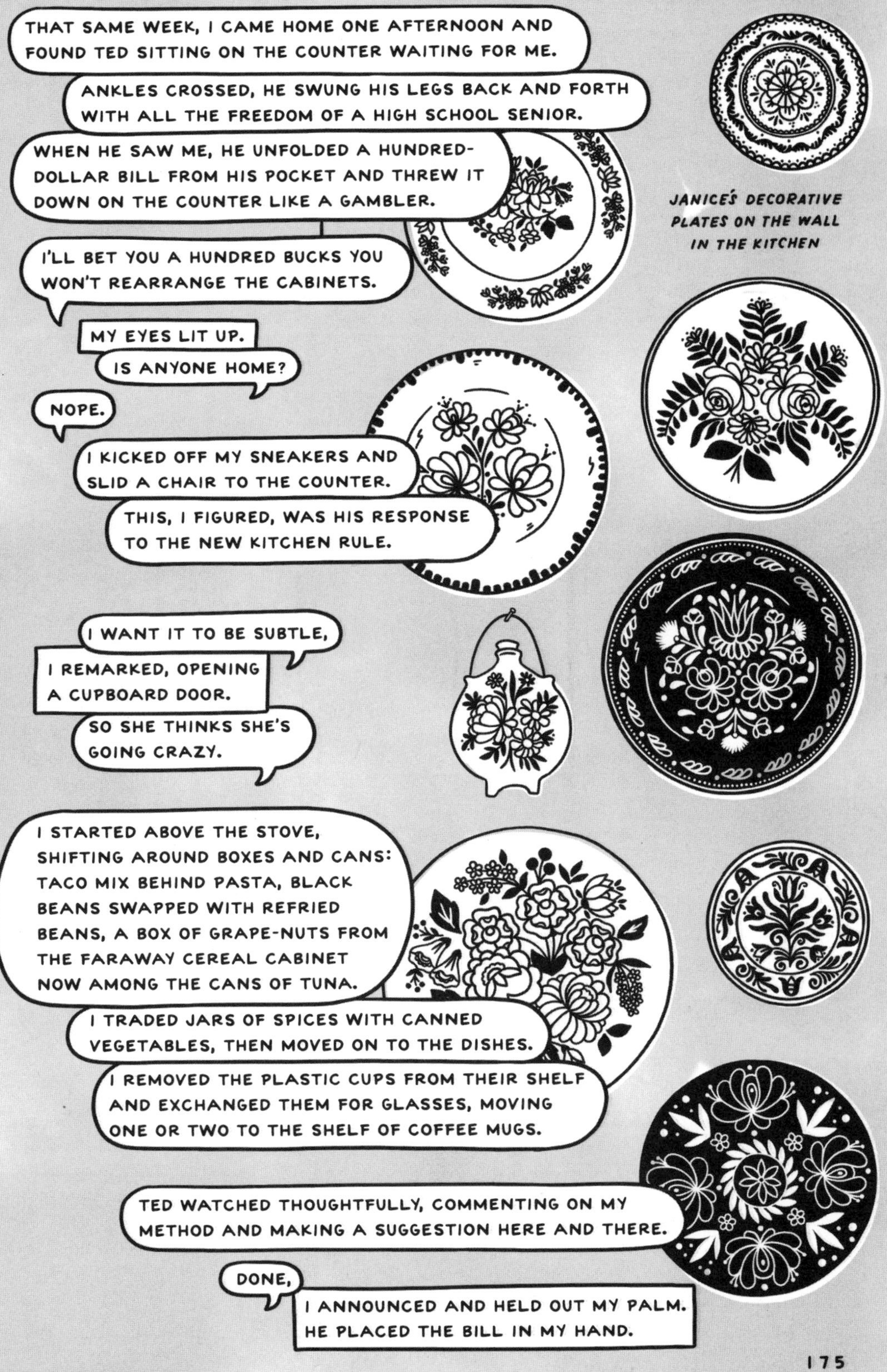
THAT SAME WEEK, I CAME HOME ONE AFTERNOON AND FOUND TED SITTING ON THE COUNTER WAITING FOR ME.
ANKLES CROSSED, HE SWUNG HIS LEGS BACK AND FORTH WITH ALL THE FREEDOM OF A HIGH SCHOOL SENIOR.
JANICE'S DECORATIVE PLATES ON THE WALL IN THE KITCHEN
WHEN HE SAW ME, HE UNFOLDED A HUNDRED-DOLLAR BILL FROM HIS POCKET AND THREW IT DOWN ON THE COUNTER LIKE A GAMBLER.
I'LL BET YOU A HUNDRED BUCKS YOU WON'T REARRANGE THE CABINETS.
MY EYES LIT UP.
IS ANYONE HOME?
NOPE.
I KICKED OFF MY SNEAKERS AND SLID A CHAIR TO THE COUNTER.
THIS, I FIGURED, WAS HIS RESPONSE TO THE NEW KITCHEN RULE.
I WANT IT TO BE SUBTLE,
I REMARKED, OPENING A CUPBOARD DOOR.
SO SHE THINKS SHE'S GOING CRAZY.
I STARTED ABOVE THE STOVE, SHIFTING AROUND BOXES AND CANS: TACO MIX BEHIND PASTA, BLACK BEANS SWAPPED WITH REFRIED BEANS, A BOX OF GRAPE-NUTS FROM THE FARAWAY CEREAL CABINET NOW AMONG THE CANS OF TUNA.
I TRADED JARS OF SPICES WITH CANNED VEGETABLES, THEN MOVED ON TO THE DISHES.
I REMOVED THE PLASTIC CUPS FROM THEIR SHELF AND EXCHANGED THEM FOR GLASSES, MOVING ONE OR TWO TO THE SHELF OF COFFEE MUGS.
TED WATCHED THOUGHTFULLY, COMMENTING ON MY METHOD AND MAKING A SUGGESTION HERE AND THERE.
DONE,
I ANNOUNCED AND HELD OUT MY PALM. HE PLACED THE BILL IN MY HAND.

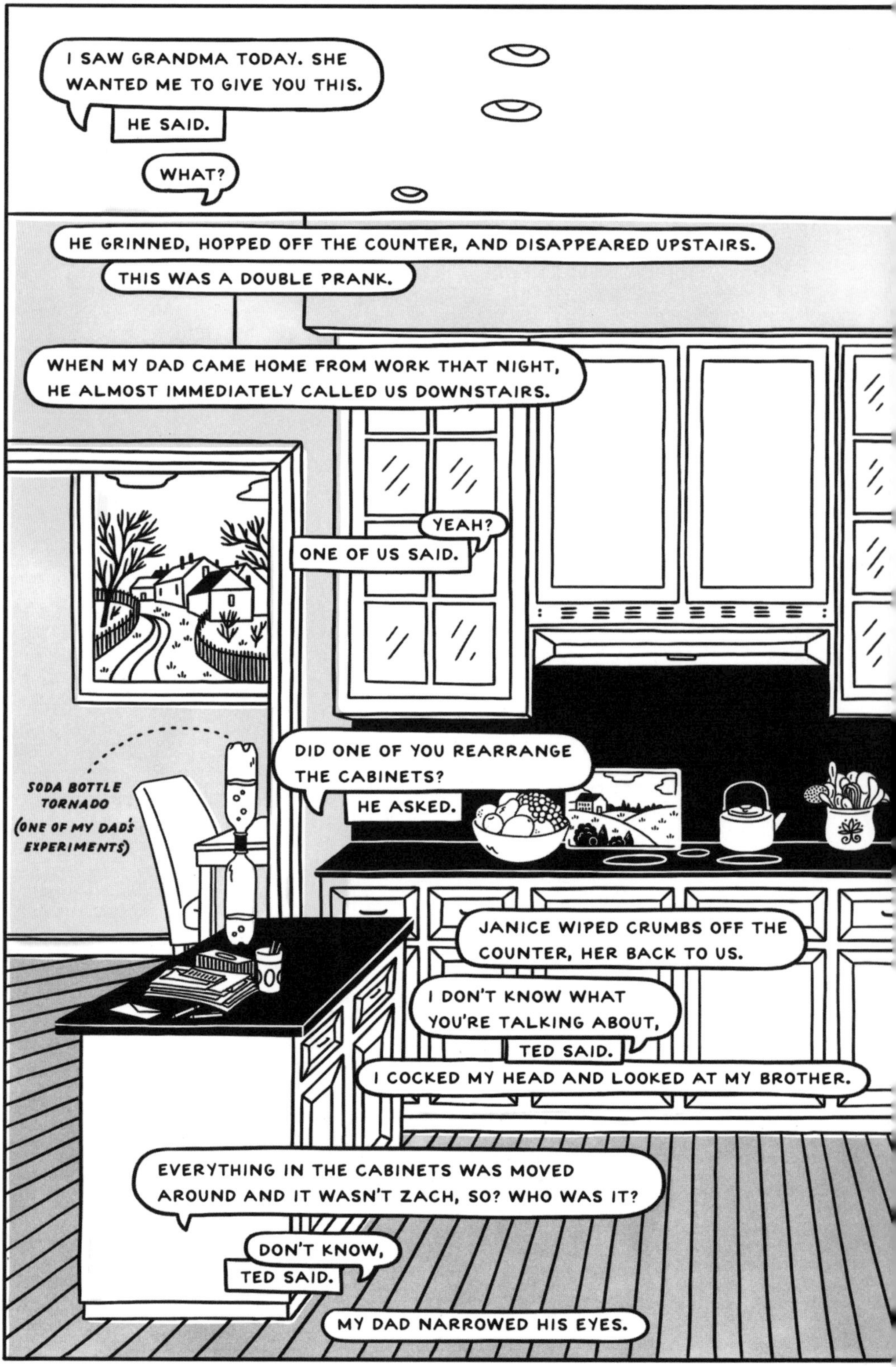
I SAW GRANDMA TODAY. SHE WANTED ME TO GIVE YOU THIS.
HE SAID.
WHAT?
HE GRINNED, HOPPED OFF THE COUNTER, AND DISAPPEARED UPSTAIRS.
THIS WAS A DOUBLE PRANK.
WHEN MY DAD CAME HOME FROM WORK THAT NIGHT, HE ALMOST IMMEDIATELY CALLED US DOWNSTAIRS.
YEAH?
ONE OF US SAID.
SODA BOTTLE TORNADO (ONE OF MY DAD'S EXPERIMENTS)
DID ONE OF YOU REARRANGE THE CABINETS?
HE ASKED.
JANICE WIPED CRUMBS OFF THE COUNTER, HER BACK TO US.
I DON'T KNOW WHAT YOU'RE TALKING ABOUT,
TED SAID.
I COCKED MY HEAD AND LOOKED AT MY BROTHER.
EVERYTHING IN THE CABINETS WAS MOVED AROUND AND IT WASN'T ZACH, SO? WHO WAS IT?
DON'T KNOW,
TED SAID.
MY DAD NARROWED HIS EYES.

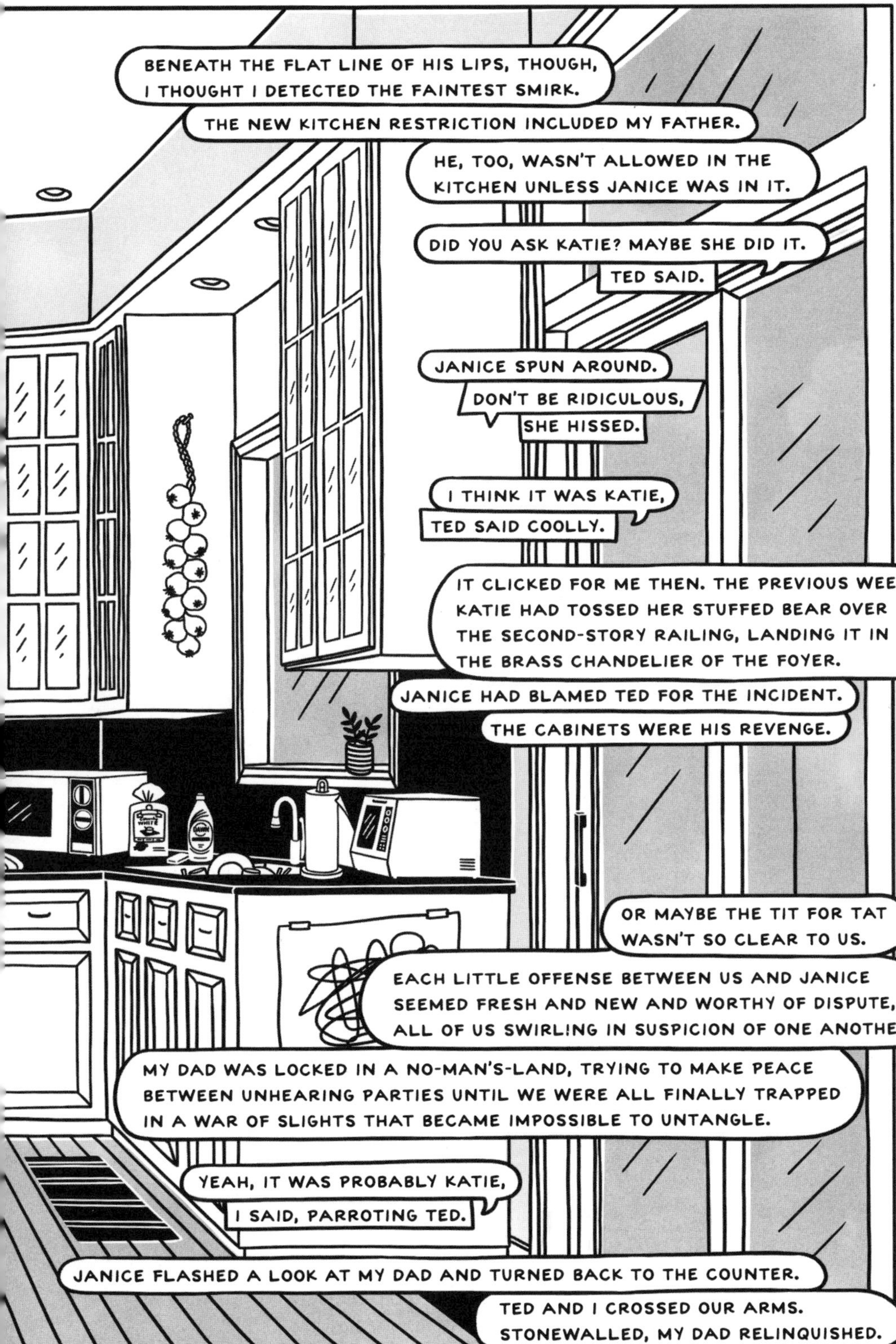
BENEATH THE FLAT LINE OF HIS LIPS, THOUGH, I THOUGHT I DETECTED THE FAINTEST SMIRK.
THE NEW KITCHEN RESTRICTION INCLUDED MY FATHER.
HE, TOO, WASN'T ALLOWED IN THE KITCHEN UNLESS JANICE WAS IN IT.
DID YOU ASK KATIE? MAYBE SHE DID IT.
TED SAID.
JANICE SPUN AROUND.
DON'T BE RIDICULOUS,
SHE HISSED.
I THINK IT WAS KATIE,
TED SAID COOLLY.
IT CLICKED FOR ME THEN. THE PREVIOUS WEEK KATIE HAD TOSSED HER STUFFED BEAR OVER THE SECOND-STORY RAILING, LANDING IT IN THE BRASS CHANDELIER OF THE FOYER.
JANICE HAD BLAMED TED FOR THE INCIDENT.
THE CABINETS WERE HIS REVENGE.
OR MAYBE THE TIT FOR TAT WASN'T SO CLEAR TO US.
EACH LITTLE OFFENSE BETWEEN US AND JANICE SEEMED FRESH AND NEW AND WORTHY OF DISPUTE, ALL OF US SWIRLING IN SUSPICION OF ONE ANOTHER.
MY DAD WAS LOCKED IN A NO-MAN'S-LAND, TRYING TO MAKE PEACE BETWEEN UNHEARING PARTIES UNTIL WE WERE ALL FINALLY TRAPPED IN A WAR OF SLIGHTS THAT BECAME IMPOSSIBLE TO UNTANGLE.
YEAH, IT WAS PROBABLY KATIE,
I SAID, PARROTING TED.
JANICE FLASHED A LOOK AT MY DAD AND TURNED BACK TO THE COUNTER.
TED AND I CROSSED OUR ARMS. STONEWALLED, MY DAD RELINQUISHED.

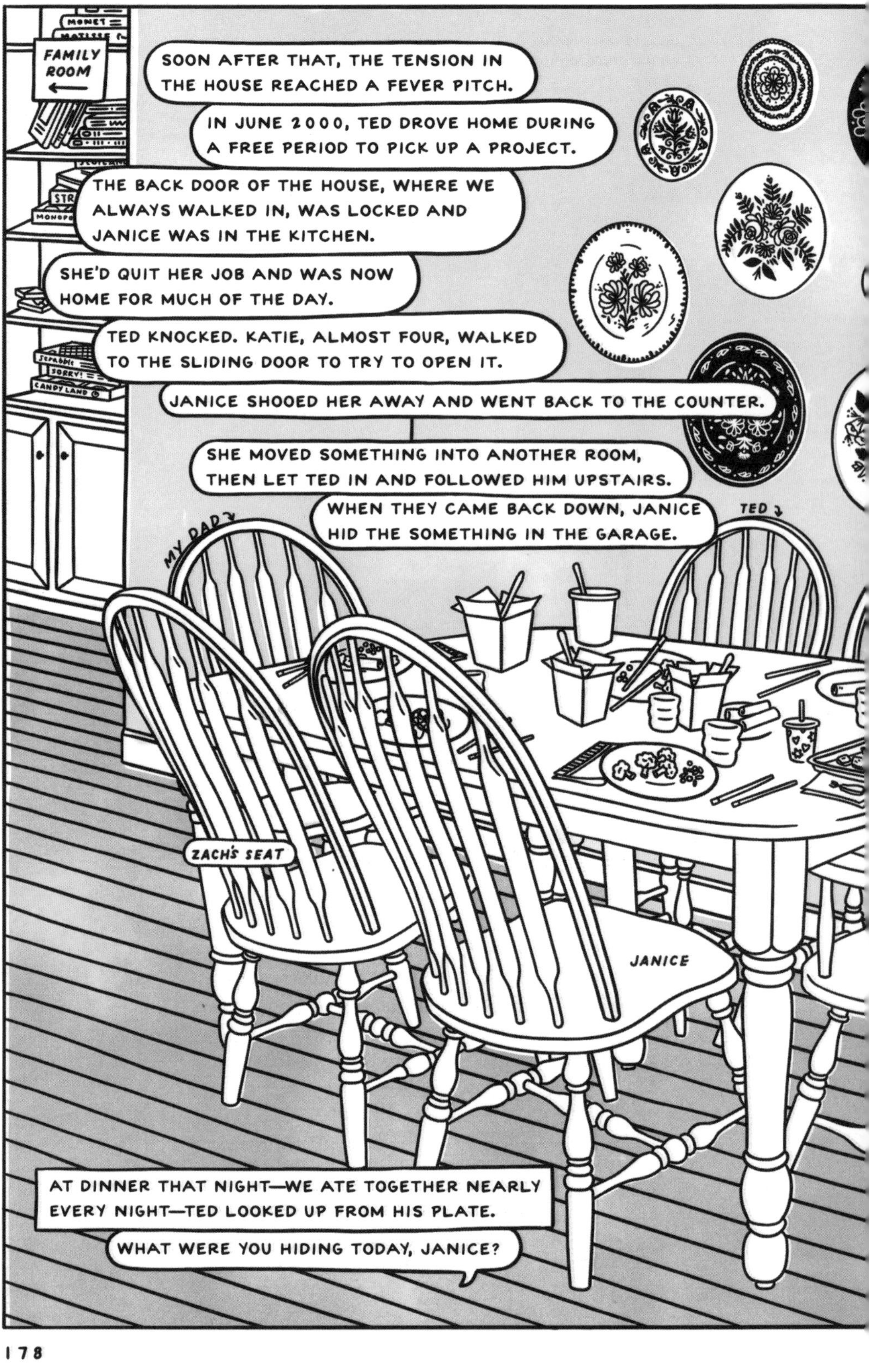
FAMILY ROOM
MONET
SOON AFTER THAT, THE TENSION IN THE HOUSE REACHED A FEVER PITCH.
IN JUNE 2000, TED DROVE HOME DURING A FREE PERIOD TO PICK UP A PROJECT.
THE BACK DOOR OF THE HOUSE, WHERE WE ALWAYS WALKED IN, WAS LOCKED AND JANICE WAS IN THE KITCHEN.
SHE'D QUIT HER JOB AND WAS NOW HOME FOR MUCH OF THE DAY.
TED KNOCKED. KATIE, ALMOST FOUR, WALKED TO THE SLIDING DOOR TO TRY TO OPEN IT.
JANICE SHOOED HER AWAY AND WENT BACK TO THE COUNTER.
SHE MOVED SOMETHING INTO ANOTHER ROOM, THEN LET TED IN AND FOLLOWED HIM UPSTAIRS.
WHEN THEY CAME BACK DOWN, JANICE HID THE SOMETHING IN THE GARAGE.
SORRY!
CANDY LAND
MY DAD
TED
ZACH'S SEAT
JANICE
AT DINNER THAT NIGHT—WE ATE TOGETHER NEARLY EVERY NIGHT—TED LOOKED UP FROM HIS PLATE.
WHAT WERE YOU HIDING TODAY, JANICE?

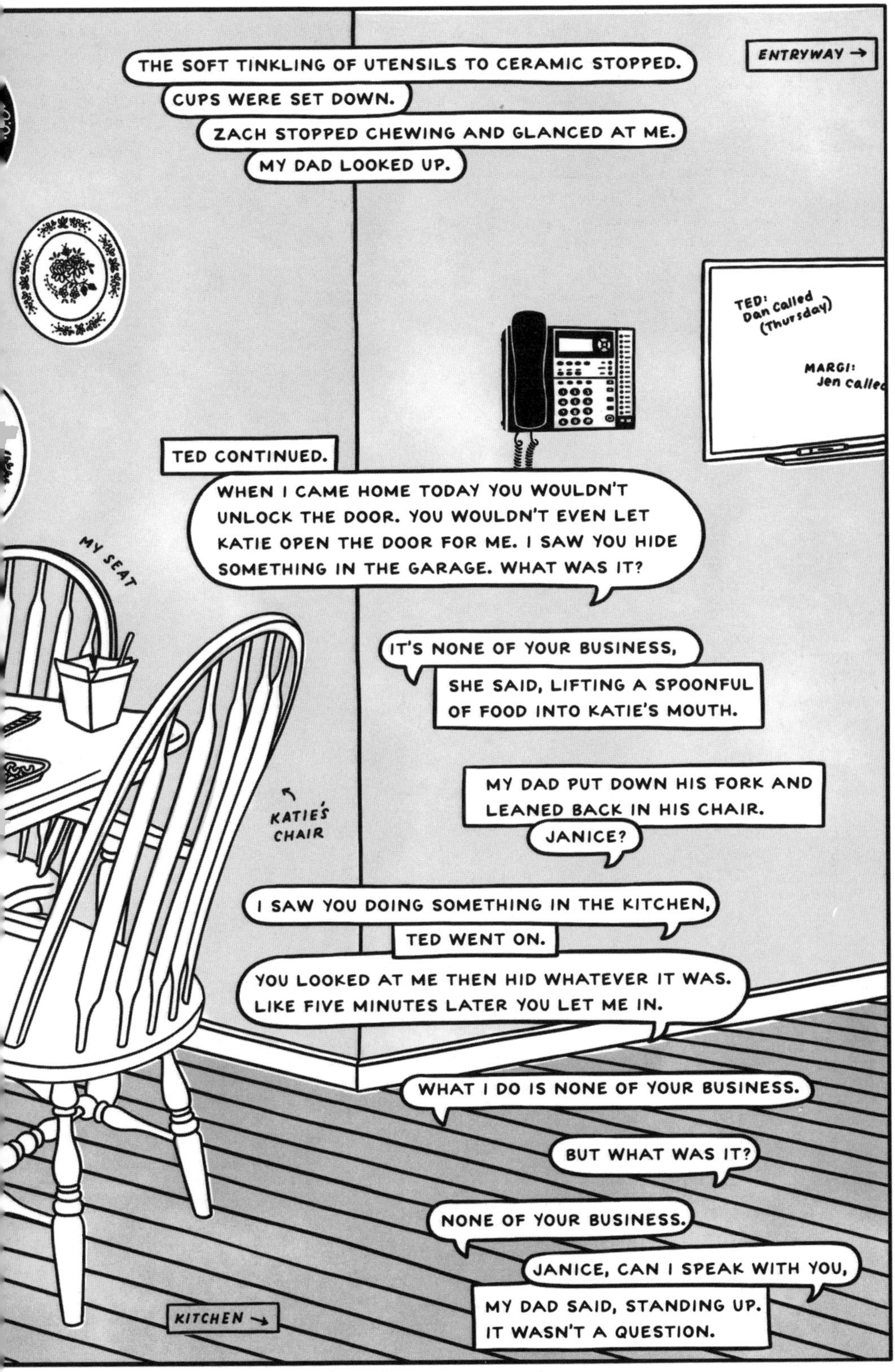

THE SOFT TINKLING OF UTENSILS TO CERAMIC STOPPED.
CUPS WERE SET DOWN.
ZACH STOPPED CHEWING AND GLANCED AT ME.
MY DAD LOOKED UP.
ENTRYWAY →
TED:
Dan called
(Thursday)
MARGI:
Jen called
TED CONTINUED.
WHEN I CAME HOME TODAY YOU WOULDN'T UNLOCK THE DOOR. YOU WOULDN'T EVEN LET KATIE OPEN THE DOOR FOR ME. I SAW YOU HIDE SOMETHING IN THE GARAGE. WHAT WAS IT?
MY SEAT
IT'S NONE OF YOUR BUSINESS,
SHE SAID, LIFTING A SPOONFUL OF FOOD INTO KATIE'S MOUTH.
MY DAD PUT DOWN HIS FORK AND LEANED BACK IN HIS CHAIR.
JANICE?
KATIE'S CHAIR
I SAW YOU DOING SOMETHING IN THE KITCHEN,
TED WENT ON.
YOU LOOKED AT ME THEN HID WHATEVER IT WAS. LIKE FIVE MINUTES LATER YOU LET ME IN.
WHAT I DO IS NONE OF YOUR BUSINESS.
BUT WHAT WAS IT?
NONE OF YOUR BUSINESS.
JANICE, CAN I SPEAK WITH YOU,
MY DAD SAID, STANDING UP. IT WASN'T A QUESTION.
KITCHEN →

THEY WENT UPSTAIRS. TED AND I CHUCKLED UNDER OUR BREATHS.

WE HAD NO IDEA THAT ENOUGH PRESSURE COULD SNAP A FAMILY INTO PARTS.

BY THAT POINT I DON'T THINK WE CARED.

ZACH, AGE THIRTEEN, LOOKED AT US BUT DIDN'T SAY ANYTHING.

A FEW MINUTES LATER THEY RETURNED TO THE TABLE.

GUYS, I SPOKE WITH JANICE. I KNOW WHAT IT WAS. IT'S FINE.

MY DAD SAID.

US ON ONE SIDE...

BUT WHAT WAS IT?
TED ASKED.

AN OLD SWEATER FROM NELLIE

LET IT GO,
MY DAD ORDERED.

THIS IS PROBABLY ONE OF THE LAST PICTURES WE TOOK TOGETHER...

ALL OF US AT TED'S GRADUATION A FEW WEEKS LATER
(MY MOM TOOK THIS PICTURE)

I NEVER FOUND OUT WHAT IT WAS. IN MY DIARY, I SUSPECTED DRUGS, SOMETHING SIMPLE LIKE WEED. IN MORE SENSATIONAL MOMENTS, I THOUGHT IT WAS COCAINE OR PROOF OF AN AFFAIR. WHAT EXACTLY DID I IMAGINE THAT EVIDENCE MIGHT BE? THIS WAS BEFORE CELL PHONES AND TEXT MESSAGES. A LETTER DESCRIBING THE ILLICIT ROMANCE? A RECORDED CONFESSION? A BAG OF DRUGS IN THE FORMAL DINING ROOM? I SUPPOSE I COULD PRESS MY DAD TO DIVULGE WHAT JANICE HID THAT DAY BUT I DON'T THINK IT MATTERS. THE SECRET ITSELF WAS THE AFFRONT, THE FACT OF ONE ADULT HIDING SOMETHING IN OUR MIDST AND REFUSING TO SAY WHAT IT WAS. ALL COUPLES HAVE PRIVATE MATTERS, BUT THIS WAS A ONE-PARENT COVER-UP, A CLANDESTINE ACT THAT MEANT DISTANCE. JANICE WAS CREATING A BOUNDARY FOR HERSELF AND A SEPARATION FROM THE REST OF US. A SECRET PUNCTURES CLOSENESS, CRATERS INTIMACY. IT LEAVES THE OTHER PARTY MYSTIFIED, SEARCHING FOR A LINK IN THE CHAIN. WHEN JANICE AND MY DAD REFUSED TO SAY MORE, OUR FRACTURING SOLIDIFIED.

SOON AFTER THAT NIGHT, TED WAS OFF TO COLLEGE, NEVER TO AGAIN CONFRONT JANICE AT A FAMILY DINNER IN OUR HOUSE.

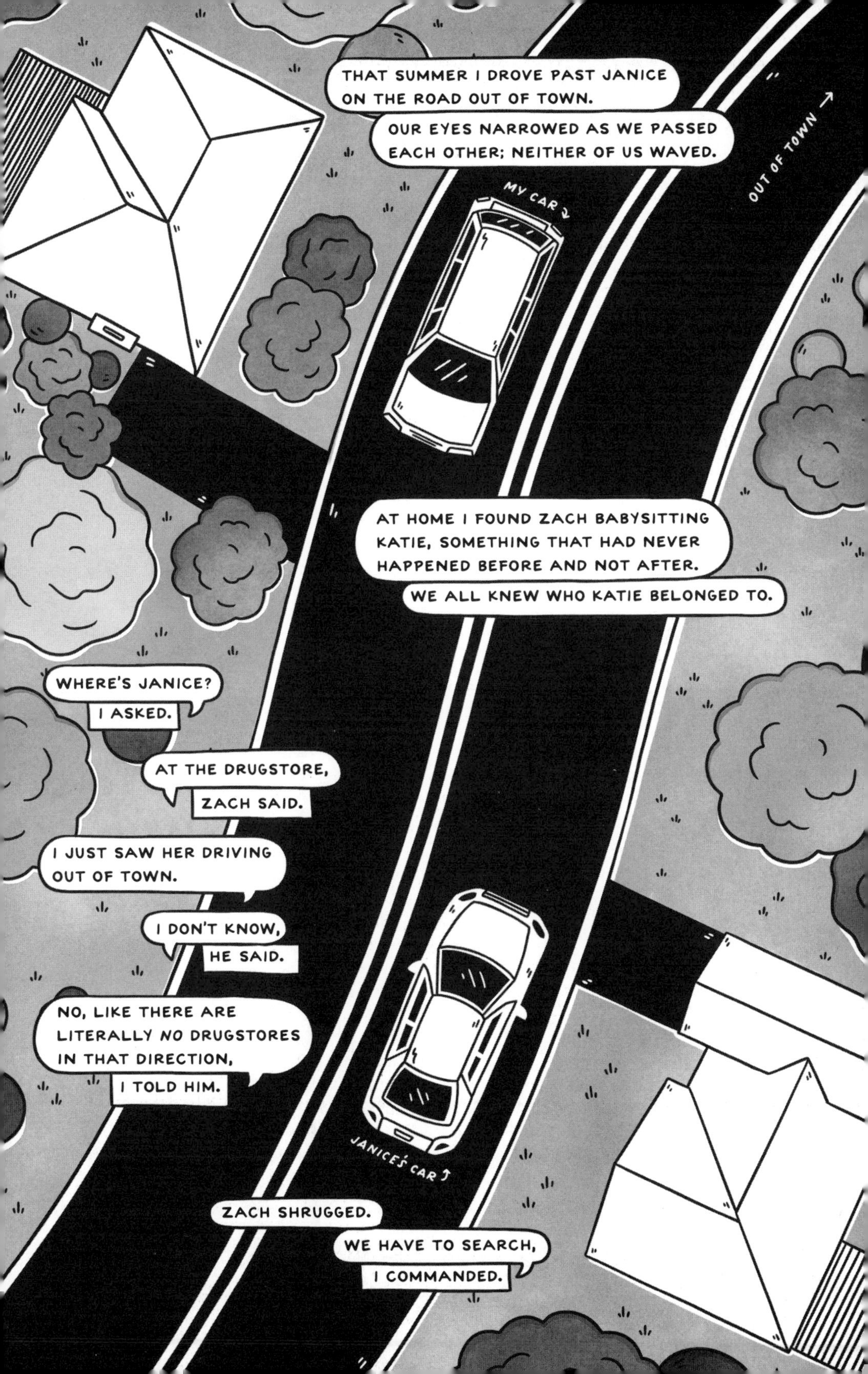
THAT SUMMER I DROVE PAST JANICE ON THE ROAD OUT OF TOWN.
OUR EYES NARROWED AS WE PASSED EACH OTHER; NEITHER OF US WAVED.
MY CAR
OUT OF TOWN →
AT HOME I FOUND ZACH BABYSITTING KATIE, SOMETHING THAT HAD NEVER HAPPENED BEFORE AND NOT AFTER.
WE ALL KNEW WHO KATIE BELONGED TO.
WHERE'S JANICE?
I ASKED.
AT THE DRUGSTORE,
ZACH SAID.
I JUST SAW HER DRIVING OUT OF TOWN.
I DON'T KNOW,
HE SAID.
NO, LIKE THERE ARE LITERALLY *NO* DRUGSTORES IN THAT DIRECTION,
I TOLD HIM.
JANICE'S CAR
ZACH SHRUGGED.
WE HAVE TO SEARCH,
I COMMANDED.

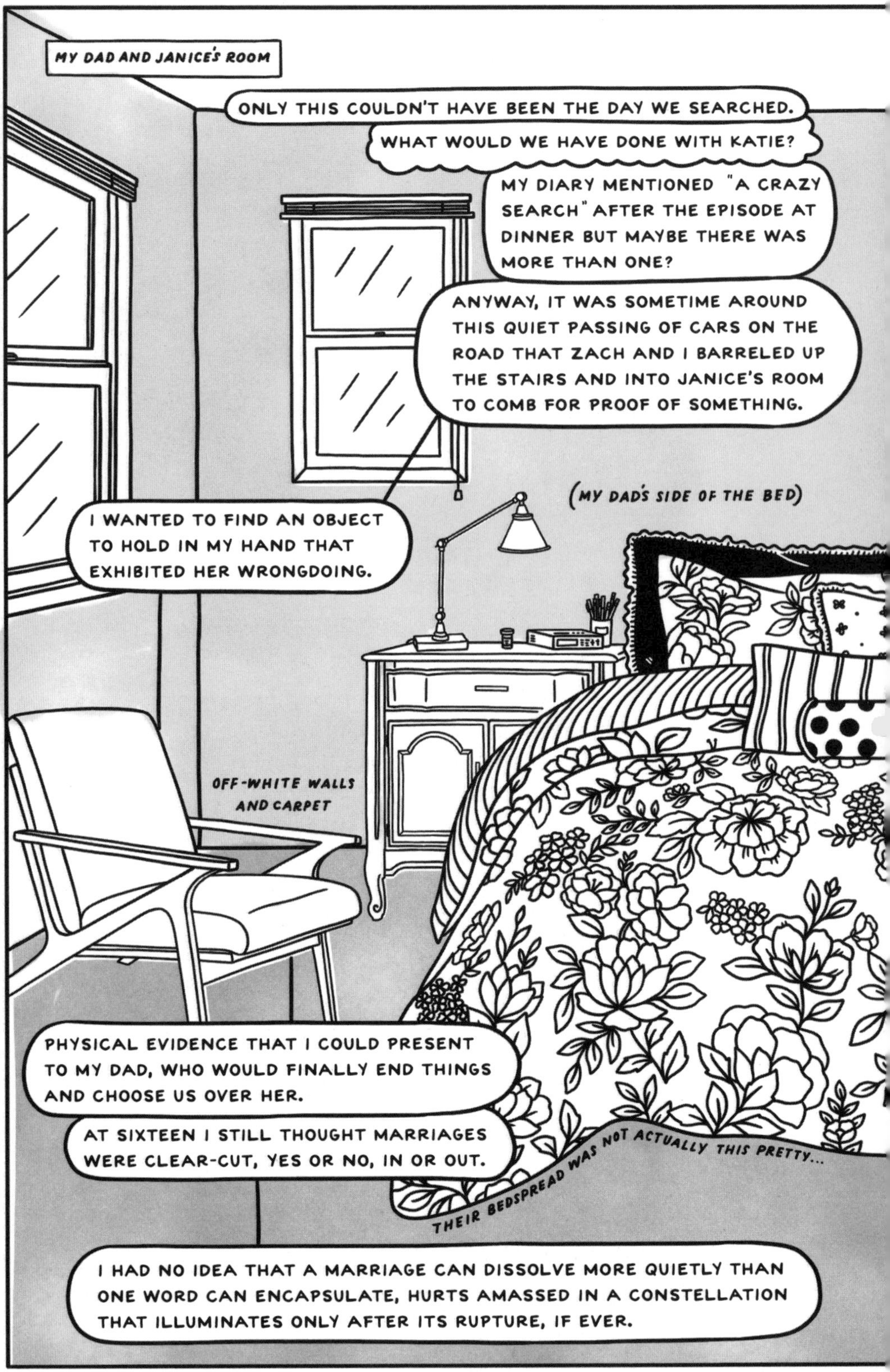
MY DAD AND JANICE'S ROOM
ONLY THIS COULDN'T HAVE BEEN THE DAY WE SEARCHED.
WHAT WOULD WE HAVE DONE WITH KATIE?
MY DIARY MENTIONED "A CRAZY SEARCH" AFTER THE EPISODE AT DINNER BUT MAYBE THERE WAS MORE THAN ONE?
ANYWAY, IT WAS SOMETIME AROUND THIS QUIET PASSING OF CARS ON THE ROAD THAT ZACH AND I BARRELED UP THE STAIRS AND INTO JANICE'S ROOM TO COMB FOR PROOF OF SOMETHING.
I WANTED TO FIND AN OBJECT TO HOLD IN MY HAND THAT EXHIBITED HER WRONGDOING.
(MY DAD'S SIDE OF THE BED)
OFF-WHITE WALLS AND CARPET
PHYSICAL EVIDENCE THAT I COULD PRESENT TO MY DAD, WHO WOULD FINALLY END THINGS AND CHOOSE US OVER HER.
AT SIXTEEN I STILL THOUGHT MARRIAGES WERE CLEAR-CUT, YES OR NO, IN OR OUT.
THEIR BEDSPREAD WAS NOT ACTUALLY THIS PRETTY...
I HAD NO IDEA THAT A MARRIAGE CAN DISSOLVE MORE QUIETLY THAN ONE WORD CAN ENCAPSULATE, HURTS AMASSED IN A CONSTELLATION THAT ILLUMINATES ONLY AFTER ITS RUPTURE, IF EVER.

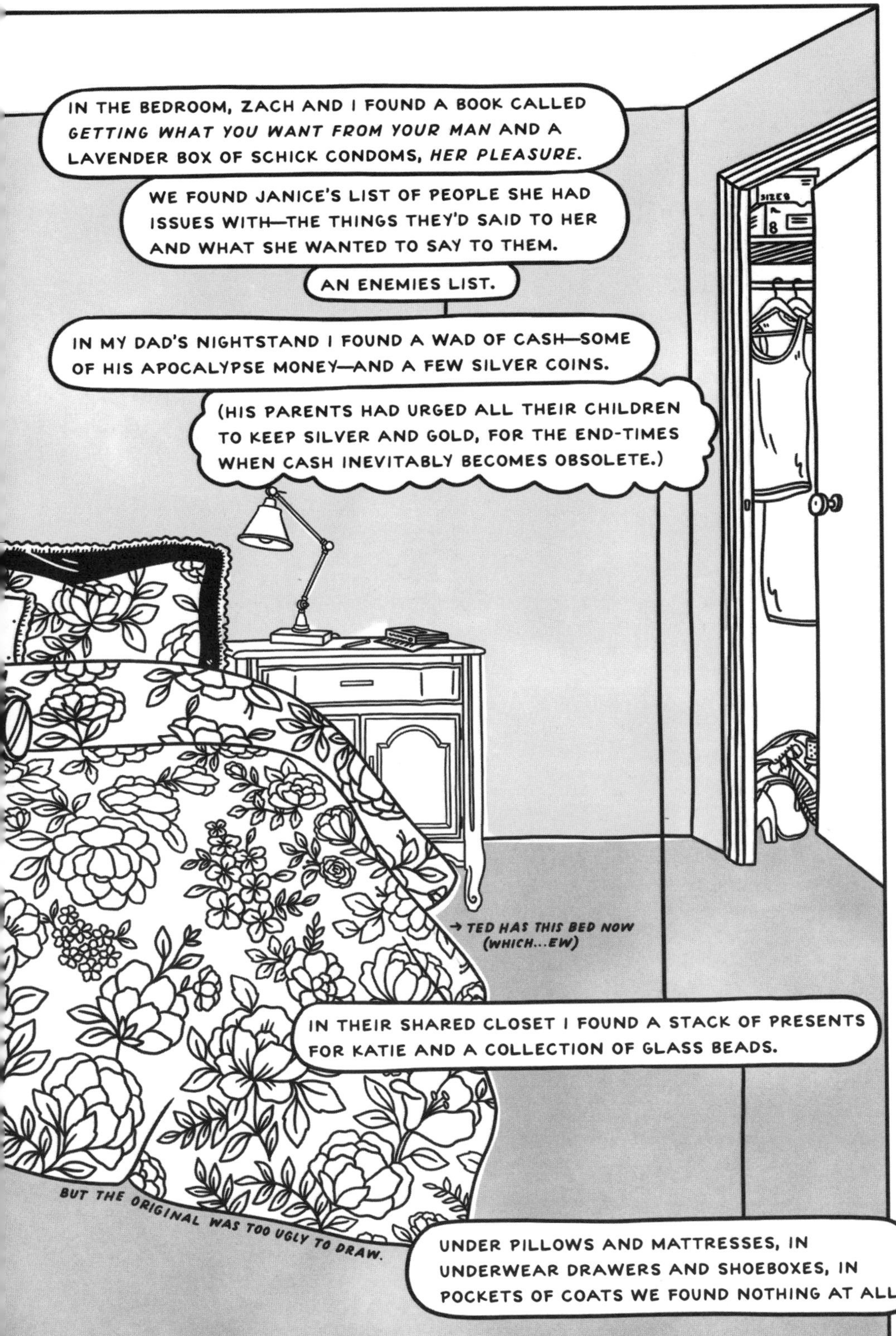

IN THE BEDROOM, ZACH AND I FOUND A BOOK CALLED *GETTING WHAT YOU WANT FROM YOUR MAN* AND A LAVENDER BOX OF SCHICK CONDOMS, *HER PLEASURE*.
WE FOUND JANICE'S LIST OF PEOPLE SHE HAD ISSUES WITH—THE THINGS THEY'D SAID TO HER AND WHAT SHE WANTED TO SAY TO THEM.
AN ENEMIES LIST.
IN MY DAD'S NIGHTSTAND I FOUND A WAD OF CASH—SOME OF HIS APOCALYPSE MONEY—AND A FEW SILVER COINS.
(HIS PARENTS HAD URGED ALL THEIR CHILDREN TO KEEP SILVER AND GOLD, FOR THE END-TIMES WHEN CASH INEVITABLY BECOMES OBSOLETE.)
SIZES
8
→ TED HAS THIS BED NOW (WHICH...EW)
IN THEIR SHARED CLOSET I FOUND A STACK OF PRESENTS FOR KATIE AND A COLLECTION OF GLASS BEADS.
BUT THE ORIGINAL WAS TOO UGLY TO DRAW.
UNDER PILLOWS AND MATTRESSES, IN UNDERWEAR DRAWERS AND SHOEBOXES, IN POCKETS OF COATS WE FOUND NOTHING AT ALL.

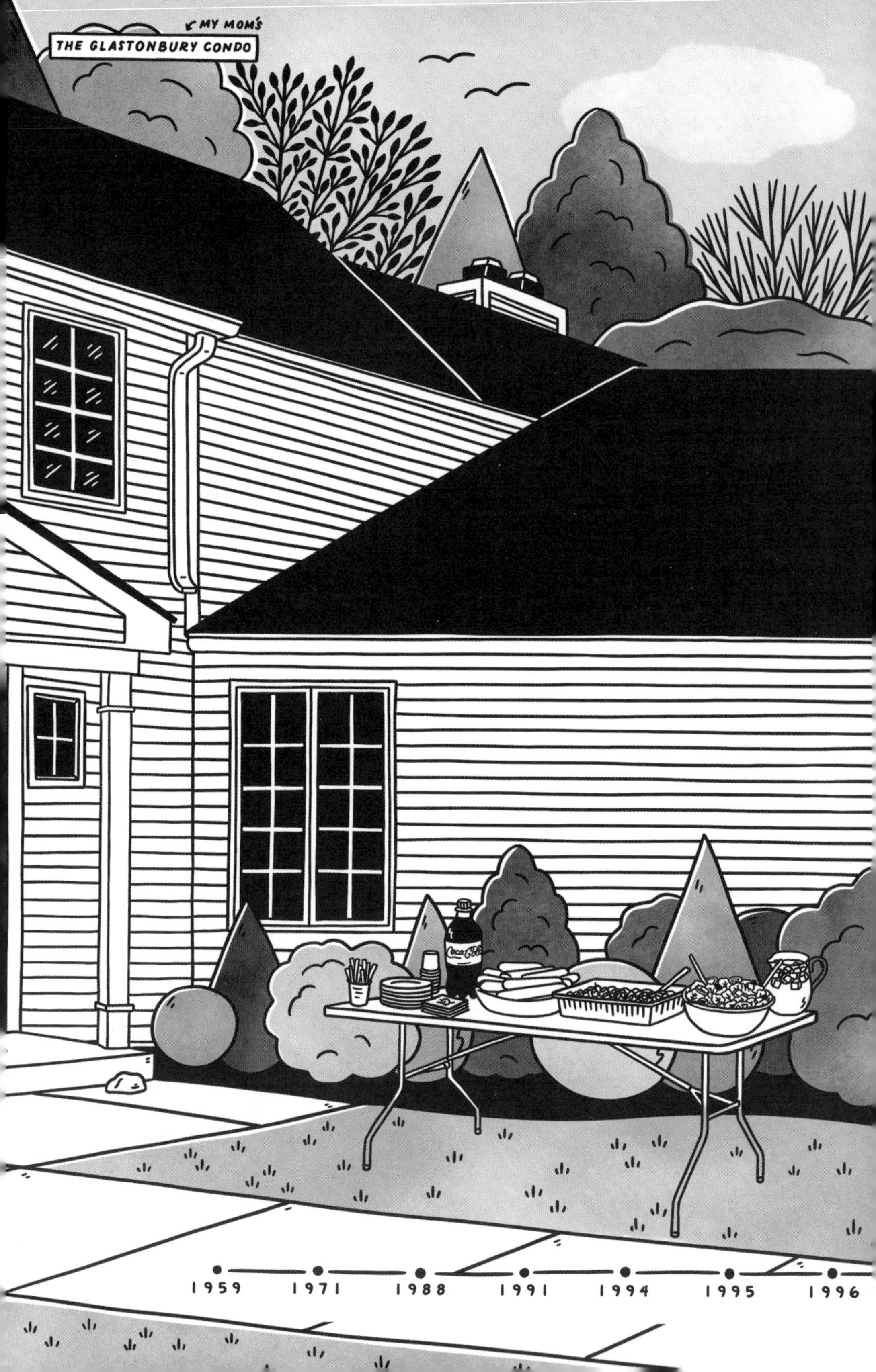

MY MOM'S
THE GLASTONBURY CONDO
Coca-Cola
1959
1971
1988
1991
1994
1995
1996

CHAPTER 14

The Dinner Party

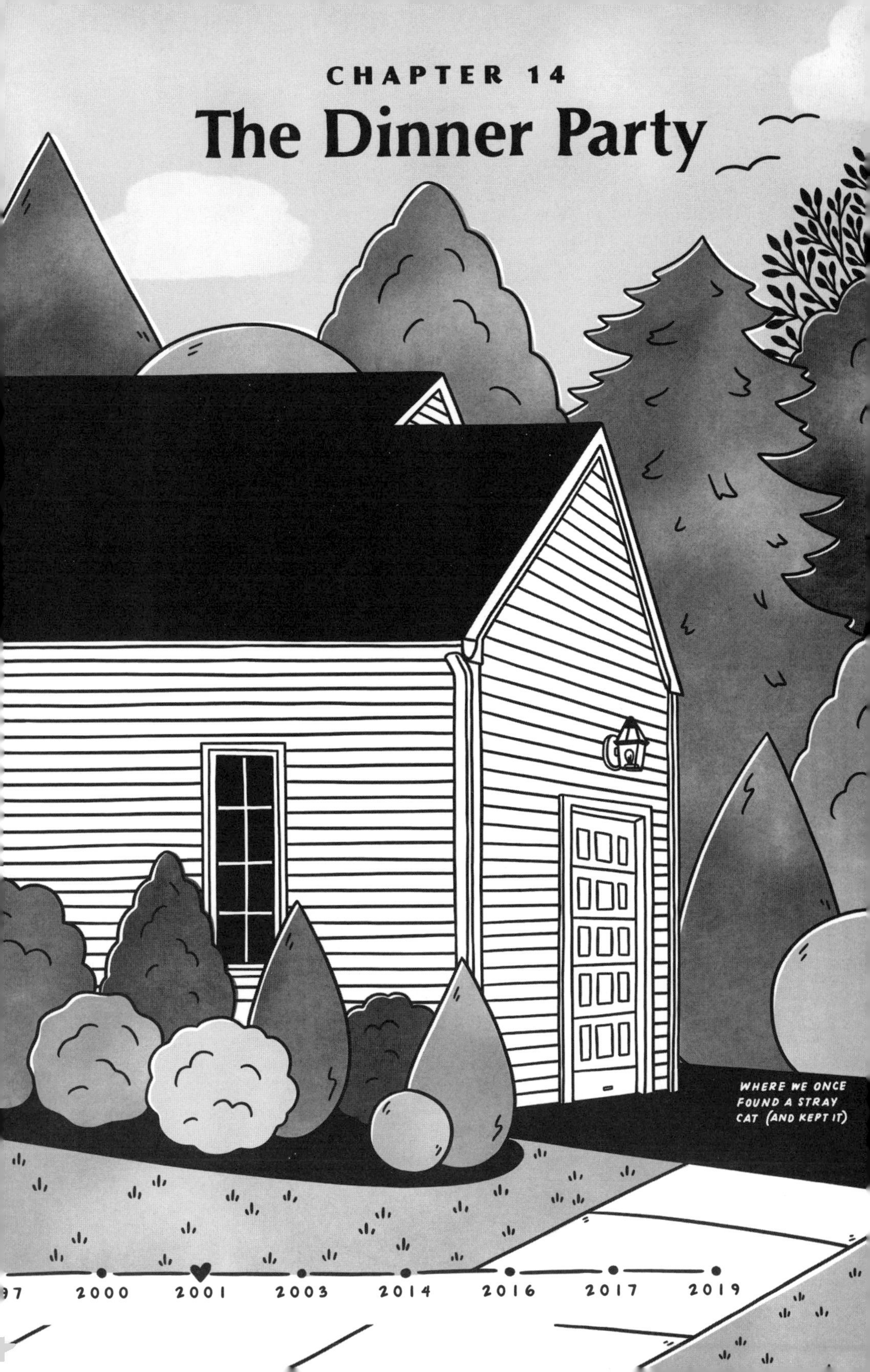
WHERE WE ONCE
FOUND A STRAY
CAT (AND KEPT IT)
2000
2001
2003
2014
2016
2017
2019

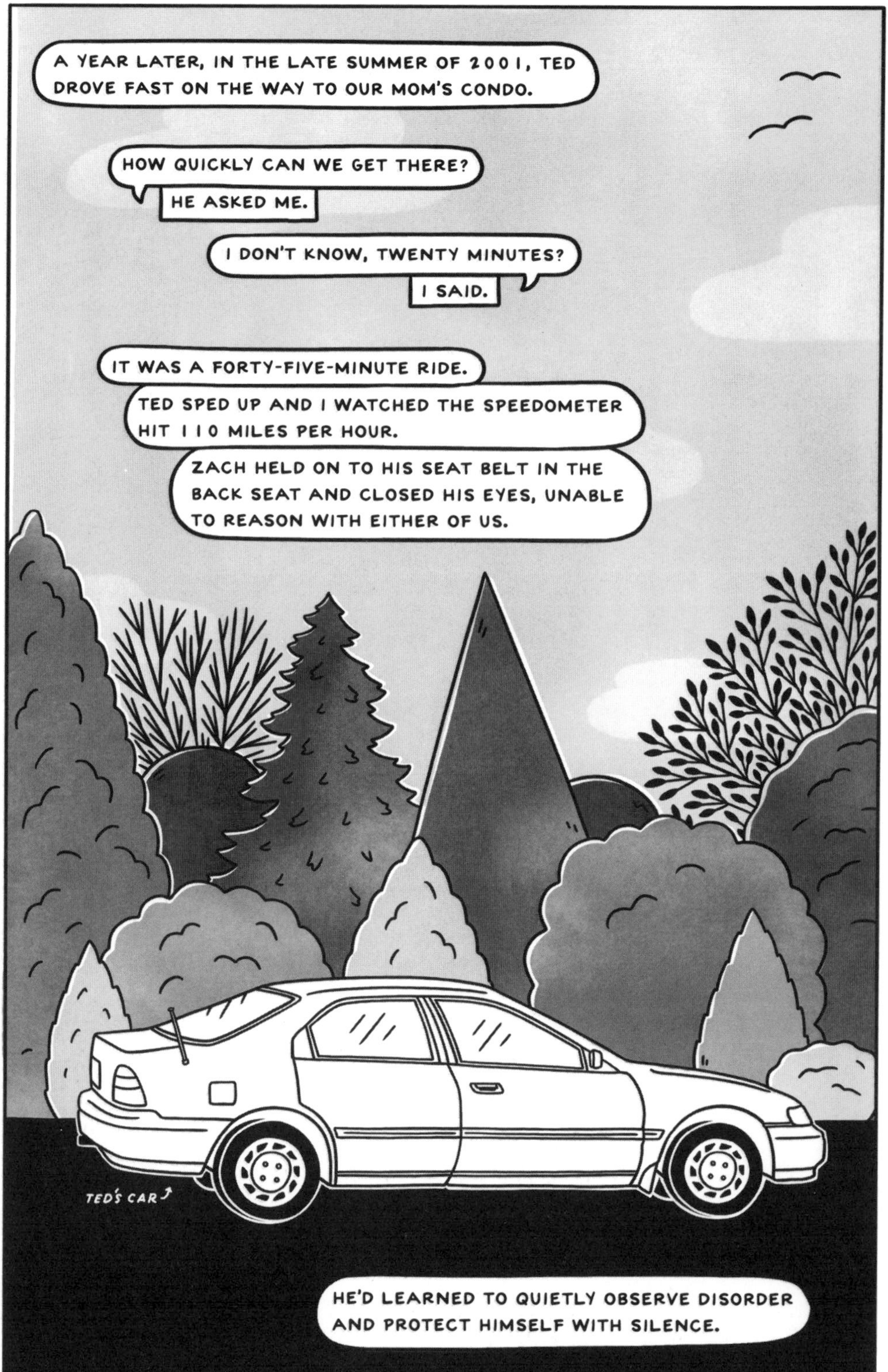
A YEAR LATER, IN THE LATE SUMMER OF 2001, TED DROVE FAST ON THE WAY TO OUR MOM'S CONDO.
HOW QUICKLY CAN WE GET THERE?
HE ASKED ME.
I DON'T KNOW, TWENTY MINUTES?
I SAID.
IT WAS A FORTY-FIVE-MINUTE RIDE.
TED SPED UP AND I WATCHED THE SPEEDOMETER HIT 110 MILES PER HOUR.
ZACH HELD ON TO HIS SEAT BELT IN THE BACK SEAT AND CLOSED HIS EYES, UNABLE TO REASON WITH EITHER OF US.
TED'S CAR
HE'D LEARNED TO QUIETLY OBSERVE DISORDER AND PROTECT HIMSELF WITH SILENCE.

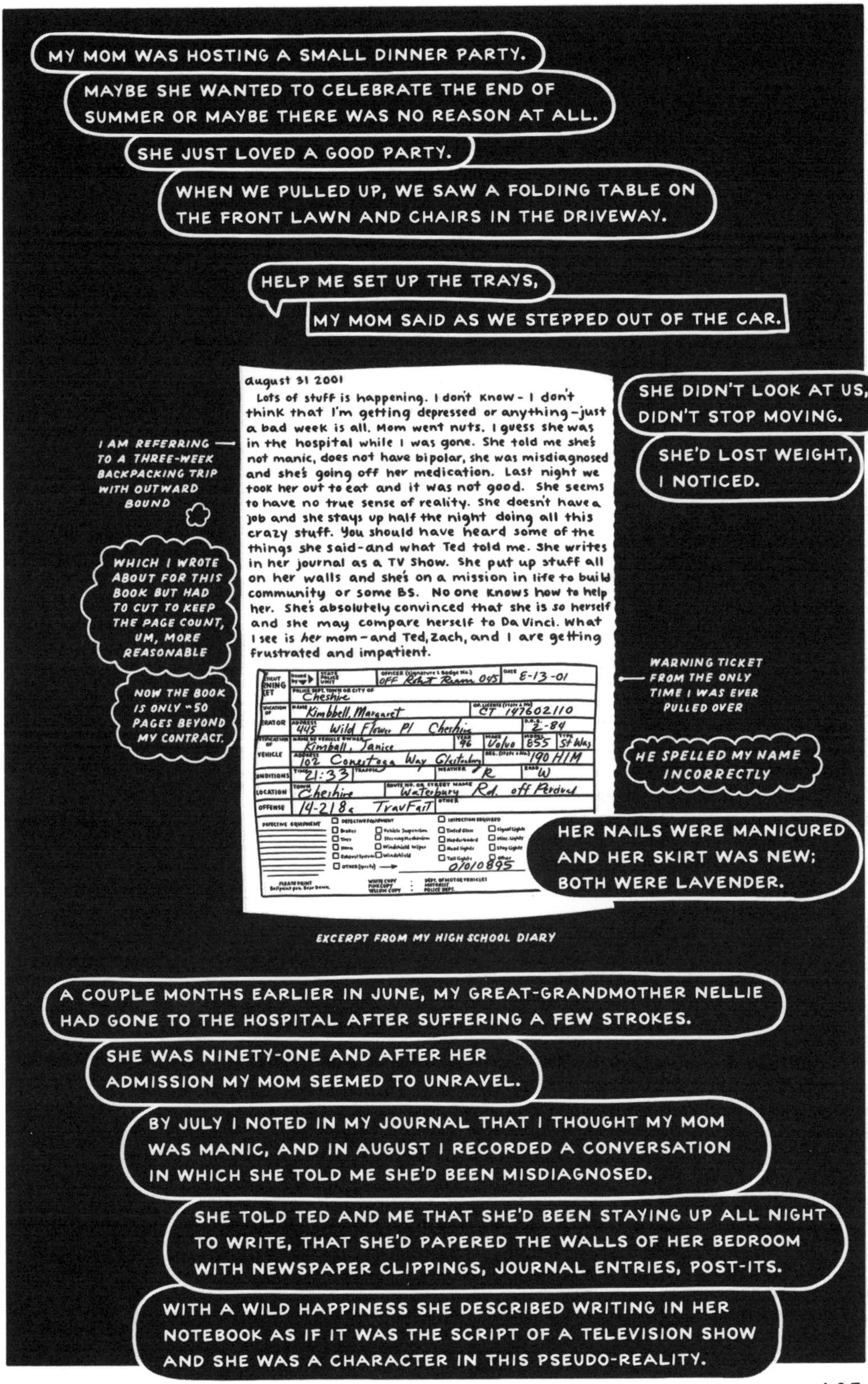

MY MOM WAS HOSTING A SMALL DINNER PARTY.
MAYBE SHE WANTED TO CELEBRATE THE END OF SUMMER OR MAYBE THERE WAS NO REASON AT ALL.
SHE JUST LOVED A GOOD PARTY.
WHEN WE PULLED UP, WE SAW A FOLDING TABLE ON THE FRONT LAWN AND CHAIRS IN THE DRIVEWAY.
HELP ME SET UP THE TRAYS,
MY MOM SAID AS WE STEPPED OUT OF THE CAR.
August 31 2001
Lots of stuff is happening. I don't know - I don't think that I'm getting depressed or anything - just a bad week is all. Mom went nuts. I guess she was in the hospital while I was gone. She told me she's not manic, does not have bipolar, she was misdiagnosed and she's going off her medication. Last night we took her out to eat and it was not good. She seems to have no true sense of reality. She doesn't have a job and she stays up half the night doing all this crazy stuff. You should have heard some of the things she said - and what Ted told me. She writes in her journal as a TV show. She put up stuff all on her walls and she's on a mission in life to build community or some BS. No one knows how to help her. She's absolutely convinced that she is so herself and she may compare herself to Da Vinci. What I see is her mom - and Ted, Zach, and I are getting frustrated and impatient.
I AM REFERRING TO A THREE-WEEK BACKPACKING TRIP WITH OUTWARD BOUND
WHICH I WROTE ABOUT FOR THIS BOOK BUT HAD TO CUT TO KEEP THE PAGE COUNT, UM, MORE REASONABLE
NOW THE BOOK IS ONLY ~50 PAGES BEYOND MY CONTRACT.
OFFICER (signature & badge no.) OFF Robt Ream 045
DATE 8-13-01
POLICE DEPT. TOWN OR CITY OF Cheshire
NAME Kimbbell, Margaret
OP. LICENSE (state & no.) CT 147602110
ADDRESS 445 Wild Flower Pl Cheshire
D.O.B. 2-84
NAME OF VEHICLE OWNER Kimball, Janice
YEAR 96 MAKE Volvo MODEL 855 TYPE St Wag
ADDRESS 102 Conestoga Way Glastonbury
REG. (state & no.) 190 HIM
CONDITIONS TIME 21:33 TRAFFIC WEATHER R ROAD W
LOCATION TOWN Cheshire ROUTE NO. OR STREET NAME Waterbury Rd. off Perdue
OFFENSE 14-218a TravFast OTHER
DEFECTIVE EQUIPMENT
0l010895
WHITE COPY - DEPT. OF MOTOR VEHICLES
PINK COPY - MOTORIST
YELLOW COPY - POLICE DEPT.
PLEASE PRINT Ballpoint pen. Bear down.
SHE DIDN'T LOOK AT US, DIDN'T STOP MOVING.
SHE'D LOST WEIGHT, I NOTICED.
WARNING TICKET FROM THE ONLY TIME I WAS EVER PULLED OVER
HE SPELLED MY NAME INCORRECTLY
HER NAILS WERE MANICURED AND HER SKIRT WAS NEW; BOTH WERE LAVENDER.
EXCERPT FROM MY HIGH SCHOOL DIARY
A COUPLE MONTHS EARLIER IN JUNE, MY GREAT-GRANDMOTHER NELLIE HAD GONE TO THE HOSPITAL AFTER SUFFERING A FEW STROKES.
SHE WAS NINETY-ONE AND AFTER HER ADMISSION MY MOM SEEMED TO UNRAVEL.
BY JULY I NOTED IN MY JOURNAL THAT I THOUGHT MY MOM WAS MANIC, AND IN AUGUST I RECORDED A CONVERSATION IN WHICH SHE TOLD ME SHE'D BEEN MISDIAGNOSED.
SHE TOLD TED AND ME THAT SHE'D BEEN STAYING UP ALL NIGHT TO WRITE, THAT SHE'D PAPERED THE WALLS OF HER BEDROOM WITH NEWSPAPER CLIPPINGS, JOURNAL ENTRIES, POST-ITS.
WITH A WILD HAPPINESS SHE DESCRIBED WRITING IN HER NOTEBOOK AS IF IT WAS THE SCRIPT OF A TELEVISION SHOW AND SHE WAS A CHARACTER IN THIS PSEUDO-REALITY.

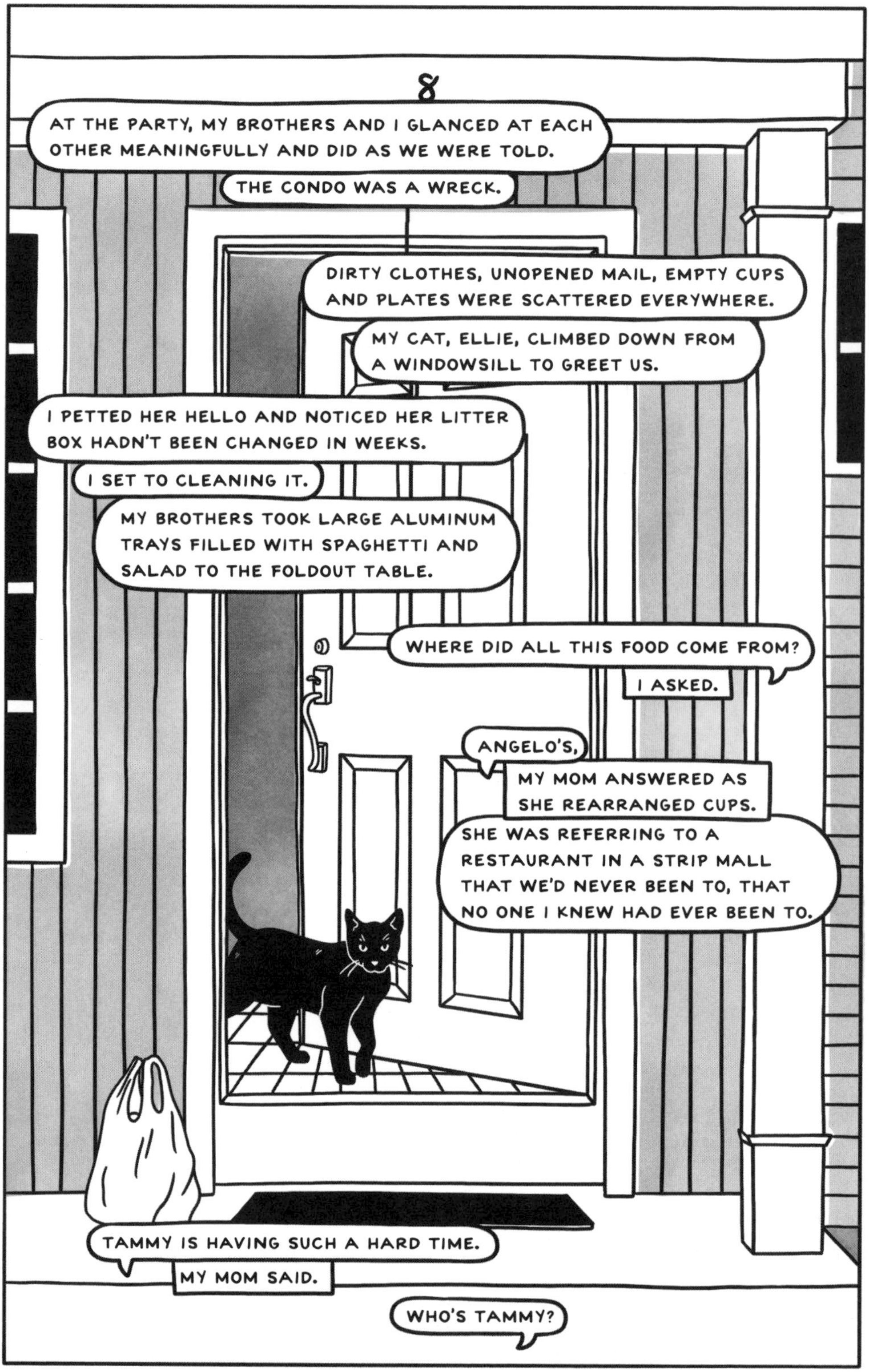
8
AT THE PARTY, MY BROTHERS AND I GLANCED AT EACH OTHER MEANINGFULLY AND DID AS WE WERE TOLD.
THE CONDO WAS A WRECK.
DIRTY CLOTHES, UNOPENED MAIL, EMPTY CUPS AND PLATES WERE SCATTERED EVERYWHERE.
MY CAT, ELLIE, CLIMBED DOWN FROM A WINDOWSILL TO GREET US.
I PETTED HER HELLO AND NOTICED HER LITTER BOX HADN'T BEEN CHANGED IN WEEKS.
I SET TO CLEANING IT.
MY BROTHERS TOOK LARGE ALUMINUM TRAYS FILLED WITH SPAGHETTI AND SALAD TO THE FOLDOUT TABLE.
WHERE DID ALL THIS FOOD COME FROM?
I ASKED.
ANGELO'S,
MY MOM ANSWERED AS SHE REARRANGED CUPS.
SHE WAS REFERRING TO A RESTAURANT IN A STRIP MALL THAT WE'D NEVER BEEN TO, THAT NO ONE I KNEW HAD EVER BEEN TO.
TAMMY IS HAVING SUCH A HARD TIME.
MY MOM SAID.
WHO'S TAMMY?

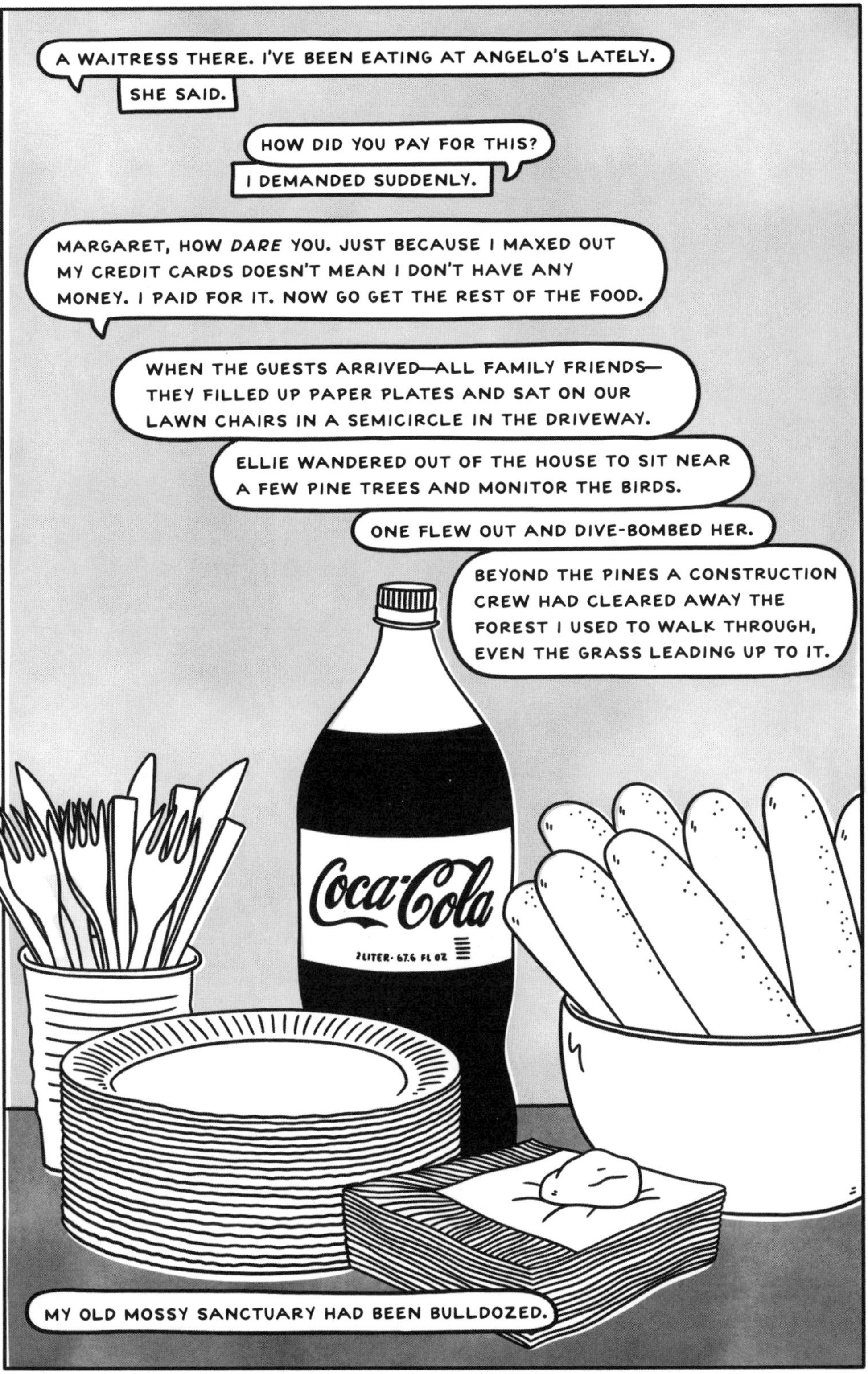
A WAITRESS THERE. I'VE BEEN EATING AT ANGELO'S LATELY.
SHE SAID.
HOW DID YOU PAY FOR THIS?
I DEMANDED SUDDENLY.
MARGARET, HOW *DARE* YOU. JUST BECAUSE I MAXED OUT MY CREDIT CARDS DOESN'T MEAN I DON'T HAVE ANY MONEY. I PAID FOR IT. NOW GO GET THE REST OF THE FOOD.
WHEN THE GUESTS ARRIVED—ALL FAMILY FRIENDS—THEY FILLED UP PAPER PLATES AND SAT ON OUR LAWN CHAIRS IN A SEMICIRCLE IN THE DRIVEWAY.
ELLIE WANDERED OUT OF THE HOUSE TO SIT NEAR A FEW PINE TREES AND MONITOR THE BIRDS.
ONE FLEW OUT AND DIVE-BOMBED HER.
BEYOND THE PINES A CONSTRUCTION CREW HAD CLEARED AWAY THE FOREST I USED TO WALK THROUGH, EVEN THE GRASS LEADING UP TO IT.
Coca-Cola
2LITER · 67.6 FL OZ
MY OLD MOSSY SANCTUARY HAD BEEN BULLDOZED.

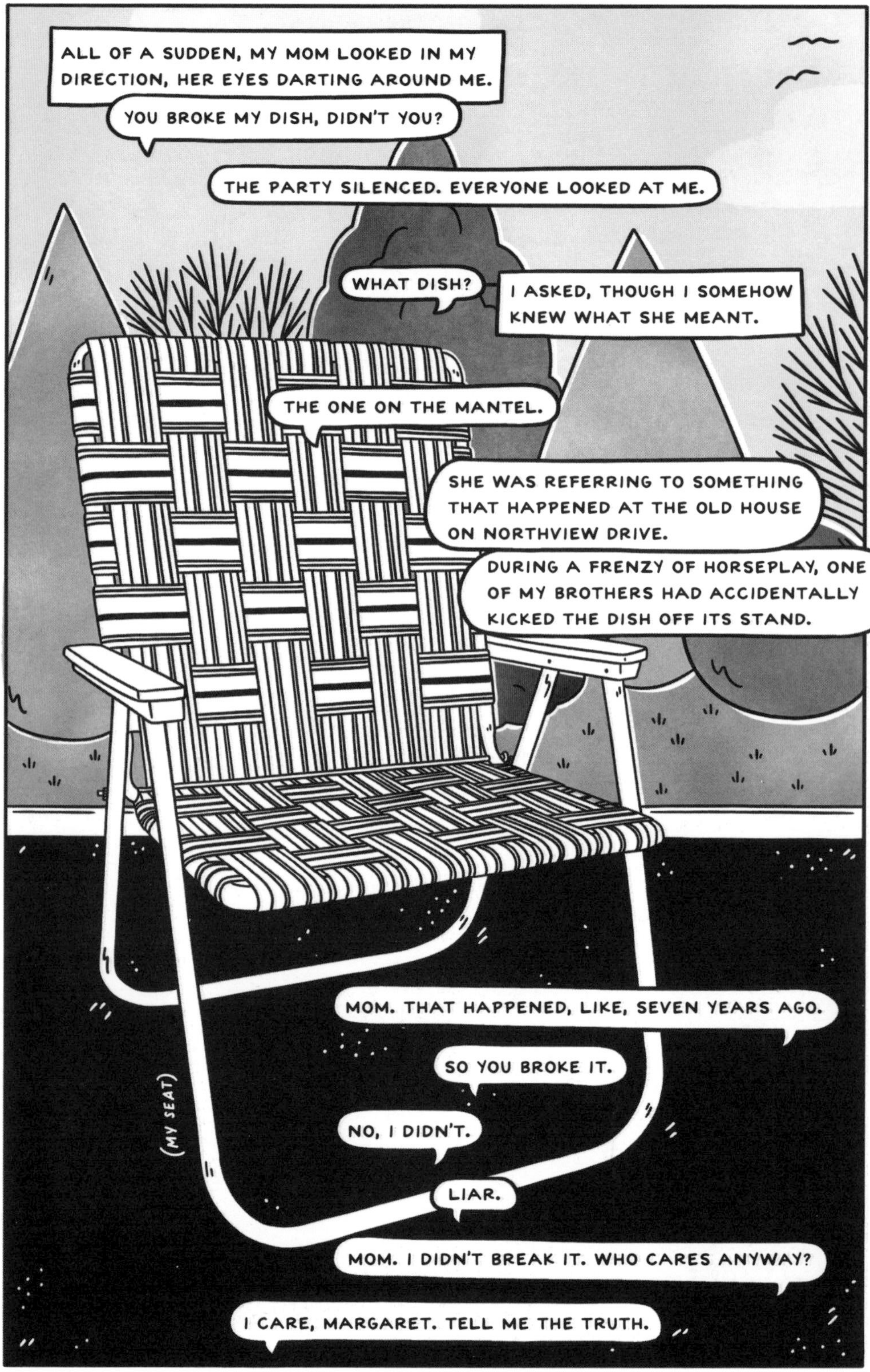
ALL OF A SUDDEN, MY MOM LOOKED IN MY DIRECTION, HER EYES DARTING AROUND ME.
YOU BROKE MY DISH, DIDN'T YOU?
THE PARTY SILENCED. EVERYONE LOOKED AT ME.
WHAT DISH?
I ASKED, THOUGH I SOMEHOW KNEW WHAT SHE MEANT.
THE ONE ON THE MANTEL.
SHE WAS REFERRING TO SOMETHING THAT HAPPENED AT THE OLD HOUSE ON NORTHVIEW DRIVE.
DURING A FRENZY OF HORSEPLAY, ONE OF MY BROTHERS HAD ACCIDENTALLY KICKED THE DISH OFF ITS STAND.
(MY SEAT)
MOM. THAT HAPPENED, LIKE, SEVEN YEARS AGO.
SO YOU BROKE IT.
NO, I DIDN'T.
LIAR.
MOM. I DIDN'T BREAK IT. WHO CARES ANYWAY?
I CARE, MARGARET. TELL ME THE TRUTH.

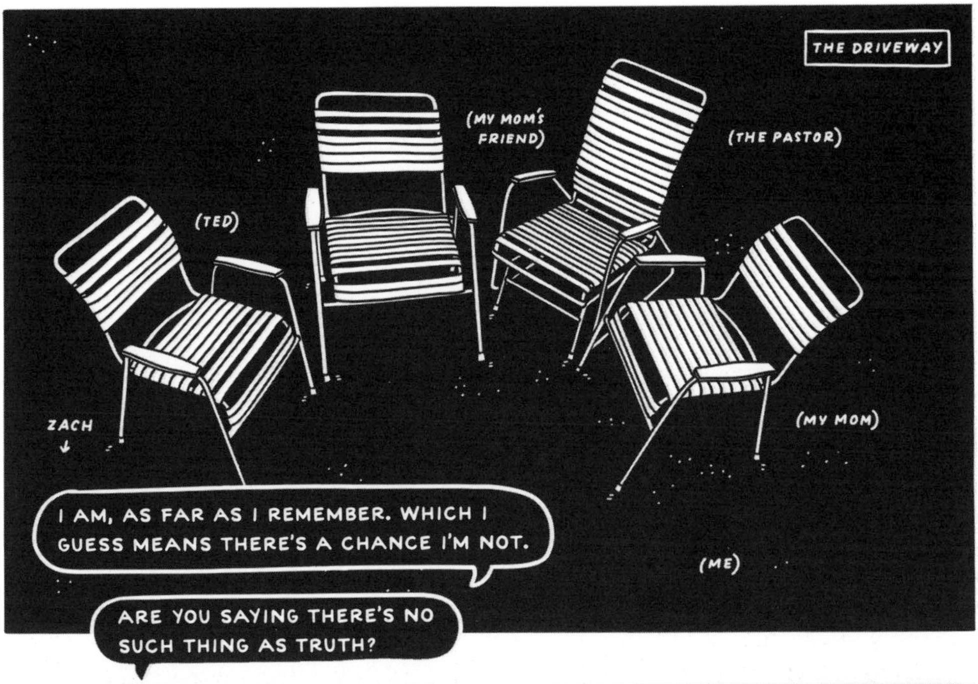
THE DRIVEWAY
(MY MOM'S FRIEND)
(THE PASTOR)
(TED)
ZACH
(MY MOM)
I AM, AS FAR AS I REMEMBER. WHICH I GUESS MEANS THERE'S A CHANCE I'M NOT.
(ME)
ARE YOU SAYING THERE'S NO SUCH THING AS TRUTH?

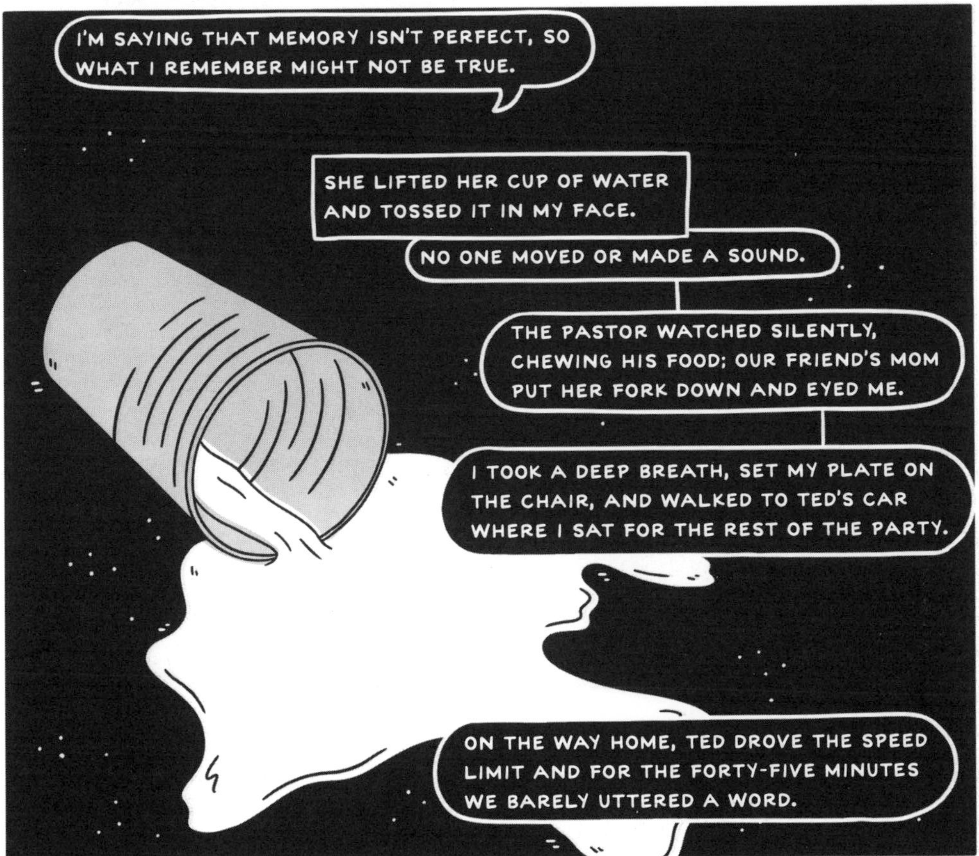
I'M SAYING THAT MEMORY ISN'T PERFECT, SO WHAT I REMEMBER MIGHT NOT BE TRUE.
SHE LIFTED HER CUP OF WATER AND TOSSED IT IN MY FACE.
NO ONE MOVED OR MADE A SOUND.
THE PASTOR WATCHED SILENTLY, CHEWING HIS FOOD; OUR FRIEND'S MOM PUT HER FORK DOWN AND EYED ME.
I TOOK A DEEP BREATH, SET MY PLATE ON THE CHAIR, AND WALKED TO TED'S CAR WHERE I SAT FOR THE REST OF THE PARTY.
ON THE WAY HOME, TED DROVE THE SPEED LIMIT AND FOR THE FORTY-FIVE MINUTES WE BARELY UTTERED A WORD.

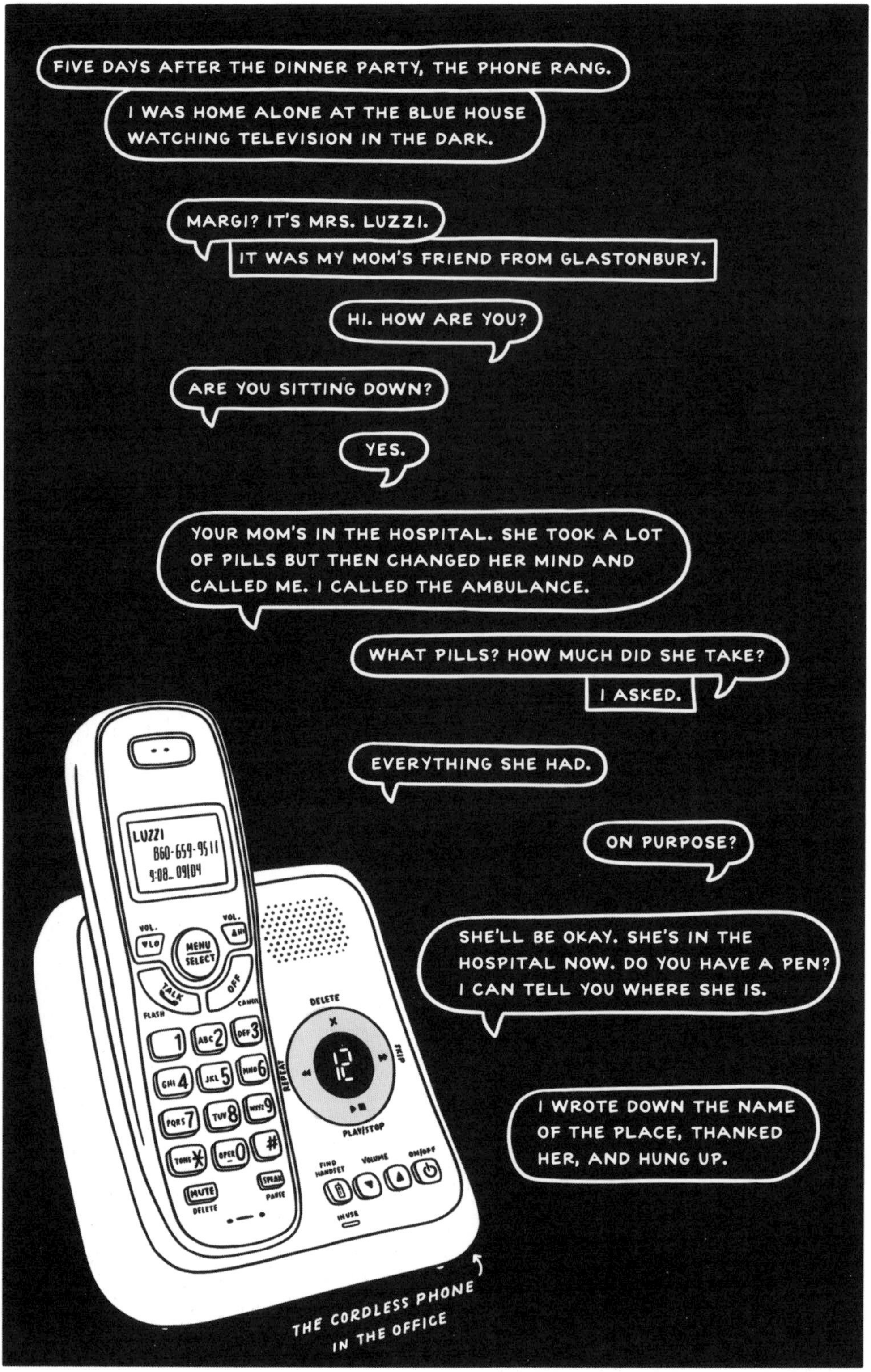
FIVE DAYS AFTER THE DINNER PARTY, THE PHONE RANG.
I WAS HOME ALONE AT THE BLUE HOUSE WATCHING TELEVISION IN THE DARK.
MARGI? IT'S MRS. LUZZI.
IT WAS MY MOM'S FRIEND FROM GLASTONBURY.
HI. HOW ARE YOU?
ARE YOU SITTING DOWN?
YES.
YOUR MOM'S IN THE HOSPITAL. SHE TOOK A LOT OF PILLS BUT THEN CHANGED HER MIND AND CALLED ME. I CALLED THE AMBULANCE.
WHAT PILLS? HOW MUCH DID SHE TAKE?
I ASKED.
EVERYTHING SHE HAD.
ON PURPOSE?
SHE'LL BE OKAY. SHE'S IN THE HOSPITAL NOW. DO YOU HAVE A PEN? I CAN TELL YOU WHERE SHE IS.
I WROTE DOWN THE NAME OF THE PLACE, THANKED HER, AND HUNG UP.
LUZZI
860-659-9511
THE CORDLESS PHONE IN THE OFFICE

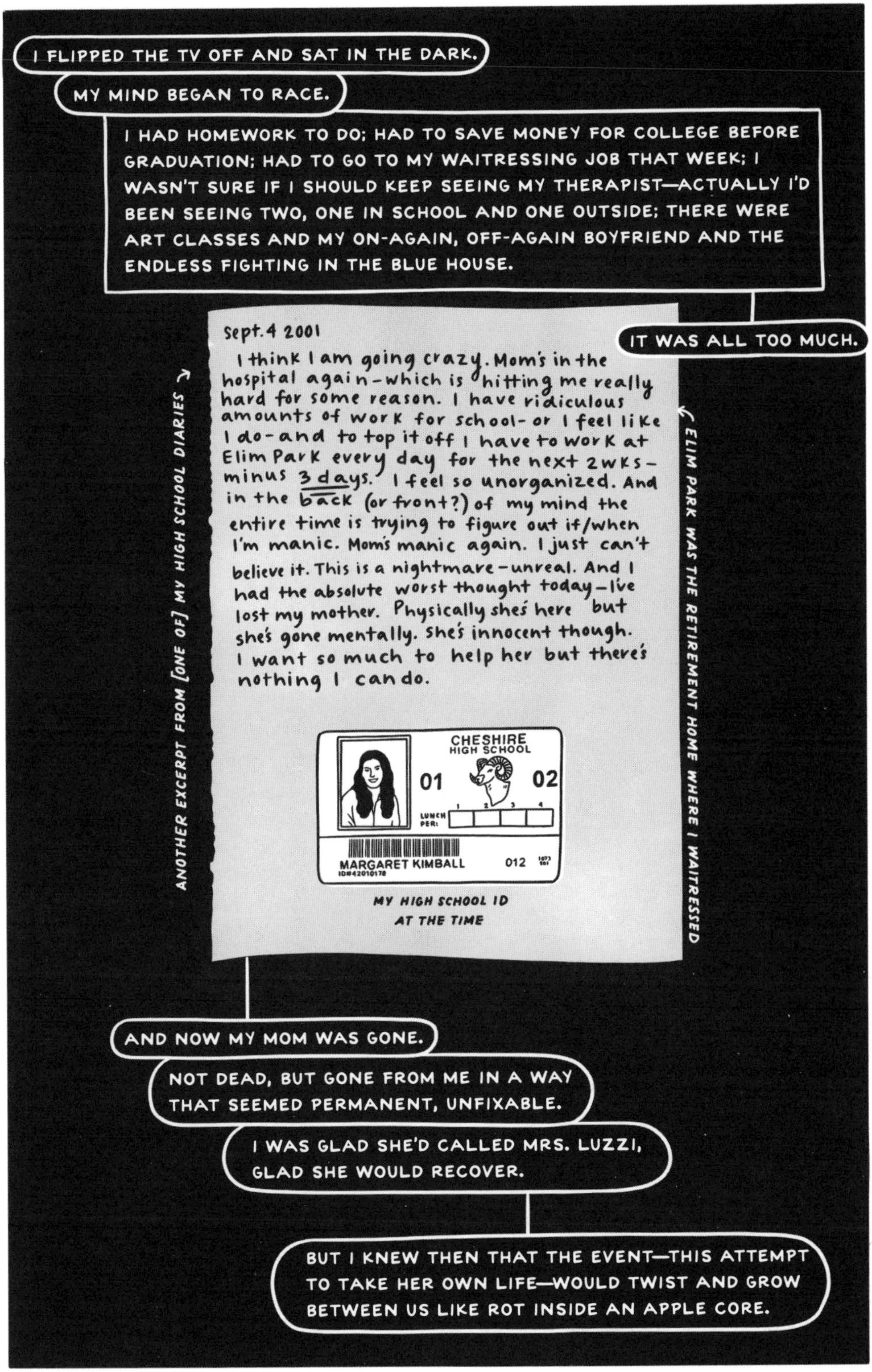
I FLIPPED THE TV OFF AND SAT IN THE DARK.
MY MIND BEGAN TO RACE.
I HAD HOMEWORK TO DO; HAD TO SAVE MONEY FOR COLLEGE BEFORE GRADUATION; HAD TO GO TO MY WAITRESSING JOB THAT WEEK; I WASN'T SURE IF I SHOULD KEEP SEEING MY THERAPIST—ACTUALLY I'D BEEN SEEING TWO, ONE IN SCHOOL AND ONE OUTSIDE; THERE WERE ART CLASSES AND MY ON-AGAIN, OFF-AGAIN BOYFRIEND AND THE ENDLESS FIGHTING IN THE BLUE HOUSE.
IT WAS ALL TOO MUCH.
ANOTHER EXCERPT FROM [ONE OF] MY HIGH SCHOOL DIARIES
Sept. 4 2001
I think I am going crazy. Mom's in the hospital again—which is hitting me really hard for some reason. I have ridiculous amounts of work for school—or I feel like I do—and to top it off I have to work at Elim Park every day for the next 2 wks—minus 3 days. I feel so unorganized. And in the back (or front?) of my mind the entire time is trying to figure out if/when I'm manic. Mom's manic again. I just can't believe it. This is a nightmare—unreal. And I had the absolute worst thought today—I've lost my mother. Physically she's here but she's gone mentally. She's innocent though. I want so much to help her but there's nothing I can do.
ELIM PARK WAS THE RETIREMENT HOME WHERE I WAITRESSED
CHESHIRE HIGH SCHOOL
01 02
LUNCH PER:
MARGARET KIMBALL
012
MY HIGH SCHOOL ID AT THE TIME
AND NOW MY MOM WAS GONE.
NOT DEAD, BUT GONE FROM ME IN A WAY THAT SEEMED PERMANENT, UNFIXABLE.
I WAS GLAD SHE'D CALLED MRS. LUZZI, GLAD SHE WOULD RECOVER.
BUT I KNEW THEN THAT THE EVENT—THIS ATTEMPT TO TAKE HER OWN LIFE—WOULD TWIST AND GROW BETWEEN US LIKE ROT INSIDE AN APPLE CORE.

CEDARCREST REGIONAL HOSPITAL IN NEWINGTON, CONNECTICUT, WAS ORIGINALLY BUILT FOR TUBERCULOSIS PATIENTS IN 1910 AND IN 1976 BECAME PART OF THE DEPARTMENT OF MENTAL HEALTH. NINE YEARS AFTER MY MOM'S ADMISSION, THE HOSPITAL CLOSED.

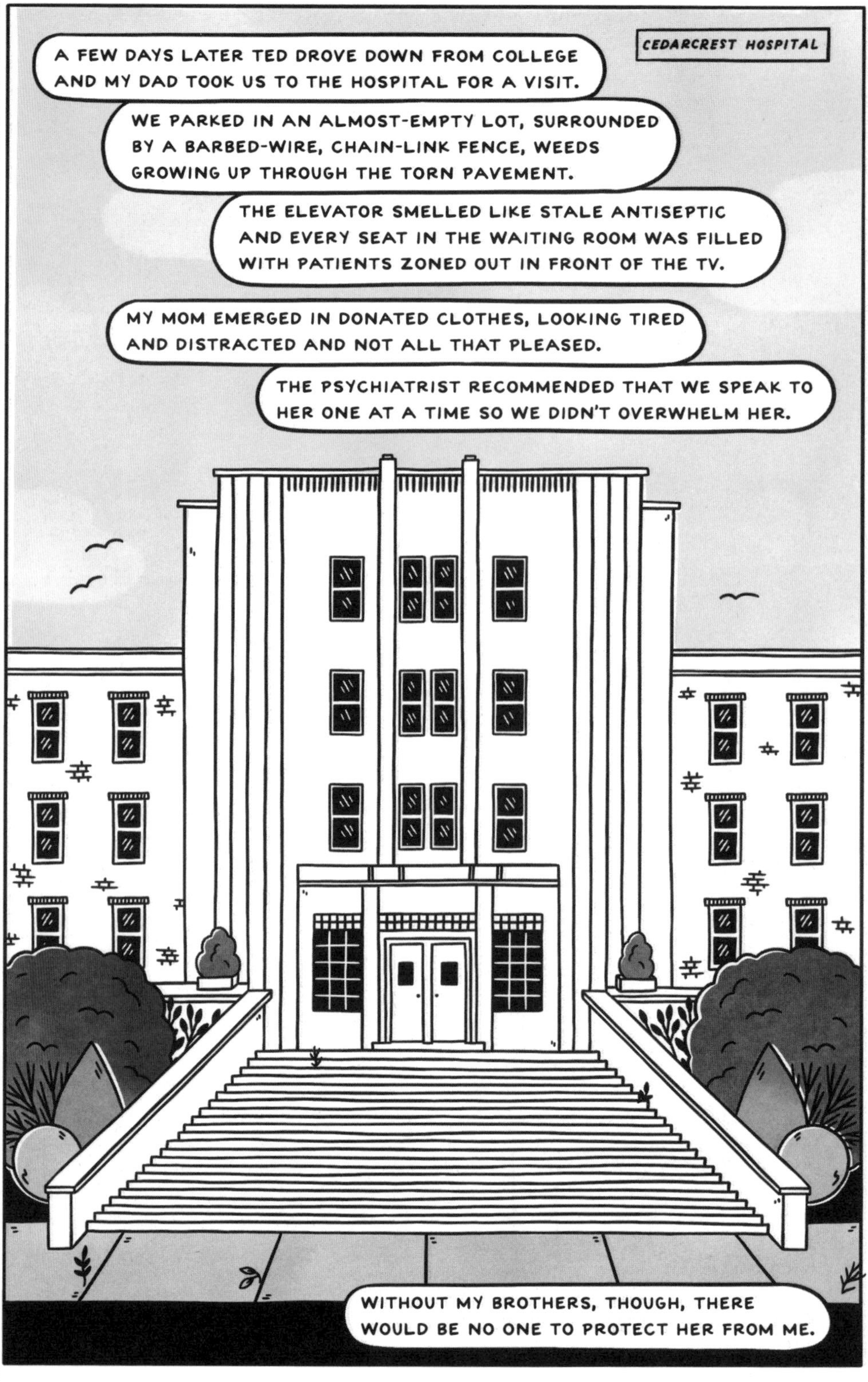
A FEW DAYS LATER TED DROVE DOWN FROM COLLEGE AND MY DAD TOOK US TO THE HOSPITAL FOR A VISIT.
CEDARCREST HOSPITAL
WE PARKED IN AN ALMOST-EMPTY LOT, SURROUNDED BY A BARBED-WIRE, CHAIN-LINK FENCE, WEEDS GROWING UP THROUGH THE TORN PAVEMENT.
THE ELEVATOR SMELLED LIKE STALE ANTISEPTIC AND EVERY SEAT IN THE WAITING ROOM WAS FILLED WITH PATIENTS ZONED OUT IN FRONT OF THE TV.
MY MOM EMERGED IN DONATED CLOTHES, LOOKING TIRED AND DISTRACTED AND NOT ALL THAT PLEASED.
THE PSYCHIATRIST RECOMMENDED THAT WE SPEAK TO HER ONE AT A TIME SO WE DIDN'T OVERWHELM HER.
WITHOUT MY BROTHERS, THOUGH, THERE WOULD BE NO ONE TO PROTECT HER FROM ME.

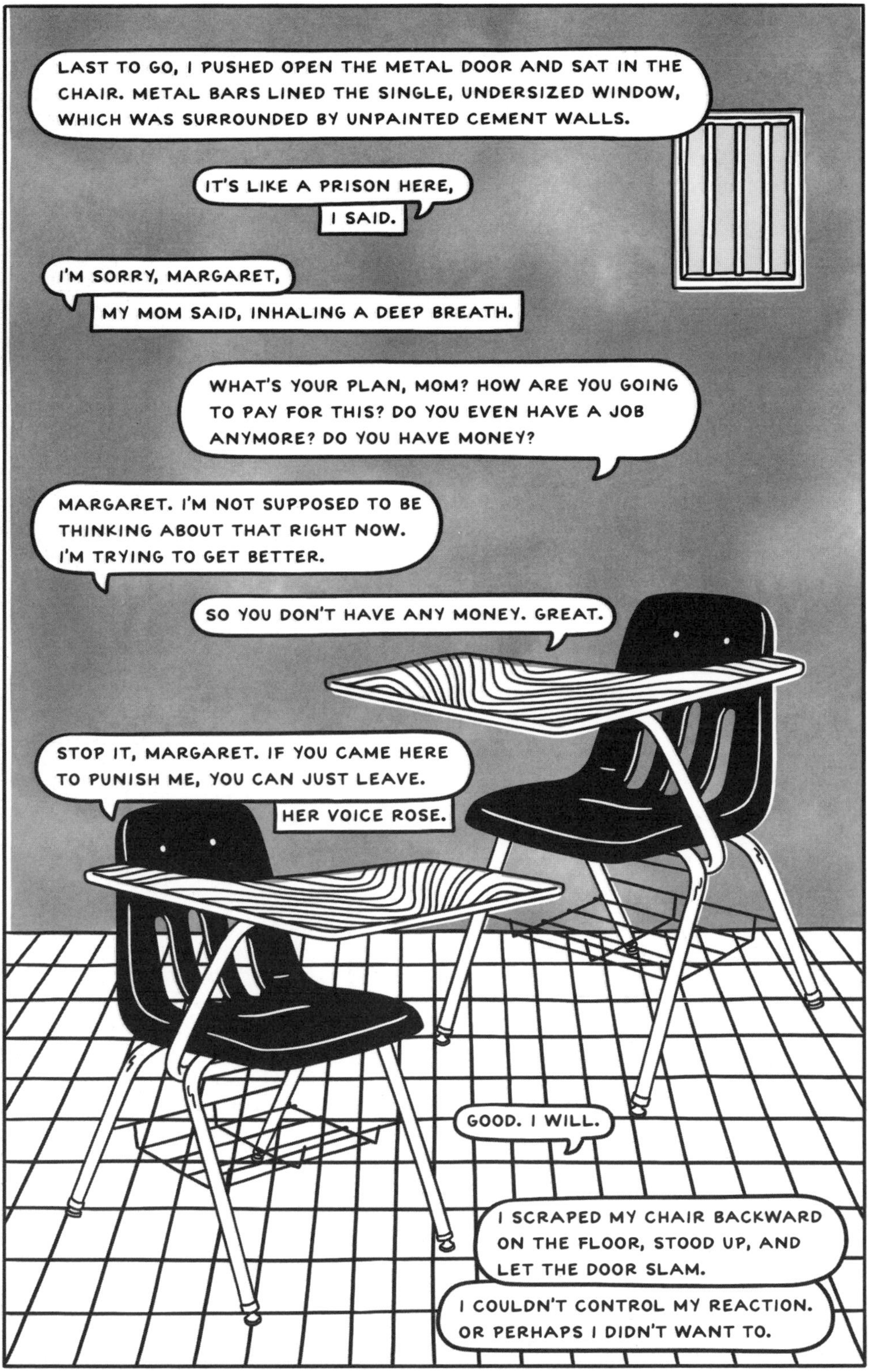
LAST TO GO, I PUSHED OPEN THE METAL DOOR AND SAT IN THE CHAIR. METAL BARS LINED THE SINGLE, UNDERSIZED WINDOW, WHICH WAS SURROUNDED BY UNPAINTED CEMENT WALLS.
IT'S LIKE A PRISON HERE,
I SAID.
I'M SORRY, MARGARET,
MY MOM SAID, INHALING A DEEP BREATH.
WHAT'S YOUR PLAN, MOM? HOW ARE YOU GOING TO PAY FOR THIS? DO YOU EVEN HAVE A JOB ANYMORE? DO YOU HAVE MONEY?
MARGARET. I'M NOT SUPPOSED TO BE THINKING ABOUT THAT RIGHT NOW. I'M TRYING TO GET BETTER.
SO YOU DON'T HAVE ANY MONEY. GREAT.
STOP IT, MARGARET. IF YOU CAME HERE TO PUNISH ME, YOU CAN JUST LEAVE.
HER VOICE ROSE.
GOOD. I WILL.
I SCRAPED MY CHAIR BACKWARD ON THE FLOOR, STOOD UP, AND LET THE DOOR SLAM.
I COULDN'T CONTROL MY REACTION. OR PERHAPS I DIDN'T WANT TO.

THE NOW-DILAPIDATED HOSPITAL

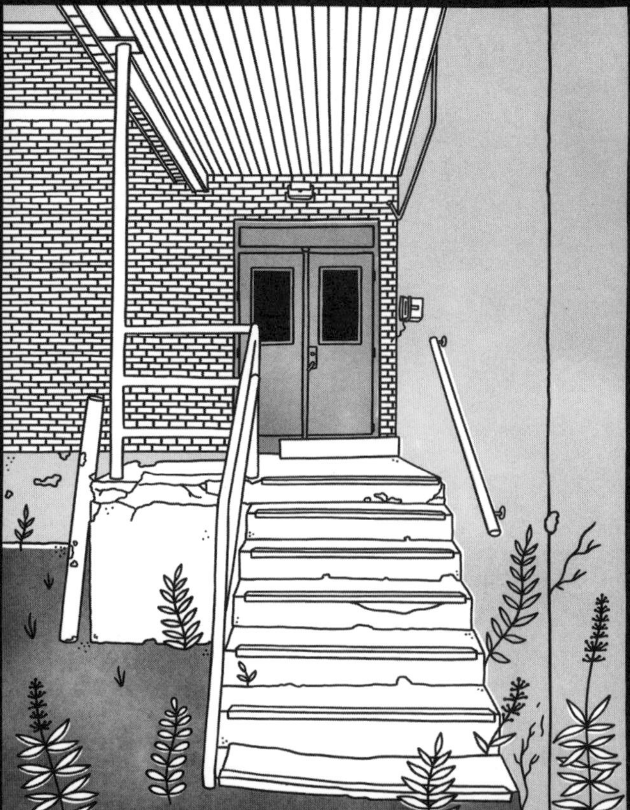

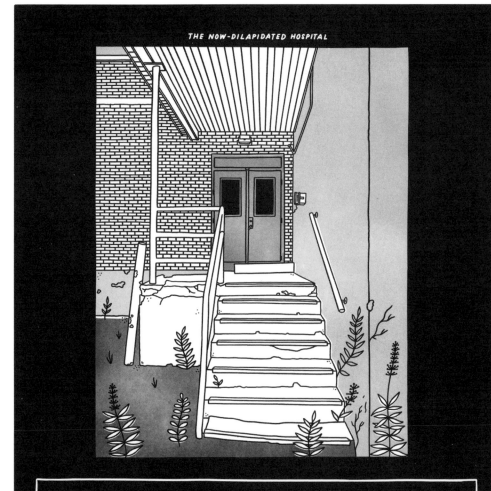

WHAT ENRAGED ME ABOUT MY MOTHER'S ILLNESS WAS NOT PRECISELY THE ISSUE OF MONEY; IT WAS THE FACT THAT SHE TRANSFORMED FROM PARENT TO STRANGER. THE MANIC EPISODES WOULD ERUPT AND TURN HER INTO A TORNADO OF DESTRUCTION. ANY MONEY SHE HAD DISAPPEARED. SHE WAS FIRED FROM JOBS, DISCRIMINATION LAWS BE DAMNED. SHE STRUCK UP FRIENDSHIPS WITH CUSTOMERS AT RANDOM PLACES. PILES OF CLUTTER BECAME MOUNTAINS IN HER HOME; WE HAD TO LITERALLY CLEAN UP THE MESS. WORST OF ALL, SHE BECAME IMPOSSIBLE TO TALK TO. HER EYES DARTED AROUND THE ROOM AND AS THE SPEED OF HER SPEECH INCREASED, WHAT SHE SAID MADE NO SENSE. SHE COULD BE MEAN, HER LANGUAGE SUDDENLY LADEN WITH SWEARS. NO ONE COULD SLOW HER DOWN OR CONNECT WITH HER AND SHE FELT GONE FROM ME. THE PERSON I KNEW WAS NOT THERE ANYMORE. WHEN THAT PERSON IS YOUR MOTHER, THE WORLD BECOMES A FRIGHTENINGLY UNCERTAIN PLACE WHERE ANYTHING IS POSSIBLE, AS IF ALL THE TREES IN ALL THE WORLD SPROUTED KNIVES FOR BRANCHES. IN THE HOSPITAL I COULDN'T SAY ANY OF THIS; MONEY WAS JUST AN EASY THING I COULD POINT TO, A WORTHLESS REBUTTAL TO THE FACT OF HER BIPOLAR DISORDER.

(FROM PHOTOS FOUND ONLINE OF THE OUTDOOR ELEVATOR)

MAXIMUM CAPACITY
750 LB. (340 KG)
1 PASSENGER + 1 ATTENDANT
OPERATING INSTRUCTIONS
1. CHECK POSITION OF CAR:
IF AT YOUR LANDING: PUSH DOOR OPEN BUTTON.
IF AT OTHER LANDING: PUSH DIRECTION BUTTON UNTIL CAR STOPS AT YOUR LANDING.
2. DOOR WILL OPEN AUTOMATICALLY.
3. ENTER CAR.

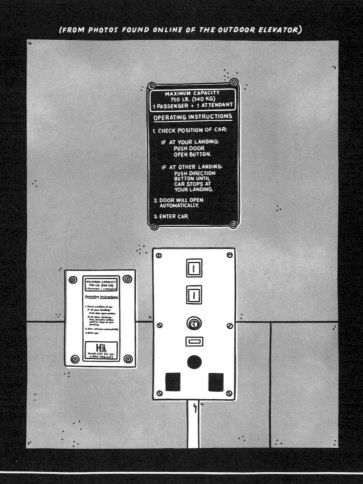

AT THE CENTER OF THIS ANGER WAS MY OWN STRUGGLE TO UNDERSTAND MENTAL ILLNESS. INTELLECTUALLY, I KNEW SHE HAD A DIAGNOSIS, I KNEW SHE WAS DEPRESSED, AND THAT REASON AND RATIONALITY WEREN'T FACTORS IN THIS EQUATION. I UNDERSTOOD THAT *IMPULSE* WAS A BETTER WORD THAN *CHOICE* TO DESCRIBE HER MANIC BEHAVIOR, BUT MY INSTINCTIVE REACTION WAS TO BE LIVID AT THE CHAOS THAT RESULTED FROM HER ATTEMPTED SUICIDE. I FIGURED SHE DIDN'T CARE ENOUGH ABOUT US TO PROTECT US FROM THE FALLOUT OF HER HOSPITALIZATION, THAT SHE THOUGHT HER CHILDREN WEREN'T WORTH LIVING FOR. BUT LOGIC PLAYED NO ROLE IN ANY OF THIS. MENTAL ILLNESS DEFIES LOGIC. THAT WAS AND PROBABLY STILL IS THE LIMITATION OF MY PATTERN-SEEKING BRAIN, A MIND THAT WANTS A CLEAR STORY—POINT A TO POINT B WITH NARRATIVE ARC AND ALL THAT.

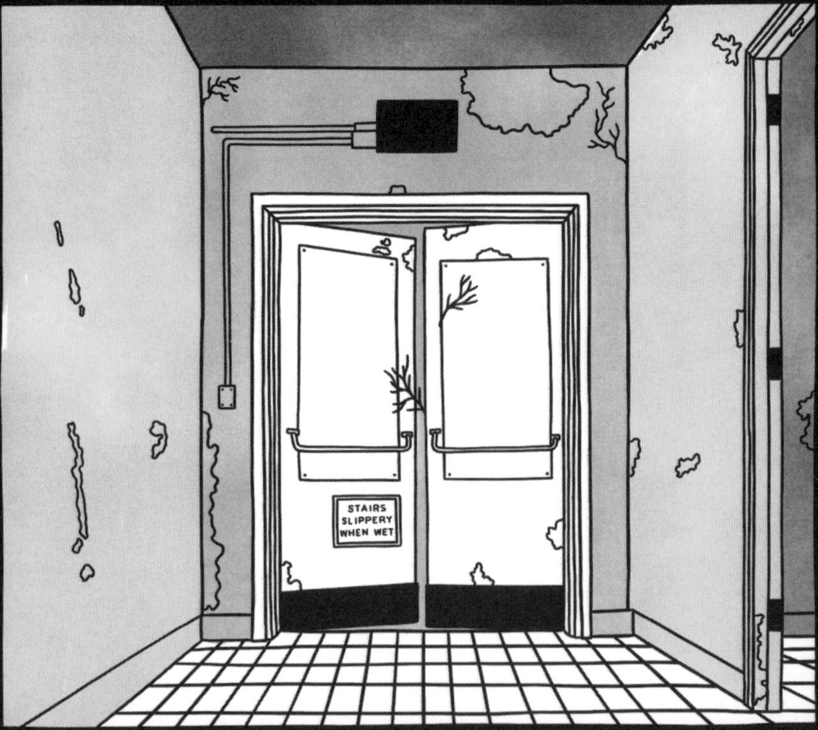
STAIRS
SLIPPERY
WHEN WET

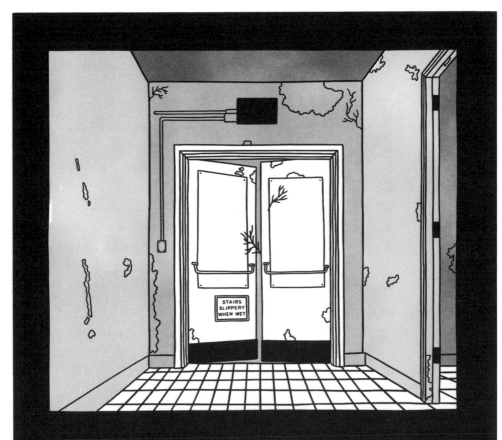

BUT THIS IS ACTUALLY WRONG. MY MOM'S BRAIN WAS EXCEEDINGLY LOGICAL DURING HER MANIC PHASE, ONLY THAT LOGIC WAS BASED ON A REALITY I DIDN'T RECOGNIZE. WHILE MANIC SHE BELIEVED THAT SHE SHOULD BE A TEACHER AT THE ELITE PRIVATE SCHOOL WHERE SHE WAS SECRETARY TO THE HEADMASTER. SHE HAD NEVER TAUGHT HIGH SCHOOL BEFORE. WHEN THE HEADMASTER TOLD HER THIS WOULD BE IMPOSSIBLE—EVEN IF SHE GOT CERTIFIED—SHE RESIGNED, FIGURING SHE'D FIND A JOB ELSEWHERE. BUT SHE WAS BEHAVING AS A MANIC PERSON BEHAVES, WITH FAST SPEECH THAT WAS IMPOSSIBLE TO FOLLOW AND BIG DREAMS UNSUPPORTED BY EXPERIENCE. SOON SOMETHING CHANGED INSIDE HER MIND.

I RETURN TO KAY REDFIELD JAMISON'S PASSAGE TO TRY AND UNDERSTAND HOW THIS FEELS: "THE FAST IDEAS ARE FAR TOO FAST, AND THERE ARE FAR TOO MANY...MEMORY GOES. HUMOR AND ABSORPTION ON FRIENDS' FACES ARE REPLACED BY FEAR AND CONCERN. EVERYTHING PREVIOUSLY MOVING WITH THE GRAIN IS NOW AGAINST—YOU ARE IRRITABLE, ANGRY, FRIGHTENED, UNCONTROLLABLE, AND ENMESHED TOTALLY IN THE BLACKEST CAVES OF THE MIND. YOU NEVER KNEW THOSE CAVES WERE THERE." AND THEN, IN MY MOM'S CASE, YOU SWALLOWED EVERY PILL IN YOUR POSSESSION.

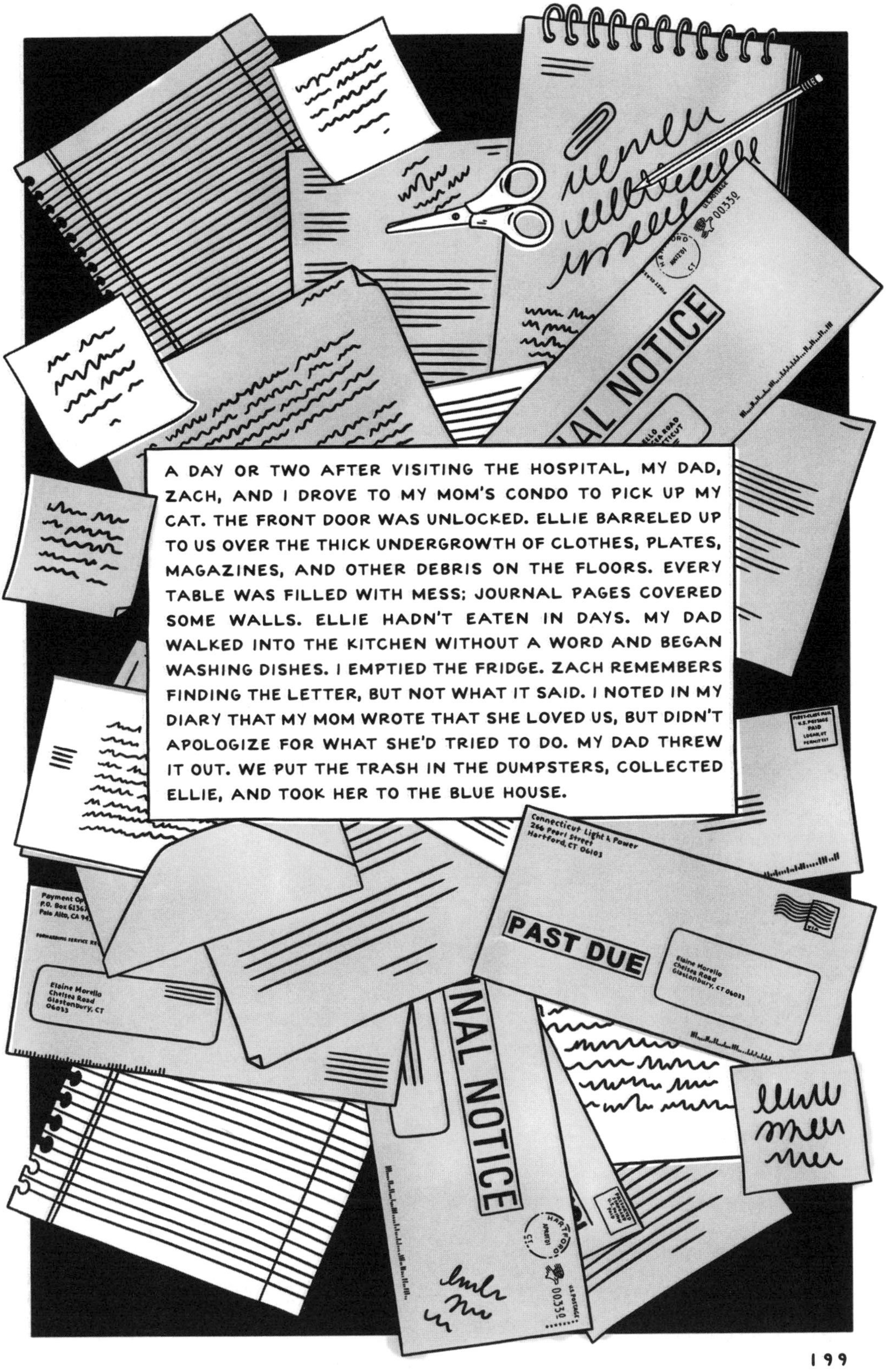
A DAY OR TWO AFTER VISITING THE HOSPITAL, MY DAD, ZACH, AND I DROVE TO MY MOM'S CONDO TO PICK UP MY CAT. THE FRONT DOOR WAS UNLOCKED. ELLIE BARRELED UP TO US OVER THE THICK UNDERGROWTH OF CLOTHES, PLATES, MAGAZINES, AND OTHER DEBRIS ON THE FLOORS. EVERY TABLE WAS FILLED WITH MESS; JOURNAL PAGES COVERED SOME WALLS. ELLIE HADN'T EATEN IN DAYS. MY DAD WALKED INTO THE KITCHEN WITHOUT A WORD AND BEGAN WASHING DISHES. I EMPTIED THE FRIDGE. ZACH REMEMBERS FINDING THE LETTER, BUT NOT WHAT IT SAID. I NOTED IN MY DIARY THAT MY MOM WROTE THAT SHE LOVED US, BUT DIDN'T APOLOGIZE FOR WHAT SHE'D TRIED TO DO. MY DAD THREW IT OUT. WE PUT THE TRASH IN THE DUMPSTERS, COLLECTED ELLIE, AND TOOK HER TO THE BLUE HOUSE.
NAL NOTICE
Connecticut Light & Power
266 Pearl Street
Hartford, CT 06103
PAST DUE
Elaine Morello
Chelsea Road
Glastonbury, CT 06033
Elaine Morello
Chelsea Road
Glastonbury, CT
06033
NAL NOTICE

grief, *n.*

Pronunciation: Brit.   /griːf/, U.S.   /grif/

Forms: Plural griefs. Forms: ME gref, ME–15 greffe, grefe, greve, ME–16 greef(e), (ME greyf)

Frequency (in current use): ●●●●●●○○

7.

a. Mental pain, distress, or sorrow. In modern use in a more
limited sense: deep or violent sorrow, caused by loss or trouble;
a keen or bitter feeling of regret for something lost, remorse for
something done, or sorrow for mishap to oneself or others.

> a1375 (▸c1350) *William of Palerne* (1867) l. 2473 So glad was he þanne, þat na gref
> vnder god gayned to his ioye.

> 1413 *Pilgr. Sowle* (1483) IV. xx. 66 How may myn eyen..Restreyne them for to shewen
> by wepyng Myn hertes greef.

> 1568 H. BILLINGSLEY tr. P. M. Vermigli *Most Learned Comm. Epist. Romanes* ix. 237 b
> Griefe (as sayth Cicero..) is a disseaue which vexeth the mind, and it is taken by
> reason of the euill which semeth to be already at hand, and to be present.

> 1599 W. SHAKESPEARE *Romeo & Juliet* V. iii. 210 Griefe of my sonnes exile hath stopt
> her breath.

GRIEF IS A SWARM OF FEELINGS THAT SWIRLS INSIDE OF YOU FOR
YOUR WHOLE LIFE; IT'S A WEIGHT THAT SETTLES AROUND THE
EYES, TRANSFORMS THE SHAPE OF A LAUGH. IT IS SADNESS MIXED
WITH A FURIOUS RAGE CHURNING IN AN OCEAN OF HELPLESSNESS.
IT'S AN OLD WORD, DATING BACK TO THE 1200s, AND ITS LATIN
ROOTS MEAN TO "MAKE HEAVY." THE FIRST SIX DEFINITIONS IN
THE *OXFORD ENGLISH DICTIONARY* DESCRIBE VARIOUS TYPES OF
HARDSHIP OR PHYSICAL PAIN. THE SEVENTH DEFINITION MAKES ME
THINK *GRIEF* IS THE CORRECT TERM FOR THE STORM OF EMOTION
I ASSOCIATE WITH MY MOM'S MENTAL ILLNESS. "MENTAL PAIN,
DISTRESS, OR SORROW...DEEP OR VIOLENT SORROW, CAUSED BY LOSS
OR TROUBLE; A KEEN OR BITTER FEELING OF REGRET FOR SOMETHING
LOST, REMORSE FOR SOMETHING DONE, OR SORROW FOR MISHAP TO
ONESELF OR OTHERS."

THE FOUR OF US SOON AFTER MY MOM RECOVERED

[TH]E GRIEF IN OUR FAMILY HAS BEEN PASSED ON AND RESHAPED THROUGH [THE] [G]ENERATIONS, EACH PERSON CONTAINING TWO SORROWS—ONE FOR HERSE[LF] [A]ND ONE FOR OTHERS. MY GREAT-GRANDMOTHER NELLIE WAS LIKELY DEPRESS[ED] [A]CCORDING TO MY MOM. YOU CAN SEE HER WORRY AND SADNESS IN THE VIDE[O] [A]S HER DAUGHTER WHIRLS MADLY AROUND. MY GRANDMOTHER FRANCES W[AS] [C]ATAPULTED BETWEEN STATES OF ELATION AND DEEP DEPRESSION, HURTL[ING] [T]HROUGH FITS OF PSYCHOSIS IN BETWEEN. MY MOM, HAVING SURVIVED H[ER] [O]WN MOTHER'S MADNESS, NOW LIVES WITH A MENTAL ILLNESS SHE DO[ES] [N]OT WANT. SHE HAS TRIED TO MAKE PEACE WITH IT AND SHE'S APOLOGIZ[ED] [F]OR IT. STILL THE FACT OF HER BIPOLAR DISORDER LURKS FOREVER IN T[HE] [B]ACKGROUND. SHE NEVER KNOWS WHEN IT WILL REAR UP. NOR DO I.

[SI]NCE THE AGE OF TEN I DESPERATELY WANTED TO BELIEVE THAT MY MO[M'S] [S]ICKNESS ENDED UPON HER BEING DISCHARGED FROM THE HOSPITAL. THAT S[HE] [W]OULD DUST HERSELF OFF AND—PHOENIXLIKE—SHE'D LIFT HER CHIN, WA[LK] [O]UT INTO THE WORLD, AND LAND A STEADY JOB, A COMFORTABLE HOME. EV[EN] [A]FTER HER STINT IN THE HOSPITAL WHEN I WAS SEVENTEEN, I HOPED A[ND] [B]ELIEVED SHE WOULD OVERCOME HER OWN BRAIN. THIS NEVER HAPPENED.

[T]HERE'S MORE TO GRIEF THAN ITS DEFINITIONS ALLOW. THE KÜBLER-RO[SS] [M]ODEL DESCRIBES FIVE STAGES OF GRIEF: DENIAL, ANGER, BARGAINI[NG,] [D]EPRESSION, AND ACCEPTANCE. DURING THIS LAST STAGE, A PERSON THIN[KS] [T]O HERSELF *IT'S GOING TO BE OKAY.* EVEN IF I'VE ACCEPTED MY MOM'S MENT[AL] [I]LLNESS—AND AFTER THREE DECADES I'M NOT ENTIRELY CERTAIN I HAVE—[THE] [S]ADNESS AND ANGER AND HELPLESSNESS HAVE NOT VANISHED. ON BETT[ER] [D]AYS I SENSE A POWERFUL RESILIENCE: I HAVE SURVIVED. ON WORSE DA[YS] [I] FEEL HOPELESS: I'VE FAILED TO HELP HER. WHAT I CAN SEE NOW IS TH[AT] [S]HE TRIED TO PROTECT ME FROM HER OWN SUFFERING. BY SENDING ME [TO] [T]HERAPISTS, ENCOURAGING MY HIKING TRIPS AND ART CLASSES, AND LETT[ING]

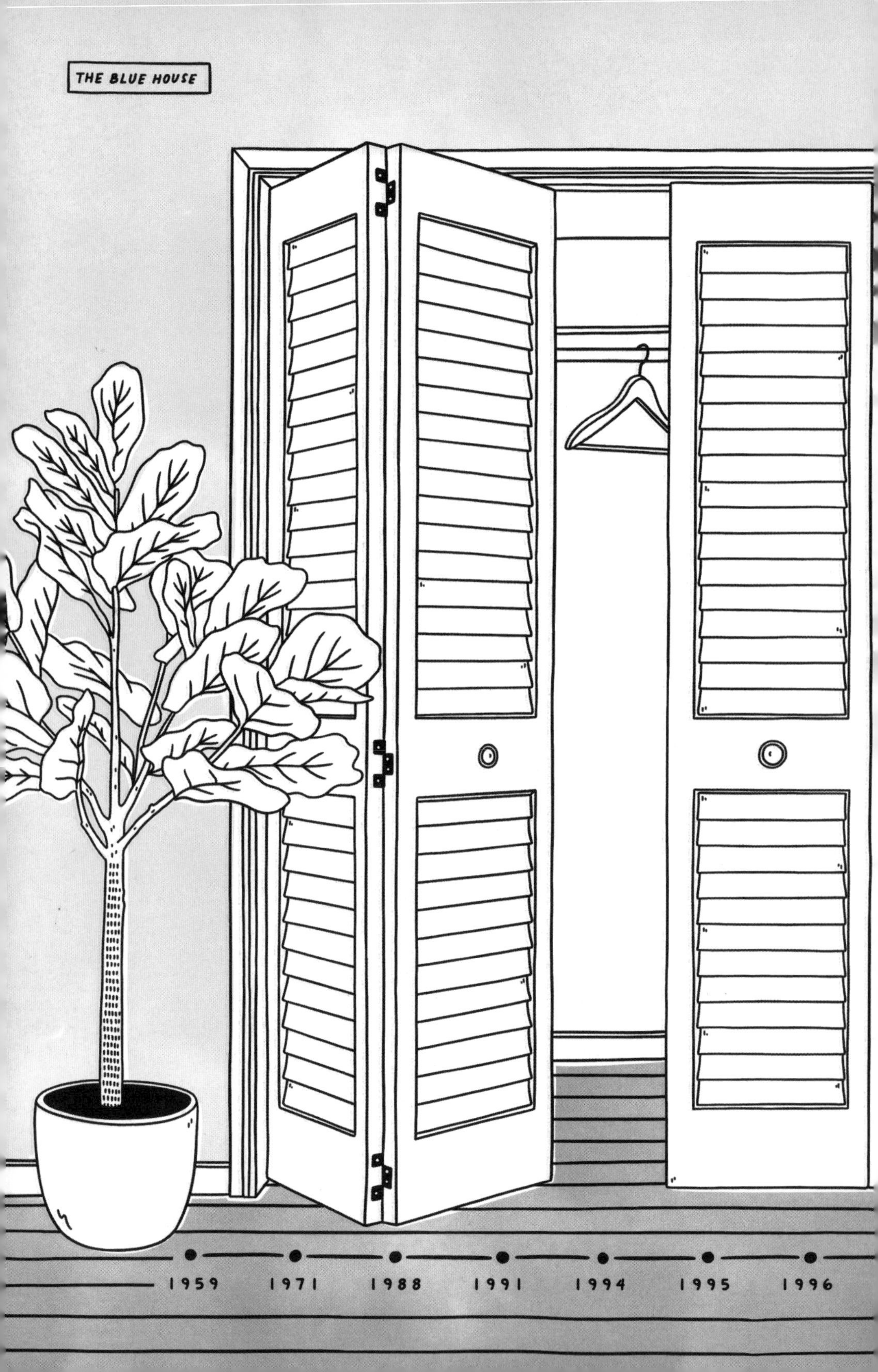
THE BLUE HOUSE
1959
1971
1988
1991
1994
1995
1996

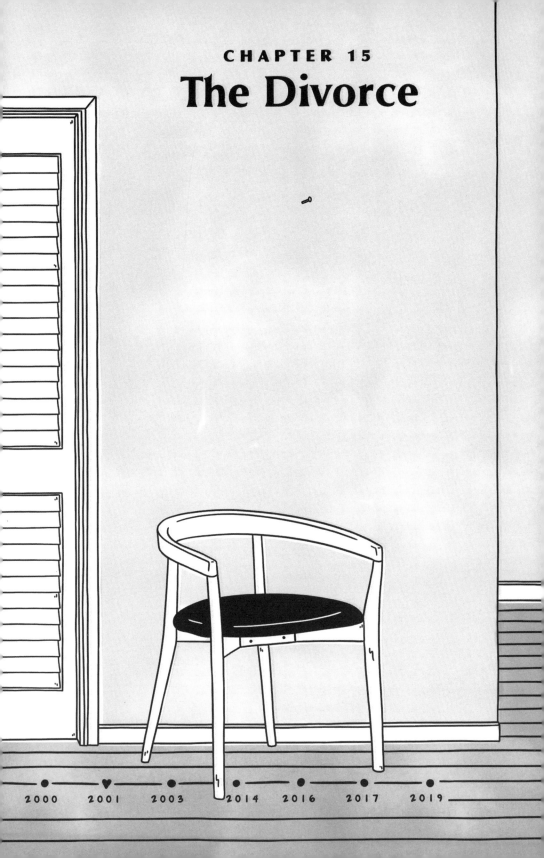

CHAPTER 15
The Divorce

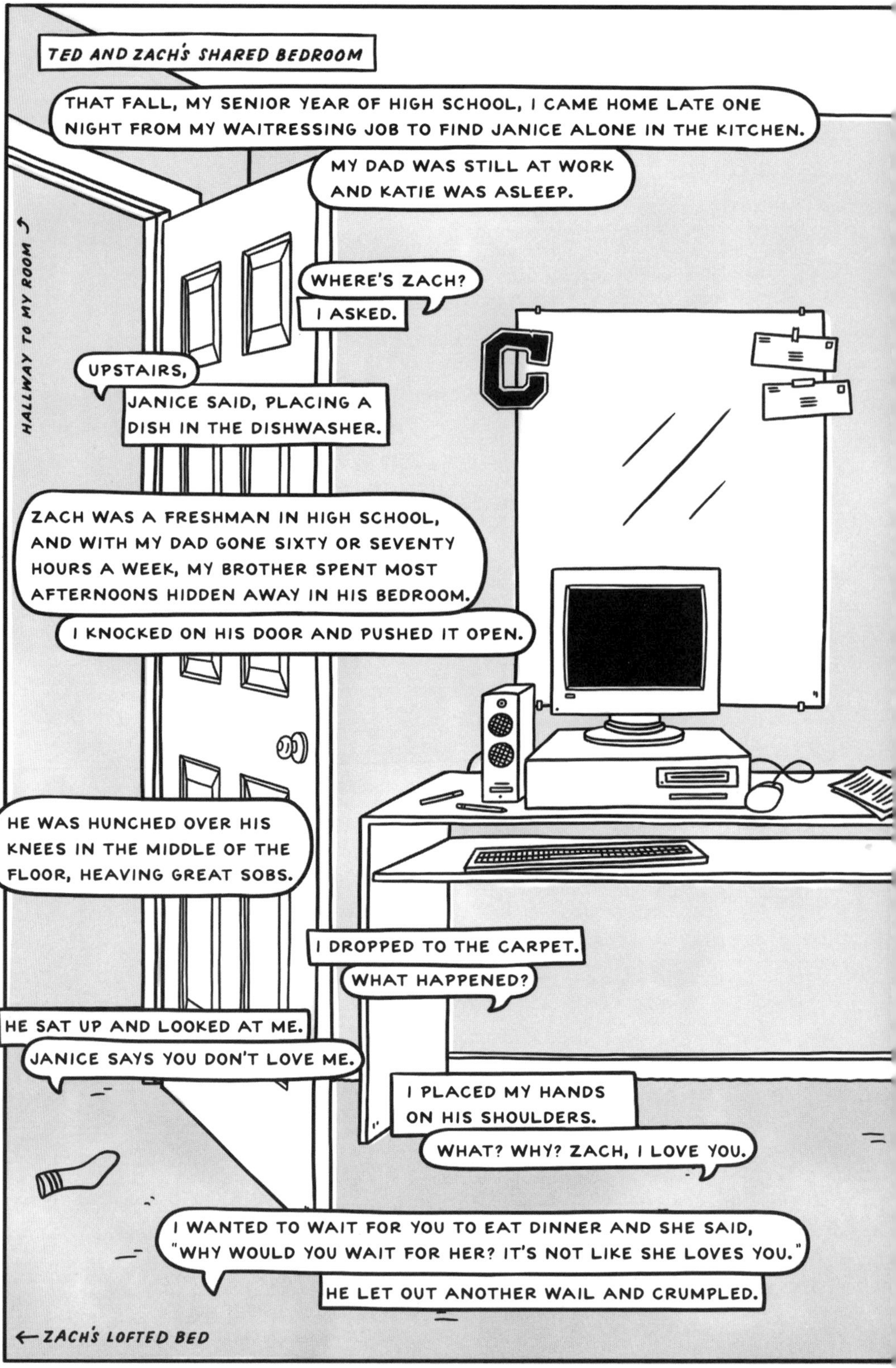
TED AND ZACH'S SHARED BEDROOM
THAT FALL, MY SENIOR YEAR OF HIGH SCHOOL, I CAME HOME LATE ONE NIGHT FROM MY WAITRESSING JOB TO FIND JANICE ALONE IN THE KITCHEN.
MY DAD WAS STILL AT WORK AND KATIE WAS ASLEEP.
HALLWAY TO MY ROOM
WHERE'S ZACH?
I ASKED.
UPSTAIRS,
JANICE SAID, PLACING A DISH IN THE DISHWASHER.
ZACH WAS A FRESHMAN IN HIGH SCHOOL, AND WITH MY DAD GONE SIXTY OR SEVENTY HOURS A WEEK, MY BROTHER SPENT MOST AFTERNOONS HIDDEN AWAY IN HIS BEDROOM.
I KNOCKED ON HIS DOOR AND PUSHED IT OPEN.
HE WAS HUNCHED OVER HIS KNEES IN THE MIDDLE OF THE FLOOR, HEAVING GREAT SOBS.
I DROPPED TO THE CARPET.
WHAT HAPPENED?
HE SAT UP AND LOOKED AT ME.
JANICE SAYS YOU DON'T LOVE ME.
I PLACED MY HANDS ON HIS SHOULDERS.
WHAT? WHY? ZACH, I LOVE YOU.
I WANTED TO WAIT FOR YOU TO EAT DINNER AND SHE SAID, "WHY WOULD YOU WAIT FOR HER? IT'S NOT LIKE SHE LOVES YOU."
HE LET OUT ANOTHER WAIL AND CRUMPLED.
← ZACH'S LOFTED BED

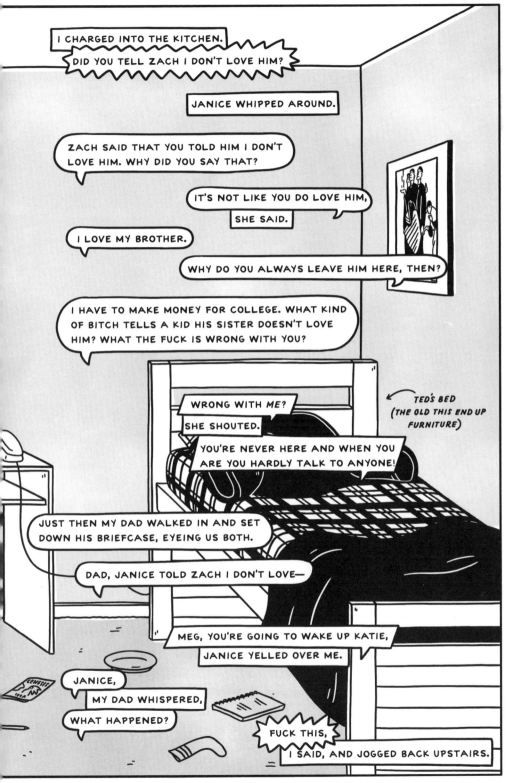

I CHARGED INTO THE KITCHEN.

DID YOU TELL ZACH I DON'T LOVE HIM?

JANICE WHIPPED AROUND.

ZACH SAID THAT YOU TOLD HIM I DON'T LOVE HIM. WHY DID YOU SAY THAT?

IT'S NOT LIKE YOU DO LOVE HIM, SHE SAID.

I LOVE MY BROTHER.

WHY DO YOU ALWAYS LEAVE HIM HERE, THEN?

I HAVE TO MAKE MONEY FOR COLLEGE. WHAT KIND OF BITCH TELLS A KID HIS SISTER DOESN'T LOVE HIM? WHAT THE FUCK IS WRONG WITH YOU?

WRONG WITH ME? SHE SHOUTED.

YOU'RE NEVER HERE AND WHEN YOU ARE YOU HARDLY TALK TO ANYONE!

TED'S BED (THE OLD THIS END UP FURNITURE)

JUST THEN MY DAD WALKED IN AND SET DOWN HIS BRIEFCASE, EYEING US BOTH.

DAD, JANICE TOLD ZACH I DON'T LOVE—

MEG, YOU'RE GOING TO WAKE UP KATIE, JANICE YELLED OVER ME.

JANICE, MY DAD WHISPERED, WHAT HAPPENED?

FUCK THIS, I SAID, AND JOGGED BACK UPSTAIRS.

205

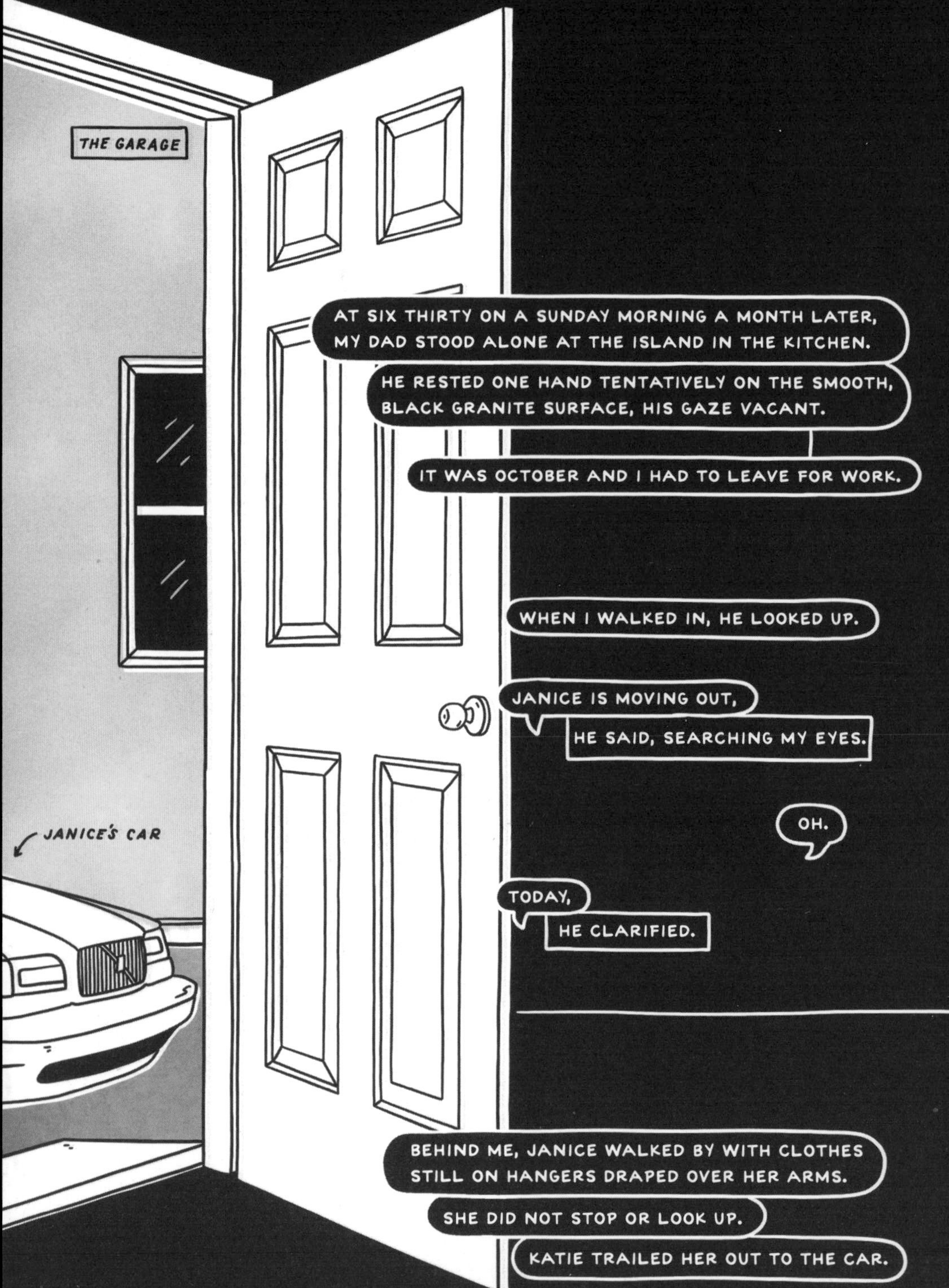
THE GARAGE
AT SIX THIRTY ON A SUNDAY MORNING A MONTH LATER, MY DAD STOOD ALONE AT THE ISLAND IN THE KITCHEN.
HE RESTED ONE HAND TENTATIVELY ON THE SMOOTH, BLACK GRANITE SURFACE, HIS GAZE VACANT.
IT WAS OCTOBER AND I HAD TO LEAVE FOR WORK.
WHEN I WALKED IN, HE LOOKED UP.
JANICE IS MOVING OUT,
HE SAID, SEARCHING MY EYES.
OH.
TODAY,
HE CLARIFIED.
JANICE'S CAR
BEHIND ME, JANICE WALKED BY WITH CLOTHES STILL ON HANGERS DRAPED OVER HER ARMS.
SHE DID NOT STOP OR LOOK UP.
KATIE TRAILED HER OUT TO THE CAR.

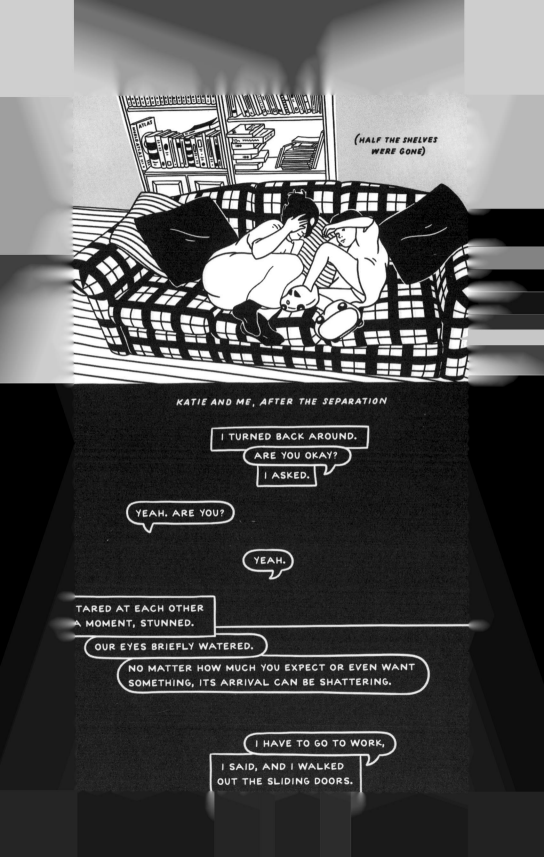

(HALF THE SHELVES WERE GONE)

KATIE AND ME, AFTER THE SEPARATION

I TURNED BACK AROUND.

ARE YOU OKAY?

I ASKED.

YEAH. ARE YOU?

YEAH.

TARED AT EACH OTHER A MOMENT, STUNNED.

OUR EYES BRIEFLY WATERED.

NO MATTER HOW MUCH YOU EXPECT OR EVEN WANT SOMETHING, ITS ARRIVAL CAN BE SHATTERING.

I HAVE TO GO TO WORK,

I SAID, AND I WALKED OUT THE SLIDING DOORS.

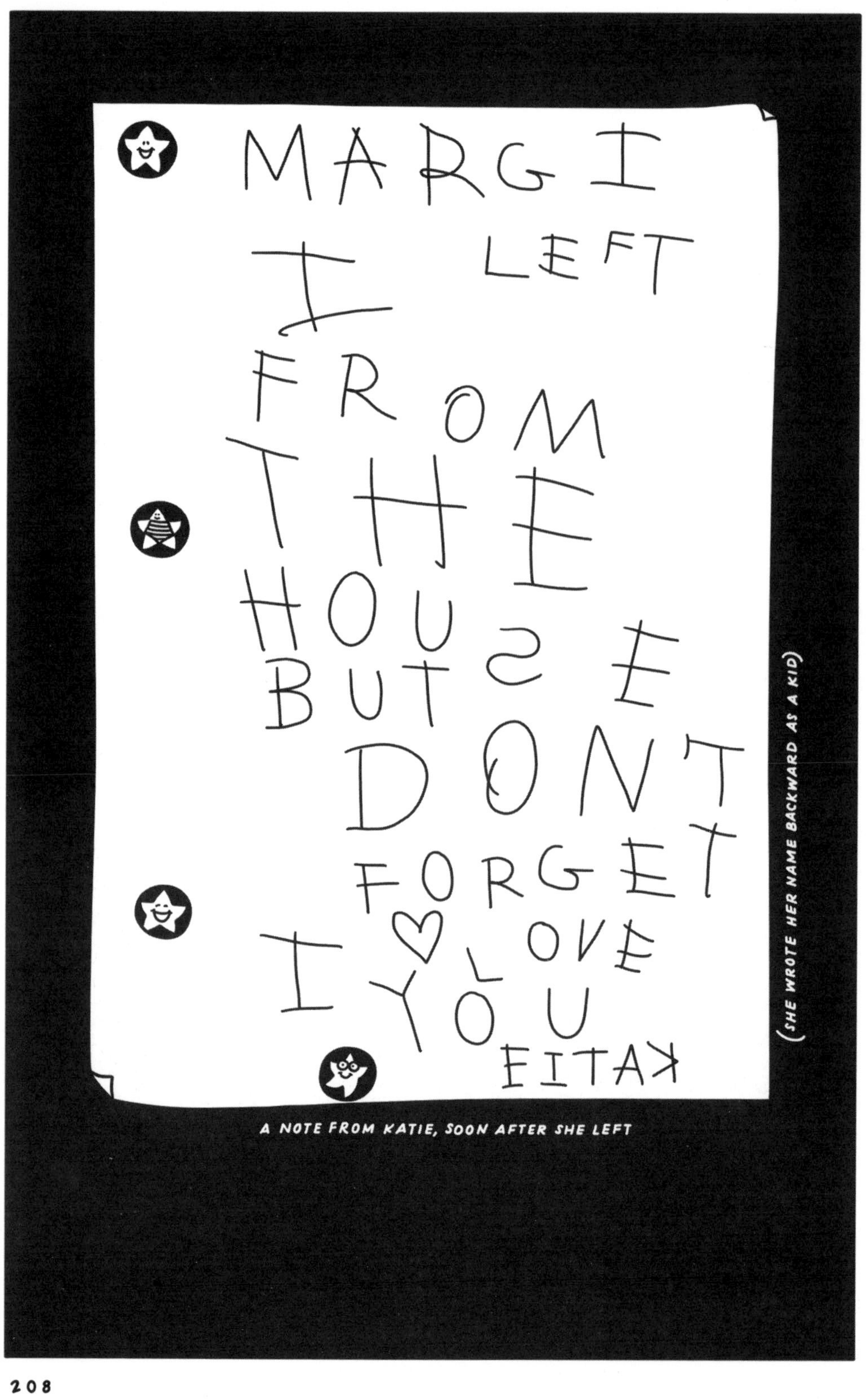
MARGI
I LEFT
FROM
THE
HOUSE
BUT
DONT
FORGET
I ♥ LOVE
YOU
EITAK

(SHE WROTE HER NAME BACKWARD AS A KID)

A NOTE FROM KATIE, SOON AFTER SHE LEFT

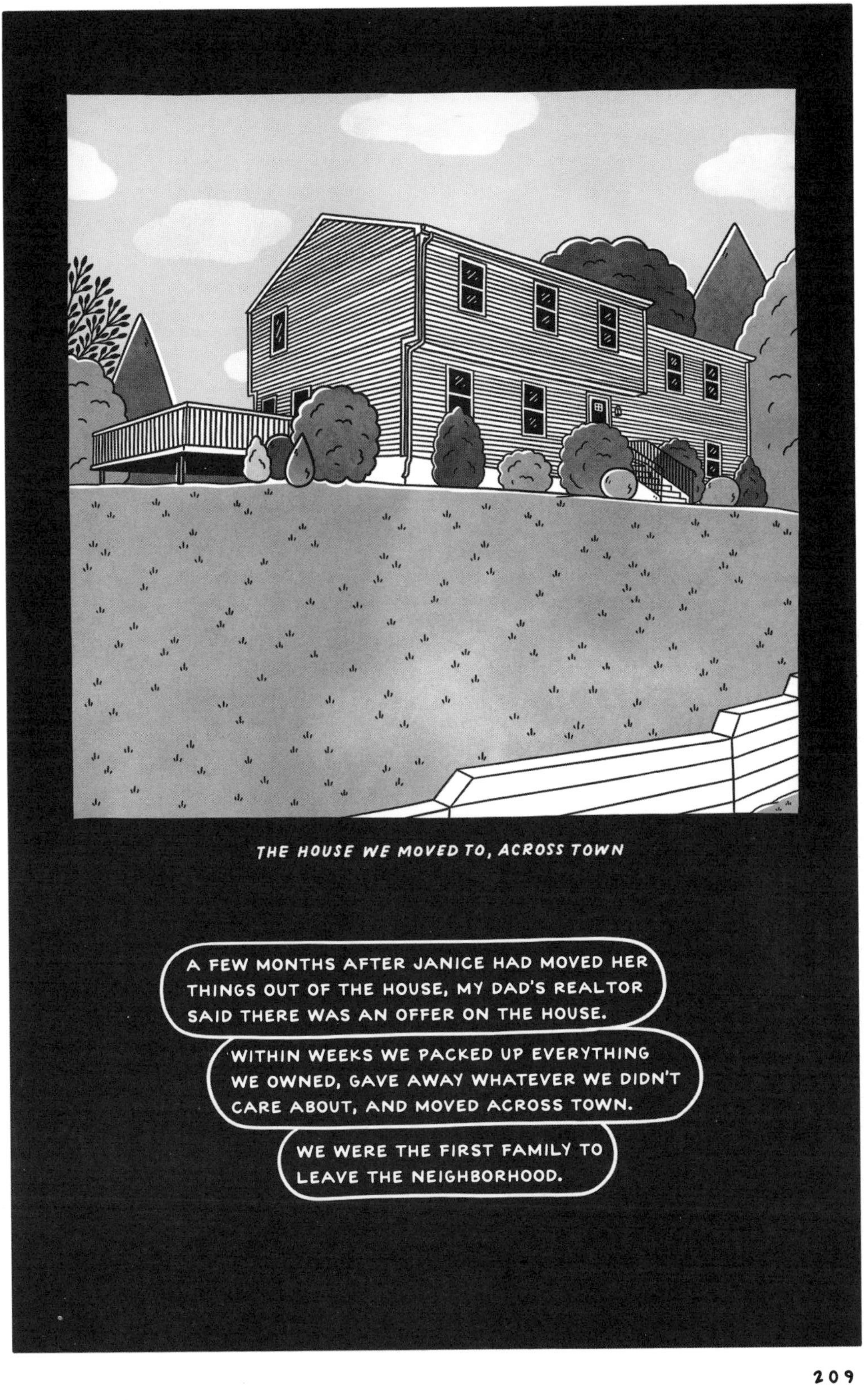
THE HOUSE WE MOVED TO, ACROSS TOWN
A FEW MONTHS AFTER JANICE HAD MOVED HER THINGS OUT OF THE HOUSE, MY DAD'S REALTOR SAID THERE WAS AN OFFER ON THE HOUSE.
WITHIN WEEKS WE PACKED UP EVERYTHING WE OWNED, GAVE AWAY WHATEVER WE DIDN'T CARE ABOUT, AND MOVED ACROSS TOWN.
WE WERE THE FIRST FAMILY TO LEAVE THE NEIGHBORHOOD.

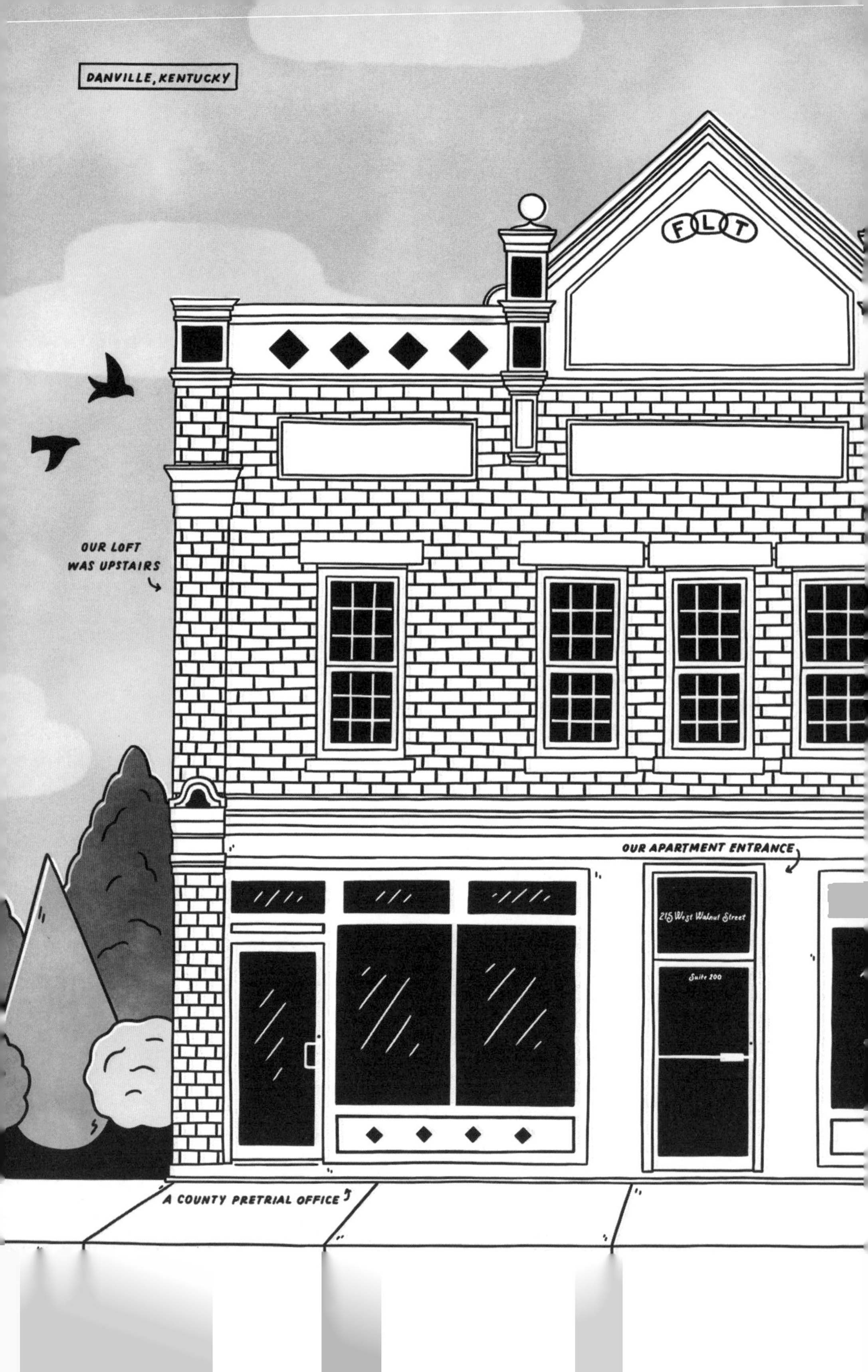
DANVILLE, KENTUCKY
FLT
OUR LOFT WAS UPSTAIRS
OUR APARTMENT ENTRANCE
215 West Walnut Street
Suite 200
A COUNTY PRETRIAL OFFICE

CHAPTER 16

The Long Weekend

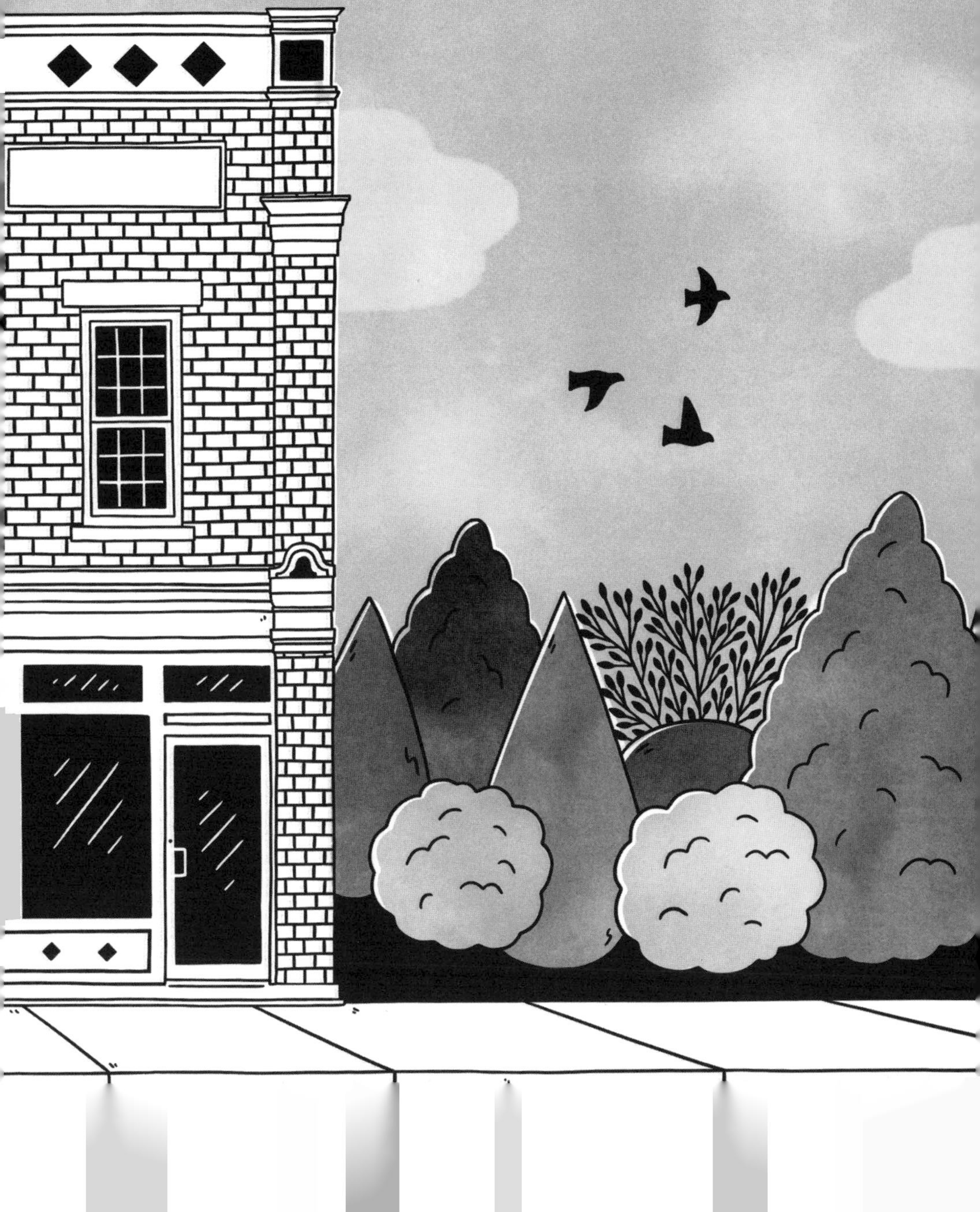

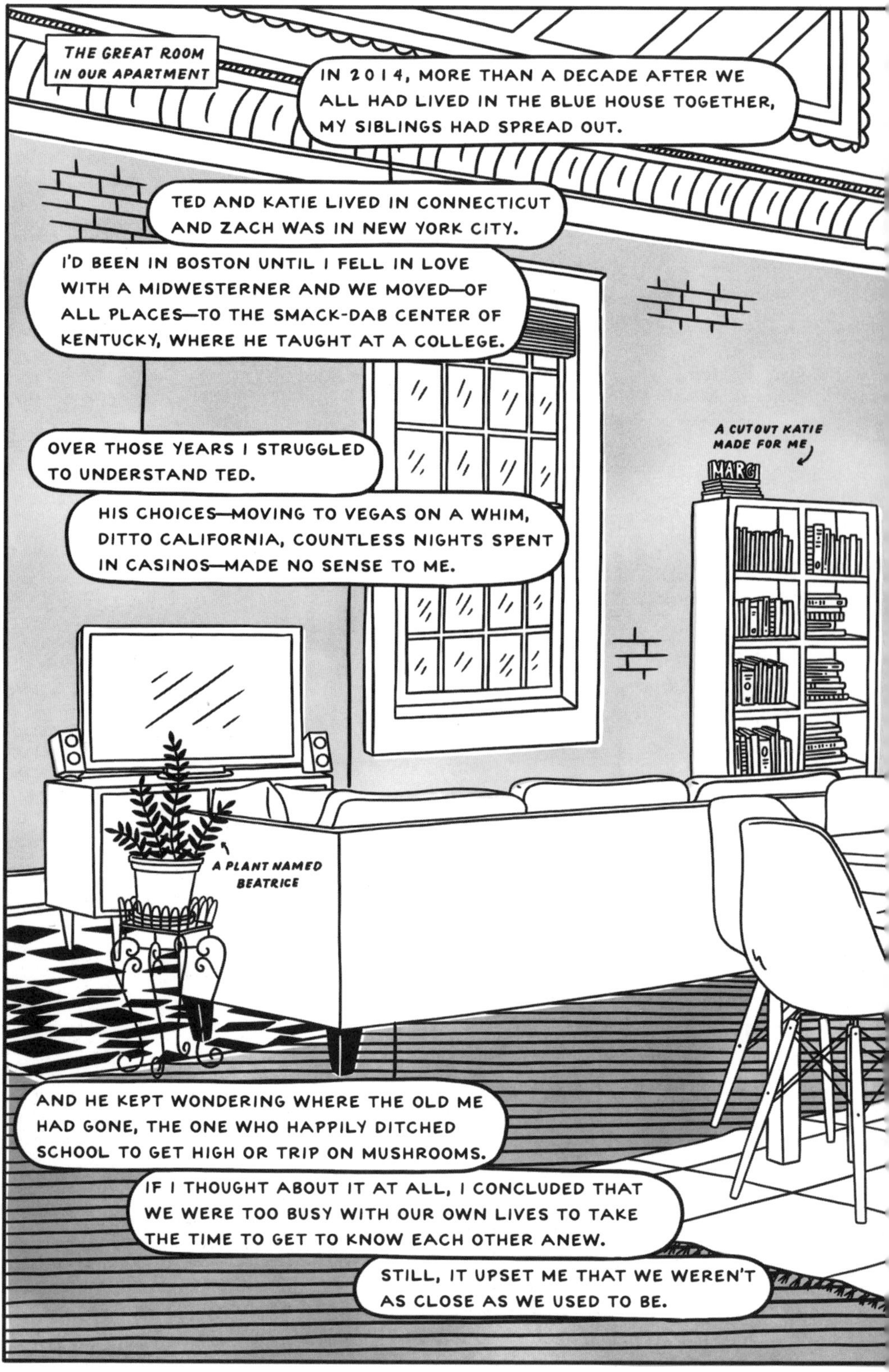
THE GREAT ROOM IN OUR APARTMENT
IN 2014, MORE THAN A DECADE AFTER WE ALL HAD LIVED IN THE BLUE HOUSE TOGETHER, MY SIBLINGS HAD SPREAD OUT.
TED AND KATIE LIVED IN CONNECTICUT AND ZACH WAS IN NEW YORK CITY.
I'D BEEN IN BOSTON UNTIL I FELL IN LOVE WITH A MIDWESTERNER AND WE MOVED—OF ALL PLACES—TO THE SMACK-DAB CENTER OF KENTUCKY, WHERE HE TAUGHT AT A COLLEGE.
OVER THOSE YEARS I STRUGGLED TO UNDERSTAND TED.
HIS CHOICES—MOVING TO VEGAS ON A WHIM, DITTO CALIFORNIA, COUNTLESS NIGHTS SPENT IN CASINOS—MADE NO SENSE TO ME.
A CUTOUT KATIE MADE FOR ME
MARGI
A PLANT NAMED BEATRICE
AND HE KEPT WONDERING WHERE THE OLD ME HAD GONE, THE ONE WHO HAPPILY DITCHED SCHOOL TO GET HIGH OR TRIP ON MUSHROOMS.
IF I THOUGHT ABOUT IT AT ALL, I CONCLUDED THAT WE WERE TOO BUSY WITH OUR OWN LIVES TO TAKE THE TIME TO GET TO KNOW EACH OTHER ANEW.
STILL, IT UPSET ME THAT WE WEREN'T AS CLOSE AS WE USED TO BE.

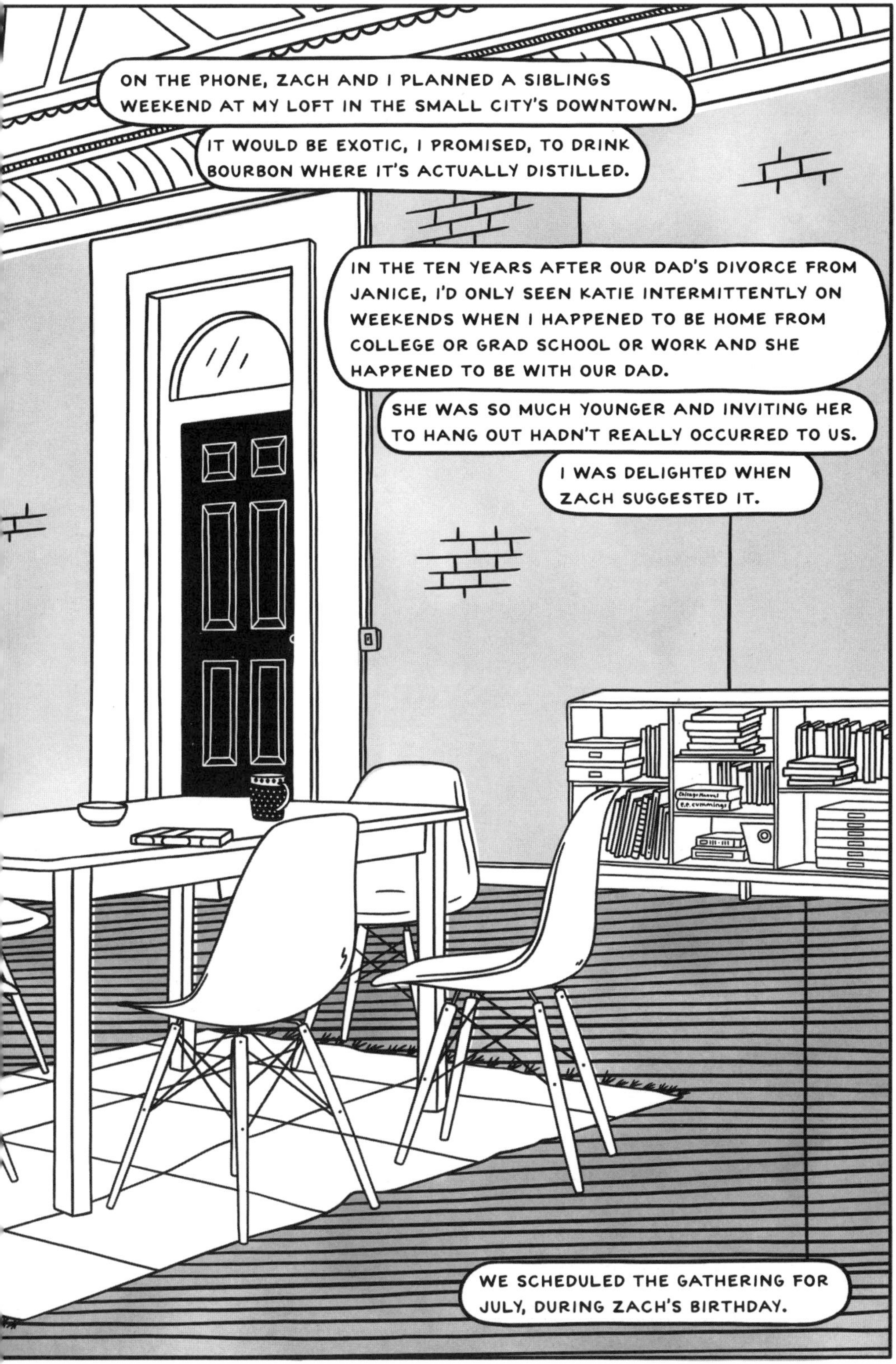
ON THE PHONE, ZACH AND I PLANNED A SIBLINGS WEEKEND AT MY LOFT IN THE SMALL CITY'S DOWNTOWN.
IT WOULD BE EXOTIC, I PROMISED, TO DRINK BOURBON WHERE IT'S ACTUALLY DISTILLED.
IN THE TEN YEARS AFTER OUR DAD'S DIVORCE FROM JANICE, I'D ONLY SEEN KATIE INTERMITTENTLY ON WEEKENDS WHEN I HAPPENED TO BE HOME FROM COLLEGE OR GRAD SCHOOL OR WORK AND SHE HAPPENED TO BE WITH OUR DAD.
SHE WAS SO MUCH YOUNGER AND INVITING HER TO HANG OUT HADN'T REALLY OCCURRED TO US.
I WAS DELIGHTED WHEN ZACH SUGGESTED IT.
WE SCHEDULED THE GATHERING FOR JULY, DURING ZACH'S BIRTHDAY.

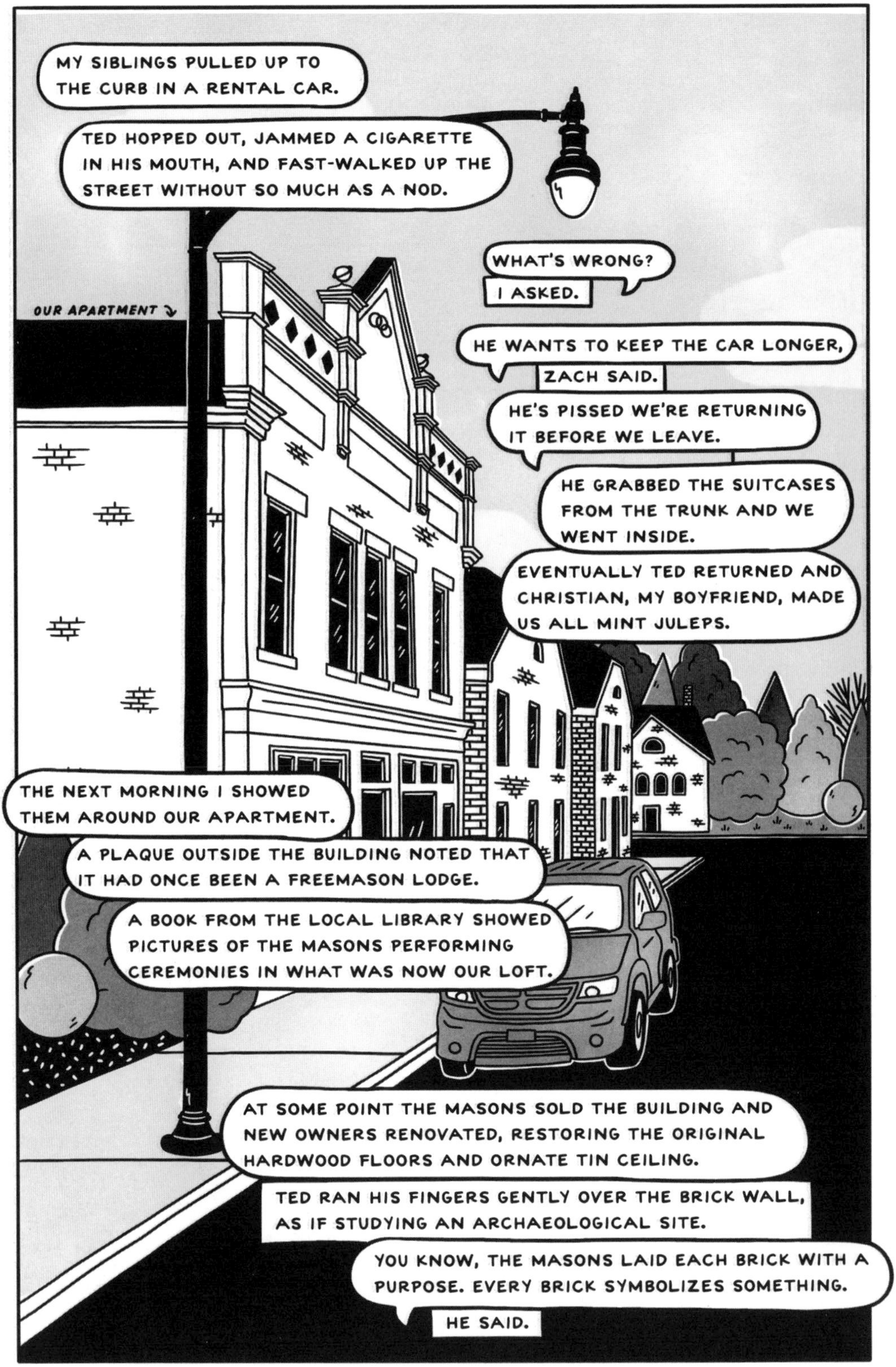
MY SIBLINGS PULLED UP TO THE CURB IN A RENTAL CAR.
TED HOPPED OUT, JAMMED A CIGARETTE IN HIS MOUTH, AND FAST-WALKED UP THE STREET WITHOUT SO MUCH AS A NOD.
OUR APARTMENT
WHAT'S WRONG?
I ASKED.
HE WANTS TO KEEP THE CAR LONGER,
ZACH SAID.
HE'S PISSED WE'RE RETURNING IT BEFORE WE LEAVE.
HE GRABBED THE SUITCASES FROM THE TRUNK AND WE WENT INSIDE.
EVENTUALLY TED RETURNED AND CHRISTIAN, MY BOYFRIEND, MADE US ALL MINT JULEPS.
THE NEXT MORNING I SHOWED THEM AROUND OUR APARTMENT.
A PLAQUE OUTSIDE THE BUILDING NOTED THAT IT HAD ONCE BEEN A FREEMASON LODGE.
A BOOK FROM THE LOCAL LIBRARY SHOWED PICTURES OF THE MASONS PERFORMING CEREMONIES IN WHAT WAS NOW OUR LOFT.
AT SOME POINT THE MASONS SOLD THE BUILDING AND NEW OWNERS RENOVATED, RESTORING THE ORIGINAL HARDWOOD FLOORS AND ORNATE TIN CEILING.
TED RAN HIS FINGERS GENTLY OVER THE BRICK WALL, AS IF STUDYING AN ARCHAEOLOGICAL SITE.
YOU KNOW, THE MASONS LAID EACH BRICK WITH A PURPOSE. EVERY BRICK SYMBOLIZES SOMETHING.
HE SAID.

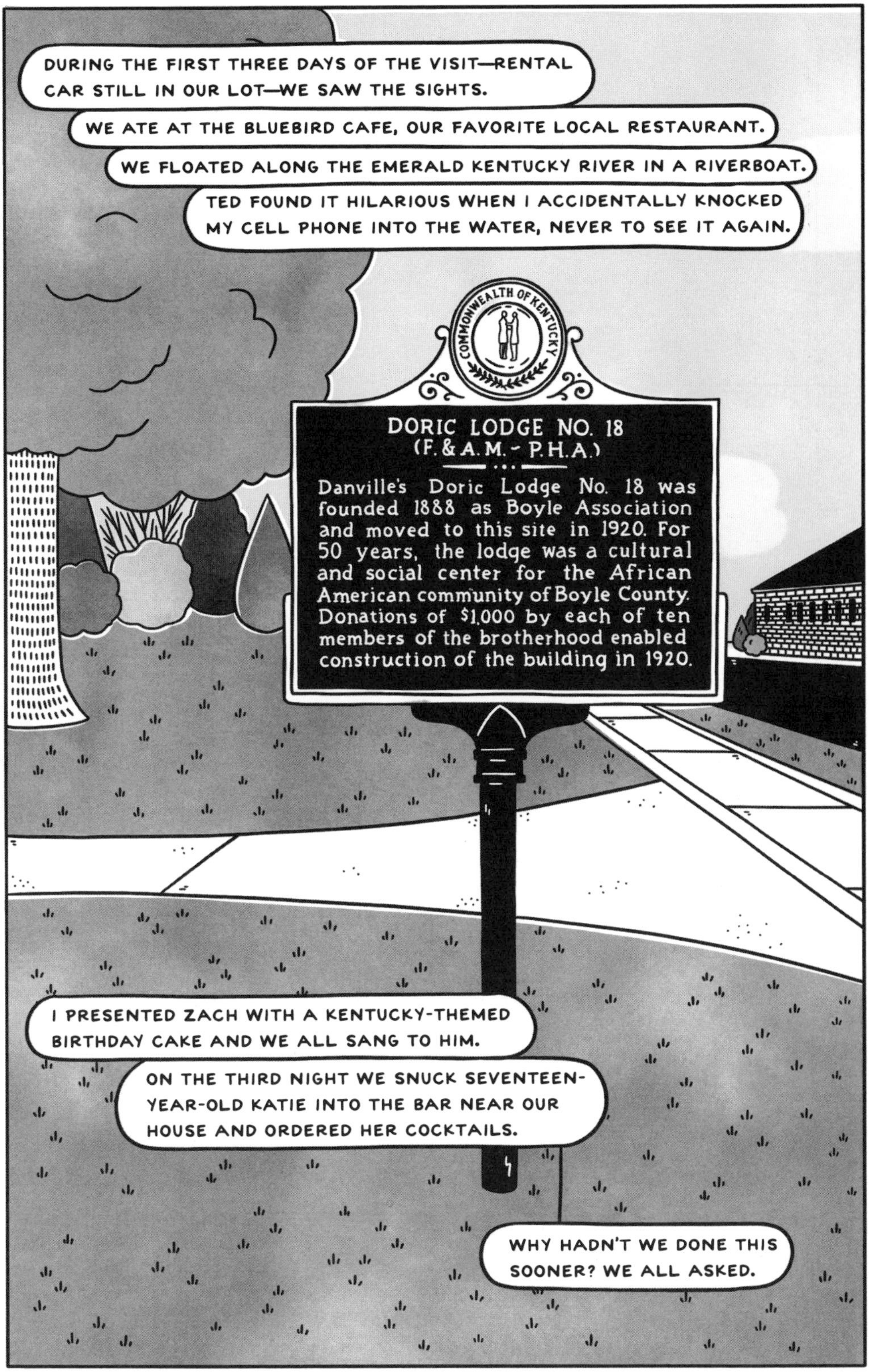
DURING THE FIRST THREE DAYS OF THE VISIT—RENTAL CAR STILL IN OUR LOT—WE SAW THE SIGHTS.
WE ATE AT THE BLUEBIRD CAFE, OUR FAVORITE LOCAL RESTAURANT.
WE FLOATED ALONG THE EMERALD KENTUCKY RIVER IN A RIVERBOAT.
TED FOUND IT HILARIOUS WHEN I ACCIDENTALLY KNOCKED MY CELL PHONE INTO THE WATER, NEVER TO SEE IT AGAIN.
COMMONWEALTH OF KENTUCKY
DORIC LODGE NO. 18
(F. & A. M. - P. H. A.)
Danville's Doric Lodge No. 18 was founded 1888 as Boyle Association and moved to this site in 1920. For 50 years, the lodge was a cultural and social center for the African American community of Boyle County. Donations of $1,000 by each of ten members of the brotherhood enabled construction of the building in 1920.
I PRESENTED ZACH WITH A KENTUCKY-THEMED BIRTHDAY CAKE AND WE ALL SANG TO HIM.
ON THE THIRD NIGHT WE SNUCK SEVENTEEN-YEAR-OLD KATIE INTO THE BAR NEAR OUR HOUSE AND ORDERED HER COCKTAILS.
WHY HADN'T WE DONE THIS SOONER? WE ALL ASKED.

ON THE FOURTH NIGHT, AFTER THE RENTAL CAR WAS RETURNED, WE SAT DOWN FOR A GAME OF KINGS.

AS IF OUR DRINKING NEEDED A PURPOSE.

IT WOULD BE ANOTHER THREE YEARS BEFORE I FINALLY RECOGNIZED ALCOHOL'S GRIP ON ME.

THAT NIGHT, THOUGH, I WAS ALL CHEERS AND BOTTOMS UP.

I SET BEERS OUT FOR EVERYONE WHILE TED JOTTED DOWN THE RULES IN HIS ALL-CAPS HANDWRITING.

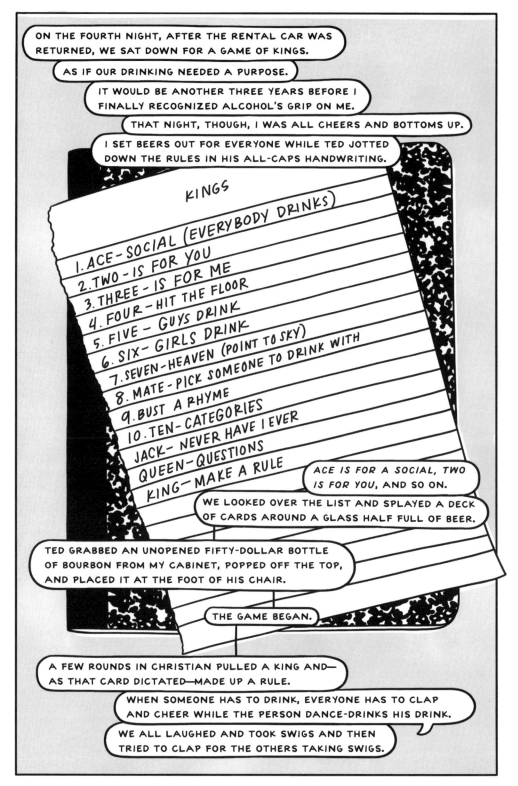

KINGS

1. ACE - SOCIAL (EVERYBODY DRINKS)
2. TWO - IS FOR YOU
3. THREE - IS FOR ME
4. FOUR - HIT THE FLOOR
5. FIVE - GUYS DRINK
6. SIX - GIRLS DRINK
7. SEVEN - HEAVEN (POINT TO SKY)
8. MATE - PICK SOMEONE TO DRINK WITH
9. BUST A RHYME
10. TEN - CATEGORIES
JACK - NEVER HAVE I EVER
QUEEN - QUESTIONS
KING - MAKE A RULE

ACE IS FOR A SOCIAL, TWO IS FOR YOU, AND SO ON.

WE LOOKED OVER THE LIST AND SPLAYED A DECK OF CARDS AROUND A GLASS HALF FULL OF BEER.

TED GRABBED AN UNOPENED FIFTY-DOLLAR BOTTLE OF BOURBON FROM MY CABINET, POPPED OFF THE TOP, AND PLACED IT AT THE FOOT OF HIS CHAIR.

THE GAME BEGAN.

A FEW ROUNDS IN CHRISTIAN PULLED A KING AND— AS THAT CARD DICTATED—MADE UP A RULE.

WHEN SOMEONE HAS TO DRINK, EVERYONE HAS TO CLAP AND CHEER WHILE THE PERSON DANCE-DRINKS HIS DRINK.

WE ALL LAUGHED AND TOOK SWIGS AND THEN TRIED TO CLAP FOR THE OTHERS TAKING SWIGS.

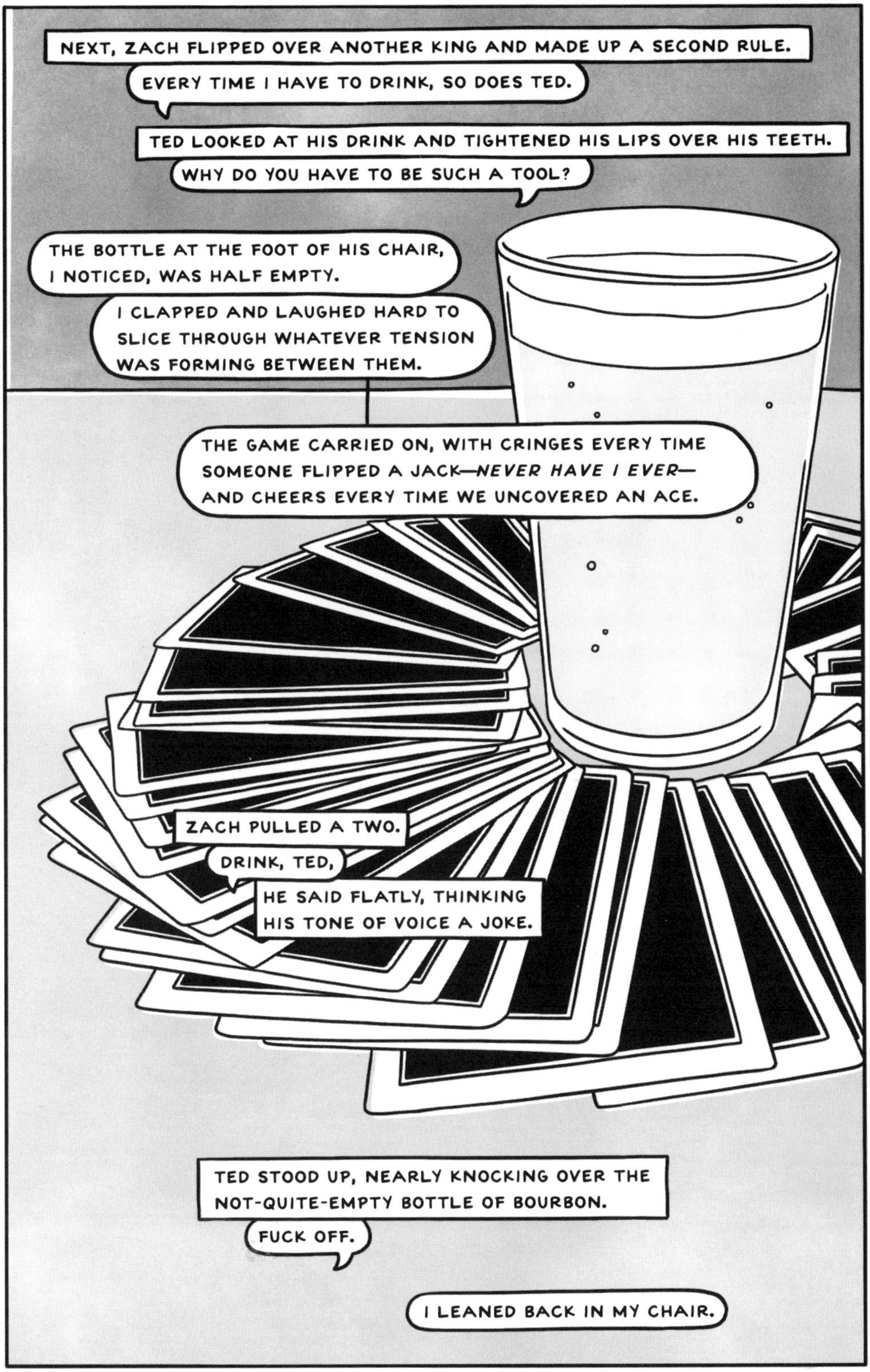
NEXT, ZACH FLIPPED OVER ANOTHER KING AND MADE UP A SECOND RULE.
EVERY TIME I HAVE TO DRINK, SO DOES TED.
TED LOOKED AT HIS DRINK AND TIGHTENED HIS LIPS OVER HIS TEETH.
WHY DO YOU HAVE TO BE SUCH A TOOL?
THE BOTTLE AT THE FOOT OF HIS CHAIR, I NOTICED, WAS HALF EMPTY.
I CLAPPED AND LAUGHED HARD TO SLICE THROUGH WHATEVER TENSION WAS FORMING BETWEEN THEM.
THE GAME CARRIED ON, WITH CRINGES EVERY TIME SOMEONE FLIPPED A JACK—*NEVER HAVE I EVER*—AND CHEERS EVERY TIME WE UNCOVERED AN ACE.
ZACH PULLED A TWO.
DRINK, TED,
HE SAID FLATLY, THINKING HIS TONE OF VOICE A JOKE.
TED STOOD UP, NEARLY KNOCKING OVER THE NOT-QUITE-EMPTY BOTTLE OF BOURBON.
FUCK OFF.
I LEANED BACK IN MY CHAIR.

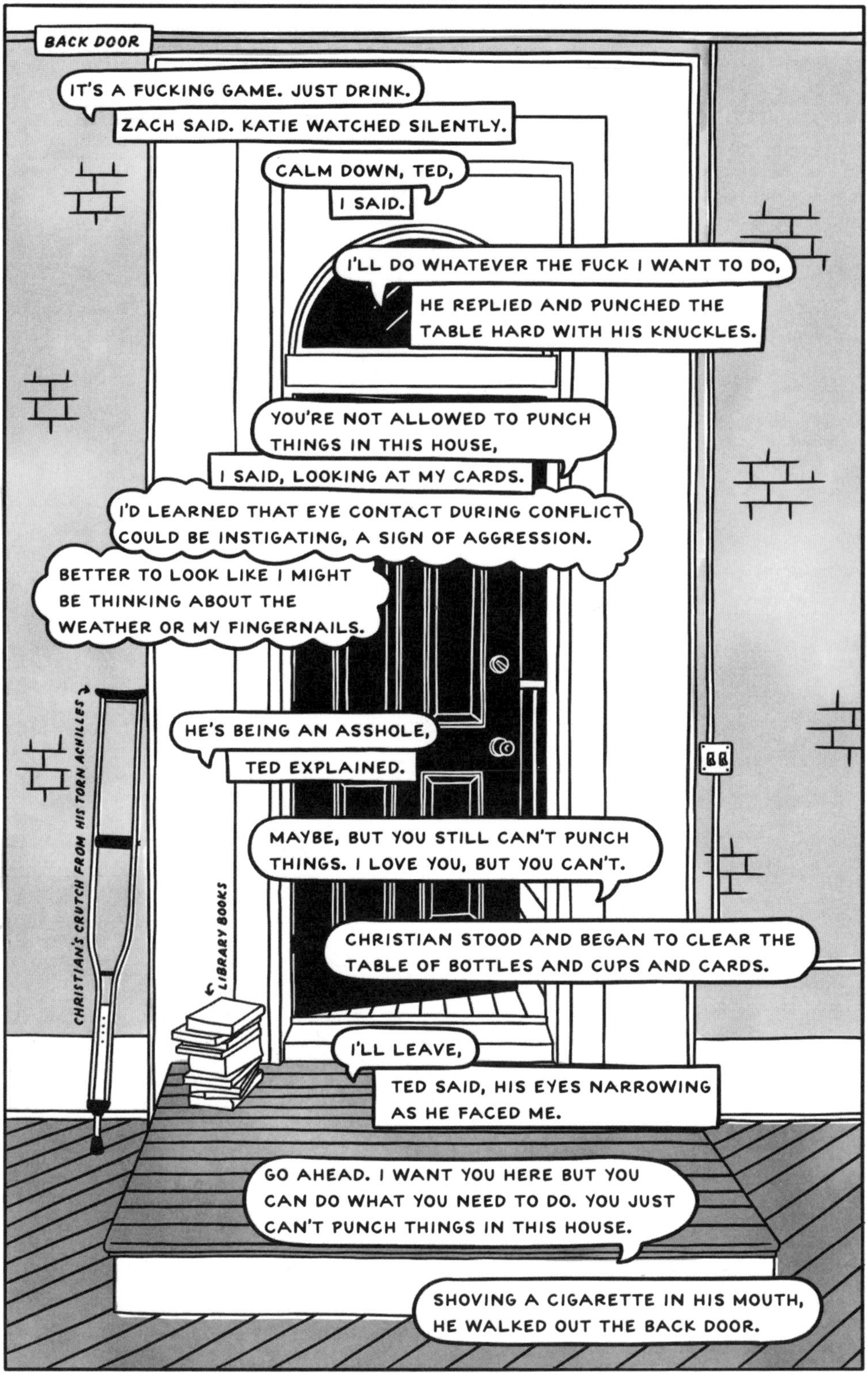
BACK DOOR
IT'S A FUCKING GAME. JUST DRINK.
ZACH SAID. KATIE WATCHED SILENTLY.
CALM DOWN, TED,
I SAID.
I'LL DO WHATEVER THE FUCK I WANT TO DO,
HE REPLIED AND PUNCHED THE TABLE HARD WITH HIS KNUCKLES.
YOU'RE NOT ALLOWED TO PUNCH THINGS IN THIS HOUSE,
I SAID, LOOKING AT MY CARDS.
I'D LEARNED THAT EYE CONTACT DURING CONFLICT COULD BE INSTIGATING, A SIGN OF AGGRESSION.
BETTER TO LOOK LIKE I MIGHT BE THINKING ABOUT THE WEATHER OR MY FINGERNAILS.
CHRISTIAN'S CRUTCH FROM HIS TORN ACHILLES
HE'S BEING AN ASSHOLE,
TED EXPLAINED.
MAYBE, BUT YOU STILL CAN'T PUNCH THINGS. I LOVE YOU, BUT YOU CAN'T.
LIBRARY BOOKS
CHRISTIAN STOOD AND BEGAN TO CLEAR THE TABLE OF BOTTLES AND CUPS AND CARDS.
I'LL LEAVE,
TED SAID, HIS EYES NARROWING AS HE FACED ME.
GO AHEAD. I WANT YOU HERE BUT YOU CAN DO WHAT YOU NEED TO DO. YOU JUST CAN'T PUNCH THINGS IN THIS HOUSE.
SHOVING A CIGARETTE IN HIS MOUTH, HE WALKED OUT THE BACK DOOR.

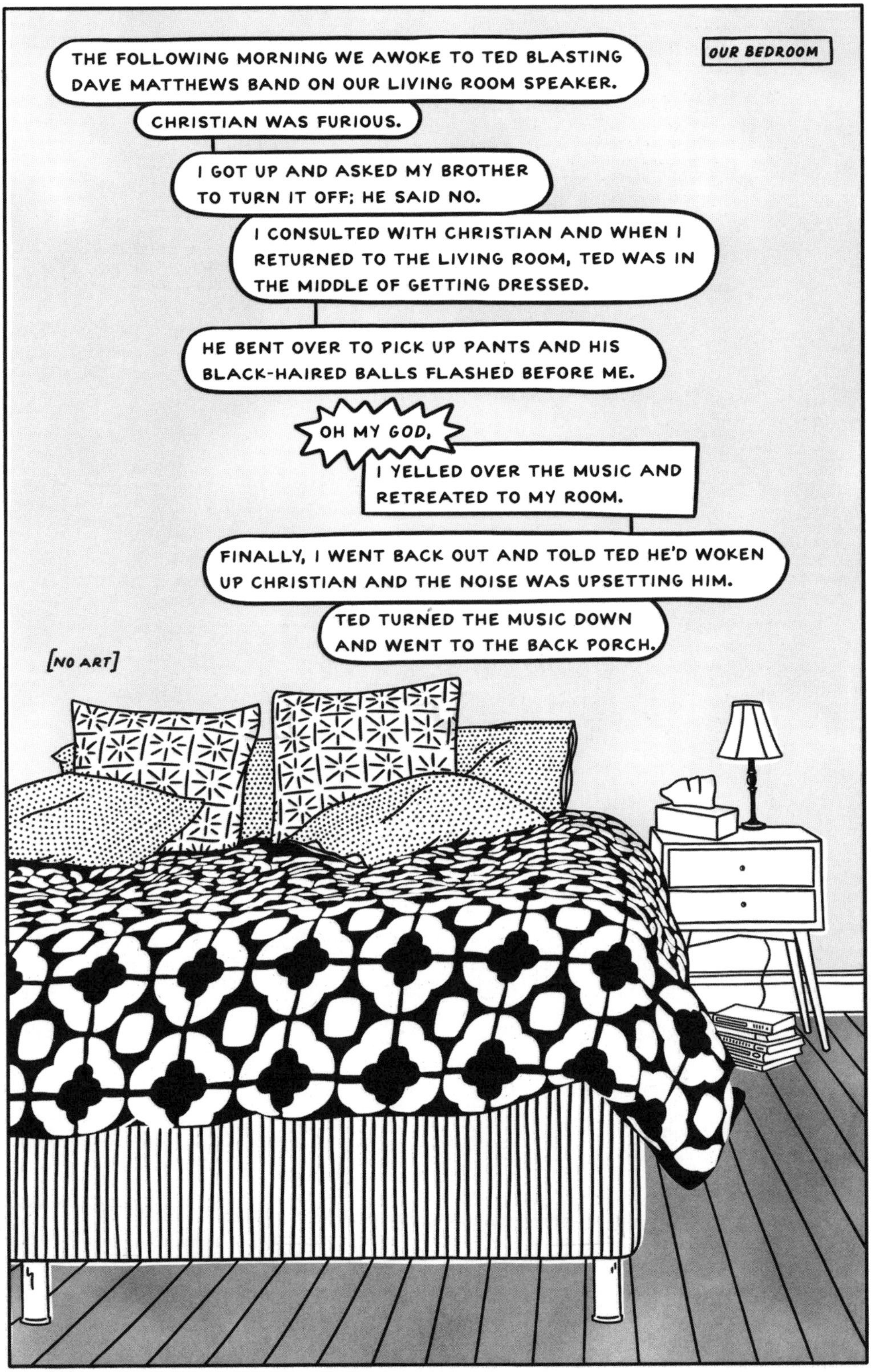
THE FOLLOWING MORNING WE AWOKE TO TED BLASTING DAVE MATTHEWS BAND ON OUR LIVING ROOM SPEAKER.
OUR BEDROOM
CHRISTIAN WAS FURIOUS.
I GOT UP AND ASKED MY BROTHER TO TURN IT OFF; HE SAID NO.
I CONSULTED WITH CHRISTIAN AND WHEN I RETURNED TO THE LIVING ROOM, TED WAS IN THE MIDDLE OF GETTING DRESSED.
HE BENT OVER TO PICK UP PANTS AND HIS BLACK-HAIRED BALLS FLASHED BEFORE ME.
OH MY GOD,
I YELLED OVER THE MUSIC AND RETREATED TO MY ROOM.
FINALLY, I WENT BACK OUT AND TOLD TED HE'D WOKEN UP CHRISTIAN AND THE NOISE WAS UPSETTING HIM.
TED TURNED THE MUSIC DOWN AND WENT TO THE BACK PORCH.
[NO ART]

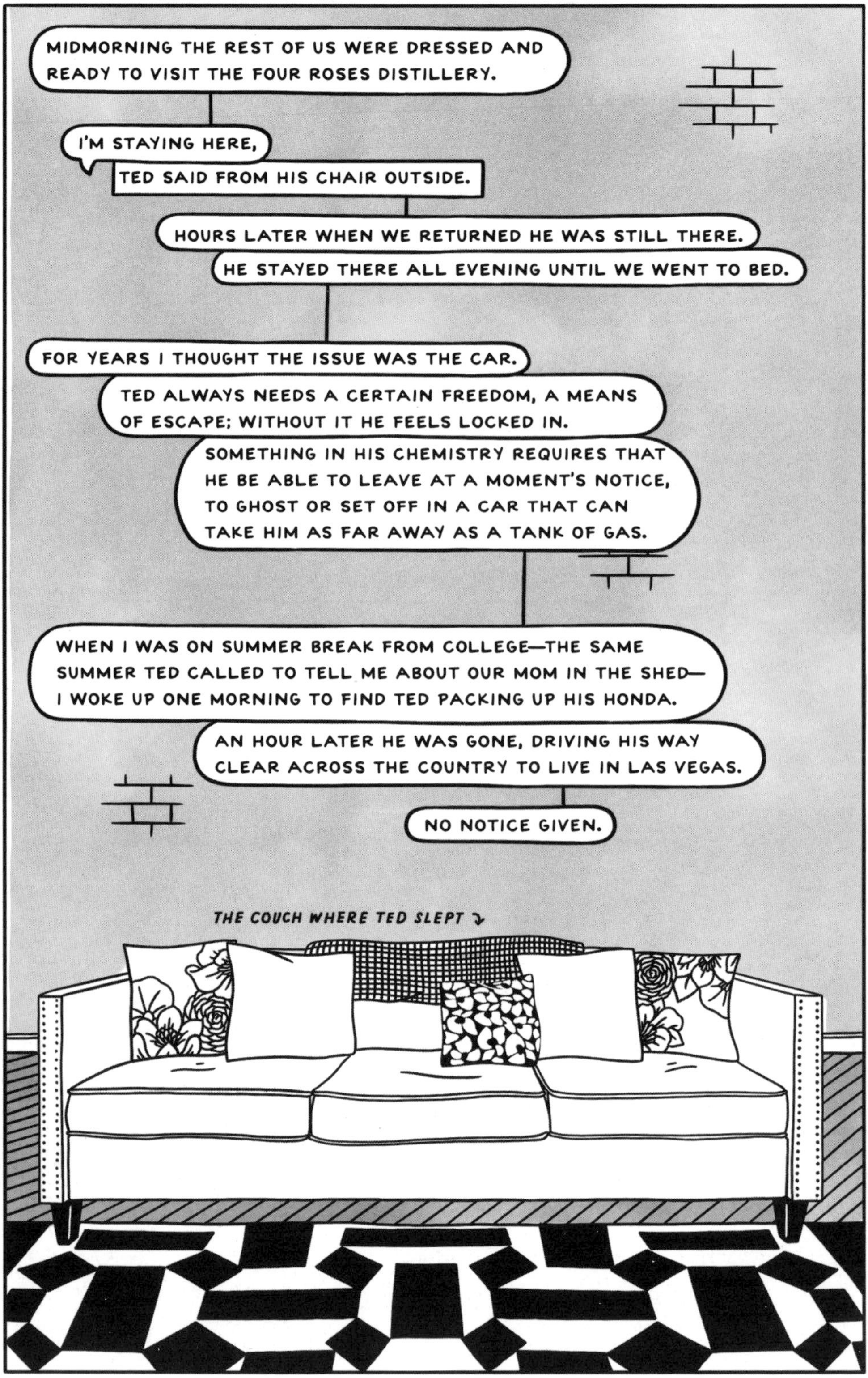
MIDMORNING THE REST OF US WERE DRESSED AND READY TO VISIT THE FOUR ROSES DISTILLERY.
I'M STAYING HERE,
TED SAID FROM HIS CHAIR OUTSIDE.
HOURS LATER WHEN WE RETURNED HE WAS STILL THERE.
HE STAYED THERE ALL EVENING UNTIL WE WENT TO BED.
FOR YEARS I THOUGHT THE ISSUE WAS THE CAR.
TED ALWAYS NEEDS A CERTAIN FREEDOM, A MEANS OF ESCAPE; WITHOUT IT HE FEELS LOCKED IN.
SOMETHING IN HIS CHEMISTRY REQUIRES THAT HE BE ABLE TO LEAVE AT A MOMENT'S NOTICE, TO GHOST OR SET OFF IN A CAR THAT CAN TAKE HIM AS FAR AWAY AS A TANK OF GAS.
WHEN I WAS ON SUMMER BREAK FROM COLLEGE—THE SAME SUMMER TED CALLED TO TELL ME ABOUT OUR MOM IN THE SHED—I WOKE UP ONE MORNING TO FIND TED PACKING UP HIS HONDA.
AN HOUR LATER HE WAS GONE, DRIVING HIS WAY CLEAR ACROSS THE COUNTRY TO LIVE IN LAS VEGAS.
NO NOTICE GIVEN.
THE COUCH WHERE TED SLEPT

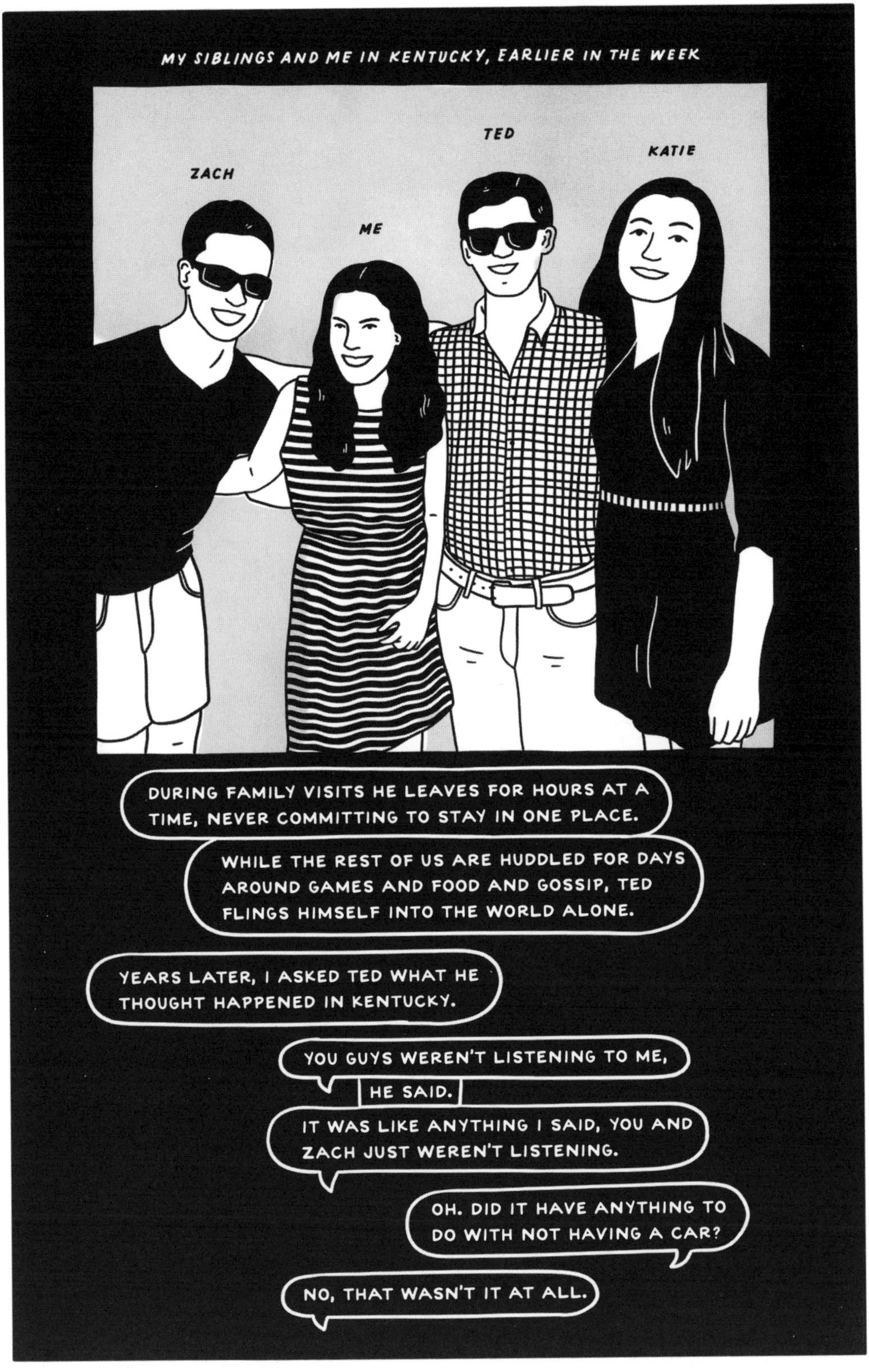
MY SIBLINGS AND ME IN KENTUCKY, EARLIER IN THE WEEK
TED
KATIE
ZACH
ME
DURING FAMILY VISITS HE LEAVES FOR HOURS AT A TIME, NEVER COMMITTING TO STAY IN ONE PLACE.
WHILE THE REST OF US ARE HUDDLED FOR DAYS AROUND GAMES AND FOOD AND GOSSIP, TED FLINGS HIMSELF INTO THE WORLD ALONE.
YEARS LATER, I ASKED TED WHAT HE THOUGHT HAPPENED IN KENTUCKY.
YOU GUYS WEREN'T LISTENING TO ME,
HE SAID.
IT WAS LIKE ANYTHING I SAID, YOU AND ZACH JUST WEREN'T LISTENING.
OH. DID IT HAVE ANYTHING TO DO WITH NOT HAVING A CAR?
NO, THAT WASN'T IT AT ALL.

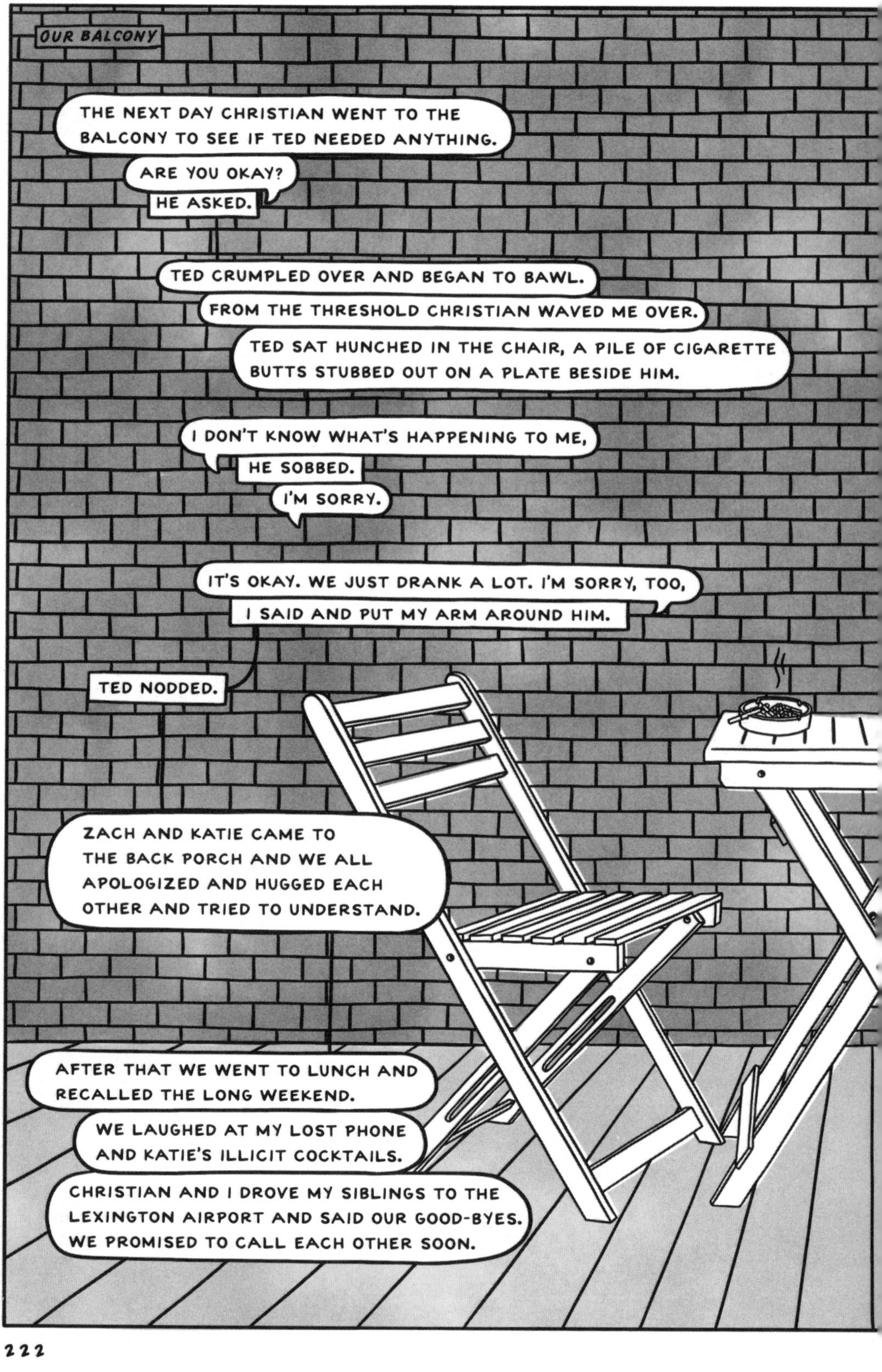
OUR BALCONY
THE NEXT DAY CHRISTIAN WENT TO THE BALCONY TO SEE IF TED NEEDED ANYTHING.
ARE YOU OKAY?
HE ASKED.
TED CRUMPLED OVER AND BEGAN TO BAWL.
FROM THE THRESHOLD CHRISTIAN WAVED ME OVER.
TED SAT HUNCHED IN THE CHAIR, A PILE OF CIGARETTE BUTTS STUBBED OUT ON A PLATE BESIDE HIM.
I DON'T KNOW WHAT'S HAPPENING TO ME,
HE SOBBED.
I'M SORRY.
IT'S OKAY. WE JUST DRANK A LOT. I'M SORRY, TOO,
I SAID AND PUT MY ARM AROUND HIM.
TED NODDED.
ZACH AND KATIE CAME TO THE BACK PORCH AND WE ALL APOLOGIZED AND HUGGED EACH OTHER AND TRIED TO UNDERSTAND.
AFTER THAT WE WENT TO LUNCH AND RECALLED THE LONG WEEKEND.
WE LAUGHED AT MY LOST PHONE AND KATIE'S ILLICIT COCKTAILS.
CHRISTIAN AND I DROVE MY SIBLINGS TO THE LEXINGTON AIRPORT AND SAID OUR GOOD-BYES. WE PROMISED TO CALL EACH OTHER SOON.

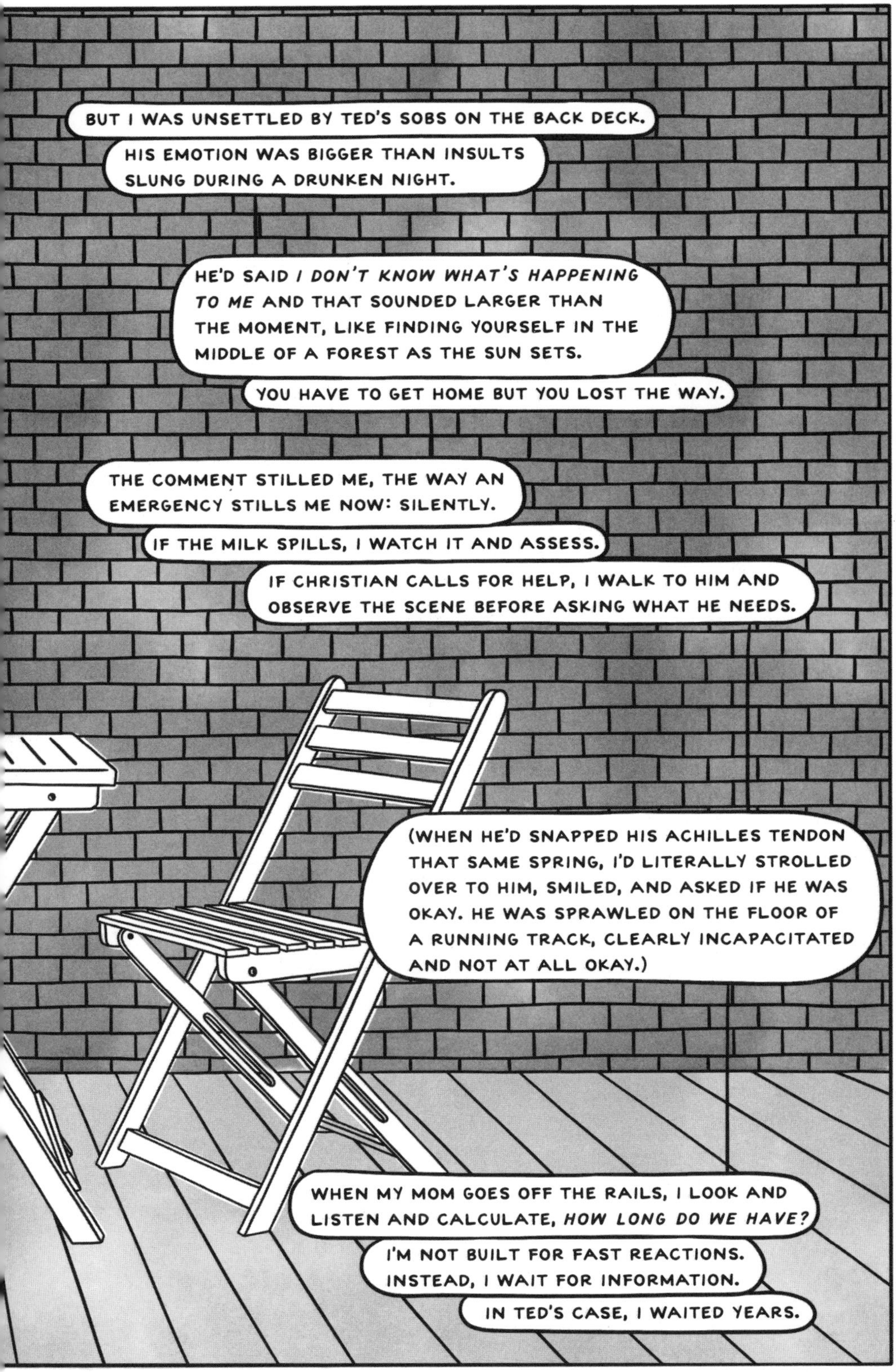
BUT I WAS UNSETTLED BY TED'S SOBS ON THE BACK DECK.
HIS EMOTION WAS BIGGER THAN INSULTS SLUNG DURING A DRUNKEN NIGHT.
HE'D SAID *I DON'T KNOW WHAT'S HAPPENING TO ME* AND THAT SOUNDED LARGER THAN THE MOMENT, LIKE FINDING YOURSELF IN THE MIDDLE OF A FOREST AS THE SUN SETS.
YOU HAVE TO GET HOME BUT YOU LOST THE WAY.
THE COMMENT STILLED ME, THE WAY AN EMERGENCY STILLS ME NOW: SILENTLY.
IF THE MILK SPILLS, I WATCH IT AND ASSESS.
IF CHRISTIAN CALLS FOR HELP, I WALK TO HIM AND OBSERVE THE SCENE BEFORE ASKING WHAT HE NEEDS.
(WHEN HE'D SNAPPED HIS ACHILLES TENDON THAT SAME SPRING, I'D LITERALLY STROLLED OVER TO HIM, SMILED, AND ASKED IF HE WAS OKAY. HE WAS SPRAWLED ON THE FLOOR OF A RUNNING TRACK, CLEARLY INCAPACITATED AND NOT AT ALL OKAY.)
WHEN MY MOM GOES OFF THE RAILS, I LOOK AND LISTEN AND CALCULATE, *HOW LONG DO WE HAVE?*
I'M NOT BUILT FOR FAST REACTIONS. INSTEAD, I WAIT FOR INFORMATION.
IN TED'S CASE, I WAITED YEARS.

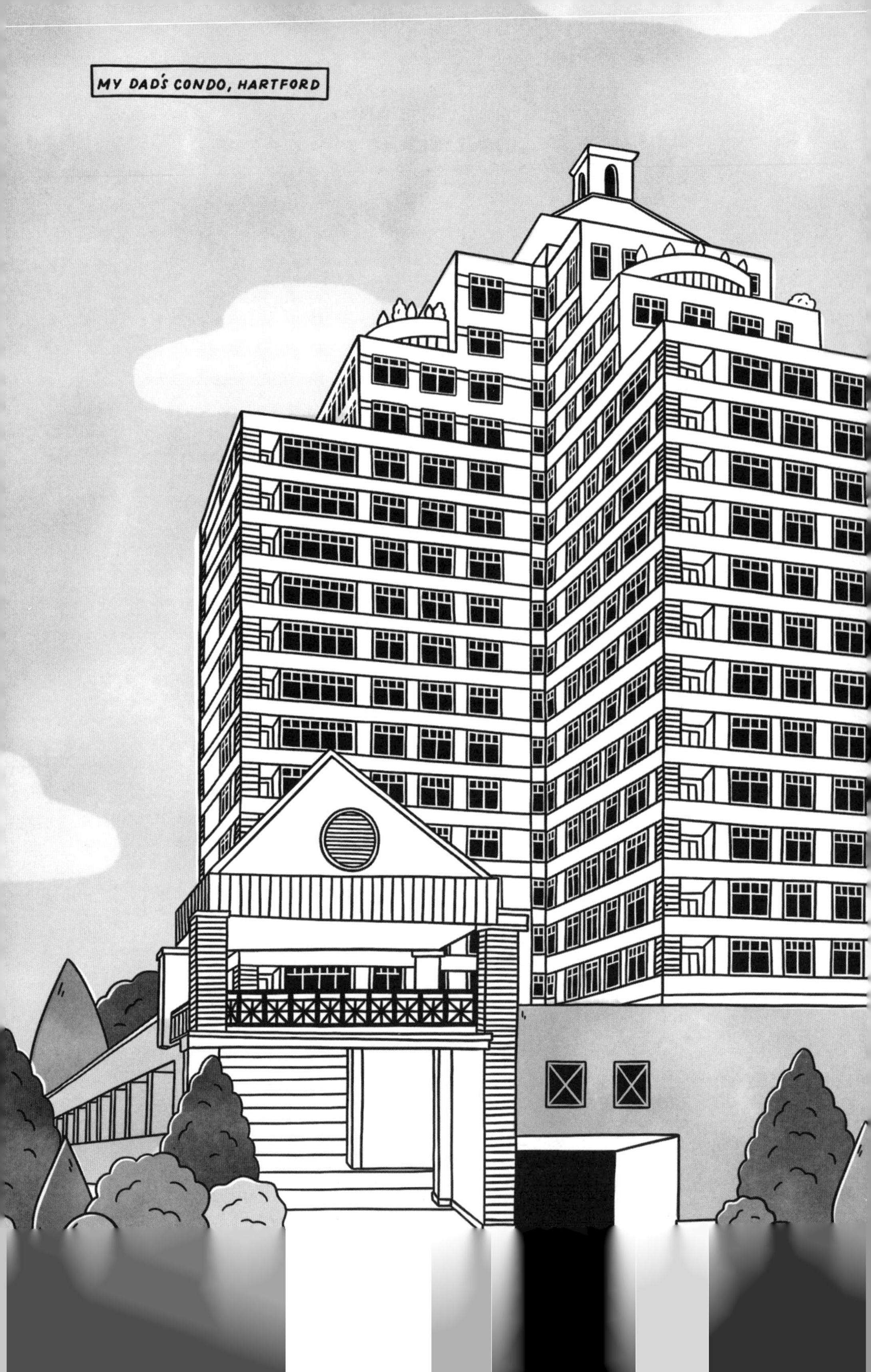
MY DAD'S CONDO, HARTFORD

CHAPTER 17
The Trip Home
PART II

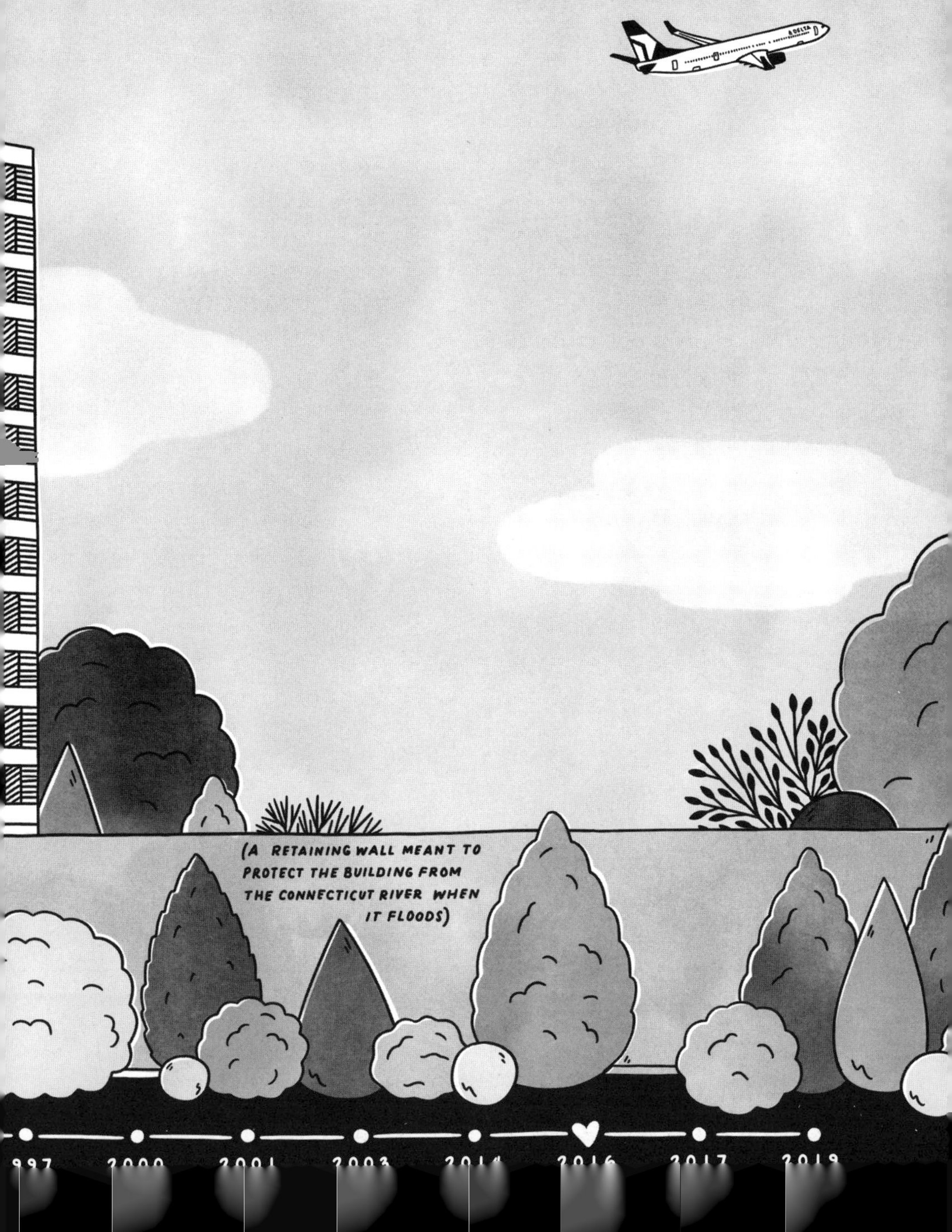
(A RETAINING WALL MEANT TO PROTECT THE BUILDING FROM THE CONNECTICUT RIVER WHEN IT FLOODS)

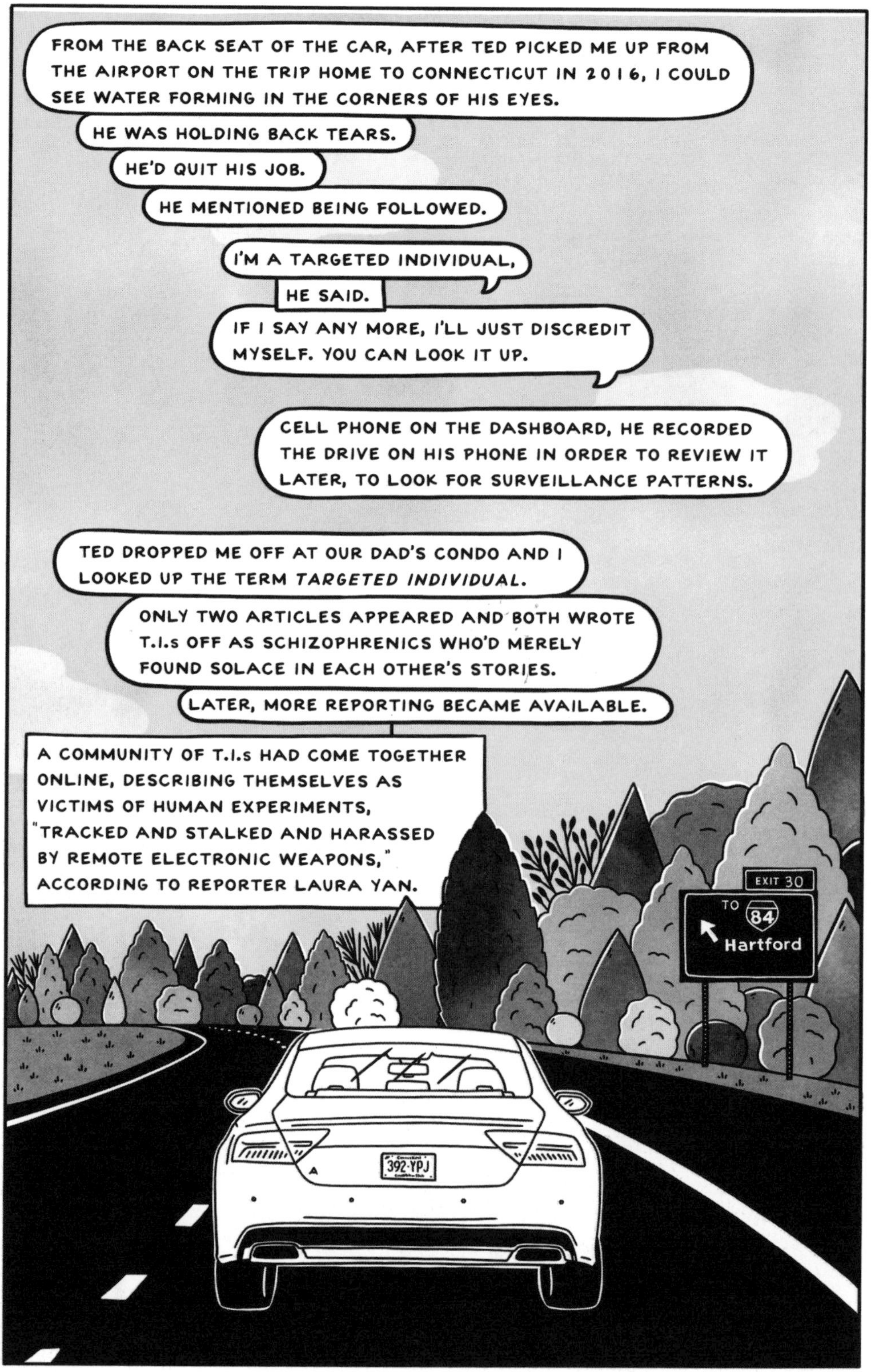
FROM THE BACK SEAT OF THE CAR, AFTER TED PICKED ME UP FROM THE AIRPORT ON THE TRIP HOME TO CONNECTICUT IN 2016, I COULD SEE WATER FORMING IN THE CORNERS OF HIS EYES.
HE WAS HOLDING BACK TEARS.
HE'D QUIT HIS JOB.
HE MENTIONED BEING FOLLOWED.
I'M A TARGETED INDIVIDUAL,
HE SAID.
IF I SAY ANY MORE, I'LL JUST DISCREDIT MYSELF. YOU CAN LOOK IT UP.
CELL PHONE ON THE DASHBOARD, HE RECORDED THE DRIVE ON HIS PHONE IN ORDER TO REVIEW IT LATER, TO LOOK FOR SURVEILLANCE PATTERNS.
TED DROPPED ME OFF AT OUR DAD'S CONDO AND I LOOKED UP THE TERM *TARGETED INDIVIDUAL*.
ONLY TWO ARTICLES APPEARED AND BOTH WROTE T.I.s OFF AS SCHIZOPHRENICS WHO'D MERELY FOUND SOLACE IN EACH OTHER'S STORIES.
LATER, MORE REPORTING BECAME AVAILABLE.
A COMMUNITY OF T.I.s HAD COME TOGETHER ONLINE, DESCRIBING THEMSELVES AS VICTIMS OF HUMAN EXPERIMENTS, "TRACKED AND STALKED AND HARASSED BY REMOTE ELECTRONIC WEAPONS," ACCORDING TO REPORTER LAURA YAN.
EXIT 30
TO 84 Hartford
392·YPJ

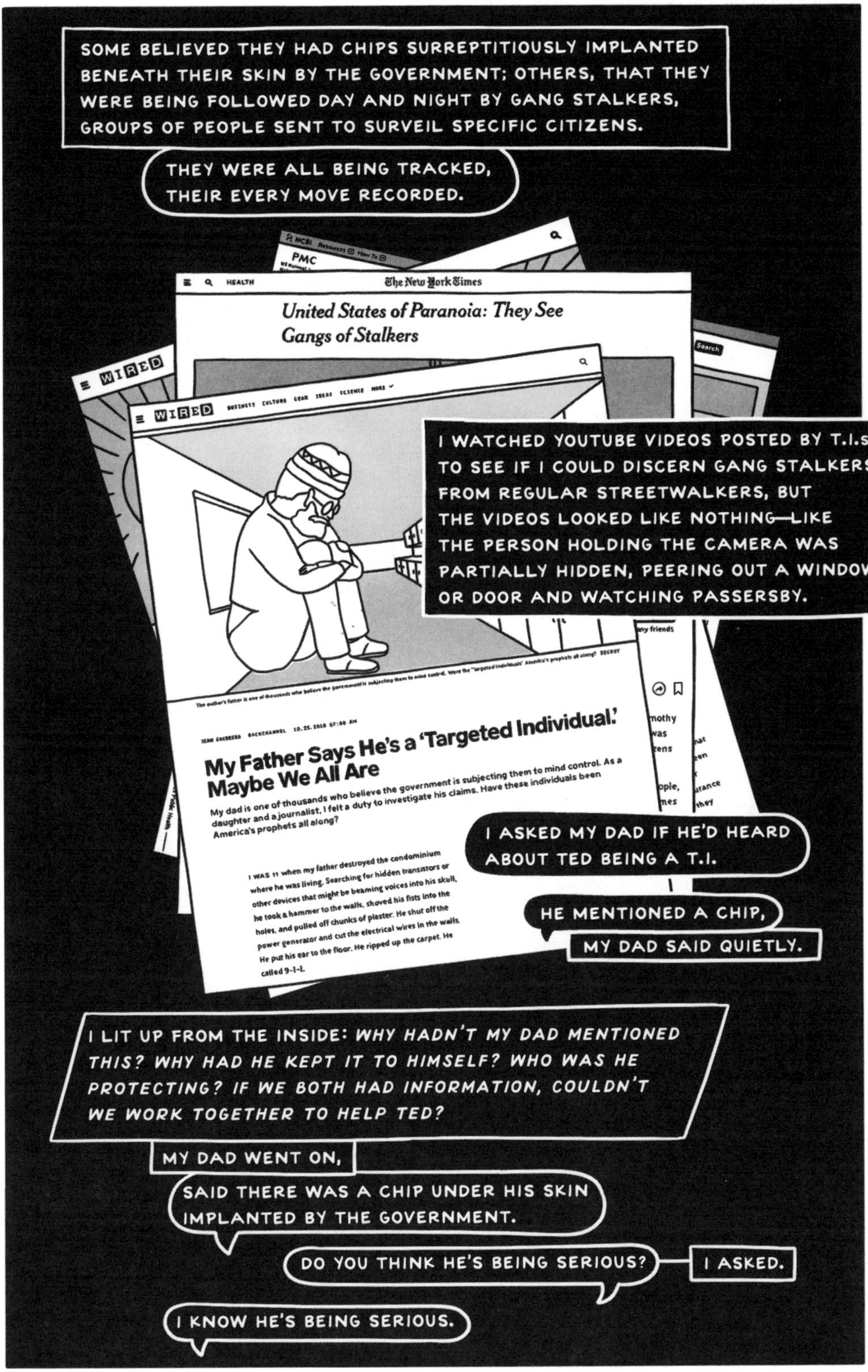
SOME BELIEVED THEY HAD CHIPS SURREPTITIOUSLY IMPLANTED BENEATH THEIR SKIN BY THE GOVERNMENT; OTHERS, THAT THEY WERE BEING FOLLOWED DAY AND NIGHT BY GANG STALKERS, GROUPS OF PEOPLE SENT TO SURVEIL SPECIFIC CITIZENS.
THEY WERE ALL BEING TRACKED, THEIR EVERY MOVE RECORDED.
HEALTH
The New York Times
United States of Paranoia: They See Gangs of Stalkers
WIRED
My Father Says He's a 'Targeted Individual.' Maybe We All Are
My dad is one of thousands who believe the government is subjecting them to mind control. As a daughter and a journalist, I felt a duty to investigate his claims. Have these individuals been America's prophets all along?
I WAS 11 when my father destroyed the condominium where he was living. Searching for hidden transistors or other devices that might be beaming voices into his skull, he took a hammer to the walls, shoved his fists into the holes, and pulled off chunks of plaster. He shut off the power generator and cut the electrical wires in the walls. He put his ear to the floor. He ripped up the carpet. He called 9-1-1.
I WATCHED YOUTUBE VIDEOS POSTED BY T.I.s TO SEE IF I COULD DISCERN GANG STALKERS FROM REGULAR STREETWALKERS, BUT THE VIDEOS LOOKED LIKE NOTHING—LIKE THE PERSON HOLDING THE CAMERA WAS PARTIALLY HIDDEN, PEERING OUT A WINDOW OR DOOR AND WATCHING PASSERSBY.
I ASKED MY DAD IF HE'D HEARD ABOUT TED BEING A T.I.
HE MENTIONED A CHIP,
MY DAD SAID QUIETLY.
I LIT UP FROM THE INSIDE: *WHY HADN'T MY DAD MENTIONED THIS? WHY HAD HE KEPT IT TO HIMSELF? WHO WAS HE PROTECTING? IF WE BOTH HAD INFORMATION, COULDN'T WE WORK TOGETHER TO HELP TED?*
MY DAD WENT ON,
SAID THERE WAS A CHIP UNDER HIS SKIN IMPLANTED BY THE GOVERNMENT.
DO YOU THINK HE'S BEING SERIOUS?
I ASKED.
I KNOW HE'S BEING SERIOUS.

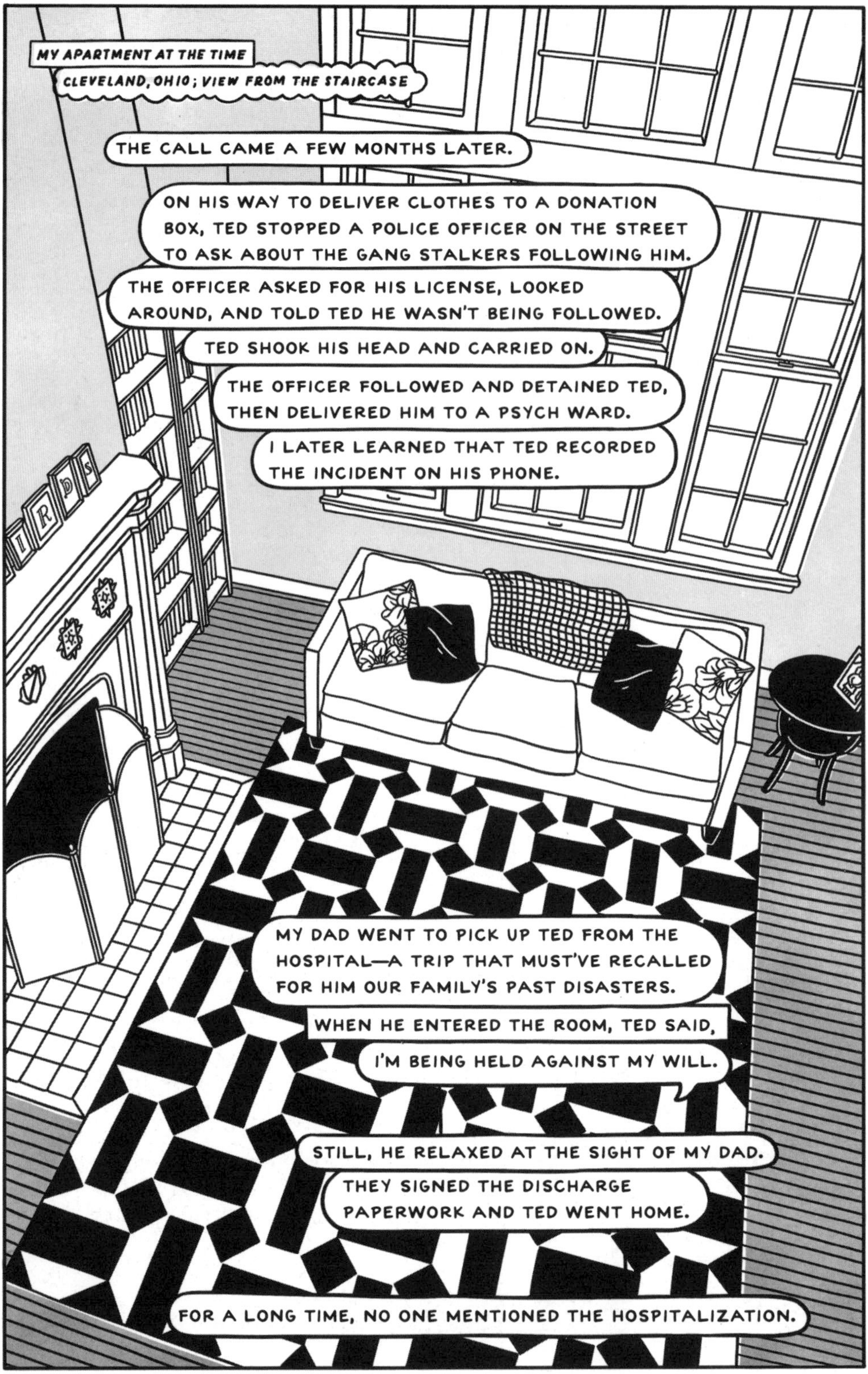
MY APARTMENT AT THE TIME
CLEVELAND, OHIO; VIEW FROM THE STAIRCASE
THE CALL CAME A FEW MONTHS LATER.
ON HIS WAY TO DELIVER CLOTHES TO A DONATION BOX, TED STOPPED A POLICE OFFICER ON THE STREET TO ASK ABOUT THE GANG STALKERS FOLLOWING HIM.
THE OFFICER ASKED FOR HIS LICENSE, LOOKED AROUND, AND TOLD TED HE WASN'T BEING FOLLOWED.
TED SHOOK HIS HEAD AND CARRIED ON.
THE OFFICER FOLLOWED AND DETAINED TED, THEN DELIVERED HIM TO A PSYCH WARD.
I LATER LEARNED THAT TED RECORDED THE INCIDENT ON HIS PHONE.
MY DAD WENT TO PICK UP TED FROM THE HOSPITAL—A TRIP THAT MUST'VE RECALLED FOR HIM OUR FAMILY'S PAST DISASTERS.
WHEN HE ENTERED THE ROOM, TED SAID,
I'M BEING HELD AGAINST MY WILL.
STILL, HE RELAXED AT THE SIGHT OF MY DAD.
THEY SIGNED THE DISCHARGE PAPERWORK AND TED WENT HOME.
FOR A LONG TIME, NO ONE MENTIONED THE HOSPITALIZATION.

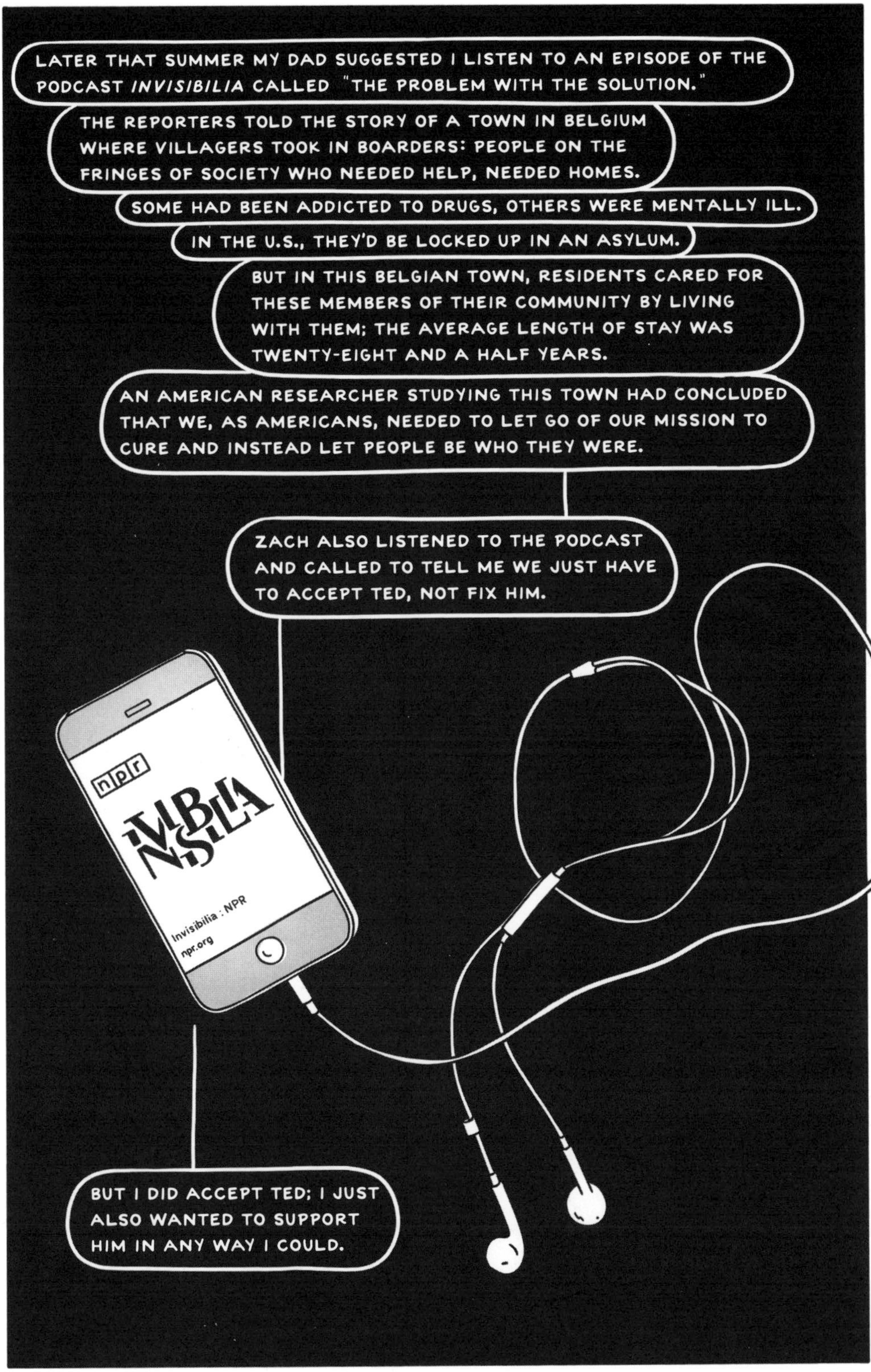
LATER THAT SUMMER MY DAD SUGGESTED I LISTEN TO AN EPISODE OF THE PODCAST *INVISIBILIA* CALLED "THE PROBLEM WITH THE SOLUTION."
THE REPORTERS TOLD THE STORY OF A TOWN IN BELGIUM WHERE VILLAGERS TOOK IN BOARDERS: PEOPLE ON THE FRINGES OF SOCIETY WHO NEEDED HELP, NEEDED HOMES.
SOME HAD BEEN ADDICTED TO DRUGS, OTHERS WERE MENTALLY ILL.
IN THE U.S., THEY'D BE LOCKED UP IN AN ASYLUM.
BUT IN THIS BELGIAN TOWN, RESIDENTS CARED FOR THESE MEMBERS OF THEIR COMMUNITY BY LIVING WITH THEM; THE AVERAGE LENGTH OF STAY WAS TWENTY-EIGHT AND A HALF YEARS.
AN AMERICAN RESEARCHER STUDYING THIS TOWN HAD CONCLUDED THAT WE, AS AMERICANS, NEEDED TO LET GO OF OUR MISSION TO CURE AND INSTEAD LET PEOPLE BE WHO THEY WERE.
ZACH ALSO LISTENED TO THE PODCAST AND CALLED TO TELL ME WE JUST HAVE TO ACCEPT TED, NOT FIX HIM.
npr
INVISIBILIA
Invisibilia : NPR
npr.org
BUT I DID ACCEPT TED; I JUST ALSO WANTED TO SUPPORT HIM IN ANY WAY I COULD.

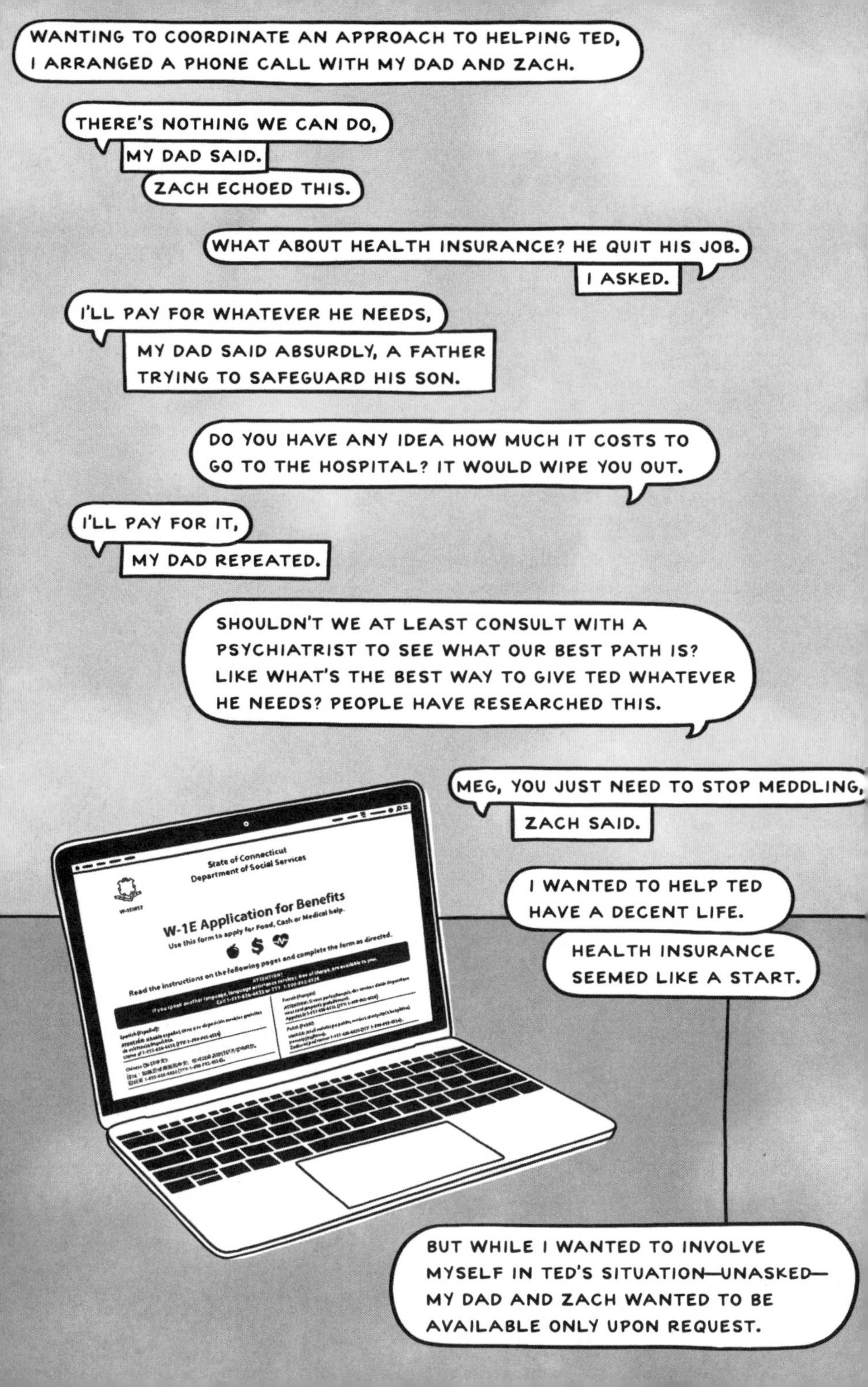
WANTING TO COORDINATE AN APPROACH TO HELPING TED, I ARRANGED A PHONE CALL WITH MY DAD AND ZACH.
THERE'S NOTHING WE CAN DO,
MY DAD SAID.
ZACH ECHOED THIS.
WHAT ABOUT HEALTH INSURANCE? HE QUIT HIS JOB.
I ASKED.
I'LL PAY FOR WHATEVER HE NEEDS,
MY DAD SAID ABSURDLY, A FATHER TRYING TO SAFEGUARD HIS SON.
DO YOU HAVE ANY IDEA HOW MUCH IT COSTS TO GO TO THE HOSPITAL? IT WOULD WIPE YOU OUT.
I'LL PAY FOR IT,
MY DAD REPEATED.
SHOULDN'T WE AT LEAST CONSULT WITH A PSYCHIATRIST TO SEE WHAT OUR BEST PATH IS? LIKE WHAT'S THE BEST WAY TO GIVE TED WHATEVER HE NEEDS? PEOPLE HAVE RESEARCHED THIS.
MEG, YOU JUST NEED TO STOP MEDDLING,
ZACH SAID.
State of Connecticut
Department of Social Services
W-1E Application for Benefits
Use this form to apply for Food, Cash or Medical help.
Read the instructions on the following pages and complete the form as directed.
I WANTED TO HELP TED HAVE A DECENT LIFE.
HEALTH INSURANCE SEEMED LIKE A START.
BUT WHILE I WANTED TO INVOLVE MYSELF IN TED'S SITUATION—UNASKED—MY DAD AND ZACH WANTED TO BE AVAILABLE ONLY UPON REQUEST.

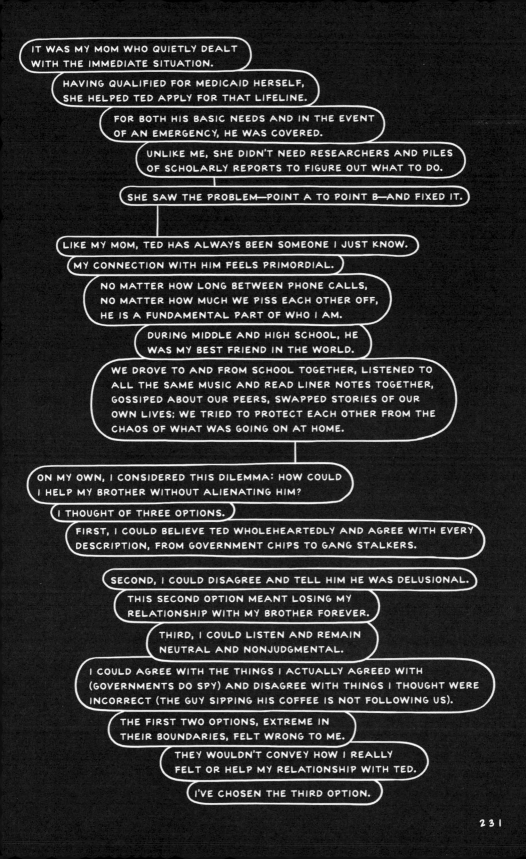

IT WAS MY MOM WHO QUIETLY DEALT WITH THE IMMEDIATE SITUATION.

HAVING QUALIFIED FOR MEDICAID HERSELF, SHE HELPED TED APPLY FOR THAT LIFELINE.

FOR BOTH HIS BASIC NEEDS AND IN THE EVENT OF AN EMERGENCY, HE WAS COVERED.

UNLIKE ME, SHE DIDN'T NEED RESEARCHERS AND PILES OF SCHOLARLY REPORTS TO FIGURE OUT WHAT TO DO.

SHE SAW THE PROBLEM—POINT A TO POINT B—AND FIXED IT.

LIKE MY MOM, TED HAS ALWAYS BEEN SOMEONE I JUST KNOW.

MY CONNECTION WITH HIM FEELS PRIMORDIAL.

NO MATTER HOW LONG BETWEEN PHONE CALLS, NO MATTER HOW MUCH WE PISS EACH OTHER OFF, HE IS A FUNDAMENTAL PART OF WHO I AM.

DURING MIDDLE AND HIGH SCHOOL, HE WAS MY BEST FRIEND IN THE WORLD.

WE DROVE TO AND FROM SCHOOL TOGETHER, LISTENED TO ALL THE SAME MUSIC AND READ LINER NOTES TOGETHER, GOSSIPED ABOUT OUR PEERS, SWAPPED STORIES OF OUR OWN LIVES; WE TRIED TO PROTECT EACH OTHER FROM THE CHAOS OF WHAT WAS GOING ON AT HOME.

ON MY OWN, I CONSIDERED THIS DILEMMA: HOW COULD I HELP MY BROTHER WITHOUT ALIENATING HIM?

I THOUGHT OF THREE OPTIONS.

FIRST, I COULD BELIEVE TED WHOLEHEARTEDLY AND AGREE WITH EVERY DESCRIPTION, FROM GOVERNMENT CHIPS TO GANG STALKERS.

SECOND, I COULD DISAGREE AND TELL HIM HE WAS DELUSIONAL.

THIS SECOND OPTION MEANT LOSING MY RELATIONSHIP WITH MY BROTHER FOREVER.

THIRD, I COULD LISTEN AND REMAIN NEUTRAL AND NONJUDGMENTAL.

I COULD AGREE WITH THE THINGS I ACTUALLY AGREED WITH (GOVERNMENTS DO SPY) AND DISAGREE WITH THINGS I THOUGHT WERE INCORRECT (THE GUY SIPPING HIS COFFEE IS NOT FOLLOWING US).

THE FIRST TWO OPTIONS, EXTREME IN THEIR BOUNDARIES, FELT WRONG TO ME.

THEY WOULDN'T CONVEY HOW I REALLY FELT OR HELP MY RELATIONSHIP WITH TED.

I'VE CHOSEN THE THIRD OPTION.

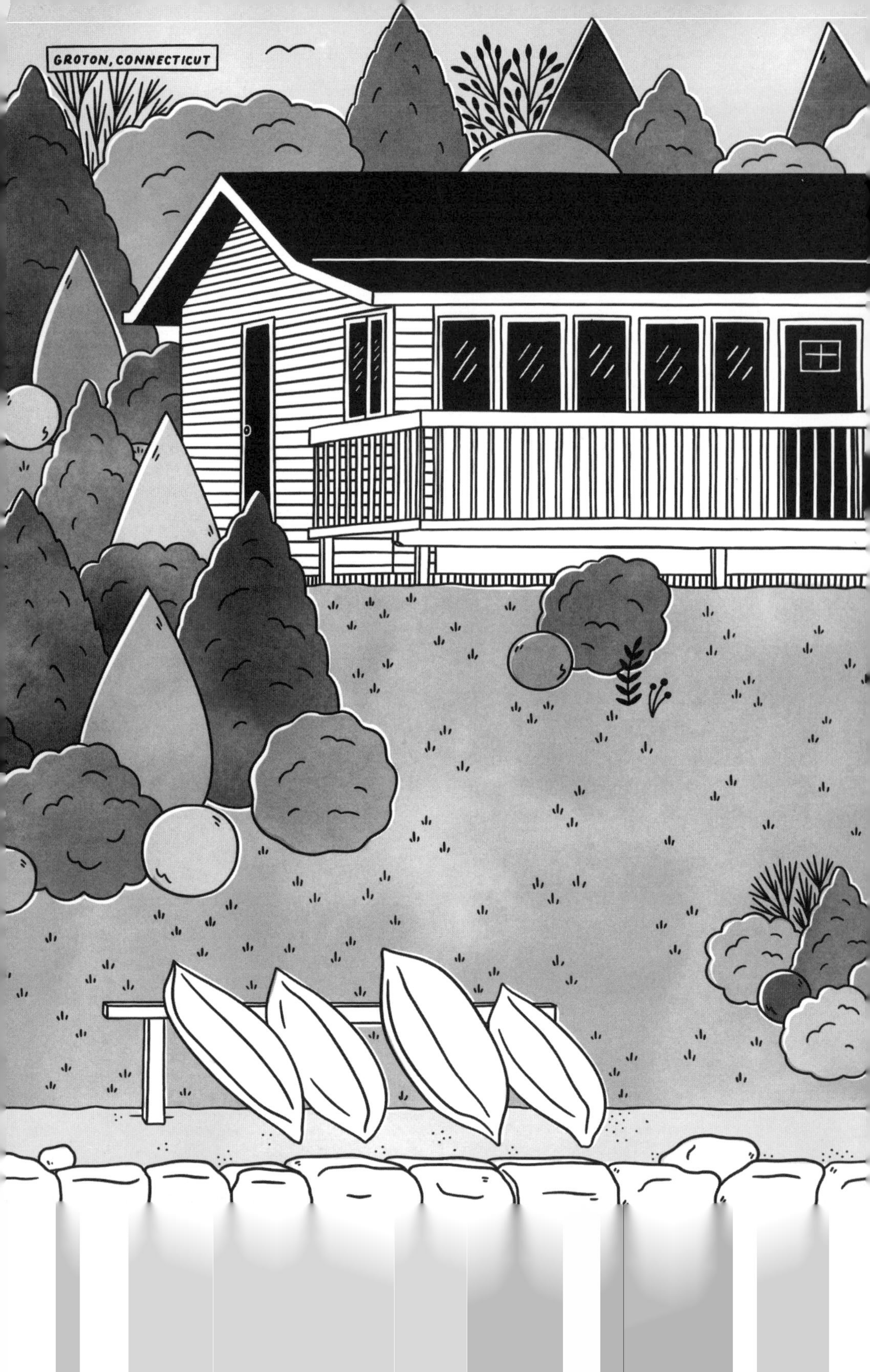
GROTON, CONNECTICUT

CHAPTER 18

The Birthday

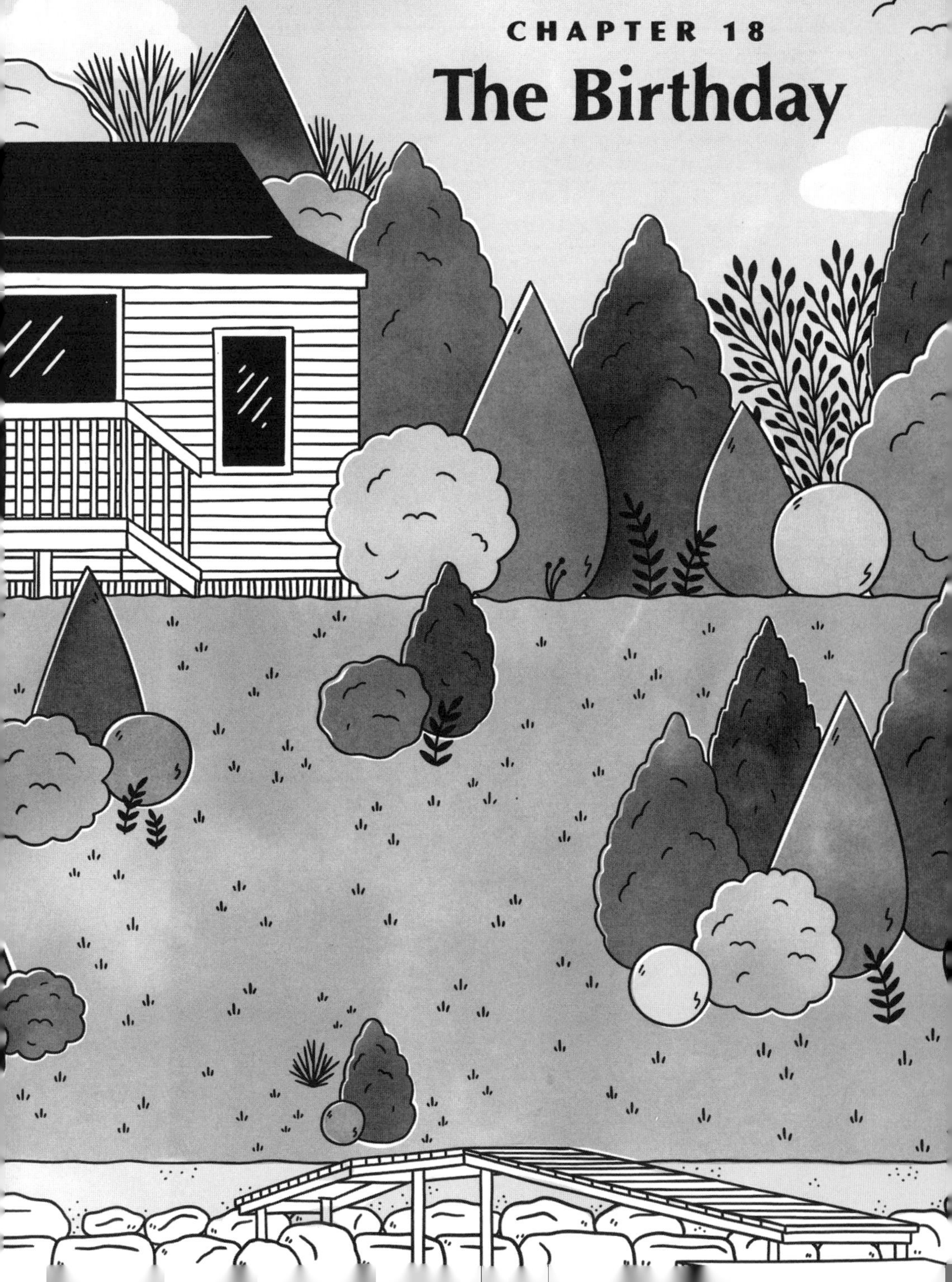

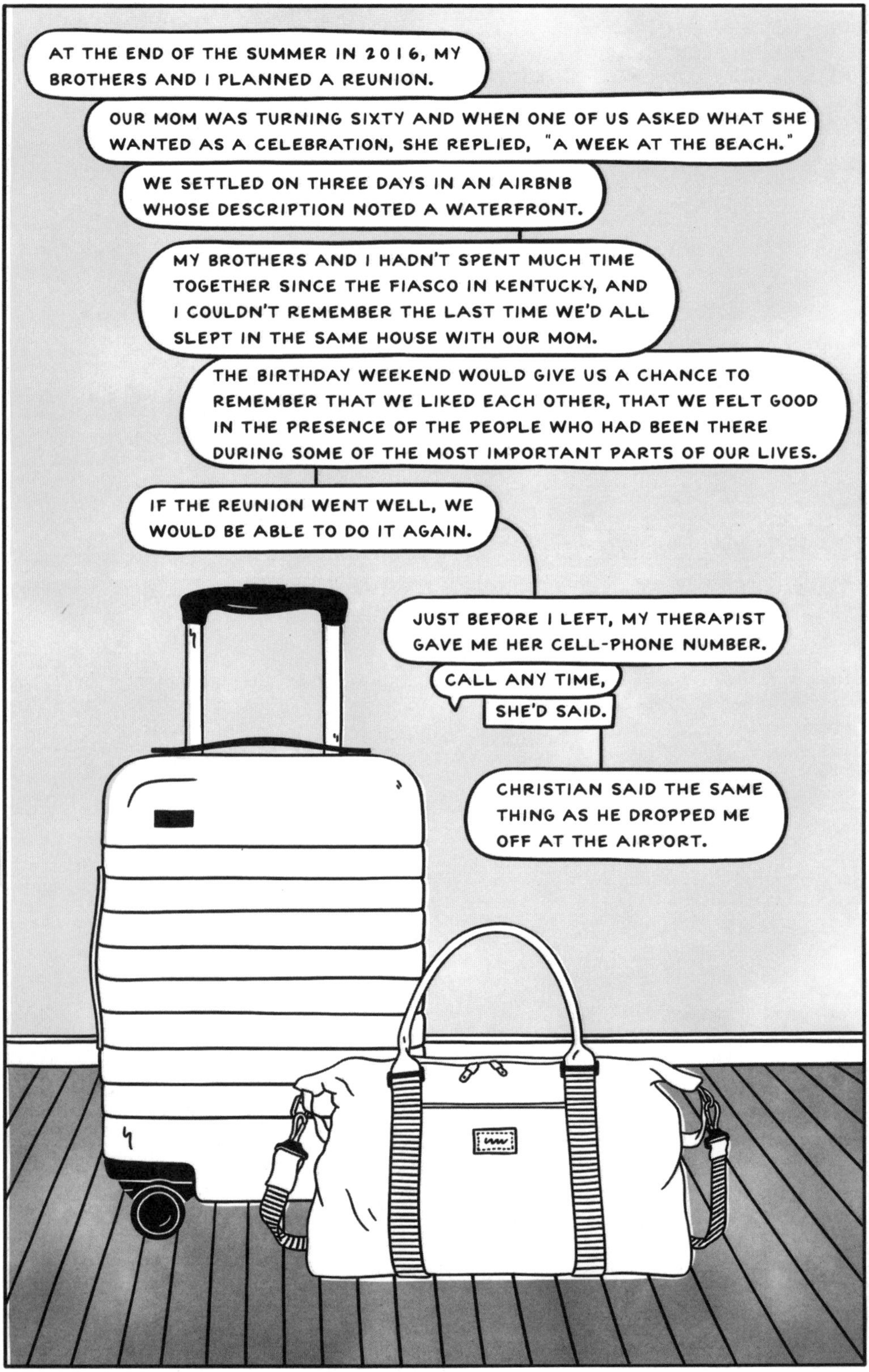
AT THE END OF THE SUMMER IN 2016, MY BROTHERS AND I PLANNED A REUNION.
OUR MOM WAS TURNING SIXTY AND WHEN ONE OF US ASKED WHAT SHE WANTED AS A CELEBRATION, SHE REPLIED, "A WEEK AT THE BEACH."
WE SETTLED ON THREE DAYS IN AN AIRBNB WHOSE DESCRIPTION NOTED A WATERFRONT.
MY BROTHERS AND I HADN'T SPENT MUCH TIME TOGETHER SINCE THE FIASCO IN KENTUCKY, AND I COULDN'T REMEMBER THE LAST TIME WE'D ALL SLEPT IN THE SAME HOUSE WITH OUR MOM.
THE BIRTHDAY WEEKEND WOULD GIVE US A CHANCE TO REMEMBER THAT WE LIKED EACH OTHER, THAT WE FELT GOOD IN THE PRESENCE OF THE PEOPLE WHO HAD BEEN THERE DURING SOME OF THE MOST IMPORTANT PARTS OF OUR LIVES.
IF THE REUNION WENT WELL, WE WOULD BE ABLE TO DO IT AGAIN.
JUST BEFORE I LEFT, MY THERAPIST GAVE ME HER CELL-PHONE NUMBER.
CALL ANY TIME,
SHE'D SAID.
CHRISTIAN SAID THE SAME THING AS HE DROPPED ME OFF AT THE AIRPORT.

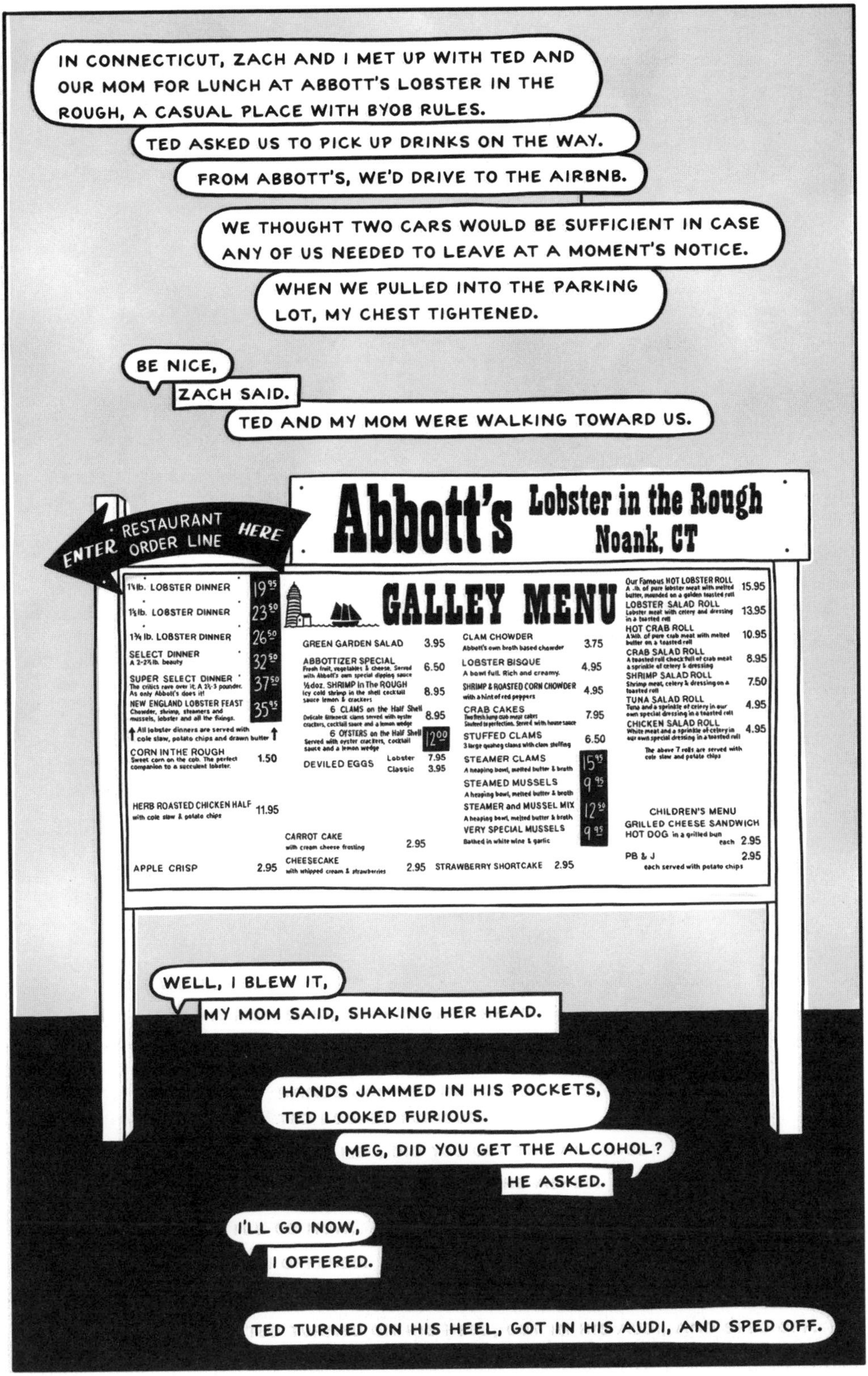
IN CONNECTICUT, ZACH AND I MET UP WITH TED AND OUR MOM FOR LUNCH AT ABBOTT'S LOBSTER IN THE ROUGH, A CASUAL PLACE WITH BYOB RULES.
TED ASKED US TO PICK UP DRINKS ON THE WAY.
FROM ABBOTT'S, WE'D DRIVE TO THE AIRBNB.
WE THOUGHT TWO CARS WOULD BE SUFFICIENT IN CASE ANY OF US NEEDED TO LEAVE AT A MOMENT'S NOTICE.
WHEN WE PULLED INTO THE PARKING LOT, MY CHEST TIGHTENED.
BE NICE,
ZACH SAID.
TED AND MY MOM WERE WALKING TOWARD US.
Abbott's Lobster in the Rough Noank, CT
ENTER RESTAURANT ORDER LINE HERE
GALLEY MENU
1¼ lb. LOBSTER DINNER 19.95
1½ lb. LOBSTER DINNER 23.50
1¾ lb. LOBSTER DINNER 26.50
SELECT DINNER 32.50
SUPER SELECT DINNER 37.50
NEW ENGLAND LOBSTER FEAST 35.95
All lobster dinners are served with cole slaw, potato chips and drawn butter
CORN IN THE ROUGH 1.50
HERB ROASTED CHICKEN HALF 11.95
APPLE CRISP 2.95
GREEN GARDEN SALAD 3.95
ABBOTTIZER SPECIAL 6.50
½ doz. SHRIMP In The ROUGH 8.95
6 CLAMS on the Half Shell 8.95
6 OYSTERS on the Half Shell 12.00
DEVILED EGGS Lobster 7.95 Classic 3.95
CARROT CAKE 2.95
CHEESECAKE 2.95
CLAM CHOWDER 3.75
LOBSTER BISQUE 4.95
SHRIMP & ROASTED CORN CHOWDER 4.95
CRAB CAKES 7.95
STUFFED CLAMS 6.50
STEAMER CLAMS 15.95
STEAMED MUSSELS 9.95
STEAMER and MUSSEL MIX 12.50
VERY SPECIAL MUSSELS 9.95
STRAWBERRY SHORTCAKE 2.95
Our Famous HOT LOBSTER ROLL 15.95
LOBSTER SALAD ROLL 13.95
HOT CRAB ROLL 10.95
CRAB SALAD ROLL 8.95
SHRIMP SALAD ROLL 7.50
TUNA SALAD ROLL 4.95
CHICKEN SALAD ROLL 4.95
The above 7 rolls are served with cole slaw and potato chips
CHILDREN'S MENU
GRILLED CHEESE SANDWICH
HOT DOG in a grilled bun each 2.95
PB & J 2.95
each served with potato chips
WELL, I BLEW IT,
MY MOM SAID, SHAKING HER HEAD.
HANDS JAMMED IN HIS POCKETS, TED LOOKED FURIOUS.
MEG, DID YOU GET THE ALCOHOL?
HE ASKED.
I'LL GO NOW,
I OFFERED.
TED TURNED ON HIS HEEL, GOT IN HIS AUDI, AND SPED OFF.

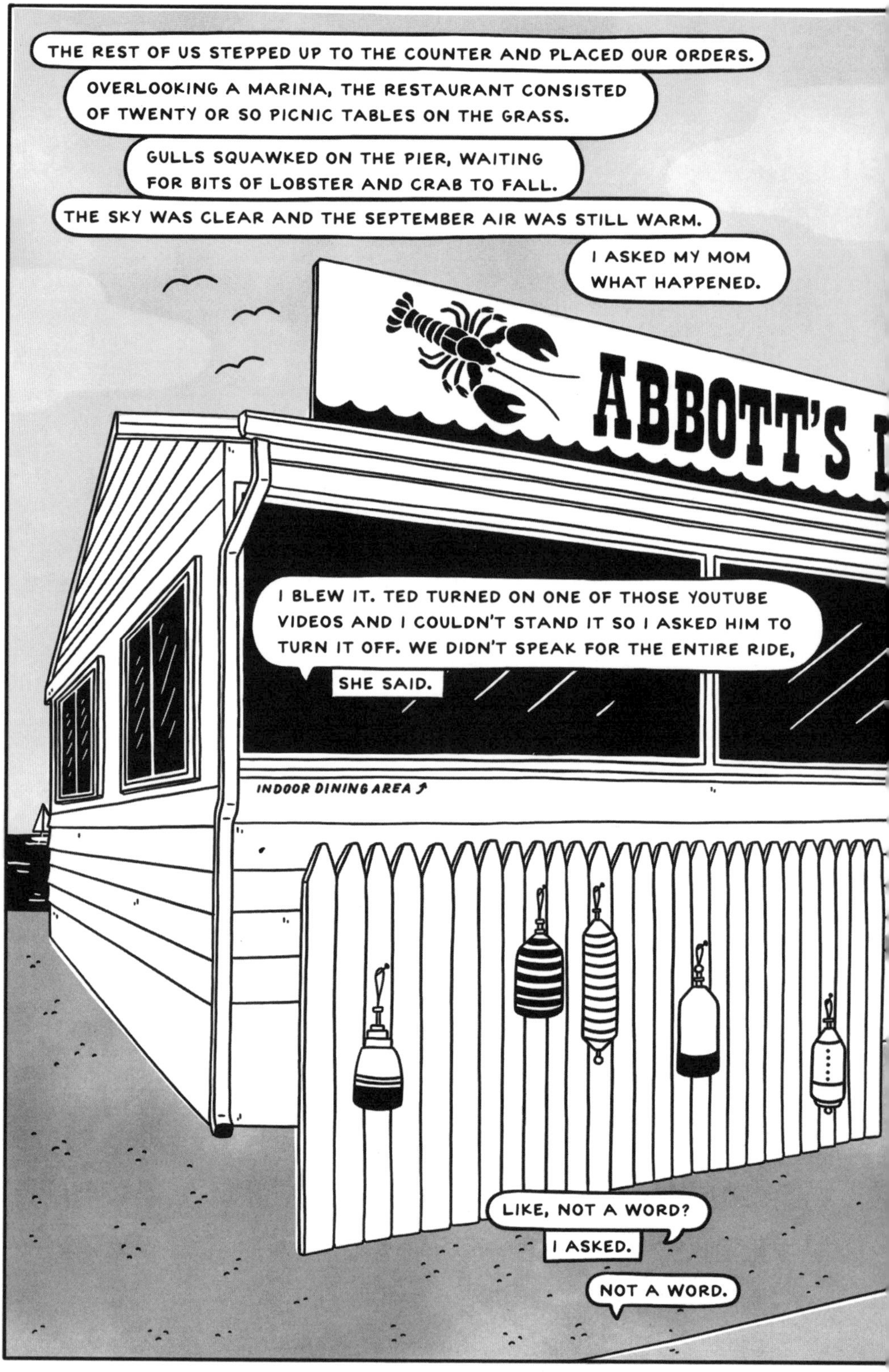
THE REST OF US STEPPED UP TO THE COUNTER AND PLACED OUR ORDERS.
OVERLOOKING A MARINA, THE RESTAURANT CONSISTED OF TWENTY OR SO PICNIC TABLES ON THE GRASS.
GULLS SQUAWKED ON THE PIER, WAITING FOR BITS OF LOBSTER AND CRAB TO FALL.
THE SKY WAS CLEAR AND THE SEPTEMBER AIR WAS STILL WARM.
I ASKED MY MOM WHAT HAPPENED.
ABBOTT'S
I BLEW IT. TED TURNED ON ONE OF THOSE YOUTUBE VIDEOS AND I COULDN'T STAND IT SO I ASKED HIM TO TURN IT OFF. WE DIDN'T SPEAK FOR THE ENTIRE RIDE,
SHE SAID.
INDOOR DINING AREA
LIKE, NOT A WORD?
I ASKED.
NOT A WORD.

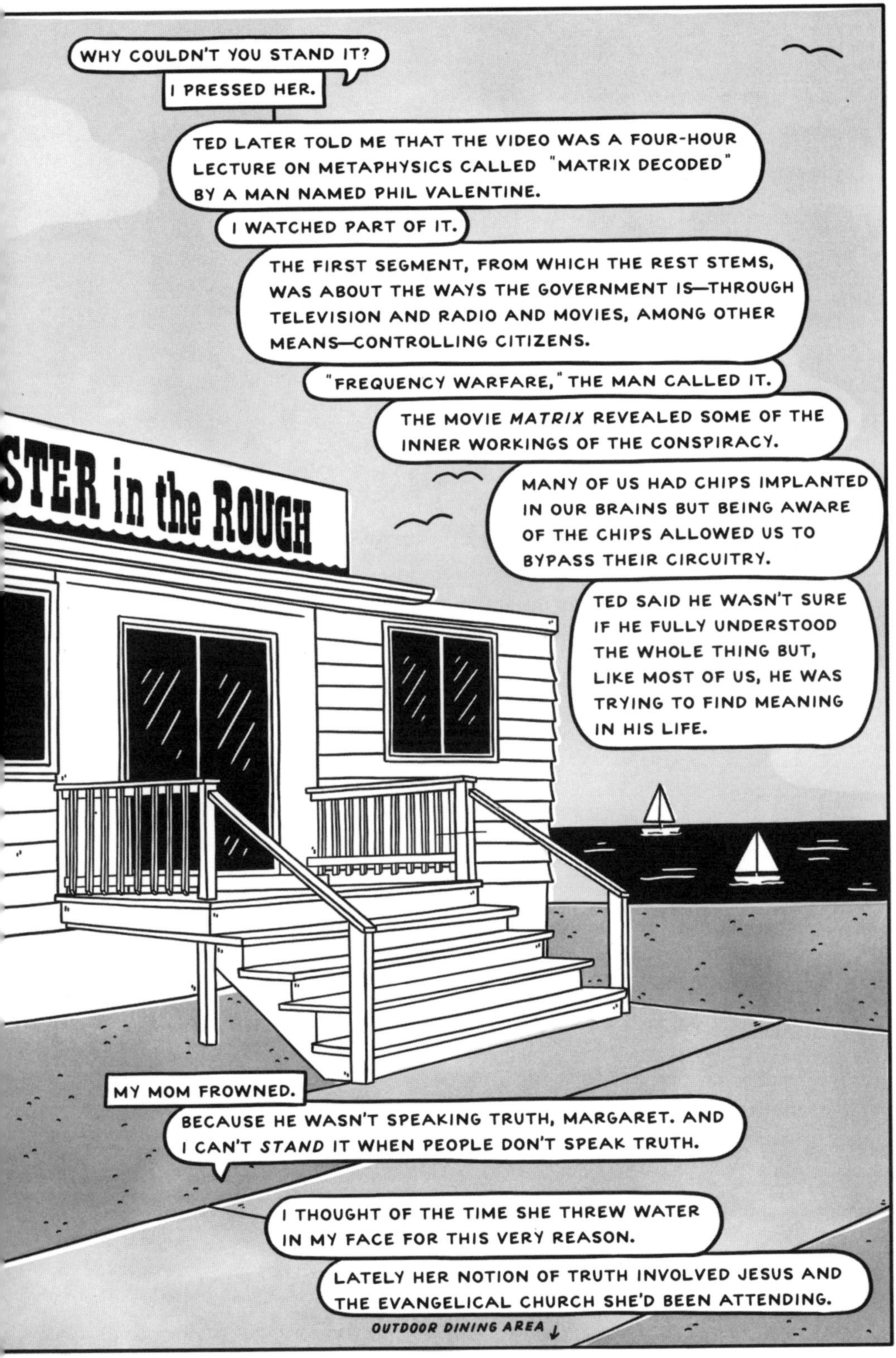
WHY COULDN'T YOU STAND IT?
I PRESSED HER.
TED LATER TOLD ME THAT THE VIDEO WAS A FOUR-HOUR LECTURE ON METAPHYSICS CALLED "MATRIX DECODED" BY A MAN NAMED PHIL VALENTINE.
I WATCHED PART OF IT.
THE FIRST SEGMENT, FROM WHICH THE REST STEMS, WAS ABOUT THE WAYS THE GOVERNMENT IS—THROUGH TELEVISION AND RADIO AND MOVIES, AMONG OTHER MEANS—CONTROLLING CITIZENS.
"FREQUENCY WARFARE," THE MAN CALLED IT.
THE MOVIE *MATRIX* REVEALED SOME OF THE INNER WORKINGS OF THE CONSPIRACY.
MANY OF US HAD CHIPS IMPLANTED IN OUR BRAINS BUT BEING AWARE OF THE CHIPS ALLOWED US TO BYPASS THEIR CIRCUITRY.
TED SAID HE WASN'T SURE IF HE FULLY UNDERSTOOD THE WHOLE THING BUT, LIKE MOST OF US, HE WAS TRYING TO FIND MEANING IN HIS LIFE.
STER in the ROUGH
MY MOM FROWNED.
BECAUSE HE WASN'T SPEAKING TRUTH, MARGARET. AND I CAN'T *STAND* IT WHEN PEOPLE DON'T SPEAK TRUTH.
I THOUGHT OF THE TIME SHE THREW WATER IN MY FACE FOR THIS VERY REASON.
LATELY HER NOTION OF TRUTH INVOLVED JESUS AND THE EVANGELICAL CHURCH SHE'D BEEN ATTENDING.
OUTDOOR DINING AREA ↓

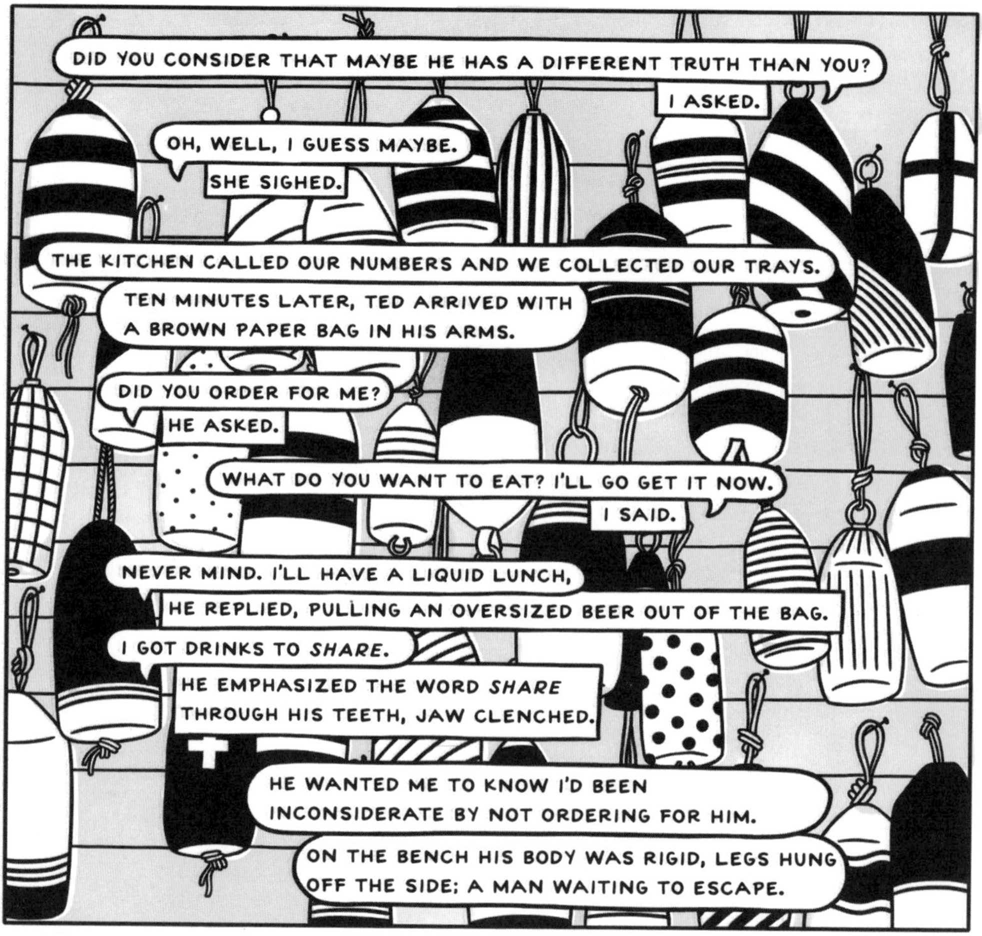
DID YOU CONSIDER THAT MAYBE HE HAS A DIFFERENT TRUTH THAN YOU?
I ASKED.
OH, WELL, I GUESS MAYBE.
SHE SIGHED.
THE KITCHEN CALLED OUR NUMBERS AND WE COLLECTED OUR TRAYS.
TEN MINUTES LATER, TED ARRIVED WITH A BROWN PAPER BAG IN HIS ARMS.
DID YOU ORDER FOR ME?
HE ASKED.
WHAT DO YOU WANT TO EAT? I'LL GO GET IT NOW.
I SAID.
NEVER MIND. I'LL HAVE A LIQUID LUNCH,
HE REPLIED, PULLING AN OVERSIZED BEER OUT OF THE BAG.
I GOT DRINKS TO *SHARE*.
HE EMPHASIZED THE WORD *SHARE* THROUGH HIS TEETH, JAW CLENCHED.
HE WANTED ME TO KNOW I'D BEEN INCONSIDERATE BY NOT ORDERING FOR HIM.
ON THE BENCH HIS BODY WAS RIGID, LEGS HUNG OFF THE SIDE; A MAN WAITING TO ESCAPE.

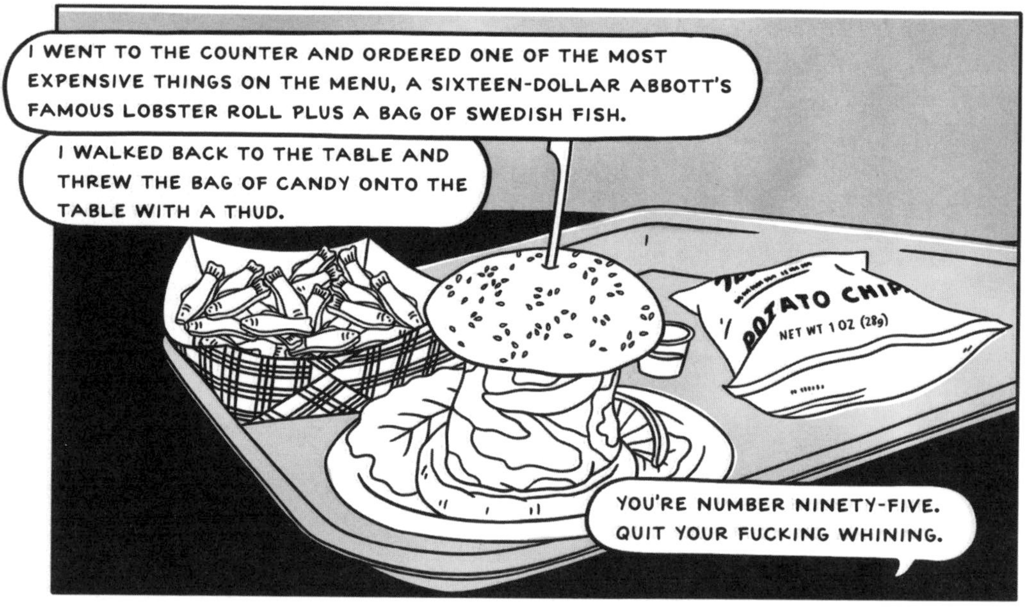
I WENT TO THE COUNTER AND ORDERED ONE OF THE MOST EXPENSIVE THINGS ON THE MENU, A SIXTEEN-DOLLAR ABBOTT'S FAMOUS LOBSTER ROLL PLUS A BAG OF SWEDISH FISH.
I WALKED BACK TO THE TABLE AND THREW THE BAG OF CANDY ONTO THE TABLE WITH A THUD.
POTATO CHIP
NET WT 1 OZ (28g)
YOU'RE NUMBER NINETY-FIVE. QUIT YOUR FUCKING WHINING.

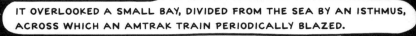

THE AIRBNB COTTAGE TURNED OUT TO BE A CONVERTED SHED.

IT OVERLOOKED A SMALL BAY, DIVIDED FROM THE SEA BY AN ISTHMUS, ACROSS WHICH AN AMTRAK TRAIN PERIODICALLY BLAZED.

BEYOND THE STRIP OF LAND A FEW EGRETS STOOD TALL IN THE MARSH, SPECKS OF WHITE PEPPERING THE GREEN AND BLUE.

WE EXPLORED THE RENTAL.

MY MOM HAD HER OWN ROOM, ZACH AND I HAD BUNK BEDS, AND TED WOULD SLEEP ON THE FUTON.

COBWEBS HUNG IN CORNERS.

A BIT OF HAIR SWIRLED IN THE SHOWER DRAIN.

A SINGLE ROLL OF TOILET PAPER SAT ON THE COUNTER.

THIS WAS THE SORT OF PLACE WHERE YOU KEPT YOUR SHOES ON, CAREFUL NOT TO TOUCH ANYTHING YOU DIDN'T ABSOLUTELY HAVE TO.

NO ONE SHOWERED ALL WEEKEND. WE WERE INSIDE OF A DAMP, THIN-WALLED SHACK.

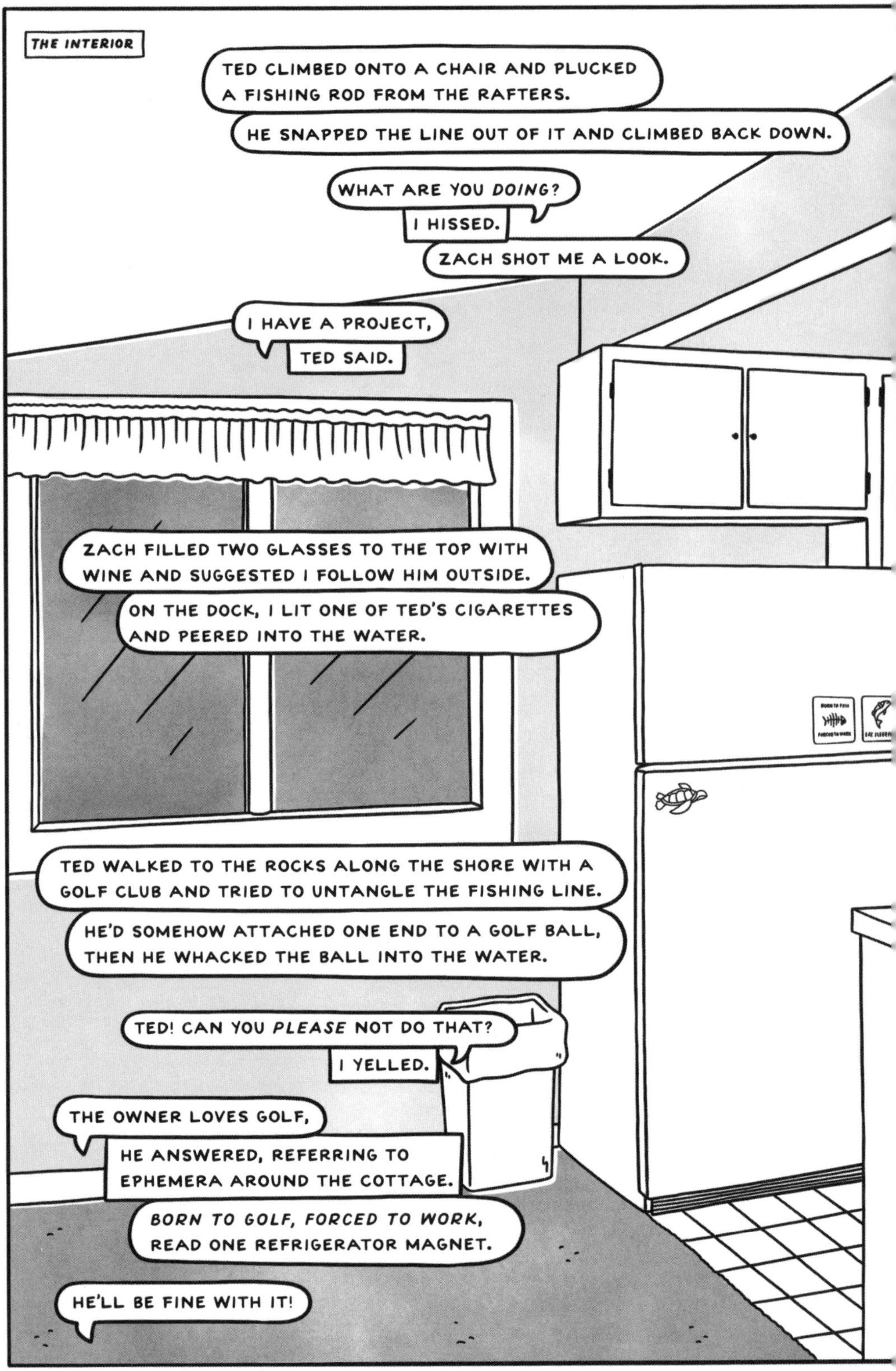
THE INTERIOR
TED CLIMBED ONTO A CHAIR AND PLUCKED A FISHING ROD FROM THE RAFTERS.
HE SNAPPED THE LINE OUT OF IT AND CLIMBED BACK DOWN.
WHAT ARE YOU *DOING*?
I HISSED.
ZACH SHOT ME A LOOK.
I HAVE A PROJECT,
TED SAID.
ZACH FILLED TWO GLASSES TO THE TOP WITH WINE AND SUGGESTED I FOLLOW HIM OUTSIDE.
ON THE DOCK, I LIT ONE OF TED'S CIGARETTES AND PEERED INTO THE WATER.
TED WALKED TO THE ROCKS ALONG THE SHORE WITH A GOLF CLUB AND TRIED TO UNTANGLE THE FISHING LINE.
HE'D SOMEHOW ATTACHED ONE END TO A GOLF BALL, THEN HE WHACKED THE BALL INTO THE WATER.
TED! CAN YOU *PLEASE* NOT DO THAT?
I YELLED.
THE OWNER LOVES GOLF,
HE ANSWERED, REFERRING TO EPHEMERA AROUND THE COTTAGE.
BORN TO GOLF, FORCED TO WORK, READ ONE REFRIGERATOR MAGNET.
HE'LL BE FINE WITH IT!

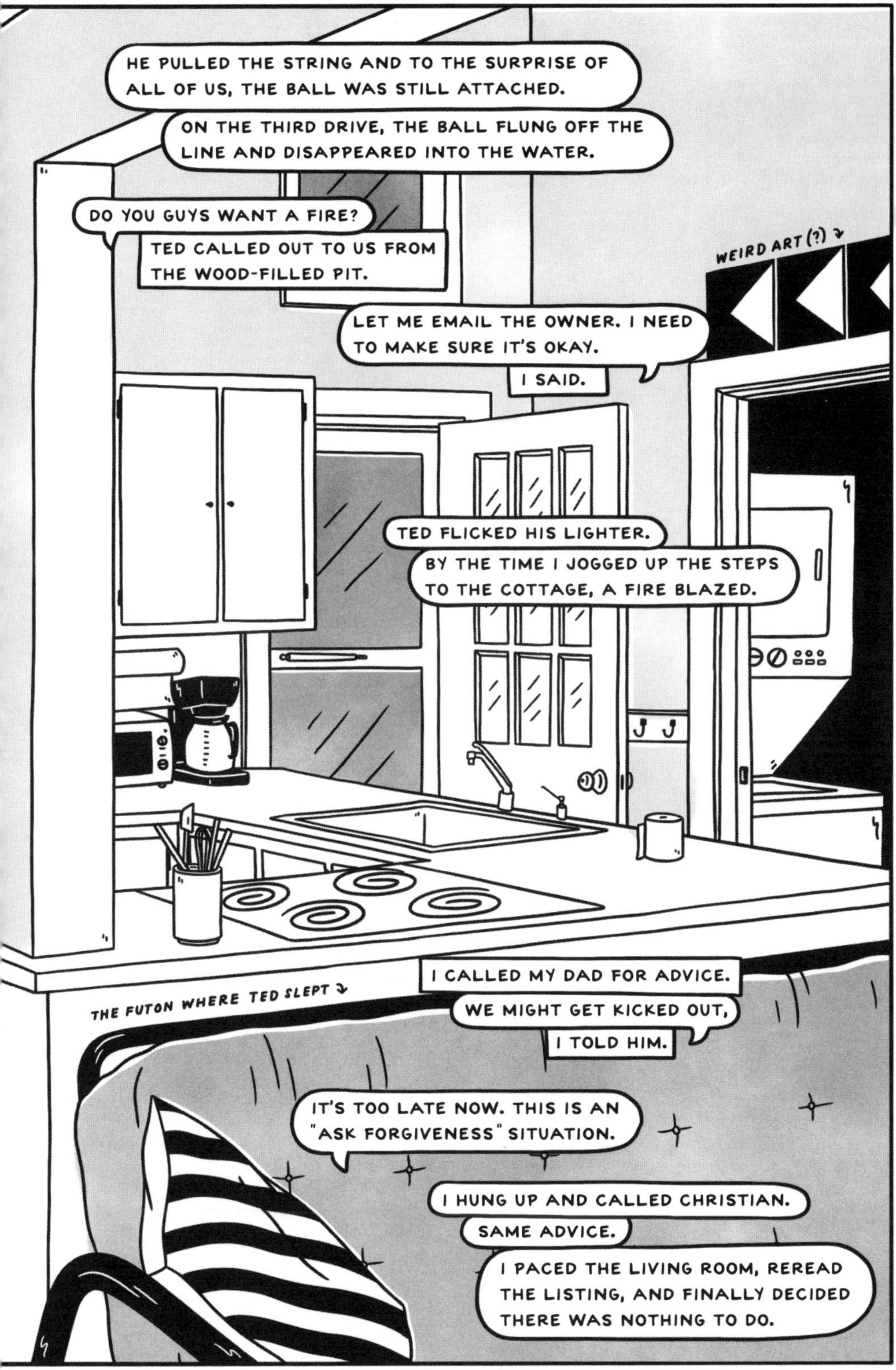
HE PULLED THE STRING AND TO THE SURPRISE OF ALL OF US, THE BALL WAS STILL ATTACHED.
ON THE THIRD DRIVE, THE BALL FLUNG OFF THE LINE AND DISAPPEARED INTO THE WATER.
DO YOU GUYS WANT A FIRE?
TED CALLED OUT TO US FROM THE WOOD-FILLED PIT.
WEIRD ART (?)
LET ME EMAIL THE OWNER. I NEED TO MAKE SURE IT'S OKAY.
I SAID.
TED FLICKED HIS LIGHTER.
BY THE TIME I JOGGED UP THE STEPS TO THE COTTAGE, A FIRE BLAZED.
THE FUTON WHERE TED SLEPT
I CALLED MY DAD FOR ADVICE.
WE MIGHT GET KICKED OUT,
I TOLD HIM.
IT'S TOO LATE NOW. THIS IS AN "ASK FORGIVENESS" SITUATION.
I HUNG UP AND CALLED CHRISTIAN.
SAME ADVICE.
I PACED THE LIVING ROOM, REREAD THE LISTING, AND FINALLY DECIDED THERE WAS NOTHING TO DO.

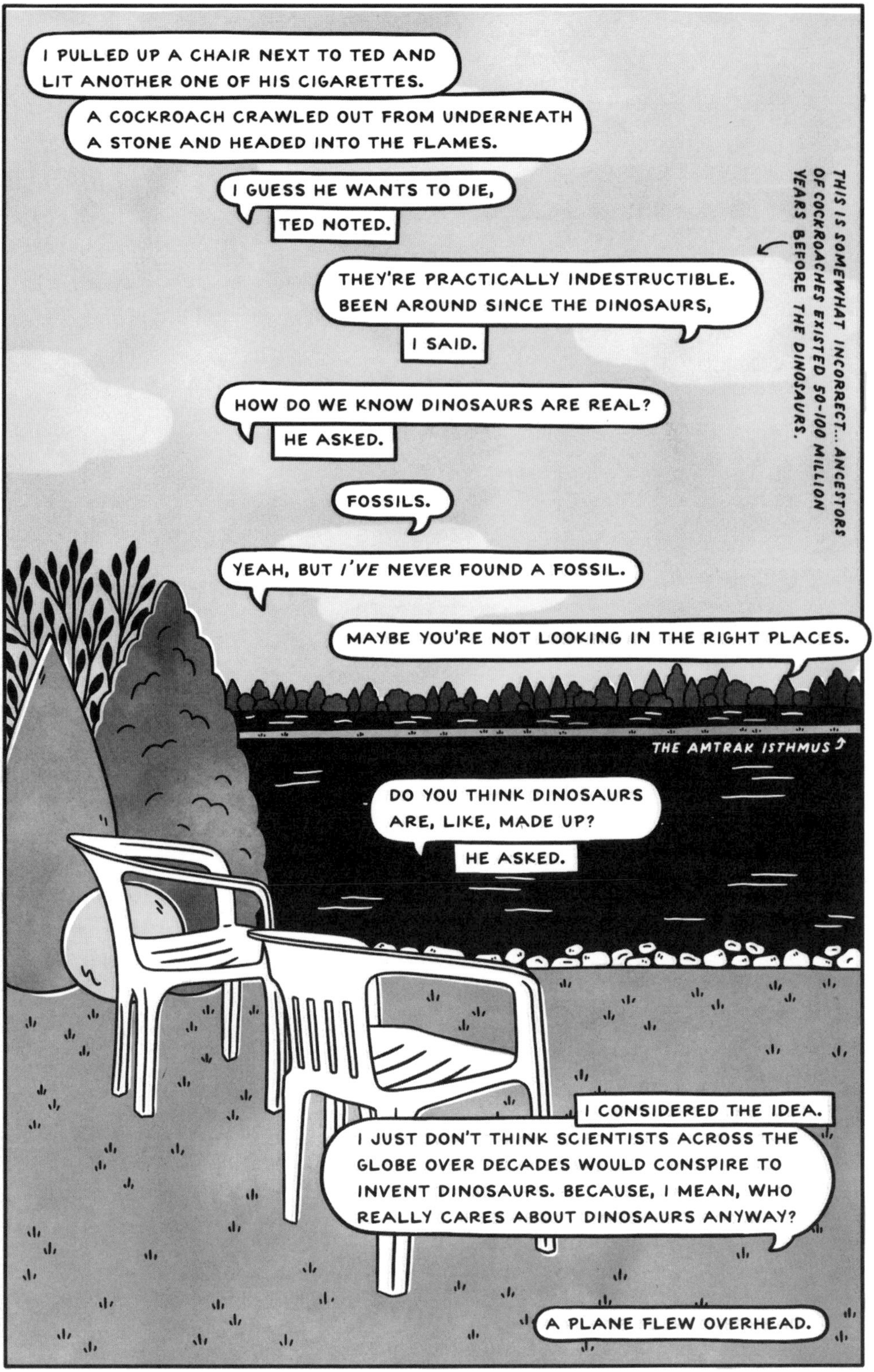
I PULLED UP A CHAIR NEXT TO TED AND LIT ANOTHER ONE OF HIS CIGARETTES.
A COCKROACH CRAWLED OUT FROM UNDERNEATH A STONE AND HEADED INTO THE FLAMES.
I GUESS HE WANTS TO DIE,
TED NOTED.
THEY'RE PRACTICALLY INDESTRUCTIBLE. BEEN AROUND SINCE THE DINOSAURS,
I SAID.
THIS IS SOMEWHAT INCORRECT... ANCESTORS OF COCKROACHES EXISTED 50-100 MILLION YEARS BEFORE THE DINOSAURS.
HOW DO WE KNOW DINOSAURS ARE REAL?
HE ASKED.
FOSSILS.
YEAH, BUT *I'VE* NEVER FOUND A FOSSIL.
MAYBE YOU'RE NOT LOOKING IN THE RIGHT PLACES.
THE AMTRAK ISTHMUS
DO YOU THINK DINOSAURS ARE, LIKE, MADE UP?
HE ASKED.
I CONSIDERED THE IDEA.
I JUST DON'T THINK SCIENTISTS ACROSS THE GLOBE OVER DECADES WOULD CONSPIRE TO INVENT DINOSAURS. BECAUSE, I MEAN, WHO REALLY CARES ABOUT DINOSAURS ANYWAY?
A PLANE FLEW OVERHEAD.

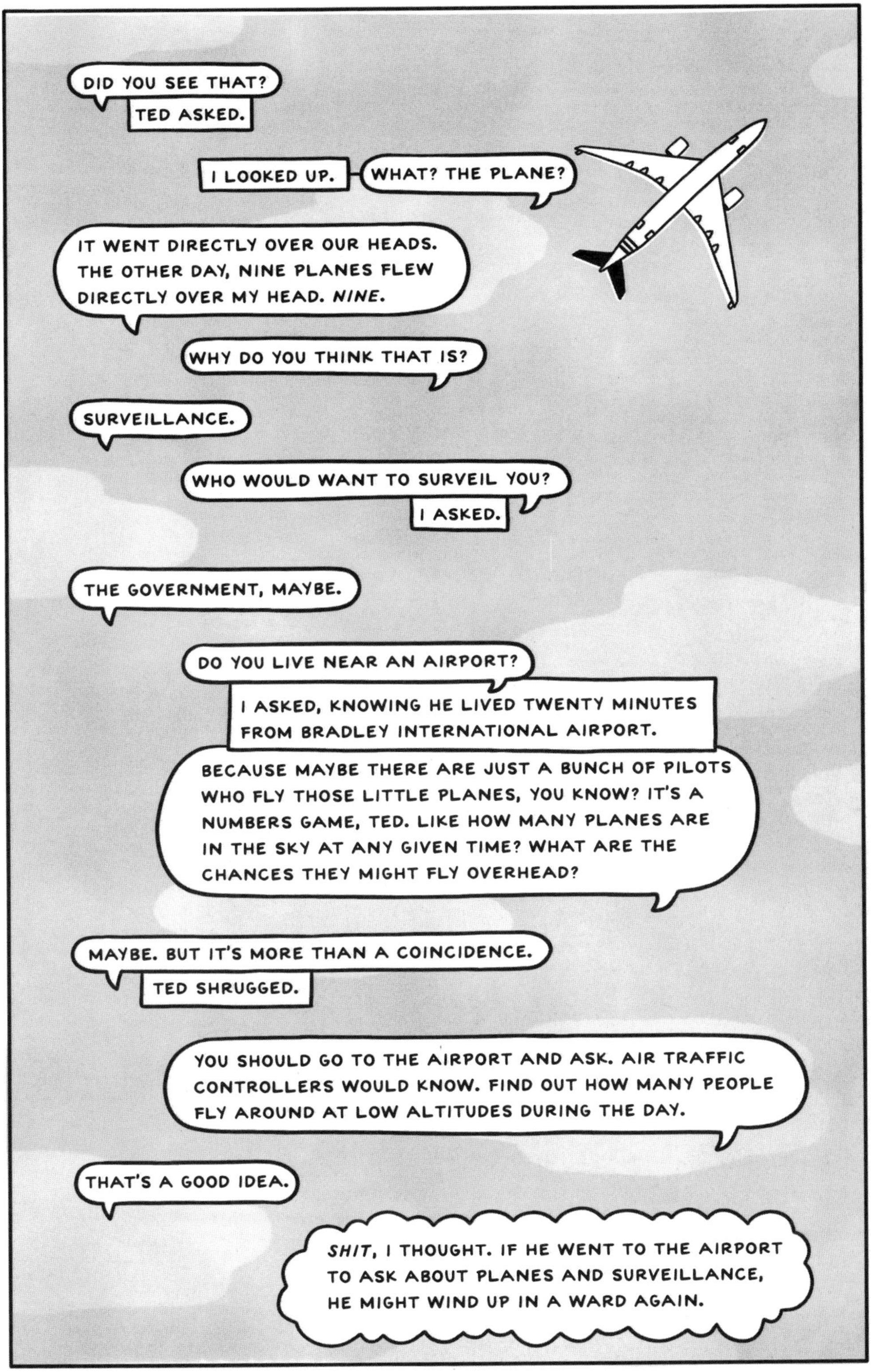
DID YOU SEE THAT?
TED ASKED.
I LOOKED UP.
WHAT? THE PLANE?
IT WENT DIRECTLY OVER OUR HEADS. THE OTHER DAY, NINE PLANES FLEW DIRECTLY OVER MY HEAD. *NINE*.
WHY DO YOU THINK THAT IS?
SURVEILLANCE.
WHO WOULD WANT TO SURVEIL YOU?
I ASKED.
THE GOVERNMENT, MAYBE.
DO YOU LIVE NEAR AN AIRPORT?
I ASKED, KNOWING HE LIVED TWENTY MINUTES FROM BRADLEY INTERNATIONAL AIRPORT.
BECAUSE MAYBE THERE ARE JUST A BUNCH OF PILOTS WHO FLY THOSE LITTLE PLANES, YOU KNOW? IT'S A NUMBERS GAME, TED. LIKE HOW MANY PLANES ARE IN THE SKY AT ANY GIVEN TIME? WHAT ARE THE CHANCES THEY MIGHT FLY OVERHEAD?
MAYBE. BUT IT'S MORE THAN A COINCIDENCE.
TED SHRUGGED.
YOU SHOULD GO TO THE AIRPORT AND ASK. AIR TRAFFIC CONTROLLERS WOULD KNOW. FIND OUT HOW MANY PEOPLE FLY AROUND AT LOW ALTITUDES DURING THE DAY.
THAT'S A GOOD IDEA.
SHIT, I THOUGHT. IF HE WENT TO THE AIRPORT TO ASK ABOUT PLANES AND SURVEILLANCE, HE MIGHT WIND UP IN A WARD AGAIN.

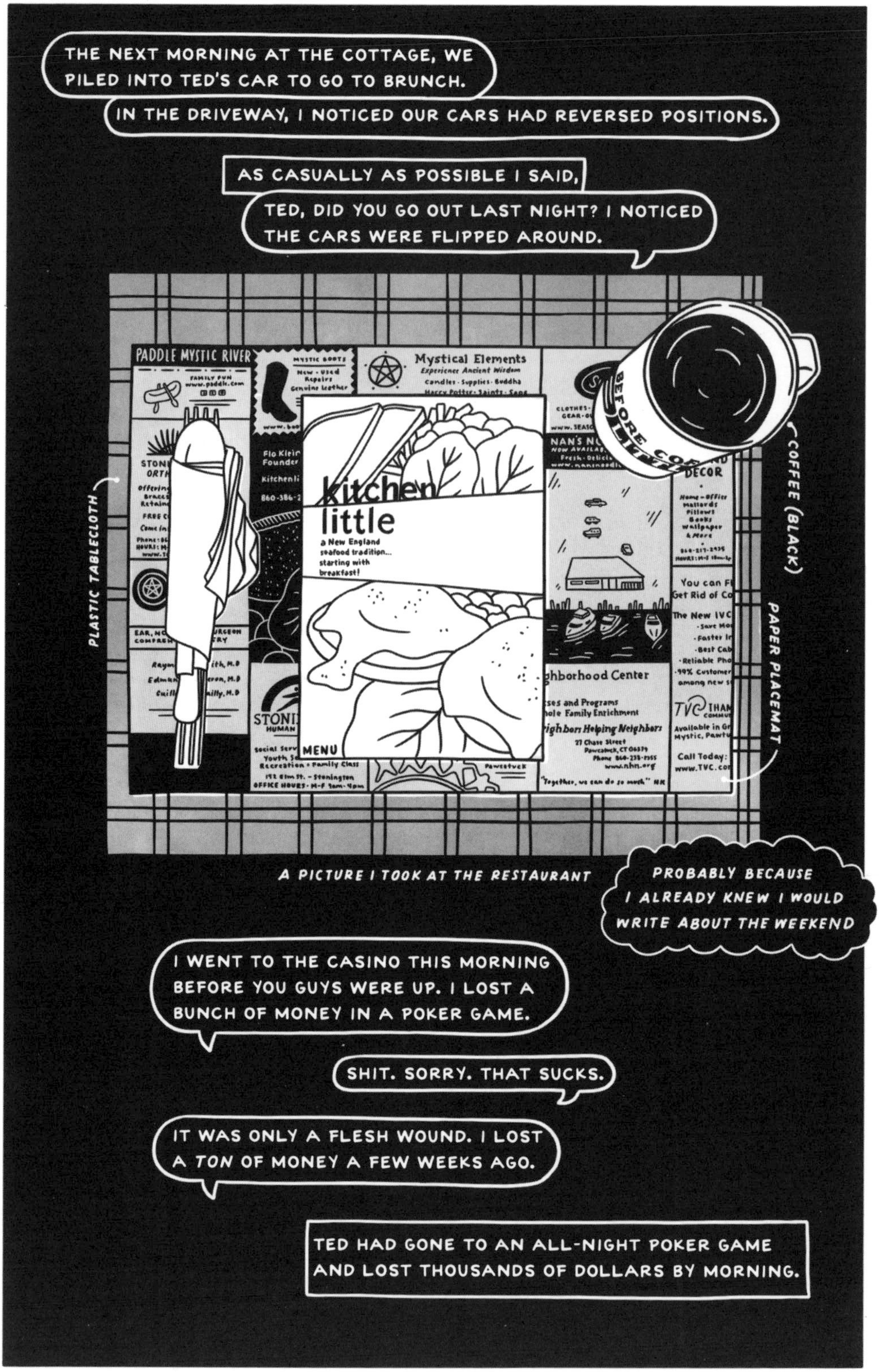
THE NEXT MORNING AT THE COTTAGE, WE PILED INTO TED'S CAR TO GO TO BRUNCH.
IN THE DRIVEWAY, I NOTICED OUR CARS HAD REVERSED POSITIONS.
AS CASUALLY AS POSSIBLE I SAID,
TED, DID YOU GO OUT LAST NIGHT? I NOTICED THE CARS WERE FLIPPED AROUND.
PADDLE MYSTIC RIVER
Mystical Elements
kitchen little
a New England seafood tradition... starting with breakfast!
MENU
PLASTIC TABLECLOTH
COFFEE (BLACK)
PAPER PLACEMAT
A PICTURE I TOOK AT THE RESTAURANT
PROBABLY BECAUSE I ALREADY KNEW I WOULD WRITE ABOUT THE WEEKEND
I WENT TO THE CASINO THIS MORNING BEFORE YOU GUYS WERE UP. I LOST A BUNCH OF MONEY IN A POKER GAME.
SHIT. SORRY. THAT SUCKS.
IT WAS ONLY A FLESH WOUND. I LOST A TON OF MONEY A FEW WEEKS AGO.
TED HAD GONE TO AN ALL-NIGHT POKER GAME AND LOST THOUSANDS OF DOLLARS BY MORNING.

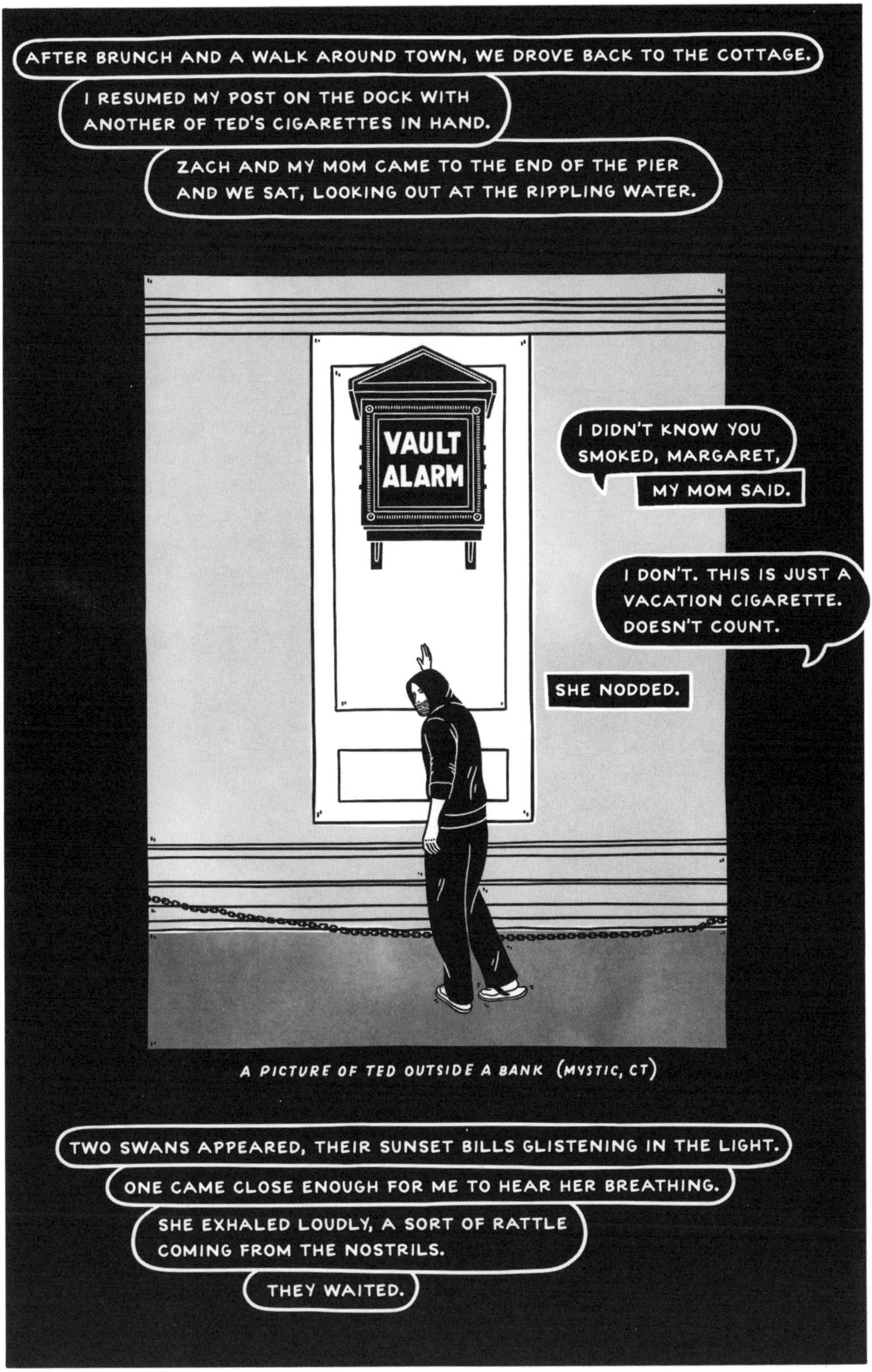
AFTER BRUNCH AND A WALK AROUND TOWN, WE DROVE BACK TO THE COTTAGE.
I RESUMED MY POST ON THE DOCK WITH ANOTHER OF TED'S CIGARETTES IN HAND.
ZACH AND MY MOM CAME TO THE END OF THE PIER AND WE SAT, LOOKING OUT AT THE RIPPLING WATER.
VAULT ALARM
I DIDN'T KNOW YOU SMOKED, MARGARET,
MY MOM SAID.
I DON'T. THIS IS JUST A VACATION CIGARETTE. DOESN'T COUNT.
SHE NODDED.
A PICTURE OF TED OUTSIDE A BANK (MYSTIC, CT)
TWO SWANS APPEARED, THEIR SUNSET BILLS GLISTENING IN THE LIGHT.
ONE CAME CLOSE ENOUGH FOR ME TO HEAR HER BREATHING.
SHE EXHALED LOUDLY, A SORT OF RATTLE COMING FROM THE NOSTRILS.
THEY WAITED.

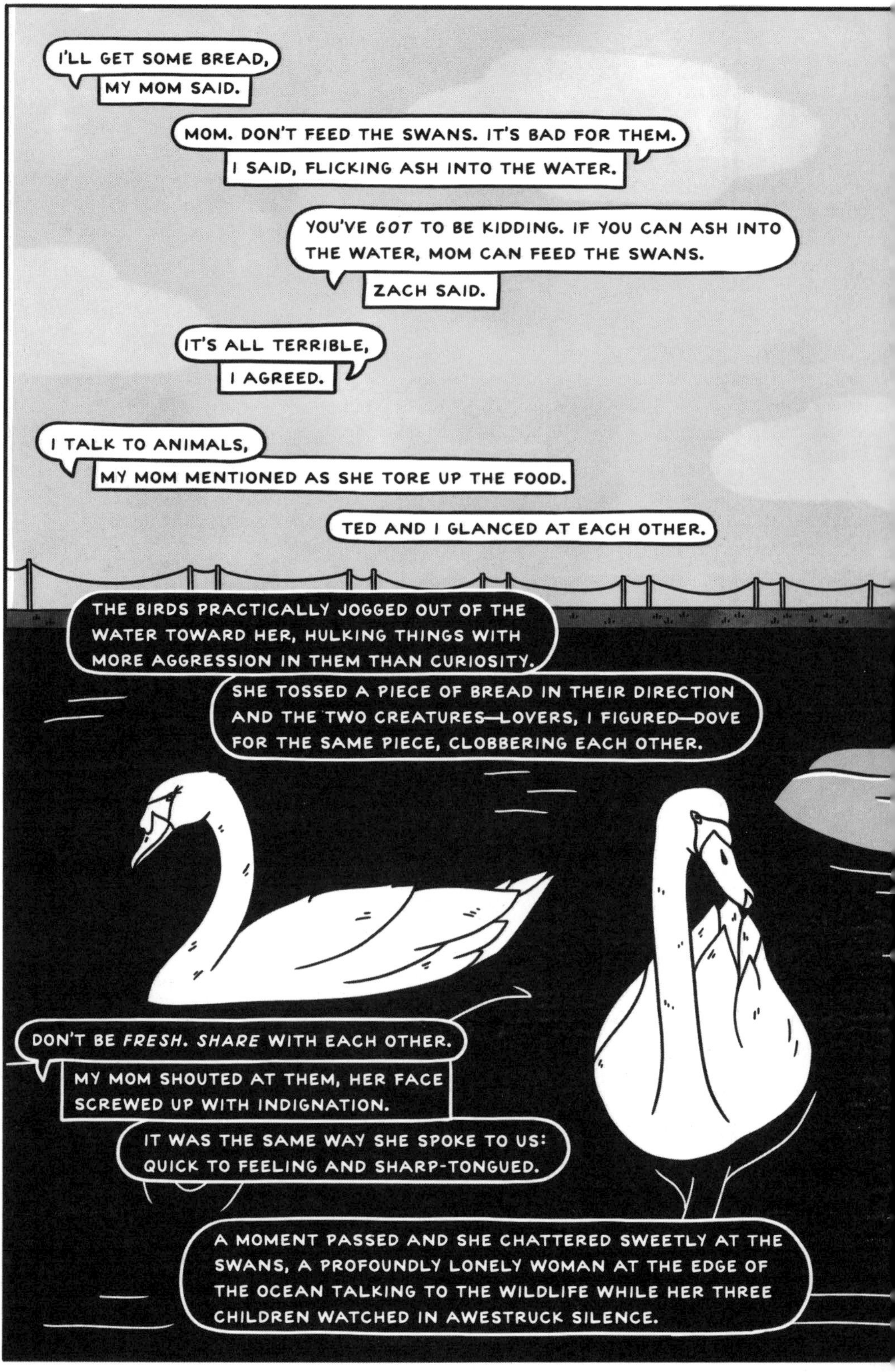
I'LL GET SOME BREAD,
MY MOM SAID.
MOM. DON'T FEED THE SWANS. IT'S BAD FOR THEM.
I SAID, FLICKING ASH INTO THE WATER.
YOU'VE *GOT* TO BE KIDDING. IF YOU CAN ASH INTO THE WATER, MOM CAN FEED THE SWANS.
ZACH SAID.
IT'S ALL TERRIBLE,
I AGREED.
I TALK TO ANIMALS,
MY MOM MENTIONED AS SHE TORE UP THE FOOD.
TED AND I GLANCED AT EACH OTHER.
THE BIRDS PRACTICALLY JOGGED OUT OF THE WATER TOWARD HER, HULKING THINGS WITH MORE AGGRESSION IN THEM THAN CURIOSITY.
SHE TOSSED A PIECE OF BREAD IN THEIR DIRECTION AND THE TWO CREATURES—LOVERS, I FIGURED—DOVE FOR THE SAME PIECE, CLOBBERING EACH OTHER.
DON'T BE *FRESH*. *SHARE* WITH EACH OTHER.
MY MOM SHOUTED AT THEM, HER FACE SCREWED UP WITH INDIGNATION.
IT WAS THE SAME WAY SHE SPOKE TO US: QUICK TO FEELING AND SHARP-TONGUED.
A MOMENT PASSED AND SHE CHATTERED SWEETLY AT THE SWANS, A PROFOUNDLY LONELY WOMAN AT THE EDGE OF THE OCEAN TALKING TO THE WILDLIFE WHILE HER THREE CHILDREN WATCHED IN AWESTRUCK SILENCE.

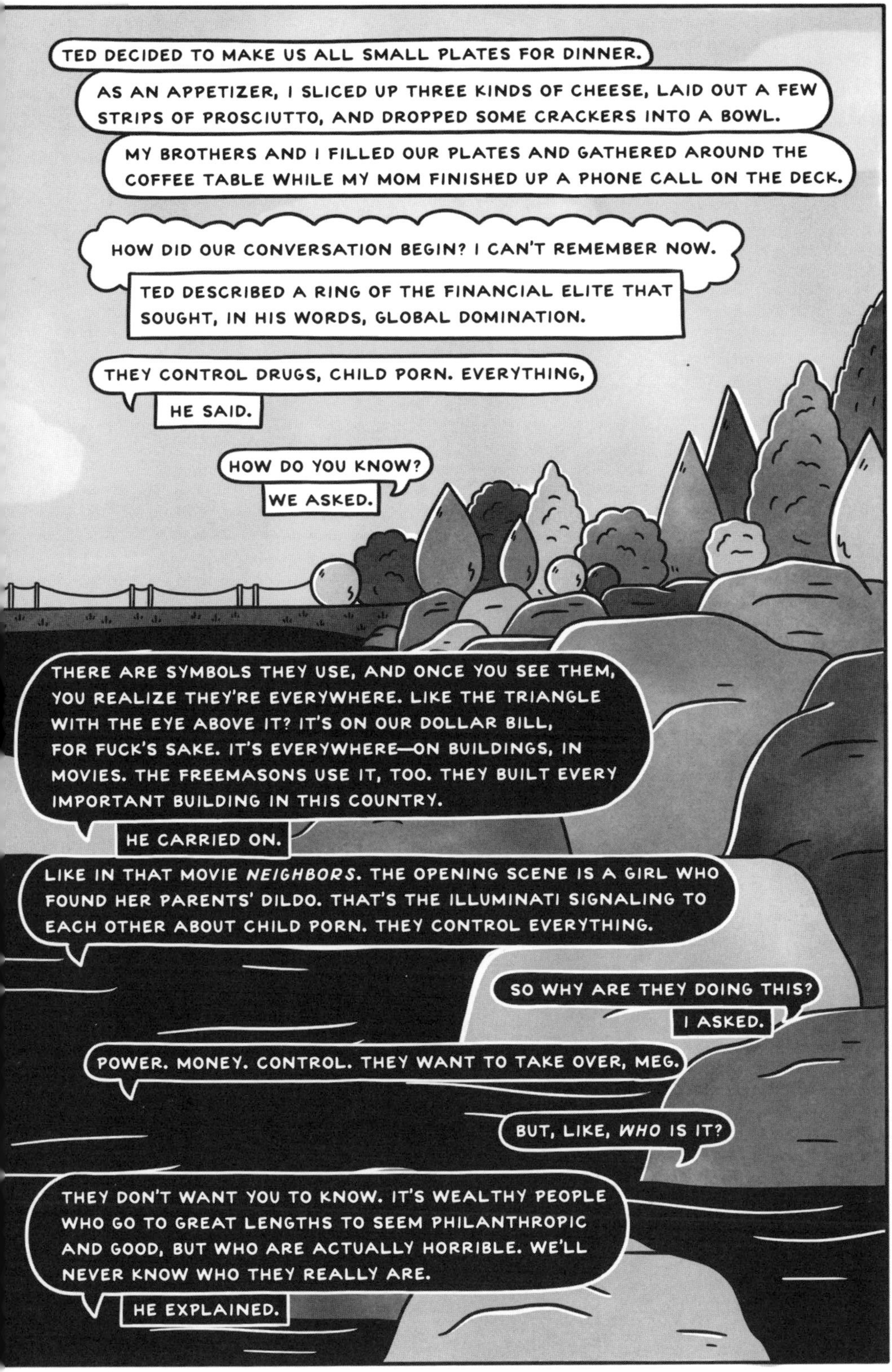
TED DECIDED TO MAKE US ALL SMALL PLATES FOR DINNER.
AS AN APPETIZER, I SLICED UP THREE KINDS OF CHEESE, LAID OUT A FEW STRIPS OF PROSCIUTTO, AND DROPPED SOME CRACKERS INTO A BOWL.
MY BROTHERS AND I FILLED OUR PLATES AND GATHERED AROUND THE COFFEE TABLE WHILE MY MOM FINISHED UP A PHONE CALL ON THE DECK.
HOW DID OUR CONVERSATION BEGIN? I CAN'T REMEMBER NOW.
TED DESCRIBED A RING OF THE FINANCIAL ELITE THAT SOUGHT, IN HIS WORDS, GLOBAL DOMINATION.
THEY CONTROL DRUGS, CHILD PORN. EVERYTHING,
HE SAID.
HOW DO YOU KNOW?
WE ASKED.
THERE ARE SYMBOLS THEY USE, AND ONCE YOU SEE THEM, YOU REALIZE THEY'RE EVERYWHERE. LIKE THE TRIANGLE WITH THE EYE ABOVE IT? IT'S ON OUR DOLLAR BILL, FOR FUCK'S SAKE. IT'S EVERYWHERE—ON BUILDINGS, IN MOVIES. THE FREEMASONS USE IT, TOO. THEY BUILT EVERY IMPORTANT BUILDING IN THIS COUNTRY.
HE CARRIED ON.
LIKE IN THAT MOVIE *NEIGHBORS*. THE OPENING SCENE IS A GIRL WHO FOUND HER PARENTS' DILDO. THAT'S THE ILLUMINATI SIGNALING TO EACH OTHER ABOUT CHILD PORN. THEY CONTROL EVERYTHING.
SO WHY ARE THEY DOING THIS?
I ASKED.
POWER. MONEY. CONTROL. THEY WANT TO TAKE OVER, MEG.
BUT, LIKE, *WHO* IS IT?
THEY DON'T WANT YOU TO KNOW. IT'S WEALTHY PEOPLE WHO GO TO GREAT LENGTHS TO SEEM PHILANTHROPIC AND GOOD, BUT WHO ARE ACTUALLY HORRIBLE. WE'LL NEVER KNOW WHO THEY REALLY ARE.
HE EXPLAINED.

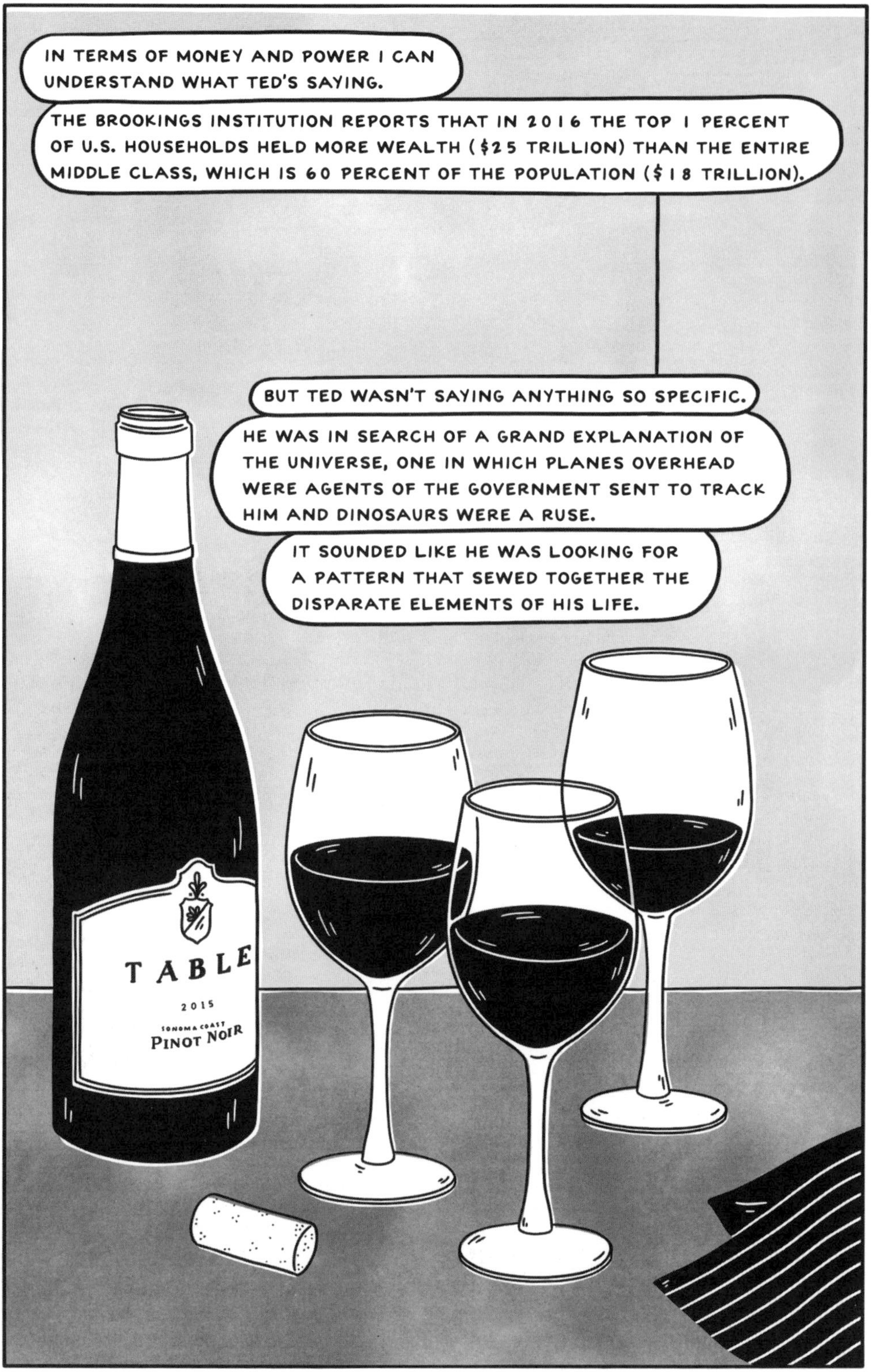
IN TERMS OF MONEY AND POWER I CAN UNDERSTAND WHAT TED'S SAYING.
THE BROOKINGS INSTITUTION REPORTS THAT IN 2016 THE TOP 1 PERCENT OF U.S. HOUSEHOLDS HELD MORE WEALTH ($25 TRILLION) THAN THE ENTIRE MIDDLE CLASS, WHICH IS 60 PERCENT OF THE POPULATION ($18 TRILLION).
BUT TED WASN'T SAYING ANYTHING SO SPECIFIC.
HE WAS IN SEARCH OF A GRAND EXPLANATION OF THE UNIVERSE, ONE IN WHICH PLANES OVERHEAD WERE AGENTS OF THE GOVERNMENT SENT TO TRACK HIM AND DINOSAURS WERE A RUSE.
IT SOUNDED LIKE HE WAS LOOKING FOR A PATTERN THAT SEWED TOGETHER THE DISPARATE ELEMENTS OF HIS LIFE.
TABLE
2015
SONOMA COAST
PINOT NOIR

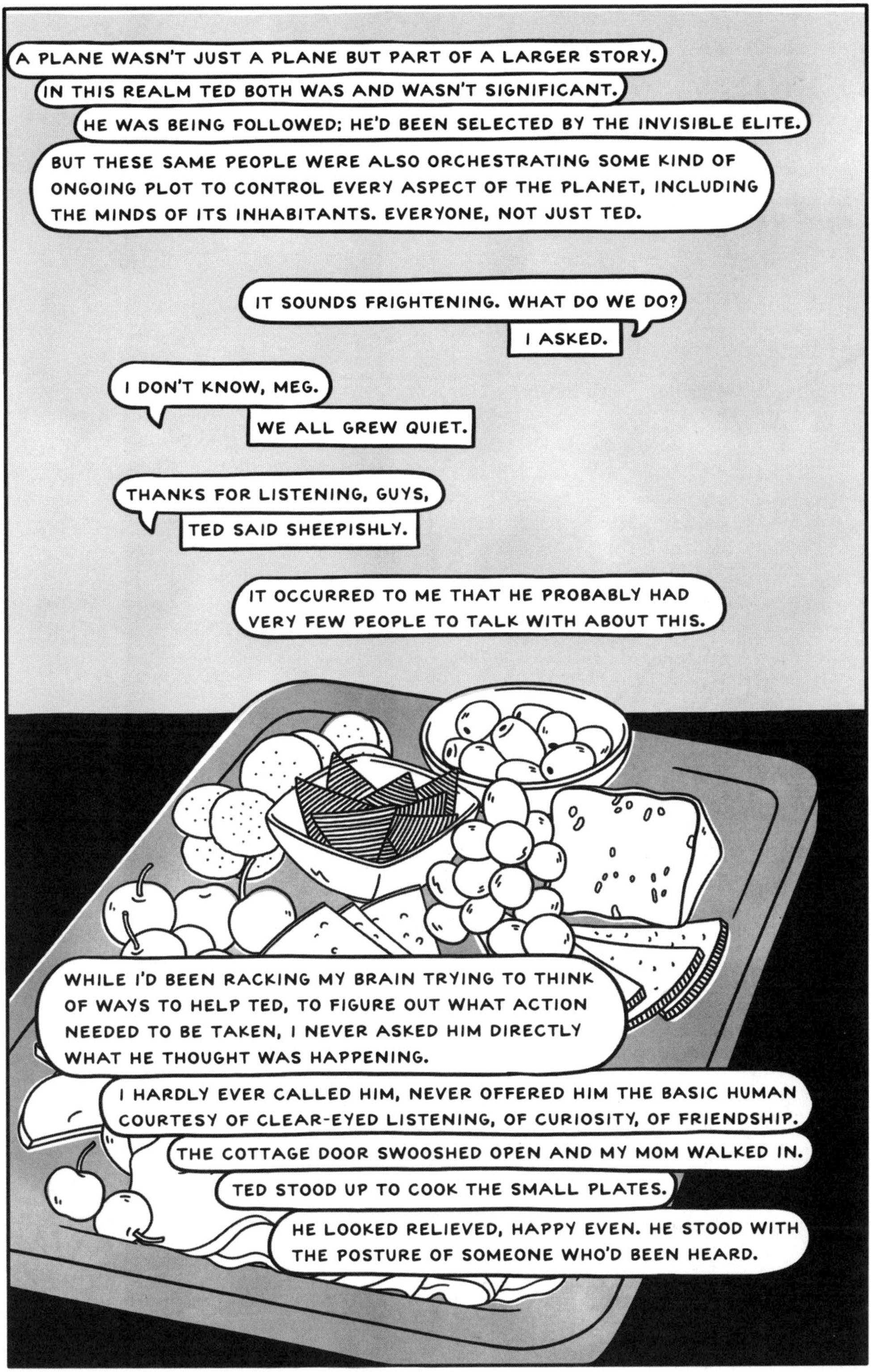
A PLANE WASN'T JUST A PLANE BUT PART OF A LARGER STORY.
IN THIS REALM TED BOTH WAS AND WASN'T SIGNIFICANT.
HE WAS BEING FOLLOWED; HE'D BEEN SELECTED BY THE INVISIBLE ELITE.
BUT THESE SAME PEOPLE WERE ALSO ORCHESTRATING SOME KIND OF ONGOING PLOT TO CONTROL EVERY ASPECT OF THE PLANET, INCLUDING THE MINDS OF ITS INHABITANTS. EVERYONE, NOT JUST TED.
IT SOUNDS FRIGHTENING. WHAT DO WE DO?
I ASKED.
I DON'T KNOW, MEG.
WE ALL GREW QUIET.
THANKS FOR LISTENING, GUYS,
TED SAID SHEEPISHLY.
IT OCCURRED TO ME THAT HE PROBABLY HAD VERY FEW PEOPLE TO TALK WITH ABOUT THIS.
WHILE I'D BEEN RACKING MY BRAIN TRYING TO THINK OF WAYS TO HELP TED, TO FIGURE OUT WHAT ACTION NEEDED TO BE TAKEN, I NEVER ASKED HIM DIRECTLY WHAT HE THOUGHT WAS HAPPENING.
I HARDLY EVER CALLED HIM, NEVER OFFERED HIM THE BASIC HUMAN COURTESY OF CLEAR-EYED LISTENING, OF CURIOSITY, OF FRIENDSHIP.
THE COTTAGE DOOR SWOOSHED OPEN AND MY MOM WALKED IN.
TED STOOD UP TO COOK THE SMALL PLATES.
HE LOOKED RELIEVED, HAPPY EVEN. HE STOOD WITH THE POSTURE OF SOMEONE WHO'D BEEN HEARD.

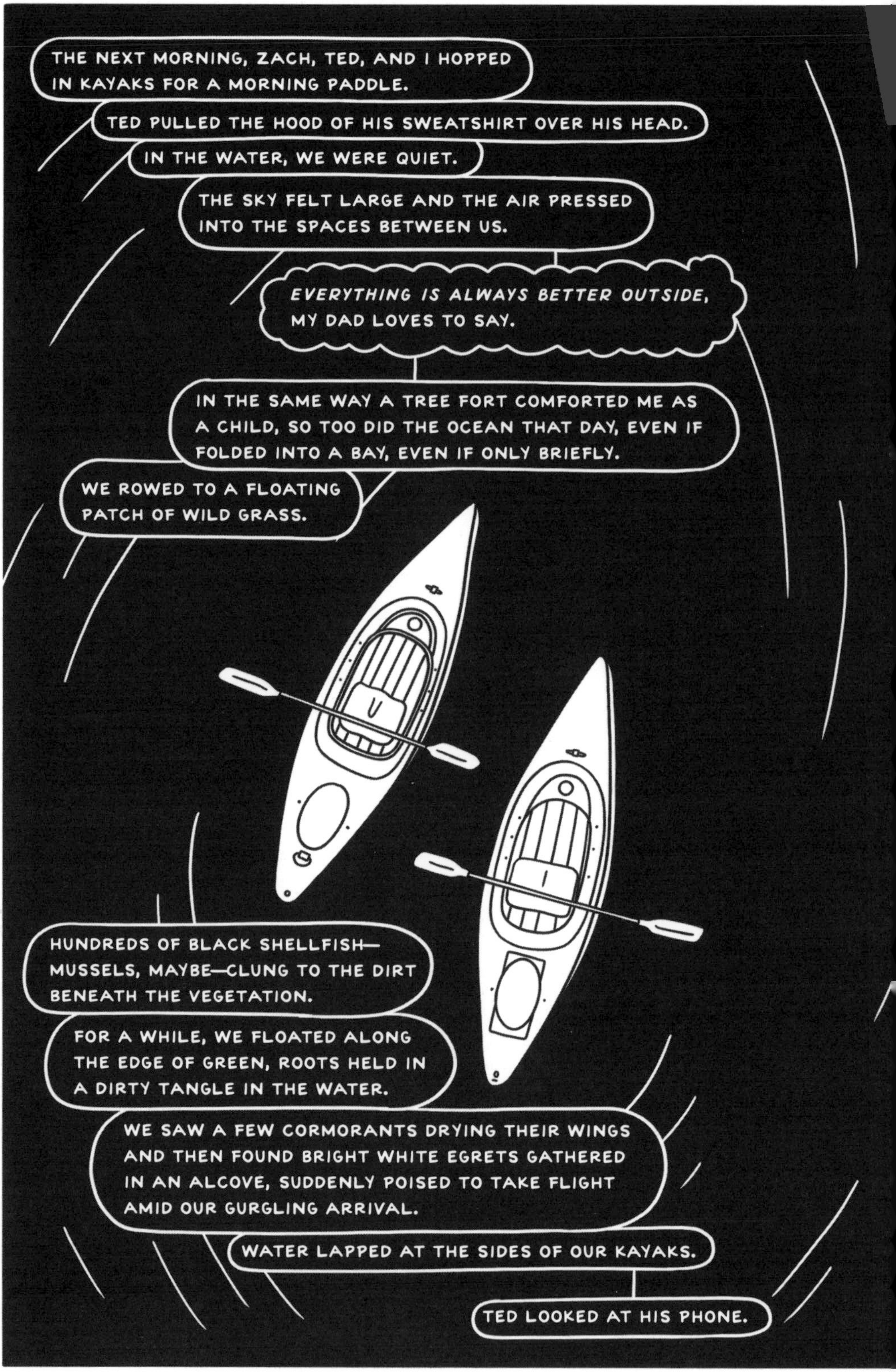
THE NEXT MORNING, ZACH, TED, AND I HOPPED IN KAYAKS FOR A MORNING PADDLE.
TED PULLED THE HOOD OF HIS SWEATSHIRT OVER HIS HEAD.
IN THE WATER, WE WERE QUIET.
THE SKY FELT LARGE AND THE AIR PRESSED INTO THE SPACES BETWEEN US.
EVERYTHING IS ALWAYS BETTER OUTSIDE, MY DAD LOVES TO SAY.
IN THE SAME WAY A TREE FORT COMFORTED ME AS A CHILD, SO TOO DID THE OCEAN THAT DAY, EVEN IF FOLDED INTO A BAY, EVEN IF ONLY BRIEFLY.
WE ROWED TO A FLOATING PATCH OF WILD GRASS.
HUNDREDS OF BLACK SHELLFISH—MUSSELS, MAYBE—CLUNG TO THE DIRT BENEATH THE VEGETATION.
FOR A WHILE, WE FLOATED ALONG THE EDGE OF GREEN, ROOTS HELD IN A DIRTY TANGLE IN THE WATER.
WE SAW A FEW CORMORANTS DRYING THEIR WINGS AND THEN FOUND BRIGHT WHITE EGRETS GATHERED IN AN ALCOVE, SUDDENLY POISED TO TAKE FLIGHT AMID OUR GURGLING ARRIVAL.
WATER LAPPED AT THE SIDES OF OUR KAYAKS.
TED LOOKED AT HIS PHONE.

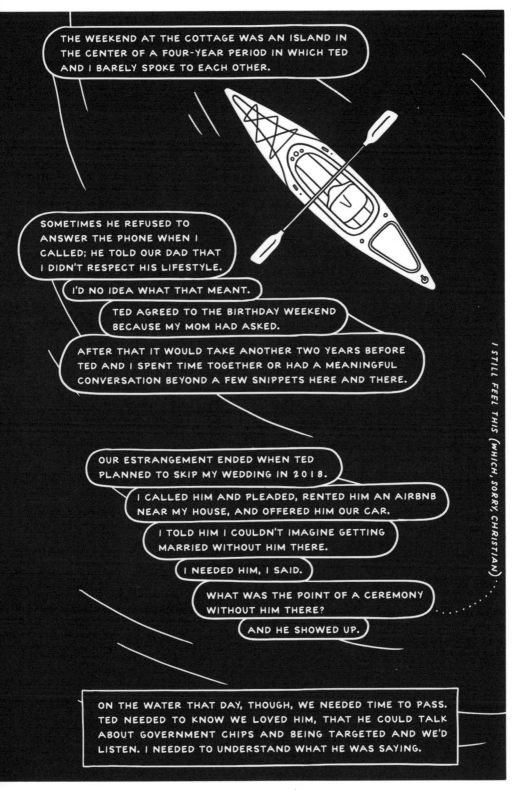

THE WEEKEND AT THE COTTAGE WAS AN ISLAND IN THE CENTER OF A FOUR-YEAR PERIOD IN WHICH TED AND I BARELY SPOKE TO EACH OTHER.

SOMETIMES HE REFUSED TO ANSWER THE PHONE WHEN I CALLED; HE TOLD OUR DAD THAT I DIDN'T RESPECT HIS LIFESTYLE.

I'D NO IDEA WHAT THAT MEANT.

TED AGREED TO THE BIRTHDAY WEEKEND BECAUSE MY MOM HAD ASKED.

AFTER THAT IT WOULD TAKE ANOTHER TWO YEARS BEFORE TED AND I SPENT TIME TOGETHER OR HAD A MEANINGFUL CONVERSATION BEYOND A FEW SNIPPETS HERE AND THERE.

I STILL FEEL THIS (WHICH, SORRY, CHRISTIAN).

OUR ESTRANGEMENT ENDED WHEN TED PLANNED TO SKIP MY WEDDING IN 2018.

I CALLED HIM AND PLEADED, RENTED HIM AN AIRBNB NEAR MY HOUSE, AND OFFERED HIM OUR CAR.

I TOLD HIM I COULDN'T IMAGINE GETTING MARRIED WITHOUT HIM THERE.

I NEEDED HIM, I SAID.

WHAT WAS THE POINT OF A CEREMONY WITHOUT HIM THERE?

AND HE SHOWED UP.

ON THE WATER THAT DAY, THOUGH, WE NEEDED TIME TO PASS. TED NEEDED TO KNOW WE LOVED HIM, THAT HE COULD TALK ABOUT GOVERNMENT CHIPS AND BEING TARGETED AND WE'D LISTEN. I NEEDED TO UNDERSTAND WHAT HE WAS SAYING.

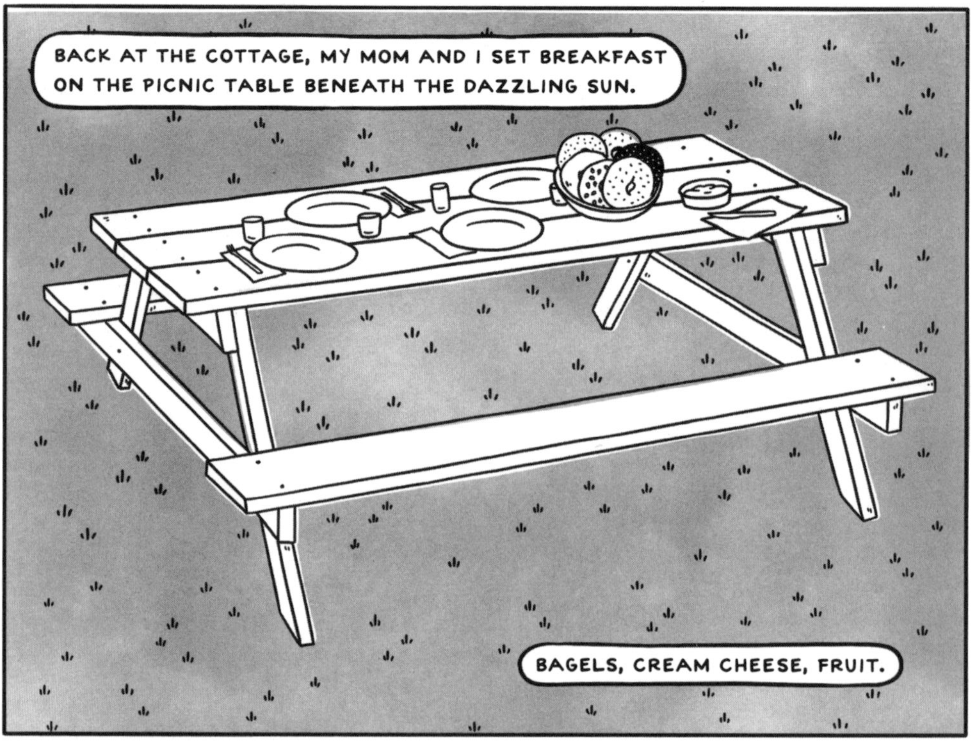
BACK AT THE COTTAGE, MY MOM AND I SET BREAKFAST ON THE PICNIC TABLE BENEATH THE DAZZLING SUN.
BAGELS, CREAM CHEESE, FRUIT.

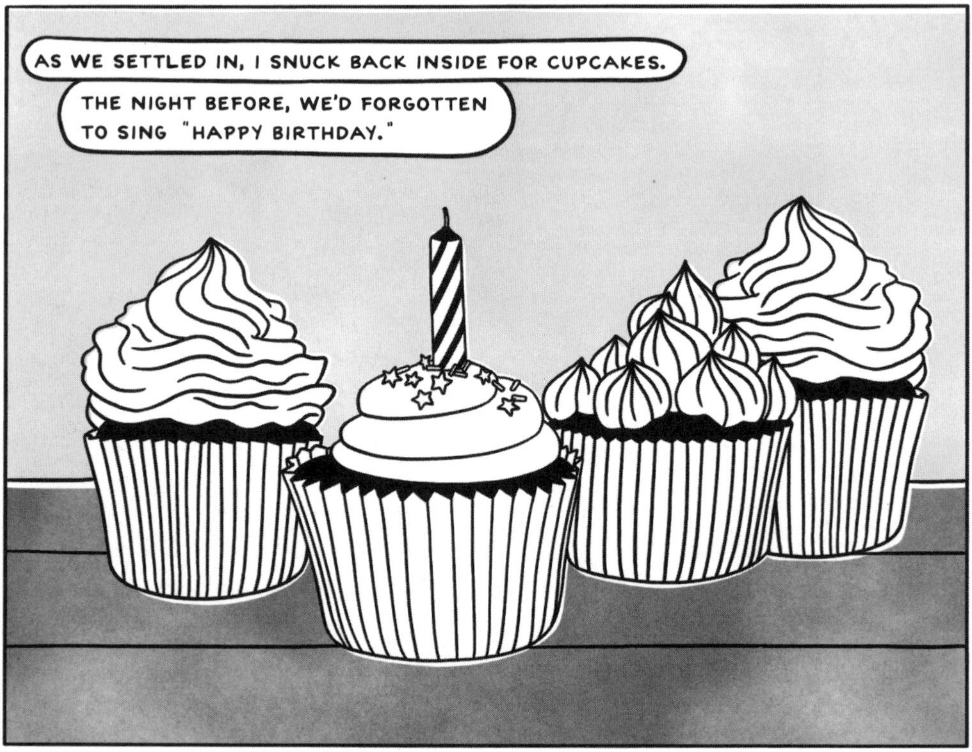
AS WE SETTLED IN, I SNUCK BACK INSIDE FOR CUPCAKES.
THE NIGHT BEFORE, WE'D FORGOTTEN TO SING "HAPPY BIRTHDAY."

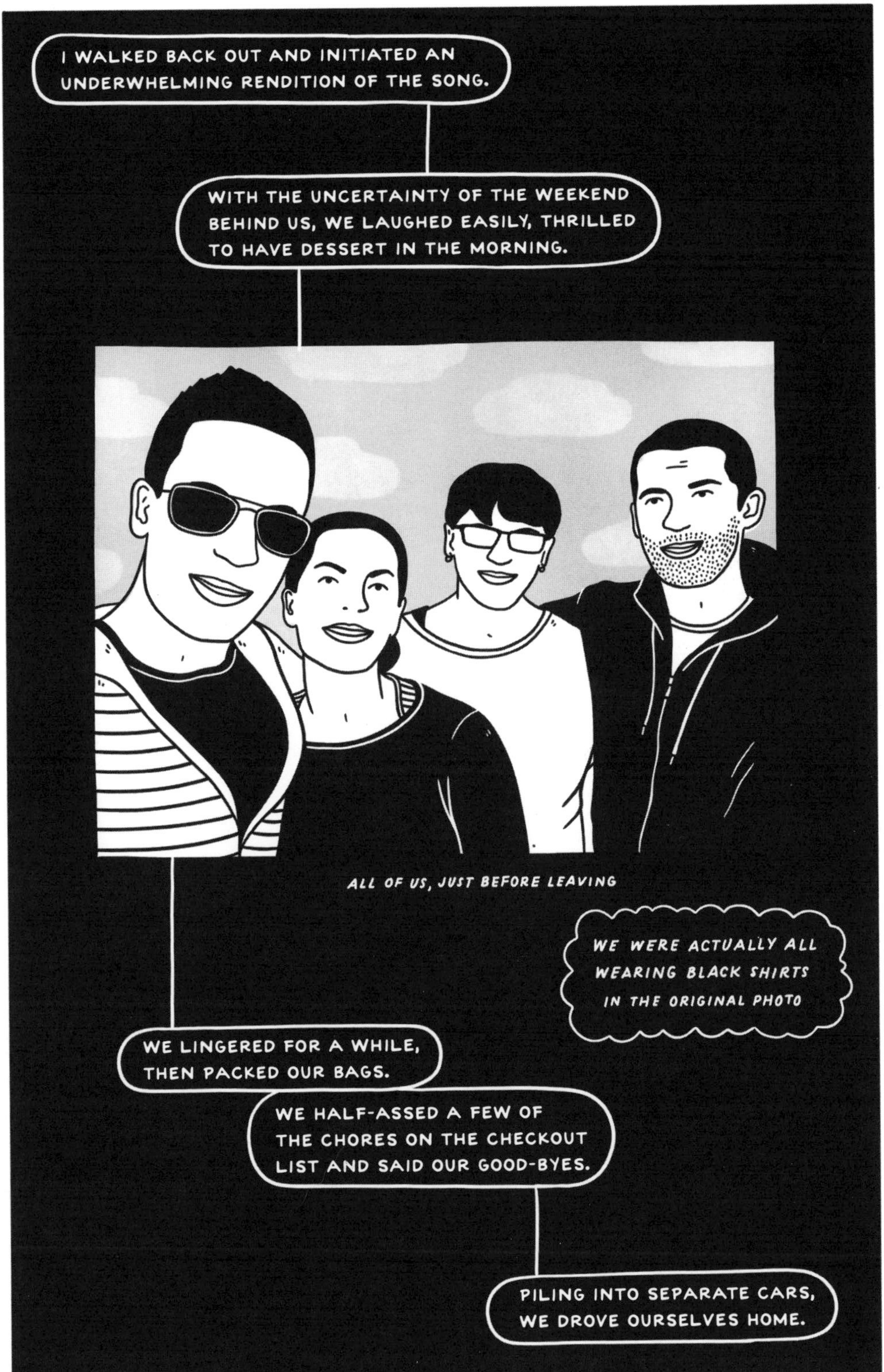
I WALKED BACK OUT AND INITIATED AN UNDERWHELMING RENDITION OF THE SONG.
WITH THE UNCERTAINTY OF THE WEEKEND BEHIND US, WE LAUGHED EASILY, THRILLED TO HAVE DESSERT IN THE MORNING.
ALL OF US, JUST BEFORE LEAVING
WE WERE ACTUALLY ALL WEARING BLACK SHIRTS IN THE ORIGINAL PHOTO
WE LINGERED FOR A WHILE, THEN PACKED OUR BAGS.
WE HALF-ASSED A FEW OF THE CHORES ON THE CHECKOUT LIST AND SAID OUR GOOD-BYES.
PILING INTO SEPARATE CARS, WE DROVE OURSELVES HOME.

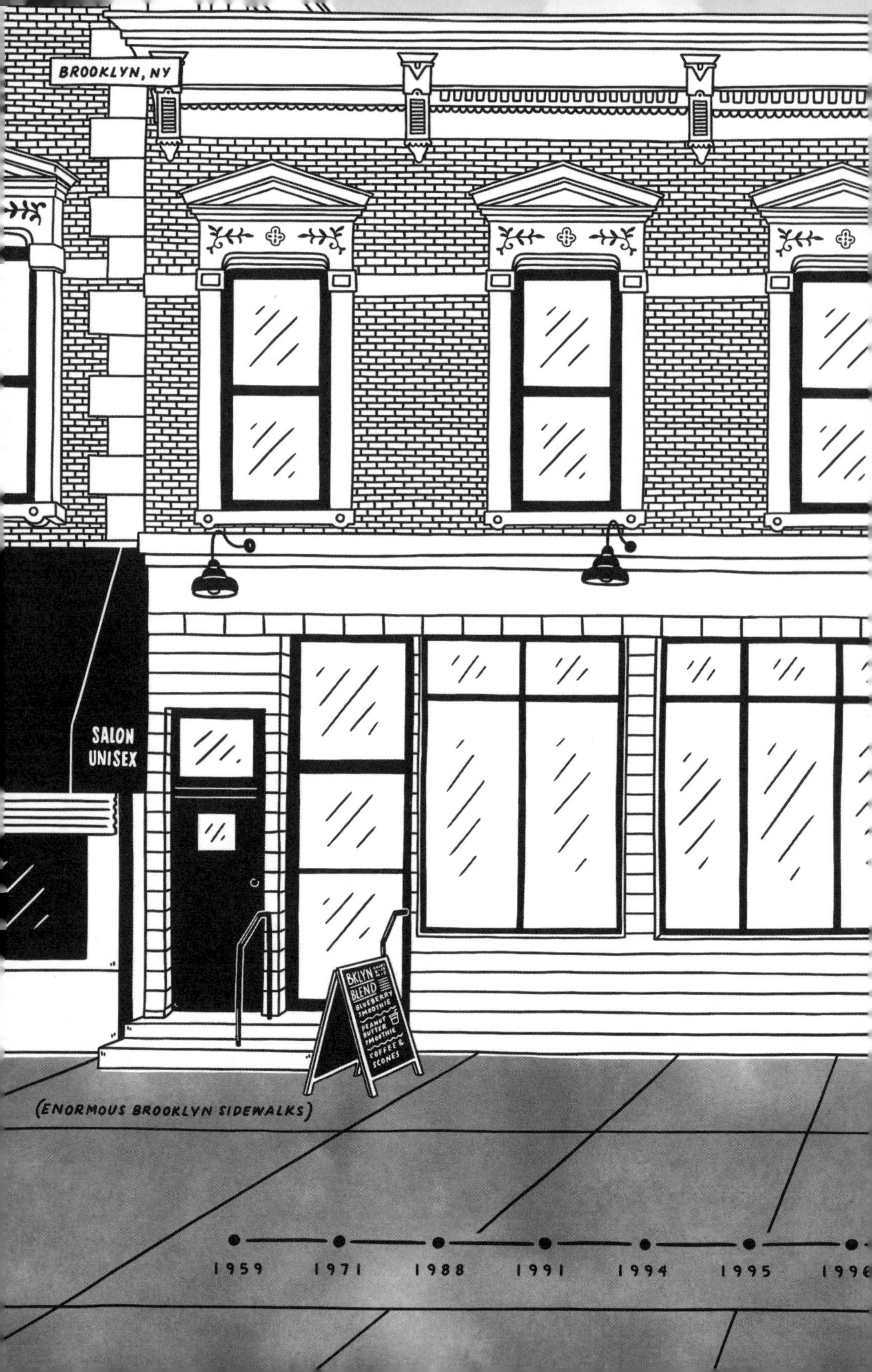
BROOKLYN, NY
SALON UNISEX
BKLYN BLEND
BLUEBERRY SMOOTHIE
PEANUT BUTTER SMOOTHIE
COFFEE & SCONES
(ENORMOUS BROOKLYN SIDEWALKS)
1959
1971
1988
1991
1994
1995
1996

CHAPTER 19

The Interview

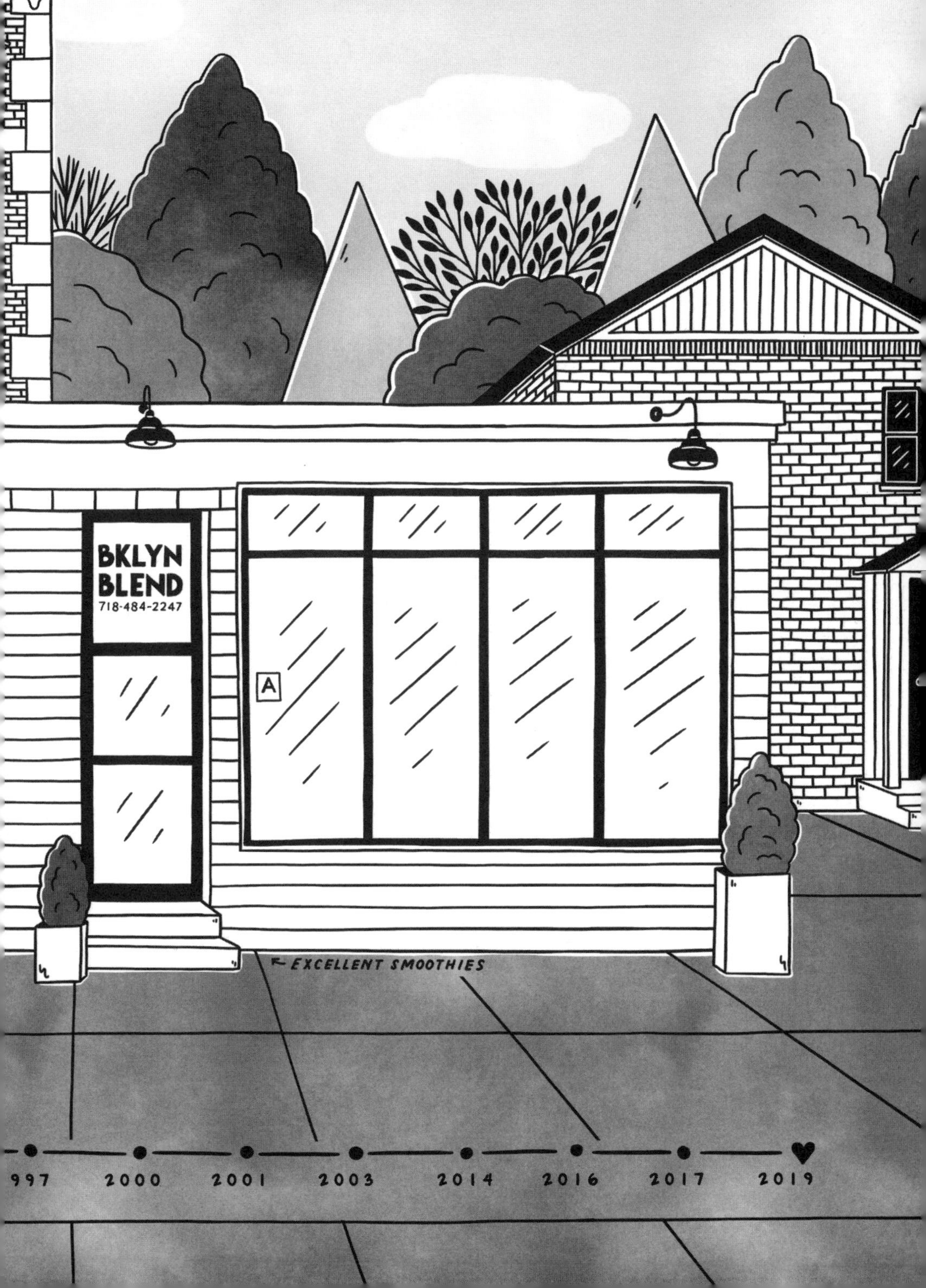
BKLYN BLEND
718-484-2247
A
EXCELLENT SMOOTHIES
997
2000
2001
2003
2014
2016
2017
2019

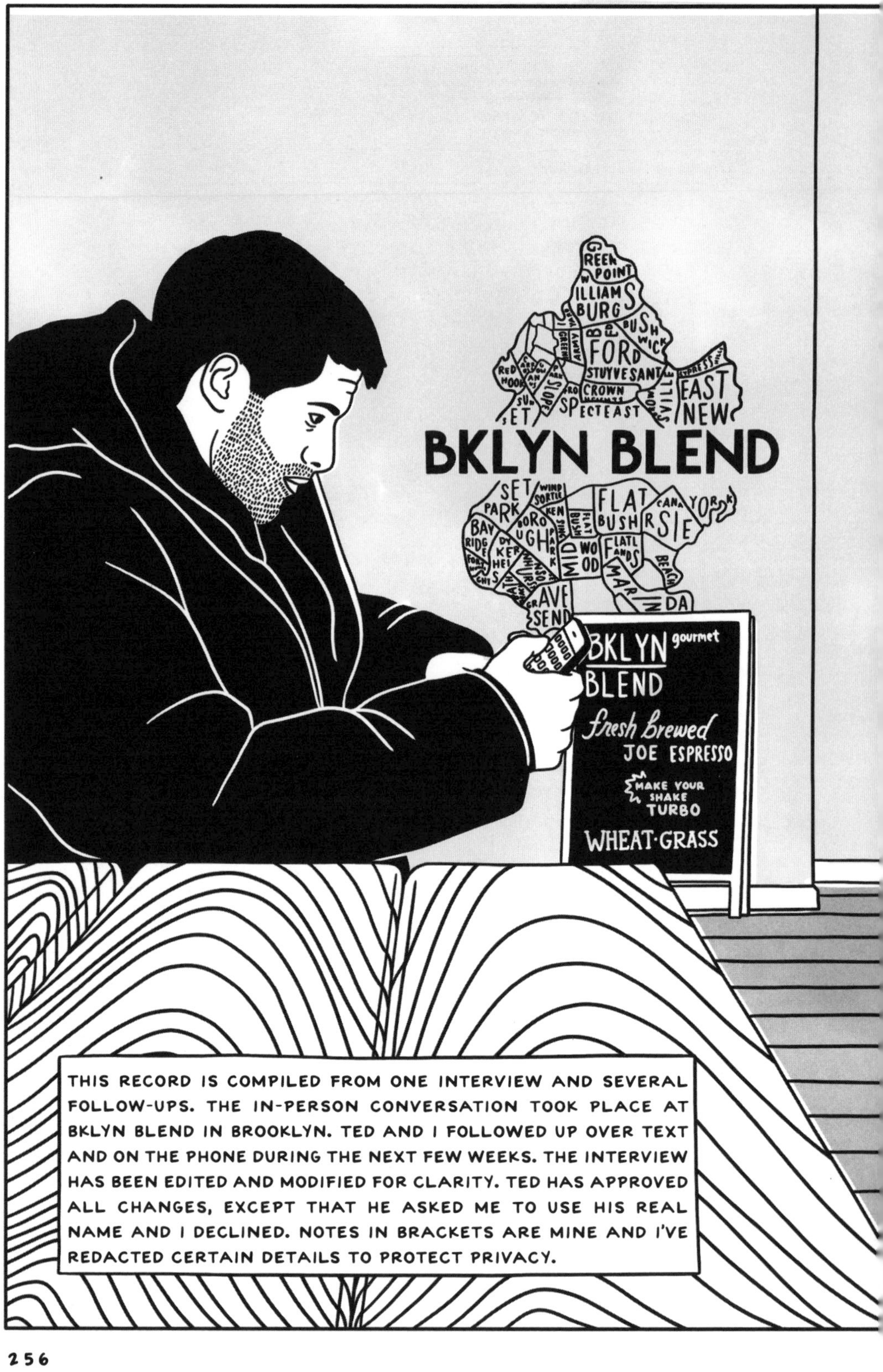
BKLYN BLEND
BKLYN gourmet
BLEND
fresh brewed
JOE ESPRESSO
MAKE YOUR SHAKE TURBO
WHEAT·GRASS
THIS RECORD IS COMPILED FROM ONE INTERVIEW AND SEVERAL FOLLOW-UPS. THE IN-PERSON CONVERSATION TOOK PLACE AT BKLYN BLEND IN BROOKLYN. TED AND I FOLLOWED UP OVER TEXT AND ON THE PHONE DURING THE NEXT FEW WEEKS. THE INTERVIEW HAS BEEN EDITED AND MODIFIED FOR CLARITY. TED HAS APPROVED ALL CHANGES, EXCEPT THAT HE ASKED ME TO USE HIS REAL NAME AND I DECLINED. NOTES IN BRACKETS ARE MINE AND I'VE REDACTED CERTAIN DETAILS TO PROTECT PRIVACY.

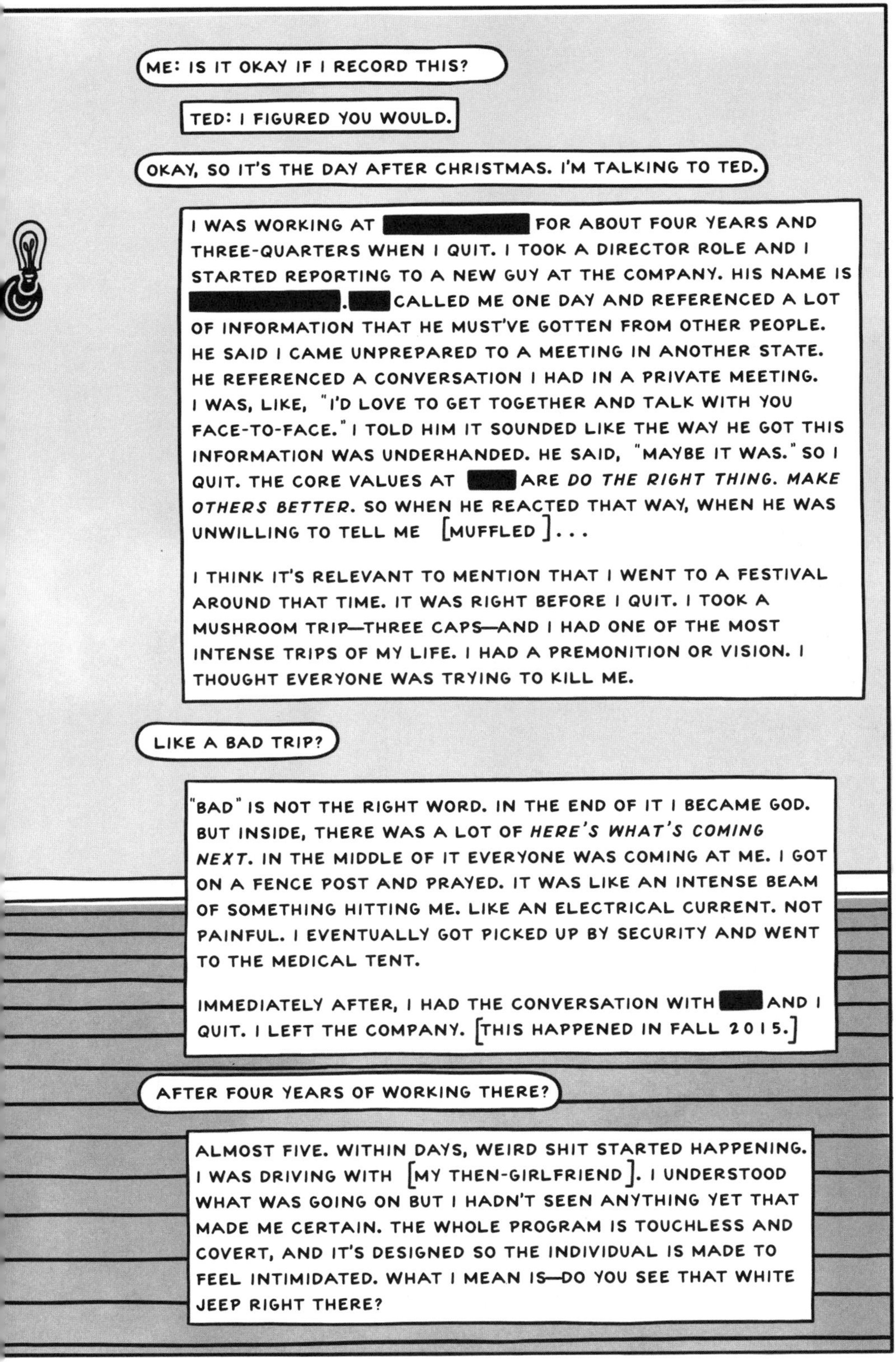
ME: IS IT OKAY IF I RECORD THIS?
TED: I FIGURED YOU WOULD.
OKAY, SO IT'S THE DAY AFTER CHRISTMAS. I'M TALKING TO TED.
I WAS WORKING AT [redacted] FOR ABOUT FOUR YEARS AND THREE-QUARTERS WHEN I QUIT. I TOOK A DIRECTOR ROLE AND I STARTED REPORTING TO A NEW GUY AT THE COMPANY. HIS NAME IS [redacted]. [redacted] CALLED ME ONE DAY AND REFERENCED A LOT OF INFORMATION THAT HE MUST'VE GOTTEN FROM OTHER PEOPLE. HE SAID I CAME UNPREPARED TO A MEETING IN ANOTHER STATE. HE REFERENCED A CONVERSATION I HAD IN A PRIVATE MEETING. I WAS, LIKE, "I'D LOVE TO GET TOGETHER AND TALK WITH YOU FACE-TO-FACE." I TOLD HIM IT SOUNDED LIKE THE WAY HE GOT THIS INFORMATION WAS UNDERHANDED. HE SAID, "MAYBE IT WAS." SO I QUIT. THE CORE VALUES AT [redacted] ARE DO THE RIGHT THING. MAKE OTHERS BETTER. SO WHEN HE REACTED THAT WAY, WHEN HE WAS UNWILLING TO TELL ME [MUFFLED]...
I THINK IT'S RELEVANT TO MENTION THAT I WENT TO A FESTIVAL AROUND THAT TIME. IT WAS RIGHT BEFORE I QUIT. I TOOK A MUSHROOM TRIP—THREE CAPS—AND I HAD ONE OF THE MOST INTENSE TRIPS OF MY LIFE. I HAD A PREMONITION OR VISION. I THOUGHT EVERYONE WAS TRYING TO KILL ME.
LIKE A BAD TRIP?
"BAD" IS NOT THE RIGHT WORD. IN THE END OF IT I BECAME GOD. BUT INSIDE, THERE WAS A LOT OF HERE'S WHAT'S COMING NEXT. IN THE MIDDLE OF IT EVERYONE WAS COMING AT ME. I GOT ON A FENCE POST AND PRAYED. IT WAS LIKE AN INTENSE BEAM OF SOMETHING HITTING ME. LIKE AN ELECTRICAL CURRENT. NOT PAINFUL. I EVENTUALLY GOT PICKED UP BY SECURITY AND WENT TO THE MEDICAL TENT.
IMMEDIATELY AFTER, I HAD THE CONVERSATION WITH [redacted] AND I QUIT. I LEFT THE COMPANY. [THIS HAPPENED IN FALL 2015.]
AFTER FOUR YEARS OF WORKING THERE?
ALMOST FIVE. WITHIN DAYS, WEIRD SHIT STARTED HAPPENING. I WAS DRIVING WITH [MY THEN-GIRLFRIEND]. I UNDERSTOOD WHAT WAS GOING ON BUT I HADN'T SEEN ANYTHING YET THAT MADE ME CERTAIN. THE WHOLE PROGRAM IS TOUCHLESS AND COVERT, AND IT'S DESIGNED SO THE INDIVIDUAL IS MADE TO FEEL INTIMIDATED. WHAT I MEAN IS—DO YOU SEE THAT WHITE JEEP RIGHT THERE?

YES.

THAT'S THE SAME KIND OF JEEP THAT MY GIRLFRIEND HAD AT THE TIME. IN ALL OF THIS, I AM MADE TO BELIEVE THAT MY INVOLVEMENT IN THE PROGRAM HAS TO DO WITH HER. WHETHER OR NOT IT DOES—I CAN'T FIGURE IT OUT. I WAS DRIVING WITH HER AND I FINALLY SAW SOMETHING THAT I COULDN'T IGNORE.

WHAT DID YOU SEE?

A CAR PULLED RIGHT IN FRONT OF ME. THEN A SECOND CAR PULLED RIGHT IN FRONT OF ME, AND THEN A THIRD CAR PULLED RIGHT IN FRONT OF ME. ONE, TWO, THREE, JUST LIKE THAT. IT WAS SYSTEMATIC, MILITARY. THE FIRST DRIVER THREW HIS ARM DOWN LIKE THIS [GESTURES] AND THEN THE SECOND DRIVER DID THE SAME MOTION.

IF YOU RESEARCH THESE TYPES OF PROGRAMS, EVERYONE DESCRIBES WHAT THEY SEE THE SAME WAY. IT'S THE SAME TACTICS, THE SAME INTIMIDATION METHODS. THEY KEEP THEIR HANDS OUT OF THE CAR POINTED DOWNWARD, LIKE, *YOU'RE GOING TO HELL*. IT'S A HAND SIGN. I'M SPECULATING ON THE DEFINITION.

THAT WAS MY FIRST ENCOUNTER WITH SOMETHING I COULDN'T IGNORE, SOMETHING THAT WAS RIGHT IN MY FACE AS A FUCK YOU.

DID [YOUR GIRLFRIEND] NOTICE IT TOO?

NO. I TRIED TO EXPLAIN IT TO HER BUT SHE WAS OBLIVIOUS TO THE WHOLE THING.

THEY TRY TO BREAK YOU DOWN. FOR THE FIRST TWO TO FOUR WEEKS I WOULD GET AN ELECTRICAL IMPULSE RIGHT AT THE MOMENT I WAS TRYING TO FALL ASLEEP. THE TIMING WAS PRECISE. RIGHT AS I WAS ABOUT TO GO INTO RAPID EYE MOVEMENT, I'D BE JOLTED AWAKE. SLEEP DEPRIVATION FOR WEEKS. THE OTHER THING THEY DO IS NOISE CAMPAIGNS. WHEN I'M COMING OR LEAVING THE HOUSE, I HEAR SIRENS AT THAT EXACT MOMENT. I'M MONITORED 24/7. ANY TIME I GO OUT OR COME IN THERE'S ACTIVITY RIGHT OUTSIDE OF MY HOUSE.

WHAT DO YOU MEAN?

I CAN'T TELL REALITY FROM—I CAN'T TELL IF IT'S ALL REAL OR NOT. HOW DEEP DOES THE INFLUENCE GO? WHAT'S COINCIDENCE AND WHAT'S NOT? I DON'T HAVE A NORMAL SCHEDULE. I GET UP AT ALL CRAZY TIMES. IT'S HARD TO TELL WHAT'S COINCIDENCE AND WHAT'S—

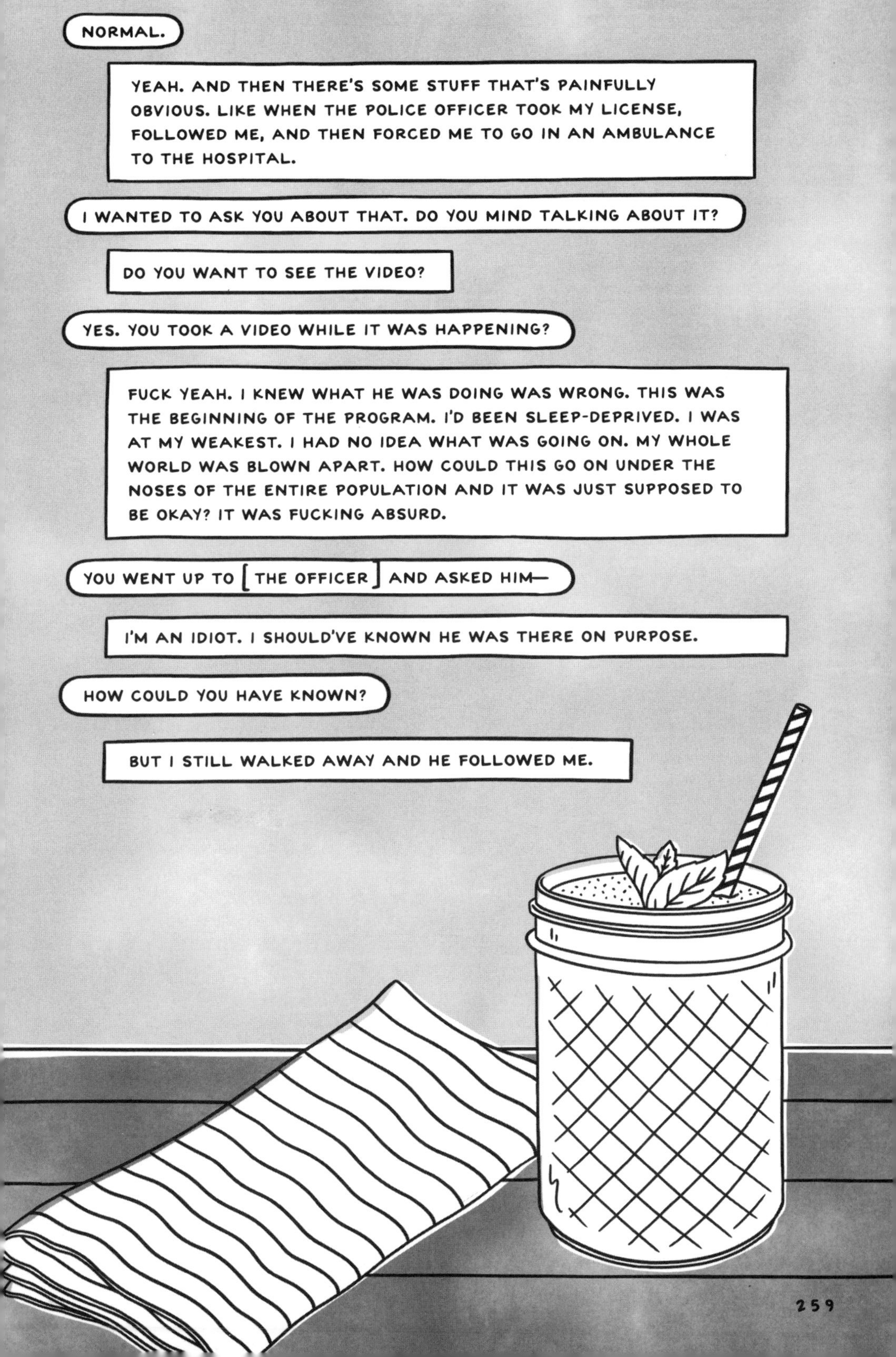
NORMAL.
YEAH. AND THEN THERE'S SOME STUFF THAT'S PAINFULLY OBVIOUS. LIKE WHEN THE POLICE OFFICER TOOK MY LICENSE, FOLLOWED ME, AND THEN FORCED ME TO GO IN AN AMBULANCE TO THE HOSPITAL.
I WANTED TO ASK YOU ABOUT THAT. DO YOU MIND TALKING ABOUT IT?
DO YOU WANT TO SEE THE VIDEO?
YES. YOU TOOK A VIDEO WHILE IT WAS HAPPENING?
FUCK YEAH. I KNEW WHAT HE WAS DOING WAS WRONG. THIS WAS THE BEGINNING OF THE PROGRAM. I'D BEEN SLEEP-DEPRIVED. I WAS AT MY WEAKEST. I HAD NO IDEA WHAT WAS GOING ON. MY WHOLE WORLD WAS BLOWN APART. HOW COULD THIS GO ON UNDER THE NOSES OF THE ENTIRE POPULATION AND IT WAS JUST SUPPOSED TO BE OKAY? IT WAS FUCKING ABSURD.
YOU WENT UP TO [THE OFFICER] AND ASKED HIM—
I'M AN IDIOT. I SHOULD'VE KNOWN HE WAS THERE ON PURPOSE.
HOW COULD YOU HAVE KNOWN?
BUT I STILL WALKED AWAY AND HE FOLLOWED ME.

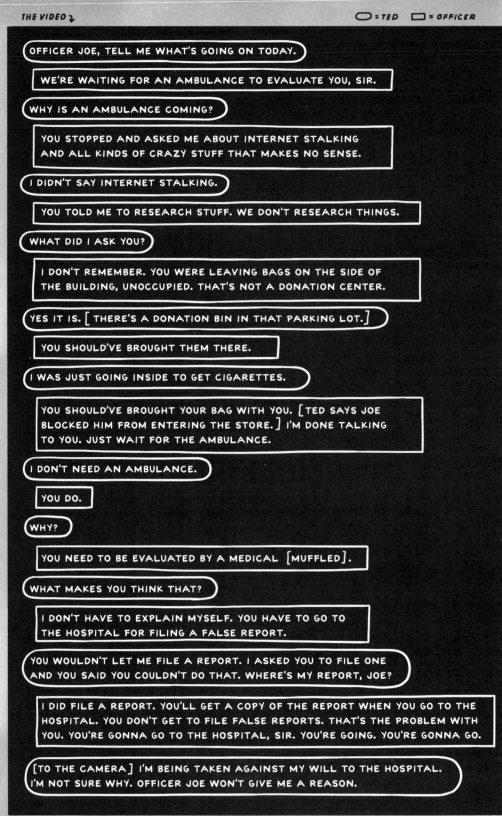

OFFICER JOE, TELL ME WHAT'S GOING ON TODAY.

WE'RE WAITING FOR AN AMBULANCE TO EVALUATE YOU, SIR.

WHY IS AN AMBULANCE COMING?

YOU STOPPED AND ASKED ME ABOUT INTERNET STALKING AND ALL KINDS OF CRAZY STUFF THAT MAKES NO SENSE.

I DIDN'T SAY INTERNET STALKING.

YOU TOLD ME TO RESEARCH STUFF. WE DON'T RESEARCH THINGS.

WHAT DID I ASK YOU?

I DON'T REMEMBER. YOU WERE LEAVING BAGS ON THE SIDE OF THE BUILDING, UNOCCUPIED. THAT'S NOT A DONATION CENTER.

YES IT IS. [THERE'S A DONATION BIN IN THAT PARKING LOT.]

YOU SHOULD'VE BROUGHT THEM THERE.

I WAS JUST GOING INSIDE TO GET CIGARETTES.

YOU SHOULD'VE BROUGHT YOUR BAG WITH YOU. [TED SAYS JOE BLOCKED HIM FROM ENTERING THE STORE.] I'M DONE TALKING TO YOU. JUST WAIT FOR THE AMBULANCE.

I DON'T NEED AN AMBULANCE.

YOU DO.

WHY?

YOU NEED TO BE EVALUATED BY A MEDICAL [MUFFLED].

WHAT MAKES YOU THINK THAT?

I DON'T HAVE TO EXPLAIN MYSELF. YOU HAVE TO GO TO THE HOSPITAL FOR FILING A FALSE REPORT.

YOU WOULDN'T LET ME FILE A REPORT. I ASKED YOU TO FILE ONE AND YOU SAID YOU COULDN'T DO THAT. WHERE'S MY REPORT, JOE?

I DID FILE A REPORT. YOU'LL GET A COPY OF THE REPORT WHEN YOU GO TO THE HOSPITAL. YOU DON'T GET TO FILE FALSE REPORTS. THAT'S THE PROBLEM WITH YOU. YOU'RE GONNA GO TO THE HOSPITAL, SIR. YOU'RE GOING. YOU'RE GONNA GO.

[TO THE CAMERA] I'M BEING TAKEN AGAINST MY WILL TO THE HOSPITAL. I'M NOT SURE WHY. OFFICER JOE WON'T GIVE ME A REASON.

DAD CAME TO THE HOSPITAL, RIGHT?

YEP. THEY KEPT ME FOR EIGHT HOURS. THE GUY TALKED TO ME FOR FIVE MINUTES AND EVALUATED ME AS SOME TYPE OF PSYCHOSIS [SIC]. IF THIS INTERVIEW EVER MAKES ANY KIND OF TRACTION, THEY'LL LOOK BACK AND SAY I'M NOT CREDIBLE. I'M PSYCHOTIC. THEY'LL DO WHATEVER THEY HAVE TO DO TO SUPPRESS THESE PROGRAMS. THEY'RE DESIGNED TO KEEP PEOPLE SILENT. THEY'LL SUPPRESS ANYBODY WHO HAS ANY TYPE OF INFORMATION FOR WHAT'S GOING ON IN THE WORLD, SO THEY CAN KEEP DOING IT.

YOU DON'T GET IT. YOU HAVE NO IDEA. NEITHER DOES ANYONE ELSE. THE WEAPONRY THEY HAVE, THE SYSTEMS THEY USE—IT'S COMPLETELY ILLEGAL. AFTER 9/11 THEY MIGHT EVEN FIND LEGAL LOOPHOLES IN TERMS OF PRIVACY.

THE PATRIOT ACT ALLOWED A LOT OF SPYING.

I DON'T KNOW IF I'LL EVER BE ABLE TO PROVE ANY OF IT. IT'S SO COVERT AND TOUCHLESS. THE WHOLE POINT IS TO GET THE PERSON TO BREAK DOWN MENTALLY AND GO KILL HIMSELF. OR FOR ME TO DO SOMETHING SO BAD THAT THEY CAN LOCK ME UP AND THROW AWAY THE KEY.

DO YOU REMEMBER THE WEEKEND IN KENTUCKY? YOU WERE LOOKING AT THE BRICKS IN THE FREEMASON LODGE I LIVED IN. WERE YOU STARTING TO SEE SIGNS THEN?

[MY FRIEND] TURNED ME ON TO SOME OF THE SYMBOLISM. I WAS PAYING ATTENTION TO IT. I WAS LOOKING AT THE NUMBERS ON BUILDINGS. IT WAS TRIPPING ME OUT.

BEFORE YOU SAY YOU WERE PUT INTO THE PROGRAM, YOU WERE SEEING THESE THINGS?

I JUST BECAME MORE AWARE OF WHAT IS HERE. THESE BUILDINGS BELONG TO THESE PEOPLE, THE SYMBOLISM OF THE NUMBERS—ALL THAT STUFF IS HERE. YOU CAN FIND IT.

DO YOU STILL CALL IT THE T.I. PROGRAM?

LOOK AT THAT GUY [POINTS OUTSIDE THE WINDOW]. DO YOU SEE HIM? DO YOU SEE HOW HE'S SIPPING HIS MUG? DID YOU SEE HOW MANY TIMES HE DID IT?

I SEE HIM. I DIDN'T SEE HOW MANY TIMES HE DID IT. I THINK HE'S JUST SINGING.

IT'S GOTTEN TO THE POINT WHERE I DON'T KNOW. IT'S ALMOST IMPOSSIBLE FOR SOMEONE NOT IN THE PROGRAM TO COMPREHEND ANY OF THIS STUFF. I HAVE A HARD TIME WRAPPING MY HEAD AROUND WHAT'S POSSIBLE. I DON'T HAVE ILLUSIONS OF CONVINCING ANYONE OF ANYTHING. IF YOU'RE ABLE TO DO SOMETHING POSITIVE WITH THIS INFORMATION AND GET IT OUT THERE, THAT'S GREAT. BUT YOU PUT YOURSELF AT RISK. THEY'LL DO EVERYTHING THEY WANT TO DO TO PROTECT THEIR WAY OF LIFE. WE'RE NOTHING TO THEM.

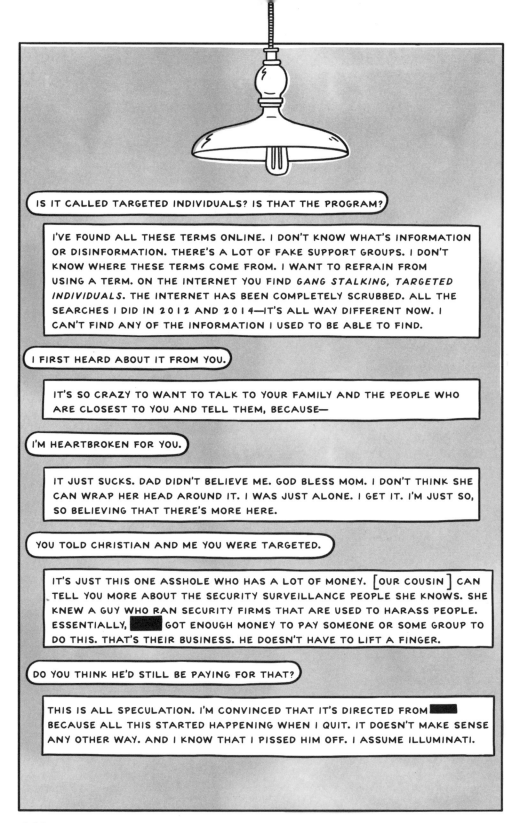

IS IT CALLED TARGETED INDIVIDUALS? IS THAT THE PROGRAM?

I'VE FOUND ALL THESE TERMS ONLINE. I DON'T KNOW WHAT'S INFORMATION OR DISINFORMATION. THERE'S A LOT OF FAKE SUPPORT GROUPS. I DON'T KNOW WHERE THESE TERMS COME FROM. I WANT TO REFRAIN FROM USING A TERM. ON THE INTERNET YOU FIND *GANG STALKING, TARGETED INDIVIDUALS.* THE INTERNET HAS BEEN COMPLETELY SCRUBBED. ALL THE SEARCHES I DID IN 2012 AND 2014—IT'S ALL WAY DIFFERENT NOW. I CAN'T FIND ANY OF THE INFORMATION I USED TO BE ABLE TO FIND.

I FIRST HEARD ABOUT IT FROM YOU.

IT'S SO CRAZY TO WANT TO TALK TO YOUR FAMILY AND THE PEOPLE WHO ARE CLOSEST TO YOU AND TELL THEM, BECAUSE—

I'M HEARTBROKEN FOR YOU.

IT JUST SUCKS. DAD DIDN'T BELIEVE ME. GOD BLESS MOM. I DON'T THINK SHE CAN WRAP HER HEAD AROUND IT. I WAS JUST ALONE. I GET IT. I'M JUST SO, SO BELIEVING THAT THERE'S MORE HERE.

YOU TOLD CHRISTIAN AND ME YOU WERE TARGETED.

IT'S JUST THIS ONE ASSHOLE WHO HAS A LOT OF MONEY. [OUR COUSIN] CAN TELL YOU MORE ABOUT THE SECURITY SURVEILLANCE PEOPLE SHE KNOWS. SHE KNEW A GUY WHO RAN SECURITY FIRMS THAT ARE USED TO HARASS PEOPLE. ESSENTIALLY, ███ GOT ENOUGH MONEY TO PAY SOMEONE OR SOME GROUP TO DO THIS. THAT'S THEIR BUSINESS. HE DOESN'T HAVE TO LIFT A FINGER.

DO YOU THINK HE'D STILL BE PAYING FOR THAT?

THIS IS ALL SPECULATION. I'M CONVINCED THAT IT'S DIRECTED FROM ███ BECAUSE ALL THIS STARTED HAPPENING WHEN I QUIT. IT DOESN'T MAKE SENSE ANY OTHER WAY. AND I KNOW THAT I PISSED HIM OFF. I ASSUME ILLUMINATI.

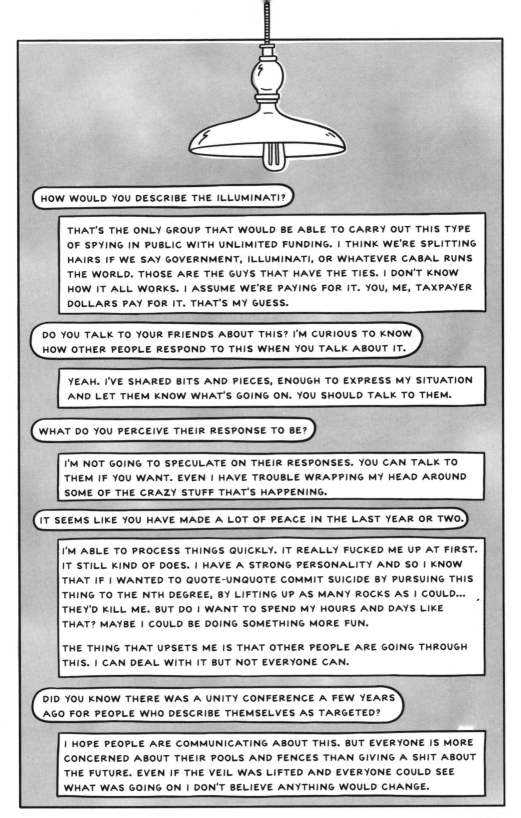

HOW WOULD YOU DESCRIBE THE ILLUMINATI?

THAT'S THE ONLY GROUP THAT WOULD BE ABLE TO CARRY OUT THIS TYPE OF SPYING IN PUBLIC WITH UNLIMITED FUNDING. I THINK WE'RE SPLITTING HAIRS IF WE SAY GOVERNMENT, ILLUMINATI, OR WHATEVER CABAL RUNS THE WORLD. THOSE ARE THE GUYS THAT HAVE THE TIES. I DON'T KNOW HOW IT ALL WORKS. I ASSUME WE'RE PAYING FOR IT. YOU, ME, TAXPAYER DOLLARS PAY FOR IT. THAT'S MY GUESS.

DO YOU TALK TO YOUR FRIENDS ABOUT THIS? I'M CURIOUS TO KNOW HOW OTHER PEOPLE RESPOND TO THIS WHEN YOU TALK ABOUT IT.

YEAH. I'VE SHARED BITS AND PIECES, ENOUGH TO EXPRESS MY SITUATION AND LET THEM KNOW WHAT'S GOING ON. YOU SHOULD TALK TO THEM.

WHAT DO YOU PERCEIVE THEIR RESPONSE TO BE?

I'M NOT GOING TO SPECULATE ON THEIR RESPONSES. YOU CAN TALK TO THEM IF YOU WANT. EVEN I HAVE TROUBLE WRAPPING MY HEAD AROUND SOME OF THE CRAZY STUFF THAT'S HAPPENING.

IT SEEMS LIKE YOU HAVE MADE A LOT OF PEACE IN THE LAST YEAR OR TWO.

I'M ABLE TO PROCESS THINGS QUICKLY. IT REALLY FUCKED ME UP AT FIRST. IT STILL KIND OF DOES. I HAVE A STRONG PERSONALITY AND SO I KNOW THAT IF I WANTED TO QUOTE-UNQUOTE COMMIT SUICIDE BY PURSUING THIS THING TO THE NTH DEGREE, BY LIFTING UP AS MANY ROCKS AS I COULD... THEY'D KILL ME. BUT DO I WANT TO SPEND MY HOURS AND DAYS LIKE THAT? MAYBE I COULD BE DOING SOMETHING MORE FUN.

THE THING THAT UPSETS ME IS THAT OTHER PEOPLE ARE GOING THROUGH THIS. I CAN DEAL WITH IT BUT NOT EVERYONE CAN.

DID YOU KNOW THERE WAS A UNITY CONFERENCE A FEW YEARS AGO FOR PEOPLE WHO DESCRIBE THEMSELVES AS TARGETED?

I HOPE PEOPLE ARE COMMUNICATING ABOUT THIS. BUT EVERYONE IS MORE CONCERNED ABOUT THEIR POOLS AND FENCES THAN GIVING A SHIT ABOUT THE FUTURE. EVEN IF THE VEIL WAS LIFTED AND EVERYONE COULD SEE WHAT WAS GOING ON I DON'T BELIEVE ANYTHING WOULD CHANGE.

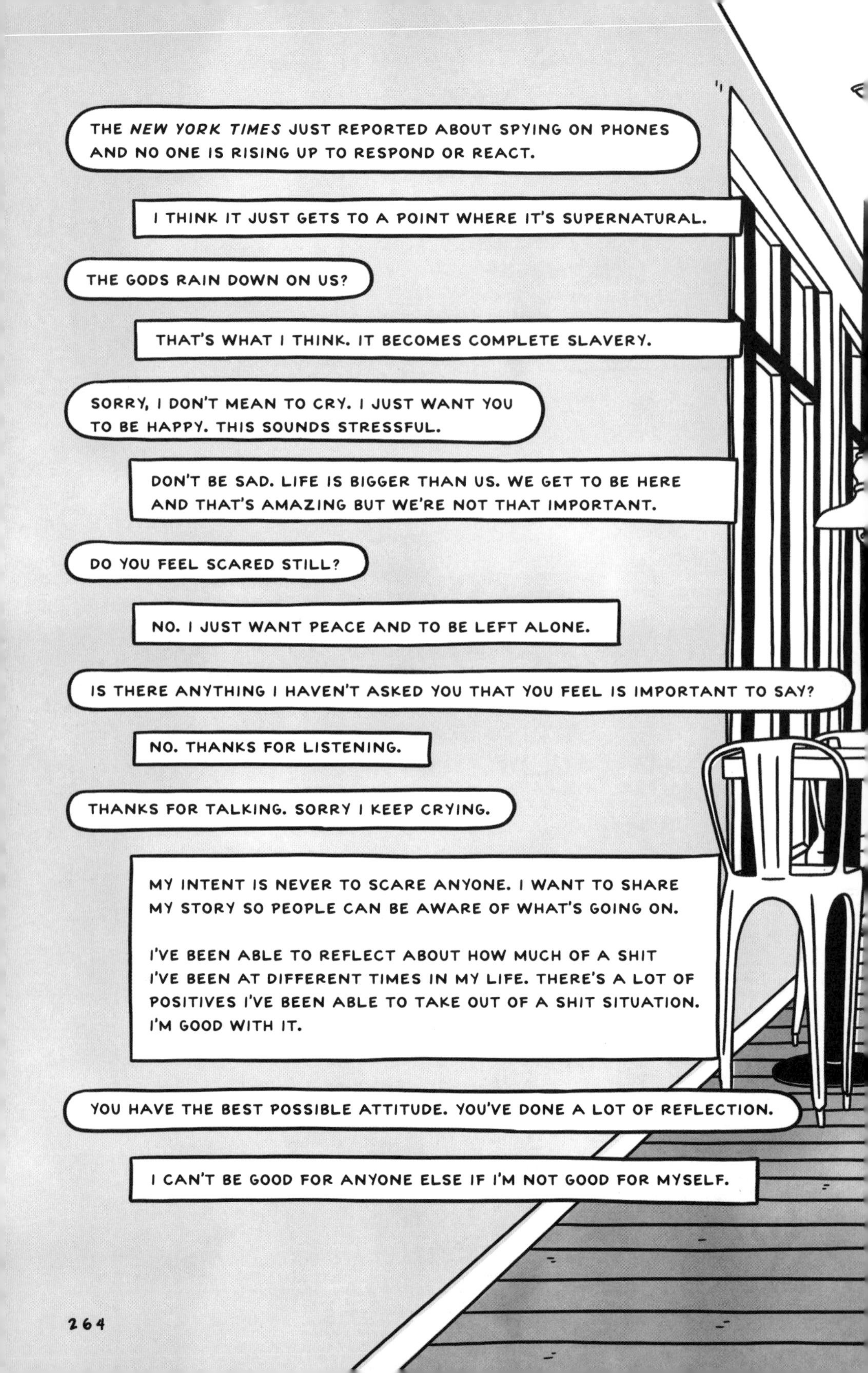
THE *NEW YORK TIMES* JUST REPORTED ABOUT SPYING ON PHONES AND NO ONE IS RISING UP TO RESPOND OR REACT.
I THINK IT JUST GETS TO A POINT WHERE IT'S SUPERNATURAL.
THE GODS RAIN DOWN ON US?
THAT'S WHAT I THINK. IT BECOMES COMPLETE SLAVERY.
SORRY, I DON'T MEAN TO CRY. I JUST WANT YOU TO BE HAPPY. THIS SOUNDS STRESSFUL.
DON'T BE SAD. LIFE IS BIGGER THAN US. WE GET TO BE HERE AND THAT'S AMAZING BUT WE'RE NOT THAT IMPORTANT.
DO YOU FEEL SCARED STILL?
NO. I JUST WANT PEACE AND TO BE LEFT ALONE.
IS THERE ANYTHING I HAVEN'T ASKED YOU THAT YOU FEEL IS IMPORTANT TO SAY?
NO. THANKS FOR LISTENING.
THANKS FOR TALKING. SORRY I KEEP CRYING.
MY INTENT IS NEVER TO SCARE ANYONE. I WANT TO SHARE MY STORY SO PEOPLE CAN BE AWARE OF WHAT'S GOING ON.
I'VE BEEN ABLE TO REFLECT ABOUT HOW MUCH OF A SHIT I'VE BEEN AT DIFFERENT TIMES IN MY LIFE. THERE'S A LOT OF POSITIVES I'VE BEEN ABLE TO TAKE OUT OF A SHIT SITUATION. I'M GOOD WITH IT.
YOU HAVE THE BEST POSSIBLE ATTITUDE. YOU'VE DONE A LOT OF REFLECTION.
I CAN'T BE GOOD FOR ANYONE ELSE IF I'M NOT GOOD FOR MYSELF.

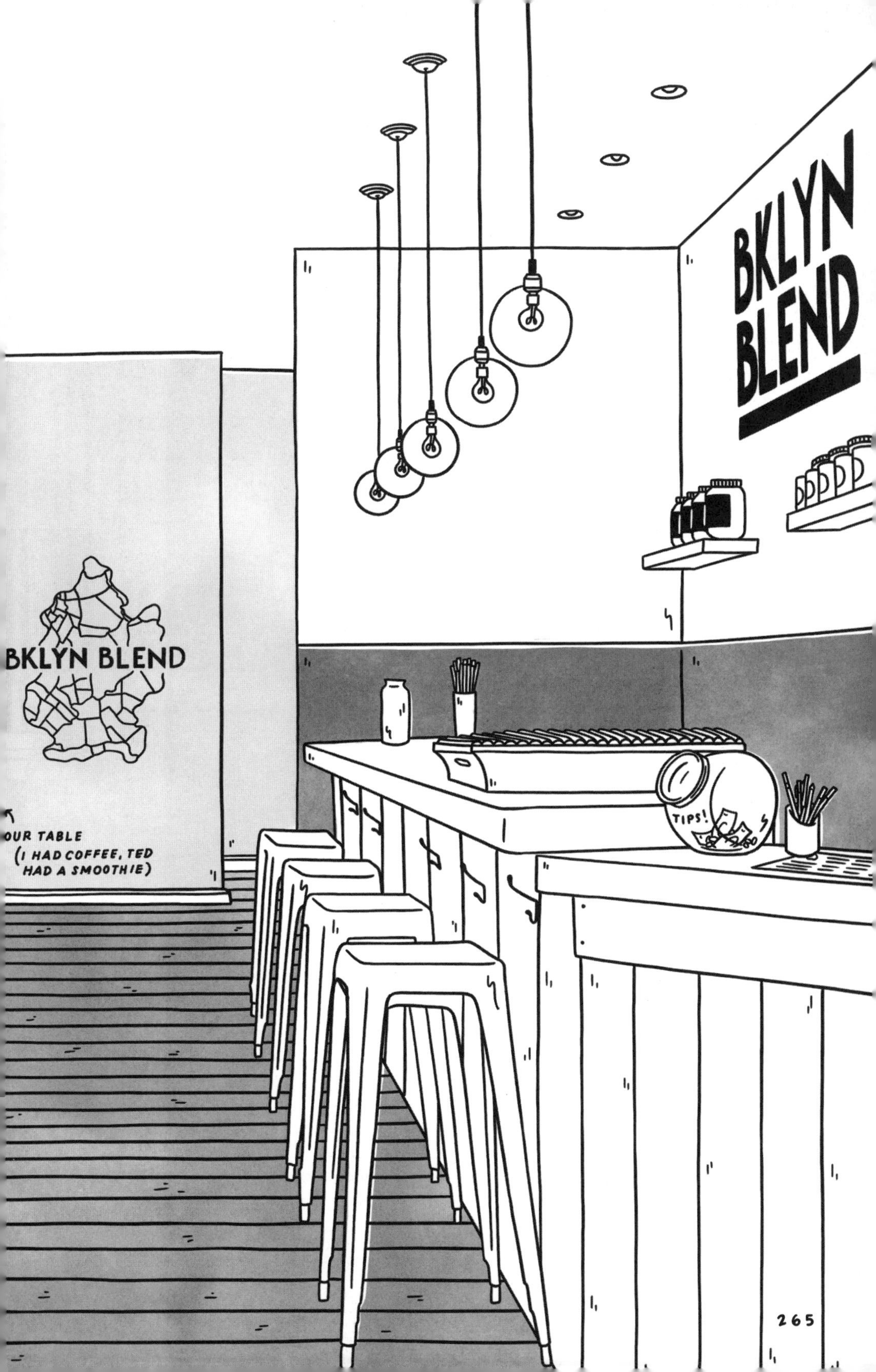
BKLYN BLEND
BKLYN BLEND
OUR TABLE
(I HAD COFFEE, TED HAD A SMOOTHIE)
TIPS!

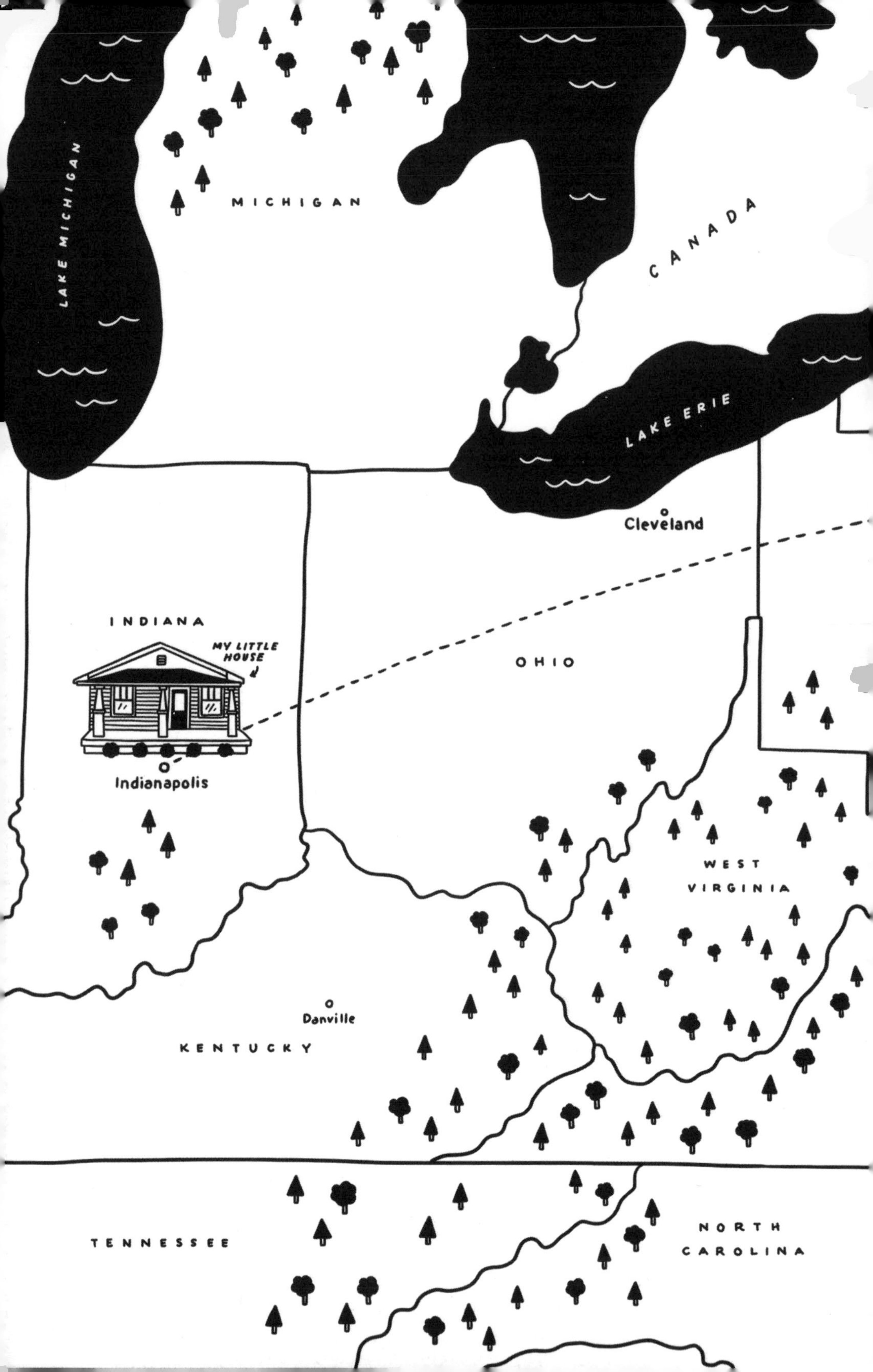
LAKE MICHIGAN
MICHIGAN
CANADA
LAKE ERIE
Cleveland
INDIANA
MY LITTLE HOUSE
OHIO
Indianapolis
WEST VIRGINIA
Danville
KENTUCKY
TENNESSEE
NORTH CAROLINA

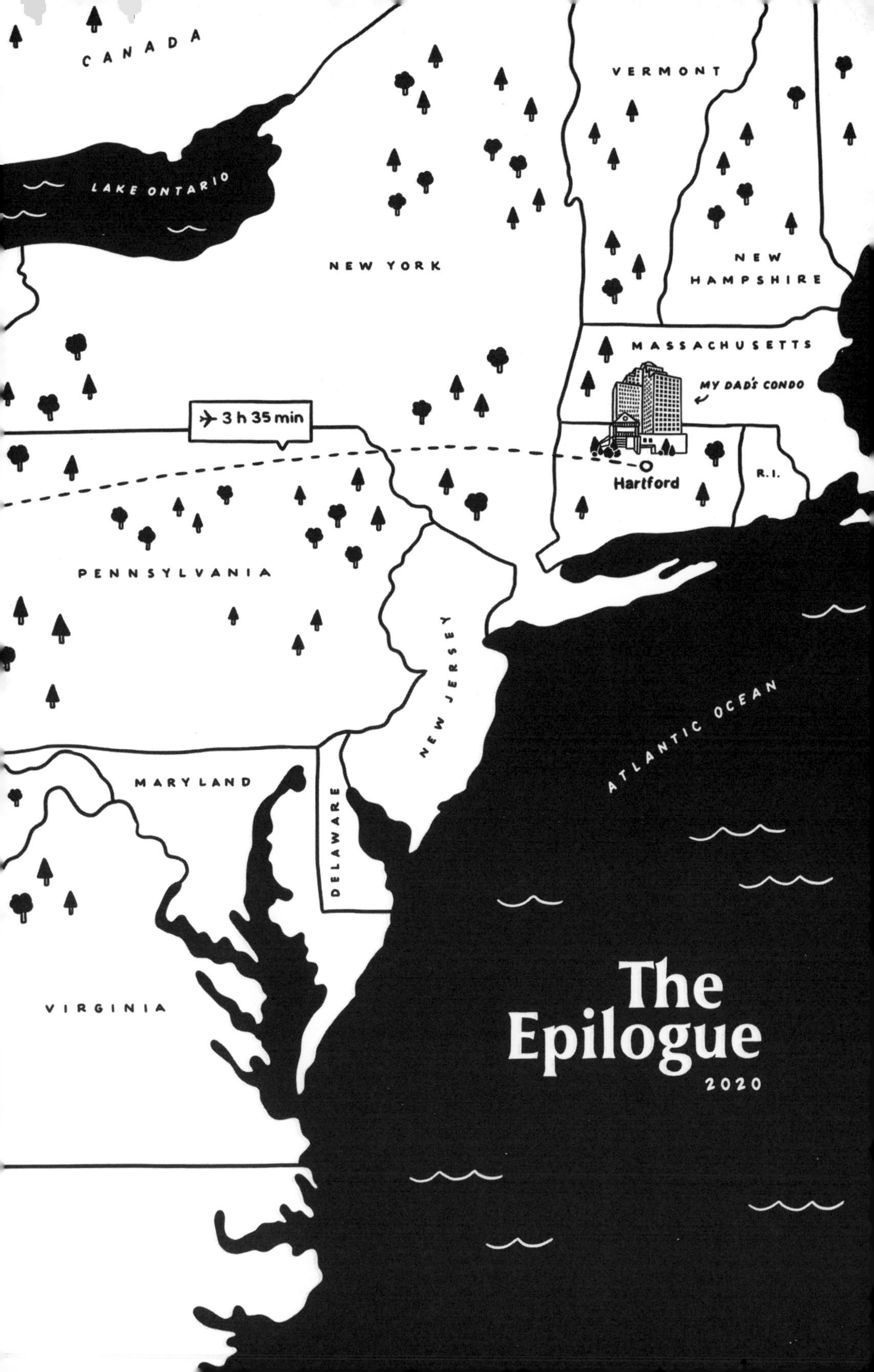
CANADA
LAKE ONTARIO
NEW YORK
VERMONT
NEW HAMPSHIRE
MASSACHUSETTS
MY DAD'S CONDO
3 h 35 min
Hartford
R.I.
PENNSYLVANIA
NEW JERSEY
ATLANTIC OCEAN
MARYLAND
DELAWARE
VIRGINIA

The Epilogue

2020

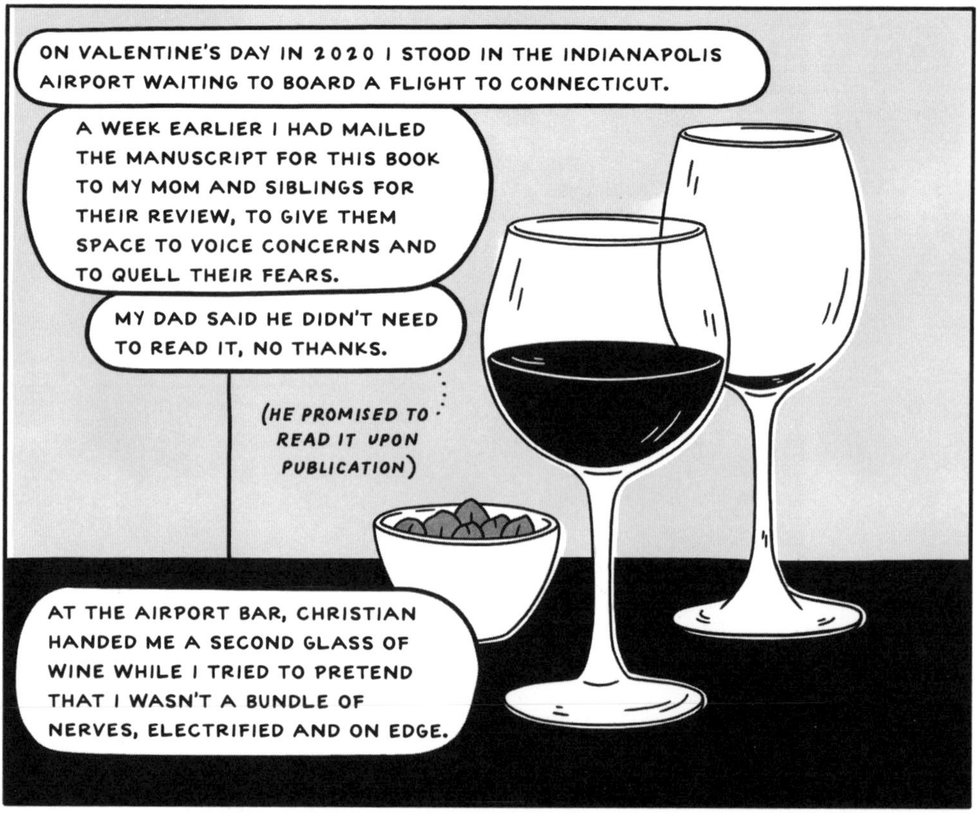
ON VALENTINE'S DAY IN 2020 I STOOD IN THE INDIANAPOLIS AIRPORT WAITING TO BOARD A FLIGHT TO CONNECTICUT.
A WEEK EARLIER I HAD MAILED THE MANUSCRIPT FOR THIS BOOK TO MY MOM AND SIBLINGS FOR THEIR REVIEW, TO GIVE THEM SPACE TO VOICE CONCERNS AND TO QUELL THEIR FEARS.
MY DAD SAID HE DIDN'T NEED TO READ IT, NO THANKS.
(HE PROMISED TO READ IT UPON PUBLICATION)
AT THE AIRPORT BAR, CHRISTIAN HANDED ME A SECOND GLASS OF WINE WHILE I TRIED TO PRETEND THAT I WASN'T A BUNDLE OF NERVES, ELECTRIFIED AND ON EDGE.

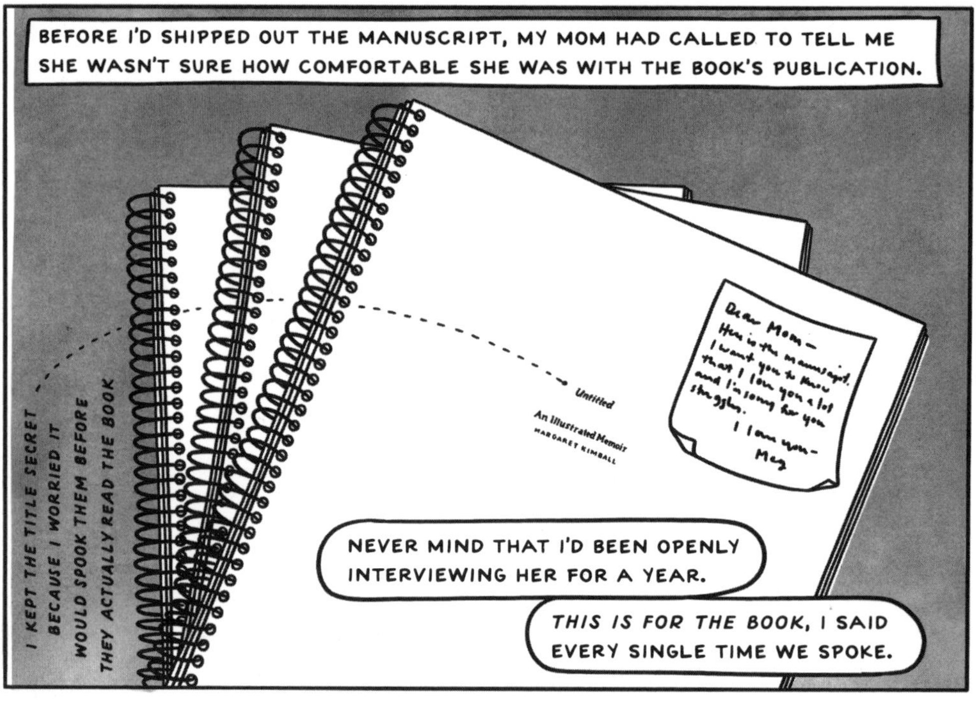
BEFORE I'D SHIPPED OUT THE MANUSCRIPT, MY MOM HAD CALLED TO TELL ME SHE WASN'T SURE HOW COMFORTABLE SHE WAS WITH THE BOOK'S PUBLICATION.
I KEPT THE TITLE SECRET BECAUSE I WORRIED IT WOULD SPOOK THEM BEFORE THEY ACTUALLY READ THE BOOK
Untitled
An Illustrated Memoir
MARGARET KIMBALL
Dear Mom— Here is the manuscript. I want you to know that I love you a lot and I'm sorry for your struggles.
I love you— Meg
NEVER MIND THAT I'D BEEN OPENLY INTERVIEWING HER FOR A YEAR.
THIS IS FOR THE BOOK, I SAID EVERY SINGLE TIME WE SPOKE.

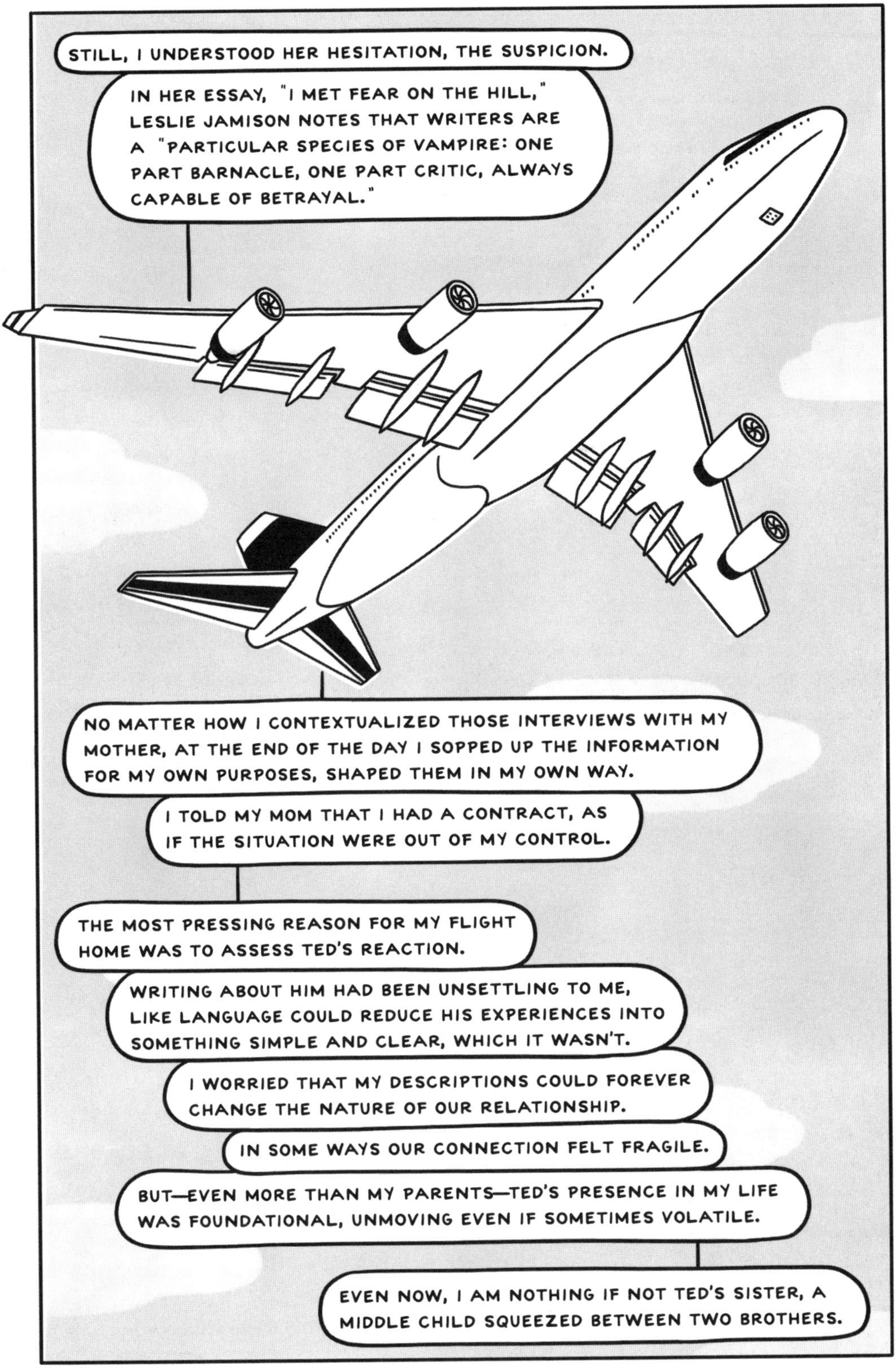
STILL, I UNDERSTOOD HER HESITATION, THE SUSPICION.
IN HER ESSAY, "I MET FEAR ON THE HILL," LESLIE JAMISON NOTES THAT WRITERS ARE A "PARTICULAR SPECIES OF VAMPIRE: ONE PART BARNACLE, ONE PART CRITIC, ALWAYS CAPABLE OF BETRAYAL."
NO MATTER HOW I CONTEXTUALIZED THOSE INTERVIEWS WITH MY MOTHER, AT THE END OF THE DAY I SOPPED UP THE INFORMATION FOR MY OWN PURPOSES, SHAPED THEM IN MY OWN WAY.
I TOLD MY MOM THAT I HAD A CONTRACT, AS IF THE SITUATION WERE OUT OF MY CONTROL.
THE MOST PRESSING REASON FOR MY FLIGHT HOME WAS TO ASSESS TED'S REACTION.
WRITING ABOUT HIM HAD BEEN UNSETTLING TO ME, LIKE LANGUAGE COULD REDUCE HIS EXPERIENCES INTO SOMETHING SIMPLE AND CLEAR, WHICH IT WASN'T.
I WORRIED THAT MY DESCRIPTIONS COULD FOREVER CHANGE THE NATURE OF OUR RELATIONSHIP.
IN SOME WAYS OUR CONNECTION FELT FRAGILE.
BUT—EVEN MORE THAN MY PARENTS—TED'S PRESENCE IN MY LIFE WAS FOUNDATIONAL, UNMOVING EVEN IF SOMETIMES VOLATILE.
EVEN NOW, I AM NOTHING IF NOT TED'S SISTER, A MIDDLE CHILD SQUEEZED BETWEEN TWO BROTHERS.

WITH MY MOM, I FELT COMPELLED TO WRITE ABOUT HER AND THAT COMPULSION FELT LIKE AN INALIENABLE RIGHT: A CHILDHOOD IS IMPRESSED UPON AN UNCHOOSING PARTICIPANT SO WHY SHOULDN'T SHE BE ABLE TO WRITE ABOUT IT?

I WANTED TO TAKE THE SINGULAR THING I KNEW ABOUT MY MOTHER—HER MENTAL ILLNESS—AND INSCRIBE COMPLEXITY UPON IT SO I COULD BETTER UNDERSTAND AND APPRECIATE HER.

(TED GREW HIS HAIR OUT)

MY BROTHERS AND ME
(THE NIGHT BEFORE MY WEDDING, 2018)

WITH MY BROTHER THE OPPOSITE IS TRUE.

I HAVE NO DESIRE TO WRITE ABOUT HIM, BUT I CAN THINK OF NO OTHER WAY TO PROCESS WHAT HE TELLS ME.

AND WHEREAS I TOOK A SIMPLE FACT ABOUT MY MOM AND TRIED TO COMPLICATE IT, WITH MY BROTHER I'VE TRIED TO STITCH TOGETHER A MILLION PIECES OF FABRIC—EVERYTHING I'VE KNOWN ABOUT HIM FOR THIRTY-SIX YEARS—AND SEW IT INTO A WELL-DESIGNED BLANKET. NEITHER APPROACH IS PERFECT OR COMPLETE.

DURING THE FIFTEEN YEARS THAT I WORKED ON THIS BOOK, TED WAS UNWAVERING IN HIS SUPPORT OF IT.

"WRITE WHATEVER YOU WANT," HE ALWAYS SAID.

BUT AFTER I'D INTERVIEWED HIM OVER THE PREVIOUS CHRISTMAS, HE ASKED ME WHAT I PLANNED TO DO WITH HIS STORY.

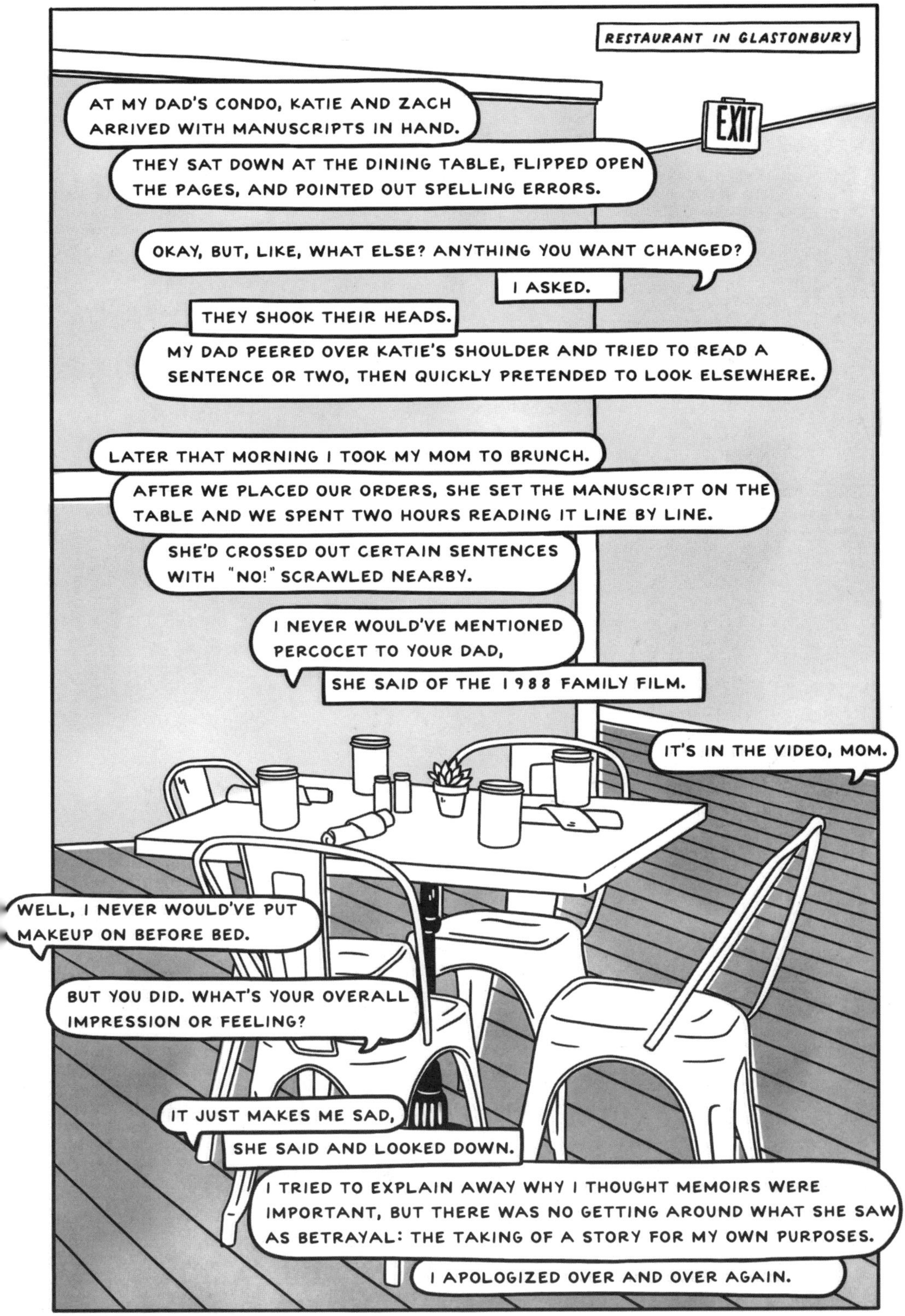
RESTAURANT IN GLASTONBURY
AT MY DAD'S CONDO, KATIE AND ZACH ARRIVED WITH MANUSCRIPTS IN HAND.
THEY SAT DOWN AT THE DINING TABLE, FLIPPED OPEN THE PAGES, AND POINTED OUT SPELLING ERRORS.
OKAY, BUT, LIKE, WHAT ELSE? ANYTHING YOU WANT CHANGED?
I ASKED.
THEY SHOOK THEIR HEADS.
MY DAD PEERED OVER KATIE'S SHOULDER AND TRIED TO READ A SENTENCE OR TWO, THEN QUICKLY PRETENDED TO LOOK ELSEWHERE.
LATER THAT MORNING I TOOK MY MOM TO BRUNCH.
AFTER WE PLACED OUR ORDERS, SHE SET THE MANUSCRIPT ON THE TABLE AND WE SPENT TWO HOURS READING IT LINE BY LINE.
SHE'D CROSSED OUT CERTAIN SENTENCES WITH "NO!" SCRAWLED NEARBY.
I NEVER WOULD'VE MENTIONED PERCOCET TO YOUR DAD,
SHE SAID OF THE 1988 FAMILY FILM.
IT'S IN THE VIDEO, MOM.
WELL, I NEVER WOULD'VE PUT MAKEUP ON BEFORE BED.
BUT YOU DID. WHAT'S YOUR OVERALL IMPRESSION OR FEELING?
IT JUST MAKES ME SAD,
SHE SAID AND LOOKED DOWN.
I TRIED TO EXPLAIN AWAY WHY I THOUGHT MEMOIRS WERE IMPORTANT, BUT THERE WAS NO GETTING AROUND WHAT SHE SAW AS BETRAYAL: THE TAKING OF A STORY FOR MY OWN PURPOSES.
I APOLOGIZED OVER AND OVER AGAIN.

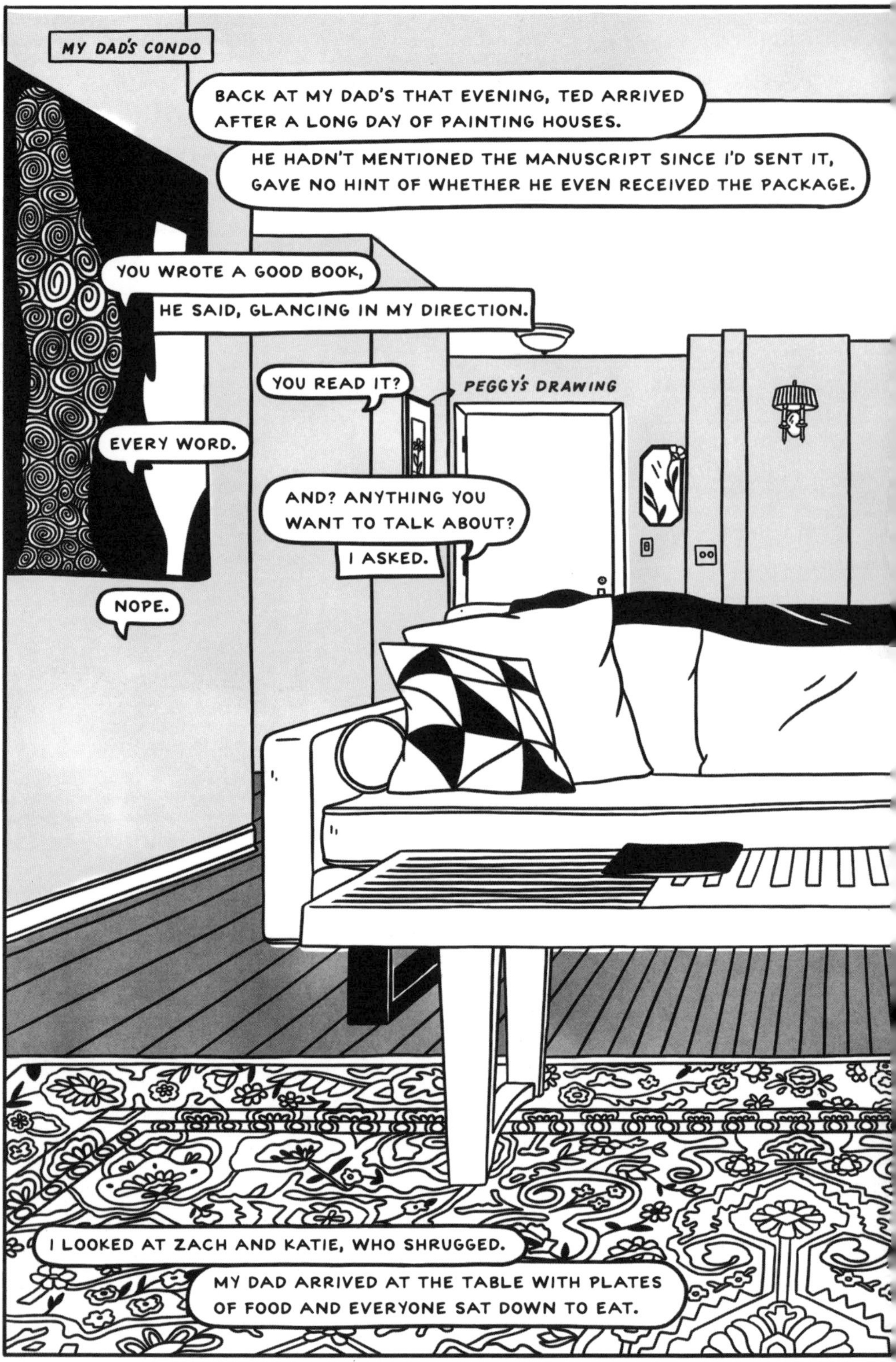
MY DAD'S CONDO
BACK AT MY DAD'S THAT EVENING, TED ARRIVED AFTER A LONG DAY OF PAINTING HOUSES.
HE HADN'T MENTIONED THE MANUSCRIPT SINCE I'D SENT IT, GAVE NO HINT OF WHETHER HE EVEN RECEIVED THE PACKAGE.
YOU WROTE A GOOD BOOK,
HE SAID, GLANCING IN MY DIRECTION.
YOU READ IT?
PEGGY'S DRAWING
EVERY WORD.
AND? ANYTHING YOU WANT TO TALK ABOUT?
I ASKED.
NOPE.
I LOOKED AT ZACH AND KATIE, WHO SHRUGGED.
MY DAD ARRIVED AT THE TABLE WITH PLATES OF FOOD AND EVERYONE SAT DOWN TO EAT.

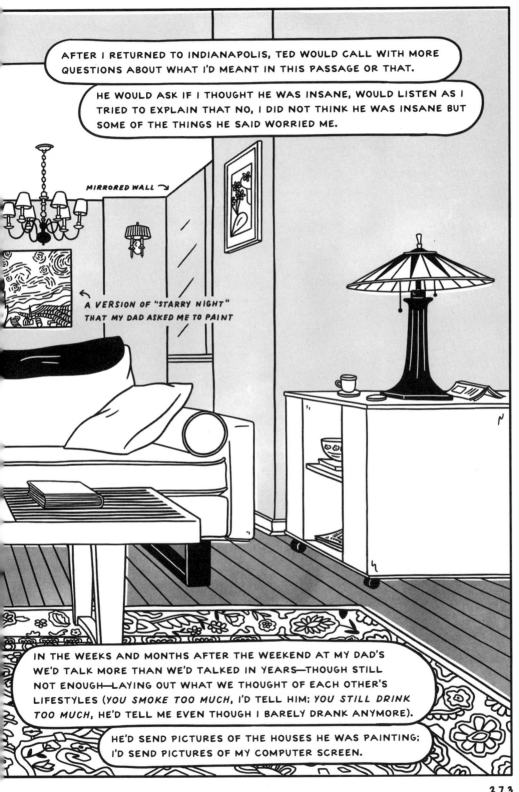

AFTER I RETURNED TO INDIANAPOLIS, TED WOULD CALL WITH MORE QUESTIONS ABOUT WHAT I'D MEANT IN THIS PASSAGE OR THAT.

HE WOULD ASK IF I THOUGHT HE WAS INSANE, WOULD LISTEN AS I TRIED TO EXPLAIN THAT NO, I DID NOT THINK HE WAS INSANE BUT SOME OF THE THINGS HE SAID WORRIED ME.

MIRRORED WALL

A VERSION OF "STARRY NIGHT" THAT MY DAD ASKED ME TO PAINT

IN THE WEEKS AND MONTHS AFTER THE WEEKEND AT MY DAD'S WE'D TALK MORE THAN WE'D TALKED IN YEARS—THOUGH STILL NOT ENOUGH—LAYING OUT WHAT WE THOUGHT OF EACH OTHER'S LIFESTYLES (*YOU SMOKE TOO MUCH*, I'D TELL HIM; *YOU STILL DRINK TOO MUCH*, HE'D TELL ME EVEN THOUGH I BARELY DRANK ANYMORE).

HE'D SEND PICTURES OF THE HOUSES HE WAS PAINTING; I'D SEND PICTURES OF MY COMPUTER SCREEN.

MY SIBLINGS AND I HAVEN'T SEEN EACH OTHER IN PERSON SINCE FEBRUARY BECAUSE OF THE COVID-19 PANDEMIC AND WE HAVEN'T TAKEN A PHOTO TOGETHER SINCE THE KENTUCKY WEEKEND IN 2014. I ASKED THEM TO SEND ME PICTURES. SO HERE WE ALL ARE IN 2020.

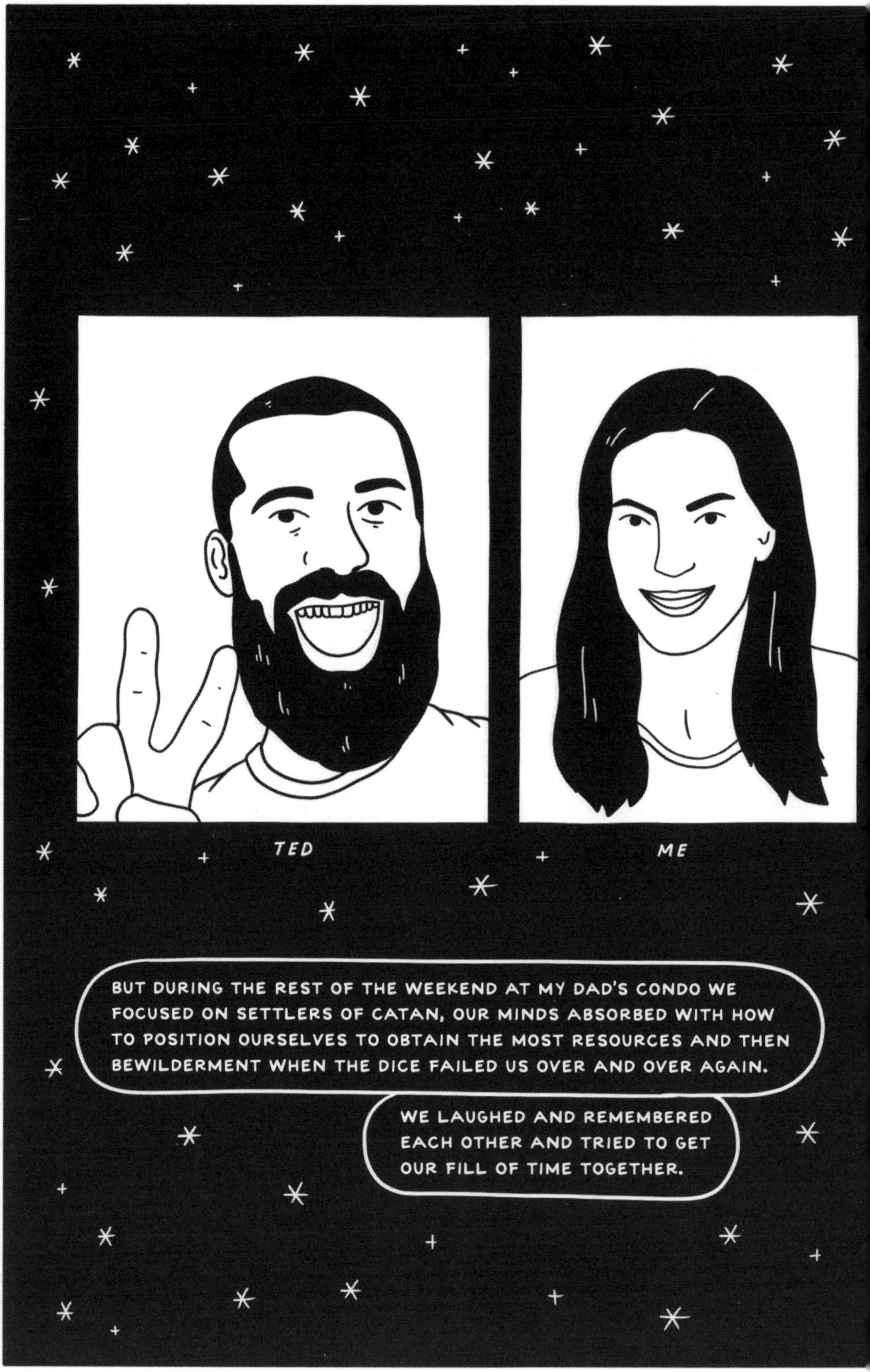
TED
ME
BUT DURING THE REST OF THE WEEKEND AT MY DAD'S CONDO WE FOCUSED ON SETTLERS OF CATAN, OUR MINDS ABSORBED WITH HOW TO POSITION OURSELVES TO OBTAIN THE MOST RESOURCES AND THEN BEWILDERMENT WHEN THE DICE FAILED US OVER AND OVER AGAIN.
WE LAUGHED AND REMEMBERED EACH OTHER AND TRIED TO GET OUR FILL OF TIME TOGETHER.

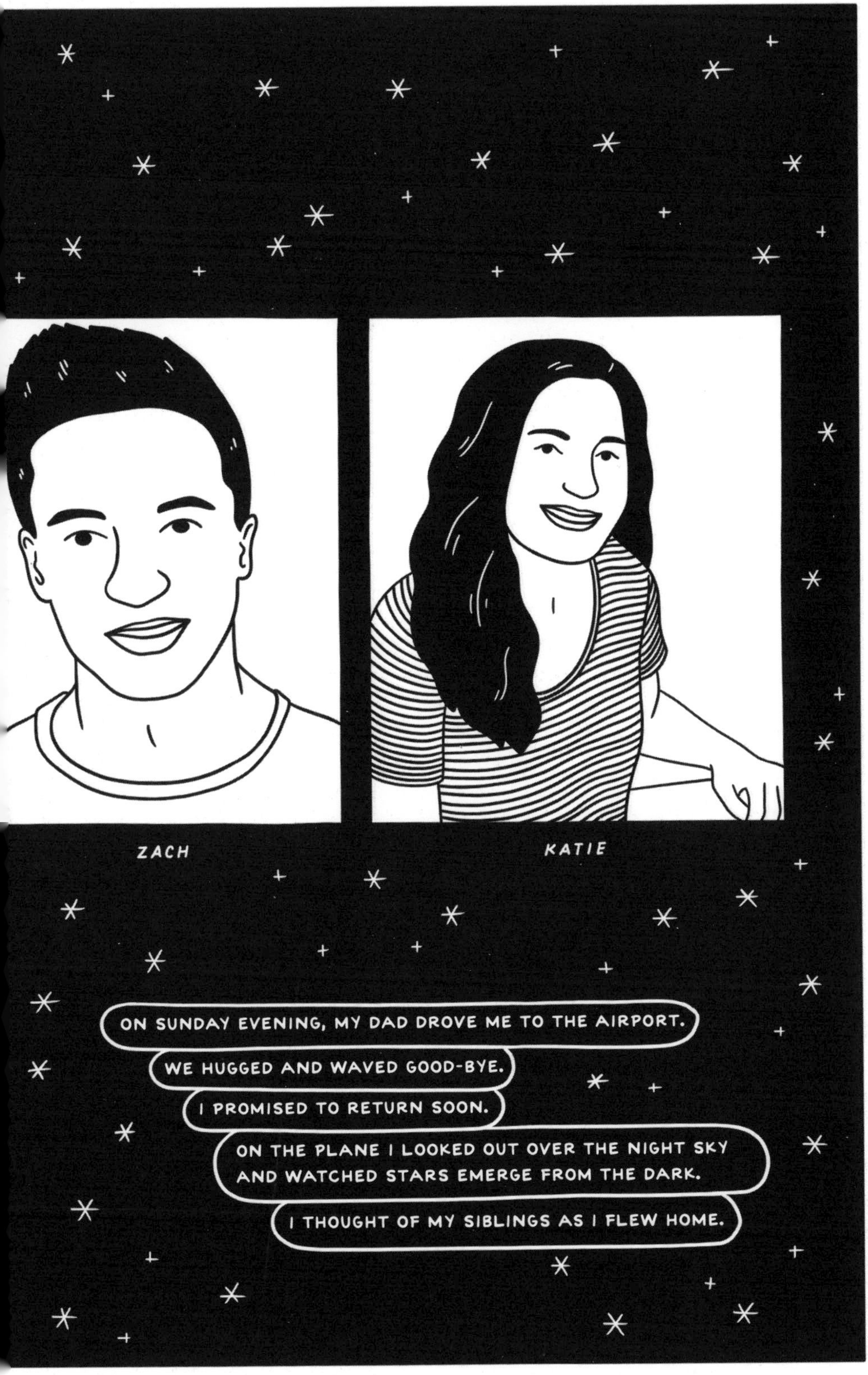
ZACH
KATIE
ON SUNDAY EVENING, MY DAD DROVE ME TO THE AIRPORT.
WE HUGGED AND WAVED GOOD-BYE.
I PROMISED TO RETURN SOON.
ON THE PLANE I LOOKED OUT OVER THE NIGHT SKY AND WATCHED STARS EMERGE FROM THE DARK.
I THOUGHT OF MY SIBLINGS AS I FLEW HOME.

ACKNOWLEDGMENTS

I AM ENORMOUSLY GRATEFUL TO A SMALL VILLAGE OF PEOPLE WHO HELPED MAKE THIS BOOK EXIST. FIRST, THANK YOU TO MY ENTHUSIASTIC AGENT, CHAD LUIBL AT JANKLOW & NESBIT, FOR SEEING POTENTIAL IN EARLY DRAFTS OF MY MANUSCRIPT AND FOR WRITING AND CALLING WITH ENCOURAGEMENT ALL THE WAY THROUGH.

THANKS ALSO TO MY FABULOUS EDITOR, HILARY SWANSON AT HARPERONE, FOR GUIDING ME THROUGH MANY EDITS WITH VAST PATIENCE AND THOUGHTFULNESS. THE ENTIRE TEAM—AIDAN MAHONEY, ADRIAN MORGAN, ANDREW JACOBS, SUZANNE QUIST, AND EVERYONE BEHIND THE SCENES—HAS BEEN A DREAM TO WORK WITH.

OVER A DECADE AGO MY ARIZONA MFA WORKSHOP FAMILY ENDURED MANY DRAFTS OF THIS BOOK, ONLY ONCE IN A WHILE ASKING *WHAT IS THIS?* OR *WHY ARE THERE PICTURES?* I'M GRATEFUL FOR THE COMMUNITY AND FEEDBACK. I AM ESPECIALLY THANKFUL TO BETHANY MAILE, WHO SENT ME A CARE PACKAGE AT THE EXACT MOMENT I NEEDED IT WHILE FINISHING UP THIS BOOK. THANKS ALSO TO B. IOSCA AND JENNIE ZEIGLER FOR LONG-AGO DINNERS AND CONVERSATIONS AND LETTERS THAT SUSTAINED ME. A SPECIAL THANKS TO MY ILLUSTRATION MFA MENTORS ELLEN MCMAHON AND PHIL AND KAREN ZIMMERMANN.

SPEAKING OF MENTORS, I'VE BEEN LUCKY FOR THE GUIDANCE OF LYNN Z. BLOOM, NATASHA PISKUNOVA, AMY WILSON, AND JOYCE KESSLER, ALL OF WHOM HELPED ME AT DIFFERENT TIMES IN MY LIFE. THANK YOU.

MY ILLUSTRATION AGENT, SCOTT HULL, HAS BEEN A GUIDING LIGHT AS I WORKED MY WAY THROUGH THIS BOOK. AND I'M ALSO GRATEFUL TO PENELOPE DULLAGHAN FOR HER KINDNESS AND FRIENDSHIP.

THANK YOU TO MACDOWELL AND YADDO FOR GIVING ME TIME TO WORK ON THIS BOOK AND FOR FEEDING ME WONDERFUL FOOD. EARLY VERSIONS OF SOME STORIES IN THIS BOOK WERE PUBLISHED IN LITERARY MAGAZINES. THANKS TO THE FOLLOWING MAGAZINES FOR YOUR SUPPORT:

MEMOIR MAGAZINE, "48 NORTHVIEW DRIVE"
SOUTH LOOP REVIEW, "10 SPEZZANO DRIVE"
BLACK WARRIOR REVIEW, "YOUR BODY BECOMES SUBMERGED"
COPPER NICKEL, "8 CHELSEA ROAD"
ECOTONE, "DAVE"